Information Security Management

HANDBOOK

4TH EDITION

OTHER AUERBACH PUBLICATIONS

A Standard for Auditing Computer Applications, Martin Krist,
ISBN: 0-8493-9983-1

Analyzing Business Information Systems, Shouhong Wang,
ISBN: 0-8493-9240-3

Broadband Networking, James Trulove, Editor, ISBN: 0-8493-9821-5

Communications Systems Management Handbook, 6th Edition,
Anura Gurugé and Lisa M. Lindgren, Editors, 0-8493-9826-6

Computer Telephony Integration, William Yarberry, Jr.,
ISBN: 0-8493-9995-5

Data Management Handbook, 3rd Edition, Sanjiv Purba, Editor,
ISBN: 0-8493-9832-0

Electronic Messaging, Nancy Cox, Editor, ISBN: 0-8493-9825-8

Enterprise Operations Management Handbook, 2nd Edition,
Steve F. Blanding, Editor, ISBN: 0-8493-9824-X

Enterprise Systems Architectures, Andersen Consulting, 0-8493-9836-3

Enterprise Systems Integration, John Wyzalek, Editor, ISBN: 0-8493-9837-1

Healthcare Information Systems, Phillip L. Davidson, Editor, ISBN: 0-8493-9963-7

Information Security Architecture, Jan Killmeyer, ISBN: 0-8493-9988-2

IS Management Handbook, 7th Edition, Carol V. Brown, Editor,
ISBN: 0-8493-9820-7

Information Technology Control and Audit, Frederick Gallegos, Sandra Allen-Senft,
and Daniel P. Manson, ISBN: 0-8493-9994-7

Internet Management, Jessica Keyes, Editor,
ISBN: 0-8493-9987-4

Local Area Network Handbook, 6th Edition, John P. Slone, Editor,
ISBN: 0-8493-9838-X

Multi-Operating System Networking: Living with UNIX, NetWare, and NT,
Raj Rajagopal, Editor, ISBN: 0-8493-9831-2

Network Manager's Handbook, 3rd Edition, John Lusa, Editor,
ISBN: 0-8493-9841-X

Project Management, Paul C. Tinnirello, Editor, ISBN: 0-8493-9998-X

Effective Use of Teams in IT Audits, Martin Krist,
ISBN: 0-8493-9828-2

Systems Development Handbook, 4th Edition, Paul C. Tinnirello, Editor,
ISBN: 0-8493-9822-3

AUERBACH PUBLICATIONS

www.auerbach-publications.com
TO Order: Call: 1-800-272-7737 • Fax: 1-800-374-3401
E-mail: orders@crcpress.com

Information Security Management

HANDBOOK

4TH EDITION

Harold F. Tipton
Micki Krause

EDITORS

AUERBACH

Boca Raton   London   New York   Washington, D.C.

Library of Congress Cataloging-in-Publication Data

Information security management handbook / Harold F. Tipton, Micki Krause, editors. — 4th ed.
   p. cm.
Revised edition of: Handbook of information security management 1999.
Includes bibliographical references and index.
ISBN 0-8493-9829-0 (alk. paper)
1. Computer security — Management — Handbooks, manuals, etc. 2. Data protection—
Handbooks, manuals, etc. I. Tipton, Harold F. 2. Krause, Micki. III.Title: Handbook of
information security management 1999.
QA76.9.A25H36 1999a
6589.0558—dc21   99-42823
                                                                  CIP

© 2000 by CRC Press LLC
Auerbach is an imprint of CRC Press LLC

No claim to original U.S. Government works
International Standard Book Number 0-8493-9829-0
Library of Congress Card Number   99-42823
Printed in the United States of America   2 3 4 5 6 7 8 9 0
Printed on acid-free paper

Contributors

STEVEN F. BLANDING, *Arthur Andersen LLP, Houston, TX*
BILL BONI, *Coopers & Lybrand LLP, Los Angeles, CA*
JAMES CANNADY, *Georgia Tech Research Institute, Atlanta, GA*
STEPHEN COBB, *Cobb Associates, Titusville, FL*
DOUGLAS G. CONORICH, *Internet Security Analyst, IBM Corp.,*
Clearfield, UT
HARRY DEMAIO, *Deloitte & Touche Enterprise Risk Services, Deerfield, IL*
JOHN DORF, *Risk Management Consulting, Ernst & Young, Chicago, IL*
JEFF FLYNN, *Jeff Flynn & Associates, Irvine, CA*
RONALD A. GOVE, PH.D, *Vice President, Science Applications International*
Corp., Columbia, MD
CARL B. JACKSON, *Principal, Ernst & Young LLP, Houston, TX*
MARTY JOHNSON, *Information Systems Assurance & Advisory Systems, Ernst &*
Young, Chicago, IL
RAY KAPLAN, *Information Systems Security Specialist, Secure Computing Corp.,*
Roseville, MN
CHRISTOPHER KING, *Information Security Engineering, Chelmsford, MA*
JOE KOVARA, *Product Development Manager, CyberSafe, Inc.,*
Redmond, WA
MICKI KRAUSE, *Manager, Information Securities Systems, PacifiCare Health*
Systems, Cypress, CA
LT. JEFFERY J. LOWDER, *Chief, Network Security Element, Air Force Network*
Control Center, USAF Academy, Colorado Springs, CO
WILLIAM HUGH MURRAY, *Executive Consultant, Information Systems Security,*
Deloitte and Touche LLP, New Canaan, CT
WILL OZIER, *President and Founder, OPA — The Integrated Risk Management*
Group, Petaluma, CA
TOM PELTIER, *Enterprise Networking Services, Detroit, MI*
RALPH SPENCER POORE, *Ernst & Young, Arlington, TX*
DONALD R. RICHARDS, *Biometric Security Consultant, IriScan, Fairfax, VA*
BEN ROTHKE, *Information Security Services, Ernst & Young, Iselin, NJ*

Contributors

E. EUGENE SCHULTZ, *Program Manager, SRI Consultants, Menlo Park, CA*

EUGENE SPAFFORD, *Professor, Department of Computer Science, Purdue University, Lafayette, IN*

BILL STACKPOLE, *Olympic Resource Management, Poulsbo, WA*

HAROLD F. TIPTON, *HFT Associates, Villa Park, CA*

JOHN R. VACCA, *Independent Consultant, Pomeroy, OH*

THOMAS WELCH, *Welch and Welch Investigations, Glenwood, NJ*

Contents

Contents

Contents

Introduction

TWO PRIMARY PURPOSES

From its inception in 1993, the Handbook of Information Security Management series was intended to be not only an everyday reference for information security practitioners but also an important document for use by practitioners in conducting the intense review necessary to prepare for the CISSP examination. As the field of information security continues to become more and more complicated, the demand by employers for those having the professional credential, Certified Information System Security Professional (CISSP), is increasing.

Currently, almost 2500 practitioners have achieved CISSP certification by the International Information Systems Security Certification Consortium (ISC^2). Several hundred take the examination annually. Preparing for the examination is a major effort because a thorough understanding of the topics contained in the Common Body of Knowledge (CBK) for the field is required. The HISM series of books have become some of the most important references used by candidates preparing for the exam.

The tables of contents for current and future editions of the handbook are purposely arranged to correspond to the 10 domains of the certification examination. This enables reviewers to easily locate topics for focused study. One or more chapters of each book address specific CBK topics in each domain. No single book is able to contain all of the CBK topics because of the broad scope of the field. Therefore, we intend to include at least 50 percent new topics in each edition to ensure that we keep up to date as the field marches ahead. Those chapters retained for a subsequent edition address important topics that haven't changed significantly from the previous year.

Domain 1 addresses access control issues and methodology. Access control involves all of the various mechanisms (physical, logical, and administrative) used to ensure that only specifically authorized persons or processes are allowed to use or access a system. This edition focuses on access control issues.

Domain 2 addresses telecommunications and network security. Two subsets are included in this edition: network security and Internet, intranet, and extranet security. This domain involves ensuring the integrity and confidentiality of information transmitted via telecommunications media as well as ensuring the availability of the telecommunications media itself.

Domain 3 addresses security management practices. These include several topics. Policies, procedures, baselines, and guidelines are needed to assure a reasonable and consistent level of security through an organization. Information classification is used to ensure that the sensitivity of information is protected. Security awareness training is important to enable an understanding of the need for compliance with policies and procedures. An understanding of organization architecture helps identify the appropriate place for the information security function. Risk management is the management tool that makes it possible to apply resources most effectively. This edition focuses on security awareness, organization architecture, and risk management.

Domain 4 addresses applications and systems development security. This edition focuses on application security. Application and system development security involves the various controls available and used within systems and applications software and the procedures used in their development.

Domain 5 addresses cryptography. This topic involves the use of secret codes to obtain desired levels of information confidentiality and integrity. This edition focuses on crypto technology and implementations from the basics to the latest, such as key management, Kerberos, and PKI.

Domain 6 addresses security architecture and models. Computer architecture deals with those aspects of computer organization and configuration that can be employed to achieve computer security. Models describe the concepts used to maintain the security of systems and information. PC and LAN security issues are also included in this domain. In this edition, the focus is on microcomputer and LAN security.

Domain 7 addresses operations security. Operations security involves data center and distributed processing security issues revolving around operator and system administrator privileges, the protection of computing resources, and the need to understand the implications of threats to these important assets. This edition concentrates on the threats posed to operations security by outside activities.

Domain 8 addresses business continuity planning and disaster recovery planning. There is considerable confusion related to the terminology used in this domain, but essentially it boils down to the planning of specific, coordinated actions to avoid or mitigate the effects of disruptions to normal business information processing functions. This edition contains chapters discussing issues related to both business continuity planning and disaster recovery planning.

Domain 9 addresses law, investigations, and ethics. Law involves the legal and regulatory issues facing an information security function. Investigation consists of guidelines and principles necessary to successfully investigate security incidents and preserve the integrity of evidence. Ethics deals with a knowledge of the difference between right and wrong and the willingness to do the right thing. This edition contains chapters in each of the three areas: law, investigation, and ethics.

Domain 10 addresses physical security. Physical security involves the provision of a safe environment for information processing activities, with a focus on preventing unauthorized physical and technical access to computing equipment. The chapter included in this edition is concerned with threats and facility requirements.

Hal Tipton
Micki Krause
Summer 1999

Domain 1
Access Control Systems and Methodology

A fundamental tenet of information security is controlling access to the critical resources that require protection from unauthorized modification or disclosure. The essence of access control is that permissions are assigned to individuals or system objects, which are authorized to access specific resources. Some access control methodologies utilize certain characteristics associated with its user, e.g., what a person knows, what a person possesses, or what a person is, and range from simple user identifiers and passwords, to hardware password generators, to technologically advanced biometric devices, e.g., retinal scanners or palm print readers.

Access controls can be invoked at various layers of a system, including the host or network operating system, database, or application layer. And in some instances, especially at the database or application layer, the lack of controls requires the imposition of access controls by third-party products.

In other instances, access controls are not invoked by hardware or software, but are administrative in nature, for example, the segregation of responsibilities.

The chapters in this domain address access control issues and the administration of those controls. They discuss advanced biometric technologies, access control standards for remote access, and the panacea that promises to reduce user account administration and introduce user friendliness, the concept of single sign-on.

Domain 1.1
Access Control Issues

Chapter 1
Biometric Identification

Donald R. Richards

Envision a day when the door to a secured office building can be opened by using an automated system for identification based on a person's physical presence, even though that person left his or her ID or access card on the kitchen counter at home. Imagine ticket-less airline travel, whereby a person can enter the aircraft based on a positive identification verified biometrically at the gateway. Picture getting into a car, starting the engine by flipping down the driver's visor, and glancing into the mirror and driving away, secure in the knowledge that only authorized individuals can make the vehicle operate.

The day when these actions are routine is rapidly approaching. Actually, implementation of fast, accurate, reliable, and user-acceptable biometric identification systems is already under way. Societal behavior patterns result in ever-increasing requirements for automated positive identification systems, and these are growing even more rapidly. The potential applications for these systems are limited only by a person's imagination. Performance claims cover the full spectrum from realistic to incredible. System implementation problems with these new technologies have been predictably high. User acceptance obstacles are on the rise. Security practitioners contemplating use of these systems are faced with overwhelming amounts of often contradictory information provided by manufacturers and dealers.

This chapter provides the security professional with the knowledge necessary to avoid potential pitfalls in selecting, installing, and operating a biometric identification system. The characteristics of these systems are introduced in sufficient detail to enable determination as to which are most important for particular applications. Historical problems experienced in organizational use of biometric systems are also discussed. Finally, the specific technologies available in the marketplace are described, including the data acquisition process, enrollment procedure, data files, user interface actions, speed, anticounterfeit information, accuracy, and unique system aspects.

BACKGROUND AND HISTORY LEADING
TO BIOMETRIC DEVELOPMENT

Since the early days of mankind, humans have struggled with the problem of protecting their assets. How can unauthorized persons effectively and efficiently be prevented from making off with the things that are considered valuable, even a cache of food? Of course, the immediate solution then, as it has always been for the highest-value assets, was to post a guard. Then, as now, it was realized that the human guard is an inefficient and sometimes ineffective method of protecting resources.

The creation of a securable space, for example, a room with no windows or other openings except a sturdy door, was a step in the right direction. From there, the addition of the lock and key was a small, but very effective move, which enabled the removal of the continuous guard. Those with authorized access to the protected assets were given keys, which was the beginning of the era of identification of authorized persons based on the fact that they had such keys. Over centuries, locks and keys were successively improved to provide better security. The persistent problem was lost and stolen keys. When these events occurred, the only solution was the replacement of the lock (later just the cylinder) and of all keys, which was time consuming and expensive.

The next major breakthrough was the advent of electronic locks, controlled by cardreaders with plastic cards as keys. This continued the era of identification of authorized persons based on things that they had (e.g., coded plastic cards). The great advancement was the ability to electronically remove the ability of lost or stolen (key) cards to unlock the door. Therefore, no locks or keys had to be changed, with considerable savings in time and cost. However, as time passed, experience proved that assets were sometimes removed before authorized persons even realized that their cards had been lost or stolen.

The addition of a Personal Identification Number (PIN) keypad to the cardreader was the solution to the unreported lost or stolen card problem. Thus began the era of identification of authorized persons based on things they had and on things they knew (e.g., a PIN). This worked well until the "bad guys" figured out that most people chose PINs that were easy for them to remember, such as birthdays, anniversaries, or other numbers significant in their lives. With a lost or stolen card, and a few trials, "bad guys" were sometimes successful in guessing the correct PIN and accessing the protected area.

The obvious solution was to use only random numbers as PINs, which solved the problem of PINs being guessed or found through trial and error. However, the difficulty in remembering random numbers caused another predictable problem. PINs (and passwords) were written on pieces of paper, post-it-notes, driver's licenses, blotters, bulletin boards, computers, or wherever they were convenient to find when needed. Sometimes they were written on the access cards themselves. In addition, because it is often easy to observe PINs being entered, "bad guys" planning a theft were sometimes able to obtain the number prior to stealing the associated card. These scenarios demonstrate that cardreaders, even those with PINs, cannot positively authenticate the identity of persons with authorized entry.

The only way to be truly positive in authenticating identity for access is to base the authentication on the physical attributes of the persons themselves (i.e., biometric identification). Because most identity authentication requirements take place when persons are fully clothed (neck to feet and wrists), the parts of the body conveniently available for this purpose are the hands, face, and eyes.

Biometric Development

Once it became apparent that truly positive identification could only be based on the physical attributes of the person, two questions had to be answered. First, what part of the body could be used? Second, how could identification be accomplished with sufficient accuracy, reliability, and speed so as to be viable in field performance? However, had the pressures demanding automated personal identification not been rising rapidly at the highest levels (making necessary resources and funds available), this research would not have occurred.

At the time, the only measurable characteristic associated with the human body that was universally accepted as a positive identifier was the fingerprint. Contact data collected using special inks, dusting powders, and tape, for example, are matched by specially trained experts. Uniquely positioned whorls, ridge endings, and bifurcations were located and compared against templates. A sensor capable of reading a print made by a finger pressed against a piece of glass was required. Matching the collected print against a stored template is a classic computer task. Fortuitously, at the time these identification questions were being asked, computer processing capabilities and speed were increasing rapidly, while size and cost were falling. Had this not been the case, even the initial development of biometric systems would not have taken place. It has taken an additional 25 years of computer and biometric advancement, and cost reduction, for biometrics to achieve widespread acceptability and field proliferation.

Predictably, the early fingerprint-identifying verification systems were not successful in the marketplace, but not because they could not do what they were designed to do. They did. Key problems were the slow decision speed and the lack of ability to detect counterfeit fingerprints. Throughput of two to three persons per minute results in waiting lines, personal frustration, and lost productive time. Failure to detect counterfeit input (i.e., rubber fingers, photo images) can result in false acceptance of impostors.

Continued comprehensive research and development and advancements in sensing and data processing technologies enabled production of systems acceptable in field use. Even these systems were not without problems, however. Some systems required high levels of maintenance and adjustment for reliable performance. Some required lengthy enrollment procedures. Some required data templates of many thousands of bytes, requiring large amounts of expensive storage media and slowing processing time. Throughput was still relatively slow (though acceptable). Accuracy rates (i.e., false accept and mostly false reject) were higher than would be acceptable today. However, automated biometric identifying verification systems were now performing needed functions in the field.

The value of fast, accurate, and reliable biometric identity verification was rapidly recognized, even if it was not yet fully available. Soon, the number of organized biometric research and development efforts exceeded 20. Many were fingerprint spinoffs: thumb print; full finger print; finger pattern (i.e., creases on the underside of the finger); and palm print. Hand topography (i.e., the side-view elevations of the parts of the hand placed against a flat surface) proved not sufficiently unique for accurate verification, but combined with a top view of the hand (i.e., hand geometry) it became one of the most successful systems in the field. Two-finger geometry is a recently marketed variation.

Other technologies that have achieved at least some degree of market acceptance include voice patterns, retina scan (i.e., the blood-vessel pattern inside the eyeball), signature dynamics (i.e., the speed, direction, and pressure of pen strokes), and iris recognition (i.e., the pattern of features in the colored portion of the eye around the pupil). Others that have reached the market, but have not remained, include keystroke dynamics (i.e., the measurable pattern of speed and time in typing words) and signature recognition (i.e., matching). Other physical characteristics that have been and are currently being investigated as potential biometric identifiers include finger length (though not sufficiently unique), wrist veins (underside), hand veins (back of the hand), knuckle creases (when grasping a bar), fingertip structure (blood vessel pattern under the skin), finger sections (between first and second joint), ear shape, and lip shape. One organization has been spending significant amounts investigating biometric identification based on body odor.

Another biometric identifying verification area receiving significant attention (and funding) is facial recognition. This partially results from the ease of acquiring facial images with standard video technology and from the perceived high payoff to be enjoyed by a successful facial recognition system. Facial thermography (i.e., heat patterns of the facial tissue) is an expensive variation because of high camera cost.

The history of the development of biometric identifying verification systems is far from complete. Entrepreneurs continue to see rich rewards for faster, more accurate, and reliable technology, and advanced development will continue. However, advancements are expected to be improvements or variations of current technologies. These will be associated with the hands, eyes, and face for the "what we are" systems and the voice and signature for the "what we do" systems.

CHARACTERISTICS OF BIOMETRIC SYSTEMS

These are the important factors necessary for any effective biometric system: accuracy, speed and throughput rate, acceptability to users, uniqueness of the biometric organ and action, resistance to counterfeiting, reliability, data storage requirements, enrollment time, intrusiveness of data collection, and subject and system contact requirements.

Accuracy

Accuracy is the most critical characteristic of a biometric identifying verification system. If the system cannot accurately separate authentic persons from impostors, it should not even be termed a biometric identification system.

False Reject Rate. The rate, generally stated as a percentage, at which authentic, enrolled persons are rejected as unidentified or unverified persons by a biometric system is termed the false reject rate. False rejection is sometimes called a Type I error. In access control, if the requirement is to keep the "bad guys" out, false rejection is considered the least important error. However, in other biometric applications, it may be the most important error. When used by a bank or retail store to authenticate customer identity and account balance, false rejection means that the transaction or sale (and associated profit) is lost, and the customer becomes upset. Most bankers and retailers are willing to allow a few false accepts as long as there are no false rejects.

False rejections also have a negative effect on throughput, frustrations, and unimpeded operations, because they cause unnecessary delays in personnel movements. An associated problem that is sometimes incorrectly attributed to false rejection is failure to acquire. Failure to acquire occurs when the biometric sensor is not presented with sufficient usable data to

9

make an authentic or impostor decision. Examples include smudged prints on a fingerprint system, improper hand positioning on a hand geometry system, improper alignment on a retina or iris system, or mumbling on a voice system. Subjects cause failure-to-acquire problems, either accidentally or on purpose.

False Accept Rate. The rate, generally stated as a percentage, at which unenrolled persons or impostors are accepted as authentic, enrolled persons by a biometric system is termed the false accept rate. False acceptance is sometimes called a Type II error. This is usually considered to be the most important error for a biometric access control system.

Crossover Error Rate (CER). This is also called the equal error rate and is the point, generally stated as a percentage, at which the false rejection rate and the false acceptance rate are equal. This has become the most important measure of biometric system accuracy.

All biometric systems have sensitivity adjustment capability. If false acceptance is not desired, the system can be set to require (nearly) perfect matches of enrollment data and input data. If tested in this configuration, the system can truthfully be stated to achieve a (near) zero false accept rate. If false rejection is not desired, this system can be readjusted to accept input data that only approximate a match with enrollment data. If tested in this configuration, the system can be truthfully stated to achieve a (near) zero false rejection rate. However, the reality is that biometric systems can operate on only one sensitivity setting at a time.

The reality is also that when system sensitivity is set to minimize false acceptance, closely matching data will be spurned, and the false rejection rate will go up significantly. Conversely, when system sensitivity is set to minimize false rejects, the false acceptance rate will go up notably. Thus, the published (i.e., truthful) data tell only part of the story. Actual system accuracy in field operations may even be less than acceptable. This is the situation that created the need for a single measure of biometric system accuracy.

The crossover error rate (CER) provides a single measurement that is fair and impartial in comparing the performance of the various systems. In general, the sensitivity setting that produces the equal error will be close to the setting that will be optimal for field operation of the system. A biometric system that delivers a CER of 2 percent will be more accurate than a system with a CER of 5 percent.

Speed and Throughput Rate

The speed and throughput rate are the most important biometric system characteristics. Speed is often related to the data processing capability of the system and is stated as how fast the accept or reject decision is annunciated. In actuality, it relates to the entire authentication procedure: stepping up to the system; inputting the card or PIN (if a verification system); inputting the physical data by inserting a hand or finger, aligning an eye, speaking access words, or signing a name; processing and matching of data files; annunciation of the accept or reject decision; and, if a portal system, moving through and closing the door.

Generally accepted standards include a system speed of 5 seconds from startup through decision annunciation. Another standard is a portal throughput rate of 6 to 10/minute, which equates to 6 to 10 seconds/person through the door. Only in recent years have biometric systems become capable of meeting these speed standards, and, even today, some marketed systems do not maintain this rapidity. Slow speed and the resultant waiting lines and movement delays have frequently caused the removal of biometric systems and even the failure of biometric companies.

Acceptability to Users

System acceptability to the people who must use it has been a little noticed but increasingly important factor in biometric identification operations. Initially, when there were few systems, most were of high security and the few users had a high incentive to use the systems; user acceptance was of little interest. In addition, little user threat was seen in fingerprint and hand systems.

Biometric system acceptance occurs when those who must use the system — organizational managers and any union present — all agree that there are assets that need protection, the biometric system effectively controls access to these assets, system usage is not hazardous to the health of the users, system usage does not inordinately impede personnel movement and cause production delays, and the system does not enable management to collect personal or health information about the users. Any of the parties can effect system success or removal. Uncooperative users will overtly or covertly compromise, damage, or sabotage system equipment. The cost of union inclusion of the biometric system in their contracts may become too costly. Moreover, management has the final decision on whether the biometric system benefits outweigh its liabilities.

Uniqueness of Biometric Organ and Action

Because the purpose of biometric systems is positive identification of personnel, some organizations (e.g., elements of the government) are specifying systems based only on a unique (i.e., no duplicate in the world) physical characteristic. The rationale is that when the base is a unique characteristic, a file match is a positive identification rather than a statement of high probability that this is the right person. Only three physical characteristics or human organs used for biometric identification are unique: the fingerprint, the retina of the eye (i.e., the blood-vessel pattern inside the back of the eyeball), and the iris of the eye (i.e., random pattern of features in the colored portion of the eye surrounding the pupil). These features include freckles, rings, pits, striations, vasculature, coronas, and crypts.

Resistance to Counterfeiting

The ability to detect or reject counterfeit input data is vital to a biometric access control system meeting high security requirements. These include use of rubber, plastic, or even hands or fingers of the deceased in hand or fingerprint systems, and mimicked or recorded input to voice systems. Entertainment media, such as the James Bond or Terminator films, have frequently shown security system failures when the heads or eyes of deceased (i.e., authentic) persons were used to gain access to protected assets or information. Because most of the early biometric identifying verification systems were designed for high security access control applications, failure to detect or reject counterfeit input data was the reason for several system or organization failures. Resistance to counterfeit data remains a criterion of high-quality, high-accuracy systems. However, the proliferation of biometric systems into other non-high-security type applications means that lack of resistance to counterfeiting is not likely to cause the failure of a system in the future.

Reliability

It is vital that biometric identifying verification systems remain in continuous, accurate operation. The system must allow authorized persons access while precluding others, without breakdown or deterioration in performance accuracy or speed. In addition, these performance standards must be sustained without high levels of maintenance or frequent diagnostics and system adjustments.

Data Storage Requirements

Data storage requirements are a far less significant issue today than in the earlier biometric systems when storage media were very expensive. Nevertheless, the size of biometric data files remains a factor of interest. Even with current ultra-high-speed processors, large data files take longer to process than small files, especially in systems that perform full identification, matching the input file against every file in the database. Biometric file size varies between 9 and 10,000 bytes, with most falling in the 256- to 1,000-byte range.

Enrollment Time

Enrollment time is also a less significant factor today. Early biometric systems sometimes had enrollment procedures requiring many repetitions and several minutes to complete. A system requiring a 5-minute enrollment instead of 2 minutes causes 50 hours of expensive nonproductive time if 1,000 users must be enrolled. Moreover, when line waiting time is considered, the cost increases several times. The accepted standard for enrollment time is 2 minutes per person. Most of the systems in the marketplace today meet this standard.

Intrusiveness of Data Collection

Originally, this factor developed because of user concerns regarding collection of biometric data from inside the body, specifically, the retina inside the eyeball. Early systems illuminated the retina with a red light beam. However, this coincided with increasing public awareness of lasers, sometimes demonstrated as red light beams cutting steel. There has never been an allegation of user injury from retina scanning, but user sensitivity expanded from resistance to red lights intruding inside the body to include any intrusion inside the body. This user sensitivity has now increased to concerns about intrusions into perceived personal space.

Subject and System Contact Requirements

This factor could possibly be considered as a next step or continuation of intrusiveness. Indications are that biometric system users are becoming increasingly sensitive to being required to make firm physical contact with surfaces where up to hundreds of other unknown (to them) persons are required to make contact for biometric data collection. These concerns include voice systems that require holding and speaking into a handset close to the lips.

There seems to be some user feeling that: "if I choose to do something, it is OK, but if an organization, or society, requires me to do the same thing, it is wrong." Whether or not this makes sense, it is an attitude spreading through society which is having an impact on the use of biometric systems. Systems using video camera data acquisition do not fall into this category.

HISTORICAL BIOMETRIC PROBLEMS

A variety of problems in the field utilization of biometric systems over the past 25 years have been identified. Some have been overcome and are seldom seen today; others still occur. These problems include performance, hardware and software robustness, maintenance requirements, susceptibility to sabotage, perceived health maladies because of usage, private information being made available to management, and skill and cooperation required to use the system.

Performance

Field performance of biometric identifying verification systems is often different than that experienced in manufacturers' or laboratory tests. There are two ways to avoid being stuck with a system that fails to deliver promised performance. First, limit consideration to technologies and systems that have been tested by an independent, unbiased testing organization. Sandia National Laboratories, located in Albuquerque, New Mexico, has done biometric system testing for the Department of Energy for many years, and some of their reports are available. Second, any system manufacturer or sales representative should be able to provide a list of organizations currently using their system. They should be able to point out those users whose application is similar to that currently contemplated (unless the planned operation is a new and unique application). Detailed discussions, and perhaps a site visit, with current users with similar application requirements should answer most questions and prevent many surprises.

Hardware and Software Robustness

Some systems and technologies that are very effective with small- to medium-sized user data bases have a performance that is less than acceptable with large data bases. Problems that occur include system slowdown and accuracy degradation. Some biometric system users have had to discard their systems and start over because their organizations became more successful, grew faster than anticipated, and the old system could not handle the growth. If they hope to "grow" their original system with the organization, system managers should at least double the most optimistic growth estimate and plan for a system capable of handling that load.

Another consideration is hardware capability to withstand extended usage under the conditions expected. An example is the early signature dynamics systems, which performed adequately during testing and early fielding periods. However, the pen and stylus sensors used to detect stroke direction, speed, and pressure were very tiny and sensitive. After months or a year of normal public use, the system performance had deteriorated to the point that the systems were no longer effective identifiers.

Maintenance Requirements

Some sensors and systems have required very high levels of preventive maintenance or diagnostics and adjustment to continue effective operations. Under certain operating and user conditions (e.g., dusty areas or with frequent users of hand lotions or creams), some fingerprint sensors needed cleaning as frequently as every day to prevent deterioration of accuracy. Other systems demanded weekly or monthly connection of diagnostic equipment, evaluation of performance parameters, and careful adjustment to retain productive performance. These human interventions not only disrupt the normal security process, but significantly increase operational costs.

Susceptibility to Sabotage

Systems with data acquisition sensors on pedestals protruding far out from walls or with many moving parts are often susceptible to sabotage or disabling damage. Spinning floor polisher handles or hammers projecting out of pockets can unobtrusively or accidentally affect sensors. These incidents have most frequently occurred when there was widespread user or union resistance to the biometric system.

Perceived Health Maladies Due to Usage

As new systems and technologies were developed and public sensitivity to new viruses and diseases such as AIDS, Ebola, and *E. coli* increased by orders of magnitude, acceptability became a more important issue. Perceptions of possible organ damage and potential spread of disease from biometric system usage ultimately had such a devastating affect on sales of one system that it had to be totally redesigned. Though thousands of the original units had been successfully fielded, whether the newly packaged technology regains popularity or even survives remains to be seen. All of this occurred without even one documented allegation of a single user becoming sick or injured as a result of system utilization.

Many of the highly contagious diseases recently publicized can be spread by simple contact with a contaminated surface. As biometric systems achieve wider market penetration in many applications, user numbers are growing logarithmically. There are developing indications that users are becoming increasingly sensitive about systems and technologies that require firm physical contact for acquisition of the biometric data.

Private Information Made Available to Management

Certain health events can cause changes in the blood vessel pattern (i.e., retina) inside the eyeball. These include diabetes and strokes. Allegations have been made that the retina-based biometric system enables management to improperly obtain health information that may be used to the detriment of system users. The scenario begins with the system failing to identify a routine user. The user is easily authenticated and re-enrolled. As a result, management will allegedly note the re-enrollment report and conclude that this user had a minor health incident (minor because the user is present the next working day). In anticipation that this employee's next health event could cause major medical cost, management might find (or create) a reason for termination. Despite the fact that there is no recorded case of actual occurrence of this alleged scenario, this folklore continues to be heard within the biometric industry.

Skill and Cooperation Required to Use the System

The performance of some biometric systems is greatly dependent on the skill or careful cooperation of the subject in using the system. Though there is an element of this factor required for data acquisition positioning for all biometric systems, it is generally attributed to the "what we do" type of systems.

BENEFITS OF BIOMETRIC IDENTIFICATION AS COMPARED WITH CARD SYSTEMS

Biometric identifying verification systems control people. If the person with the correct hand, eye, face, signature, or voice is not present, the identification and verification cannot take place and the desired action (i.e., portal passage, data or resource access) does not occur.

As has been demonstrated many times, adversaries and criminals obtain and successfully use access cards, even those that require the addition of a PIN. This is because these systems control only pieces of plastic (and sometimes information), rather than people. Real asset and resource protection can only be accomplished by people, not cards and information, because unauthorized persons can (and do) obtain the cards and information.

Further, life-cycle costs are significantly reduced because no card or PIN administration system or personnel are required. The authorized person does not lose physical characteristics (i.e., hands, face, eyes, signature, or voice), but cards and PINs are continuously lost, stolen, or forgotten. This is why card access systems require systems and people to administer, control, record, and issue (new) cards and PINs. Moreover, the cards are an expensive and recurring cost.

Card System Error Rates

The false accept rate is 100% when the access card is in the wrong hands, lost, or stolen. It is a false reject when the right card is swiped incorrectly or just does not activate the system. (Think about the number of times to retry hotel room access cards to get the door to unlock.) Actually, it is also a false reject when a card is forgotten and that person cannot get through the door.

BIOMETRIC DATA UPDATES

Some biometric systems, using technologies based on measuring characteristics and traits that may vary over time, work best when the data base is updated with every use. These are primarily the "what we do" technologies (i.e., voice, signature, and keystroke). Not all systems do this. The action measured by these systems changes gradually over time. The voice changes as people age. It is also affected by changes in weight and by certain health conditions. Signature changes over time are easily documented. For example, look at a signature from Franklin D. Roosevelt at the beginning of his first term as president. Each name and initial is clearly discernible. Then, compare it with his signature in his third term, just 8 years later. To those familiar with it, the strokes and lines are clearly the president's signature, but to others, they bear no relationship to his name or any other words. Keystroke patterns change similarly over time, particularly depending on typing frequency.

Systems that update the database automatically average the current input data into the database template after the identification transaction is complete. Some also delete an earlier data input, making that database a moving average. These gradual changes in input data may not affect user identification for many months or years. However, as the database file and the input data become further apart, increasingly frequent false rejections will cause enough inconvenience that re-enrollment is dictated, which is another inconvenience.

DIFFERENT TYPES OF BIOMETRIC SYSTEMS AND THEIR CHARACTERISTICS

This section describes the different types of biometric systems: fingerprint systems, hand geometry systems, voice pattern systems, retina pattern systems, iris pattern systems, and signature dynamics systems. For each system these characteristics are described: the enrollment procedure and time, the template or file size, the user action required, the system response time, any anticounterfeit method, accuracy, field history, problems experienced, and unique system aspects.

Fingerprint Systems

The information in this section is a compilation of information about several biometric identifying verification systems whose technology is based on the fingerprint.

Data Acquisition. Fingerprint data is acquired when subjects firmly press their fingers against a glass or polycarbonate plate. The fingerprint image is not stored. Information on the relative location of the ridges, whorls, lines, bifurcations, and intersections is stored as an enrolled user database file and later compared with user input data.

Enrollment Procedure and Time. As instructed, subject enters a 1- to 9-digit PIN on the keypad. As cued, the finger is placed on the reader plate and then removed. A digitized code is created. As cued, the finger is placed and removed four more times for calibration. The total enrollment time required is less than 2 minutes.

17

Template or File Size. Fingerprint user files are generally between 500 and 1,500 bytes.

User Actions Required. Nearly all fingerprint-based biometrics are verification systems. The user states identification by entering a PIN through a keypad or by using a card reader, then places a finger on the reader plate.

System Response Time. Visual and audible annunciation of the confirmed and not confirmed decision occurs in 5 to 7 seconds.

Accuracy. Some fingerprint systems can be adjusted to achieve a false accept rate of 0.0%. Sandia National Laboratories tests of a top-rated fingerprint system in 1991 and 1993 produced a three-try false reject rate of 9.4% and a crossover error rate of 5%.

Field History. Thousands of units have been fielded for access control and identity verification for disbursement of government benefits, for example.

Problems Experienced. System operators with large user populations are often required to clean sensor plates frequently to remove built-up skin oil and dirt that adversely affect system accuracy.

Unique System Aspects. To avoid the dirt build-up problem, a newly developed fingerprint system acquires the fingerprint image with ultrasound. Claims are made that this system can acquire the fingerprint of a surgeon wearing latex gloves. A number of companies are producing fingerprint-based biometric identification systems.

Hand Geometry System

Hand geometry data, the three-dimensional record of the length, width, and height of the hand and fingers is acquired by simultaneous vertical and horizontal camera images.

Enrollment Procedure and Time. The subject is directed to place the hand flat on a grid platen, positioned against pegs between the fingers. Four finger-position lights ensure proper hand location. A digital camera records a single top and side view from above, using a 45° mirror for the side view. The subject is directed to withdraw and then reposition the hand twice more. The readings are averaged into a single code and given a PIN. Total enrollment time is less than 2 minutes.

Template or File Size. The hand geometry user file size is nine bytes.

User Actions Required. The hand geometry system operates only as an identification verifier. The user states identification by entering a PIN on a keypad or by using a card reader. When the "place hand" message appears on the unit display, the user places the hand flat on the platen against the pegs. When all four lights confirm correct hand position the data are acquired and a "remove hand" message appears.

System Response Time. Visual and audible annunciation of the confirm or not confirm decision occurs in 3 to 5 seconds.

Anticounterfeit Method. The manufacturer states that "the system checks to ensure that a live hand is used."

Accuracy. Sandia National Laboratories tests have produced a one-try false accept rate less than 0.1 percent, a three-try false reject rate less than 0.1 percent, and crossover error rates of 0.2 and 2.2 percent (i.e., two tests).

Field History. Thousands of units have been fielded for access control, college cafeterias and dormitories, and government facilities. Hand geometry was the original biometric system of choice of the Department of Energy and the Immigration and Naturalization Service. It was also used to protect the Athlete's Village at the 1996 Olympics in Atlanta.

Problems Experienced. Some of the field applications did not perform up to the accuracy results of the initial Sandia test. There have been indications that verification accuracy achieved when user databases are in the hundreds deteriorates when the database grows into the thousands.

Unique System Aspects. The hand geometry user file code of nine bytes is by far the smallest of any current biometric system. Hand geometry identification systems are manufactured by Recognition Systems, Inc. A variation, a two-finger geometry identification system, is manufactured by BioMet Partners.

Voice Pattern Systems

Up to seven parameters of nasal tones, larynx and throat vibrations, and air pressure from the voice are captured by audio and other sensors.

Enrollment Procedure and Time. Most voice systems use equipment similar to a standard telephone. As directed, the subject picks up the handset and enters a PIN on the telephone keypad. When cued through the handset, the subject speaks his or her access phrase, which may be his or her PIN and name or some other four- to six-word phrase. The cue and the access phrase are repeated up to four times. Total enrollment time required is less than 2 minutes.

Template or File Size. Voice user files vary from 1,000 to 10,000 bytes, depending on the system manufacturer.

User Actions Required. Currently, voice systems operate only as identification verifiers. The user states identification by entering the PIN on the telephone-type keypad. As cued through the handset (i.e., recorded voice stating "please say your access phrase"), the user speaks into the handset sensors.

System Response Time. Audible response (i.e., "accepted, please enter" or "not authorized") is provided through the handset. Some systems include visual annunciation (e.g., red and green lights or LEDs). Total transaction time is up to 10 to 14 seconds.

Anticounterfeit Method. Various methods are used including measuring increased air pressure when "p" or "t" sounds are spoken. Some sophisticated systems require the user to speak different words from a list of 10 or more enrolled words in a different order each time the system is used.

Accuracy. Sandia National Laboratories has reported crossover errors over 10% for two systems they have tested. Other voice tests are being planned.

Field History. Over 100 systems have been installed, with over 1,000 door access units, at colleges, hospitals, laboratories, and offices.

Problems Experienced. Background noise can affect the accuracy of voice systems. Access systems are located at entrances, hallways, and doorways, which tend to be busy, high-traffic, and high-noise-level sites.

Unique System Aspects. Some voice systems can also be used as an intercom or to leave messages for other system users. There are several companies producing voice-based biometric identification systems.

Retina Pattern System

The system records elements of the blood-vessel pattern of the retina on the inside rear portion of the eyeball by using a camera to acquire the image.

Enrollment Procedure and Time. The subject is directed to position his or her eye an inch or two from the system aperture, keeping a pulsing green dot inside the unit centered in the aperture, and remain still. An ultra-low-intensity invisible light enables reading 320 points on a 450° circle on the retina. A PIN is entered on a unit keypad. Total enrollment time required is less than 2 minutes.

Template or File Size. The retina pattern digitized waveform is stored as a 96-byte template.

User Actions Required. If verifying, the user enters the PIN on the keypad. The system automatically acquires data when an eye is positioned in front of the aperture and centered on the pulsing green dot. Acceptance or non-acceptance is indicated in the LCD display.

System Response Time. Verification system decision time is about 1.5 seconds. Recognition decision time is less than 5 seconds with a 1,500-file data base. Average throughput time is 4 to 7 seconds.

Anticounterfeit Method. The system "requires a live, focusing eye to acquire pattern data," according to the manufacturer.

Accuracy. Sandia National Laboratories' test of the previous retina model produced no false accepts and a crossover error rate of 1.5%. The new model, System 2001, is expected to perform similarly.

Field History. Hundreds of the original binocular-type units were fielded before those models were discontinued. They were used for access control and identification in colleges, laboratories, government facilities, and jails. The new model, System 2001, is now on sale.

Problems Experienced. Because persons perspiring or having watery eyes could leave moisture on the eyecups of the previous models, some users were concerned about acquiring a disease through the transfer of body fluids. Because the previous models used a red light beam to acquire pattern data, some users were concerned about possible eye damage from the "laser." No allegations were made that any user actually became injured or diseased through the use of these systems. Because some physical conditions such as diabetes and heart attacks can cause changes in the retinal pattern, which can be detected by this system, some users were concerned that management would gain unauthorized medical information that could be used to their detriment. No cases of detrimental employee personnel actions resulting from retina system information have been reported.

Unique System Aspects. Some potential system users remain concerned about potential eye damage from using the new System 2001. They state that, even if they cannot see it, the system projects a beam inside the eye to read the retina pattern. Patents for retina-based identification are owned by EyeDentify Inc.

Iris Pattern System

The iris (i.e., the colored portion of the eye surrounding the pupil) has rich and unique patterns of striations, pits, freckles, rifts, fibers, filaments, rings, coronas, furrows, and vasculature. The images are acquired by a standard 1/3 inch CCD video camera capturing 30 images per second, similar to a camcorder.

Enrollment Procedure and Time. The subject looks at a mirror-like LCD feedback image of his or her eye, centering and focusing the image as directed. The system creates zones of analysis on the iris image, locates the features within the zones, and creates an IrisCode. The system processes three images, selects the most representative, and stores it upon approval of the operator. A PIN is added to the administrative (i.e., name, address) data file. Total enrollment time required is less than 2 minutes.

Template or File Size. The IrisCode occupies 256 bytes.

User Actions Required. The IriScan system can operate as a verifier, but is normally used in full identification mode because it performs this function faster than most systems verify. The user pushes the start button, tilts the optical unit if necessary to adjust for height, and looks at the LCD feedback image of his or her eye, centering and focusing the image. If the system is used as a verifier, a keypad or cardreader is interconnected.

System Response Time. Visual and audible annunciation of the identified or not identified decision occurs in 1 to 2 seconds, depending on the size of the data base. Total throughput time (i.e., start button to annunciation) is 2.5 to 4 seconds with experienced users.

Anticounterfeit Method. The system ensures that data input is from a live person by using naturally occurring physical factors of the eye.

Accuracy. Sandia National Laboratories' test of a preproduction model had no false accepts, low false rejects, and the system "performed extremely well." Sandia has a production system currently in testing. British Telecommunications recently tested the system in various modes and will publish a report in its engineering journal. They report 100% correct performance on over 250,000 IrisCode comparisons. "Iris recognition is a reliable and robust biometric. Every eye presented was enrolled. There were no False Accepts, and every enrolled eye was successfully recognized." Other tests have reported a crossover error rate of less than 0.5%.

Field History. Units have been fielded for access control and personnel identification at military and government organizations, banks, telecommunications firms, prisons and jails, educational institutions, manufacturing companies, and security companies.

Problems Experienced. Because this is a camera-based system, the optical unit must be positioned such that the sun does not shine directly into the aperture.

Unique System Aspects. The iris of the eye is a stable organ that remains virtually unchanged from 1 year of age throughout life. Therefore, once enrolled, a person will always be recognized, absent certain eye injuries or diseases. IriScan Inc. has the patents worldwide on iris recognition technology.

Signature Dynamics Systems

The signature pen-stroke speed, direction, and pressure are recorded by small sensors in the pen, stylus, or writing tablet.

Enrollment Procedure and Time. As directed, the subject signs a normal signature by using the pen, stylus, or sensitive tablet provided. Five signatures are required. Some systems record three sets of coordinates vs. time patterns as the template. Templates are encrypted to preclude signature reproduction. A PIN is added through using a keypad. Total enrollment time required is less than 2 minutes.

Template or File Size. Enrollment signature input is averaged into a 1,000- to 1,500-byte template.

User Actions Required. The user states identification through PIN entry on a keypad or cardreader. The signature is then written by using the instrument or tablet provided. Some systems permit the use of a stylus without paper if a copy of the signature is not required for a record.

System Response Time. Visual and audible annunciation of the verified or not verified decision is annunciated after about 1 second. The total throughput time is in the 5- to 10-second range, depending on the time required to write the signature.

Anticounterfeit Method. This feature is not applicable for signature dynamics systems.

Accuracy. Data collection is under way at pilot projects and beta test sites. Current signature dynamics biometric systems have not yet been tested by an independent agency.

Field History. Approximately 100 units are being used in about a dozen systems operated by organizations in the medical, pharmaceutical, banking, manufacturing, and government fields.

Problems Experienced. Signature dynamics systems, which previously performed well during laboratory and controlled tests, did not stand up to rigorous operational field use. Initially acceptable accuracy and reliability rates began to deteriorate after months of system field use. Although definitive failure information is not available, it is believed that the tiny, super-accurate sensors necessary to measure the minute changes in pen speed, pressure, and direction did not withstand the rough handling of the public.

It is too early to tell whether the current generation of signature systems has overcome these shortcomings.

Unique System Aspects. Among the various biometric identification systems, bankers and lawyers advocate signature dynamics because legal documents and financial drafts historically have been validated by signature. Signature dynamics identification systems are not seen as candidates for access control and other security applications. There are several companies producing signature dynamics systems.

INFORMATION SECURITY APPLICATIONS

The use of biometric identification systems in support of information security applications falls into two basic categories: controlling access to hard-copy documents and to rooms where protected information is discussed; and controlling computer use and access to electronic data.

Access Control

Controlling access to hard-copy documents and to rooms where protected information is discussed can be accomplished by using the systems and technologies previously discussed. This applies also to electronic data tape and disk repositories.

Computer and Electronic Data Protection

Controlling access to computers, the data they access and use, and the functions they can perform is becoming more vitally important with each passing day. Because of the ease of electronic access to immense amounts of information and funds, losses in these areas have rapidly surpassed losses resulting from physical theft and fraud. Positive identification of the computer operators who are accessing vital programs and data files and performing vital functions is becoming imperative as it is the only way to eliminate these losses.

The use of passwords and PINs to control computer boot-up and program and data file call-up is better than no control at all, but is subject to all the shortcomings previously discussed. Simple, easy-to-remember codes are easy for the "bad guys" to figure out. Random or obtuse codes are difficult to remember and nearly always get written down in some convenient and vulnerable place. In addition, and just as important, is that these controls are only operative at the beginning of the operation or during access to the program or files.

What is needed is a biometric system capable of providing continuing, transparent, and positive identification of the person sitting at the computer keyboard. This system would interrupt the computer boot-up until the operator is positively identified as a person authorized to use that computer or terminal. This system would also prevent the use of controlled programs or data files until the operator is positively identified as a person authorized for such access. This system would also provide continuing, periodic (e.g., every 30 seconds) positive identification of the operator as long as these controlled programs or files were in use. If this system did not verify the presence of the authorized operator during a periodic check, the screen could be cleared of data. If this system verified the presence of an unauthorized or unidentified operator, the file and program could be closed.

Obviously, the viability of such a system is dependent on software with effective firewalls and programmer access controls to prevent tampering, insertion of unauthorized identification files, or bypasses. However, such software already exists. Moreover, a biometric identification system replacing the log-on password already exists. Not yet available is a viable, independently tested, continuing, and transparent operator identification system.

System Currently Available. Identix' TouchSafe™ provides verification of enrolled persons who log on or off the computer. It comes with an IBM-compatible plug-in electronics card and a 5.4" × 2.5" × 3.6" fingerprint reader unit with cable. This unit can be expected to be even more accurate than the normal fingerprint access control systems previously described because of a more controlled operating environment and limited user list. However, it does not provide for a continuing or transparent identification. Every time that identification is required, the operator must stop activity and place a finger on the reader.

Systems Being Developed. Only a camera-based system can provide the necessary continuing and transparent identification. With a small video camera mounted on a top corner of the computer monitor, the system could be programmed to check operator identity every 30 or 60 seconds. Because the operator can be expected to look at the screen frequently, a face or iris identification system would be effective without ever interrupting the operator's work. Such a system could be set to have a 15-second observation window to acquire an acceptable image and identify the operator. If the operator did not look toward the screen or was not present during the 15-second window, the screen would be cleared with a screen saver. The system would remain in the observation mode so that when the operator returned to the keyboard or looked at the screen and was identified, the screen would be restored. If the operator at the keyboard was not authorized or was unidentified, the program and files would be saved and closed.

The first development system that seems to have potential for providing these capabilities is a face recognition system from Miros Inc. Miros is working on a line of products called TrueFace. At this time, no independent test data are available concerning the performance and accuracy of Miros' developing systems. Face recognition research has been under way for many years, but no successful systems have yet reached the marketplace. Further, the biometric identification industry has a history of promising developments that have failed to deliver acceptable results in field use. Conclusions regarding Miros' developments must wait for performance and accuracy tests by a recognized independent organization.

IriScan Inc. is in the initial stages of developing an iris recognition system capable of providing the desired computer or information access control capabilities. IriScan's demonstrated accuracy gives this development the potential to be the most accurate information user identification system.

SUMMARY

The era of fast, accurate, cost-effective biometric identification systems has arrived. Societal activities increasingly threaten individuals' and organizations' assets, information, and, sometimes, even their existence. Instant, positive personal identification is a critically important step in controlling access to and protecting society's resources. Effective tools are now available.

There are more than a dozen companies manufacturing and selling significant numbers of biometric identification systems today. Even more organizations are conducting biometric research and development and hoping to break into the market or are already selling small numbers of units. Not all biometric systems and technologies are equally effective in general, nor specifically in meeting all application requirements. Security managers are advised to be cautious and thorough in researching candidate biometric systems before making a selection. Independent test results and the reports of current users with similar applications are recommended. On-site tests are desirable. Those who are diligent and meticulous in their selection and installation of a biometric identification system will realize major increases in asset protection levels.

Chapter 2
Single Sign-On for the Enterprise

John R. Vacca

Password synchronization vs. single sign-on; shared systems; authentication; password synchronization; advantages of password synchronization; advantages of single sign-on; remote log-on; password protection; enforcing password change policy; auditing and alarms; single sign-on encryption; integration of other authentication techniques; scope of the single sign-on standard; functional objectives; user sign-on interface; user account management interface; nonfunctional objectives; and, security objectives.

PAYOFF IDEA

In many enterprises, employees typically require access to many computers in the normal course of their work. In most cases, this requires that they hold usernames and passwords for each computer they need to access and results in too many passwords for individuals to remember as they move from system to system. Consequently, stories abound of passwords being written on notes stuck to terminals and work stations. Given that users move or otherwise change jobs, the management of these user accounts is an arduous and expensive task. This chapter discusses how security enterprises such as The Open Group, Mercury Information Technology, Inc., Platinum Technology IP, Inc., and Schumann Security Software, Inc., are developing an industry-wide product standard for single sign-on (SSO). This standard will enable a user to log on once to the enterprise, instead of requiring an individual log-on to each individual system for which access is required. In this chapter you will learn how single sign-on programs are used to allow a user to authenticate himself once, and from then on be able to access additional network resources without providing additional passwords.

INTRODUCTION

As IT systems proliferate to support enterprise processes, users and system administrators are faced with an increasingly complicated interface to accomplish their job functions. Users typically have to sign on to multiple systems, necessitating an equivalent number of sign-on dialogues, each of which may involve different user names and authentication information. System administrators are faced with managing user accounts within each of the multiple systems to be accessed in a coordinated manner in order to maintain the integrity of security policy enforcement. This legacy approach to user sign-on to multiple systems is illustrated in Figure 2.1.[1]

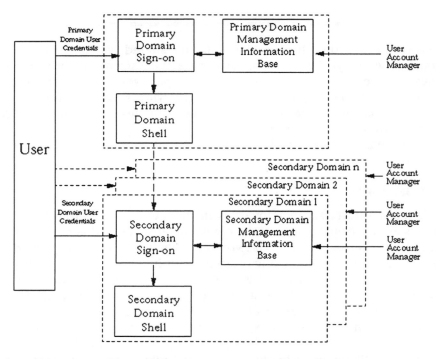

Exhibit 2.1. Legacy Approach to User Sign-On to Multiple Systems

Historically, a distributed system has been assembled from components that act as independent security domains. These components comprise individual platforms with associated operating system and applications.

The components also act as independent domains in the sense that an end user has to identify and authenticate himself or herself independently to each of the domains with which he wishes to interact. This scenario is illustrated in Figure 2.1. The end user initially interacts with a primary domain to establish a session with that primary domain. This is termed the primary domain sign-on, as shown in Figure 2.1, and requires the end user to supply a set of user credentials applicable to the primary domain, for example a username and password. The primary domain session is typically represented by an operating system session shell executed on the end user's work station within an environment representative of the end user (process attributes, environment variables, and home directory). From this primary domain session shell, the user is able to invoke the services of the other domains, such as platforms or applications.

To invoke the services of a secondary domain, an end user is required to perform a secondary domain sign-on. This requires the end user to supply a further set of user credentials applicable to that secondary domain. An end user has to conduct a separate sign-on dialogue with each secondary domain that he needs to use. The secondary domain session is typically represented by an operating system shell or an application shell, again within an environment representative of the end user. From the management perspective, the legacy approach requires independent management of each domain and the use of multiple user account management interfaces. Considerations of both usability and security give rise to a need to coordinate and, where possible, integrate user sign-on functions and user account management functions for the multitude of different domains now found within an enterprise. A service that provides such coordination and integration can provide real cost benefits to an enterprise through:

- Improved security through the enhanced ability of system administrators to maintain the integrity of user account configuration, including the ability to inhibit or remove an individual user's access to all system resources in a coordinated and consistent manner.
- Improved security through the reduced need for a user to handle and remember multiple sets of authentication information.
- Reduced time taken, and improved response, by system administrators in adding and removing users to the system or modifying their access rights.
- Reduced time taken by users in sign-on operations to individual domains, including reducing the possibility of such sign-on operations failing.[1]

Such a service has been termed single sign-on after the end-user perception of the impact of this service. However, both the end-user and management aspects of the service are equally important. This approach is illustrated in Figure 2.2.[1] In the single sign-on approach, the system is required to collect from the user, as part of the primary sign-on, all the identification and user credential information necessary to support the authentication of the user to each of the secondary domains the user may potentially need to interact with. The information supplied by the user is

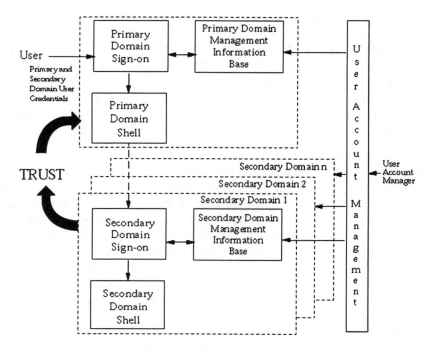

Exhibit 2.2. Single User Sign-On to Multiple Services

then used by single sign-on services within the primary domain to support the authentication of the end user to each of the secondary domains with which the user actually requests to interact. The information supplied by the end user as part of the primary domain sign-on procedure may be used in support of secondary domain sign-on in several ways:

- Directly, the information supplied by the user is passed to a secondary domain as part of a secondary sign-on.
- Immediately, to establish a session with a secondary domain as part of the initial session establishment. This implies that application clients are automatically invoked and communications established at the time of the primary sign-on operation.
- Indirectly, the information supplied by the user is used to retrieve other user identification and credential information stored within a single sign-on management information base. The retrieved information is then used as the basis for a secondary domain sign-on operation.
- Temporarily, stored or cached and used at the time a request for the secondary domain services is made by the end user.[1]

From a management perspective the single sign-on model provides a single user account management interface through which all the component domains may be managed in a coordinated and synchronized manner. Two significant security aspects or approaches to single sign-on systems are:

- The authentication credentials have to be protected when transferred between the primary and secondary domains against threats arising from interception or eavesdropping leading to possible masquerade attacks.
- The secondary domains have to trust the primary domain to: correctly assert the identity and authentication credentials of the end user and protect the authentication credentials used to verify the end user's identity to the secondary domain from unauthorized use.[1]

With that in mind, let's discuss how security enterprises like The Open Group, Mercury Information Technology, Inc., Platinum Technology IP, Inc., MEMCO Software, and Schumann Security Software, Inc., are developing industry-wide product standards and new technologies for single sign-on (SSO). I'll start with The Open Group.

SCOPE OF THE SINGLE SIGN-ON STANDARD

The Open Group defines the scope of the single sign-on standard (SSOS) as services in support of the development of applications to provide a common, single end-user sign-on interface for an enterprise. It is further defined as services in support of the development of applications for the coordinated management of multiple-user account management information bases maintained by an enterprise.

Functional Objectives: User Sign-On Interface

The following functional objectives have been defined for the SSOS in support of a user sign-on interface. For example, change of user-controlled authentication information shall be supported. This is interpreted as initially being restricted to change of user password, although capability for future extension shall not be precluded.

Furthermore, provision of a service to enable a caller to notify the SSOS implementation of a change of user-controlled authentication information by an application other than the SSOS implementation is an optional requirement and may be supported. Also, SSOS shall not predefine the timing of secondary sign-on operations.

In addition, support for the initiation of cleanup services on session termination, or sign-off, shall be supported. Also, support shall be provided for a caller to establish a default user profile. User selection from a set of available user profiles is not required to be supported but shall not be precluded as a future extension. Finally, the interface shall be independent of the type of authentication of information handled.*

User Account Management Interface

The following functional objectives have been defined for the SSOS in support of a user account management interface are, for instance, that the creation, deletion, and modification of user accounts shall be supported. Also, the setting of attributes for individual user accounts shall be supported. The attributes to be supported will include, as a minimum, those necessary to support the SSOS.

Nonfunctional Objectives

The nonfunctional objectives of the SSOS are, for example, that the SSOS shall be authentication-technology independent. The interface shall not prescribe the use of a specific authentication technology, nor preclude the use of any appropriate authentication technology.**

SSOS shall also be independent of platform or operating system. Also, SSOS shall not preclude the integration of common desktops or common services, including mainframes. Finally, there is no expectation that such desktops or servers will be capable of integration within SSOS without modification.

Security Objectives

There are many security objectives to be met by an implementation of SSOS. These objectives are:

- An SSOS implementation shall audit all security-relevant events that occur within the context of the SSOS.
- An SSOS implementation shall protect all security-relevant information supplied to or generated by the SSOS implementation such that other services may adequately trust the integrity and origin of all security information provided to them as part of a secondary sign-on operation.

* This means that SSOS shall not require that all sign-on operations are performed at the same time as the primary sign-on operation. This would result in the creation of user sessions with all possible services even though those services may not actually be required by the user.
** Some authentication technology, for example, those based upon challenge–response mechanisms of which a user-held device is a component, may not be appropriate for use as part of secondary sign-on functions.

- SSOS shall not adversely affect the resilience of the system within which it is deployed.
- SSOS shall not adversely affect the availability of any individual system service.
- SSOS shall not provide access by principals to user account information to which they would not be permitted access within the controlling security domain for that information.
- The SSOS shall provide protection to security-relevant information when exchanged between its own constituent components and between those components and other services.[1]

Out of Scope

Finally, there are also many aspects that are not considered to be within the current scope of SSOS. These aspects are:

- Configuration and management of alternative sets of user profiles.
- Graphical and command line user interfaces to SSOS-based services. These are the province of applications written to utilize the SSOS.
- Maintenance of the integrity of the single sign-on user account information base with underlying individual service user account information bases when the latter are modified by means other than SSOS-provided functionality.
- Selection of alternative user profiles on user sign-on.
- Support for single sign-on across enterprise system boundaries.
- User-initiated change of nonuser configured authentication information, for example, magnetic badges, smart cards, etc.[1]

Now, let's very briefly discuss how Mercury Information Technology, Inc., is developing an industry-wide product standard and technology for single sign-on (SSO).[2] This part of the chapter briefly defines two authentication-related technologies developed by Mercury Information Technology, Inc.: password synchronization and their individual strengths and weaknesses. Before we go there, let's look at shared systems first.

SHARED SYSTEMS

Mercury Information Technology, Inc., defines enterprise networks as including servers that provide the following services to multiple users:

- Database management
- Electronic messaging
- File sharing
- Printer sharing
- Remove access
- Run centralized applications[2]

Most of these systems require users to identify themselves before servicing their requests.

Authentication

Shared systems on a network are either open to all users or restricted to access by authorized users only. When systems are restricted to authorized users only, they normally determine whether a given user may access a specific function based on that user's identity.

For access control based on user identity to be effective, users must be identified reliably. Authentication is the process of identifying users in a manner that makes it difficult for one user to impersonate another.

A number of technologies are available for user authentication. The most popular authentication systems are:

- Biometric devices (fingerprints, retina scans, head scans, etc.)
- Secret passwords
- Smart cards[2]

Password Synchronization

Most shared systems use passwords to authenticate users. In a network where users access multiple shared resources, they must remember a password for every system they access. Users frequently forget their passwords and must ask the enterprise help desk to reset them. Also, password synchronization software is used to ensure that each of a user's multiple passwords is set to the same value, so that users need not remember multiple passwords for multiple systems.

Single Sign-On

Single sign-on programs are used to allow a user to authenticate himself once, and from then on be able to access additional network resources without providing additional passwords. In practice, most single sign-on systems operate as follows:

First of all, the user provides a user-ID and password to a primary login program, which authenticates the user against a *master* system. Once authenticated, the user may request access to additional systems. When he or she does so, the single sign-on system retrieves the user's password for the new system, and starts a session with the new system using that password.

ADVANTAGES OF PASSWORD SYNCHRONIZATION

Password synchronization is characterized by the following advantages:

- Improved security
- Less intrusive
- Lower cost

Improved Security

A user must still enter his password to access a shared system. If a work station is left unattended, only the systems currently being accessed are vulnerable to access by someone who can reach the work station. By implementing a single point from which passwords are changed, it is possible to apply stringent requirements for what constitutes a valid password, and so make passwords much harder to guess.

Less Intrusive

Password synchronization does not require any new servers on the network. Furthermore, password synchronization can be implemented without installing any new software on existing servers.

Lower Cost

Finally, password synchronization can be implemented for about one tenth the cost of single sign-on technology. With that in mind, how does SSO measure up to password synchronization? Let's take a very brief look.

ADVANTAGES OF SINGLE SIGN-ON

SSO is characterized by the advantages of convenience and centralized administration. Let's take a brief look at those advantages:

Convenience

Using single sign-on, users only have to type their password once when they first log in. Users can also access additional systems by just pressing a button, and without entering their ID and password again.

Centralized Administration

Some single sign-on systems are built around a unified server administration system. These systems allow a single administrator to add and delete accounts across the entire network from one user interface.

Now, let's briefly discuss how Platinum Technology IP, Inc., is developing an industry-wide product standard and technology for single sign-on.[3] More important, let's take a look at Platinum Technology IP, Inc.'s SSO solution: ProVision AutoSecure Single Sign on (SSO) remote log on and password protection; as well as other authentication techniques and how to use an enterprise SSO.

AN SSO ENTERPRISE SOLUTION

The benefits of the client/server revolution have brought with them a new generation of challenges and security risks. The Platinum SSO solution (like many of the SSO solutions just discussed) addresses the shift toward distributed computing that has dispersed information traditionally stored in a central mainframe into a network of interconnecting LANs—with multivendor server, many different applications and services, complex login routines, and a multitude of passwords. Platinum's ProVision AutoSecure Single Sign On (SSO) further addresses these problems by:

- Enforcing password security policy by managing the password change process and ensuring that content rules are maintained.
- Increasing user productivity by allowing users to access all their authorized applications and services with a single user name and password — without having to log into each individually.
- Protecting information by authenticating all users and authorizing which applications and services they can use.
- Reducing administrator and help desk workloads by cutting the number of passwords a user needs — and by logging users transparently into the applications and services they need to use.
- Reducing the system administrator's workload by providing facilities that allow an unskilled administrator to set up and delete user accounts on different platforms from a single point.[3]

Using an Enterprise SSO

With an enterprise SSO, users sign on to the SSO client using their SSO user name, SSO password, and (optionally) a role. The SSO client sends the information (in encrypted form) to that user's security server, where it is validated against defined security policies. Successful authentication means that the user's credentials are acceptable and that the user is allowed that role from that particular work station.

Following this, the user is presented with a desktop containing all the applications they are authorized to use in that role. Desktops are constructed in user-friendly GUI or text format, depending on the type of terminal or work station being used.

Users can then select an application or service from the desktop, and they are transparently logged into that application or service by the Service Access Procedures (SAPs). No further authentication is needed. Users can also, optionally, be logged onto network servers.

If authentication fails, the enterprise SSO prevents the user from gaining access to the enterprise's applications and services. The defined security policy determines whether the user is given an explanation for the failure or not. After a predetermined number of consecutive failed log-on attempts by the user, the work station can be disabled pending specific intervention by the local administrator.

Remote Log On

An enterprise SSO offers its entire set of capabilities to mobile users, who can log on to the network via a modem from remote locations. They should be presented with their own desktops, enabling them to use their usual set of applications.

Password Protection

To protect its passwords from interception and misuse, an enterprise SSO offers a range of controls and encryption techniques. Where security requirements are less stringent, the requirement for password authentication can be overridden by defining roles whose users can simply log on through a user name.

Enforcing Password Change Policy

An enterprise SSO provides options as to how password changes are handled. The system can be set up to allow users to select the passwords to their applications and services. An enterprise SSO can also be used to generate random passwords on their behalf. In the latter case, the user never knows the passwords to the individual applications and services. This can provide increased security, since the only way a user can gain access is via the enterprise SSO system, preventing backdoor access.

Facilities are also available to accommodate an enterprise that wants all the passwords for a user's applications and services to be the same. This approach, however, is not recommended, because it can undermine security by providing a means of access that circumvents the enterprise SSO systems and the associated auditing and alert processes.

Auditing and alarms

An enterprise SSO's audit capability keeps track of all the actions carried out by users. Auditing capabilities ensure that security policies are enforced and that users are accountable for their activities. For example, the security policy may specify a maximum of three password attempts to log on to the network. When an enterprise SSO senses the fourth attempt, it will take whatever action has been stipulated. It could, for example, close the work station down or raise an alert. An enterprise SSO can even raise a *silent* alert that allows the attacker to continue the break-in attempt unaware that he has been detected. This allows time to trace the offender.

The record of events can be analyzed to identify where breaches of security and policy may have occurred. For events where immediate attention is required, the audit facility can trigger alarms that can be directed to any number of places, including administrators' work stations, a pager or e-mail system, or an event management system. Examples of information that can be audited include:

- End of user session
- Failed log-on attempts
- Inactivity periods for work stations
- Lock-outs of users and terminals
- Services and applications used
- Start of a user session and role adopted by the user
- System start-up and close-down
- Use of administration utilities[3]

A logged event can also specify the user, role, and work station or terminal used, as well as the date, time, and session. Audit administrators have considerable control over configuration of alarm capabilities and can set parameters on some 600 events to trigger the following actions:

- Enter the event in an audit file
- Ignore the event
- Raise an alert[3]

In addition to the deterrent of audit facilities the audit log can be used to access damage and recover data caused by breeches of security. It can also provide insight into the method of attack used, which can form the basis of effective future defense.

Furthermore, the security administration tools provide methods to access the audit file via various filters. In addition, the audit data can be moved into popular databases where *ad hoc* inquiries and various reports can be run.

SSO Encryption

All enterprise SSO components include encryption facilities that the system uses to enhance security. Techniques used include one-way encryption algorithms for password protection and two-way algorithms for functions such as password access control (PAC) and script-variable protection.

Integration of Other Authentication Techniques

An enterprise SSO itself offers standard authentication via password. It can also support additional or alternative authentication techniques, such as magnetic stripe cards and smart tokens (Security Dynamics SecurID card).[4] If required, these may be associated with specific roles. In addition to an enterprise SSO's password authentication method, it also provides APIs to other authentication facilities to enable an enterprise to integrate its own choice of authentication method.

Now, let's briefly discuss other single sign-on solutions. In particular, let's look at MEMCO Software's Proxima SSO.[5]

OTHER SSO SOLUTIONS

Finally, with the proliferation of client/server technologies over the past years, information has gradually migrated from centralized computers to heterogeneous, distributed environments. This trend toward open and diverse systems has impacted today's enterprises by requiring that end users remember a number of IDs and passwords to gain access to various computing platforms and applications. The necessity for multiple passwords, while designed to increase security, has instead compromised enterprise productivity and security, as well as increased the costs of managing a diverse computing environment.

How can multiple passwords compromise both productivity and security?[6]* The amount of time it takes for a user to recall and enter multiple passwords to access various platforms and applications can translate to tens of thousands of dollars a year. Users who desire to be more *efficient* by writing down their numerous passwords for swift recall can create a significant security breach. Add to both these scenarios the fact that today's help desk administrators routinely claim that up to 50% of their time is spent resetting forgotten passwords. It all translates into a waste of time and productivity in a system that is far less secure than anyone can imagine.

MEMCO's Proxima SSO is one of many SSOs described in this chapter that also addresses these concerns. As previously discussed, SSO reduces the frustration of end users by enabling them to easily access multiple platforms and applications through use of a single password. It eases the burden of password administration for the help desk or system administrators by consolidating user account administration. It also offers enterprises the assurance that access across distributed computing environments remains secure.

* The Schumann answer for the dilemma of multiple sign-ons is Secure Single Sign-On (SAM/SSSO). This fully scalable solution uses a tamper-proof smart card (other tokens are possible)) and a single sign-on PIN to access an environment from client/server to legacy. All logins and passwords are encrypted into the card's integrated circuit. Only possession of the card and knowledge of the single sign-on PIN will allow it function. The smart card operates by presenting all logins and passwords immediately and automatically to applications in use, creating large gains in productivity and security.

Choosing the Right Single Sign-On Solution

The truth is, there aren't many single sign-on solutions designed to fully adapt to the number of diverse operating systems and authentication methods available today. SSOs should be capable of handling a diverse security infrastructure, and provide a seamless interface across platforms and applications to allow administrators to learn one system rather than many. The following are key components that should be part of any well-designed single sign-on solution:

- Open architecture
- Open authentication
- Support for multiple login methods, including one-time passwords
- Credentials forwarding
- Support for multiple servers, clients, and hosts
- Seamless user and administrative interface
- Central administration

Open Architecture

An SSO solution designed for today and tomorrow is based on open standards. Open architecture ensures that the solution can be easily extended as an enterprise's security policy evolves. As standards change, an open architecture adapts with them.

Open Authentication

Support for a diverse range of authentication methods is critical. Popular platforms must be supported, such as NetWare, UNIX, and Windows NT. Broker-based authentication, such as digital certificates, must be supported, along with hardware (smart card) and software token-based methods. And — perhaps even more critical — such support must be easy to weave into an existing security infrastructure, because many enterprises are planning to move to one or more of these systems in the near future.

Support for Multiple Login Methods

With all of the diverse systems in use today, SSO must support login methods from passwords to tokens. Due to the all-too-common use of *sniffers* to detect passwords sent in plain text over the Internet and intranet, support for one-time passwords (OTP) is an important means of providing enhanced system security.

Credentials Forwarding

In the past, SSO solutions relied on scripts to forward passwords to various and diverse applications and platforms. Today's solutions use Application Programming Interfaces (APIs) and easy-to-use Login Dialogs. A well-designed solution must allow these forwarding methods to work in parallel to suit the needs of a heterogeneous computing environment.

Support for Multiple Servers, Clients, and Hosts

Today's most popular platforms, including UNIX, Windows (3.x, 95, 98, 2000, and NT), and MVS, must be supported. Legacy systems must also be supported as well.

Seamless User and Administrative Interface

A Windows 95/NT, 98/NT, or 2000/NT *look and feel* eases the learning curve for administrators and end users. The SSO solution could maintain a consistent *look and feel* across platforms. It must appear integrated with the operating system and transparent to the end user.

Central Administration

Finally, security or system administrators must be able to manage the SSO solution from a central location. The interface, again, must be seamless with the operating system, enabling the administrator to easily learn the process and become proficient quickly and efficiently.

CONCLUSION AND SUMMARY

In today's heterogeneous computing environments, end users frequently need access to applications and network resources running on multiple platforms and systems to perform their day-to-day responsibilities. As a result, end users must use multiple sign-on routines, user-IDs, and passwords. This cumbersome management problem impedes productivity and compromises security when end users resort to writing down their passwords in an effort to keep track of them.

With that in mind, this chapter was directed toward enterprise executives, IT managers, security administrators, and others who want to know more about how different types SSOs are designed to be simple to administer in even the largest, most complex, networks. Different types of SSO tools were presented which allow effective administration of:

- Applications
- Menus
- Roles
- SAP variables
- Users
- Work stations

Most SSOs should provide a highly flexible set of rules that enable a clear definition of users' access authority, as well as the construction of roles that encompass numerous capabilities. Relationships between the different administrative functions should be vital elements in an SSO's ability to define which services can be accessed by individual users. The system should embody these relationships in the following ways:

- An application definition can refer to SAP variables (SVs).
- Any role can be restricted to a single application or initial menu.
- Applications and menus are allocated to these roles.
- Menus contain lists of applications and other menus.
- SAP variable values can be assigned to users, roles, or specific applications.
- Users are allocated roles according to their needs.

Work stations identifiable by an SSO server can be permitted or denied access by specific roles; users can only use such work stations to run roles permitted on that work station.

Also presented in this chapter was a high-level overview of SSO technology requirements to meet the diverse needs of the end user, the help desk/security administrator, and the security officer who sets overall enterprise security policy. The enterprise SSO should be able to meet these needs by increasing user productivity, reducing administrative overhead, and increasing overall security throughout the enterprise. Its flexible, open architecture should ensure that it is designed to meet the requirements of today's ever-involving computing environment.

SSOs should also be able to automate user login to applications and platforms by supplying an application *Launch Pad* that acts as a familiar desktop for users and simplifies login, reducing it to a simple *point and click* process. End users authenticate once and are presented with a customized desktop of authorized applications, which they can access quickly and efficiently. This simple process should enable an enterprise to flexibly move from password-based logins to strong authentication methods without visibly affecting the login process for the end user.

SSOs should be able to consolidate security administration by providing a centralized database of user IDs, applications dialogs, access paths, and preferred *credentials forwarding* information. An additional tier of administration enables central management of user access to applications and platforms across the enterprise.

An SSO should also be able to act as a mediator between users and applications, matching the best available security with application capabilities and requirements. Most of the SSOs discussed in this article offer a hybrid approach to support SSO for a wide range of applications and systems, from legacy applications requiring proprietary passwords to one-time passwords to encrypted tickets. Finally, their architecture should be able to meet the requirements of the most complicated computing environments by providing a secure method of single sign-on that includes:

- A flexible use of current credentials-forwarding methods and adaptability to future security standards.
- The ability for a phased implementation approach to ease the introduction of enhanced security standards across an enterprise.
- An effective and secure response that meets the SSO expectations of end users, administrators, and security officers alike.

John Vacca is an information technology consultant and internationally known author based in Pomeroy, Ohio. Since 1982, John has authored 27 books and more than 330 articles in the areas of Internet and intranet security, programming, systems development, rapid application development, multimedia, and the Internet. John was also a configuration management specialist, computer specialist, and the computer security official for NASA's space station program (Freedom) and the International Space Station Program, from 1988 until his early retirement from NASA in 1995. His most recent books include: *Internet Security Secrets* (IDG Books/Published Date: 1-96/Translations: Russian, German, Spanish and French); *VRML: Bringing Virtual Reality to the Internet* (AP Professional/Published Date: 4-96/Translations: German); *JavaScript Development: Bringing Development and Customization to Intranets and the Internet* (AP Professional/Published Date: 11-96/Translations: German); *Official Netscape LiveWire Pro Book* (Ventana/Published Date: 3-97); *Intranet Security* (Charles River Media/Published Date: 8-97/Translations: Russian); *VRML Clearly Explained — 2nd Edition* (AP Professional/Published date 1-17-97); *The Cabling Handbook*, (Prentice Hall/Publication date: 9-98); and *MCSE Implementing and Supporting Microsoft Systems Management Server 2.0*, (Prentice Hall/Publication date: 2-99). His most recent articles from Auerbach Publications include: "Data Center Security: Useful Intranet Security Methods And Tools," (Enterprise Operations Management: 46-40-23). John can be reached on the Internet at jvacca@hti.net.

References

1. The Open Group, 1010 El Camino Real, Suite 380, Menlo Park CA 94025-4345, 1999.
2. M-Tech Mercury Information Technology, Inc., Suite 750, 910 7th Avenue S.W., Calgary, Alberta, T2P 3N8, Canada, 1999.
3. Platinum Technology IP, Inc., 1815 South Meyers Road, Oakbrook Terrace, IL 60181-5421, USA, 1999.
4. Security Dynamics Technologies, Inc., 20 Crosby Drive, Bedford, MA 01730, 1999.
5. MEMCO Software, 12 East 49th Street, 32nd Floor, New York, NY 10017, 1999.
6. Schumann Security Software, Inc., 8101 Sandy Spring Road, Laurel, MD 20707, 1999.

Domain 2
Telecommunications and Network Security

This domain is by far the largest since the computing environment has extended beyond the glass-housed mainframe to the network and networked networks. Being able to secure the network requires a good understanding of the various communications protocols, their vulnerabilities and the mechanisms that can be deployed to improve network controls. In this domain, we report on the popular protocols and network services, illustrate their security properties, and make recommendations for their use or the implementation of mitigating controls that offset their weaknesses.

If the network is ubiquitous, then the controls must be as well. However, implementing security services in a layered communications architecture is a complicated endeavor and raises significant issues. Regardless, organizations are compelled to extend their networks by connecting to trading partners, suppliers, customers, and the public at large. The extended networked environment forces the need for additional security safeguards that were likely not needed in the glass house. Many of these safeguards are addressed in the chapters of this domain, where the application of controls at the network layer, transport layer, and application layer are capably described.

If a business is not on the Internet today, it is perceived to be behind the eight ball. The explosion of the Internet has all but demanded that a business entity desiring longevity utilize the Internet to perform electronic commerce. Thankfully, Internet security offerings are abundant. The market is rich with encryption, firewalls, and Web-enabled application development products that provide for user identification, authentication, and access controls. This domain details the countermeasures that are available for deployment in the Web world, the Internet, the intranet, and the extranet.

Domain 2.1
Network Security

Chapter 3
Secured Connections to External Networks

Steven F. Blanding

A private network that carries sensitive data between local computers requires proper security measures to protect the privacy and integrity of the traffic. When such a network is connected to other networks, or when telephone access is allowed into that network, the remote terminals, phone lines, and other connections become extensions of that private network and must be secured accordingly. In addition, the private network must be secured from outside attacks that could cause loss of information, breakdowns in network integrity, or breaches in security.

Many organizations have connected or want to connect their private local area networks (LANs) to the Internet so that their users can have convenient access to Internet services. Since the Internet as a whole is not trustworthy, their private systems are vulnerable to misuse and attack. Firewalls are typically used as a safeguard to control access between a trusted network and a less trusted network. A firewall is not a single component; it is a strategy for protecting an organization's resources from the Internet. A firewall serves as the gatekeeper between the untrusted Internet and the more trusted internal networks. Some organizations are also in the process of connecting their private networks to other organizations' private networks. Firewall security capabilities should also be used to provide protection for these types of connections as well.

This chapter identifies areas of security that should be considered with connections to external networks. Security policies must be developed for user identification and authorization, software import controls, encryption, and system architecture, which include the use of Internet firewall security capabilities. These sections discuss security policy statements that address connections to external networks including the Internet. Each section contains multiple sample policies for use at the different risk profiles. Some areas provide multiple examples at the same risk level to show the different presentation methods that might be used to get the message across.

This first section discusses the risks and assumptions that should be acknowledged before a security analysis can be performed.

RISKS AND ASSUMPTIONS

An understanding of the risks and assumptions is required before defining security policies for external connections. It is beyond the scope of this chapter to quantify the probability of the risks; however the risks should cover a broad, comprehensive area. The following are the risks and assumptions.

- The data being protected, while not classified, is highly sensitive and would do damage to the organization and its mission if disclosed or captured.
- The integrity of the internal network directly affects the ability of the organization to accomplish its mission.
- The internal network is physically secure; the people using the internal network are trustworthy.
- PCs on the internal network are considered to be unsecured. Reliance is placed on the physical security of the location to protect them.
- Whenever possible, employees who are connected from remote sites should be treated as members of the internal network and have access to as many services as possible without compromising internal security.
- The Internet is assumed to be unsecured; the people using the Internet are assumed to be untrustworthy.
- Employees are targets for spying; information they carry or communicate is vulnerable to capture.
- Passwords transmitted over outside connections are vulnerable to capture.
- Any data transmitted over outside connections are vulnerable to capture.
- There is no control over e-mail once it leaves the internal network; e-mail can be read, tampered with, and spoofed.
- Any direct connection between a PC on the internal network and one on the outside can possibly be compromised and used for intrusion.
- Software bugs exist and may provide intrusion points from the outside into the internal network.
- Password protection on PCs directly reachable from the outside can be compromised and used for intrusion.
- Security through obscurity is counter-productive. Easy-to-understand measures are more likely to be sound, and are easier to administer.

SECURITY POLICIES

Security policies fall into two broad categories: technical policies to be carried out by hardware or software, and administrative policy to be carried out by people using and managing the system. The final section of this chapter discusses Internet firewall security policies in more detail.

Identification and Authentication

Identification and authentication are the processes of recognizing and verifying valid users or processes. Identification and authentication information is generally then used to determine what system resources a user or process will be allowed to access. The determination of who can access what should coincide with a data categorization effort.

The assumption is that there is connectivity to internal systems from external networks or the Internet. If there is no connectivity, there is no need for identification and authentication controls. Many organizations separate Internet-accessible systems from internal systems through the use of firewalls and routers.

Authentication over the Internet presents several problems. It is relatively easy to capture identification and authentication data (or any data) and replay it in order to impersonate a user. As with other remote identification and authorization controls, and often with internal authorization systems, there can be a high level of user dissatisfaction and uncertainty, which can make this data obtainable via social engineering. Having additional authorization controls for use of the Internet may also contribute to authorization data proliferation, which is difficult for users to manage. Another problem is the ability to hijack a user session after the identification and authorization have been performed.

There are three major types of authentication available: static, robust, and continuous. Static authentication includes passwords and other techniques that can be compromised through replay attacks. They are often called reusable passwords. Robust authentication involves the use of cryptography or other techniques to create one-time passwords that are used to create sessions. These can be compromised by session hijacking. Continuous authentication prevents session hijacking.

Static Authentication. Static authentication only provides protection against attacks in which an impostor cannot see, insert or alter the information passed between the claimant and the verifier during an authentication exchange and subsequent session. In these cases, an impostor can only attempt to assume a claimant's identity by initiating an access control session as any valid user might do and trying to guess a legitimate user's authentication data. Traditional password schemes provide this level of

51

protection, and the strength of the authentication process is highly depen-dent on the difficulty of guessing password values and how well they are protected.

Robust Authentication. This class of authentication mechanism relies on dynamic authentication data that changes with each authenticated session between a claimant and verifier. An impostor who can see information passed between the claimant and verifier may attempt to record this infor-mation, initiate a separate access control session with the verifier, and replay the recorded authentication data in an attempt to assume the claim-ant's identity. This type of authentication protects against such attacks, because authentication data recorded during a previous session will not be valid for any subsequent sessions.

However, robust authentication does not provide protection against active attacks in which the impostor is able to alter the content or flow of information between the claimant and verifier after they have established a legitimate session. Since the verifier binds the claimant's identity to the logical communications channel for the duration of the session, the verifier believes that the claimant is the source of all data received through this channel.

Traditional fixed passwords would fail to provide robust authentication because the password of a valid user could be viewed and used to assume that user's identity later. However, one-time passwords and digital signa-tures can provide this level of protection.

Continuous Authentication. This type of authentication provides protec-tion against impostors who can see, alter, and insert information passed between the claimant and verifier even after the claimant/verifier authenti-cation is complete. These are typically referred to as active attacks, since they assume that the impostor can actively influence the connection between claimant and verifier. One way to provide this form of authentica-tion is to apply a digital signature algorithm to every bit of data that is sent from the claimant to the verifier. There are other combinations of cryptog-raphy that can provide this form of authentication, but current strategies rely on applying some type of cryptography to every bit of data sent. Oth-erwise, any unprotected bit would be suspect.

Applying Identification and Authorization Policies. Although passwords are easily compromised, an organization may find that a threat is not likely, would be fairly easy to recover from, or would not affect critical systems (which may have separate protection mechanisms). In low-risk connec-tions, only static authentication may be required for access to corporate systems from external networks or the Internet.

In medium-risk connections, Internet access to information and processing (low impact if modified, unavailable, or disclosed) would require a password, and access to all other resources would require robust authentication. Telnet access to corporate resources from the Internet would also require the use of robust authentication.

Internet access to all systems behind the firewall would require robust authentication. Access to information and processing (high impact if modified, unavailable, or disclosed) would require continuous authentication.

PASSWORD MANAGEMENT POLICIES

The following are general password policies applicable for Internet use. These are considered to be the minimum standards for security control.

- Passwords and user log-on IDs will be unique to each authorized user.
- Passwords will consist of a minimum of 6 alphanumeric characters (no common names or phrases). There should be computer-controlled lists of proscribed password rules and periodic testing (e.g., letter and number sequences, character repetition, initials, common words, and standard names) to identify any password weaknesses.
- Passwords will be kept private i.e., not shared, coded into programs, or written down.
- Passwords will be changed every 90 days (or less). Most operating systems can enforce password change with an automatic expiration and prevent repeated or reused passwords.
- User accounts will be frozen after 3 failed log-on attempts. All erroneous password entries will be recorded in an audit log for later inspection and action, as necessary.
- Sessions will be suspended after 15 minutes (or other specified period) of inactivity and require the password to be reentered.
- Successful log-ons should display the date and time of the last log-on and log-off.
- Log-on IDs and passwords should be suspended after a specified period of non-use.
- For high-risk systems, after excessive violations, the system should generate an alarm and be able to simulate a continuing session (with dummy data, etc.) for the failed user (to keep this user connected while personnel attempt to investigate the incoming connection).

Robust Authentication Policy. The decision to use robust authentication requires an understanding of the risks, the security gained, and the cost of user acceptance and administration. User acceptance will be dramatically improved if users are appropriately trained in robust authentication and how it is used.

There are many technologies available that provide robust authentication including dynamic password generators, cryptography-based challenge/ response tokens and software, and digital signatures and certificates. If digital signatures and certificates are used, another policy area is opened up: the security requirements for the certificates.

Users of robust authentication must receive training prior to use of the authentication mechanism. Employees are responsible for safe handling and storage of all company authentication devices. Authentication tokens should not be stored with a computer that will be used to access corporate systems. If an authentication device is lost or stolen, the loss must be immediately reported to security so that the device can be disabled.

Digital Signatures and Certificates. If identification and authorization makes use of digital signatures, then certificates are required. They can be issued by the organization or by a trusted third party. Commercial public key infrastructures (PKI) are emerging within the Internet community. Users can obtain certificates with various levels of assurance. For example, level 1 certificates verify electronic mail addresses. This is done through the use of a personal information number that a user would supply when asked to register. This level of certificate may also provide a name as well as an electronic mail address; however, it may or may not be a genuine name (i.e., it could be an alias). Level 2 certificates verify a user's name, address, social security number, and other information against a credit bureau database. Level 3 certificates are available to companies. This level of certificate provides photo identification (e.g., for their employees) to accompany the other items of information provided by a Level 2 certificate.

Once obtained, digital certificate information may be loaded into an electronic mail application or a web browser application to be activated and provided whenever a web site or another user requests it for the purposes of verifying the identity of the person with whom they are communicating. Trusted certificate authorities are required to administer such systems with strict controls, otherwise fraudulent certificates could easily be issued.

Many of the latest web servers and web browsers incorporate the use of digital certificates. Secure Socket Layer (SSL) is the technology used in most Web-based applications. SSL version 2.0 supports strong authentication of the Web server, while SSL 3.0 adds client-side authentication. Once both sides are authenticated, the session is encrypted, providing protection against both eavesdropping and session hijacking. The digital certificates used are based on the X.509 standard and describe who issued the certificate, the validity period, and other information.

Oddly enough, passwords still play an important role even when using digital certificates. Since digital certificates are stored on a computer, they can only be used to authenticate the computer, rather than the user, unless the user provides some other form of authentication to the computer. Passwords or "passphrases" are generally used; smart cards and other hardware tokens will be used in the future.

Any company's systems making limited distribution data available over the Internet should use digital certificates to validate the identity of both the user and the server. Only Company-approved certificate authorities should issue certificates. Certificates at the user end should be used in conjunction with standard technologies such as Secure Sockets Layer to provide continuous authentication to eliminate the risk of session hijacking. Access to digital certificates stored on personal computers should be protected by passwords or passphrases. All policies for password management must be followed and enforced.

SOFTWARE IMPORT CONTROL

Data on computers is rarely static. Mail arrives and is read. New applications are loaded from floppy, CD-ROM, or across a network. Web-based interactive software downloads executables that run on a computer. Each modification runs the risk of introducing viruses, damaging the configuration of the computer, or violating software-licensing agreements. Organizations need to protect themselves with different levels of control depending on the vulnerability to these risks. Software Import Control provides an organization with several different security challenges:

- Virus and Trojan Horse Prevention, Detection, and Removal
- Controlling Interactive Software (Java, ActiveX)
- Software Licensing

Each challenge can be categorized according to the following criteria:

- Control — who initiates the activity, and how easily can it be determined that software has been imported
- Threat type — executable program, macro, applet, violation of licensing agreement
- Cleansing Action — scanning, refusal of service, control of permissions, auditing, deletion

When importing software onto a computer, one runs the risk of getting additional or different functionality than one bargained for. The importation may occur as a direct action, or as a hidden side effect, which is not readily visible. Examples of direct action are:

- File Transfer — utilizing FTP to transfer a file to a computer
- Reading e-mail — causing a message which has been transferred to a computer to be read, or using a tool (e.g., Microsoft Word) to read an attachment
- Downloading software from a floppy disk or over the network can spawn indirect action. Some examples include (1) reading a Web page which downloads a Java applet to your computer and (2) executing an application such as Microsoft Word and opening a file infected with a Word Macro Virus.

Virus Prevention, Detection, and Removal. A virus is a self-replicating program spread from executables, boot records, and macros. Executable viruses modify a program to do something other than the original intent. After replicating itself into other programs, the virus may do little more than print an annoying message, or it could do something as damaging as deleting all of the data on a disk. There are different levels of sophistication in how hard a virus may be to detect.

The most common "carrier" of viruses has been the floppy disk, since "sneaker net" was the most common means of transferring software between computers. As telephone-based bulletin boards became popular, viruses travelled more frequently via modem. The Internet provides yet another channel for virus infections, one that can often bypass traditional virus controls.

For organizations that allow downloading of software over the Internet (which can be via Internet e-mail attachments) virus scanning at the firewall can be an appropriate choice — but it does not eliminate the need for client and server based virus scanning, as well. For several years to come, viruses imported on floppy disks or infected vendor media will continue to be a major threat.

Simple viruses can be easily recognized by scanning for a signature of byte strings near the entry point of a program, once the virus has been identified. Polymorphic viruses modify themselves as they propagate. Therefore, they have no signature and can only be found (safely) by executing the program in a virtual processor environment. Boot record viruses modify the boot record such that the virus is executed when the system is booted.

Applications that support macros are at risk for macro viruses. Macro viruses are commands that are embedded in data. Vendor applications, such as Microsoft Word, Microsoft Excel, or printing standards such as Postscript are common targets. When the application opens the data file the infected macro virus is instantiated.

The security service policy for viruses has three aspects:

- Prevention — policies which prevent the introduction of viruses into a computing environment,
- Detection — determination that an executable, boot record, or data file is contaminated with a virus, and
- Removal — deletion of the virus from the infected computing system may require reinstallation of the operating system from the ground up, deleting files, or deleting the virus from an infected file.

There are various factors that are important in determining the level of security concern for virus infection of a computer. Viruses are most prevalent on DOS, Windows (3.x, 95), and NT operating systems. However some UNIX viruses have been identified.

The frequency that new applications or files are loaded on to the computer is proportional to the susceptibility of that computer to viruses. Configuration changes resulting from exposure to the Internet, exposure to mail, or receipt of files from external sources are more at risk for contamination.

The greater the value of the computer or data on the computer, the greater the concern should be for ensuring that virus policy as well as implementation procedures are in place. The cost of removal of the virus from the computing environment must be considered within your organization as well as from customers you may have infected. Cost may not always be identified as monetary; company reputation and other considerations are just as important.

It is important to note that viruses are normally introduced into a system by a voluntary act of a user (e.g., installation of an application, executing a file, etc.). Prevention policies can therefore focus on limiting the introduction of potentially infected software and files to a system. In a high-risk environment, virus-scanning efforts should be focused on when new software or files are introduced to maximize protection.

Controlling Interactive Software. A programming environment evolving as a result of Internet technology is Interactive Software, as exemplified by Java and ActiveX. In an Interactive Software environment, a user accesses a server across a network. The server downloads an application (applet) onto the user's computer that is then executed. There have been various claims that when utilizing languages such as Java, it is impossible to introduce a virus because of restrictions within the scripting language for file system access and process control. However, security risks using Java and ActiveX have been documented.

Therefore, there are several assumptions of trust that a user must make before employing this technology:

- The server can be trusted to download trustworthy applets;
- The applet will execute in a limited environment restricting disk reads and writes to functions which do not have security;
- The applet can be scanned to determine if it is safe; and
- Scripts are interpreted, not precompiled.

FIREWALL POLICY

Firewalls are critical to the success of secured connections to external networks as well as the Internet. The main function of a firewall is to centralize access control. If outsiders or remote users can access the internal networks without going through the firewall, its effectiveness is diluted. For example, if a traveling manager has a modem connected to his office PC that he or she can dial into while traveling, and that PC is also on the protected internal network, an attacker who can dial into that PC has circumvented the controls imposed by the firewall. If a user has a dial-up Internet account with a commercial Internet Service Provider (ISP), and sometimes connects to the Internet from his office PC via modem, he is opening an unsecured connection to the Internet that circumvents the firewall.

Firewalls can also be used to secure segments of an organization's Intranet, but this document will concentrate on the Internet aspects of firewall policy.

Firewalls provide several types of protection.

- They can block unwanted traffic.
- They can direct incoming traffic to more trustworthy internal systems.
- They hide vulnerable systems, which can't easily be secured from the Internet.
- They can log traffic to and from the private network.
- They can hide information like system names, network topology, network device types, and internal user IDs from the Internet.
- They can provide more robust authentication than standard applications might be able to do.

Each of these functions is described in more detail below.

As with any safeguard, there are tradeoffs between convenience and security. Transparency is the visibility of the firewall to both inside users and outsiders going through a firewall. A firewall is transparent to users if they do not notice or stop at the firewall in order to access a network. Firewalls are typically configured to be transparent to internal network users (while going outside the firewall); on the other hand, firewalls are configured to be non-transparent for outside network coming through the firewall. This generally provides the highest level of security without placing an undue burden on internal users.

Firewall Authentication

Router-based firewalls don't provide user authentication. Host-based firewalls can provide various kinds of authentication. *Username/password authentication* is the least secure, because the information can be sniffed or shoulder-surfed. *One-time passwords* use software or hardware tokens and generate a new password for each session. This means that old passwords cannot be reused if they are sniffed or otherwise borrowed or stolen. Finally, *Digital Certificates* use a certificate generated using public key encryption.

Routing Versus Forwarding

A clearly defined policy should be written as to whether or not the firewall will act as a router or a forwarder of Internet packets. This is trivial in the case of a router that acts as a packet filtering gateway because the firewall (router in this case) has no option but to route packets. Applications gateway firewalls should generally not be configured to route any traffic between the external interface and the internal network interface, since this could bypass security controls. All external to internal connections should go through the application proxies.

Source Routing. Source routing is a routing mechanism whereby the path to a target machine is determined by the source, rather than by intermediate routers. Source routing is mostly used for debugging network problems but could also be used to attack a host. If an attacker has knowledge of some trust relationship between your hosts, source routing can be used to make it appear that the malicious packets are coming from a trusted host. Because of this security threat, a packet filtering router can easily be configured to reject packets containing source route option.

IP Spoofing. IP spoofing is when an attacker masquerades his machine as a host on the target's network (i.e., fooling a target machine that packets are coming from a trusted machine on the target's internal network). Policies regarding packet routing need to be clearly written so that they will be handled accordingly if there is a security problem. It is necessary that authentication based on source address be combined with other security schemes to protect against IP spoofing attacks.

Types of Firewalls

There are different implementations of firewalls, which can be arranged in different ways. These include packet filtering gateways, application gateways, and hybrid or complex gateways.

Packet Filtering Gateways. Packet filtering firewalls use routers with packet filtering rules to grant or deny access based on source address, destination address, and port. They offer minimum security but at a very low cost, and can be an appropriate choice for a low-risk environment. They are fast, flexible, and transparent. Filtering rules are not often easily maintained on a router, but there are tools available to simplify the tasks of creating and maintaining the rules.

Filtering gateways do have inherent risks including:

- The source and destination addresses and ports contained in the IP packet header are the only information that is available to the router in making a decision whether or not to permit traffic access to an internal network;
- They don't protect against IP or DNS address spoofing;
- An attacker will have a direct access to any host on the internal network once access has been granted by the firewall;
- Strong user authentication isn't supported with packet filtering gateways; and
- They provide little or no useful logging.

Application Gateways. An application gateway uses server programs called proxies that run on the firewall. These proxies take external requests, examine them, and forward legitimate requests to the internal host that provides the appropriate service. Application gateways can support functions such as user authentication and logging.

Because an application gateway is considered the most secure type of firewall, this configuration provides a number of advantages to the medium-high risk site:

- The firewall can be configured as the only host address that is visible to the outside network, requiring all connections to and from the internal network to go through the firewall;
- The use of proxies for different services prevents direct access to services on the internal network, protecting the enterprise against insecure or misconfigured internal hosts;
- Strong user authentication can be enforced with application gateways; and
- Proxies can provide detailed logging at the application level. Application level firewalls shall be configured such that outbound network traffic appears as if the traffic had originated from the firewall (i.e., only the firewall is visible to outside networks). In this manner, direct access to network services on the internal network is not allowed. All incoming requests for different network services such as Telnet, FTP, HTTP, RLOGIN, etc., regardless of which host on the internal network will be the final destination, must go through the appropriate proxy on the firewall.

Applications gateways require a proxy for each service, such as FTP, HTTP, etc., to be supported through the firewall. When a service is required that is not supported by a proxy, an organization has three choices.

- Deny the service until the firewall vendor has developed a secure proxy — This is the preferred approach, as many newly introduced Internet services have unacceptable vulnerabilities.
- Develop a custom proxy — This is a fairly difficult task and should be undertaken only by very sophisticated technical organizations.
- Pass the service through the firewall — Using what are typically called "plugs," most application gateway firewalls allow services to be passed directly through the firewall with only a minimum of packet filtering. This can limit some of the vulnerability but can result in compromising the security of systems behind the firewall.

Hybrid or Complex Gateways. Hybrid gateways combine two or more of the above firewall types and implement them in series rather than in parallel. If they are connected in series, then the overall security is enhanced; on the other hand, if they are connected in parallel, then the network security perimeter will be only as secure as the least secure of all methods used. In medium- to high-risk environments, a hybrid gateway may be the ideal firewall implementation.

Suggested ratings are identified in Exhibit 3.1 for various firewall types.

Firewall Architecture	High-Risk Environment e.g. Hospital	Medium-Risk Environment e.g. University	Low-Risk Environment e.g. Florist Shop
Packet Filtering	Unacceptable	Minimal Security	Recommended
Application Gateways	Effective Option	Recommended	Acceptable
Hybrid Gateways	Recommended	Effective Option	Acceptable

Exhibit 3.1. Firewall Security Risk

Firewall Architectures

Firewalls can be configured in a number of different architectures, providing various levels of security at different costs of installation and operation. Organizations should match their risk profile to the type of firewall architecture selected. The following describes typical firewall architectures and sample policy statements.

Multi-homed host. A multi-homed host is a host (a firewall in this case) that has more than one network interface, with each interface connected to logically and physically separate network segments. A dual-homed host (host with two interfaces) is the most common instance of a multi-homed host.

A dual-homed firewall is a firewall with two network interface cards (NICs) with each interface connected to different networks. For instance, one network interface is typically connected to the external or untrusted network, while the other interface is connected to the internal or trusted network. In this configuration, a key security tenet is not to allow traffic coming in from the untrusted network to be directly routed to the trusted network, that is, the firewall must always act as an intermediary. Routing by the firewall shall be disabled for a dual-homed firewall so that IP packets from one network are not directly routed from one network to the other.

Screened Host. A screened host firewall architecture uses a host (called a bastion host) to which all outside hosts connect, rather than allow direct connection to other, less secure internal hosts. To achieve this, a filtering router is configured so that all connections to the internal network from the outside network are directed towards the bastion host. If a packet filtering gateway is to be deployed, then a bastion host should be set up so that all connections from the outside network go through the bastion host to prevent direct Internet connection between the internal network and the outside world.

Screened Subnet. The screened subnet architecture is essentially the same as the screened host architecture, but adds an extra stratum of security by creating a network at which the bastion host resides (often call perimeter network) which is separated from the internal network. A screened subnet is deployed by adding a perimeter network in order to separate the internal network from the external. This assures that if there is a successful attack on the bastion host, the attacker is restricted to the perimeter network by the screening router that is connected between the internal and perimeter network.

Intranet

Although firewalls are usually placed between a network and the outside untrusted network, in large companies or organizations, firewalls are often used to create different subnets of the network, often called an intranet. Intranet firewalls are intended to isolate a particular subnet from the overall corporate network. The reason for the isolation of a network segment might be that certain employees can access subnets guarded by these firewalls only on a need-to-know basis. An example could be a firewall for the payroll or accounting department of an organization.

The decision to use an intranet firewall is generally based on the need to make certain information available to some but not all internal users, or to provide a high degree of accountability for the access and use of confidential or sensitive information.

For any systems hosting internal critical applications, or providing access to sensitive or confidential information, internal firewalls or filtering routers should be used to provide strong access control and support for auditing and logging. These controls should be used to segment the internal network to support the access policies developed by the designated owners of information.

Firewall Administration

A firewall, like any other network device, has to be managed by someone. Security policy should state who is responsible for managing the firewall.

Two firewall administrators (one primary and one secondary) shall be designated by the Chief Information Security Officer (or other manager) and shall be responsible for the upkeep of the firewall. The primary administrator shall make changes to the firewall, and the secondary shall only do so in the absence of the former so that there is no simultaneous or contradictory access to the firewall. Each firewall administrator shall provide their home phone number, pager number, cellular phone number, and other numbers or codes in which they can be contacted when support is required.

Qualification of the Firewall Administrator. Two experienced people are generally recommended for the day-to-day administration of the firewall. In this manner availability of the firewall administrative function is largely ensured. It should be required that on-call information about each firewall administrator be written down so that one may be contacted in the event of a problem.

Security of a site is crucial to the day-to-day business activity of an organization. It is therefore required that the administrator of the firewall have a sound understanding of network concepts and implementation. For instance, since most firewalls are TCP/IP based, a thorough understanding of this protocol is compulsory. An individual that is assigned the task of firewall administration must have good hands-on experience with networking concepts, design, and implementation so that the firewall is configured correctly and administered properly. Firewall administrators should receive periodic training on the firewalls in use and in network security principles and practices.

Remote Firewall Administration. Firewalls are the first line of defense visible to an attacker. By design, firewalls are generally difficult to attack directly, causing attackers to often target the administrative accounts on a firewall. The username/password of administrative accounts must be strongly protected.

The most secure method of protecting against this form of attack is to have strong physical security around the firewall host and to only allow firewall administration from an attached terminal. However, operational concerns often dictate that some form of remote access for firewall administration be supported. In no case should remote access to the firewall be supported over untrusted networks without some form of strong authentication. In addition, to prevent eavesdropping, session encryption should be used for remote firewall connections.

User Accounts. Firewalls should never be used as general purpose servers. The only user accounts on the firewall should be those of the firewall administrator and any backup administrators. In addition, only these administrators should have privileges for updating system executables or other system software. Only the firewall administrator and backup administrators will be given user accounts on the COMPANY firewall. Any modification of the firewall system software must be done by the firewall administrator or backup administrator and requires approval of the cognizant Manager.

Firewall Backup. To support recovery after failure or natural disaster, a firewall, like any other network host, has to have some policy defining system backup. Data files as well as system configuration files need to be components of a backup and recovery plan in case of firewall failure.

The firewall (system software, configuration data, database files, etc.) must be backed up daily, weekly, and monthly so that in case of system failure, data and configuration files can be recovered. Backup files should be stored securely on read-only media so that data in storage is not over-written inadvertently, and locked up so that the media is only accessible to the appropriate personnel.

Another backup alternative would be to have another firewall configured as one already deployed and kept safely in case there is a failure of the current one. This backup firewall would simply be turned on and used as the firewall while the previous one is undergoing a repair. At least one firewall should be configured and reserved (not-in-use) so that in case of a firewall failure, this backup firewall can be switched in to protect the network.

OTHER FIREWALL POLICY CONSIDERATIONS

Firewall technology has only been around for the last five years. In the past two years, however, firewall products have diversified considerably and now offer a variety of technical security controls that can be used in ever more complex network connections.

This section discusses some of the firewall policy considerations in the areas of network trust relationships, virtual private networks, DNS and mail resolution, system integrity, documentation, physical firewall security, firewall incident handling, service restoration, upgrades, and audit trail logging.

Network Trust Relationships

Business networks frequently require connections to other business networks. Such connections can occur over leased lines, proprietary Wide Area Networks, Value Added Networks (VANs), or over public networks such as the Internet. For instance, many local governments use leased lines or dedicated circuits to connect regional offices across the state. Many businesses use commercial VANs to connect business units across the country or the world.

The various network segments involved may be under control of different organizations and may operate under a variety of security policies. By their very nature, when networks are connected the security of the resulting overall network drops to the level of the weakest network. When decisions are made for connecting networks, trust relationships must be defined to avoid reducing the effective security of all networks involved.

Trusted networks are defined as networks that share the same security policy or implement security controls and procedures that provide an agreed upon set of common security services. Untrusted networks are those that do not implement such a common set of security controls, or where the level of security is unknown or unpredictable. The most secure policy is to only allow connection to trusted networks, as defined by an appropriate level of management. However, business needs may force temporary connections with business partners or remote sites that involve the use of untrusted networks.

Virtual Private Networks (VPN)

Virtual Private Networks allow a trusted network to communicate with another trusted network over untrusted networks such as the Internet. Since some firewalls provide VPN capability, it is necessary to define policy for establishing VPNs. The following are recommended policy statements:

- Any connection between firewalls over public networks shall use encrypted Virtual Private Networks to ensure the privacy and integrity of the data passing over the public network.
- All VPN connections must be approved and managed by the Network Services Manager.
- Appropriate means for distributing and maintaining encryption keys must be established prior to operational use of VPNs.

DNS and Mail Resolution

On the Internet, the Domain Name Service provides the mapping and translation of domain names to IP addresses, such as "mapping server1. acme.com to 123.45.67.8". Some firewalls can be configured to run as a primary, secondary, or caching DNS server.

Deciding how to manage DNS services is generally not a security decision. Many organizations use a third party, such as an Internet Service Provider, to manage their DNS. In this case, the firewall can be used as a DNS caching server, improving performance but not requiring your organization to maintain its own DNS database.

If the organization decides to manage its own DNS database, the firewall can (but doesn't have to) act as the DNS server. If the firewall is to be configured as a DNS server (primary, secondary, or caching), it is necessary that other security precautions be in place. One advantage of implementing the firewall as a DNS server is that it can be configured to hide the internal host information of a site. In other words, with the firewall acting as a DNS server, internal hosts get an unrestricted view of both internal and external DNS data. External hosts, on the other hand, do not have access to information about internal host machines. To the outside world all connections to any host in the internal network will appear to have originated from the firewall. With the host information hidden from the outside, an attacker will not know the host names and addresses of internal hosts that offer service to the Internet. A security policy for DNS hiding might state: If the firewall is to run as a DNS server, then the firewall must be configured to hide information about the network so that internal host data is not advertised to the outside world.

System Integrity

To prevent unauthorized modifications of the firewall configuration, some form of integrity assurance process should be used. Typically, checksums, cyclic redundancy checks, or cryptographic hashes are made from the run-time image and saved on protected media. Each time the firewall configuration has been modified by an authorized individual (usually the firewall administrator), it is necessary that the system integrity online database be updated and saved onto a file system on the network or removable media. If the system integrity check shows that the firewall configuration files have been modified, it will be known that the system has been compromised.

The firewall's system integrity database shall be updated each time the firewall's configuration is modified. System integrity files must be stored on read only media or off-line storage. System integrity shall be checked on a regular basis on the firewall in order for the administrator to generate a listing of all files that may have been modified, replaced, or deleted.

Documentation

It is important that the operational procedures for a firewall and its configurable parameters be well documented, updated, and kept in a safe and secure place. This assures that if a firewall administrator resigns or is otherwise unavailable, an experienced individual can read the documentation and rapidly pick up the administration of the firewall. In the event of a break-in such documentation also supports trying to recreate the events that caused the security incident.

Physical Firewall Security

Physical access to the firewall must be tightly controlled to preclude any authorized changes to the firewall configuration or operational status, and to eliminate any potential for monitoring firewall activity. In addition, precautions should be taken to assure that proper environment alarms and backup systems are available to assure the firewall remains online.

The firewall should be located in a controlled environment, with access limited to the Network Services Manager, the firewall administrator, and the backup firewall administrator. The room in which the firewall is to be physically located must be equipped with heat, air-conditioner, and smoke alarms to assure the proper working order of the room. The placement and recharge status of the fire extinguishers shall be checked on a regular basis. If uninterruptible power service is available to any Internet-connected systems, such service should be provided to the firewall as well.

Firewall Incident Handling

Incident reporting is the process whereby certain anomalies are reported or logged on the firewall. A policy is required to determine what type of report to log and what to do with the generated log report. This should be consistent with Incident Handling policies detailed previously. The following policies are appropriate to all risk environments.

- The firewall shall be configured to log all reports on daily, weekly, and monthly bases so that the network activity can be analyzed when needed.
- Firewall logs should be examined on a weekly basis to determine if attacks have been detected.
- The firewall administrator shall be notified at anytime of any security alarm by e-mail, pager, or other means so that he may immediately respond to such alarm.
- The firewall shall reject any kind of probing or scanning tool that is directed to it so that information being protected is not leaked out by the firewall. In a similar fashion, the firewall shall block all software

types that are known to present security threats to a network (such as ActiveX and Java) to better tighten the security of the network.

Restoration of Services

Once an incident has been detected, the firewall may need to be brought down and reconfigured. If it is necessary to bring down the firewall, Internet service should be disabled or a secondary firewall should be made operational. Internal systems should not be connected to the Internet without a firewall. After being reconfigured, the firewall must be brought back into an operational and reliable state. Policies for restoring the firewall to a working state when a break-in occurs are needed.

In case of a firewall break-in, the firewall administrator(s) are responsible for reconfiguring the firewall to address any vulnerabilities that were exploited. The firewall shall be restored to the state it was before the break-in so that the network is not left wide open. While the restoration is going on, the backup firewall shall be deployed.

Upgrading the Firewall

It is often necessary that the firewall software and hardware components be upgraded with the necessary modules to assure optimal firewall performance. The firewall administrator should be aware of any hardware and software bugs, as well as firewall software upgrades that may be issued by the vendor. If an upgrade of any sort is necessary, certain precautions must be taken to continue to maintain a high level of operational security. Sample policies that should be written for upgrades may include the following:

- To optimize the performance of the firewall, all vendor recommendations for processor and memory capacities shall be followed.
- The firewall administrator must evaluate each new release of the firewall software to determine if an upgrade is required. All security patches recommended by the firewall vendor should be implemented in a timely manner.
- Hardware and software components shall be obtained from a list of vendor-recommended sources. Any firewall specific upgrades shall be obtained from the vendor. NFS shall not be used as a means of obtaining software components. The use of virus checked CD-ROM or FTP to a vendor's site is an appropriate method.
- The firewall administrator(s) shall monitor the vendor's firewall mailing list or maintain some other form of contact with the vendor to be aware of all required upgrades. Before an upgrade of any of the firewall components, the firewall administrator must verify with the vendor that an upgrade is required. After any upgrade the firewall shall be tested to verify proper operation prior to going operational.

Given the rapid introduction of new technologies and the tendency for organizations to continually introduce new services, firewall security policies should be reviewed on a regular basis. As network requirements change, so should security policy.

Logs and Audit Trails (Audit/Event Reporting and Summaries)

Most firewalls provide a wide range of capabilities for logging traffic and network events. Some security-relevant events that should be recorded on the firewall's audit trail logs are: hardware and disk media errors, login/logout activity, connect time, use of system administrator privileges, inbound and outbound e-mail traffic, TCP network connect attempts, inbound and outbound proxy traffic type.

SUMMARY

Connections to external networks and to the Internet are rapidly becoming commonplace in today's business community. These connections must be effectively secured to protect internal trusted networks from misuse and attack. The security policies outlined above should provide an effective guideline for implementing the appropriate level of controls to protect internal networks from outside attack.

Domain 2.2
Internet, Intranet, and Extranet Security

Chapter 4
Firewalls: An Effective Solution for Internet Security

E. Eugene Schultz

The Internet has presented a new, complex set of challenges that even the most sophisticated technical experts have not been able to solve adequately. Achieving adequate security is one of the foremost of these challenges. The major security threats that the Internet community faces are described in this chapter. It also explains how firewalls —potentially one of the most effective solutions for Internet security—can address these threats, and it presents some practical advice for obtaining the maximum advantages of using firewalls.

INTERNET SECURITY THREATS

The vastness and openness that characterizes the Internet presents an extremely challenging problem—security. Although many claims about the number and cost of Internet-related intrusions are available, valid, credible statistics about the magnitude of this problem will not be available until scientific research is conducted. Exacerbating this dilemma is that most corporations that experience intrusions from the Internet and other sources do not want to make these incidents known for fear of public relations damage and, worse yet, many organizations fail to even detect most intrusions. Sources, such as Carnegie Mellon University's Computer Emergency Response Team, however, suggest that the number of Internet-related intrusions each year is very high and that the number of intrusions reported to CERT (which is one of dozens of incident response teams) is only the tip of the iceberg. No credible statistics concerning the total amount of financial loss resulting from security-related intrusions are available, but judging from the amount of money corporations and government agencies are spending to implement Internet and other security controls, the cost must be extremely high.

0-8493-9829-0/00/$0.00+$.50
© 2000 by CRC Press LLC

Many types of Internet security threats exist. One of the most serious methods is IP spoofing. In this type of attack, a perpetrator fabricates packets that bear the address of origination of a client host and sends these packets to the server for this client. The server acknowledges receiving these packets by returning packets with a certain sequence number. If the attacker can guess this packet sequence number and incorporate it into another set of fabricated packets that are then sent back to the server, the server can be tricked into setting up a connection with a fraudulent client. The intruder can subsequently use attack methods, such as use of trusted host relationships, to intrude into the server machine.

A similar threat is domain name service (DNS) spoofing. In this type of attack, an intruder subverts a host within a network and sets up this machine to function as an apparently legitimate name server. The host then provides bogus data about host identities and certain network services, enabling the intruder to break into other hosts within the network.

Session hijacking is another Internet security threat. The major tasks for the attacker who wants to hijack an ongoing session between remote hosts are locating an existing connection between two hosts and fabricating packets that bear the address of the host from which the connection has originated. By sending these packets to the destination host, the originating host's connection is dropped, and the attacker picks up the connection.

Another Internet security threat is network snooping, in which attackers install programs that copy packets traversing network segments. The attackers periodically inspect files that contain the data from the captured packets to discover critical log-on information, particularly user IDs and passwords for remote systems. Attackers subsequently connect to the systems for which they possess the correct log-on information and log on with no trouble. Attackers targeting networks operated by Internet service providers (ISPs) have made this problem especially serious, because so much information travels these networks. These attacks demonstrate just how vulnerable network infrastructures are; successfully attacking networks at key points, where router, firewalls, and server machines are located, is generally the most efficient way to gain information allowing unauthorized access to multitudes of host machines within a network.

A significant proportion of attacks exploit security exposures in programs that provide important network services. Examples of these programs include sendmail, Network File System (NFS), and Network Information Service (NIS). These exposures allow intruders to gain access to remote hosts and to manipulate services supported by these hosts or even to obtain superuser access. Of increasing concern is the susceptibility of World Wide Web services and the hosts that house these services to successful attack. The ability of intruders to exploit vulnerabilities in the HTTP and in Java, a programming language used to write WWW applications, seems to be growing at an alarming rate.

Until a short time ago, most intruders have attempted to cover up indications of their activity, often by installing programs that selectively eliminated data from system logs. These also avoided causing system crashes or causing massive slowdowns or disruption. However, a significant proportion of the perpetrator community has apparently shifted its strategy by increasingly perpetrating denial-of-service attacks. For example, many types of hosts crash or perform a core dump when they are sent a packet internet groper or ping packet that exceeds a specified size limit or when they are flooded with synchronize (SYN) packets that initiate host-to-host connections. (Packet internet groper, or ping, is a service used to determine whether a host on a network is up and running.) These denial-of-service attacks make up an increasing proportion of observed Internet attacks. They represent a particularly serious threat, because many organizations require continuity of computing and networking operations to maintain their business operations.

Not to be overlooked is another type of security threat called social engineering. Social engineering is fabricating a story to trick users, system administrators, or help desk personnel into providing information required to access systems. Intruders usually solicit passwords for user accounts, but information about the network infrastructure and the identity of individual hosts can also be the target of social engineering attacks.

INTERNET SECURITY CONTROLS

As previously mentioned, Internet security threats pose a challenge because of their diversity and severity. An added complication is an abundance of potential solutions.

Encryption

Encryption is a process of using an algorithm to transform cleartext information into text that cannot be read without the proper key. Encryption protects information stored in host machines and transmitted over networks. It is also useful in authenticating users to hosts or networks. Although encryption is an effective solution, its usefulness is limited by the difficulty in managing encryption keys (i.e., of assigning keys to users and recovering keys if they are lost or forgotten), laws limiting the export and use of encryption, and the lack of adherence to encryption standards by many vendors.

One-Time Passwords

Using one-time passwords is another way in which to challenge security threats. One-time passwords captured while in transit over networks become worthless, because each password can only be used once. A captured password has already been used by the legitimate user who has initiated a remote log-on session by the time the captured password can be employed. Nevertheless, one-time passwords address only a relatively small proportion of the total range of Internet security threats. They do not, for example, protect against IP spoofing or exploitation of vulnerabilities in programs.

Installing fixes for vulnerabilities in all hosts within an Internet-capable network does not provide an entirely suitable solution because of the cost of labor, and, over the last few years, vulnerabilities have surfaced at a rate far faster than that at which fixes have become available.

Firewalls

Although no single Internet security control measure is perfect, the firewall has, in many respects, proved more useful overall than most other controls. Simply, a firewall is a security barrier between two networks that screens traffic coming in and out of the gate of one network to accept or reject connections and service requests according to a set of rules. If configured properly, it addresses a large number of threats that originate from outside a network without introducing any significant security liabilities. Because most organizations are unable to install every patch that CERT advisories describe, these organizations can nevertheless protect hosts within their networks against external attacks that exploit vulnerabilities by installing a firewall that prevents users from outside the network from reaching the vulnerable programs in the first place. A more sophisticated firewall also controls how any connection between a host external to a network and an internal host occurs. Moreover, an effective firewall hides information, such as names and addresses of hosts within the network, as well as the topology of the network which it is employed to protect.

Firewalls can defend against attacks on hosts (including spoofing attacks), application protocols, and applications. In addition, firewalls provide a central method for administering security on a network and for logging incoming and outgoing traffic to allow for accountability of user actions and for triggering incident response activity if unauthorized activity occurs.

Firewalls are typically placed at gateways to networks to create a security perimeter, as shown in Exhibit 4.1, primarily to protect an internal network from threats originating from an external one (particularly from the

Internet). This scheme is successful to the degree that the security perimeter is not accessible through unprotected avenues of access. The firewall acts as a choke component for security purposes. Exhibit 4.1 displays routers that are located in front and in back of the firewall. The first router (shown above the firewall) is an external one used initially to route incoming traffic, to direct outgoing traffic to external networks, and to broadcast information that enables other network routers (as well as the router on the other side of the firewall) to know how to reach the host network. The other internal router (shown below the firewall) sends incoming packets to their destination within the internal network, directs outgoing packets to the external router, and broadcasts information on how to reach the internal network and the external router. This belt-and-suspenders configuration further boosts security by preventing the broadcast of information about the internal network outside the network the firewall protects. An attacker finding this information can learn IP addresses, subnets, servers, and other information which is useful in perpetrating attacks against the network. Hiding information about the internal network is much more difficult if the gate has only one router.

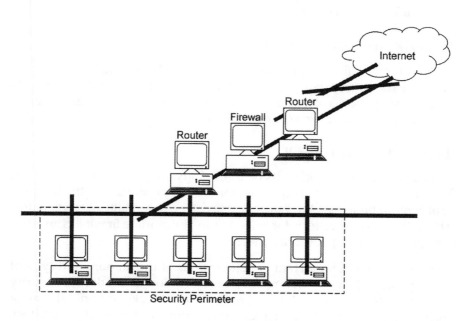

Exhibit 4.1. A Typical Gate-Based Firewall Architecture

Another way in which firewalls are deployed (though less frequently) is within an internal network—at the entrance to a subnet within a network—rather than at the gateway to the entire network. The purpose of this configuration (shown in Exhibit 4.2) is to segregate a subnetwork (a screened subnet) from the internal network at large, a wise strategy if the subnet has tighter security requirements than the rest of the security perimeter. This type of deployment more carefully controls access to data and services within a subnet than is otherwise allowed within the network. The gate-based firewall, for example, may allow file transfer protocol (FTP) access to an internal network from external sources. However, if a subnet contains hosts that store information, such as lease bid data or salary data, allowing FTP access to this subnet is less advisable. Setting up the subnet as a screened subnet may provide suitable security control, that is, the internal firewall that provides security screening for the subnet is configured to deny all FTP access, regardless of whether the access requests originated from outside or inside the network.

Simply having a firewall, no matter how it is designed and implemented, does not necessarily protect against externally originated security threats. The benefits of firewalls depend to a large degree on the type used and how it is deployed and maintained.

USING FIREWALLS EFFECTIVELY

To ensure that firewalls perform their intended function, it is important to choose the appropriate firewall and to implement it correctly. Establishing a firewall policy is also a critical step in securing a system, as is regular maintenance of the entire security structure.

Choosing the Right Firewall

Each type of firewall offers its own set of advantages and disadvantages. Combined with the vast array of vendor firewall products and the possibility of custom-building a firewall, this task can be potentially overwhelming. Establishing a set of criteria for selecting an appropriate firewall is an effective aid in narrowing down the choices.

One of the most important considerations is the amount and type of security needed. For some organizations with low to moderate security needs, installing a packet-filtering firewall that blocks out only the most dangerous incoming service requests often provides the most satisfactory solution, because the cost and effort are not likely to be great. For other organizations, such as banks and insurance corporations, packet-filtering firewalls do not generally provide the granularity and control against unauthorized actions usually needed for connecting customers to services that reside within a financial or insurance corporation's network.

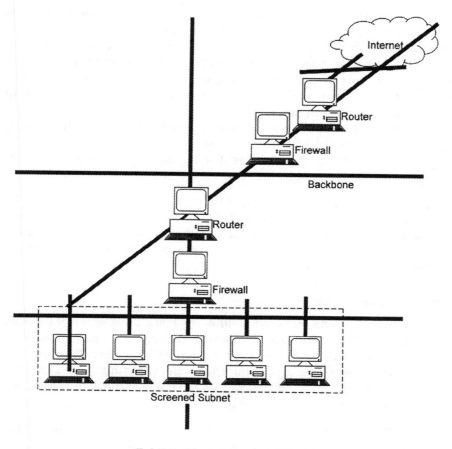

Exhibit 4.2. A Screened Subnet

Additional factors, such as the reputation of the vendor, the arrangements for vendor support, the verifiability of the firewall's code (i.e., to confirm that the firewall does what the vendor claims it does), the support for strong authentication, the ease of administration, the ability of the firewall to withstand direct attacks, and the quality and extent of logging and alarming capabilities should also be strong considerations in choosing a firewall.

The Importance of a Firewall Policy

The discussion to this point has focused on high-level technical considerations. Although these considerations are extremely important, too often security professionals overlook other considerations that, if neglected, can render firewalls ineffective. The most important consideration in effectively using firewalls is developing a firewall policy.

A firewall policy is a statement of how a firewall should work—the rules by which incoming and outgoing traffic should be allowed or rejected. A firewall policy, therefore, is a type of security requirements document for a firewall. As security needs change, firewall policies must change accordingly. Failing to create and update a firewall policy for each firewall almost inevitably results in gaps between expectations and the actual function of the firewall, resulting in uncontrolled security exposures in firewall functionality. For example, security administrators may think that all incoming HTTP requests are blocked, but the firewall may actually allow HTTP requests from certain IP addresses, leaving an unrecognized avenue of attack.

An effective firewall policy should provide the basis for firewall implementation and configuration; needed changes in the way the firewall works should always be preceded by changes in the firewall policy. An accurate, up-to-date firewall policy should also serve as the basis for evaluating and testing a firewall.

Security Maintenance

Many organizations that employ firewalls feel a false sense of security once the firewalls are in place. Properly designing and implementing firewalls can be difficult, costly, and time consuming. It is critical to remember, however, that firewall design and implementation are simply the beginning points of having a firewall. Firewalls that are improperly maintained soon lose their value as security control tools.

One of the most important facets of firewall maintenance is updating the security policy and rules by which each firewall operates. Firewall functionality invariably must change as new services and applications are introduced in (or sometimes removed from) a network. Undertaking the task of daily inspections of firewall logs to discover attempted and possibly successful attacks on both the firewall and the internal network that it protects should be an extremely high priority. Evaluating and testing the adequacy of firewalls for unexpected access avenues to the security perimeter and vulnerabilities that lead to unauthorized access to the firewall should also be a frequent, high-priority activity.

Firewall products have improved considerably over the past several years and are likely to continue to improve. Several vendor products, for example, are not network addressable, which makes breaking into these platforms by someone who does not have physical access to them virtually impossible. At the same time, however, recognizing the limitations of firewalls and ensuring that other appropriate Internet security controls are in place is becoming increasingly important because of such problems as third-party connections to organizations' networks that bypass gate-based security mechanisms altogether. Therefore, an Internet security strategy that includes firewalls in addition to host-based security mechanisms is invariably the most appropriate direction for achieving suitable levels of Internet security.

CONCLUSION

Internet connectivity can be extremely valuable to an organization, but it involves many security risks. A firewall is a key tool in an appropriate set of security control measures to protect Internet-capable networks. Firewalls can be placed at the gateway to a network to form a security perimeter around the networks that they protect or at the entrance to subnets to screen the subnets from the rest of the internal network.

Developing an accurate and complete firewall policy is the most important step in using firewalls effectively. This policy should be modified and updated as new applications are added within the internal network protected by the firewall and as new security threats emerge. Maintaining firewalls properly and regularly examining the log data that they provide are almost certainly the most neglected aspects of using firewalls. Yet, these activities are among the most important in ensuring the defenses are adequate and that incidents are quickly detected and handled. Performing regular security evaluations and testing the firewall to identify any exploitable vulnerabilities or misconfigurations are also essential activities. Establishing a regular security procedure minimizes the possibility of system penetration by an attacker.

Chapter 5
Internet Security: Securing the Perimeter

Douglas G. Conorich

The Internet has become the fastest growing tool organizations have ever had that can help them become more productive. In spite of its usefulness, there have been many debates as to whether the Internet can be used, in light of the many security issues. Today, more than ever before, computing systems are vulnerable to unauthorized access. Given the right combination of motivation, expertise, resources, time, and social engineering, an intruder will be able to access any computer that is attached to the Internet.

The Corporate Community has, in part, created this problem for themselves. The rapid growth of the Internet with all the utilities now available to Web surf, combined with the number of users who now have easy access through all the various Internet providers, make every desktop, including those in homes, schools, and libraries, places where an intruder can launch an attack. Surfing the Internet began as a novelty. Users were seduced by the vast amounts of information they could find. In many cases, it has become addictive.

Much of the public concern with the Internet has been focused on the inappropriate access to websites by children from their homes or schools. A business, however, is concerned with the bottom-line. How profitable a business is can be directly related to the productivity of its employees. Inappropriate use of the Internet in the business world can decrease that productivity in many ways. The network bandwidth — how much data can flow across a network segment at any time — is costly to increase, because of the time involved and the technology issues. Inappropriate use of the Internet can slow the flow of data and create the network approximation of a log jam.

There are also potential legal or public relations implications of inappropriate employee usage. One such issue is the increasing prevalence of "sin surfing" — browsing the pornographic websites. One company reported that 37 percent of their Internet bandwidth was taken up by "sin surfing." Lawsuits can be generated and, more importantly, the organization's image can be damaged by employees using the Internet to distribute inappropriate materials. To legally curtail the inappropriate use of the Internet, an organization must have a policy that defines what is acceptable, what is not, and what can happen if those who misuse the Internet are caught.

As part of the price of doing business, companies continue to span the bridge between the Internet and their own intranets with mission-critical applications. This makes them more vulnerable to new and unanticipated security threats. Such exposures can place organizations at risk at every level — down to the very credibility upon which they build their reputations.

Making the Internet safe and secure for business requires careful management by the organization. Companies will have to use existing and new, emerging technologies, security policies tailored to the business needs of the organization, and employee training in order to accomplish this goal. IBM has defined four phases of Internet adoption by companies as they do business on the Internet: Access, Presence, Integration, and E-Business. Each of these phases has risks involved.

- Access — In this first phase of adoption, a company has just begun to explore the Internet and to learn about its potential benefits. A few employees are using modems connected to their desktop PCs to dial into either a local Internet service provider, or a national service such as America Online. In this phase, the company is using the Internet as a resource for getting information only — all requests for access are in the outbound direction, and all information flow is in the inbound direction. Exchanging electronic mail and browsing the Web make up the majority of activities in this phase.
- Presence — In this phase, the company has begun to make use of the Internet not only as a resource for getting information, but also as a means of providing information to others. Direct connection of the company's internal network means that now all employees have the ability to access the Internet (although this may be restricted by policy), allowing them to use it as an information resource, and also enabling processes such as customer support via e-mail. The creation of a Web server, either by the company's own staff or through a content hosting service, allows the company to provide static information such as product catalogs and data sheets, company background information, software updates, etc., to its customers and prospects.
- Integration — In this phase, the company has begun to integrate the Internet into its day-to-day business processes, by connecting its Web

server directly (through a firewall or other protection system) to its back-office systems. In the previous phase, updates to the Web server's data were made manually, via tape or other means. In this phase, the Web server can obtain information on-demand, as users request it. To use banking as an example, this phase enables the bank's customers to obtain their account balances, find out when checks cleared, and other information retrieval functions.

- E-business — In the final phase, the company has enabled bidirectional access requests and information flow. This means that not only can customers on the Internet retrieve information from the company's back-office systems, but they can also add to or change information stored on those systems. At this stage, the company is conducting business electronically — customers can place orders, transfer money (via credit cards or other means), check on shipments, and so forth. Business partners can update inventories, make notes in customer records, etc. In short, the entire company has become accessible via the Internet.

While a company may follow this road to the end, as described by IBM, they are most likely somewhere on it, either in one of the phases or in transition between them.

INTERNET PROTOCOLS

Communication between two people is made possible by their mutual agreement to a common mode of transferring ideas from one person to the other. Each person must know exactly how to communicate with the other if this is to be successful. The communication may be in the form of a verbal or written language, such as English, Spanish, or German. It could also take the form of physical gestures like sign language. It can even be done through pictures or music. Regardless of the form of the communications, it is paramount that the meaning of an element, say a word, has the same meaning to both parties involved. The medium used for the communications is also important. Both parties must have access to the same communication medium. You cannot talk to someone via telephone, if only one of you has a telephone.

With computers, communications over networks is made possible by what are known as protocols. A protocol is a well-defined message format. The message format defines what each position in the message means. One possible message format could define the first four bits as the version number, the next four bits as the length of the header, and then eight bits for the service being used. As long as both computers agree on this format, communications can take place.

Network communications use more than one protocol. Sets of protocols used together are known as protocol suites or layered protocols. One well-known protocol suite is the Transport Control Protocol/ InternetProtocol (TCP/IP) suite. It is based on the International Standards Organization's (ISO) Open Systems Interconnection (OSI) Reference Model (see Exhibit 5.1).

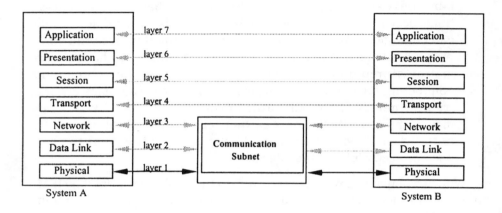

Exhibit 5.1. The ISO Model

The ISO Reference Model is divided into seven layers:

- The Physical Layer is the lowest layer in the protocol stack. It consists of the "physical" connection. This may be copper wire or fiber optic cables and the associated connection hardware. The sole responsibility of the Physical Layer is to transfer the bits from one location to another.
- The second layer is the Data Link Layer. It provides for the reliable delivery of data across the physical link. The Data Link Layer creates a checksum of the message that can be used by the receiving host to ensure that the entire message was received.
- The Network Layer manages the connections across the network for the upper four layers and isolates them from the details of addressing and delivery of data.
- The Transport Layer provides the end-to-end error detection and correction function between communicating applications.
- The Session Layer manages the sessions between communicating applications.

- The Presentation Layer standardizes the data presentation to the application level.
- The Application Layer consists of application programs that communicate across the network. This is the layer with which most users interact.

Network devices can provide different levels of security depending on how far up the stack they can read. Repeaters are used to connect two Ethernet segments.

The repeater simply copies the electrical transmission and sends it on to the next segment of the network. Since the repeater only reads up through the Data Link Layer, no security can be added by its use.

The bridge is a computer that is used to connect two or more networks. The bridge differs from the repeater in that it can store and forward entire packets, instead of just repeating electrical signals. Since it reads up through the Network Layer of the packet, the bridge can add some security. It could allow the transfer of only packets with local addresses. A bridge uses physical addresses, not IP addresses. The physical address, also know as the Ethernet address, is the actual address of the Ethernet hardware. It is a 48-bit number.

Routers and Gateways are computers that determine which of the many possible paths a packet will take to get to the destination device. These devices read up through the Transport Layer and can read IP addresses, including port numbers. They can be programmed to allow, disallow, and/or re-route IP datagrams determined by the IP address of the packet.

As previously mentioned, TCP/IP is based on the ISO model, but it groups the seven layers of the ISO model into four layers, as displayed in Exhibit 5.2.

Application Layer   consists of applications and   processes that use the network.
Host-to-Host Transport Layer   provides end-to-end data   delivery service.
Internet Layer   defines the datagram and handles   the routing of data.
Network Access Layer   consists of routines for accessing   physical networks.

Exhibit 5.2. The TCP/IP protocol architecture

The Network Access Layer is the lowest layer of the TCP/IP protocol stack. It provides the means of delivery and has to understand how the network transmits data from one IP address to another. The Network Access Layer, basically, provides the functionality of the first three layers of the ISO model.

TCP/IP provides a scheme of IP addressing that uniquely defines every host connected to the Internet. The Network Access Layer provides the functions that encapsulate the datagrams and maps the IP addresses to the physical addresses used by the network.

The Internet Layer has at its core the Internet Protocol (RFC791). IP provides the basic building blocks of the Internet. It provides:

- The datagram definition scheme
- The Internet addressing scheme
- The means of moving data between the Network Access Layer and the Host-to Host Layer
- The means for datagrams to be routed to remote hosts
- The function of breaking apart and reassembling packets for transmission.

IP is a connectionless protocol. This means that it relies on other protocols within the TCP/IP stack to provide the connection-oriented services. The connection-oriented services (i.e., TCP) take care of the handshake — the exchange of control information. The IP Layer contains the Internet Control Message Protocol (ICMP).

The Host-to Host Transport Layer houses two protocols: the Transport Control Protocol (TCP) and the User Datagram Protocol (UDP). Its primary function is to deliver messages between the Application layer and the Internet Layer. TCP is a reliable protocol. This means that it guarantees that the message will arrive as sent. It contains error detection and correction features. UDP does not have these features and is, therefore, unreliable. For shorter messages, where it is easier to resend the message than worry about the overhead involved with TCP, UDP is used.

The Application Layer contains the various services that users will use to send data. The Application Layer contains such user programs as the Network Terminal Protocol (TELNET), File Transfer Protocol (FTP), and Simple Mail Transport Protocol (SMTP). It also contains protocols not directly used by users, but required for system use, e.g., Domain Name Service (DNS), Routing Information Protocol (RIP), and Network File System (NFS).

Attacks

As previously mentioned, TCP is a reliable messaging protocol. This means that TCP is a connection-oriented protocol. TCP uses what is known as a "three-way" handshake. A handshake is simply the exchange of control information between the two computers. This information enables the computers to determine which packets go where and ensure that all the information in the message has been received.

When a connection is desired between two systems, Host A and Host B, using TCP/IP, a three-way handshake must occur. The initiating host, Host A (the client), sends the receiving host, Host B (the server), a message with the SYN (synchronize sequence number) bit set. The SYN contains information needed by Host B to setup the connection. This message contains the IP address of both Host A and Host B and the port numbers they will talk on. The SYN tells Host B what sequence number the client will start with, seq=x. This number is important to keep all the data transmitted in the proper order and can be used to notify Host B that a piece of data is missing. The sequence number is found starting at bit 32 to 63 of the header.

When Host B receives the SYN, it sends the client an ACK (Acknowledgment message). This message contains the sequence number that Host B will start with, SYN, seq=y, and the sequence number of Host A incremented, the ACK, x+1. The Acknowledgment number is bits 64 through 95 of the header.

The three-way handshake is completed when Host A receives the ACK from Host B and sends an ACK, y+1, in return. Now data can flow back and forth between the two hosts. This connection is now known as a socket. A socket is usually identified as Host_A_IP:Port_Number, Host_B_IP:Port_Number.

There are two attacks that use this technology; SYN Flood and Sequence Predictability.

SYN Flood Attack. The SYN Flood attack uses a TCP connection request (SYN). The SYN is sent to the target computer with the source IP address in the packet "spoofed," or replaced with an address that is not in use on the Internet, or that belongs to another computer. When the target computer receives the connection request, it allocates resources to handle and track the new connection. A "SYN_RECEIVED" state is stored in a buffer register awaiting the return response (ACK) from the initiating computer which would complete the three-way handshake. It then sends out a "SYN-ACK." If the response is sent to the "spoofed," nonexistent IP address, there will never be a response. If the "SYN-ACK" is sent to a real computer, it checks to see if it has a SYN in the buffer to that IP address. Since it doesn't, it ignores the request. The target computer retransmits the "SYN-ACK" a number of times. After a finite amount of wait time, the original SYN request is purged from the buffer of the target computer. This condition is known as a half-open socket.

As an example, the default configuration for a Windows NT 3.5x or 4.0 computer is to retransmit the SYN-ACK five times, doubling the time-out value after each retransmission. The initial time-out value is three seconds, so retries are attempted at 3, 6, 12, 24, and 48 seconds. After the last retransmission, 96 seconds are allowed to pass before the computer gives up on receiving a response and deallocates the resources that were set aside earlier for the connection. The total elapsed time that resources are in use is 189 seconds.

An attacker will send many of these TCP SYNs to tie up as many resources as possible on the target computer. Since the buffer-size for the storage of SYNs is a finite size, numerous attempts can cause a buffer over-flow. The effect of tying up connection resources varies, depending upon the TCP/IP stack and applications listening on the TCP port. For most stacks, there is a limit on the number of connections that can be in the half-open SYN_RECEIVED state. Once the limit is reached for a given TCP port, the target computer responds with a reset to all further connection requests until resources are freed. Using this method, an attacker can cause a denial-of-services on several ports.

Finding the source of a SYN Flood attack can be very difficult. A network analyzer may be used to try to track the problem down, and it may be necessary to contact your Internet Service Provider for assistance in attempting to trace the source. Firewalls should be set up to reject packets from the external network with any IP address from the internal network.

Sequence Predictability. The ability to guess sequence numbers is very useful to intruders, because they can create a short-lived connection to a host without having to see the reply packets. This ability, taken in combination with the fact that: many hosts have trust relationships that use IP addresses as authentication; that packets are easily spoofed; and that individuals can mount denial of service attacks; means you can impersonate the trusted systems to break into such machines without using source routing.

If an intruder wants to spoof a connection between two computers so that the connection seems as if it is coming from B to A, using your computer C, it works like this:

1. First, the intruder uses computer C to mount a SYN flood attack on the ports on computer B where the impersonating will take place.
2. Then, computer C sends a normal SYN to a port on A.
3. Computer A returns a SYN-ACK to computer C containing computer A's current Initial Sequence Number (ISN).
4. Computer A internally increments the ISN. This incrementation is done differently in different operating systems (OSs). Operating

systems such as BSD's, HPUX, Irix, SunOS (not Solaris), and others, usually increment by $FA00 for each connection and double each second. With this information, the intruder can now guess the ISN that computer A will pick for the next connection. Now comes the spoof.

5. Computer C sends a SYN to computer A, using the source IP spoofed as computer B.

6. Computer A sends a SYN-ACK back to computer B, containing the ISN. The intruder on computer C doesn't see this, but the intruder has guessed the ISN.

7. At this point, computer B would respond to computer A with an RST. This occurs since computer B does not have an SYN_RECEIVED from computer A. Since the intruder used a SYN flood attack on computer B, it won't respond.

8. The intruder on computer C sends an ACK to computer A, using the source IP spoofed as computer B, containing the guessed ISN+1. If the guess was correct, computer A now thinks there has been a successful three-way handshake and the TCP connection between computer A and computer B is fully set up. Now the spoof is complete. The intruder on computer C can do anything, but blindly.

9. Computer C sends 'echo + + >>/.rhosts' to port 514 on computer A.

10. If root on computer A had computer B in its /.rhosts file, the intruder has root.

11. Computer C now sends a FIN to computer A.

12. Computer C could be brutal and send an RST to computer A just to clean things up.

13. Computer C could also send an RST to the SYN flooded port on B, leaving no traces.

To prevent such attacks, you should NEVER TRUST ANYTHING FROM THE INTERNET. Routers and firewalls should filter out any packets that are coming from the external, sometimes known as the red, side of the firewall that has an IP address of a computer on the internal, sometimes known as the blue, side. This only stops Internet trust exploits; it won't stop spoofs that build on intranet trust. Companies should avoid using rhosts files, wherever possible.

ICMP

A major component of the TCP/IP's Internet Layer is the Internet Control Message Protocol (ICMP). ICMP is used for flow control, detecting unreachable destinations, re-direction routes, and checking remote hosts. Most users are interested in the last of these functions. Checking a remote host is accomplished by sending an ICMP Echo Message. The ping command is used to send these messages.

When a system receives one of these ICMP Echo Messages, it places the message in a buffer, then re-transmits the message from the buffer back to the source. Due to the buffer size, the ICMP Echo message size cannot exceed 64K. UNIX hosts, by default, will send an ICMP Echo Message that is 64 bytes long. They will not allow a message of over 64K. With the advent of Microsoft Windows NT, longer messages can be sent. The Windows NT hosts do not place an upper limit on these messages. Intruders have been sending messages of 1MB and larger. When these messages are received, they cause a buffer overflow on the target host. Different operating systems will react differently to this buffer overflow. The reactions range from re-booting to a total system crash.

Firewalls

The first line of defense between the Internet and your Intranet should be a firewall. A firewall is a multi-homed host that is placed in the Internet route, such that it stops and can make decisions about each packet that wants to get through. A firewall performs a function different from that of a router. A router can be used to filter out certain packets that meet a specific criterion, i.e., an IP address. A router processes the packets up through the IP Layer. A firewall stops all packets. All packets are processed up through the Application Layer. Routers cannot perform all the functions of a firewall. A firewall should meet, at least, the following criteria:

- In order for an internal or external host to connect to the other network, they first have to log in on the firewall host.
- All electronic mail is sent to the firewall, which in turn distributes it.
- Firewalls should not mount file systems via NFS, nor should any of its file systems be mounted.
- Firewalls should not run (Network Information Systems) NIS.
- Only required users should have accounts on the Firewall host.
- The Firewall host should not be trusted nor trust any other host.
- The Firewall host is the only machine with Anonymous FTP.
- Only the minimum service should be enabled on the Firewall in the file inetd.conf.
- All system logs on the Firewall should log to a separate host.
- Compilers and loaders should be deleted on the Firewall.
- System directories permissions on the Firewall host should be 711 or 511.

The DMZ

Most companies today are finding out that it is imperative to have an Internet presence. This Internet presence takes on the form of Anonymous FTP sites and a World Wide Web (www) site. In addition to these, companies are setting up hosts to act as a proxy server for Internet mail and a

Domain Name Server (DNS). The host that sponsors these functions cannot be on the inside of the firewall. Therefore, companies are creating what has become known as the DeMilitarized Zone (DMZ) or Perimeter Network, a segment between the router that connects to the Internet and the firewall.

Proxy Servers

A proxy host is a dual-homed host that is dedicated to a particular service or set of services, such as mail. All external requests to that service directed toward the internal network are routed to the proxy. The proxy host then evaluates the request and either passes the request on to the internal service server or discards it. The reverse is also true. Internal requests are passed to the proxy from the service server before they are passed on to the Internet.

One of the functions of the proxy hosts is to protect the company from advertising its internal network scheme. Most proxy software packages contain Network Address Translation (NAT). Take for example a mail server. The mail from Albert_Smith@starwars.abc.com would be translated to smith@proxy.abc.com as it went out to the Internet. Mail sent to smith@proxy.abc.com would be sent to the mail proxy. Here it would be readdressed to Albert_Smith@starwars.abc.com and sent to the internal mail server for final delivery.

Testing the Perimeter

A company cannot use the Internet without taking risks. It is important to recognize these risks, and it is important not to exaggerate them. You cannot cross the street without taking a risk. But by recognizing the dangers, and taking the proper precautions (such as looking both ways before stepping off the curb), millions of people cross the street safely every day.

The Internet and intranets are in a state of constant change — new protocols, new applications, and new technologies — and a company's security practices must be able to adapt to these changes. To adapt, the security process should be viewed as forming a circle. The first step is to assess the current state of security within your intranet and along the perimeter. Once you understand where you are, you can deploy a security solution. If you don't monitor that solution by enabling some detection and devising a response plan, the solution is useless. It would be like putting an alarm on your car, but never checking it when the alarm goes off. As we monitor and test the solution, we are going to find further weaknesses. This brings us back to the assessment stage, and the process is repeated. Those new weaknesses are then learned about and dealt with, and a third round begins. This continuous improvement ensures that your corporate assets are always protected.

As part of this process, a company must employ some sort of vulnerability checking on a regular basis. This can be done by the company, or they may choose to have an independent group do the testing. The company's security policy should state how the firewall and the other hosts in the DMZ are to be configured. These configurations need to be validated and then periodically checked to ensure that the configurations have not changed. The vulnerability test may find additional weakness with the configurations, and then the policy needs to be changed.

Security is achieved through the combination of technology and policy. The technology must be kept up to date and the policy must outline the procedures. An important part of a good security policy is to ensure that there are as few information leaks as possible.

One source of information can be DNS records. There are two basic DNS services: lookups and zone transfers. Lookup activities are used to resolve IP addresses into host names or to do the reverse. A zone transfer happens when one DNS server (a secondary server) asks another DNS server (the primary server) for all the information that it knows about a particular part of the DNS tree (a zone). These zone transfers only happen between DNS servers that are supposed to be providing the same information. Users can also request a zone transfer.

A zone transfer is accomplished using the nslookup command in interactive mode. The zone transfer can be used to check for information leaks. This procedure can show hosts, their IP addresses and operating systems. A good security policy is to disallow zone transfers on external DNS servers. This information may be used by an intruder to attack or spoof other hosts. If this is not operationally possible, as a general rule, DNS servers outside of the firewall (on the red side) should not list hosts within the firewall (on the blue side). Listing internal hosts only helps an intruder gain network mapping information and gives them an idea of the internal IP addressing scheme.

In addition to trying to do a zone transfer, the DNS records should be checked to ensure that they are correct and that they have not changed. Domain Information Gofer (DIG) is a flexible command-line tool that is used to gather information from the Domain Name System servers.

The ping command, as previously mentioned, has the ability to determine the status of a remote host by using the ICMP ECHO Message. If a host is running and is reachable by the message, the ping program will return an "alive" message. If the host is not reachable and the host name can be resolved by DNS, the program returns a "host not responding" message. Otherwise, you get an "unknown host" message. An intruder can use the ping program to set up a "war dialer." This is a program that systematically goes through the IP addresses one after another, looking for "alive" or "not responding" hosts. To prevent intruders from mapping your internal networks, the firewall should screen out ICMP messages. This can be done by not allowing ICMP messages to go through to the internal network or go out from the internal network. The former is the preferred method. This would keep intruders from using ICMP attacks, such as the Ping O'Death or Loki tunnelling.

The traceroute program is another useful tool to use to test the corporate perimeter. Since the Internet is a large aggregate of networks and hardware connected by various gateways, traceroute is used to check the "time to live" (ttl) parameter and routes. Traceroute sends a series of three UDP packets with an ICMP packet incorporated during its check. The ttl of each packet is similar. As the ttl expires, it sends the ICMP packet back to the originating host with the IP address of the host where it expired. Each successive broadcast uses a longer ttl. By continuing to send longer ttl's, trace-route pieces together the successive jumps. Checking the various jumps not only shows the routes, but it can show possible problems that may give an intruder information or leads. This information might show a place where an intruder might successfully launch an attack. A "*" return shows that a particular hop has exceeded the three-second timeout. These are hops that could be used by intruders to create DoS's. Duplicate entries for successive hops are indications of bugs in the kernel of that gateway or looping within the routing table.

Checking the open ports and services available is another important aspect of firewall and proxy server testing. There are a number of programs like the freeware program strobe, IBM's Network Services Auditor (NSA), ISS's Internet Scanner™, and AXENT Technologies' NetRecon™ that can perform a selective probe of the target UNIX® or Windows NT™ network communication services, operating systems, and key applications. These programs use a comprehensive set of penetration tests. The software searches for weaknesses most often exploited by intruders to gain access to a network. They analyze security risks and provide a series of highly informative reports and recommended corrective actions.

There have been numerous attacks in the past year that have been directed at specific ports. The teardrop, newtear, oob, and land.c are only a few of the recent attacks. Firewalls and proxy hosts should have only the minimum number of ports open. By default, the following ports are open as shipped by the vendor, and should be closed:

    o echo on TCP port 7.
    o echo on UDP port 7.
    o discard on TCP port 9.
    o daytime on TCP port 13.
    o daytime on UDP port 13.

o chargen on TCP port 19.
o chargen on UDP port 19.
o NetBIOS-NS on UDP port 137.
o NetBIOS-ssn on TCP port 139.

Other sources of information leaks are the Telnet, FTP, and sendmail programs. They all, by default, advertise the operating system or service type and version. They also may advertise the host name. This "feature" can be turned off and a more appropriate warning message should be put in their place.

Sendmail has a feature that will allow the administrator to expand or verify users. This feature should not be turned on on any host in the DMZ. An intruder would only have to telnet to the sendmail port to obtain user account names. There are a number of well-known user accounts that an intruder would test. This method works even if the finger command is disabled.

VRFY and EXPN allows an intruder to determine if an account exists on a system and can provide a significant aid to a brute force attack on user accounts. If you are running Sendmail, add the line "Opnovrfy" and "Opnoexpn" to your Sendmail configuration file, usually located in /etc/sendmail.cf. With other mail servers, contact your vendor for information on how to disable the verify command.

```
# telnet xxx.xxx.xx.xxx
Trying xxx.xxx.xx.xxx...
Connected to xxx.xxx.xx.xxx.
Escape character is '^]'.
220 proxy.abc.com Sendmail 4.1/SMI-4.1 ready at Thu, 26 Feb 98 12:50:05
        CST
expn root
250- John Doe <jdoe>
250 Jane User <juser>
vrfy root
250- John Doe <jdoe>
250 Jane User <juser>
vrfy jdoe
250 John Doe <john_doe@mailserver.internal.abc.com>
vrfy juser
250 John User <jane_user@mailserver.internal.abc.com>
    ^]
```

Another important check that needs to be run on these hosts in the DMZ is a validation that the system and important application files are valid and not hacked. This is done by running a checksum or a cyclic redundancy check (CRC) on the files. Since these values are not stored anywhere on the host, external applications need to be used for this function. Some suggested security products are: freeware applications such as COPS and Tripwire, or third-party commercial products like AXENT Technologies' Enterprise Security Manager™ (ESM), ISS's RealSecure™, or Kane Security Analyst™.

SUMMARY

The assumption must be made that we are not going to be able to stop everyone from getting into our computers. An intruder only has to succeed once. Security practitioners, on the other hand, have to succeed every time. Once we come to this conclusion, then, the only strategy we have left is to secure the Perimeter the best we can while allowing business to continue and have some means to detect the intrusions as they happen. If we can do this, we can limit what the intruder can do.

Chapter 6
Extranet Access Control Issues

Christopher King

Many businesses are discovering the value of networked applications with business partners and customers. Extranets allow trading partners to exchange information electronically by extending their intranets. The security architecture necessary to allow this type of communication must provide adequate protection of corporate data and the proper separation of data among users (e.g., confidential partner information). The information security technologies must minimize the risk to the intranet while keeping the extranet configuration flexible. Corporations are acting as service providers, providing a common network and resources to be shared among the user base. The Web server is evolving into a universal conduit to corporate resources. Without adequate security controls, extranet security will become unmanageable.

INTRODUCTION

Most extranets are used for business-to-business (BTB) and electronic commerce applications between trading partners and external customers. Historically, these applications used value-added networks (VAN) with electronic data exchange (EDI) transactions. The VANs provided a private point-to-point connection between the enterprises, and EDI's security was inherent in the format of the data and the manual process after transmission. VANs, by design, were outsourced to VAN providers (e.g., Sterling, IBM, GEIS, and Harbinger). With the advent of virtual private network (VPN) technology, providing a private channel over a public network (i.e., the Internet), VAN-based EDI growth is currently at a standstill. A new data interchange format based on extensible markup language (XML) is rivaling EDI for Internet-enabled applications.

0-8493-9829-0/00/$0.00+$.50
© 2000 by CRC Press LLC

Companies can use an extranet to:

- Supplement and possibly replace existing VANs using EDI.
- Project management and control for companies that are part of a common work project.
- Provide a value-added service to their customers that are difficult to replace.
- Share product catalogs exclusively with wholesalers or those "in the trade."
- Collaborate with other companies on joint development efforts.

There are two distinct types of extranets: a one-to-many and a many-to-many. A one-to-many is more common, linking many companies to a single resource (e.g., home banking). A many-to-many extranet is viewed as the intersection of a number of different company intranets (e.g., the Automotive Network Exchange). Extranets are soaring because they facilitate a seamless flow of information and commerce among employees, suppliers, and customers and because they sharply reduce communication costs. Extranet connectivity can be used for short- and long-term business relationships. This chapter concentrates on the access control mechanism and the administration aspects of extending one's intranet. The access control enforcement mechanisms generally fall into the following categories: **network** — VPN, firewall, intrusion detection; **authentication** — certificate, token, password; **platform** — intrusion detection, compliance management, Web-to-Web server, Web agent, monitoring, and auditing.

For an extranet to be successful it must be contained within a secure environment and add value to the existing line of business. Organizations that are currently implementing intranets should consider a security infrastructure that allows them to securely extend the intranet to form an extranet. This will allow them to leverage information sharing between trading partners.

WHO IS ON THE WIRE?

Intranet, extranet, and the Internet are all networks of networks. The major difference between the three classes of networks is the aspect of network traffic control (i.e., who are the participants in the network). Intranets are owned by individual organizations (i.e., intraenterprise systems). Some organizations operate their own network, and some outsource that function to network operations groups (e.g., EDS, AT&T Data Solutions, etc.). A key characteristic of intranet implementation is that protected applications are not visible to the Internet at large. Intranet access control relies heavily on the physical access point to the corporate LAN. Once physical access is gained into a corporate site, application access controls are the only constraint on access to corporate resources. Secure intranets are separated from the Internet by means of a firewall system. Inbound Internet traffic is NOT allowed into the corporate security perimeter except for e-mail. Outbound network traffic destined to the Internet from the intranet is not usually filtered. Some corporations constrain outbound traffic to allow only Web-based protocols (e.g., HTTP, FTP, and IIOP).

The rise in remote access usage is making the reliance on physical proximity to the corporate LAN a moot point. With a growing number of access points in today's corporate intranets, network and application security has to become more stringent to provide adequate protection for corporate resources. The lines between the intranet and other classes of networks are becoming blurred.

A one-to-many (e.g., provider-centric) extranet is a *secure* extension of an enterprise intranet. A many-to-many (e.g., user-centric) extranet is a secure extension of two or more enterprise intranets. This secure extension allows well-defined interactions between the participating organizations. This private network uses the Internet protocols and possibly the public network as a transport mechanism. "Private" means that this network is not publicly accessible. Only the extranet providers' suppliers, vendors, partners, and customers are allowed onto this network. Once access is gained to the network, fine-grained application and platform controls must exist (i.e., a combination of network and application security must be in place) to further restrict access to data and resources. The technology for building an extranet is essentially the same as that for intranets (e.g., Web-based). This doesn't mean that access to extranet resources will allow an extranet user to communicate with the provider's intranet directly. There must be a secure partition between the extranet and the provider's intranet. Extranet security must be tight, so corporations can develop stronger business relationships and forge closer ties with individuals who need differing levels of access to information or resources on their network. The challenge is to develop a proper security architecture that allows semi-trusted users to *share* a network with other individual organizations. These organizations could be competitors, so access control is of the utmost importance.

Internet applications that employ application-level security do not constitute an extranet. There must be a *clear separation* between the extranet resources (e.g., database, application logic or platforms) and the Internet and intranet. An extranet requires a higher level of security and privacy than traditional intranets. Most corporations have strong perimeter security and lenient security controls once inside the intranet (i.e., hard and crunchy outside and soft and chewy middle). The extranet also has to be designed with industry-standard development techniques (e.g., IP, SQL, LDAP, S/MIME, RADIUS, and especially Web).

INTERNET, INTRANET, AND EXTRANET SECURITY

The Internet is a global network of networks providing ubiquitous access to an increasing user base. Enterprises use the Internet and its technologies to save money and to generate revenue. The Internet technology (e.g., Web) has influenced the other classes of networks. Web development tools are plentiful and come at a relatively low cost with a short development cycle. The problems with the current state of the Internet are security and reliability. Enterprises should not rely too heavily on the Internet for time-sensitive or critical applications.

Some of the differences between an intranet and the Internet are the quality of service (QOS) or lack of service level agreements (SLA) which describe availability, bandwidth, latency, and response time. Most Internet service providers (ISPs) and networking device vendors are developing an Internet level of service capability. This will allow for classes of services with a price differential (see Exhibit 6.1).

EXTRANET SECURITY POLICY

The goal of an extranet security policy is to act as the foundation upon which all information-security related activities are based. In order for this security policy to be effective, it must receive approval and support from all the extranet participants (i.e., senior management). The security policy must keep up with the technological pace of the information systems technology. In other words, as access to corporate resources changes with the technology, the security must be updated. The security policy must balance the organization's operational requirements with the state-of-the-art in security solutions. Since both of these are under constant change, the policy must stay current. Some of the high-level statements in an extranet policy follow.

The extranet security architecture supports the following statements:

- The extranet must be securely partitioned from the corporate intranet.
- Secure network connectivity must be provided using a dedicated line or using a VPN.
- Extranet users must be uniquely identified using adequate authentication techniques.
- Authorization must adhere to the least-privilege principle.
- Extranet managers will receive monthly access reports to verify the proper use of the network.
- The extranet must NOT provide a routable path to the participant networks (i.e., the extranet provider's network should not allow packets to flow between partner networks).
- A real-time monitoring, auditing, and alerting facility must be employed to detect fraud and abuse.

ENFORCEMENT	INTRANET	EXTRANET	INTERNET
Security policy enforcement	The enterprise-wide security policy is enforced by the intranet security architecture.	The majority is provided by the network facilitator and agreed upon by the extranet user base.	The Internet is under no auspices for security policy enforcement.
Physical/Platform access enforcement	Highly controlled — only data center personnel have physical access to application server and network equipment.	Highly controlled — only the enterprise hosting the data center personnel has physical access to application server and network equipment. If a business partner owns a piece of equipment, it is shared between both organizations.	No physical access is provided to external users.
Network access enforcement	Private — only corporate personnel have access to this network via WAN and remote access methods. All network protocols are allowed.	Semi-private — only extranet users (e.g., business partners) have access to this network. Network protocols must be filtered to protect the intranet.	Public — All external users have ubiquitous access to an organization's public information. No network protocols other than e-mail and Web are allowed.
Application access enforcement	Semi-private — application provides some level of access control. In most cases it is a very lax security environment.	Private — Users must be authenticated and authorized to perform operations depending on their rights (i.e., least privilege).	None — Web-based applications are used to disseminate static information. There are some instances of protected access pages using basic authentication.
Quality of service guarantee	High — with the proper networking equipment (e.g., smart switches and advanced routing protocols).	Depends on the extranet provider network and participating client network provider.	None — SLA between ISPs does not exist, yet. It is in the works.

Exhibit 6.1. Security Enforcement Categories for Each Network Classification

Before the extranet can be connected to the outside world, the extranet provider must understand its network and the application vulnerabilities of extranet users and internal intranet users. This usually involves a detailed risk assessment by a certified third party. It also includes a formal review of the baseline security policy and security architecture that it meets. The assessments should be periodic, exhaustive, and include all of the member organizations of the extranet.

Secure extranet applications provide a well-defined set of data and resources to a well-defined set of authenticated individuals. To properly design authorization into an application, some basic security concepts must be employed such as: separation of duties, least-privilege, and individual accountability. Separation of duties is the practice of dividing the steps in a critical function (e.g., direct DBMS access, JAVA applet updates) among different individuals. The least privilege principle is the practice of restricting a user's access (DMBS updates or remote administration), or type of access (read, write, execute, delete) to the minimum necessary to perform the job. Individual accountability consists of holding someone responsible for his actions. Accountability is normally accomplished by identifying and authenticating users of the system and subsequently tracing actions on the system to the user who initiated them.

NETWORK PARTITIONING

To enforce the proper separation of networks, a commercial suite of network access control devices must be used. Separating the networks from each other offers one level of security necessary for a secure extranet solution. The proper network topology must exist to further protect the networks. A combination of firewalls and real-time intrusion detection configured to be as stringent as possible should adequately control network traffic flow. Exhibit 6.2 depicts such a topology.

Each network is protected using a commercial firewall product (e.g., Checkpoint Firewall-1, Cisco PIX). There is no direct connection from the Internet to the intranet. The firewall closest to the Internet (FWA) only allows encrypted traffic into the VPN gateway. Most commercial firewalls have been around since 1994; VPN devices started appearing in early 1998. Since VPN devices are latecomers to the Internet, it is better to protect them with a firewall than to leave them unprotected from current and future Internet threats. Since the data is decrypted after the VPN gateway, it should be filtered before entering the extranet (FWB). The provider's intranet is protected from any extranet threats using an additional firewall (FWC).

Extranet users gain access to the extranet by traditional means (e.g., leased lines) or by using VPNs. In a one-to-many extranet, clients must not

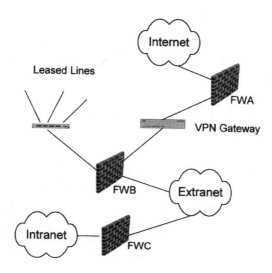

Exhibit 6.2. Extranet Network Topology

be able to communicate directly with each other via the extranet. The network routing rules must enforce a non-loop back policy (i.e., a network route between two clients).

EXTRANET AUTHENTICATION

User accountability is the ability to bind critical data functions to a single user. It holds users responsible for their actions. The extranet security architecture must enforce user accountability. At the network level, user accountability is impossible because of proxy servers, application gateway firewalls, and address translation. All the users from an organization will have the same IP address. Authentication must be performed at the application layer.

Extranet authentication is not a trivial task due to its political nature, not due to its technology. Most users already have too many passwords to remember to access their own system. Since user administration is typically distributed to the partnering organization, once users have authenticated themselves to their own organization, they should not have to authenticate themselves again to the extranet. The extranet application should leverage the authentication information and status from the user's originating organization using a proxy authentication mechanism. This allows the user to gain access to the extranet resources once they have authenticated themselves to their local domain.

Device authentication includes VPN gateways and public key infrastructure (PKI)-aware servers (e.g., Web and directory servers using secure sockets layer, SSL). VPN gateways optionally can use a shared secret instead of certificates, but this technique is unmanageable if the device count is too high.

Specific examples of proxy authentication techniques are NT domain authentication, cross certification with digital certificates, RADIUS, and a shared directory server.

EXTRANET AUTHORIZATION

Once network access is granted, it is up to the application (most likely Web-based with a database backend) to provide further authentication and authorization. Most Web server access control is provided using basic authentication. The user's rights (i.e., Web files and directories they have access to) and authentication information combined is called a user's profile. This information is stored and enforced locally on the Web server. Local Web access controls are not a scalable solution, if the user base is large, then this type of solution is unmanageable. Access to Web files and directories is sufficient for static content security. New Web development tools ease the access into database, mainframe, and BackOffice systems. Web applications are starting to look more and more like traditional client/server applications of a few years ago. The Web server is becoming a universal conduit to corporate resources.

There are many access control enforcement points between the Web server and the data being accessed, such as, the browser, the firewall, the application server, or the DBMS.

Exhibit 6.3 depicts how third-party Web access control (WAC) products such as Encommerce getAccess, Netegrity Siteminder, and Axent Webdefender provide Web login, authentication, authorization, personal navigation, and automated administration. Due to the Web's stateless nature, cookies are used to keep state between the browsers and the server. To prevent modification of the cookie by the end user, it is encrypted. The Web server must be modified to include a Web agent. The Web agent uses the Web server API (e.g., NSAPI for Netscape Enterprise Server and ISAPI for Microsoft's Internet Information Server). Access control information is controlled from a single point. Once a change is made in the security rulebase, it is replicated to all of the protected Web servers.

EXTRANET ADMINISTRATION

Extranet system administration is performed by the organization providing the service. However, user administration remains a touchy subject. The user administration of the Extranet is dictated by the relationships

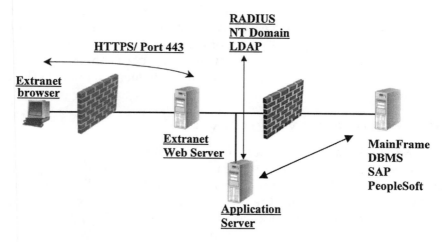

Exhibit 6.3. Web Access Control Architecture

---

between the participating organizations. Extranet managers are the points-of-contact at each organization and are legally responsible for their users. For example, is user authentication centrally administered by the extranet provider, or is it distributed among the participants, leveraging it off their existing authentication database? It would be difficult to manage 1000 business partners with 1000 users each.

Corporate users are already inundated with username/password pairs. If Extranet access were provided over the corporate network, another authentication scheme would only complicate the issue. Several questions that need to be addressed come to mind: (1) How can we integrate with an external business partner's security infrastructures? (2) How do we leverage the participants' existing security infrastructure?

Authentication is only a piece of the pie; what about authorization? Do we provide authorization at the user level, or use the concept of roles, grouping users into functions, for example, business managers, accountants, user administrators, clerks, etc.?

The way users get access to sensitive resources (i.e., items you wish to protect) is by a role-resource and user-role relationship. The extranet authorization model consists of the totality of all the user-role and role-resource relationships. This information is usually stored within a relational DBMS or a directory server. The extranet's system administrator, with input from the resource owners, is responsible for creating and maintaining this model.

The principle of least privilege will be used when an administrator assigns users to the system. Least privilege requires that an administrator grant only the most restrictive set of privileges necessary to perform authorized tasks. In other words, users will access their necessary resources to perform their job function with a minimum amount of system privileges.

EXTRANET CONNECTION AGREEMENTS

Allowing access to private data from external business partners could pose some liability issues. One of the major problems is that the legal systems lag significantly behind the advances in technology. From an insurance coverage standpoint, the problem that underwriters have is the inability to calculate the security exposure for a given information system. The best defense is a proper security architecture derived from a detailed security policy. This solves the enterprise security problem, but in most cases the corporate security policy cannot be extended outside the enterprise. A separate extranet data connection agreement must be developed and adhered to by all participants. This agreement would specify the basic terms and conditions for doing business together in a secure fashion.

The following lists some considerations for data connection agreements:

- A description of the applications and information that will be accessible by the external partner.
- A point of contact(s) for each participating organization, to be contacted in the event of a security incident.
- The legal document (e.g., non-disclosure, and security procedures) signed by partners and the external customer's authorized representative.
- The term or length (days), and start and end date, of the service.
- A protection of information statement that details the safeguard requirements (e.g., copying, transmitting to third parties, precautions, destruction) of the data transmitted.
- The sharing of responsibilities by both parties. This includes the necessary access for a physical security audit and a logical security audit (e.g., network penetration tools) at each facility.
- An indemnification statement that each party agrees to compensate the other party for any loss or damages incurred as a result of unauthorized access to the data facilities and misuse of information.
- A termination statement that is executed if either party fails to adhere to the data connection agreement provisions.
- Security awareness training for users at external or partner sites.

EXTRANET MONITORING

Extranet monitoring is important for security and business reasons. Frequent analysis of audit data is useful in case questions arise about improper systems access and to generate marketing report data (i.e., how many times were my resources accessed and by whom).

Security monitoring usually occurs wherever access control decisions are being made, for example, the firewall, authentication server, and the application itself. The problem with monitoring is that there is no real-time analysis of the data, just log entries in some file or database. Data reduction from raw data logs is not a trivial task. No standards exist for data storage or formats, and users must compile diverse logs of information and produce their own reports from the application, firewall, or network operating system. The audit trail entries must contain a specific user ID, time stamp, function and requested data. Using a scripting language such as PERL, a security manager will have to write a set of scripts to generate reports of log-in times, data accessed, and services used. In more security-intensive applications, the enterprise should install some real-time analysis tools (e.g., Internet Security Systems' RealSecure or Cisco's Net Ranger) to generate additional data and monitor for anomalous behavior.

EXTRANET SECURITY INFRASTRUCTURE

The Extranet security infrastructure consists of all the supporting security services that are required to field a security architecture. Such an architecture would include a directory server, a certificate server, an authentication server, and Web security servers. These require firewall server management; the issuance and use of digital certificates or similar means of user authentication; encryption of messages; and the use of virtual private networks (VPNs) that tunnel through the public network.

VPN TECHNOLOGY

Virtual Private Network technology allows external partners to securely participate in the extranet using public networks as a transport (i.e., Internet). VPNs rely on tunneling and encapsulation techniques, which allow the Internet Protocol (IP) to carry a wide range of popular non-IP traffic (e.g., IPX, NetBEUI). VPN technology provides encryption and authentication features within an ancillary network device to firewalls and routers called a VPN gateway. Performance enhancements in the Internet backbone and access equipment now provide the throughput needed to compete with private networks. All of these enabling technologies are based on standards that yield end-to-end interoperability. Finally, preparing Points of Presence (POPs) for VPNs is relatively simple and inexpensive. Low costs with high margin VPNs are good business.

Because VPN technology uses encryption as the basis for its security, interoperability among vendors is a major issue. The Internet Engineering Task Force (IETF) IP Security (IPSEC) specification was chosen to alleviate this problem. The IETF developed IPSEC as a security protocol for the next generation IPv6. IPSEC is an optional extension for the implementation of the current version, IPv4. IPv4 is widespread on the Internet and in corporate networks, but its design does not include any security provisions. IPSEC provides confidentiality and integrity to information transferred over IP networks through network layer encryption and authentication. IPSEC protects networks from IP network attacks, including denial of service, man-in-the-middle, and spoofing. Refer to Requests for Comment (RFC)2401 through 2412 for full details.

Before VPN devices can communicate, they must negotiate a mutually agreeable way of securing their data. As part of this negotiation, each node has to verify that the other node is actually the node it claims to be. VPN authentication schemes use digital certificate or a shared secret between communicating devices. A shared secret is a password agreed upon by the two device administrators in advance. When the administrators try to communicate, each must supply the agreed-upon password. Authentication based on certificates is more secure than password-based authentication because of distribution and formation. Passwords have to be difficult to guess and shared in a secure fashion. Since certificates are based on public key technology, they are immune to this problem.

With all of this said, using VPNs has the following drawbacks:

DRAWBACK	DESCRIPTION
Not fault tolerant	VPN devices are not fault tolerant. The IPSEC protocol does not currently support failover. This should be addressed and implemented before the end of 2000.
Performance	There are many implementation choices for VPNs (e.g., software, black box, and outboard cryptographic processors). Software solutions tend to be used for clients. Since VPN gateways are aggregating many simultaneous connections, a software-only gateway cannot keep up. Outboard cryptographic processors are used to assist in the intense cryptographic function by host-based devices (e.g., PCI slot). None of these solutions can compete with a dedicated hardware device (e.g., black box).
Reliable transport	The Internet service providers are not yet capable of providing adequate, peak or scalable bandwidth at a reasonable cost. Cisco and some of the large ISP are testing a technology called Multiprotocol label switching. MPLS allows the ISPs to offer different levels of service to their customer base.
Network placement	Most enterprises manage their own or outsource control over their Internet firewall. Where should the VPN gateway be placed? In front of, behind, parallel with, or on the firewall? These are questions with many tradeoffs.

DRAWBACK	DESCRIPTION
Addressing	Networks are not generally additive. Special care has to be taken in terms of addressing before joining two or more disparate networks. If two or more of the networks are using private address space (e.g., 10.x.x.x) with any overlap, routing can be tricky.
Key management (PKI)	VPN formation requires cryptographic information. Shared secrets between points are not scalable. The only solution is certificates. The problem that exists is that this technology is about six to nine months behind the VPN technology, which was finalized in November 1998.
Interoperability	IPSEC compliance is a term that is overused by VPN vendors. The only real compliance is an interoperability report among heterogeneous vendors. As of this writing there are only six vendors who can fully interoperate.

RESIDUAL RISKS/LIABILITY

There is no such thing as complete security. There is an associated cost with providing an adequate level of security; the adequacy is measured against the best business practices in the industry. The addition of more security safeguards comes at a high cost and only offers a minor increase in the overall security level. Extranet security has the additional burden of providing even more security and privacy from participants who are competitors. Unauthorized access to repositories of information and applications could, in the wrong hands, prove detrimental to their participants. The resolution is to manage the risk and to weigh the benefits against the resultant risk. As a supplement to all of the security mechanisms, a lawyer should be involved in the extranet data agreement. The lawyer can draw up necessary warnings to deter casual intruders as well as agreements to protect your company in the event of misuse of the data. An alternative might be to outsource the extranet to a service provider.

EXTRANET OUTSOURCING

Many ISPs and telcos are offering extranet services that provide a managed network with controlled access. Extranet service providers have a strong technical knowledge of networking and security. They also have invested in the infrastructure required to manage an extranet, for example, a PKI with an X.500 directory service. Another advantage is that the service provider can offer better network reliability and bandwidth (e.g., service level agreements). If all the extranet participants utilize this existing service provider, an SLA can be negotiated. See Exhibit 6.4 for an example architecture of an outsourced extranet.

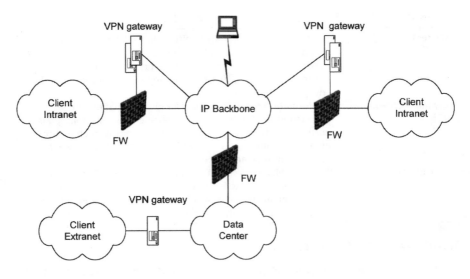

Exhibit 6.4. Extranet Network Topology

AUTOMOTIVE NETWORK EXCHANGE

The Automotive Network eXchange (ANX) is a many-to-many extranet between Chrysler Corp., General Motors Corp., and Ford Motor Company and their suppliers. This extranet utilizes VPN technology. ANX will be used to electronically route product shipment schedules, order information, engineering and drawing files for product designs, purchase orders, and other financial information. ANX replaces 50 to 100 direct-dial connections to the automakers, reducing telecommunication costs up to 70 percent, but the real payoffs are in the speed and ease of communications between suppliers and manufacturers. The real benefit is monetary savings estimated in the billions from the traditional supply chain costs and the speed of new automotive designs to less than a three-year design cycle. The improved exchange of information should result in new business practices between vendors and manufacturers.

SUMMARY

Extranets have indeed arrived and may well mean changes to how business relationships are viewed. The key to maximizing participation is to make the extranet as accessible to as many partners as possible, regardless of their technical adeptness. The more participants there are, the greater the rates of return from the system. Major enterprise resource planning (ERP) systems (e.g., Baan and SAP) are providing hooks to allow external business partners to connect with automated back-office systems.

The network boundaries (extra, intra, and Inter) continue to erode so one will have to depend on application layer security. The problem is providing a common, or standard, protection scheme for applications. This is another emerging field of security, probably with a two- or more-year development and integration cycle.

The desire to provide an enhanced layer of security, reliability, and quality of service on top of the Internet will be the primary driver of VPNs as a subset of electronic commerce extranet deployment. These features are not offered by most ISPs. Next-generation Internet and Internet2 research and development projects are testing very high-speed (gigabit) networks. Large telephone companies are laying the foundation for the networks into which the Internet may eventually evolve, as well as the support equipment (routers, switches, hubs, and network interface cards) needed to drive networks at such high speeds. Network security and virtual private network technologies will be improved, which will facilitate future extranets.

GLOSSARY

ANX	Automotive Network eXchange
BTB	Business-to-Business
DBMS	Database Management System
EDI	Electronic Data Interchange
FTP	File Transfer Protocol
HTTP	Hyper Text Transfer Protocol
IETF	Internet Engineering Task Force
IIOP	Internet Inter-ORB Protocol
IP	Internet Protocol
IPSEC	IP Security
ISAPI	Internet Server Application Program Interface
LDAP	Lightweight Directory Access Protocol
MPLS	Multiprotocol Label Switching
NSAPI	Netscape Server Application Program Interface
PCI	Peripheral Component Interconnect
PKI	Public Key Infrastructure
QOS	Quality of Service

RADIUS	Remote Authentication Dial-In User Service
RSA	Rivest, Shamir, and Adleman
S/MIME	Secure Multi-purpose Internet Mail Extension
SLA	Service Level Agreement
SQL	Structured Query Language
SSL	Secure Sockets Layer
VAN	Value Added Network
VPN	Virtual Private Network
WAC	Web Access Control
XML	Extensible Markup Language

Chapter 7

Firewall Management and Internet Attacks

Lt. Jeffery J. Lowder

Network connectivity can be both a blessing and a curse. On the one hand, network connectivity can enable users to share files, exchange e-mail, and pool physical resources. Yet network connectivity can also be a risky endeavor, if the connectivity grants access to would-be intruders. The Internet is a perfect case in point. Designed for a trusted environment, many contemporary exploits are based upon vulnerabilities inherent to the protocol itself. According to a recent dissertation by John Howard on Internet unauthorized access incidents reported to the Computer Emergency Response Team (CERT), there were 4,567 incidents between 1989 and 1996, with the number of incidents increasing each year at a rate of 41 to 62 percent. In light of this trend, many organizations are implementing firewalls to protect their internal network from the untrusted Internet.

Indeed, many people incorrectly believe that a firewall is a panacea for their network security concerns; many more believe that they have configured their firewalls correctly when in fact they have not. This chapter addresses the security issues specific to firewall management: choosing a firewall, how to lay the groundwork for a firewall, implementing a firewall, conducting firewall operations, and establishing and enforcing firewall policy and standards.

LAYING THE GROUNDWORK FOR A FIREWALL

Obtaining management support for a firewall prior to implementation can be very useful after the firewall is implemented. When a firewall is implemented on a network for the first time, it will almost surely be the source of many complaints. For example:

- Organizations that have never before had firewalls almost never have the kind of documentation necessary to support user requirements.

- If the firewall hides information about the internal network from the outside network, this will break any network transactions in which the remote system uses an access control list, and the address of the firewall is not included in that list.
- Certain types of message traffic useful in network troubleshooting (e.g., PING, TRACEROUTE) may no longer work.

All of these problems can be solved, but the point is that coordination with senior management *prior to* installation can make life much easier for firewall administrators.

Benefits of Having a Firewall

So how does one obtain management support for implementation of a firewall? The security practitioner can point out the protection that a firewall provides: protection of the organization's network from intruders, protection of external networks from intruders within the organization, and protection from "due care" lawsuits. But the security practitioner can also list the *positive* benefits a firewall can provide:

- *Increased ability to enforce network standards and policies.* Without a firewall or similar device, it is easy for users to implement systems that the Information Services (IS) department doesn't know about, that are in violation of organizational standards or policies, or both. In contrast, organizations find it very easy to enforce both standards and policies with a firewall that blocks all network connections *by default.* Indeed, it is not uncommon for organizations to discover undocumented systems when they implement such a firewall for the first time.
- *Centralized internetwork audit capability.* Since all or most traffic between the two networks must pass through the firewall (see below), the firewall is uniquely situated to provide audit trails of all connections between the two networks. These audit trails can be extremely useful for investigating suspicious network activity, troubleshooting connectivity problems, measuring network traffic flows, and even investigating employee fraud, waste, and abuse.

Limitations of a Firewall

But even with all of these benefits, firewalls still have their limitations. It is important that the security practitioner understand these limitations because if these limitations allow risks which are unacceptable to management, it is up to the security practitioner to present additional safeguards to minimize these risks. The security practitioner must not allow management to develop a false sense of security simply because a firewall has been installed.

- *Firewalls provide no data integrity.* It is simply not feasible to check all incoming traffic for viruses. There are too many file formats, and often files are sent in compressed form. Any attempt to scan incoming files for viruses would severely degrade performance. Firewalls have plenty of processing requirements without taking on the additional responsibility of virus detection and eradication.

- *Firewalls don't protect traffic that is not sent through them.* Firewalls cannot protect against unsecured, dial-up modems attached to systems inside the firewall; against internal attacks; against social engineering attacks; or against data that is routed around them. It is not uncommon for an organization to install a firewall, then pass data from a legacy system around the firewall because their firewall did not support the existing system.
- *Firewalls may not protect anything if they have been compromised.* Although this statement should be obvious, many security practitioners fail to educate senior management on its implications. All too often senior management approves – either directly or through silence – a security posture which positively *lacks* an internal security policy. Security practitioners cannot allow perimeter security via firewalls to become a substitute for internal security.
- *Firewalls cannot authenticate datagrams at the transport or network layers.* A major security problem with the TCP/IP protocol is that any machine can forge a packet claiming to be from another machine. This means that the firewall has literally no control over how the packet was created. Any authentication must be supported in one of the higher layers.
- *Firewalls provide limited confidentiality.* Many firewalls have the ability to encrypt connections between two firewalls (using a so-called "virtual private network" or "VPN"), but they typically require that the firewall be manufactured by the same vendor.

A firewall is no replacement for good host security practices and procedures. Individual system administrators still have the primary responsibility for preventing security incidents.

FIREWALLS AND THE LOCAL SECURITY POLICY

Cheswick and Bellovin (1994) define a firewall as a system with the following set of characteristics:

1. All traffic between the two networks must pass through the firewall.
2. Only traffic that is authorized by the local security policy will be allowed to pass.
3. The firewall itself is immune to penetration.

Like any security tool, a firewall merely provides the *capability* to *increase* the security of the path between two networks. It is the responsibility of the firewall administrator to take advantage of this capability; and no firewall can guarantee *absolute* protection from outside attacks. The risk analysis should define the level of protection that can be expected from the firewall; the local security policy should provide general guidelines on how this protection will be achieved; and both the assessment and revised policy should be accepted by top management prior to firewall implementation.

Despite the fact that, according to (1), *all* traffic between the two networks must pass through the firewall, in practice this is not always technically feasible or convenient. Network administrators supporting legacy or proprietary systems may find that getting them to communicate through the firewall may not be as easy as firewall vendors claim, if even possible. And even if there are no technical obstacles to routing all traffic through the firewall, users may still complain that the firewall is inconvenient or slows down their systems. Thus, the local security policy should specify the process by which requests for exceptions (1) will be considered.

As (2) states, the local security policy defines what the firewall is supposed to enforce. If a firewall is going to allow only "authorized" traffic between two networks, then the firewall has to know what traffic is "authorized." The local security policy should define "authorized" traffic, and it should do so at a somewhat technical level. The policy should also state a default rule for evaluating requests: either all traffic is denied except that which is specifically authorized, or all traffic is allowed except that which is specifically denied.

Network devices which protect other network devices should themselves be protected against intruders. (If the protection device were not secure, intruders could compromise the device and then compromise the system[s] that the device was supposed to protect.)

FIREWALL EVALUATION CRITERIA

Choosing the right firewall for an organization can be a daunting task, given the complexity of the problem and the wide variety of products to choose from. Yet the following criteria should help the security practitioner narrow the list of candidates considerably:

- *Performance.* Firewalls *always* impact the performance of the connection between the local and remote networks. Adding a firewall creates an additional "hop" for network packets to travel through; if the firewall must authenticate connections, that creates an additional delay. The firewall machine should be powerful enough to make these delays negligible.
- *Requirements Support.* A firewall should support all of the applications that an organization wants to use across the two networks. Virtually all firewalls support fundamental protocols like SMTP, TELNET, FTP, and HTTP; strong firewalls should include some form of circuit proxy

or generic "packet relay." The security practitioner should decide what other applications are required (e.g., Real Audio, VDOLive, S-HTTP, etc.) and evaluate firewall products accordingly.

- *Access Control.* Even the simplest firewalls support access control based on IP addresses; strong firewalls will support user-based access control and authentication. Large organizations should pay special attention to whether a given firewall product supports a large number of user profiles and ensure that the firewall can accommodate increased user traffic.

- *Authentication.* The firewall must support the authentication requirements of the local security policy. If implementation of the local security policy will entail authenticating large numbers of users, the firewall should provide convenient yet secure enterprise-wide management of the user accounts. Some firewalls only allow the administrator to manage user accounts from a single console; this "solution" isn't good enough for organizations with thousands of users who each need their own authentication account. Moreover, there are logistical issues which need to be thought out. For example, suppose the local security policy requires authentication of all inbound TELNET connections. How will geographically separated users obtain the proper authentication credentials (e.g., passwords, hard tokens, etc.)?

- *Physical Security.* The local security policy should stipulate the location of the firewall, and the hardware should be physically secured to prevent unauthorized access. The firewall must also be able to interface with surrounding hardware at this location.

- *Auditing.* The firewall must support the auditing requirements of the local security policy. Depending on network bandwidth and the level of event logging, firewall audit trails can become quite large. Superior firewalls will include a data reduction tool for parsing audit trails.

- *Logging and Alarms.* What logging and alarms does your security policy require? If the security policy dictates that a potential intrusion event trigger an alarm and mail message to the administrator, the system must accommodate this requirement.

- *Customer Support.* What level of customer support does the firewall vendor provide? If your organization requires 24-hour-a-day, 365-days-a-year technical support, is it available? Does the vendor provide training courses? Is self-help online assistance, such as a Web page or a mailing list, available?

- *Transparency.* How transparent is the firewall to your users? The more transparent your firewall is to your users, the more likely they will be to support it. On the other hand, the more confusing or cumbersome your firewall, the more likely your users are to resist it.

FIREWALL TECHNIQUES

There are three different techniques available to firewalls to enforce the local security policy: packet filtering, circuit gateways, and application proxies. These techniques are not mutually exclusive; in practice, firewalls tend to implement multiple techniques to varying extents. This section will define these firewall techniques.

Packet Filtering

Packet filters allow or drop packets according to the source or destination address or port. The administrator makes a list of acceptable and unacceptable machines and services, and configures the packet filter accordingly. This makes it very easy for the administrator to filter access at the network or host level, but impossible to filter access at the user level (see Exhibit 7.1).

rule number	action	local host	local port	remote host	remote port
0	deny	*	*	*	*
1	allow	www-server	80	*	*

Exhibit 7.1. Sample Packet Filter Configuration

The packet filter applies the rules in order from top to bottom. Thus, in Exhibit 7.1, rule 0 blocks all network traffic by default; rule 1 creates an exception to allow unrestricted access on port 80 to the organization's Web server.

But what if the firewall administrator wanted to allow telnet access to the Web server by the Webmaster? The administrator could configure the packet filter as shown in Exhibit 7.2.

rule number	action	local host	local port	remote host	remote port
0	deny	*	*	*	*
1	allow	www-server	80	*	*
2	allow	www-server	23	<machine room>	*

Exhibit 7.2. Packet Filter Configuration to Allow Telnet Access from <machine room> to <www-server>

The packet filter would thus allow telnet access (port 23) to the web server from the address or addresses represented by <machine room>, but the packet filter has no concept of user authentication. Thus, unauthorized individuals originating from the <machine room> address(es) would be allowed telnet access to the www-server, while authorized individuals originating from non-<machine room> address(es) would be denied access. In both cases, the lack of user authentication would prevent the packet filter from enforcing the local security policy.

Application-Level Gateways

Unlike packet filters, application-level gateways do not enforce access control lists. Instead, application-level gateways attempt to enforce *connection integrity* by ensuring that all data passed on a given port is in accordance with the protocol for that port. This is very useful for preventing transmissions prohibited by the protocol, but not handled properly by the remote system. Consider, for example, the Hyper Text Transmission Protocol (HTTP) used by World Wide Web servers to send and receive information, normally on port 80. Intruders have been able to compromise numerous servers by transmitting special packets outside the HTTP specification. Pure packet filters are ineffective against such attacks because they can only *restrict access* to a port based on source and destination address, but an application gateway could actually prevent such an attack by *enforcing the protocol specification* for all traffic on the related port.

The application gateway relays connections in a manner similar to that of the circuit-level gateway (see below), but it provides the additional service of checking individual packets for the particular application in use. They also have the additional ability to log all inbound and outbound connections.

CIRCUIT-LEVEL GATEWAYS

A circuit-level gateway creates a virtual circuit between the local and remote networks by relaying connections. The originator opens a connection on a port to the gateway, and the gateway in turn opens a connection on that same port to the remote machine. The gateway machine relays data back and forth until the connection is terminated.

Because circuit-level gateways relay packets without inspecting them, they normally provide only minimal audit capabilities and no application-specific controls. Moreover, circuit-level gateways require new or modified client software that does not attempt to establish connections with the remote site directly; the client software must allow the circuit relay to do its job.

Firewall Technique	Advantages	Disadvantages
Packet Filtering	• completely transparent • easy to filter access at the host or network level • inexpensive: can use existing routers to implement	• reveals internal network topology • does not provide enough granularity for most security policies • difficult to configure • does not support certain traffic • susceptible to address-spoofing • limited or no logging, alarms • no user authentication
Application-Level Gateways	• application-level security • strong user access control • strong logging and auditing support • ability to conceal internal network	• requires specialized proxy for each service • slower to implement new services • inconvenient to end users • no support for client software that does not support redirection
Circuit-Level Gateways	• transparent to user • excellent for relaying outbound connections	• inbound connections risky • must provide new client programs

Exhibit 7.3.   Advantages and Disadvantages of Firewall Techniques

Still, circuit relays are transparent to the user. They are well-suited for outbound connections in which authentication is important but integrity is not.

See Exhibit 7.3 for a comparison of these firewall techniques.

DEVELOPING A FIREWALL POLICY AND STANDARDS

Reasons for Having Firewall Policy and Standards

There are a number of reasons for writing formal firewall policies and standards, including:

- *Properly-written firewall policies and standards will address important issues which may not be covered by other policies.* Having a generic corporate policy on information systems security isn't good enough. There are a number of specific issues that apply to firewalls but would not be addressed, or addressed in adequate detail, by generic security policies.
- *A firewall policy can clarify how the organization's security objectives apply to the firewall.* For example, a generic organizational policy on information protection might state that "access to information is granted on a need to know basis." A firewall policy would *interpret* this objective by stating that "all traffic is denied except that which is explicitly authorized."
- *An approved set of firewall standards makes configuration decisions much more objective.* A firewall, especially one with a restrictive configuration,

can become a hot *political* topic if the firewall administrator wants to block traffic that a user really wants. Specifying the decision-making process for resolving such issues in a formal set of standards will make the process much more consistent to *all* users. Everyone may not always get what they want, but at least the issue will be decided through a process that was adopted *in advance.*

Policy and Standards Development Process

The following process is recommended as an efficient, comprehensive way to develop a firewall policy. If the steps of this process are followed in order, the security practitioner may avoid making time-wasting oversights and errors in the policy. (See also Exhibit 7.4.)

1. *Risk analysis.* An organization really ought to perform a risk analysis *prior to* developing a policy or a set of standards. The risk analysis will not only help policy-makers identify specific issues to be addressed in the document itself, but the relative weight the policy-makers should assign to those issues.
2. *Identify list of topics to cover.* A partial listing of topics is suggested under Policy Structure later in this chapter; security policy-makers should also identify any other relevant issues which may be relevant to the organization's firewall implementation.
3. *Assign responsibility.* An organization must define the roles and responsibilities of those accountable for administering the firewall. If necessary, modify job descriptions to reflect the additional responsibility for implementing, maintaining, and administering the firewall, as well as establishing, maintaining, and enforcing policy and standards.
4. *Define the audience.* Is the policy document intended to be read by IS personnel only? Or is the document intended to be read by the entire organization? The document's audience will determine its scope, as well as its degree of technical and legal detail.
5. *Write the policy.* Since anyone may read the document, write without regard to the reader's position within the organization. When it is necessary to refer to other organizational entities, use functional references whenever possible (e.g., "Public Relations" instead of "Tom Smith, Public Relations"). And be sure to list a contact person for readers who may have questions about the policy.
6. *Identify mechanisms to foster compliance.* A policy is ineffective if it does not encourage employees to comply with the policy. Therefore, the individual(s) responsible for developing or maintaining the policy must ensure that adequate *mechanisms* for enforcement exist. These enforcement mechanisms should not be confused with the clause(s) of a policy which specify the *consequences* for noncompliance. Rather, enforcement mechanisms should include such administrative

procedures as awareness and training, obtaining employee signatures on an agreement that specifies the employee has read and understands the policy and will comply with the intent.

7. *Review.* New policies should be reviewed by representatives of all major departments of the organization, not just IS personnel. A special effort should be made to resolve any disagreements at this stage: the more low- and mid-level support that exists for a policy, the easier it will be to implement that policy.

(a) Risk analysis.
(b) Identify list of topics to cover.
(c) Assign responsibility for policy.
(d) Define the audience.
(e) Write the policy.
(f) Identify mechanisms to foster compliance.
(g) Review.

Exhibit 7.4. Policy Development Process

After the policy has been coordinated with (and hopefully endorsed by) department representatives, the policy should be submitted to senior management for approval. It is extremely important that the most senior-level manager possible sign the policy. This will give the IS-security staff the authority they need to enforce the policy.

Once the policy is adopted, it should be reviewed on *at least* an annual basis. A review may have one of three results: no change, revisions to the policy, or abandoning the policy.

Policy Structure

A policy is normally understood to be a high-level document which outlines management's general instructions on how things are to be run. Therefore, an organizational firewall policy should outline that management expects other departments to support the firewall, the importance of the firewall to the organization, etc. The structure of a firewall policy should look as follows:

- Background: how does the importance of the firewall relate to overall organizational objectives, e.g., the firewall secures information assets against the threat of unauthorized external intrusion.
- Scope: to whom and what does this policy apply?
- Definitions: what is a firewall? What role does it play within the enterprise?
- Responsibilities: what resources and respective responsibilities need to be assigned to support the firewall? If the default configuration of the firewall shall be to block everything that is not specifically allowed, who is responsible for requesting exceptions? Who is authorized to approve these requests? On what basis will those decisions be made?
- Enforcement: what are the consequences of failing to meet the administrative responsibilities? How is noncompliance addressed?
- Frequency of Review: how often will this policy be reviewed? With which functions in the organization?
- Policy Coordinator: who is the point of contact for this policy?
- Date of Last Revision: when was this policy last revised?

FIREWALL STANDARDS

Firewall standards may be defined minimally as a set of configuration options for a firewall. (Although firewall standards can and should address more than mere configuration issues, all firewall standards cover *at least* this much.) Exhibit 7.5 presents a sample outline for firewall standards. Since all firewalls come with default configurations, all firewalls have default standards. The job of the security practitioner is to draft a comprehensive set of standards governing all aspects of firewall implementation, usage, and maintenance, including but not limited to:

- protection of logs against unauthorized modification
- frequency of log reviews
- how long will logs be retained?
- when will the logs be backed up?
- to whom will the alarms be sent?

LEGAL ISSUES CONCERNING FIREWALLS

If firewall audit trails need to be capable of being presented as evidence in a court of law, it is worthwhile to provide a "warning banner" to warn users about what sort of privacy they can expect. Many firewalls can be configured to display a warning banner on TELNET and FTP sessions. Exhibit 7.6 shows an example of such a warning.

I. Definition of Terms
II. Responsibilities of the Firewall Administrator
III. Statement of Firewall Limitations
    a. Inability to enforce data integrity
    b. Inability to prevent internal attacks
IV. Firewall Configuration
    a. Default policy (allow or deny) on network connections
    b. Physical location of firewall.
    c. Logical location of firewall in relation to other network nodes
    d. Firewall system access policy.
        1. Authorized individuals
        2. Authentication methods
        3. Policy on remote configuration
    e. Supported services
        1. Inbound
        2. Outbound
    f. Blocked services
        1. Inbound
        2. Outbound
    g. Firewall configuration change management policy
V. Firewall Audit Trail Policy
    a. Level of granularity (e.g., we will have one entry for each FTP or HTTP download)
    b. Frequency of review (e.g., we will check the logs once a day)
    c. Access control (e.g., access to firewall audit trails will be limited to the following individuals)
VI. Firewall Intrusion Detection Policy
    a. Alarms
        1. Alarm thresholds
        2. Alarm notifications (e.g., e-mail, pager, etc.)
    b. Notification Procedures
        1. Top management
        2. Public relations
        3. System administrators
        4. Incident response teams
        5. Law enforcement
        6. Other sites
    c. Response priorities (e.g., human safety, containment, public relations)
    d. Documentation procedures
VII. Backups
    a. Frequency of incremental backups
    b. Frequency of system backups
    c. Archive of backups (e.g., we will keep backups for 1 year)
    d. Off-site backup requirements
VIII. Firewall Outage Policy
    a. Planned outages
    b. Unplanned outages
        1. Reporting procedures
IX. Firewall Standards Review Policy (e.g., this policy shall be reviewed every six months)

Exhibit 7.5. Sample Outline of Firewall Standards

```
Per AFI 33-219 requirement:

                        Welcome to USAFAnet
                   United States Air Force Academy

This is an official Department of Defense (DoD) computer system for
authorized use only. All data contained on DoD computer systems is owned
by DoD and may be monitored, intercepted, recorded, read, copied, or
captured in any manner and disclosed in any manner by authorized
personnel. THERE IS NO RIGHT TO PRIVACY ON THIS SYSTEM. Authorized
personnel may give any potential evidence of crime found on DoD computer
systems to law enforcement officials. USE OF THIS SYSTEM BY ANY USER,
AUTHORIZED OR UNAUTHORIZED, CONSTITUTES EXPRESS CONSENT TO THIS
MONITORING, INTERCEPTION, RECORDING, READING, COPYING, OR CAPTURING, AND
DISSEMINATION BY AUTHORIZED PERSONNEL. Do not discuss, enter, transfer,
process, or transmit classified/sensitive national security information
of greater sensitivity than this system is authorized. USAFAnet is not
accredited to process classified information. Unauthorized use could
result in criminal prosecution. If you do not consent to these
conditions, do not log in!
```

Exhibit 7.6.   Sample Warning Banner

FIREWALL CONTINGENCY PLANNING

Firewall Outage

What would be the impact on your organization if your firewall was unavailable? If your organization has routed all of its Internet traffic through a firewall (as it should), then a catastrophic hardware failure of your firewall machine would result in a lack of Internet connectivity until the firewall machine is repaired or replaced. How long can your organization tolerate an outage? If the outage were a catastrophic hardware failure, do you know *how* you would repair or replace the components? Do you know *how long* it would take to repair or replace the components?

If your organization has a firewall, the odds are that a firewall outage would have a significant impact on your organization. (If the connection between the two networks was not important to your organization, why would your organization have the connection and protect it with a firewall?) Therefore the security practitioner must also develop contingency plans for responding to a firewall outage. These contingency plans must address three types of failures: hardware, software, and evolutionary (failure to keep pace with increasing usage requirements).

In the case of a hardware failure, the security practitioner has three options: repair, replacement, or removal. Firewall removal is a drastic measure that is not encouraged: it drastically reduces security while disrupting any user services which were specially configured around the firewall (e.g., Domain Name Service, proxies, etc.). Smaller organizations may choose to

127

repair their hardware because it is cheaper. Yet, this may not always be an option and may not be quick enough to satisfy user requirements. Conversely, access may be restored quickly by swapping in a "hot spare," but the cost of purchasing and maintaining such redundancy may be prohibitive to smaller organizations.

Significant Attacks, Probes, and Vulnerabilities

To be effective, the firewall administrator must understand not only how attacks and probes work, but must be able to recognize the appropriate alarms and audit trail entries.

There are three attacks in particular that any Internet firewall administrator should be familiar with.

Internet Protocol (IP) Source Address Spoofing. IP Source Address Spoofing is not an attack itself. It is a vulnerability that can be exploited to launch attacks (e.g., session hijacking). First described by Robert T. Morris in 1985 and explained in more detail by Steven Bellovin in 1989, the first known use of IP Source Address Spoofing was in 1994. Since then, hackers have made spoofing tools publicly available so that one need not be a Transmission Control Protocol (TCP)/IP expert in order to exploit this vulnerability.

IP Source Address Spoofing is used to defeat *address-based authentication*. Many services, including *rlogin* and *rsh*, rely on IP addresses for authentication. Yet, as this vulnerability illustrates, this form of authentication is extremely weak and should only be used in trusted environments. (IP addresses provide identification, not authentication.) By its very nature, the IP protocol allows anyone to send packets claiming to be from *any* IP address. Of course, when an attacker sends forged packets to a target machine, the target machine will send its replies to the legitimate client, not the attacker. In other words, the attacker can send commands but will not see any output. As described below, in some cases this is enough to cause serious damage.

Although there is no way to totally eliminate IP Source Address Spoofing, there are ways to reduce such activity. For example, a packet filter can be configured to drop all outbound packets which do not have an "inside" source address. Likewise, a firewall can block all inbound packets that have an internal address as the source address. However, such a solution will only work at the network and subnet levels. There is no way to prevent IP Source Address Spoofing *within* a subnet.

TCP Hijacking. TCP Hijacking is used to defeat authenticated connections. It is only an attack option if the attacker has access to the packet flow. In a TCP Hijacking attack, (1) the attacker is located logically between the client and the server, (2) the attacker sends a "killer packet" to the client, terminating the client's connection to the server, (3) the attacker then continues the connection.

Denial of Service. A strength of public networks like the Internet lies in the fact that anyone can create a public service (e.g., a Web server or anonymous File Transfer Protocol [FTP]server) and allow literally anyone else, anonymously to access that service. But this unrestricted availability can also be exploited in a denial-of-service attack. A denial-of-service attack exploits this unrestricted availability by overwhelming the service with requests. Although it is relatively easy to block a denial of service attack if the attack is generated by a single address, it is much more difficult, if not impossible, to stop a denial-of-service attack originating from spoofed, *random* source IP addresses.

There are two forms of denial-of-service attacks that are worth mentioning: TCP SYN Attack and ICMP Echo Flood.

1. TCP SYN Attack — The attacker floods a machine with TCP "half-open" connections, preventing the machine from providing TCP-based services while under attack and for some time after the attack stops. What makes this attack so significant is that it exploits an inherent characteristic of the TCP protocol; there is not yet a complete defense to this attack.

Under the TCP protocol (used by Simple Mail Transfer Protocol [SMTP], TELNET, HTTP, FTP, Gopher, etc.), whenever a client attempts to establish a connection to a server, there is a standard "handshake" or sequence of messages they exchange before data can be exchanged between the client and the server. In a normal connection, this handshake looks similar to the example displayed in Exhibit 7.7.

The potential for attack arises at the point where the server has sent an acknowledgment (SYN-ACK) back to the client but has not yet received the ACK message. This is what is known as a *half-open connection*. The server maintains, in a memory, a list of all half-open connections. Unfortunately, servers allocate a finite amount of memory for storing this list, and an attacker can cause an overflow by deliberately creating too many partially open connections.

The SYN Flooding is easily accomplished with IP Source Address Spoofing. In this scenario, the attacker sends SYN messages to the target (victim) server masquerading a client system that is unable to respond to the SYN-ACK messages. Therefore, the final ACK message is never sent to the target server.

	Client	Server
	SYN -------------------------	
	->	
	<------------------------	SYN-
		ACK
	ACK ------------------------	
	->	

Exhibit 7.7.   Normal TCP Handshake

Whether or not the SYN attack is used in conjunction with IP Source Address Spoofing, the effect on the target is the same. The target system's list of half-open connections will eventually fill; then the system will be unable to accept any new TCP connections until the table is emptied out. In some cases, the target may also run out of memory or crash.

Normally, half-open connections timeout after a certain amount of time; however, an attacker can generate new half-open connections faster than the target system's timeout.

2. Internet Control Message Protocol (ICMP) Echo (Ping) Flood — The   ping flood attack is where the attacker sends large amounts of ICMP ping requests from an intermediary or "bounce" site to a victim, which can cause network congestion or outages. The attack is also known as the "smurf" attack because of a hacker tool called "smurf," which enables the hacker to launch this attack with relatively little networking knowledge.

Like the SYN attack, the ping flood attack relies upon IP Source Address Spoofing to add another level of indirection to the attack. In a SYN attack with IP Source Address Spoofing, the spoofed source address receives all of the replies to the ping requests. While this does not cause an overflow on the victim machine, the *network path* from the bounce site to the victim becomes congested and potentially unusable. The bounce site may suffer for the same reason.

There are automated tools which allow attackers to use multiple bounce sites *simultaneously.* Attackers can also use tools to look for network routers that do not filter broadcast traffic and networks where multiple hosts respond.

Solutions:

1. Disable IP-directed broadcasts at your router.
2. Configure your operating system to prevent the machine from responding to ICMP packets sent to IP broadcast addresses.
3. Prevent IP source address spoofing by dropping packets which contain a source address for a different network.

CONCLUSION

A firewall can only reduce the risk of a breach of security; the only guaranteed way to prevent a compromise is to disconnect the network and physically turn all machines off. Moreover, a firewall should always be viewed as a *supplement* to host security; the primary security emphasis should be on host security. Nonetheless, a firewall is an important security device which should be used whenever an organization needs to protect one network from another.

The views expressed in this article are those of the author and do not reflect the official policy or position of the United States Air Force, Department of Defense, or the US government.

References

Atkins, Derek, et al., *Internet Security Professional Reference*, 2nd ed., New Riders, Indianapolis, Indiana, 1997.

Bellovin, Steven M. "Security Problems in the TCP/IP Protocol Suite" *Computer Communications Review* 19:2, April 1989, pp. 32-48. Available on the World Wide Web at ftp://ftp.research.att.com/dist/internet_security/ipext.ps.Z

Bernstein, Terry, Anish B. Bhimani, Eugene Schultz, and Carol Siegel. *Internet Security for Business*, John Wiley & Sons, New York, 1996.

Cheswick, W.R. and Bellovin, S.M. *Firewalls and Internet Security: Repelling the Wily Hacker*, Addison-Wesley, Reading, Massachusetts, 1994.

Garfinkel, Simson and Gene Spafford. *Practical Unix & Internet Security*, Sebastopol, California, 1995.

Huegen, Craig A. "The Latest in Denial of Service Attacks: 'Smurfing'", Oct. 18, 1998. Available on the World Wide Web at http://www.quadrunner.com/~chuegen/smurf.txt

Howard, John D. "An Analysis of Security Incidents on the Internet 1989 - 1995", Ph.D. dissertation, Carnegie Mellon University, Pittsburgh, Pennsylvania, 1997.

Morris, Robert T. "A Weakness in the 4.2BSD Unix TCP/IP Software" *Bell Labs Computer Science Technical Report* #117, Feb. 25, 1985. Available on the World Wide Web at ftp://ftp.research.att.com/dist/internet_security/117.ps.Z

Wood, Charles Cresson. Policies from the ground up, *Infosecurity News*, March/April 1997, pp. 24-29.

Chapter 8
Network Layer Security

Steven F. Blanding

INTRODUCTION

Modern computer networks today are characterized by layered protocol architectures, allowing network designs to accommodate unlimited applications and interconnection techniques. This layered approach allows protocols to become modularized, that is, developed independently and put together with other protocols in such a way as to create one complete protocol. The recognized basis of protocol layering is the Open Systems Interconnection (OSI) architecture. The OSI standards establish the architectural model and define specific protocols to fit into this model, which defines seven layers. Protocols from each of the layers are grouped together into an OSI layer stack, which is designed to fulfill the communications requirements of an application process.

Standards are also needed to adequately support security in the OSI layered communications architecture. A broad, coordinated set of standards is required to ensure necessary security functionality and still provide a cost-effective implementation. Because of the complexity and flexibility of the OSI model, security must be carefully defined to avoid an increased potential for functions being duplicated throughout the architecture and incompatible security features being used in different parts of the architecture. There is also a possibility that different and potentially contradictory security techniques can be used in different applications or layers, where fewer techniques would provide the required results with less complexity and more economy.

Security standards were added to the OSI architecture to provide a broad, coherent, and coordinated approach to applying security functionality. The security standards can be grouped into categories as follows: (1) security architecture and framework standards, (2) security techniques standards, (3) layer security protocol standards, (4) application-specific security standards, and (5) security management standards. This chapter will focus primarily on Network Layer Security, which is part of the family of layer security protocol standards. However, because the standards are closely interrelated, a brief overview of the security architecture and framework standards is required. These standards serve as a reference base for building standards in the other categories, including Network Layer Security.

NETWORK LAYER STRUCTURE, SERVICE, AND PROTOCOL

The Network Layer of the OSI model accommodates a variety of subnetwork technologies and interconnection strategies, making it one of the most complex of the seven layers in the model. The Network Layer must present a common service interface to the Transport Layer and coordinate between subnetworks of different technologies. There are also two styles of operation, connection-oriented and connectionless, that significantly contribute to this complexity.

There are three ISO standards that describe the Network Layer services, including ISO/IEC 8648, ISO/IEC 8880, and ISO/IEC 8348. The internal organization of the Network Layer is explained by the ISO/IEC 8648 standard. The general principles and the provision and support of the connection-mode and connectionless-mode network services are explained by the ISO/IEC 8880 standard. The network service definition, which includes the connection-mode, connectionless-mode addendum, and addressing addendum, is explained by the ISO/IEC 8348 standard. This standard also describes the concepts of *end system* and *intermediate system*. An end system models hardware across a complete seven-layer OSI communications model, while an intermediate system, which is located in the Network Layer, only functions across the lowest three OSI layers. Communications by an end system can occur directly with another end system or through several intermediate systems.

Intermediate systems can also include or refer to a real subnetwork, an internetworking unit connecting two or more real subnetworks, or a mix of both a real subnetwork and an internetworking unit. A collection of hardware and physical links that connect real systems is called a *real subnetwork*. Examples of real systems include local area networks or public packet-switching networks. With this foundation, many different Network Layer protocols can be established. Because the protocol can exist at the subnetwork level within the Network Layer, they do not need to be designed to specifically support the OSI standard. As a result, support for all the functions required by the Network Layer service does not need to be provided by the basic protocol of a subnetwork. To achieve OSI standard functionality, further sublayers of protocol can be provided above the subnetwork protocol.

Regardless of the type of interconnection designed, one of three roles is performed by a Network Layer protocol. These roles are subnetwork-independent convergence protocol (SNICP), subnetwork-dependent convergence protocol (SNDCP), and subnetwork-access protocol (SNAcP). The SNICP role provides functions to support the OSI network service over a well-defined set of underlying capabilities, which are not specifically based on any particular subnetwork. The role is to convey addressing and routing information over multiple interconnected networks and commonly applies to the interconnecting protocol used. The SNDCP role operates over a protocol to provide the SNAcP role in order to add capabilities required by an SNICP protocol or needed to provide the full OSI network service. The SNAcP role provides a subnetwork service at its end points, which may or may not be equivalent to the OSI network service. This protocol is inherently part of a particular type of subnetwork.

ISO/IEC 8473 identifies another protocol that is very important to the Network Layer — the Connectionless Network Protocol (CLNP). This protocol provides connectionless-mode network service within a SNICP role. The definition for how this protocol operates over X.25 packet-switched subnetworks or LAN subnetworks is contained within the ISO/IEC 8473 standard.

SECURITY SERVICE ARCHITECTURAL PLACEMENT

When designing security, significant decisions need to be made as to the layers(s) where data item or connection-based protection should be applied. Implementing security services in a layered communications architecture can be a complicated endeavor and can raise significant issues. The concept of protocol layering implies that data items can be embedded within data items and connections can be embedded within connections, with potentially multiple layers of nesting.

Guidance for where security services should be applied within the OSI model is identified in standard ISO/IEC 7498-2. As the first formal standard addressing layer assignment of security services, this standard, while providing guidance as to which OSI layers are appropriate for providing security services, does allow for many options. The security required is application dependent. Some services may need to be provided in different layers in different application scenarios, while some may even need to be provided in multiple layers in the same scenario. The complexity of these security services can be illustrated by a pair of end systems communicating with each other through a series of subnetworks.

An end system is typically defined as one piece of equipment, either a PC work station, minicomputer, or mainframe computer. An end system is described as having only one policy authority for security purposes. A collection of communications facilities employing the same communications technology is a subnetwork. An example of a subnetwork is a local area network (LAN) or wide area network (WAN). A subnetwork is described as having only one policy authority for security purposes. Each subnetwork, however, typically has a different security environment and, as a result, will probably have a different policy authority. Also, an end system and the subnetwork to which it is connected may or may not have the same policy authority.

Another complication typically found in end systems is that they often simultaneously support multiple applications, such as e-mail, file access, and directory access for multiple users. These applications often need considerably different security requirements. Not only may security requirements differ among end systems and for subnetworks, but they may also vary within a subnetwork. Subnetworks generally comprise multiple links connecting multiple subnetwork components, and different links may pass through different security environments. As a result, individual links may need to be protected through a security mechanism.

To reduce the complexity, security services can be described more simply and effectively within a four-level model. The four levels at which specific and distinct requirements for security protocol elements arise include the application, end system, subnetwork, and the direct-link levels. In the application level, security protocol elements are application dependent. In the end-system level, security protocol elements provide protection on an end system-to-end system basis. In the subnetwork level, security protocol elements provide protection internal to a subnetwork, which is considered less trusted than other parts of the network environment. In the direct-link level, security protocol elements provide protection internal to a subnetwork, over a link that is considered less trusted than other parts of the subnetwork environment.

When determining where to locate security services within these four basic architectural layers, some general properties must first be examined that vary between higher and lower levels. These general properties include traffic mixing, route knowledge, number of protection points, protocol header protection, and source/sink binding.

Traffic mixing is a term used to describe the mix of data traffic between higher and lower levels of the OSI layer architecture. With the introduction of multiplexing, lower levels tend to have a greater tendency toward data items from different source and destination applications and users mixed in the data stream than at higher levels. The type of security policy can significantly alter this factor. In instances where the security policy tends to leave individual applications or users to specify the data protection required, placing security services at a higher level tends to be better.

Individual applications or users will have inadequate protection where security is specified at lower levels. In addition, some data would also be unnecessarily protected because of the security requirements of other data sharing the data stream.

Route knowledge is also an important factor in security placement. There tends to be more knowledge of the security characteristics of different routes and links at lower levels than at higher levels. Placing security at lower levels can have effectiveness and efficiency benefits in an environment where such characteristics vary significantly. Where protection is unnecessary on subnetworks or links, security costs can be eliminated, while targeted security services are specifically employed as appropriate.

The number of protection points can vary significantly depending on where security protection is placed. If security were placed at a very high level, such as the application layer, then security would also need to be placed in every sensitive application in every end system. If security were placed at a very low level, such as the direct-link level, then security would also need to be placed at the ends of every network link. If security were placed closer to the middle of the architecture, then security features would tend to need to be placed at significantly fewer points.

To have adequate protocol header protection, security services need to be placed at a low level. If security services were placed at higher levels, lower-level protocol headers would not receive protection, which in some environments may be sensitive.

Source/sink binding is the association of data with its source or sink. Implementation of data origin authentication and nonrepudiation security services depends on this binding. These security services are most effectively achieved at higher levels, especially at the application level. However, subject to special constraints, it can sometimes be achieved at lower levels.

END SYSTEM-LEVEL SECURITY

End system-level security relates to either the Transport Layer or subnetwork-independent Network Layer protocols. Standards have been developed supporting both options, ISO/IEC 10736 for the Transport Layer and ISO/IEC 11577 for the Network Layer. The types of security requirements that are suitable for an end system-level security solution fall into three broad categories. The first includes requirements relating to network connections that are not linked to any particular application. The second includes requirements dictated by the end-system authority that are to be enforced upon all communications regardless of the application. Finally, the third includes requirements based on the assumption that the end systems are trusted, but that all underlying communications network(s) are untrusted.

In choosing between the Transport Layer or Network Layer for placement of end-level security protection, factors favoring the Network Layer approach include: (1) the ease of transparently inserting security devices at standardized physical interface points, (2) the ability to support any upper-layer architecture, including OSI, Internet, and proprietary architectures, and (3) the ability to use the same solution at the end-system and subnetwork levels.

SUBNETWORK-LEVEL SECURITY

Subnetwork-level security provides protection across one or more specific subnetworks. Subnetwork-level security needs to be distinguished from end system-level security for two important reasons. First, equipment and operational costs for subnetwork-level security solutions may be much lower than those for end system-level solutions because the number of end systems usually far exceeds the number of subnetwork gateways. Second, subnetworks close to end systems are trusted to the same extent as the end systems themselves since they are on the same premises and administered under the same conditions. As a result, subnetwork-level security should always be considered as a possible alternative to end system level security. In the OSI architecture, subnetwork-level security maps to the Network Layer.

NETWORK-LAYER SECURITY PROTOCOL

The network layer is among the complex of layers within the OSI model. As a result, several OSI standards are required to specify transmission, routing, and internetworking functions for this layer. The ISO/IEC 8880 standard describes an overview of the Network Layer. Two other standards, ISO/IEC 8348 and 8648, define the network service and describe the internal organization of the Network Layer, respectively. The most recent standard published is ISO/IEC 11577, which describes the Network-Layer Security Protocol (NLSP).

Different sublayers make up the Network Layer, each performing different roles, such as subnetwork access protocol (SNAcP) and subnetwork-dependent convergence protocol (SNDCP). The architectural placement of the NLSP can be in any of several different locations within the Network Layer, functioning as a sublayer. Above its highest layer is the Transport Layer, or possibly a router where a relay or routing function is in place.

Two service interfaces, the NLSP service interface and the underlying network (UN) service interface, are contained within the Network-Layer

Security Protocol. The NLSP service is the interface presented to an entity or sublayer above, and the UN service is the interface to a sublayer below. These service interfaces are specified in such a way as to appear like the network service, as defined in ISO/IEC 8348. The Network-Layer Security Protocol can also be defined in two different forms or variations, connection-oriented and connectionless. In the connection-oriented NLSP, the NLSP service and the UN service are connection oriented, whereas in the connectionless NLSP, these services are connectionless. The flexibility of the architecture results from the ability of the NLSP to support both end system-level or subnetwork-level security services.

For example, in a connection-oriented NLSP, suppose we defined X.25 as the underlying subnetwork technology. In this configuration, the NLSP is placed at the top of the Network Layer (just below the Transport Layer and just above the X.25 subnetwork), allowing the NLSP service to equate to a secure version of the OSI network service. In this example, the X.25 protocol is not aware that security is provided from above.

The NLSP can also provide subnetwork level security. In instances where the subnetwork is untrusted, the NLSP adds the necessary security, which can equate to either the OSI network service in the end system or to the network internal layer service (NILS) in a relay system. In connectionless cases, several configurations with practical applications are possible, such as the transfer of fully unencrypted connectionless network protocol (CLNP) headers, encrypted CLNP addresses with parts of the header not encrypted, or fully encrypted CLNP headers.

SECURE DATA TRANSFER

Encapsulation is a security function used to protect user data and sensitive parameters. In both connection-oriented and connectionless NLSP, the primary function is to provide this protection originating on request or response primitives issued at the NLSP service. The encapsulation function applies this security by generating data values for corresponding request or response primitives issued at the UN service, which is then reversed at the receiving end. This is very similar to the process used in the TLSP, where the generation and processing of the Security Encapsulation PDU occurs.

Different encapsulation functions are available for different environments within the NLSP. This provision includes the basic encapsulation function, which is very similar to the encapsulation function defined in the TLSP. The NLSP does have some additional features included in the basic function. Each octet string to be protected contains a string of fields including: (1) address parameters requiring protection, (2) quality-of-service parameters requiring protection, (3) an indicator of the type of primitive (e.g., connect request, connect response, disconnect, etc.), (4) user data requiring protection, (5) test data for use in testing cryptographic system operation, and (6) security label.

When compared to the TLSP, the protection process is the same, with the exception of two additional fields included within the generated PDU. These are an integrity sequence number (ISN) and a traffic padding field. The integrity sequence number is used to support sequence integrity. Because transport protocol sequence numbers could serve this purpose in the TLSP, this feature was not required within that layer. The traffic padding field is used to support the traffic flow confidentiality service, which is a requirement of the NLSP but not the TLSP.

The encapsulation function can include either a clear header process or, as an alternative to the basic encapsulation function, a no-header process. In the clear header feature, a clear header is prefixed to the resulting protected octet string to give an NLSP secure data transfer PDU, which contains the security association identifier. The no-header encapsulation feature is also available for optional use only with connection-oriented NLSP. The no-header option can be used when the only security mechanism applied is encryption and when the encryption–decryption processes do not change the data lengths. In the no-header alternative, the secure data transfer PDU is replaced by an encrypted version of the data requiring protection. This allows the NLSP to be inserted transparently within the Network Layer. The data characteristics of the underlying services, such as data rates, packet sizes, and bandwidth, are not affected. As a result, security functions can easily be added to an existing service without changing the network architecture. However, the range of services that can be supported is greatly reduced because ICV, ISN, padding, and security labels cannot be used. Integrity services can still be maintained where the data has sufficient natural redundancy and if cryptographic chaining is used. Basic confidentiality is also not compromised and can still be supported.

The mapping of the same type of NLSP service primitives to UN service primitives, with the exception of connection establishment and release, is how the NLSP operates. If fields do not require protection, they are copied directly from one service primitive to the other. Those NLSP fields that do require protection are processed by the encapsulation function. The encapsulated result, or secure data transfer PDU, is mapped to a user data parameter of the UN service primitive. The application of the encapsulation function may result in data expansion, which could require the use of segmentation.

CONNECTION ESTABLISHMENT AND RELEASE

As mentioned previously, special procedures are required to handle connection establishment with connection-oriented NLSP. The NLSP is similar to the TLSP in that it not only supports internal security protocol, but also security associations managed by other means. The use of special procedures is dependent upon whether or not security association establishment needs to occur in conjunction with connection establishment.

Even where a suitable security association already exists (in other words, a situation not involving security association establishment), there is a requirement for a special NLSP protocol exchange at connection establishment time. This is needed to perform peer entity authentication, establish particular encryption and integrity keys for use on the connection, and to establish starting integrity sequence numbers. In this case, a connection security control PDU is defined in the NLSP to convey this information. At connection establishment, a two-way exchange of these PDUs occurs. The type of connection authentication mechanism specified for the particular security association determines the variation in the precise contents of the PDU. The PDU fields would include a security label, key reference or key derivation information, and encrypted versions of two integrity sequence numbers, one for each direction in traffic. Successful decryption of the integrity sequence number field can simultaneously provide protection against replay attacks on authentication, demonstrate key knowledge for authentication purposes, and confirm starting integrity sequence numbers.

The data exchanges may be much more complex where security association establishment is to occur in conjunction with connection establishment. This additional complexity is typically addressed through the definition of a separate security association PDU. This separate PDU is used to handle the need for more than a two-way exchange for authentication and key derivation purposes, as well as substantial attribute negotiation. Again, like the TLSP, the NLSP does not require a particular security association establishment technique. Instead, one suitable technique based on the Authenticated Diffie–Hellman exchange is described.

The last area of discussion in this section is a description of how the protocol exchanges for NLSP connection establishment map onto the UN service. Mapping directly onto the UN connection establishment primitives would be the ideal situation. However, in reality the required NLSP protocol exchanges add substantial overhead and prevent this possibility. There may not be space in the UN connection establishment PDUs for all the data that needs to be transferred since user data fields of network protocols are commonly limited in length. In addition to this, a multi-way protocol exchange may be needed to establish a security association.

These conditions require that two basic mapping alternatives be defined. An NLSP connection establishment can map directly to UN connection establishment where only a two-way exchange is necessary, and all required data can fit in the user data fields of the UN connect primitives. If these conditions do not exist, the required data transfers map to UN data exchanges following UN connection establishment. Additional complications may occur where data transfers map to UN data exchanges. There is a possibility that the throughput, window size, quality-of-service, and other service parameters eventually negotiated do not match the characteristics of the UN connection. When this occurs, a new UN connection is established with the required, now known, characteristics, and the original UN connection is released.

Mapping problems may also occur where, upon release of an NLSP connection, user data on the disconnect needs to be protected by the encapsulating function and the resultant PDU cannot fit in the user data parameter of UN disconnect. The NLSP PDU must map to a UN data exchange prior to UN disconnect in this scenario. The NLSP is a powerful and complex protocol because of the large number of possible mapping scenarios.

SUMMARY

In general, lower-layer security protocols support end system-level, direct-link-level, and subnetwork-level security services. Security services at the subnetwork and end system levels support confidentiality, integrity, access control, and authentication services. Security services at the direct-link level support confidentiality only. These services differ according to whether the environment is connection oriented or connectionless.

Throughout the lower layers, the concepts of protection quality-of-service and security associations are used. To signal protection requirements across layer boundaries and to negotiate requirements between two ends, protection quality-of-service is used. To provide a consistent type of protection to a sequence of data transfers between two systems, a security association is used to model the collection of related attribute information maintained between those systems. A security association can be established through Application Layer protocol exchanges, lower-layer protocol exchanges in the same layer that uses the security exchange, or through nonstandard methods.

The NLSP is very flexible, functioning at either the end-system or subnetwork level. The NLSP can be positioned at any of several places in the Network Layer, functioning as a sublayer. NLSP is able to conceal trusted subnetwork protocol information while this information travels through an untrusted subnetwork, depending on its positioning within the Network

Layer. Variations of NLSP include connection-oriented and connectionless. The connection-oriented variant works in conjunction with such protocols as X.25, and the connectionless variant works in conjunction with the Connectionless Network Protocol (CLNP). An encapsulation process very similar to that of TLSP is used by NLSP. To provide for the establishment of security associations, optional protocol support is used.

Chapter 9
Transport Layer Security

Steven F. Blanding

INTRODUCTION

The Transport Layer of the OSI model ensures that a reliable end-to-end data transmission capability of the quality demanded by the session layer is offered to that layer, regardless of the nature of the underlying network over which the data will be transferred. This chapter will examine the services offered to transport service (TS) users and the security associated with the Transport Layer.

The basic Transport Layer standards are found in the ISO (International Organization for Standardization) /IEC (International Electrotechnical Commission) 8072 transport service definition, the ISO/IEC 8073 connection-oriented transport protocol specification, and the ISO/IEC 8602 connectionless transport protocol specification. These documents were first published in 1986 and 1987. Subsequent to these publications, security functionality was added to the Transport Layer with the completion of the Transport Layer Security Protocol (TLSP) standard, ISO/IEC 10736, in 1993. The U.S. government project initiated by the National Security Agency (NSA), Secure Data Network System (SDNS), produced specification Security Protocol 4 (SP4), which became the primary input to the development of the TLSP. SP4, which was a product of both industry and government, specifies security services, mechanisms, and protocols for protecting user data in networks based on the OSI model. The TLSP, even with additional contributions made toward it, is still based mostly on SP4.

Before the Transport Layer Security Protocol is presented, an overview of the Transport Layer is provided in order for the reader to have a basic understanding of the material, which is necessary to understand the security architecture.

0-8493-9829-0/00/$0.00+$.50
© 2000 by CRC Press LLC

TRANSPORT LAYER OVERVIEW

The transport service is defined in the ISO service definition document 8072. The transport service is in one of three phases at any time: (1) transport connection (TC) establishment, (2) data transfer, or (3) transport connection release. In the TC establishment phase, a connection is established between peer TS users (session entities). The session entity initiating the TC specifies the quality of service required of the connection, in terms of reliability and other aspects of the service. Once a TC is established, the session entities can exchange Transport Service Data Units (TSDUs) transparently over the connection. In the release phase, the TC is unconditionally released by either TS user.

The reliable end-to-end transmission of data is provided by the T-DATA service element, and the expedited data is provided by the T-EXPEDITED-DATA service element. The required level of service of the TC is dictated to the initiating transport entity in the quality-of-service (QOS) parameter of the T-CONNECT request. This is used as a basis for negotiation, during TC establishment, of an acceptable and attainable QOS between the end systems. The TS provider throughout the lifetime of the connection must then maintain this negotiated QOS.

The parameters associated with each TS primitive include *called address, calling address, expedited data option, quality of service, TS user data, responding address*, and *disconnect reason*. The called address and calling address are TSAP addresses and identify the TS user initiating the TC and the intended responder. The responding address conveys the TSAP as the called address, only differing from it when that address has been supplied by the initiating TS user in some generic form. Such a form results in a selection, by the responding end system, of a specific TSAP address, which is based upon the provided generic. It is this selection that is returned in the parameter. The expedited data option parameter is used to negotiate the availability of transport-expedited data service over the TC. If the calling TS user or TS provider does not offer this service, which is apparent in the T-CONNECT indication, then the called TS user may not insist upon it by including it on the response.

TS user data is a parameter that, in the case of T-DATA and T-EXPEDITED-DATA, is the mechanism for provision of transparent, reliable, TSDU exchange over a TC between peer TS users. In the case of the other services, this parameter enables a limited amount of transparent user data to be passed between TS users, which may qualify the services in question. TS user data is restricted in length according to service element type: a maximum of 32 octets for T-CONNECT, 64 octets for T-DISCONNECT, 16 octets for T-EXPEDITED-DATA, and no restriction for T-DATA.

The unconstrained size of normal data TSDUs will often not apply in practice. Constraints on implementation or on the operational environment of a transport entity, such as the size available buffering, lead to a limit being imposed on TSDUs. Such a limit will have repercussions on the higher layers, but these can be overcome by the use of segmentation by the peer session entities. Segmentation is the facility by which a Session Service Data User (SSDU), as an object of a data request, can be transmitted between peer session entities not in a single Session Protocol Data Unit (SPDU) but in segments, that is, in several consecutive SPDUs.

The quality of service parameter is itself a "list" of parameters. It is, on the T-CONNECT request, a statement by the initiating TS user concerning the level of service it requires of the, as yet unestablished, TC. It is concerned with such things as acceptable error rates and minimum acceptable data throughput. Both the calling and called transport entities may amend the QOS to a level they regarded as feasible, given knowledge of aspects of the network not necessarily visible to the initiating TS user. In the course of establishing the connection, the QOS is passed to the responding TS user in the indication. Acceptance of the connection results in a T-CONNECT confirmation, which carries a final QOS. If this is modified to an unacceptable level, the initiating TS user has the option of terminating the established connection by issuing a T-DISCONNECT request with an appropriate reason parameter value and also qualifying user data, such as "QOS negotiated to unacceptable level."

The reason parameter of the T-DISCONNECT indication gives the cause of the TC release. It shows whether the release was user or provider initiated, and could include the possible values "quality of service fallen below level agreed for this TC," "congestion or failure of local or remote TS provider," "unknown reason," "called TSAP address not valid," or "called TSAP address not available."

SUBNETWORK RELIABILITY

Errors originating in a subnetwork and consequently observed by the transport layer are of two types, *signaled* and *residual*. A signaled error is one detected by the network layer but where no steps are taken within that layer for recovery. The event is just signaled to the transport layer for recovery. Two examples are network disconnection (the network connection is lost) and network reset (the network connection is reset to a known state, possibly with loss of data in transit, but the connection remains available for use).

Residual errors are those apart from signaled errors. In effect, the network layer has not detected them. Examples are loss, corruption, duplication, and delivery out of sequence of TSDUs.

147

Subnetworks that are analyzed in terms of these two types of errors are categorized as either (1) a subnetwork where the rates of both types of errors are acceptable, (2) a subnetwork where the rate of residual errors is acceptable but not that of signaled errors, or (3) a subnetwork where the rate of residual errors is unacceptable. A network connection offered over a number of subnetworks of different error categories should expect a level of service that is the poorest level of service of the subnetworks over which it operates.

As part of transport connection establishment, the peer transport entities must establish the level of network service enhancement that must be undertaken in order to provide the agreed QOS for this connection. This involves the selection of the set of procedures that will be used during the connection. This selection is achieved as part of the connection establishment procedure in parallel with QOS negotiation.

TRANSPORT CLASSES

There is a set of five basic levels or classes of network service enhancement available from the Transport Layer. Each class is in some way related to the three categories of subnetwork identified above. Transport entities during TC establishment perform the procedure negotiation described above by agreeing on a transport to be used over the network for this particular TC. Inherent in a choice of class is a set of associated transport procedures.

Class 0, the simple class, provides the most minimal overhead, a basic transport connection designed to be used with network service where the rates of both types of errors are acceptable. Given that this type of network service provides reliable data transmission, only a basic level of transport activity is required. Class 1, the basic error recovery class, provides, with minimal overhead, a basic transport connection designed to be used with network services where the rate of residual errors is acceptable but not that of signaled errors. It handles signaled errors such as network disconnect without involving the TS user. Class 2, the multiplexing class, is as class 0 but with additional mechanisms to support the multiplexing of transport connections onto single network connections. Class 3, the error detection and recovery class, is as class 1 but with additional multiplexing mechanisms. Class 4, the error detection and recovery class, provides all the capability of class 3 together with mechanisms required to detect and recover from errors not signaled by the NS provider. This class also provides for increased throughput and for additional resilience against NS provider failure. It is designed to be used over a type of network where the rate of residual errors is unacceptable.

148

TRANSPORT PROCEDURES

The transport protocol is defined as a set of procedures, each of which relates to a particular activity. Implicit in the final negotiated transport class is the choice of a subset of those procedures that is necessary to provide the functionality of that class. An examination of the procedures will reveal that many are fundamental to basic transport service provision. These form a set of procedures common to all transport classes. These procedures include, but are not limited to, the following: assignment to a network connection; transport protocol data unit transfer; segmentation and reassembling; concatenation and separation; connection establishment; connection refusal; normal release; error release; association of TPDUs with transport connections; TPDU numbering; expedited data transfer; reassignment after failure; retention until acknowledgment of TPDUs; resynchronization; multiplexing and demultiplexing; explicit flow control; checksum; frozen references; retransmission on timeout; resequencing; inactivity control; treatment of protocol errors; and splitting and recombining.

Assignment to a network connection is a procedure that is common to all classes. Until an assignment is made, a transport class connection cannot be established. Assignment is the association of a TC with a network connection (NC). In the TC establishment stage, establishment cannot proceed until an assignment is made. However, once made and the TC established, the TC can be retained and assigned to a different NC. In either case, the transport entity may choose to establish a new NC or use a suitable existing NC.

The *transport protocol data unit transfer* procedure coordinates the conveyance of TPDUs between peer transport entities. It uses the network normal and expedited data service elements N-DATA and N-EXPEDITED-DATA. This procedure is common to all classes of transport. In the transport data PDUs, DaTa (DT) and Expedited Data (ED), the structure is such that the control section of the PDU, the protocol control information (PCI), comprises an identifier together with the length parameter giving the length of the PCI within the PDU. However, there is no length indication for the data field and the PDU. The whole is passed to the NS provider as NSDU, and it is from the overall length of this NSDU that the receiving transport entity can determine the size of the data field, which is calculated as the NSDU length minus the PCI length.

Segmentation and reassembling may also occur within the transport layer. A TSDU requested for transfer by a TS user may exceed the limit placed upon the amount of data that can be conveyed between peer transport entities in a single data (DT) TPDU. Such a limit reflects constraints within the network service on NSDUs associated with the N-DATA service

149

element. In this case, segmentation is invoked to break the TSDU into a series of appropriately sized DT TPDUs. On receipt by the peer transport entity, the sequence of DT TPDUs representing a segmented TSDU will be reassembled into the single TSDU. When this complete TSDU has been received, a data service indication is issued to the complete TS user. The End of Transport (EOT) parameter in each DT TPDU is only set when a complete TSDU has been transferred, and is used to recognize a segmented TSDU by a receiving transport entity. Where TSDUs are contained entirely within DT TPDUs, the EOT is set on every DT TPDU.

The transport layer also provides for *concatenation and separation* of TPDUs. A number of TPDUs can be concatenated into a single NSDU for transmission and separation by the receiving transport entity on receipt. If a data TPDU is one of the group of concatenated TPDUs, then it must be the last TPDU of the concatenation, and as a result, it can be the only TPDU.

The *connection establishment* procedure is available in all classes of transport to establish a TC after successful assignment to a network connection. A transport connection is established by negotiation between peers by the exchange of appropriate PDUs, which is conveyed by the use of network normal data, N-DATA. As a result of negotiation, the QOS to be maintained and the transport class to be used over the network are determined. There are optional procedures associated with particular classes that are in themselves optional within the class, and so negotiation of these optional features is also carried out at this time. For example, "Expedited Data Transfer" and "Retention Until Acknowledgment of TPDU" are both optional features in Class 1.

Connection refusal is a procedure that is initiated by the responding transport entity in response to either a T-DISCONNECT request from the responding TS user, or an inability to conform to the requirements of the initiating transport entity conveyed in the CR TPDU. Connection refusal is achieved by sending a Disconnect Request (DR) TPDU to the initiator using network normal data.

There are two types of release procedures — *normal release* and *error release*. A normal release can be described through two variants — implicit and explicit. In Class 0, the implicit variant of the normal release is achieved by disconnecting the NC using the N-DISCONNECT request, the receipt of which is considered to imply the release of the associated TC. The explicit variant of normal release is associated with all other classes. Under the explicit variant, the TC is released by a confirmed activity involving the exchange between peers of Disconnect Request (DR) and Disconnect Confirm (DC) TPDUs, using network normal data. An error release is used only in Classes 0 and 2. This is used to release the transport connection after a signaled error has been received from the NS provider. The TS user is notified of the release by a T-DISCONNECT indication.

The *association of TPDUs* with transport connections is a procedure used in all classes while data is being received. Three actions are taken when a transport entity receives an NSDU from an NS provider. First, a check is made to determine that the NSDU can be decoded into one or more concatenation of TPDUs. Second, if concatenation is detected, then the separation procedure is invoked. Finally, where multiple TCs are associated with an NC over which the NSDU is received, ensure the TPDUs are associated with the appropriate TC.

TPDU numbering is a feature required to ensure that certain procedures are successfully performed. This is a sequence number, identified as a parameter in the PCI, which is carried in each DT TPDU. The procedures include those involving flow control, resequencing, and recovery.

The *expedited data transfer* procedure places the TS user data provided by a T-EXPEDITED-DATA request into the data field of an Expedited Data (ED) TPDU. Although the transport expedited data service is unconfirmed, transport protocol demands that the peer entity procedure be confirmed, and so each ED TPDU must be acknowledged by the receiving peer transport entity by use of an expedited data acknowledge (EA) TPDU. No more than one acknowledged ED TPDU can be outstanding for each data flow direction of the TC at any time.

The *reassignment after failure* procedure is invoked when a network signaled error is received, indicating the loss of the NC to which a TC is assigned. The result will be that the TC is assigned to a different NC, which either already existed and was owned by the transport entity or is newly created for the purpose. The procedure, resynchronization, is invoked when this reassignment is achieved; however, should a reassignment not be achieved, the TC will be considered released and the transport reference frozen. The *frozen reference* procedure (described below in a paragraph on *frozen references*) is then used to ensure that a reference is not reassigned to another TC after being frozen.

Retention until acknowledgment of TPDUs provides mechanisms whereby the transmitting transport entity can retain "copies" of TPDUs until an explicit acknowledgment is received from the peer. Should no acknowledgment be received after a certain period of time has elapsed, or should a signaled error occur, then the TPDUs can be retransmitted. The persistent loss of TPDUs will cause the QOS to fall below the negotiated acceptable level and the TC to be terminated.

Resynchronization is a procedure used to restore the TC to normal after reassignment of a TC after NC failure or after a signaled event from the NS provider, which indicates a problem in the NC. The purpose of the resynchronizing transport entity is to resume the activity on the TC that was outstanding at the time of the triggering event. Resynchronization is only attempted by the initiating transport entity of the TC. The peer takes only a passive role in the resynchronization process. Since both entities are aware of the need for resynchronization, one of the peer transport entities must take a passive role or the resynchronization by both peers would result in unnecessary event collision resolutions. The passive entity responds by setting a timer for resynchronization-related TPDUs to be received from the TC initiator. If resynchronization does not occur, the timer expires and the entity considers the TC released and the reference frozen.

Multiplexing and demultiplexing procedures are available to Classes 2, 3, and 4. This process allows more than one TC to share a single NC. Multiplexing takes place where a transport entity transmits or receives TPDUs belonging to different TCs over the same NC. The transport entity receiving the TPDUs must perform demultiplexing. Demultiplexing is accomplished by invoking the association of TPDUs procedure where the TC to which individual TPDUs belong is determined. Network efficiencies are obtained where both multiplexing and concatenation procedures are used together, and a single NSDU is transferred containing concatenated TPDUs for different TCs.

Explicit flow control is a procedure available to Classes 2, 3, and 4. In Class 2 explicit flow control is optional and in Classes 3 and 4 it is mandatory. This procedure regulates the flow of DT TPDUs between peer transport entities over a TC within the transport layer and acts independently of flow control available in the network.

Checksum is an optional procedure used only in Class 4. The checksum is a value calculated according to an algorithm defined in the protocol specification, which has the octets comprising the TPDU with which it is associated as its arguments. The checksum is identified in the TPDU as the checksum parameter. After transmission over the network, the checksum is recalculated and compared to the value in the TPDU parameter. Corruption is assumed if the values are different. In this situation, the TPDU is discarded, no acknowledgment is sent, and the transmitting transport entity retransmits the TPDU.

Frozen references are used by Classes 1, 3, and 4. They are used to ensure that a reference is not reassigned to another TC after being frozen. References are information relating to the identity of a TC. *Retransmission on timeout* is a procedure used to provide retransmission by the sender of

TPDUs that appear to have become lost. In this situation, the transmitting transport entity detects lost TPDUs when it does not receive an acknowledgment during a fixed time period and when acknowledgments are known to be outstanding. When this happens, the first TPDU in the sequence of unacknowledged TPDUs is retransmitted, and the timer is reset and left to expire. After several retransmissions without acknowledgment, the sending transport entity will invoke the release procedure and inform the TS user of the failure. Only Class 4 uses this procedure.

The *resequencing* procedure is used to sort misordered DT TPDUs by the NS provider. This provides for correctly ordered octets delivered to the TS user by each TPDU regardless of the inconsistencies of the network, which may cause out-of-order TPDUs. Misordering can occur when a TPDU is segmented by the transport entity into many TPDUs and where splitting results in these TPDUs traveling between end systems spread over a number of network connections.

The procedure that addresses unsignaled termination of a network connection is *inactivity control*. This procedure, which is used only in Class 4, is invoked on the expiry of an inactivity timer maintained by the transport entity. It times the period over which no TPDU is received. Inactivity control expires after a fairly lengthy interval and then invokes the *normal release* procedure. To protect against termination because of inactivity due to traffic congestion, the interval must be long enough to avoid timing out a good connection.

The *treatment of protocol errors* procedure is used when a TPDU is received that cannot be interpreted under the rules of the standard, when no error has been received and there are no checksum errors. Several different appropriate actions are possible depending on the operational details of the errors. This procedure is used in all classes.

The TC is enabled to make use of multiple NCs through the procedure *splitting and recombining*. The result of this can be increased throughput or greater resilience against failure in particularly unreliable networks. Once an association exists between one TC and many NCs, TPDUs of that TC can be transmitted over any of the NCs. As a result, TPDUs may arrive at the peer transport entity out of sequence. This procedure is only available to Class 4.

EXPEDITED DATA

Expedited data is a special form of data transfer where data is guaranteed to arrive at the receiving user before any data subsequently transmitted by a call on any data service. The intention is that data transferred by the use of expedited data will arrive before normal data already submitted for transmission by the user that has not yet been delivered; however, it will not arrive before any previously submitted, undelivered expedited data. While expedited data is known only generally at higher levels of the OSI model, it is at the Transport Layer where the mechanics of expedited data become visible.

Expedited data is class dependent. That is, expedited data is provided entirely within Classes 2, 3, and 4 but is not provided in Class 0. In these classes, expedited TSDUs are sent as ED TPDUs over network normal data service. In Class 1, the expedited effect is provided by the expedited mechanism within the Transport Layer, together with the use of the network expedited data service to convey ED TPDUs. If this network service is not available, then the network normal data service is used.

QUALITY OF SERVICE

An application signals its lower-layers communications requirements using the concept of quality of service (QOS). This signaling occurs via a QOS parameter, which accompanies a connection establishment request or connectionless data item passed from the upper layers to the lower layers across the Transport Layer service boundary. The Transport Layer uses a similar QOS parameter in a connection-establishment request or connectionless data item it passes to the Network Layer. If the Network Layer cannot provide an adequate QOS, the Transport Layer should upgrade the provided QOS to the requisite level by adding value in its own protocol. This is done by selecting the appropriate transport protocol class and options.

The QOS parameter can convey a great deal of information covering such requirements as throughput, residual error rate, and connection failure probability. QOS can be expressed as a set of performance criteria. They generally fall into two groups: speed and accuracy/reliability. The connection establishment phase criteria include QOS parameters for *establishment delay* and *establishment failure probability*. The connection release phase criteria consists of the QOS parameters *release delay* and *release failure probability*. The data transfer phase criteria include the QOS parameters *throughput, transit delay, residual error rate, connection resilience,* and *transfer failure probability*.

The component of QOS relevant to security is called protection QOS. It is used to indicate the security services that need to be invoked and the strength of the mechanism that needs to be used to support a security service. TLSP and NLSP use a definition of protection QOS which includes a component for each relevant security service. For each component, it is possible to specify an integer value which indicates a required level for that service. The range of integers available and the meanings of the particular values are not specified in a standard. They are implied by the particular agreed-upon set of security rules for the security association in use. The use of integers implies an ordering relationship between levels, with a higher level implying a stronger mechanism.

The level-based approach to protection QOS can be supplemented by the passing of a security label between the layers, such as between the transport and network service layers. This label serves as an indicator of required QOS. The security labels used for this purpose may be the same labels used to support access control, but they would have a different meaning. For example, the label "unclassified but sensitive" might imply use of a commercial-grade confidentiality mechanism based on DES encryption, where the label "secret" implies use of a confidentiality mechanism with a higher-grade classified encryption algorithm.

At either the Transport Layer or Network Layer, the establishment of QOS for a connection involves negotiation between the two peer entities, with the aim of best matching the QOS requirements of the two service users with the capabilities of the two service providers. With protection QOS, another element is introduced. Either peer entity may inject, at the service-provider level, administration protection QOS constraints. These are minimum-security requirements imposed by system administration in order to satisfy the local system security policy. For example, a user application may request a connection with no security protection at all but, depending upon circumstances, the local system administration at one or both peer entities may upgrade the required QOS to make confidentiality protection of a certain level mandatory. The negotiation of protection QOS can take place partly in security association establishment and partly in the regular exchange of QOS parameters in the connection establishment protocol.

SECURITY ARCHITECTURE

The transport layer security protocol (TLSP) is located completely within the Transport Layer. Except for the passing of protection QOS parameters, the existence and operation of TLSP are completely transparent to both the upper layers and the underlying Network Layer. TLSP is designed to supplement the regular Transport Layer protocols rather than change them. The TLSP is designed to work in conjunction with the transport protocol data unit (TPDU) and associated processing procedures of the TPDU without any modification to procedures or formats by effectively adding another protocol sublayer. Regular TPDUs are protected by being encapsulated within TLSP PDUs at the sending end prior to being passed to the Network Layer. The encapsulation is removed at the receiving end to produce the regular TPDU, which then continues under normal protocol processing.

The processing procedures are explained in ISO/IEC 8073 for connection-oriented processing and in ISO/IEC 8602 for connectionless-oriented processing. The protection of all regular PDUs associated with one transport connection is governed by one security association in the connection-oriented case. In other words, the same form of protection is applied to all PDUs. The protection scheme, however, can become more complex where Transport Layer multiplexing is located below the TLSP. In this instance, different transport connections or different connectionless TPDUs can be provided with different types of protection, even though the PDUs may be multiplexed onto one network connection between the two end systems. Where Transport Layer concatenation procedures are used, the same security association must protect all the concatenated PDUs. Concatenation procedures are located above the TLSP. The concatenated sequence of TPDUs is processed by the TLSP similarly to a single TPDU without concatenation.

SECURITY MECHANISMS

The encapsulation function of the TLSP supports the provision of several security services and can involve any required combination of security mechanisms. These mechanisms are *security label, direction indicator, integrity check-value (ICV), encryption padding*, and *encryption*.

A *security label* is prefixed to the TPDU to support the provision of an access control service. Fields are provided to define a unique defining authority identifier plus a label value in a format controlled by the defining authority. No particular label format is defined in the OIS. A *direction indicator* is a flag field prefix containing a bit indicating the direction of the TPDU transfer. This prefix contains a reference to a recognized initiator/responder relationship determined at security association establishment and is used to repulse reflection attacks. The ICV is a value that is computed and appended involving a process where padded octets are added to the data before the ICV computation. The ICV is the primary mechanism for providing both connection integrity and connectionless integrity services. *Encryption padding* is the padding of octets into the data where it is required by the encryption algorithm or for purposes of hiding lengths of protected PDUs. *Encryption* is the mechanism for providing connection or connectionless confidentiality and for providing necessary protection to information generated by other security mechanisms.

For the connection-oriented case, some security services are provided through the combined behavior of the TLSP encapsulation function and the normal procedures of the Transport Layer. Sequence integrity is achieved using the sequence numbers provided by Class 2, 3, or 4 transport protocol, together with connection integrity. Separate sequence numbering systems are maintained for normal data and expedited data flows.

Integrity recovery is accomplished using the Class 4 transport protocol recovery procedures, in conjunction with connection integrity. Sequence integrity cannot be used with Class 0 or Class 1 transport protocol.

Entity authentication is effectively a two-stage process. The first stage is security association establishment, which results in each transport entity knowing a key that it can use to verify the other entity of its identity. With security association establishment complete, the second stage is entity authentication on connection establishment. This is accomplished through each entity demonstrating knowledge of the applicable key by using that key for ICV generation or encryption in the encapsulation of the connect request TPDU. As protection against replay, the connect request and connect confirm TPDUs use connection reference values which must be unique within the lifetime of the key. This is most easily achieved by having a sequential component in the connection references. The system would then increment this component for each new connection establishment attempted.

For the connectionless case, the same basic two-stage process is used for data origin authentication. The key used in the encapsulation process is used to obtain the required authentication for a connectionless TPDU by providing a demonstrated knowledge of that key. With the key used for authentication purposes, peer addresses in connection establishment or connectionless TPDUs are also required to be checked for consistency as further protection against masquerade attacks.

SECURITY ASSOCIATION ATTRIBUTES

The TLSP also incorporates features including *security association attributes* and *agreed set of security rules (ASSR)*. The term *security association* is used to model the collections of related information maintained in two or more systems for purposes of providing the same type of protection to a sequence of distinct data transfers. The information items maintained in a security association are known as attributes of that security association. *Security association identifiers* include a local identifier and a remote identifier, which are octet strings of a length determined by the ASSR.

The term *ASSR* is used to describe an agreement between two or more systems as to which security mechanisms are to be used and which values are to be applied to parameters of those mechanisms. This avoids having to negotiate mechanism details with every security association establishment by using an agreed-upon set of security rules in a predefined package of security mechanism information. These security rules are registered and assigned a unique identifier, which is then made known to all potential users.

Other security association attributes held by a TLSP entity include *integrity sequence numbers, ICV mechanisms, encryption mechanisms, initiator/responder indicator, protection QOS, label mechanism, security mechanism,* and *peer TLSP entity address.* The last sequence numbers sent or received for normal and expedited data streams are *integrity sequence number attributes. ICV mechanism attributes* and *encryption mechanism attributes* include an algorithm, key granularity, key reference, and block size for determining necessary padding. In setting the direction, the *initiator/responder indicator* indicates which TLSP entity takes the role of initiator and which takes the role of responder. As mentioned previously, the *protection QOS indicator* is defined as a QOS label plus an integer level value for each entity service. The ASSR defines the range of integer values and the QOS label format. The set of allowable security labels for the security association is referred to as *label mechanism attributes. Security mechanism attributes* indicate which security mechanisms are used (e.g., entity authentication, security labels, integrity check values, integrity sequence numbers, and encryption). Finally, the *peer TLSP entity address* is the connection reference that is stored if the security association is tied to a particular transport connection.

SECURITY ASSOCIATION PROTOCOL

A security association may be established through Application Layer protocol exchanges (even though the security exchange is used by a lower-layer protocol), or through protocol exchanges at the same architectural layer that uses the security exchange, or through unspecified means (which may or may not involve online data communications). In order to accommodate protocol exchanges at the same architectural layer that uses the security exchange, an optional *security association protocol* in the TLSP is used.

PDU formats capable of supporting security association establishment, security association release, and the establishment of a new data key (rekeying) within a live security association is defined by the security association protocol. Establishing initial data keys and values for all security association attributes is the function of security association establishment.

LIST OF FREQUENTLY USED ACRONYMS

ASSR	Agreed Set of Security Rules
DC	Disconnect Confirm
DR	Disconnect Request
DT	Data Transport

ED	Expedited Data
ICV	Integrity Check-Value
IEC	International Electronic Commission
ISO	International Organization for Standardization
NC	Network Connection
NS	Network Service
NSDU	Network Service Data Unit
PDU	Protocol Data Unit
QOS	Quality of Service
SPDU	Session Protocol Data Unit
SSDU	Session Service Data User
TC	Transport Connection
TLSP	Transport Layer Security Protocol
TPDU	Transport Protocol Data Unit
TS	Transport Service
TSAP	Transport Service Address Protocol
TSDU	Transport Service Data Unit

Chapter 10
Application-Layer Security Protocols for Networks
Bill Stackpole

WE'RE NOT IN KANSAS ANYMORE

The incredible growth of Internet usage has shifted routine business transactions from fax machine and telephones to e-mail and E-commerce. This shift can be attributed in part to the economical worldwide connectivity of the Internet but also to the Internet capacity for more sophisticated types of transactions. Security professionals must understand the issues and risks associated with these transactions if they want to provide viable and scalable security solutions for Internet commerce.

Presence on the Internet makes it possible to conduct international, multiple-party and multiple-site transactions regardless of time or language differences. This level of connectivity has, however, created a serious security dilemma for commercial enterprises. How can a company maintain transactional compatibility with thousands of different systems and still ensure the confidentiality of those transactions? Security measures once deemed suitable for text-based messaging and file transfers seem wholly inadequate for sophisticated multimedia and E-commerce transfers. Given the complexity of these transactions, even standardized security protocols like IPSEC are proving inadequate.

This chapter covers three areas that are of particular concern: electronic messaging, World Wide Web (WWW) transactions, and monetary exchanges. All are subject to potential risk of significant financial losses as well as major legal and public relations liabilities. These transactions require security well beyond the capabilities of most lower-layer security protocols. They require application-layer security.

A LAYER-BY-LAYER LOOK AT SECURITY MEASURES

Before going into the particulars of application-based security it may be helpful to look at how security is implemented at the different ISO layers. Exhibit 10.1 depicts the ISO model divided into upper-layer protocols (those associated with the application of data) and lower-layer protocols (those associated with the transmission of data). Examples of some of the security protocols used at each layer are listed on the right. Let's begin with layer one.

ISO Seven Layer Model

7	Applications	PEM, S-HTTP, SET
6	Presentation	
5	Session	SSL
4	Transport	IPSEC
3	Network	PPTP, swIPe
2	Data Link	VPDN, L2F, L2TP
1	Physical	Fiber Optics

Exhibit 10.1.

These are common methods for providing security at the physical layer:

- Securing the cabling conduits — encase them in concrete.
- Shielding against spurious emissions — TEMPEST.
- Using media that are difficult to tap — fiber optics.

While effective, these methods are limited to things within your physical control.

Common Layer-2 measures include physical address filtering and tunneling (i.e., L2F, L2TP). These measures can be used to control access and provide confidentiality across certain types of connections but are limited to segments where the end points are well known to the security implementer. Layer-3 measures provide for more sophisticated filtering and tunneling (i.e., PPTP) techniques. Standardized implementations like IPSEC can provide a high degree of security across multiple platforms. However, Layer-3 protocols are ill-suited for multiple-site implementations because they are limited to a single network. Layer-4 transport-based protocols overcome the single network limitation but still lack the sophistication required for multiple-party transactions. Like all lower-layer protocols, transport-based protocols do not interact with the data contained in the payload, so they are unable to protect against payload corruption or content-based attacks.

APPLICATION-LAYER SECURITY — ALS 101

This is precisely the advantage of upper-layer protocols. Application-based security has the capability of interpreting and interacting with the information contained in the payload portion of a datagram. Take, for example, the application proxies used in most firewalls for FTP transfers. These proxies have the ability to restrict the use of certain commands even though the commands are contained within the payload portion of the packet. When an FTP transfer is initiated, it sets up a connection for passing commands to the server. The commands you type (e.g., LIST, GET, PASV) are sent to the server in the payload portion of the command packet as illustrated in Exhibit 10.2. The firewall proxy — because it is application-based — has the ability to "look" at these commands and can therefore restrict their use.

ETHERNET HEADER	IP HEADER	TCP HEADER	PAYLOAD
0040A0...40020A	10.1.2.1...10.2.1.2	FTP (Command)	List...

Exhibit 10.2. File Transfer Protocol – Command – Packet

Lower-layer security protocols like IPSEC do not have this capability. They can encrypt the commands for confidentiality and authentication, but they cannot restrict their use.

But what exactly is application-layer security? As the name implies, it is security provided by the application program itself. For example, a data warehouse using internally maintained access control lists to limit user access to files, records, or fields is implementing application-based security. Applying security at the application level makes it possible to deal with any number of sophisticated security requirements and accommodate additional requirements as they come along. This scenario works particularly well when all your applications are contained on a single host or secure intranet, but it becomes problematic when you attempt to extend its functionality across the Internet to thousands of different systems and applications. Traditionally, security in these environments has been addressed in a proprietary fashion within the applications themselves, but this is rapidly changing. The distributed nature of applications on the Internet has given rise to several standardized solutions designed to replace these *ad hoc*, vendor-specific security mechanisms.

INTEROPERABILITY — THE KEY TO SUCCESS FOR ALS

Interoperability is crucial to the success of any protocol used on the Internet. Adherence to standards is crucial to interoperability. Although the ALS protocols discussed in this chapter cover three distinctly different areas, they are all based on a common set of standards and provide similar security services. This section introduces some of these common elements. Not all common elements are included, nor are all those covered found in every ALS implementation, but there is sufficient commonality to warrant their inclusion.

Cryptography is the key component of all modern security protocols. However, the management of cryptographic keys has in the past been a major deterrent to its use in open environments like the Internet. With the advent of digital certificates and public key management standards, this deterrent has been largely overcome. Standards like the Internet Public Key Infrastructure X.509 (pkix) and the Simple Public Key Infrastructure (spki) provide the mechanisms necessary to issue, manage, and validate cryptographic keys across multiple domains and platforms. All of the protocols discussed in this chapter support the use of this Public Key Infrastructure.

Standard Security Services — Maximum Message Protection

All the ALS protocols covered in this chapter provided these four standard security services:

- Confidentiality (a.k.a privacy) — The assurance that only the intended recipient can read the contents of the information sent to them.
- Integrity — The guarantee that the information received is exactly the same as the information that was sent.
- Authentication — The guarantee that the sender of a message or transmission is really who they claim to be.
- Nonrepudiation — The proof that a message was sent by its originator even if the originator claims it was not.

Each of these services relies on a form of cryptography for its functionality. Although the service implementations may vary, they all use a fairly standard set of algorithms.

Algorithms Tried and True

The strength of a cryptographic algorithm can be measured by its longevity. Good algorithms continue to demonstrate high cryptographic strength after years of analysis and attack. The ALS protocols discussed here support three types of cryptography — symmetric, asymmetric, and hashing — using time-tested algorithms.

Symmetric (also called secret key) *cryptography* is primarily used for confidentiality functions because it has high cryptographic strength and can process large volumes of data quickly. In ALS implementations, DES is the most commonly supported symmetric algorithm. *Asymmetric or public key cryptography* is most commonly used in ALS applications to provide confidentiality during the initialization or set-up portion of a transaction. Public keys and digital certificates are used to authenticate the participation parties to one another and exchange the symmetric keys used for remainder of the transaction. The most commonly supported asymmetric algorithm in ALS implementations is RSA.

Cryptographic hashing is used to provide integrity and authentication in ALS implementations. When used separately, authentication validates the sender and the integrity of the message, but using them in combination provides proof that the message was not forged and therefore cannot be refuted (nonrepudiation). The three most commonly used hashes in ALS applications are MD2, MD5, and SHA. In addition to a common set of algorithms, systems wishing to interoperate in an open environment must be able to negotiate and validate a common set of security parameters. The next section introduces some of the standards used to define and validate these parameters.

Standardized Gibberish Is Still Gibberish!

For applications to effectively exchange information they must agree upon a common format for that information. Security services, if they are to be trustworthy, require all parties to function in unison. Communication parameters must be established, security services, modes, and algorithms agreed upon, and cryptographic keys exchanged and validated. To facilitate these processes the ALS protocols covered in this chapter support the following formatting standards:

- X.509 — The X.509 standard defines the format of digital certificates used by certification authorities to validate public encryption keys.
- PKCS — The Public Key Cryptography Standard defines the underlying parameters (object identifiers) used to perform the cryptographic transforms and to validate keying data.
- CMS — The Cryptographic Message Syntax defines the transmission formats and cryptographic content types used by the security services. CMS defines six cryptographic content types ranging from no security to signed and encrypted content. They are data, signedData, envelopedData, signedAndEnvelopedData, digestData, and encryptedData.
- MOSS — The MIME Object Security Services defines two additional cryptographic content types for multipart MIME (Multimedia Internet

Mail Extensions) objects that can be used singly or in combination. They are multipart-signed and multipart-encrypted.

Encryption is necessary to ensure transaction confidentiality and integrity on open networks, and the Public Key/Certification Authority architecture provides the infrastructure necessary to manage the distribution and validation of cryptographic keys. Security mechanisms at all levels now have a standard method for initiating secure transactions, thus eliminating the need for proprietary solutions to handle secure multiple-party, multiple-site, or international transactions. A case in point is the new SET credit card transaction protocol.

SETTING THE EXAMPLE — VISA'S SECURE ELECTRONIC TRANSACTION PROTOCOL

SET (Secure Electronic Transaction) is an application-based security protocol jointly developed by Visa and MasterCard. It was created to provide secure payment card transactions over open networks. SET is the electronic equivalent of a face-to-face or mail-order credit card transaction. It provides confidentially and integrity for payment transmissions and authenticates all parties involved in the transaction. Let's walk through a SET transaction to see how this application-layer protocol handles a sophisticated multiparty financial transaction.

A SET transaction involves five different participants: the *cardholder*, the *issuer* of the payment card, the *merchant*, the *acquirer* that holds the merchant's account, and a *payment gateway* that processes SET transactions on behalf of the acquirer. The policies governing how transactions are conducted are established by a sixth party, the *brand* (i.e., Visa), but they do not participate in payment transactions.

A SET transaction requires two pairs of asymmetric encryption keys and two digital certificates; one for exchanging information and the other for digital signatures. The keys and certificates can be stored on a "smart" credit card or embedded into any SET-enabled application (i.e., Web browser). The keys and certificates are issued to the cardholder by a certification authority (CA) on behalf of the issuer. The merchant's keys and digital certificates are issued to them by a certification authority on behalf of the acquirer. They provide assurance that the merchant has a valid account with the acquirer. The cardholder and merchant certificates are digitally signed by the issuing financial institution to ensure their authenticity and to prevent them from being fraudulently altered. One interesting feature of this arrangement is that the cardholder's certificate doesn't contain his account number or expiration date. That information is encoded using a secret key that is only supplied to the payment gateway during the payment authorization. Now that we know all the players, let's get started.

Step 1

The cardholder goes shopping, selects his merchandise, and sends a purchase order to the merchant requesting a SET payment type. (The SET specification does not define how shopping is accomplished so it has no involvement in this portion of the transaction.) The cardholder and merchant, if they haven't already, authenticate themselves to each other by exchanging certificates and digital signatures. During this exchange the merchant also supplies the payment gateway's certificate and digital signature information to the cardholder. You will see how this is used later. Also established in this exchange is a pair of randomly generated symmetric keys that will be used to encrypt the remaining cardholder–merchant transmissions.

Step 2.

Once the above exchanges have been completed, the merchant contacts the payment gateway. Part of this exchange includes language selection information to ensure international interoperability. Once again certificate and digital signature information is used to authenticate the merchant to the gateway and establish random symmetric keys. Payment information (PI) is then forwarded to the gateway for payment authorization. Notice that only the *payment* information is forwarded. This is done to satisfy regulatory requirements regarding the use of strong encryption. Generally, the use of strong cryptography by financial institutions is not restricted if the transactions *only contain monetary values*.

Step 3.

Upon receipt of the PI, the payment gateway authenticates the cardholder. Notice that the cardholder is authenticated without contacting the purchase gateway directly. This is done through a process called dual-digital signature. The information required by the purchase gateway to authenticate the cardholder is sent to the merchant with a different digital signature than the one used for merchant–cardholder exchanges. This is possible because the merchant sent the purchase gateway certificates to the cardholder in an earlier exchange! The merchant simply forwards this information to the payment gateway as part of the payment authorization request. Another piece of information passed in this exchange is the secret key the gateway needs to decrypt the cardholder's account number and expiration date.

Step 4.

The gateway reformats the payment information and forwards it via a private circuit to the issuer for authorization. When the issuer authorizes the transaction, the payment gateway notifies the merchant, who notifies the cardholder, and the transaction is complete.

Step 5.

The merchant finalizes the transaction by issuing a Payment Capture request to the payment gateway causing the cardholder's account to be debited, and the merchant's account to be credited for the transaction amount.

A single SET transaction like the one outlined above is incredibly complex, requiring more than 59 different actions to take place successfully. Such complexity requires application-layer technology to be managed effectively. The beauty of SET, however, is its ability to do just that in a secure and ubiquitous manner. Other protocols are achieving similar success in different application areas.

FROM POSTCARDS TO LETTERS — SECURING ELECTRONIC MESSAGES

Electronic messaging is a world of postcards. As messages move from source to destination they are openly available (like writing on a postcard) to be read by those handling them. If postcards aren't suitable for business communications, it stands to reason that electronic mail on an open network isn't either. Standard business communications require confidentiality, and other more sensitive communications require additional safeguards like proof of delivery or sender verification, features that are not available in the commonly used Internet mail protocols. This has lead to the development of several security-enhanced messaging protocols. PEM is one such protocol.

Privacy Enhanced Mail (PEM) is an application-layer security protocol developed by the IETF (Internet Engineering Task Force) to add confidentiality and authentication services to electronic messages on the Internet. The goal was to create a standard that could be implemented on any host, be compatible with existing mail systems, support standard key management schemes, protect both individually addressed and list-addressed mail, and not interfere with nonsecure mail delivery. When the standard was finalized in 1993 it had succeeded on all counts. PEM supports all four standard security services, although all services are not necessarily part of every message. PEM messages can be MIC-CLEAR messages that provide integrity and authentication only; MIC-ONLY messages that provide integrity and authentication with support for certain gateway implementations;

or ENCRYPTED messages that provide integrity, authentication, and confidentiality.

These are some of PEM's key features:

- End-to-end confidentiality — Messages are protected against disclosure from the time they leave the sender's system until they are *read* by the recipient.
- Sender and forwarder authentication — PEM digital signatures authenticate both senders and forwarders and ensure message integrity. PEM utilizes an integrity check that allows messages to be received in any order and still be verified — an important feature in environments like the Internet where messages can be fragmented during transit.
- Originator nonrepudiation — This feature authenticates the *originator* of a PEM message. It is particularly useful for forwarded messages because a PEM digital signature only authenticates the last sender. Nonrepudiation verifies the originator no matter how many times the message is forwarded.
- Algorithm independence — PEM was designed to easily accommodate new cryptographic and key management schemes. Currently PEM supports common algorithms in four areas: DES for data encryption, DES and RSA for key management, RSA for message integrity, and RSA for digital signatures.
- PKIX support — PEM fully supports interoperability on open networks using the Internet Public Key Infrastructure X.509.
- Delivery system independence — PEM achieves delivery-system independence because its functions are contained in the body of a standard message and use a standard character set as illustrated in Exhibit 10.3.
- X.500 distinguished name support — PEM uses the distinguished name (DN) feature of the X.500 directory standard to identify senders and recipients. This feature separates mail from specific individuals allowing organizations, lists, and systems to send and receive PEM messages.

RIPEM (Riordan's Internet Privacy Enhanced Mail) is a public domain implementation of the PEM protocol although not in its entirety. Since the author, Mark Riordan, placed the code in the public domain, it has been ported to a large number of operating systems. Source and binaries are available via FTP to U.S. and Canadian citizens from **ripem.msu.edu**. Read the **GETTING_ACCESS** file in the **/pub/crypt/** directory before attempting any downloads.

Secure/Multipurpose Internet Mail Extensions (S/MIME) is another application-layer protocol that provides all four standard security services

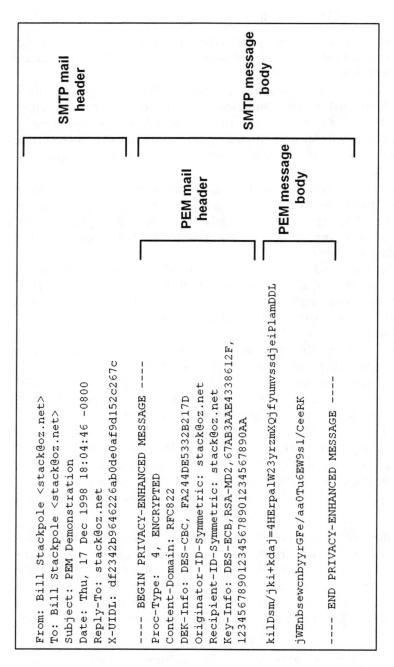

```
From: Bill Stackpole <stack@oz.net>
To: Bill Stackpole <stack@oz.net>
Subject: PEM Demonstration
Date: Thu, 17 Dec 1998 18:04:46 -0800
Reply-To: stack@oz.net
X-UIDL: df2342b964226ab0de0af9d152c267c

----- BEGIN PRIVACY-ENHANCED MESSAGE -----
Proc-Type: 4, ENCRYPTED
Content-Domain: RFC822
DEK-Info: DES-CBC, FA244DE5332B217D
Originator-ID-Symmetric: stack@oz.net
Recipient-ID-Symmetric: stack@oz.net
Key-Info: DES-ECB, RSA-MD2, 67AB3AAE4338612F,
12345678901234567890123456789AA

kilDsm/jki+kdaj=4HErpalW23yrzmXQjfyumvssdjeiPlamDDL

jWEnbsewcnbyyrGFe/aa0Tu6EW9sl/CeeRK

----- END PRIVACY-ENHANCED MESSAGE -----
```

SMTP mail header

SMTP message body

PEM mail header

PEM message body

Exhibit 10.3.

for electronic messages. Originally designed by RSA Data Security, the S/MIME specification is currently managed by the IETF S/MIME Working Group. Although S/MIME is not an IETF standard, it has already garnered considerable vendor support, largely because it is based on well-proven standards that provide a high degree of interoperability. Most notable is, of course, the popular and widely used MIME standard, but S/MIME also utilizes the CMS, PKCS, and X.509 standards. Like PEM, S/MIME is compatible with most existing Internet mail systems and does not interfere with the delivery of nonsecure messages. However, S/MIME has the added benefit of working seamlessly with other MIME transports (i.e., HTTP) and can even function in mixed-transport environments. This makes it particularly attractive for use with automated transfers like EDI and Internet FAX.

There are two S/MIME message types: *signed*, and *signed and enveloped*. Signed messages provide integrity and sender authentication, while signed and enveloped messages provide integrity, authentication, and confidentiality. The remaining features of S/MIME are very similar to PEM and do not warrant repeating here.

A list of commercial S/MIME products that have successfully completed S/MIME interoperability testing is available on the RSA Data Security web site at: **www.rsa.com/smime/html/interop_center.html.** A public domain version of S/MIME written in PERL by Ralph Levien is available at: **www.c2.org/~raph/premail.html**.

Open Pretty Good Privacy (OpenPGP), sometimes called PGP/MIME, is another emerging ALS protocol on track to becoming an IETF standard. It is based on PGP, the most widely deployed message security program on the Internet. OpenPGP is very similar in features and functionality to S/MIME, but the two are not interoperable because they use slightly different encryption algorithms and MIME encapsulations. A list of PGP implementations and other OpenPGP information is available at: **http://www-ns.rutgers.edu/~mione/openpgp/**. Freeware implementations of OpenPGP are available at the North American Cryptography Archives (**www.cryptography.org**).

TAMING HTTP — WEB APPLICATION SECURITY

Web-based applications are quickly becoming the standard for all types of electronic transactions because they are easy to use and highly interoperable. These features are also their major security failing. Web transactions traverse the network in well-known and easily intercepted formats, making them quite unsuitable for most business transactions. This section will cover some of the mechanisms used to overcome these Web security issues.

Secure HyperText Transfer Protocol (S/HTTP) is a message-oriented security protocol designed to provide end-to-end confidentiality, integrity, authentication, and nonrepudiation services for HTTP clients and servers. It was originally developed by Enterprise Integration Technologies (now Verifone, Inc.) in 1995. At this writing, S/HTTP is still an IETF draft standard, but it is already widely used in Web applications. Its success can be attributed to a flexible design that is rooted in established standards. The prominent standard is, of course, HTTP, but the protocol also utilizes the NIST Digital Signature Standard (DSS), CMS, MOSS, and X.509 standards. S/HTTP's strict adherence to the HTTP messaging model provides delivery-system independence and makes it easy to integrate S/HTTP functions into standard HTTP applications. Algorithm independence and the ability to negotiate security options between participating parties assures S/HTTP's interoperability for years to come. Secure HTTP modes of operation include message protection, key management, and a transaction freshness mechanism.

Secure HTTP protection features include the following:

- Support for MOSS and CMS — Protections are provided in both content domains using the CMS "application/s-http" content-type or the MOSS "multipart-signed" or "multipart-encrypted" header.
- Syntax compatibility — Protection parameters are specified by extending the range of HTTP message headers, making S/HTTP messages syntactically the same as standard HTTP messages, except the range of the headers is different and the body is usually encrypted.
- Recursive protections — Protections can be used singly or applied one layer after another to achieve higher levels of protection. Layering the protections makes it easier for the receiving system to parse them. The message is simply parsed one protection at a time until it yields a standard HTTP content type.
- Algorithm independence — The S/HTTP message structure can easily incorporate new cryptographic implementations. The current specification requires supporting MD5 for message digests, MD5-HMAC for authentication, DES-CBC for symmetric encryption, and NIST-DSS for signature generation and verification.
- Freshness feature — S/HTTP uses a simple challenge–response to ensure that the data being returned to the server is "fresh." In environments like HTTP, where long periods of time can pass between messages, it is difficult to track the state of a transaction. To overcome this problem, the originator of an HTTP message sends a freshness value (nonce) to the recipient along with the transaction data. The recipient returns the nonce with a response. If the nonces match, the data is fresh, and the transaction can continue. Stale data indicates an error condition.

Secure HTTP Key management modes include:

- Manual exchange — Shared secrets are exchanged through a simple password mechanism like PAP. The server simply sends the client a dialog box requesting a userID and password then authenticates the response against an existing list of authorized users.
- Public key exchange — Keys are exchanged using the Internet Public Key Infrastructure with full X.509 certificate support. S/HTTP implementations are required to support Diffie–Hellman for in-band key exchanges.
- Out-of-band key exchange — Symmetric keys can be prearranged through some other media (i.e., snail mail). This feature, unique to the S/HTTP, permits parties that do not have established public keys to participate in secure transactions.
- In-band symmetric key exchange — S/HTTP can use public-key encryption to exchange random symmetric keys in instances where the transaction would benefit from the higher performance of symmetric encryption.

Many commercial web browsers and servers implement the S/HTTP protocol, but the author was unable to find any public domain implementations. A full implementation of S/HTTP including the C source code is available in the SecureWeb Toolkit™ from Terisa (www.spyrus.com). The kit also contains the source code for SSL.

Secure Socket Layer (SSL) is a client–server protocol designed by Netscape to provide secure communications for their Web browser and server products. It was quickly adopted by other vendors and has become the *de facto* standard for secure Web transactions. However, SSL is not limited to Web services; it can provide confidentiality, integrity, authentication, and nonrepudiation services between any two communicating applications. The current version of SSL (SSL V3.0) is on track to becoming an IETF standard. While included here as an application-layer protocol, SSL is actually designed to function at the session and application-layers. The SSL Record protocol provides security services at the session layer — the point where the application interfaces to the TCP/IP transport sockets. It is used to encapsulate higher-layer protocols and data for compression and transmission. The SSL Handshake protocol is an application-based service used to authenticate the client and server to each other and negotiate the security parameters for each communication session.

The SSL Handshake Protocol utilizes public key encryption with X.509 certificate validation to negotiate the symmetric encryption parameters used for each client–server session. SSL is a stateful protocol. It transitions through several different states during connection and session operations. The handshake protocol is used to coordinate and maintain these states.

One SSL session may include multiple connections, and participating parties may have multiple simultaneous sessions. The session state maintains the peer certificate information, compression parameters, cipher parameters and the symmetric encryption key. The connection state maintains the MAC and asymmetric keys for the client and server as well as the vectors (if required) for symmetric encryption initialization. SSL was designed to be fully extensible and can support multiple encryption schemes. The current version requires support for these schemes:

- DES, RC2, RC4, and IDEA for confidentiality
- RSA and DSS for peer authentication
- SHA and MD5 for message integrity
- X.509 and FORTEZZA certificates for key validation
- RSA, Diffie–Hellman, and FORTEZZA for key exchange

SSL also supports NULL parameters for unsigned and unencrypted transmissions. This allows the implementer to apply an appropriate amount of security for their application. The support for the FORTEZZA hardware encryption system is unique to the SSL as is the data compression requirement. SSL uses a session caching mechanism to facilitate setting up multiple sessions between clients and servers and resuming disrupted sessions.

There is an exceptional public domain implementation of SSL created by Eric Young and Tim Hudson of Australia called SSLeay. It includes a full implementation of Netscape's SSL version 2 with patches for Telnet, FTP, Mosaic, and several Web servers. The current version is available from the SSLeay Web site at www.ssleay.org. The site includes several SSL white papers and an excellent *Programmers' Reference*.

DON'T SHOW ME THE MONEY — MONETARY TRANSACTION SECURITY

The success of commerce on the Internet depends upon its ability to conduct monetary transactions securely. Although purchasing seems to dominate this arena, bill payment, fund and instrument transfers, and EDI are important considerations. The lack of standards for electronic payment has fostered a multitude of proprietary solutions, including popular offerings from Cybercash (Cybercoin), Digital (Millicent), and Digicash. However, proprietary solutions are not likely to receive widespread success in a heterogeneous environment like the Internet. This section will concentrate on standardized solutions. Since the SET protocol has been covered in some detail already, only SET implementations will be mentioned here.

Secure Payment (S/PAY) is a developer's toolkit based on the SET protocol. It was developed by RSA Data Security, although the marketing rights currently belong to the Trintech Group (www.trintech.com). The S/Pay library fully implements the SET v1.0 cardholder, merchant, and acquirer functions and the underlying encryption and certificate management functions for Windows95/NT and major UNIX platforms. Included in the code is support for hardware-based encryption engines, smart card devices, and long-term private key storage. Trintech also offers full implementations of SET merchant, cardholder, and acquirer software. This includes their Pay-Ware Net-POS product, which supports several combinations of SSL and SET technologies aimed at easing the transition from Web SSL transactions to fully implemented SET transactions.

Open Financial Exchange (OFX) is an application-layer protocol created by Checkfree, Intuit, and Microsoft to support a wide range of consumer and small business banking services over the Internet. OFX is an open specification available to any financial institution or vendor desiring to implement OFX services. OFX uses SSL with digital certificate support to provide confidentiality, integrity, and authentication services to its transactions. The protocol has gained considerable support in the banking and investment industry because it supports just about every conceivable financial transaction. Currently, the OFX committee is seeking to expand OFX's presence through interoperability deals with IBM and other vendors. Copies of the OFX specification are available from the Open Financial Exchange Web site (www.ofx.net).

Micro Payment Transfer Protocol (MPTP) is part of The World Wide Web Consortium (W3C) Joint Electronic Payment Initiative. Currently, MPTP is a W3C working draft. The specification is based on variations of Rivest and Shamir's Pay-Word, Digital's Millicent, and Bellare's iKP proposals. MPTP is a very flexible protocol that can be layered upon existing transports like HTTP or MIME to provide greater transaction scope. It is highly tolerant of transmission delays allowing much of the transaction processing to take place off-line. MPTP is designed to provide payments through the services of a third-party broker. In the current version, the broker must be common to both the customer and the vendor, although Inter–broker transfers are planned for future implementations. This will be necessary if MPTP is going to scale effectively to meet Internet demands.

Customers establish an account with a broker. Once established, they are free to purchase from any vendor common to their broker. The MPTP design takes into consideration the majority of risks associated with electronic payment and provides mechanisms to mitigate those risks, but it does not implement a specific security policy. Brokers are free to define policies that best suit their business requirements.

MPTP relies on S/Key technology using MD5 or SHA algorithms to authorize payments. MPTP permits the signing of messages for authentication, integrity, and nonrepudiation using public or secret key cryptography and fully supports X.509 certificates. Although MPTP is still in the draft stages, its exceptional design, flexibility, and high performance destine it to be a prime contender in the electronic payment arena.

Java Electronic Commerce Framework (JECF) is our final item of discussion. JECF is not an application protocol. It is a framework for implementing electronic payment processing using active-content technology. Active-content technology uses an engine (i.e., a JAVA virtual machine) installed on the client to execute program components (e.g., applets) sent to it from the server. Current JECF active-content components include the Java Commerce Messages, Gateway Security Model, Commerce JavaBeans, and Java Commerce Client (JCC).

JECF is based around the concept of an electronic wallet. The wallet is an extensible client-side mechanism capable of supporting any number of E-commerce transactions. Vendors create Java applications consisting of service modules (applets) called Commerce JavaBeans that plug in to the wallet. These applets implement the operations and protocols (i.e., SET) necessary to conduct transactions with the vendor. There are several significant advantages of this architecture:

- Vendors are not tied to specific policies for their transactions. They are free to create modules containing policies and procedures best suited to their business.
- Clients are not required to have specialized applications. Since Java-Bean applets are active content, they can be delivered and dynamically loaded on the customer's system as the transaction is taking place.
- Applications can be updated dynamically. Transaction applets can be updated or changed to correct problems or meet growing business needs without having to send updates to all the clients. The new modules will be loaded over the old during their next transaction.
- Modules can be loaded or unloaded on-the-fly to accommodate different payment, encryption, or language requirements. OFX modules can be loaded for banking transactions and later unloaded when the customer requires SET modules to make a credit card purchase.
- JavaBean modules run on any operating system, browser, or application supporting Java. This gives vendors immediate access to the largest possible customer base.

The flexibility, portability, and large Java user-base make the Java Electronic Commerce Framework (JECF) a very attractive E-commerce solution. It is sure to become a major player in the electronic commerce arena.

IF IT'S NOT ENCRYPTED NOW. . .

The Internet has dramatically changed the way we do business, but that hasn't come without a price. Security for Internet transactions and messaging is woefully lacking, making much of what we are doing on the Internet an open book for all to read. This can't continue. Despite the complexity of the problems we are facing, there are solutions. The technologies outlined in this chapter provide real solutions for mitigating Internet business risks. We can secure our messages, web applications, and monetary exchanges. Admittedly, some of these applications are not as polished as we would like, and some are difficult to implement and manage, but they are nonetheless effective and most certainly a step in the right direction.

Someday all of our business transactions on the Internet will be encrypted, signed, sealed, and delivered, but I'm not sure we can wait for that day. Business transactions on the Internet are increasing, and new business uses for the Internet are going to be found. Waiting for things to get better is only going to put us further behind the curve. Someone has let the Internet bull out of the cage and we are either going to take him by the horns or get run over! ALS now!

Bibliography

Crocker, S., Freed, N., Galvan, J., and Murphy, S., RFC 1848 — MIME object security services, *IETF,* October 1995.

Dusse, Steve and Matthews, Tim, S/MIME: anatomy of a secure e-mail standard, *Messaging Magazine,* 1998.

Freier, Alan O., Karlton, Philip, and Kocher, Paul C., "INTERNET-DRAFT — The SSL Protocol Version 3.0," November 18, 1996.

Hallam-Baker, Phillip, "Micro Payment Transfer Protocol (MPTP) Version 1.0," Joint Electronic Payment Initiative — W3C, November 1995.

Hirsch, Frederick, Introducing SSL and certificates using SSLeay, the Open Group Research Institute, *World Wide Web Journal,* Summer 1997.

Hudson, T.J. and Young, E.A., *SSL Programmers Reference,* July 1, 1995.

Lundblade, Laurence, *A Review of E-mail Security Standards,* Qualcomm Inc., 1998.

Pearah, David, *Micropayments,* Massachusetts Institute of Technology, April 23, 1997.

PKCS #7: Cryptographic Message Syntax Standard, RSA Laboratories Technical Note Version 1.5, RSA Laboratories, November 1, 1993.

Ramsdell, Blake, "INTERNET-DRAFT — S/MIME Version 3 Message Specification," Worldtalk Inc., August 6, 1998.

Resorla, E. and Schiffman, A., "INTERNET-DRAFT — The Secure HyperText Transfer Protocol," Terisa Systems, Inc., June 1998.

Schneier, Bruce, *E-Mail Security: How to Keep Your Electronic Messages Private,* John Wiley & Sons, 1995.

SET Secure Electronic Transaction Specification, Book 1: Business Description, Setco, Inc., May 31, 1997.

Resources

E-Payments Resource Center, Trintech Inc., www.trintech.com
The Electronic Messaging Association, www.ema.org
Information Society Project Office (ISPO), www.ispo.cec.be
The Internet Mail Consortium (IMC), www.inc.org
Java Commerce Products, http://java.sun.com
SET Reference Implementation (SETREF), Terisa Inc., www.terisa.com
SET — Secure Electronic Transaction LLC, www.setco.org
S/MIME Central, http://www.rsa.com/smime/
Transaction Net and the Open Financial Exchange, www.ofx.net

Chapter 11
Security of Communication Protocols and Services

William Hugh Murray

The information security manager is confronted with a wide variety of communications protocols and services. At one level, the manager would like to be able to ignore how the information gets from one place to another; he would like to be able to *assume* security. At another, he understands that he has only limited control over how the information moves; because the user may be able to influence the choice of path, the manager prefers not to rely upon it. However, that being said, the manager also knows that there are differences in the security properties of the various protocols and services that he may otherwise find useful.

This chapter describes the popular protocols and services, talks about their intended uses and applications, and describes their security properties and characteristics. It compares and contrasts similar protocols and services, makes recommendations for their use, and also recommends compensating controls or alternatives for increasing security.

INTRODUCTION

For the last century, we have trusted the dial-switched voice-analog network. It was operated by one of the most trusted enterprises in the history of the world. It was connection-switched and point-to-point. While there was some eavesdropping, most of it was initiated by law enforcement and was, for the most part, legitimate. While a few of us carefully considered what we would say, most of us used the telephone automatically and without worrying about being overheard. Similarly, we were able to recognize

0-8493-9829-0/00/$0.00+$.50
© 2000 by CRC Press LLC

most of the people who called us; we trusted the millions of copies of the printed directories; and we trusted the network to connect us only to the number we dialed. While it is not completely justified, we have transferred much of that automatic trust to the modern digital network and even to the Internet.

All other things being equal, the information security manager would like to be able to ignore how information moves from one place to another. He would like to be able to assume that he can put it into a pipe at point A and have it come out reliably only at B. Of course, in the real world of the modern integrated network, this is not the case. In this world the traffic is vulnerable to eavesdropping, misdirection, interference, contamination, alteration, and even total loss.

On the other hand, relatively little of this happens; the vast majority of information is delivered when and how it is intended and without any compromise. This happens in part in spite of the way the information is moved and in part because of how it is moved. The various protocols and services have different security properties and qualities. Some provide error detection, corrective action such as retransmission, error correction, guaranteed delivery, and even information hiding.

The different levels of service exist because they have different costs and performance. They exist because different traffic, applications, and environments have different requirements. For example, the transfer of a program file has a requirement for bit-for-bit integrity; in some cases, if you lose a bit, it is as bad as losing the whole file. On the other hand, a few seconds, or even tens of seconds, of delay in the transfer of the file may have little impact. However, if one is moving voice traffic, the loss of tens of bits may be perfectly acceptable, while delay in seconds is intolerable. These costs must be balanced against the requirements of the application and the environment.

While the balance between performance and cost is often struck without regard to security, the reality is that there are security differences. The balance between performance, cost, and security is the province of the information security manager. Therefore, he needs to understand the properties and characteristics of the protocols so he can make the necessary tradeoffs or evaluate those that have already been made.

Finally, all protocols have limitations and many have fundamental vulnerabilities. Implementations of protocols can compensate for such vulnerabilities only in part. Implementers may be faced with hard design choices, and they may make errors resulting in implementation-induced vulnerabilities. The manager must understand these so he will know when and how to compensate.

PROTOCOLS

A protocol is an agreed-upon set of rules or conventions for communicating between two or more parties. "Hello" and "goodbye" for beginning and ending voice phone calls are examples of a simple protocol. A slightly more sophisticated protocol might include lines that begin with tags, like "This is (name) calling."

Protocols are to codes as sentences and paragraphs are to words. In a protocol, the parties may agree to addressing, codes, format, packet size, speed, message order, error detection and correction, acknowledgments, key exchange, and other things.

This section will deal with a number of common protocols. It will describe their intended use or application, characteristics, design choices, and limitations.

INTERNET PROTOCOL

The Internet Protocol, IP, is a primitive and application-independent protocol for addressing and routing packets of data within a network. It is the "IP" in TCP/IP, the protocol suite that is used in and defines the Internet. It is intended for use in a relatively flat, mesh, broadcast, connectionless, packet-switched net like the Internet.

IP is analogous to a post card in the 18th century. The sender wrote the message on one side of the card and the address and return address on the other. He then gave it to someone who was going in the general direction of the intended recipient. The message was not confidential; everyone who handled it could read it and might even make an undetected change to it.

IP is a "best efforts" protocol; it does not guarantee message delivery nor provide any evidence as to whether or not the message was delivered. It is unchecked; the receiver does not know whether or not he received the entire intended message or whether or not it is correct. The addresses are unreliable; the sender cannot be sure that the message will go only where he intends or even when he intends. The receiver cannot be sure that the message came from the address specified as the return address in the packet.

The protocol does not provide any checking or hiding. If the application requires these, they must be implied or specified someplace else, usually in a higher (i.e., closer to the application) protocol layer.

IP specifies the addresses of the sending or receiving hardware device,* but if that device supports multiple applications, IP does not specify which of those it is intended for.

The IP protocol uses 32-bit addresses. However, the use or meaning of the bits within the address depends upon the size and use of the network. Addresses are divided into five classes. Each class represents a different design choice between the number of networks and the number of addressable devices within the class. Class A addresses are used for very large networks where the number of such networks is expected to be low but the number of addressable devices is expected to be very high. Class A addresses are used for nation states and other very large domains such as .mil, .gov, and .com. As shown in Exhibit 11.1, a zero in bit position 0 of an address specifies it as a class A address. Positions 1 through 7 are used to specify the network, and positions 8 through 31 are used to specify devices within the network. Class C is used for networks where the possible number of networks is expected to be high but the number of addressable devices in each net is less than 128. Thus, in general, class B is used for enterprises, states, provinces, or municipalities, and class C is used for LANs. Class D is used for multicasting, and Class E is reserved for future uses.

NETWORK CLASS	DESCRIPTION	ADDRESS CLASS	NETWORK ADDRESS	DEVICE ADDRESS
A	National	0 in bit 0	1–7	8–31
B	Enterprise	10 in bits 0–1	2–15	16–31
C	LAN	110 in 0–2	3–23	24–31
D	Multicast	1110 in 0–3	4–31	
E	Reserved	1111 in 0–3		

Exhibit 11.1. IP Network Address Formats

You will often see IP addresses written as nnn.nnn.nnn.nnn.

While security is certainly not IP's long suit, it is responsible for much of the success of the Internet. It is fast and simple. In practice, the security limitations of IP simply do not matter much. Applications rely upon higher-level protocols for security.

* There is a convention of referring to all network addressable devices as "hosts." Such usage in other documents equates to the use of device or addressable device here. IPv6 defines "host."

Internet Protocol v6.0 (IPng)

IPv6 or "next generation" is a backwardly compatible new version of IP. It is intended to permit the Internet to grow both in terms of the number of addressable devices, particularly class A addresses, and in quantity of traffic. It expands the address to 128 bits, simplifies the format header, improves the support for extensions and options, adds a "quality-of-service" capability, and adds address authentication and message confidentiality and integrity. IPv6 also formalizes the concepts of packet, node, router, host, link, and neighbors that were only loosely defined in v4.

In other words, IPng addresses most of the limitations of IP, specifically including the security limitations. It provides for the use of encryption to ensure that information goes only where it is intended to go. This is called secure-IP. Secure-IP may be used for point-to-point security across an arbitrary network. More often, it is used to carve virtual private networks (VPNs) or secure virtual networks (SVNs)* out of such arbitrary networks.

Many of the implementations of secure-IP are still proprietary and do not guarantee interoperability with all other such implementations.

User Datagram Protocol (UDP)

The UDP protocol is similar to IP in that it is connectionless and offers "best effort" delivery service, and it is similar to TCP in that it is both checked and application specific.

Exhibit 11.2 shows the format of the UDP datagram. Unless the UDP source port is on the same device as the destination port, the UDP packet will be encapsulated in an IP packet. The IP address will specify the physical device, while the UDP address will specify the logical port or application on the device.

BIT POSITIONS	USAGE
0–15	Source Port Address
16–31	Destination Port Address
32–47	Message Length (n)
48–63	Checksum
64–n	Data

Exhibit 11.2. UDP Datagram

---

* VPN is used here to refer to the use of encryption to connect private networks across the public network, gateway-to-gateway. SVN is used to refer to the use of encryption to talk securely, end-to-end, across arbitrary networks. While the term VPN is sometimes used to describe both applications, different implementations of secure-IP may be required for the two applications.

UDP implements the abstraction of "port," a named logical connection or interface to a specific application or service within a device. Ports are identified by a positive integer. Port identity is local to a device, i.e., the use or meaning of port number is not global. A given port number can refer to any application that the sender and receiver agree upon. However, by convention and repeated use, certain port numbers have become identified with certain applications. Exhibit 11.3 lists examples of some of these conventional port assignments.

PORT NUMBER	APPLICATION	DESCRIPTION
23	Telnet	
53	DNS	Domain name service
43		Whois
69	TFTP	Trivial file transfer service
80	HTTP	Web service
119	Net News	
137		Netbios name service
138		Netbios datagrams
139		Netbios session data

Exhibit 11.3. Sample UDP Ports

Transmission Control Protocol (TCP)

TCP is a sophisticated composition of IP that compensates for many of its limitations. It is a connection-oriented protocol that enables two applications to exchange streams of data synchronously and simultaneously in both directions. It guarantees both the delivery and order of the packets. Since packets are given a sequence number, missing packets will be detected, and packets can be delivered in the same order in which they were sent; lost packets can be automatically resent. TCP also adapts to the latency of the network. It uses control flags to enable the receiver to automatically slow the sender so as not to overflow the buffers of the receiver.

TCP does not make the origin address reliable. The sequence number feature of TCP resists address spoofing. However, it does not make it impossible. Instances of attackers pretending to be trusted nodes have been reported to have tool kits that encapsulate the necessary work and special knowledge to implement such attacks.

Like many packet-switched protocols, TCP uses path diversity. This means some of the meaning of the traffic may not be available to an eavesdropper. However, eavesdropping is still possible. For example, user identifiers and pass-phrases usually move in the same packet. "Password grabber" programs have been detected in the network. These programs simply store the first 256 or 512 bits of packets on the assumption that many will contain passwords.

Finally, like most stateful protocols, some TCP implementations are vulnerable to denial-of-service attacks. One such attack is called *SYN flooding*. Requests for sessions, SYN flags, are sent to the target, but the acknowledgments are ignored. The target allocates memory to these requests and is overwhelmed.

Telnet

The Telnet protocol describes how commands and data are passed from one machine on the network to another over a TCP/IP connection. It is described in RFC 855. It is used to make a terminal or printer on one machine and an operating system or application on another appear to be local to each other. The user invokes the Telnet client by entering its name or clicking its icon on his local system and giving the name or address and port number of the system or application that he wishes to use. The Telnet client must listen to the keyboard and send the characters entered by the user across the TCP connection to the server. It listens to the TCP connection and displays the traffic on the user's terminal screen. The client and server use an escape sequence to distinguish between user data and their communication with each other.

The Telnet service is a frequent target of attack. By default, the Telnet service listens for login requests on port 23. Connecting this port to the public network can make the system and the network vulnerable to attack. When connected to the public net, this port should expect strong authentication or accept only encrypted traffic.

File Transfer Protocol (FTP)

FTP is the protocol used on the Internet for transferring files between two systems. It divides a file into IP packets for sending it across the Internet. The object of the transfer is a file. The protocol provides automatic checking and retransmission to provide for bit-for-bit integrity. (See section titled Services below.)

Serial Line Internet Protocol (SLIP)

SLIP is a protocol for sending IP packets over a serial line connection. It is described in RFC 1055. SLIP is often used to extend the path from an IP-addressable device, like a router at an ISP, across a serial connection, e.g., a dial connection, to a non-IP device, e.g., a serial port on a PC. It is a mechanism for attaching non-IP devices to an IP network.

SLIP encapsulates the IP packet and bits in the code used on the serial line. In the process, the packet may gain some redundancy and error correction. However, the protocol itself does not provide any error detection or correction. This means that errors may not be detected until the traffic gets to a higher layer. Because SLIP is usually used over relatively slow (56kb) lines, this may make error correction at that layer expensive. On the other hand, the signaling over modern modems is fairly robust. Similarly, SLIP traffic may gain some compression from devices, e.g., modems, in the path but does not provide any compression of its own.

Since the serial line has only two end points, the protocol does not contain any address information; i.e., the addresses are implicit. However, this limits the connection to one application; any distinctions in the intended use of the line must be handled at a higher layer.

Since SLIP is used on point-to-point connections, it may be slightly less vulnerable to eavesdropping than a shared-media connection like Ethernet. However, because it is closer to the end point, the data may be more meaningful. This observation also applies to PPP below.

Point-to-Point Protocol (PPP)

PPP is used for applications and environments similar to those for SLIP but is more sophisticated. It is described in RFC 1661, July 94. It is *the* Internet standard for transmission of IP packets over serial lines. It is more robust than SLIP and provides error-detection features. It supports both asynchronous and synchronous lines and is intended for simple links that deliver packets between two peers. It enables the transmission of multiple network-layer protocols, e.g., ip, ipx, spx, simultaneously over a single link. For example, a PC might run a browser, a Notes client, and an e-mail client over a single link to the network.

To facilitate all this, PPP has a Link Control Protocol (LCP) to negotiate encapsulation formats, format options, and limits on packet format.

Optionally, a PPP node can require that its partner authenticate itself using CHAP or PAP. This authentication takes place after the link is set up and before any traffic can flow. (See CHAP and PAP below.)

Hyper-Text Transfer Protocol (http)

HTTP is used to move data objects, called pages, between client applications, called browsers, running on one machine, and server applications, usually on another. HTTP is the protocol that is used on and that defines the World Wide Web. The pages moved by HTTP are compound data objects composed of other data and objects. Pages are specified in a language called hyper-text markup language, or HTML. HTML specifies the appearance of the page and provides for pages to be associated with one another by cross-references called hyper links.

The fundamental assumption of HTTP is that the pages are public and that no data-hiding or address reliability is necessary. However, because many electronic commerce applications are done on the World Wide Web, other protocols, described below, have been defined and implemented.

SECURITY PROTOCOLS

Most of the traffic that moves in the primitive TCP/IP protocols is public, i.e., none of the value of the data derives from its confidentiality. Therefore, the fact that the protocols do not provide any data-hiding does not hurt anything. The protocols do not add any security, but the data does not need it. However, there is some traffic that is sensitive to disclosure and which does require more security than the primitive protocols provide. The absolute amount of this traffic is clearly growing, and its proportion may be growing also. In most cases, the necessary hiding of this data is done in alternate or higher-level protocols.

A number of these secure protocols have been defined and are rapidly being implemented and deployed. This section will describe some of those protocols.

Secure Socket Layer (SSL)

Arguably, the most widely used secure protocol is SSL. It is intended for use in client–server applications in general. More specifically, it is widely used between browsers and Web servers on the www. It uses a hybrid of symmetric and asymmetric key cryptography, in which a symmetric algorithm is used to hide the traffic and an asymmetric one, RSA, is used to negotiate the symmetric keys.

SSL is a session-oriented protocol, i.e., it is used to establish a secure connection between the client and the server that lasts for the life of the session or until terminated by the application.

SSL comes in two flavors and a number of variations. At the moment, the most widely used of the two flavors is *one-way SSL*. In this implementation, the server side has a private key, a corresponding public key, and a certificate for that key pair. The server offers its public key to the client. After reconciling the certificate to satisfy itself as to the identity of the server, the client uses the public key to securely negotiate a session key with the server. Once the session key is in use, both the client and the server can be confident that only the other can see the traffic.

The client side has a public key for the key pair that was used to sign the certificate and can use this key to verify the bind between the key pair and the identity of the server. Thus, the one-way protocol provides for the authentication of the server to the client but not the other way around. If the server cares about the identity of the client, it must use the secure session to collect evidence about the identity of the client. This evidence is normally in the form of a user identifier and a pass-phrase or similar, previously shared, secret.

The other flavor of SSL is *two-way SSL*. In this implementation both the client and the server know the public key of the other and have a certificate for this key. In most instances the client's certificate is issued by the server, while the server's certificate was issued by a mutually trusted third party.

Secure-http (S-http)

S-http is a secure version of HTTP designed to move individual pages securely on the World Wide Web. It is page oriented as contrasted to SSL, which is connection or session oriented. Most browsers (thin clients) that implement SSL also implement S-http, may share key-management code, and may be used in ways that are not readily distinguishable to the end user. In other applications, S-http gets the nod where very high performance is required and where there is limited need to save state between the client and the server.

Secure File Transfer Protocol (S-ftp)

Most of the applications of the primitive file transfer protocol are used to transfer public files in private networks. Much of it is characterized as "anonymous," i.e., one end of the connection may not even recognize the other. However, as the net spreads, FTP is increasingly used to move private data in public networks.

S-ftp adds encryption to the FTP protocol to add data-hiding to the integrity checking provided in the base protocol.

Secure Electronic Transaction (SET)

SET is a special protocol developed by the credit card companies and vendors and intended for use in multiparty financial transactions like credit card transactions across the Internet. It provides not only for hiding credit card numbers as they cross the network but also for hiding them from some of the parties to the transaction and for protecting against replay.

One of the limitations of SSL when used for credit card numbers is that the merchant must become party to the entire credit card number and must make a record of it to use in the case of later disputes. This creates a vulnerability to the disclosure and reuse of the credit card number. SET uses public key cryptography to guarantee the merchant that he will be paid without his having to know or protect the credit card number.

Point-to-Point Tunneling* Protocol (PPTP)

PPTP is a protocol (from the PPTP Forum) for hiding the information in IP packets, including the addresses. It is used to connect (portable computer) clients across the dial-switched point-to-point network to the Internet and then to a (MS) gateway server to a private (enterprise) network or to (MS) servers on such a network. As its name implies, it is a point-to-point protocol. It is useful for implementing end-to-end secure virtual networks (SVNs) but less so for implementing any-gateway-to-any-gateway virtual private networks (VPNs).

It includes the ability to:

- Query the status of Comm Servers
- Provide in-band management
- Allocate channels and place outgoing calls
- Notify server on incoming calls
- Transmit and Receive user data with flow control in both directions
- Notify server on disconnected calls.

One major advantage of PPTP is that it is included in MS 32-bit operating systems. (At this writing, the client-side software is included on 32-bit MS Windows operating systems Dial Up Networking [rel. 1.2 and 1.3]. The server-side software is included in the NT Server operating system. See L2TP below.) A limitation of PPTP, when compared to secure-IP or SSL, is that it does not provide authentication of the end points. That is, the nodes know that other nodes cannot see the data passing between but must use other mechanisms to authenticate addresses or user identities.

Layer 2 Forwarding (L2F)

L2F is another mechanism for hiding information on the Internet. The encryption is provided from the point where the dial-switched point-to-point network connects the Internet Service Provider (ISP) to the gateway on the private network. The advantage is that no additional software is required on the client computer; the disadvantage is that the data is protected only on the Internet and not on the dial-switched network.

L2F is a router-to-router protocol used to protect data from acquisition by an ISP provider, across the public digital packet-switched network (Internet) to receipt by a private network. It is used by the ISP to provide data-hiding servers to its clients. Because the protocol is implemented in

---

* Tunneling is a form of encapsulation in which the encrypted package, the passenger, is encapsulated inside a datagram of the carrier protocol.

the routers (Cisco), its details and management are hidden from the end users.

Layer 2 Tunneling Protocol (L2TP)

L2TP is a proposal by MS and Cisco to provide a client-to-gateway data-hiding facility that can be operated by the ISP. It responds to the limitations of PPTP (must be operated by the owner of the gateway) and L2F (does not protect data on the dial-switched point-to-point net). Such a solution could protect the data on both parts of the public network but as a service provided by the ISP rather than by the operator of the private network.

Secure Internet Protocol (Secure-IP or IPSEC)

IPSEC is a set of protocols to provide for end-to-end encryption of the IP packets. It is being developed by the Internet Engineering Task Force (IETF). It is to be used to bind end points to one another and to implement VPNs and SVNs.

Internet Security Association Key Management Protocol (ISAKMP)

ISAKMP is a proposal for a public-key certificate-based key-management protocol for use with IPSEC. Because in order to establish a secure session the user will have to have both a certificate and the corresponding key and because the session will not be vulnerable to replay or eavesdropping, ISAKMP provides "strong authentication." What is more, since the same mechanism can be used for encryption as for authentication, it provides economy of administration.

Password Authentication Protocol (PAP)

As noted above, the PPP protocol provides for the parties to identify and authenticate each other. One of the protocols for doing this is PAP. (See also CHAP below). PAP works very much like traditional login using a shared secret. A sends a prompt or a request for authentication to B, and B responds with an identifier and a shared secret. If the pair of values meets A's expectation, then A acknowledges B.

This protocol is vulnerable to a replay attack. It is also vulnerable to abuse of B's identity by a privileged user of A.

Challenge Handshake Authentication Protocol (CHAP)

CHAP is a standard challenge–response peer-to-peer authentication mechanism. System A chooses a random number and passes it to B. B encrypts this challenge under a secret shared with A and returns it to A. A also computes the value of the challenge encrypted under the shared secret and compares this value to the value returned by B. If this response meets A's expectation, then A acknowledges B.

Many implementations of PPP/CHAP provide that the remote party be periodically reauthenticated by sending a new challenge. This resists any attempt at "session stealing."

SERVICES

Telnet

File Transfer

FTP is the name of a protocol, but it is also the name of a service that uses the protocol to deliver files. The service is symmetric in that either the server or the client can initiate a transfer in either direction, either can get a file or send a file, either can do a get or a put. The client may itself be a server. The server may or may not recognize its user, may or may not restrict access to the available files.

Where the server does restrict access to the available files, it usually does that through the use of the control facilities of the underlying file system. If the file server is built upon the UNIX operating system and file system or the Windows operating systems, then it will use the rules-based file access controls of the file system. If the server is built upon the NT operating system, then it will use the object-oriented controls of the NT file system. If the file service is built on MVS, and yes that does happen, then it is the optional access control facility of MVS that will be used.

Secure Shell (SSH 2)

Secure Shell is a UNIX-to-UNIX client–server program that uses strong cryptography for protecting all transmitted data, including passwords, binary files, and administrative commands between systems on a network. One can think of it as a client–server command processor or shell. While it is used primarily for system management, it should not be limited to this application.

It implements Secure IP and ISAKMP at the application layer, as contrasted to the network layer, to provide a secure network computing environment. It provides node identification and authentication, node-to-node encryption, and secure command and file transfer. It compensates for most of the protocol limitations noted above. It is now preferred to and used in place of more limited or application-specific protocols or implementations such as secure-ftp.

CONCLUSIONS

Courtney's first law says that nothing useful can be said about the security of a mechanism except in the context of an application and an environment. Of course, the converse of that law says that, in such a context, one can say quite a great deal.

The Internet is an open, not to say hostile, environment in which most everything is permitted. It is defined almost exclusively by its addresses and addressing schema and by the protocols that are honored in it. Little else is reliable.

Nonetheless, most sensitive applications can be done there as long as one understands the properties and limitations of those protocols and carefully chooses among them. We have seen that there are a large number of protocols defined and implemented on the Internet. No small number of them are fully adequate for all applications. On the other hand, the loss in performance, flexibility, generality, and function in order to use those that are secure for the intended application and environment are small. What is more, as the cost of performance falls, the differences become even less significant.

The information security manager must understand the needs of his applications, know the tools, protocols, and what is possible in terms of security. Then he must choose and apply those protocols and implementations carefully.

Domain 3
Security Management Practices

It is said that people and organizational issues are more important than technical matters, and if properly addressed, can yield powerful results. This domain deals with these types of issues. The savvy information security practitioner knows that a good security awareness program will provide a greater return on investment than most technical programs or devices. Moreover, the success of the security program increases exponentially as it is adopted and embraced by each user in an organization.

In order to succeed, the security program must communicate to the users the significance of the organization's security policies, standards, and guidelines — their intent, their rationale — in addition to the value proposition that is established by complying with policy. Further, the consequences of noncompliance must be well understood. Thus, a well-written, well-defined, and well-communicated security architecture is imperative as a first step.

Likewise, the implementation of security technologies, i.e., the technical security architecture, must support and enforce the security policies and standards, and should be developed or purchased and implemented by those responsible within the organization whenever providing information systems and services.

Of course, the cost and extent of protection should be commensurate with the value of the information resource. The analysis that is done to calculate the benefit of a safeguard against the value of the resource is the process known as risk management. This concept is addressed within the chapters of this domain, as is an interesting treatise on high-technology espionage and the application of information security within the healthcare industry.

Domain 3.1
Security Awareness

Chapter 12
Security Awareness Program
Tom Peltier

INTRODUCTION

Development of security policies, standards, procedures, and guidelines is only the beginning of an effective information security program. A strong security architecture will be less effective if there is no process in place to make certain that the employees are aware of their rights and responsibilities. All too often, security professionals implement the "perfect" security program, and then forget to factor the customer into the formula. In order for the product to be as successful as possible, the information security professional must find a way to sell this product to the customers. An effective security awareness program could be the most cost-effective action management can take to protect its critical information assets.

Implementing an effective security awareness program will help all employees understand why they need to take information security seriously, what they will gain from its implementation, and how it will assist them in completing their assigned tasks. The process should begin at new-employee orientation and continue annually for all employees at all levels of the organization.

KEY GOALS OF AN INFORMATION SECURITY PROGRAM

For security professionals there are three key elements for any security program: *integrity, confidentiality*, and *availability*. Management wants information to reflect the real world and to have confidence in the information available to them so they can make informed business decisions. One of the goals of an effective security program is to ensure that the organization's information and its information processing resources are properly protected.

The goal of confidentiality extends beyond just keeping the bad guys out; it also ensures that those with a business need have access to the resources they need to get their jobs done. Confidentiality ensures that controls and reporting mechanisms are in place to detect problems or possible intrusions with speed and accuracy.

DELOITTE & TOUCHE	RATE 1–3	ERNST & YOUNG
1	**Availability**	2
3	**Confidentiality**	3
2	**Integrity**	1

1 = Most Important, 2 = next, 3 = least

**Exhibit 12.1. Fortune 500 Managers Rate the Importance
of Information**

In a pair of recent surveys, the Big Four Accounting firms of Ernst & Young and Deloitte & Touche interviewed Fortune 500 managers and asked them to rank (in importance to them) information availability, confidentiality, and integrity. As can be seen from Exhibit 12.1, the managers felt that information needed to be available when they needed to have access to it. Implementing access control packages that rendered access difficult or overly restrictive is a detriment to the business process. Additionally, other managers felt that the information must reflect the real world. That is, controls should be in place to ensure that the information is correct. Preventing or controlling access to information that was incorrect was of little value to the enterprise.

An effective information security program must review the business objectives or the mission of the organization and ensure that these goals are met. Meeting the business objectives of the organization and understanding the customers' needs are what the goal of a security program is all about. An awareness program will reinforce these goals and will make the information security program more acceptable to the employee base.

KEY ELEMENTS OF A SECURITY PROGRAM

The starting point with any security program is the implementation of policies, standards, procedures, and guidelines. As important as the written word is in defining the goals and objectives of the program and the organization, the fact is that most employees will not have the time or the desire to read these important documents. An awareness program will ensure that the messages identified as important will get to all of those who need them.

Having individuals responsible for the implementation of the security program is another key element. To be most effective, the enterprise will need to have leadership at a minimum of two levels. There is a strong need to identify a senior level manager to assume the role of Corporate Information Officer (CIO). In a supporting capacity, an information security coordinator responsible for the day-to-day implementation of the information security program and reporting to the CIO is the second key player in the overall security program. Because a security program is more than just directions from the IT organization, each business unit should have its own coordinator responsible for the implementation of the program within that business unit.

The ability to classify information assets according to their relative value to the organization is the third key element in an information security program. Knowing what information an organization has that is sensitive will allow the informed implementation of controls and will allow the business units to use their limited resources where they will provide the most value. Understanding classification levels, employee responsibilities (owner, custodian, user), intellectual property requirements (copyright, trade secret, patent), and privacy rights is critical. An effective awareness program will have to take this most confusing message to all employees and provide training material for all nonemployees needing access to such resources.

The fourth key element is the implementation of the basic security concepts of separation of duties and rotation of assignments. *Separation of duties* — No single individual should have complete control of a business process or transaction from inception to completion. This control concept limits the potential error, opportunity, and temptation of personnel, and can best be defined as segregating incompatible functions (e.g., accounts payable activities with disbursement). The activities of a process are split among several people. Mistakes made by one person tend to be caught by the next person in the chain, thereby increasing information integrity. Unauthorized activities will be limited since no one person can complete a process without the knowledge and support of another. *Rotation of assignments* — Individuals should alternate various essential tasks involving business activities or transactions periodically. There are always some assignments that can cause an organization to be at risk unless proper controls are in place. To ensure that desk procedures are being followed and to provide for staff backup on essential functions, individuals should be assigned to different tasks at regular intervals.

One of the often-heard knocks against rotation of assignments is that it reduces job efficiency. However, it has been proven that an employee's interest declines over time when doing the same job for extended periods. Additionally, employees sometimes develop dangerous shortcuts when they have been in a job too long. By rotating assignments, the organization can compare the different ways of doing the task and determine where changes should be made.

The final element in an overall security program is an employee awareness program. Each of these elements will ensure that an organization meets its goals and objectives. The employee security awareness program will ensure that the program has a chance to succeed.

SECURITY AWARENESS PROGRAM GOALS

In order to be successful, a security awareness program must stress how security will support the enterprise's business objectives. Selling a security program requires the identification of business needs and how the security program supports those objectives. Employees want to know how to get things accomplished and to whom to turn for assistance. A strong awareness program will provide those important elements.

All personnel need to know and understand management's directives relating to the protection of information and information processing resources. One of the key objectives of a security awareness program is to ensure that all personnel get this message. It must be presented to new employees as well as existing employees. The program must also work with the Purchasing people to ensure that the message of security is presented to contract personnel. It is important to understand that contract personnel need to have this information, but it must be handled through their contract house. Work with Purchasing and Legal to establish the proper process.

All too often the security program fails because there is little or no follow-up. There is usually a big splash with all the fanfare that kicks off a new program. Unfortunately this is where many programs end. Employees have learned that if they wait long enough, the new programs will die from lack of interest or follow-up. It is very important to keep the message in front of the user community and to do this on a regular basis. To assist you in this process, there are a number of "Days" that can be used in conjunction with your awareness program.

- May 10 — International Emergency Response Day
- September 8 — Computer Virus Awareness Day
- November 30 — International Computer Security Day

Keeping the message in front of the user community is not enough. The message must make the issues of security alive and important to all employees. It is important to find ways to tie the message in with the goals and objectives of each department. Every department has different objectives and different security needs. The awareness message needs to reflect those concerns. We will discuss this in more detail shortly.

Find ways to make the message important to employees. When discussing controls, identify how they help protect the employee. When requiring employees to wear identification badges, many security programs tell the employees that this has been implemented to meet security objectives. What does this really mean? What the employees should be told is that the badges ensure that only authorized persons have access to the workplace. By doing this, the company is attempting to protect the employees. Finding out how controls support or protect the company's assets (including the employees) will make the security program message more acceptable.

Finally, a security program is meant to reduce losses associated with either intentional or accidental information disclosure, modification, destruction, and or denial of service. This can be accomplished by raising the consciousness of all employees regarding ways to protect information and information processing resources. By ensuring that these goals are met, the enterprise will be able to improve employee efficiency and productivity.

IDENTIFY CURRENT TRAINING NEEDS

To be successful, the awareness program should take into account the needs and current levels of training and understanding of the employees and management. There are five keys to establishing an effective awareness program. These include:

- Assess the current level of computer usage:
- Determine what the managers and employees want to learn.
- Examine the level of receptiveness to the security program.
- Map out how to gain acceptance.
- Identify possible allies.

To assess the current level of computer usage, it will be necessary to ask questions of the audience. While sophisticated work stations may be found in employees' work areas, their understanding of what these devices can do may be very limited. Ask questions as to what the jobs are and how the tools available are used to support these tasks. It may come as a surprise to find that the most sophisticated computer is being used as a glorified 3270 terminal.

Be an effective listener. Listen to what the users are saying and scale the awareness and training sessions to meet their needs. In the awareness field, one size (or plan) does not fit everyone.

Work with the managers and supervisors to understand what their needs are and how the program can help them. It will become necessary for you to understand the language of the business units and to interpret their needs. Once you have an understanding, you will be able to modify the program to meet these special needs. No single awareness program will work for every business unit. There must be alterations and a willingness to accept suggestions from nonsecurity personnel.

Identify the level of receptiveness to the security program. Find out what is accepted and what is meeting resistance. Examine the areas of noncompliance and try to find ways to alter the program if at all possible. Do not change fundamental information security precepts just to gain unanimous acceptance; this is an unattainable goal. Make the program meet the greater good of the enterprise and then work with pockets of resistance to lessen the impact.

The best way to gain acceptance is to make your employees and managers partners in the security process. Never submit a new control or policy to management without sitting down with them individually and reviewing the objectives. This will require you to do your homework and to understand the business process in each department. It will be important to know the peak periods of activity in the department and what the manager's concerns are. When meeting with the managers, be sure to listen to their concerns and be prepared to ask for their suggestions on how to improve the program. Remember the key here is to partner with your audience.

Finally, look for possible allies. Find out what managers support the objectives of the security program and identify those who have the respect of their peers. This means that it will be necessary to expand the area of support beyond physical security and the audit staff. Seek out business managers who have a vested interest in seeing this program succeed. Use their support to springboard the program to acceptance.

A key point in this entire process is to never refer to the security program or the awareness campaign as "my program." The enterprise has identified the need for security, and you and your group are acting as the catalysts for moving the program forward. When discussing the program with employees and managers, it will be beneficial to refer to it as "their program" or "our program." Make them feel that they are key stakeholders in this process.

In a presentation used to introduce the security concept to the organization, it may be beneficial to say something like:

> Just as steps have been to taken to ensure the safety of the employees in the workplace, the organization is now asking that the employees work to protect the second most important enterprise asset — information. If the organization fails to protect its information from unauthorized access, modification, disclosure, or destruction, the organization faces the prospect of loss of customer confidence, com-

petitive advantage, and possibly jobs. All employees must accept the need and responsibility to protect our property and assets.

Involve the user community and accept their comments whenever possible. Make information security their program. Use what they identify as important in the awareness program. By having them involved, the program truly becomes theirs and they are more willing to accept and internalize the process.

SECURITY AWARENESS PROGRAM DEVELOPMENT

Not everyone needs the same degree or type of information security awareness to do their jobs. An awareness program that distinguishes between groups of people, and presents only information that is relevant to that particular audience will have the best results. Segmenting the audiences by job function, familiarity with systems, or some other category can improve the effectiveness of the security awareness and acceptance program. The purpose of segmenting audiences is to give the message the best possible chance of success. There are many ways in to segment the user community. Some of the more common methods are provided for you here.

- *Level of Awareness* — Employees may be divided up based on their current level of awareness of the information security objectives. One method of determining levels of awareness is to conduct a "walk-about." A walkabout is conducted after normal working hours and looks for certain key indicators. Look for just five key indicators:
  1. Offices locked
  2. Desks and cabinets locked
  3. Work stations secured
  4. Information secured
  5. Recording media (diskettes, tapes, CDs, cassettes, etc.) Secured
- *Job category* — Personnel may be grouped according to their job functions or titles.
  1. Senior managers (including officers and directors)
  2. Middle management
  3. Line supervision
  4. Employees
  5. Others
- *Specific job function* — Employees and personnel may be grouped according to:
  1. Service providers
  2. Information owners
  3. Users
- *Information processing knowledge* — As discussed above, not every employee has the same level of knowledge on how computers work. A security message for technical support personnel may be very differ-

ent from that for data entry clerks. Senior management may have a very different level of computer skills than their office administrator.

- *Technology, system, or application used* — To avoid "religious wars," it may be prudent to segment the audience based on the technology used. Mac users and users of Intel-based systems often have differing views, as do MVS users and UNIX users. The message may reach the audience faster if the technology used is considered.

Once the audience has been segmented, it will be necessary to establish the roles expected of the employees. These roles may include information owners, custodians of the data and systems, and general users. For all messages it will be necessary to employ the KISS process. That is, Keep It Simple, Sweetie. Inform the audience, but try to stay away from commandments or directives. Discuss the goals and objectives using real-world scenarios. Whenever possible, avoid quoting policies, procedures, standards, or guidelines.

Policies and procedures are boring, and if employees want more information, they can access the documents on the organization intranet. If you feel that you must resort to this method, you have missed the most important tenet of awareness: to identify the business reason *why*. Never tell employees that something is being implemented to "be in compliance with audit requirements." This is, at best, a cop out and fails to explain in business terms why something is needed.

METHODS USED TO CONVEY THE AWARENESS MESSAGE

How do people learn and where do people obtain their information? These are two very important questions to understand when developing an information security awareness program. Each one is different. If we were implementing a training program, we would be able to select from three basic methods of training:

- Buy a book and read about the subject
- Watch a video on the subject
- Ask someone to show you how

For most employees, the third method is best for training. They like the hands-on approach and want to have someone there to answer their questions. With security awareness, the process is a little different. According to findings reported in *USA Today*, over 90 percent of Americans obtain their news from television or radio. To make an awareness program work, it will be necessary to tap into that model.

There are a number of different ways to get the message out to the user community. The key is to make the message stimulating to the senses of the audience. This can be accomplished by using posters, pictures, and videos. Because so many of our employees use television as their primary source of information, it is important to use videos to reinforce the message. The use of videos will serve several purposes.

With the advent of the news-magazine format so popular in television today, our employees are already conditioned to accept the information presented as factual. This allows us to use the media to present the messages we consider important. Because the audience accepts material presented in this format, the use of videos allows us to bring in an informed outsider to present the message. Many times our message fails because the audience knows the messenger. Being a fellow worker, our credibility may be questioned. A video provides an expert on the subject.

There are a number of organizations that offer computer and information security videos (a listing of how to contact them is included at the end of this chapter). You might want to consider having a senior executive videotape a message that can be run at the beginning of the other video. Costs for creating a quality in-house video can be prohibitive. A 20-minute video that is more than just "talking heads" can run $90,000 to $100,000. Check out the quality and messages of the vendors discussed later in this chapter.

An effective program will also take advantage of brochures, newsletters, or booklets. In all cases, the effectiveness of the medium will depend on how well it is created and how succinct the message is. One major problem with newsletters is finding enough material to fill the pages each time you want to go to print. One way to present a quality newsletter is to look for vendors to provide such material. The Computer Security Institute offers a document titled *Frontline.* This newsletter is researched and written every quarter by CSI's own editorial staff. It provides the space for a column written by your organization to provide information pertinent for your organization. Once the materials are ready, CSI sends out either camera-ready or PDF format versions of the newsletter. The customer is then authorized to make unlimited copies.

As we discussed above, many organizations are requiring business units to name information protection coordinators. One of the tasks of these coordinators is to present awareness sessions for their organizations. An effective way to get a consistent message out is to "train the trainers." Create a security awareness presentation and then bring in the coordinators to train them in presenting the corporate message to their user community. This will ensure that the message presented meets the needs of each organization and that they view the program as theirs.

It will be necessary to identify those employees who have not attended awareness training. By having some form of sign-in or other recording mechanism, the program will be assured of reaching most of the employees. By having the coordinator submit annual reports on the number of employees trained, the enterprise will have a degree of comfort in meeting its goals and objectives.

PRESENTATION KEY ELEMENTS

While every organization has its own style and method for training, it might help to review some important issues when creating an awareness program. One very important item to keep in mind is that the topic of information security is very broad. Do not get overwhelmed with the prospect of providing information on every facet of information security in one meeting. Remember the old adage, "How do you eat an elephant? One bite at a time."

Prioritize your message for the employees. Start small and build on the program. Remember you are going to have many opportunities to present your messages. Identify where to begin, present the message, reinforce the message, and then build to the next objective. Keep the training session as brief as possible. It is normally recommended to limit these sessions to no more than 50 minutes. There are a number of reasons for this: biology (you can only hold coffee for so long), attention spans, and productive work needs. Start with an attention-grabbing piece and then follow up with additional information.

Tailor the presentations to the vocabulary and skill of the audience. Know to whom you are talking and provide them with information they can understand. This will not be a formal doctoral presentation. The awareness session must take into account the audience and the culture of the organization. Understand the needs, knowledge, and jobs of the attendees. Stress the positive and business side of security — protecting the assets of the organization. Provide the audience with a reminder (booklet, brochure, or trinket) of the objectives of the program.

TYPICAL PRESENTATION FORMAT

In a program that hopes to modify behavior, the three keys are: tell them what you are going to say; say it; and then remind them of what you said. A typical agenda appears in Exhibit 12.2.

Start with an introduction of what information security is about and how it will impact their business units and departments. Follow with a video that will reinforce the message and present the audience with an external expert supporting the corporate message. Discuss any methods that will be employed to monitor compliance to the program and provide the audience with the rationale for the compliance checking. Provide them with a time for questions and ensure that every question either gets an answer or is recorded and the answer provided as soon as possible. Finally, give them some item that will reinforce the message.

Information Security Awareness
Date
Time
Place

Agenda:

Introduction	**CIO**
Goals and Objectives	**ISSO**
Video	
Questions/Answer	**All**
Next Steps	**ISSO**

Exhibit 12.2. Typical Security Awareness Meeting Agenda

WHEN TO DO AWARENESS

Any awareness program must be scheduled around the work patterns of the audience. Take into account busy periods for the various departments and make certain that the sessions do not impact their peak periods. The best times for having these sessions is in the morning on Tuesday, Wednesday, and Thursday. A meeting first-thing Monday morning will impact those trying to get the week's work started. Having the session on Friday afternoon will not be as productive as you would like. Scheduling anything right after lunch is always a worry. The human physiological clock is at its lowest productivity level right after lunch. If you turn out the lights to show a movie, the snoring may drown out the audio. Also, schedule sessions during off-shift hours. Second- and third-shift employees should have the opportunity to view the message during their work hours just as those on the day shift do.

SENIOR MANAGEMENT PRESENTATIONS

While most other sessions will last about an hour, senior management has less time, even for issues as important as this. Prepare a special brief, concise presentation plus in-depth supporting documents. Unlike other presentations, senior management often does not want the "dog and pony show." They may not even want presentation foils to be used. They prefer that you sit with them for a few minutes and discuss the program and how it will help them meet their business objectives.

Quickly explain the purpose of the program, identify any problem areas and what solutions you propose. Suggest a plan of action. Do not go to them with problems for which you do not have a solution. Do not give them a number of solutions and ask them to choose. You are their expert and they are expecting you to come to them with your informed opinion on how the organization should move forward.

GROUP	BEST TECHNIQUES	BEST APPROACH	EXPECTED RESULTS
Senior Management	Cost justification Industry comparison Audit report Risk analysis	Presentation Video Violation reports	Funding Support

Line Supervisors	Demonstrate job
	  performance benefits
	Perform security
	  reviews
		Presentation
		Circulate news articles
		Video
			Support
			Resource help
			Adherence

Users	Sign responsibility
	  statements
	Policies and
	  procedures
		Presentation
		Newsletters
		Video
			Adherence
			Support

Exhibit 12.3. Three Groups

Senior management — will be expecting a sound, rational approach to information security. They will be interested in the overall cost of implementing the policies and procedures and how this program stacks up against others in the industry. A key concern will be how their policies and procedures will be viewed by the audit staff and that the security program will give them an acceptable level of risk.

Line supervisors — These individuals are focused on getting their job done. They will not be interested in anything that appears to slow down their already tight schedule. To win them over, it will be necessary to demonstrate how the new controls will improve their job performance process. As we have been stressing since the beginning, the goal of security is to assist management in meeting the business objectives or mission.

It will be self-defeating to tell supervisors that the new policies are being implemented to allow the company to be in compliance with audit requirements. This is not the reason to do anything, and a supervisor will find this reason useless. Stress how the new process will give the employees the tools they need (access to information and systems) in a timely and efficient manner. Show them where the problem-resolution process is and who to call if there are any problems with the new process.

Employees — are going to be skeptical. They have been through so many company initiatives that they have learned to wait. If they wait long enough and do nothing new, the initiative will generally die on its own. It will be necessary to build employees' awareness of the information security policies and procedures. Identify what is expected of them and how it will assist them in gaining access to the information and systems they need to complete their tasks. Point out that by protecting access to information, they can have a reasonable level of assurance (remember, never use absolutes) that their information assets will be protected from unauthorized access, modification, disclosure, or destruction.

The type of approach chosen will be based on whether your organization has an information security program in place and how active it is. For those organizations with no information security program, it will be necessary to convince management and employees of its importance. For organizations with an existing or outdated program, the key will be convincing management and employees that there is a need for change.

THE INFORMATION SECURITY MESSAGE

The employees need to know that information is an important enterprise asset and is the property of the organization. All employees have a responsibility to ensure that this asset, like all others, must be protected and used to support management-approved business activities. To assist them in this process, employees must be made aware of the possible threats and what can be done to combat those threats. The scope of the program must be identified. Is the program dealing only with computer-held data or does it reach to all information wherever it resides? Make sure the employees know the total scope of the program. Enlist their support in protecting this asset. The mission and business of the enterprise may depend on it.

INFORMATION SECURITY SELF-ASSESSMENT

Each organization will have to develop a process by which to measure the compliance level of the information security program. As part of the awareness process, staff should be made aware of the compliance process. Included for you here is an example of how an organization might evaluate the level of information security within a department or throughout the enterprise.

INFORMATION PROTECTION PROGRAM AND ADMINISTRATION
ASSESSMENT QUESTIONNAIRE

Rating Scale

1 = Completed
2 = Being implemented
3 = In development
4 = Under discussion
5 = Haven't begun

FACTORS	RATING/VALUE 1 2 3 4 5
A. ADMINISTRATION	
1. A Corporate Information Officer (CIO) or equivalent level of authority has been named and is responsible for implementing and maintaining an effective IP program.	1 2 3 4 5
2. An individual has been designated as the organization information protection coordinator (OIPC) and has been assigned overall responsibility for the IP program.	1 2 3 4 5
3. The OIPC reports directly to the CIO or equivalent.	1 2 3 4 5
4. IP is identified as a separate and distinct budget item (minimally 1 to 3 percent of the overall ISO budget).	1 2 3 4 5
5. Senior management is aware of the business need for an effective program and is committed to its success.	1 2 3 4 5
6. Each business unit, department, agency, etc., has designated an individual responsible for implementing the IP program for the organization.	1 2 3 4 5
B. PROGRAM	
1. The IP program supports the business objectives or mission statement of the enterprise.	1 2 3 4 5
2. An enterprise-wide IP policy has been implemented.	1 2 3 4 5
3. The IP program is an integral element of the enterprise's overall management practices.	1 2 3 4 5
4. A formal risk analysis process has been implemented to assist management in making informed business decisions.	1 2 3 4 5
5. Purchase and implementation of IP countermeasures are based on cost/benefit analysis utilizing risk analysis input.	1 2 3 4 5
6. The IP program is integrated into a variety of areas both inside and outside the "computer security" field.	1 2 3 4 5
7. Comprehensive information-protection policies, procedures, standards, and guidelines have been created and disseminated to all employees and appropriate third parties.	1 2 3 4 5
8. An ongoing IP awareness program has been implemented for all employees.	1 2 3 4 5
9. A positive, proactive relationship between IP and audit has been established and is actively cultivated.	1 2 3 4 5
C. COMPLIANCE	
1. Employees are made aware that their data processing activities may be monitored.	1 2 3 4 5

FACTORS	RATING/VALUE 1 2 3 4 5
2. An effective program to monitor IP program-related activities has been implemented.	1 2 3 4 5
3. Employee compliance with IP-related issues is a performance appraisal element.	1 2 3 4 5
4. The ITD Project Team members have access to individuals who have leading-edge hardware/software expertise to help the Project Team, as needed.	1 2 3 4 5
5. The application development methodology addresses IP requirements during all phases, including the initiation or analysis (first) phase.	1 2 3 4 5
6. The IP program is reviewed annually and modified where necessary.	1 2 3 4 5

OTHER FACTORS

1.	1 2 3 4 5
2.	1 2 3 4 5
3.	1 2 3 4 5
TOTAL SCORE	

Interpreting the Total Score: Use this table of risk assessment question-naire score ranges to assess resolution urgency and related actions.

IF THE SCORE IS...	AND...	THE ASSESSMENT RATE IS ...	ACTIONS MIGHT INCLUDE...
21 to 32	• Most activities have been implemented • Most employees are aware of the program	Superior	• Annual reviews and reports to management • Annual recognition days (Computer Security Awareness Day) • Team recognition may be appropriate!
32 to 41	• Many activities have been implemented • Many employees are aware of the program and its objectives	Excellent	• Formal action plan must be implemented • Obtain appropriate sponsorship • Obtain senior management commitment
42 to 62	• Some activities are under development • An IP team has been identified	Solid	• Identify IP program goals • Identify management sponsor • Implement IP policy
63 to 83	• There is a plan to begin planning • Some benchmarking has begun	Low	• Identify roles and responsibilities • Conduct formal risk analysis
84 to 105	• Policies, standards, procedures are missing or not implemented • Management and employees are unaware of the need for a program	Poor	• Conduct risk assessment • Prioritize program elements • Obtain budget commitment • Identify OIPC

CONCLUSION

Information security is more than just policies, standards, procedures, and guidelines. It is more than audit comments and requirements. It is a cultural change for most employees. Before any employee can be required to comply with a security program, he first must become aware of the program. Awareness is an ongoing program that employees must have contact with on at least an annual basis.

Information security awareness does not require huge cash outlays. It does require time and proper project management. Keep the message in front of the employees. Use different methods and means. Bring in outside speakers whenever possible, and use videos to your best advantage.

Video Sources

Commonwealth Films, Inc.
223 Commonwealth Ave.
Boston, MA 02116
617.262.5634
www.commonwealthfilms.com

Mediamix Productions
6812(F) Glenridge Dr.
Atlanta, GA 770.512.7007
www.mediamixus.com

Domain 3.2
Organization Architecture

Chapter 13
Enterprise Security Architecture
William Hugh Murray

INTRODUCTION

Sometime during the 1980s we crossed a line from a world in which the majority of computer users were users of multi-user systems to one in which the majority were users of single-user systems. We are now in the process of connecting all computers in the world into the most complex mechanism that humans have ever built. While for many purposes we may be able to do this on an *ad hoc* basis, for purposes of security, audit, and control it is essential that we have a rigorous and timely design. We will not achieve effective, much less efficient, security without an enterprise-wide design and a coherent management system.

Enterprise

If you look in the dictionary for the definitions of enterprise, you will find that an enterprise is a project, a task, or an undertaking; or, the readiness for such, the motivation, or the moving forward of that undertaking. The dictionary does not contain the definition of the enterprise as we are using it here. For our purposes here, the enterprise is defined as the largest unit of business organization, that unit of business organization that is associated with ownership. If the institution is a government institution, then it is the smallest unit headed by an elected official. What we need to understand is that it is a large, coordinated, and independent organization.

ENTERPRISE SECURITY IN THE 1990s

Because the scale of the computer has changed from one scaled to the enterprise to one scaled to the application or the individual, the computer security requirements of the enterprise have changed. The new requirement can best be met by an architecture or a design.

We do not do design merely for the fun of it or even because it is the "right" thing to do. Rather, we do it in response to a problem or a set of requirements. While the requirements for a particular design will be those for a specific enterprise, there are some requirements that are so pervasive as to be typical of many, if not most, enterprises. This section describes a set of observations by the author to which current designs should respond.

Inadequate expression of management intent — One of these is that there is an inadequate expression of management's intent. Many enterprises have no written policy at all. Of those that do, many offer inadequate guidance for the decisions that must be made. Many say little more than "do good things." They fail to tell managers and staff how much risk general management is prepared or intends to accept. Many fail to adequately assign responsibility or duties or fix the discretion to say who can use what resources. This results in inconsistent risk and inefficient security, i.e., some resources are overprotected and others are underprotected.

Multiple sign-ons, IDs, and passwords — Users are spending tens of minutes per day logging on and logging off. They may have to log on to several processes in tandem in order to access an application. They may have to log off of one application in order to do another. They may be required to remember multiple user identifiers and coordinate many passwords. Users are often forced into insecure or inefficient behavior in futile attempts to compensate for these security measures. For example, they may write down or otherwise record identifiers and passwords. They may even automate their use in macros. They may postpone, or even forget tasks so as not to have to quit one application in order to do another. This situation is often not obvious to system managers. They tend to view the user only in the context of the systems that they manage rather than in the context of the systems he uses. He may also see this cost as "soft money," not easily reclaimed by him. On the other hand, it is very real money to the enterprise, which may have thousands of such users and which might be able to get by with fewer if they were not engaged in such activity. Said another way, information technology management overlooks what general management sees as an opportunity.

Multiple points of control — Contrary to what we had hoped and worked for in the 1980s, data are proliferating and spreading throughout the enterprise. We did not succeed in bringing all enterprise data under a single access control system. Management is forced to rely upon multiple processes to control access to data. This often results in inconsistent and incomplete control. Inconsistent control is usually inefficient. It means that management is spending too much or too little for protection. Incomplete control is ineffective. It means that some data are completely unprotected and unreliable.

Unsafe defaults — In order to provide for ease of installation and avoid deadlocks, systems are frequently shipped with security mechanisms set to the unsafe conditions by default. The designers are concerned that even before the system is completely installed, management may lose control. The administrator might accidentally lock himself out of his own system with no remedy but to start over from scratch. Therefore, the system may be shipped with controls defaulted to their most open settings. The intent is that after the systems are configured and otherwise stable, the administrator will reset the controls to the safe condition. However, in practice and so as not to interfere with running systems, administrators are often reluctant to alter these settings. This may be complicated by the fact that systems which are not securely configured are, by definition, unstable. The manager has learned that changes to an already unstable system tend to aggravate the instability.

Complex administration — The number of controls, relations between them, and the amount of special knowledge required to use them may overwhelm the training of the administrator. For example, in order to properly configure the password controls for a Novell server, the administrator may have to set four different controls. The setting of one requires not only knowledge of how the others are set but how they relate to each other. The administrator's training is often focused on the functionality of the systems rather than on security and control. The documentation tends to focus on the function of the controls while remaining silent on their use to achieve a particular objective or their relationship to other controls.

Late recognition of problems — In part because of the absence of systematic measurement and monitoring systems, many problems are being detected and corrected late. Errors that are not detected or corrected may be repeated. Attacks are permitted to go on long enough to succeed. If permitted to continue for a sufficient length of time without corrective action, any attack will succeed. The cost of these problems is greater than it would be if they were detected on a more timely basis.

Increasing use, users, uses, and importance — Most important for our purposes here, security requirements arise in the enterprise as the result of increasing use of computers, increasing numbers of users, increasing numbers of uses and applications, and increasing importance of those applications and uses to the enterprise. All of these things can be seen to be growing at a rate that dwarfs our poor efforts to improve security. The result is that relative security is diminishing to the point that we are approaching chaos.

ARCHITECTURE DEFINED

In response to these things we must increase not only the effectiveness of our efforts but also their efficiency. Because we are working on the scale of the enterprise, *ad hoc* and individual efforts are not likely to be successful. Success will require that we coordinate the collective efforts of the enterprise according to a plan, design, or architecture.

Architecture can be defined as that part of design that deals with what things look like, what they do, where they are, and what they are made of. That is, it deals with appearance, function, location, and materials. It is used to agree on what is to be done and what results are to be produced so that multiple people can work on the project in a collaborative and cooperative manner and so that we can agree when we are through and the results are as expected.

The design is usually reflected in a picture, model, or prototype; in a list of specified materials; and possibly in procedures to be followed in achieving the intended result. When dealing in common materials, the design usually references standard specifications. When using novel materials, the design must describe these materials in detail.

In information technology we borrow the term *architecture* from the building and construction industry. However, unlike this industry, we do not have 10,000 years of tradition, conventions, and standards behind us. Neither do we share the rigor and discipline that characterize them.

TRADITIONAL IT ENVIRONMENT

Computing environments can be characterized as traditional and modern. Each has its own security requirements but, in general and all other things being equal, the traditional environment is easier to secure than its modern equivalent.

Closed — Traditional IT systems and networks are closed. Only named parties can send messages. The nodes and links are known in advance. The insertion of new ones requires the anticipation and cooperation of others. They are closed in the sense that their uses or applications are determined in advance by their design, and late changes are resisted.

Hierarchical — Traditional IT can be described as hierarchical. Systems are organized and controlled top down, usually in a hierarchical or tree structure. Messages and controls flow vertically better than they do horizontally. Such horizontal traffic as exists is mediated by the node at the top of the tree, for example, a mainframe.

Point-to-point — Traffic tends to flow directly from point to point along nodes and links which, at least temporarily, are dedicated to the traffic. Traffic flows directly from one point to another; what goes in at node A will come out only at node B.

Connection switched — The resources that make up the connection between two nodes are dedicated to that connection for the life of the communication. When either is to talk to another, the connection is torn down and a new one is created. The advantage is in speed of communication and security, but capacity may not be used efficiently.

Host-dependent work stations — In traditional computing, work stations are incapable of performing independent applications. They are dependent upon cooperation with a host or master in order to be able to perform any useful work.

Homogeneous components — In traditional networks and architectures, there is a limited number of different component types from a limited number of vendors. Components are designed to work together in a limited number of ways. That is to say, part of the design may be dictated by the components chosen.

MODERN IT ENVIRONMENT

Open — By contrast, modern computing environments are open. Like the postal system, for the price of a stamp anyone may send a message. For the price of an accommodation address, anyone can get an answer back. For not much more, anyone can open his own post office. Modern networks are open in the sense that nodes can be added late and without the permission or cooperation of others. They are open in the sense that their applications are not predetermined.

Flat — The modern network is flat. Traffic flows with equal ease between any two points in the network. It flows horizontally as well as it does vertically. Traffic flows directly and without any mediation. If one were to measure the bandwidth between any two points in the network, chosen arbitrarily, it would be approximately equal to that between any other two points chosen the same way. While traffic may flow faster between two points that are close to each other, taken across the collection of all pairs, it flows with the same speed.

Broadcast — Modern networks are broadcast. While orderly nodes accept only that traffic which is intended for them, traffic will be seen by multiple nodes in addition to the one for which it is intended. Thus, confidentiality may depend in part upon the fact that a large number of otherwise unreliable devices all behave in an orderly manner.

Packet-switched — Modern networks are packet-switched rather than circuit-switched. In part this means that the messages are broken into packets and each packet is sent independent of the others. Two packets sent from the same origin to the same destination may not follow the same path and may not arrive at the destination in the same order that they were sent. The sender cannot rely upon the safety of the path or the arrival of the message at the destination, and the receiver cannot rely upon the return address. In part, it means that a packet may be broadcast to multiple nodes, even to all nodes, in an attempt to speed it to its destination. By design it will be heard by many nodes other than the ones for which it is intended.

Intelligent work stations — In modern environments, the work stations are intelligent, independently programmable, and capable of performing independent work or applications. They are also vulnerable both to the leakage of sensitive information and to the insertion of malicious programs. These malicious programs may be untargeted viruses or they may be password grabbers that are aimed at specific work stations, perhaps those used by privileged users.

Heterogeneousness — The modern network is composed of a variety of nodes and links from many different vendors. There may be dozens of different work stations, servers, and operating systems. The links may be of many speeds and employ many different kinds of signaling. This makes it difficult to employ an architecture that relies upon the control or behavior of the components.

OTHER SECURITY ARCHITECTURE REQUIREMENTS

IT architecture — The information security architecture is derivative of and subordinate to the information technology architecture. It is not independent. One cannot do a security architecture except in the context of and in response to an IT architecture. An information technology architecture describes the appearance, function, location, and materials for the use of information technology. Often one finds that the IT architecture is not sufficiently well thought out or documented to support the development of the security architecture. That is to say, it describes fewer than all four of the things that an architecture must describe. Where it is documented at all, one can expect to find that it describes the materials but not appearance, location, or function.

Policy or management intent — The security architecture must document and respond to a policy or an expression of the level of risk that management is prepared to take. This will influence materials chosen, the roles assigned, the number of people involved in sensitive duties, etc.

Industry and institutional culture — The architecture must document and respond to the industry and institutional culture. The design that is appropriate to a bank will not work for a hospital, university, or auto plant.

Other — Likewise, it must respond to the management style — authoritarian or permissive, prescriptive or reactive — of the institution, to law and regulation, to duties owed to constituents, and to good practice.

SECURITY ARCHITECTURE

The security architecture describes the appearance of the security functions, what is to be done with them, where they will be located within the organization, its systems, and its networks, and what materials will be used to craft them. Among other things, it will describe the following.

Duties, roles, and responsibilities — It will describe who is to do what. It specifies who management relies upon and for what. For every choice or degree of freedom within the system, the architecture will identify who will exercise it.

How objects will be named — It will describe how objects are named. Specifically, it will describe how users are named, identified or referred to. Likewise it will describe how information resources are to be named within the enterprise.

What authentication will look like — It must describe how management gains sufficient confidence in these names or identifiers. How does it know that a user is who he says he is and that the data returned for a name are the expected data? Specifically, the architecture describes what evidence the user will present to demonstrate her identity. For example, if the user is to be authenticated based upon something that she knows, what are the properties (length and character set) of that knowledge?

Where it will be done — Similarly, the architecture will describe where the instant data are to be collected, where the reference data will be stored, and what process will reconcile the two.

What the object of control will be — The architecture must describe what it is that will be controlled. In the traditional IT architecture this was usually a file or a dataset, or sometimes a procedure such as a program or a transaction type. In modern systems it is more likely to be a database object such as a table or a view.

Where access will be controlled — The architecture will describe where, i.e., what processes, will exercise control over the objects. In the traditional IT architecture we tried to centralize all access control in a single process, scaled to the enterprise. In more modern systems access will be controlled in a large number of places. These places will be scaled to departments, applications, and other ways of organizing resources. They may be exclusive or they may overlap. How they are related and where they are located is the subject of the design.

Generation and distribution of warnings and alarms — Finally, the design must specify what events or combinations of events require corrective action, what process will detect them, who is responsible for the action, and how the warning will be communicated from the detecting process to the party responsible for the correction.

POLICY

A Statement of Management's Intent

Among other things, a policy is a statement of management's intent. Among other things, a security policy describes how much risk management intends to take. This statement must be adequate for managers to be able to figure out what to do in a given set of circumstances. It should be sufficiently complete that two managers will read it the same way, reach similar conclusions, and behave in similar ways.

It should speak to how much risk management is prepared to take. For example, management expects to take normal business risk, or acceptable and accepted risk. Alternately or in addition, management can specify the intended level of control. For example, management can say that controls must be such that multiple people must be involved in sensitive duties or material fraud.

The policy should state what management intends to achieve, for example, data integrity, availability, and confidentiality, and how it intends to do it. It should clearly state who is to be responsible for what. It should state who is to have access to what information. Where such access is to be restricted or discretionary, then the policy should state who will exercise the discretion.

The policy should be such that it can be translated into an access control policy. For example, it might say that read access to confidential data must be restricted to those authorized by the owner of the data. The architecture will describe how a given platform or a network of platforms will be used to implement that policy.

IMPORTANT SECURITY SERVICES

The architecture will describe the security mechanisms and services that will be used to implement the access control policy. These will include but not be limited to the following.

User name service — The user name service is used for assigning unique names to users and for resolving aliases where necessary. It can be thought of as a database, database application, or database service. The server can encode and decode user names into user identifiers. For the distinguished user name it returns a system user identifier or identifiers. For the system user identifier it returns a distinguished user name. It can be used to store information about the user. It is often used to store other descriptive data about the user. It may store office location, telephone number, department name, and manager's name.

Group name service — The group name service is used for assigning unique group names and for associating users with those groups. It permits the naming of any arbitrary but useful group such as member of department m, employees, vendors, consultants, users of system 1, users of application A, etc. It can also be used to name groups of one, such as the payroll manager. For the group name, it returns the names, identifiers, or aliases of members of the group. For a user name, it returns a list of the groups of which that user is a member. A complete list of the groups of which a user is a member is a description of his role or relationship to the enterprise. Administrative activity can be minimized by assigning authority, capabilities, and privileges to groups and assigning users to the groups. While this is indirect it is also usually efficient.

Authentication server — The authentication server reconciles evidence of identity. Users are enrolled along with the expectation, i.e., the reference data, for authenticating their identity. For a user identifier and an instance of authenticating data, the server returns *true* if the data meets its expectation, i.e., matches the reference data, and *false* if it does not. If *true*, the server will vouch to its clients for the identity of the user. The authentication server must be trusted by its client, and the architecture must provide the basis for that trust. The server may be attached to its client by a trusted path or it may give its client a counterfeit-resistant voucher (ticket or encryption-based logical token).

Authentication service products — A number or authentication services are available off the shelf. These include Kerberos, SESAME, NetSP, and Open Software Foundation Distributed Computing Environment (OSF/DCE). These products can meet some architectural requirements in whole or in part.

Single point of administration — One implication of multiple points of control is that there may be multiple controls that must be administered. The more such controls there are, the more desirable it becomes to minimize the points of administration. Such points of administration may simply provide for a common interface to the controls or may provide for a single database of its own. There are a number of standard architectures that are useful here. These include SESAME and the Open Software Foundation Distributed Computing Environment.

RECOMMENDED ENTERPRISE SECURITY ARCHITECTURE

This section makes some recommendations about enterprise security architecture. It describes those choices which, all other things being equal, are to be preferred over others.

Single-user name space for the enterprise — Prefer a single-user name space across all systems. Alternatively, have an enterprise name server that relates all of a user's aliases to his distinguished name. This server should be the single point of name assignment. In other words it is a database application or server for assigning names.

Prefer strong authentication — Strong authentication should be preferred by all enterprises of interest. Strong authentication is characterized by two kinds of evidence, at least one of which is resistant to replay. Users should be authenticated using two kinds of evidence. Evidence can be something that only one person knows, has, is, or can do. The most common form of strong authentication is something that the user knows, such as a password, pass-phrase, or personal identification number (PIN), plus something that they carry, such as a token. The token generates a one-time password that is a function of time or a challenge. Other forms in use include a token plus palm geometry or a PIN plus the way the user speaks.

Prefer single sign-on — Prefer single sign-on. A user should have to log on only once per work station per enterprise per day. A user should not be surprised that if he changes work stations, crosses an enterprise boundary, or leaves for the day, that he should have to log on again. However, he should not have to log off one application to log on to another or log on to multiple processes to use one application.

Application or service as point of control — Prefer the application or service as the point of control. The first applicable principle is that the closer to the data the control is, the fewer instances of it there will be, the less subject it will be to user interference, the more difficult it will be to bypass, and consequently, the more reliable it will be. This principle can be easily understood by contrasting it to the worst case — the one where the control is on the desktop. Multiple copies must be controlled, they are very vulnerable to user interference, not to say complete abrogation, and the more people there are who are already behind the control. The second principle is that application objects are both specific, i.e., their behavior is intuitive, predictable from their name, and obvious as to their intended use. Contrast "update name and address of customer" to "write to customer database." One implication of the application as the point of control is that there will be more than one point of control. However, there will be fewer than if the control were even closer to the user.

Multiple points of control — Each server or service should be responsible for control of access to all of its dynamically allocated resources. Prefer that all such resources be of the same resource type. To make its access decision, the server may use local knowledge or data or it may use a common service that is sufficiently abstract to include its rules. One implication of the server or service as the point of control is that there will be multiple points of control. That is to say, there are multiple repositories of data and multiple mechanisms that management must manipulate to exercise control. This may increase the requirement for special knowledge, communication, and coordination.

Limited points of administration — Therefore, prefer a limited number of points of administration that operate across a number of points of control. These may be relatively centralized to respond to a requirement for a great deal of special knowledge about the control mechanism. Alternatively it can be relatively decentralized to meet a requirement for special knowledge about the users, their duties, and responsibilities.

Single resource name space for enterprise data — Prefer a single name space for all enterprise data. Limit this naming scheme to enterprise data; i.e., data that are used and meaningful across business functions or that are related to the business strategy. It is not necessary to include all business functional data, project data, departmental data, or personal data.

Object, table, or view as unit of control — Prefer capabilities, objects, tables, views, rows, columns, and files, in that order, as objects of control. This is the order in which the data are most obvious as to meaning and intended use.

Arbitrary group names with group-name service — It is useful to be able to organize people into affinity groups. These may include functions, departments, projects, and other units of organization. They may also include such arbitrary groups as employees, nonemployees, vendors, consultants, contractors, etc. The architecture should deal only with enterprise-wide groups. It should permit the creation of groups which are strictly local to a single organizational unit or system. Enterprise group names should be assigned and group affinities should be managed by a single service across the enterprise and across all applications and systems. This service may run as part of the user name service. Within reasonable bounds any user should be able to define a group for which he is prepared to assume ownership and responsibility. Group owners should be able to manage group membership or delegate it. For example, the human resources manager might wish to restrict the ability to add members to the group *payroll department* while permitting any manager to add users to the group *employee* or the group *nonemployee*.

Rules-based (as opposed to list-based) access control — Prefer rules-based to list-based access control. For example, "access to data labelled confidential is limited to employees" should be preferred to "user A can access dataset 1." While the latter is more granular and specific, the former covers more data in a single rule. The latter will require much more administrative activity to accomplish the same result as the former. Similarly, it can be expressed in far less data. While the latter may permit only a few good things to happen, the former forbids a large number of bad things. This recommendation is counterintuitive to those of us who are part of the tradition of "least possible privilege." This rule implies that a user should be given access to only those resources required to do their job and that all access should be explicit. The rule of least privilege worked well in a world in which the number of users, data objects, and relations between them was small. It begins to break down rapidly in the modern world of tens of millions of users and billions of resources.

Data-based rules — Access control rules should be expressed in terms of the name and other labels of the data rather than in terms of the procedure to be performed. They should be independent of the procedures used to access the data or the environment in which they are stored. That is, it is better to say that a user has *read* access to *filename* than to say that he has *execute* access to *word.exe*. It makes little sense to say that a user is restricted to a procedure that can perform arbitrary operations on an unbounded set of objects. This is an accommodation to the increase in the number of data objects and the decreasing granularity of the procedures.

Prefer single authentication service — Evidence of user identity should be authenticated by a single central process for the entire enterprise and across all systems and applications. These systems and applications can be clients of the authentication server, or the server can issue trusted credentials to the user that can be recognized and honored by the using systems and applications.

Prefer a single standard interface for invoking security services — All applications, services, and systems should invoke authentication, access control, monitoring, and logging services via the same programming interface. The generalized system security application programming interface (GSSAPI) is preferred in the absence of any other overriding considerations. Using a single interface permits the replacement or enhancement of the security services with a minimum of disruption.

Encryption services — Standard encryption services should be available on every platform. These will include encryption, decryption, key management, and certificate management services. The Data Encryption Standard algorithm should be preferred for all applications, save key management, where RSA is preferred. A public key server should be available in the network. This service will permit a user or an application to find the public key of any other.

Automate and hide all key management functions — All key management should be automated and hidden from users. No keys should ever appear in the clear or be transcribed by a user. Users should reference keys only by name. Prefer dedicated hardware for the storage of keys. Prefer smart cards, tokens, PCMCIA cards, other removable media, laptops, or access-controlled single-user desktops, in that order. Only keys belonging to the system manager should be stored on a multi-user system.

Use firewalls to localize and raise the cost of attacks — The network should be compartmented with firewalls. These will localize attacks, prevent them from spreading, increase their cost, and reduce the value of success.

Firewalls should resist attack traffic in both directions. That is, each sub-network should use a firewall to connect to any other. A subnet manager should be responsible for protecting both his own net and connecting nets from any attack traffic. A conservative firewall policy is indicated. That is, firewalls should permit only that traffic which is necessary for the intended applications and should hide all information about one net from the other.

Access control begins on the desktop — Access control should begin on the desktop and be composed up rather than begin on the mainframe and spread down. The issue here is to prevent the insertion of malicious programs more than to prevent the leakage of sensitive data.

APPENDIX I

PRINCIPLES OF GOOD DESIGN

Prefer broad solutions to point solutions — Prefer broad security solutions which work across the enterprise, multiple applications, multiple resources, and against multiple hazards to those which are limited to or specific to one of these. Such practices are almost always more efficient than a collection of mechanisms that are specific to applications, resources, or hazards.

Prefer end-to-end solutions to point-by-point solutions — Similarly, prefer encryption-based end-to-end security solutions that are independent of the network. The more sensitive the application and the more hostile the network, the greater this preference. Such solutions are more robust and more efficient than those that attempt to identify and fix all of the vulnerabilities between the ends of the path.

Design top down, implement bottom up — Design by functional decomposition and successive refinement. Implement by composition from the bottom. Prefer early deployment of those services and servers which will be required over the long haul.

Do it right the first time — When building infrastructure, build for the ages. Do it right the first time. This strategy is more effective and more efficient than the "assess and patch" strategy that has been the approach to security in the past.

Prefer planning to fixing — Similarly, work by plan and design rather than by experimentation. Necessary experimentation should be carefully identified, contained, and controlled.

Prefer long term to short — Applications are becoming more sensitive and the environment more hostile. While one may consent to a plan that permits an early deployment of an application with a plan to deploy the agreed-upon security function by a date certain, do not take a "wait and see" approach.

Justify across the enterprise and time — Security measures must be justified across the entire enterprise and across the life of the application or the mechanism. By definition, security prefers predictable, regular, prevention costs to unpredictable, irregular, remedial costs. They should be justified across a time frame that is consistent with the normal frequency of the events that it addresses. Security measures are relatively easy to justify in this manner and difficult to justify locally or in the short term. In justifying security measures, weight should be given to the fact that applications are becoming more sensitive, more interoperable, and more important, and that the environment in which they operate is becoming less reliable and more hostile.

Provide economy of safe use — Using the system safely should require as little user effort as possible. For example, a user should have to log on only once per enterprise, per work station, per day.

Provide consistent presentation and appearance — Security should look the same across the enterprise, i.e., applications, systems, and platforms.

Make control predictable and intuitive — Systems should be supportive. They should encapsulate the special knowledge required by the manager and user to operate them. They should make this information available to the manager and user at the time of use.

Provide ease of safe use — Design in such a way that it is easy to do the right thing. Penalties should be associated with doing the wrong thing (e.g., economy of log-on, user should have to log on only once per work station, per enterprise, per day.)

Prefer mechanisms that are obvious as to their intent — Avoid mechanisms which are complex or obscure, which might cause error, or be used to conceal malice. For example, prefer online transactions, EDI, secure formatted e-mail, formatted e-mail, e-mail, and file transfer in that order. The online transaction is always obvious and predictable; for a given set of inputs one can predict the outputs. While the intent of a file transfer may be obvious, it is not necessarily so.

Encapsulate necessary special knowledge — Necessary special knowledge should be included in documentation or programs.

Prefer simplicity; hide complexity — For example, all other things being equal, simple mechanisms should be preferred to complex ones. Prefer a single mechanism to two, a single instance of a mechanism should be preferred to multiple ones. For example, prefer a single appearance of administration, like CA Unicenter Star to the appearance of all the systems which may be hidden by it. Similarly, prefer a single point of administration such as SAM or RAS to Unicenter Star.

Place controls close to the resource — As a rule and all other things being equal, controls should be as close to the resource as possible. The closer to the resource, the more reliable the control, the more resistant to interference, and the more resistant to bypass. Controls should be server-based, rather than client-based.

Place operation of the control as close as possible to where the knowledge is and where the effect can be observed — For example, prefer controls operated by the owner of the resource, the manager of the group, the manager of the system, and the manager of the user rather than by a surrogate such as a security administrator. While a surrogate has the necessary special knowledge to operate the control, he knows less about the intent and the effect of the control. He cannot observe the effect and take corrective action. Surrogates are often compensation for a missing, complex, or poorly designed control.

Prefer localized control and data — As a general rule and all other things being equal, prefer solutions that place reliance on as few controls in as few places as possible. Not only are such solutions more effective and efficient but they are also more easily apprehended, comprehended, and demonstrated. Distribute function and data as required or indicated for performance, reliability, availability, and use or control.

APPENDIX II

REFERENCES

IBM Security Architecture [SC28-8135-01]
ECMA 138 (SESAME) (see http://www.esat.kuleuven.ac.be/cosic/sesame3_2.html)
Open Systems Foundation Distributed Computing Architectures
    (see http://www.osf.org/tech_foc.htm)

APPENDIX III

GLOSSARY

Architecture — That part of design that deals with appearance, function, location, and materials.

Authentication — The testing or reconciliation of evidence; reconciliation of evidence of user identity.

Cryptography — The art of secret writing; the translation of information from a public code to a secret one and back again for the purpose of limiting access to it to a select few.

Distinguished User Name — User's full name so qualified as to be unique within a population. Qualifiers may include such things as enterprise name, organization unit, date of birth, etc.

Enterprise — The largest unit of organization; usually associated with ownership. (In government it is associated with sovereignty or democratic election.)

Enterprise Data — Data which are defined, meaningful, and used across business functions or for the strategic purposes of the enterprise.

Name Space — All of the possible names in a domain, whether used or not.

PIN — Personal Identification Number; evidence of personal identity when used with another form.

APPENDIX IV

PRODUCTS OF INTEREST

Secure authentication products — A number of clients and servers share a protocol for secure authentication. These include Novell Netware, Windows NT, and Oracle Secure Network Services. A choice of these may meet some of the architectural requirements.

Single sign-on products — Likewise, there are a number of products on the market that meet some or all of the requirements for limited or single sign-on. These include SSO DACS from Mergent International, NetView Access Services from IBM, and NetSP.

- SSO DACS (Mergent International) (see http://www. pilgrim.umass.edu/pub/security/mergent.html)
- NetView Access Services (IBM) (see http://www.can.ibm.com/ mainframe/software/sysman/p32.html)
- SuperSession (see http://www.candle.com/product_info/ solutions/SOLCL.HTM)
- NetSP (IBM) (see http://www.raleigh.ibm.com/dce/dcesso.html)

Authentication services — A number of standard services are available for authenticating evidence of user identity. These include:

- Ace Server (see http://www.securid.com/ID188.100543212874/ Security/ACEdata.html)
- TACACS (see http://sunsite.auc.dk/RFC/rfc/rfc1492.html)
- Radius (see http://www.tribe.com/support/TribeLink/RADIUS/ RADIUSpaper.html)

Administrative services — There are a number of products that are intended for creating and maintaining access control data across a distributed computing environment. These include:

- Security Administration Manager (SAM) (Schumann, AG) (see http://www.schumann-ag.de/deutsch/sam/sam.html)
- RAS (Technologic) (see http://www.technologic.com/RAS/rashome.html)
- Omniguard Enterprise Security Manager (Axent) (http://www.axent.com:80/axent/products/products.html)
- Mergent Domain DACS (http://www.mergent.com/html/products.html)
- RYO ("Roll yer own")

Chapter 14

An Introduction to IPSEC

Bill Stackpole

The IP Security Protocol Working Group (IPSEC) was formed by the Internet Engineering Task Force (IETF) in 1992 to develop a standardized method for implementing privacy and authentication services on IP version 4 and the emerging version 6 protocols. There were several specific goals in mind. For the architecture to be widely adopted it would have to be flexible. It must be able to accommodate changes in cryptographic technology as well as the international restrictions on cryptographic use. Second, the architecture must support all the client IP protocols (i.e., Transmission Control Protocol or TCP, User Datagram Protocol or UDP) in standard or cast (i.e., multicast) modes. Third, it must be able to secure communications between two hosts or multiple hosts, two subnets or multiple subnets, or a combination of hosts and subnets. Finally, there had to be a method for automatically distributing the cryptographic keys. This chapter will cover the key features of the IPSEC security architecture, its major components, and the minimum mandatory requirements for compliance.

FEATURES

The goals of IPSEC were transformed into the following key architectural features.

Separate Privacy and Authentication Functions with Transform Independence.

IPSEC privacy and authentication services are independent of each other. This simplifies their implementation and reduces their performance impact upon the host system. It also gives end users the ability to select the appropriate level of security for their transaction. The security functions are independent of their cryptographic transforms. This allows new encryption technologies to be incorporated into IPSEC without changing the base architecture and avoids conflicts with location-specific use and exportation restrictions. It also makes it possible for end users to implement transforms that best meet their specific security requirements.

Users can select authentication services using hashed cryptography which have low implementation costs, minimal performance impacts, and few international use restrictions. These implementations can be widely distributed and they provide a substantial improvement in security for most of today's Internet transactions. Or, users can select privacy functions based on private key cryptography. These are more difficult to implement, have higher performance impacts, and are often subject to international use restrictions, so although they provide a much higher level of security, their distribution and use is often limited. Or they can combine these functions to provide the highest possible level of security.

Network Layer (IP) Implementation with Unidirectional Set-Up. Introducing security functionality at the network layer means all the client IP protocols can operate in a secure manner without individual customization. Routing protocols like Exterior Gateway Protocol (EGP) and Border Gateway Protocol (BGP) as well as connection and connectionless transport protocols like TCP and UDP can be secured. Applications using these client protocols require no modifications to take advantage of IPSEC security services. The addition of IPSEC services makes it possible to secure applications with inherent security vulnerabilities (e.g., clear-text password) with a single system modification. And this modification will secure any such application regardless of the IP services or transports it utilizes.

This capability even extends to streaming services using multicast and unicast packets where the destination address is indeterminate. IPSEC makes this possible by using a unidirectional initialization scheme to set up secure connections. The sending station passes a set-up index to the receiving station. The receiving station uses this index to reference the table of security parameters governing the connection. The receiving station does not need to interact with the sending station to establish a secure unidirectional connection. For bidirectional connections the process is reversed. The receiving station becomes the sender, passing its set-up index back to the originator. Sending and receiving stations can be either hosts or security gateways.

Host and Gateway Topologies. IPSEC supports two basic connection topologies, host-to-host and gateway-to-gateway. In the host (sometimes called end-to-end) topology the sending and receiving systems are two or more hosts that establish secure connections to transmit data among themselves. In the gateway (also called subnet-to-subnet) topology, the sending and receiving systems are security gateways that establish connection to external (untrusted) systems on behalf of trusted hosts connected to their own internal (trusted) subnetwork(s). A trusted subnetwork is defined as a communications channel (e.g., Ethernet) containing one or more hosts that trust each other not to be engaged in passive or active attacks. A gateway-to-gateway connection is often referred to as a tunnel or a Virtual Private Network (VPN). A third scenario, host-to-gateway is also possible. In this instance the security gateway is used to establish connection between external hosts and trusted hosts on an internal subnet(s). This scenario is particularly useful for traveling workers or telecommuters who require access to applications and data on internal systems via untrusted networks like the Internet.

Key Management. The ability to effectively manage and distribute encryption keys is crucial to the success of any cryptographic system. The IP Security Architecture includes an application-layer key management scheme that supports public and private key-based systems and manual or automated key distribution. It also supports the distribution of other principle session parameters. Standardizing these functions makes it possible to use and manage IPSEC security functions across multiple security domains and vendor platforms.

Two other key features of the IPSEC security architecture are support for systems with Multi-Level Security (MLS) and the use of IANA (Internet Assigned Numbers Authority) assigned numbers for all standard IPSEC type codes.

IMPLEMENTATION AND STRUCTURES

The IPSEC security architecture is centered around two IP header constructs, the Authentication Header (AH) and the Encapsulation Security Payload (ESP) header. To fully understand how these mechanisms function it is first necessary to look at the concept of security associations. In order to achieve algorithm independence, a flexible method for specifying session parameters had to be established. Security associations (SA) became that method.

Security Associations (SA)

A security association is a table or database record consisting of a set of security parameters that govern security operations on one or more network connections. Security associations are part of the unidirectional initialization scheme mentioned above. The SA tables are established on the receiving host and referenced by the sending host using an index parameter known as the Security Parameters Index (SPI). The most common entries in an SA are:

- The type and operating mode of the transform, for example DES in block chaining mode. This is a required parameter. Remember IPSEC was designed to be transform independent so this information must be synchronized between the end points if any meaningful exchange of data is going to take place.

- The key or keys used by the transform algorithm. For obvious reasons this is also a mandatory parameter. The source of the keys can vary. They can be entered manually when the SAS is defined on the host or gateway. They can be supplied via a key distribution system or — in the case of asymmetric encryption — the public key is sent across the wire during the connection set-up.
- The encryption algorithm's synchronization or initialization vector. Some encryption algorithms, in particular those that use chaining, may need to supply the receiving system with an initial block of data to synchronize the cryptographic sequence. Usually, the first block of encrypted data serves this purpose, but this parameter allows for other implementations. This parameter is required for all ESP implementations but may be designated as "absent" if synchronization is not required.
- The life span of the transform key(s). The parameter can be an expression of duration or a specific time when a key change is to occur. There is no predefined life span for cryptographic keys. The frequency with which keys are changed is entirely at the discretion of the security implementers at the end points. Therefore this parameter is only recommended, not required.
- The life span of the security association. There is no predefined life span for a security association. The length of time a security association remains in effect is at the discretion of the end point implementers. Therefore this parameter is also recommended, but not required.
- Source address of the security association. A security association is normally established in one direction only. A communications session between two end points will usually involve two security associations. When more than one sending host is using this security association, the parameter may be set to a wild-card value. Usually this address is the same as the source address in the IP header; therefore, this parameter is recommended, but not required.
- The sensitivity level of the protected data. This parameter is required for hosts implementing multilevel security and recommended for all other systems. The parameter provides a method of attaching security labels (e.g., Secret, Confidential, Unclassified) to ensure proper routing and handling by the end points.

Security associations are normally set up in one direction only. Before a secure transmission can be established the SA's must be created on the sending and receiving hosts. These security associations can be configured manually or automatically via a key management protocol. When a datagram destined for a (secure) receiving host is ready to be sent, the sending system looks up the appropriate security association and passes the resulting index value to the receiving host. The receiving host uses the SPI and the destination address to look up the corresponding SA on its system. In the case of multilevel security, the security label also becomes part of the SA selection process. The receiving system then uses those SA parameters to process all subsequent packets from the sending host. To establish a fully authenticated communications session the sending and receiving hosts would reverse roles and establish a second SAS in the reverse direction.

One advantage to this unidirectional SA selection scheme is support for broadcast types of traffic. Security associations can still be established even in this receive-only scenario by having the receiving host select the SPI. Unicast packets can be assigned a single SPI value, and multicast packets can be assigned an SPI for each multicast group. However, the use of IPSEC for broadcast traffic does have some serious limitations. The key management and distribution is difficult, and the value of cryptography is diminished because the source of the packet cannot be positively established.

Security Parameters Index (SPI)

The Security Parameters Index is a 32-bit pseudo-random number used to uniquely identify a security association (SA). The source of an SPI can vary. They can be entered manually when the SA is defined on the host or gateway, or they can be supplied via an SA distribution system. Obviously for the security function to work properly, the SPIs must be synchronized between the end points. SPI values 1-255 have been reserved by the IANA for use with openly specified (i.e., standard) implementations. SPIs require minimal management but some precautions should be observed to ensure that previously assigned SPIs are not reused too quickly after their associated SA has been deleted. An SPI value of zero (0) specifies that no security association exists for this transaction. On host-to-host connections the SPI is used by the receiving host to look up the security association. On a gateway-to-gateway, unicast, or multicast transaction, the receiving system combines the SPI with the destination address (and in an MLS system, with the security label) to determine the appropriate SA. Now we will look at how IPSEC authentication and privacy functions utilize SAs and SPIs.

Authentication Function

IPSEC authentication uses a cryptographic hashing function to provide strong integrity and authentication for IP datagrams. The default algorithm is keyed Message Digest version 5 (MD5), which does not provide non-repudiation. Nonrepudiation can be provided by using a cryptographic algorithm that supports it (e.g., RSA). The IPSEC authentication function does not provide confidentiality nor traffic analysis protection.

The function is computed over the entire datagram using the algorithm and keys(s) specified in the security association (SA). The calculation takes place prior to fragmentation, and fields that change during transit (e.g., ttl or hop count) are excluded. The resulting authentication data is placed into the Authentication Header (AH) along with the Security Parameter Index (SPI) assigned to that SA. Placing the authentication data in its own payload structure (the AH) rather than appending it to the original datagram means the user datagram maintains its original format and can be read and processed by systems not participating in the authentication. Obviously there is no confidentiality, but there is also no need to change the Internet infrastructure to support the IPSEC authentication function. Systems not participating in the authentication can still process the datagrams normally.

The authentication header (AH) is inserted into the datagram immediately following the IP header (IPv4) or the hop-by-hop header (IPv6) and prior to the ESP header when used with the confidentiality function, as seen in Exhibit 14.1.

IPv4 Header	AH Header	Upper Protocol (e.g. TCP, UDP)

Exhibit 14.1.   IPv4 Placement Example

The header type is IANA assigned number 51 and is identified in the next header or the protocol field of the preceding header structure. There are five parameter fields in an authentication header, four of which are currently in use (see also Exhibit 14.2):

- The next header field — used to identify the IP protocol (IANA assigned number) used in the next header structure.
- The payload length — the number of 32-bit words contained in the authentication data field.
- The reserved field — intended for future expansion. This field is currently set to zero (0).
- The SPI field — The value that uniquely identifies the security association (SA) used for this datagram.
- The authentication data field — the data output by the cryptographic transform padded to the next 32-bit boundary.

Next Header	Length	RESERVED
Security Parameter Index		
Authentication Data (variable number of 32-bit words)		
1 2 3 4 5 6 7 8 1 2 3 4 5 6 7 8 1 2 3 4 5 6 7 8 1 2 3 4 5 6 7 8		

Exhibit 14.2.   IP Authentication Header Structure

IP version 4 systems claiming AH compliance must implement the IP Authentication Header with at least the MD5 algorithm using a 128-bit key. Implementation of AH is mandatory for all IP version 6 hosts and must also implement the MD5 algorithm with a 128-bit key. All AH implementations have an option to support other additional authentication algorithms (e.g., SHA-1). In fact, well-known weaknesses in the current MD5 hash functions (see Hans Dobbertin, Cryptanalysis of MD5 Compress) will undoubtedly lead to its replacement in the next version of the AH specification. The likely replacement is HMAC-MD5. HMAC is an enhanced method for calculating Hashed Message Authentication Codes that greatly increased the cryptographic strength of the underlying algorithm. Because HMAC is an enhancement rather than a replacement, it can be easily added to existing AH implementations with little impact upon the original algorithm's performance. Systems using MLS are required to implement AH on packets containing sensitivity labels to ensure the end-to-end integrity of those labels.

The calculation of hashed authentication data by systems using the Authentication Header does increase processing costs and communications latency; however, this impact is considerably less than that of a secret key cryptographic system. The Authentication Header function has a low implementation cost and is easily exportable because it is based on hashing algorithm. Nevertheless it would still represent a significant increase in security for most of the current Internet traffic.

Confidentiality Function

IPSEC confidentiality uses keyed cryptography to provide strong integrity and confidentiality for IP datagrams. The default algorithm uses the Cipher Block Chaining mode of the US Data Encryption Standard (DES CBC), which does not provide authentication or nonrepudiation. It is possible to provide authentication by using a cryptographic transform that supports it. However, it is recommended that implementation requiring authentication or nonrepudiation use the IP Authentication Header for that purpose. The IPSEC confidentiality function does not provide protection from traffic analysis attacks.

There are two modes of operation, tunnel and transport. In tunnel-mode the entire contents of the original IP datagram are encapsulated into the Encapsulation Security Payload (ESP) using the algorithm and key(s) specified in the Security Association (SA). The resulting encrypted ESP along with the Security Parameter Index (SPI) assigned to this SA become the payload portion of a second datagram with a clear-text IP header. This clear-text header is usually a duplicate of the original header for host-to-host transfers, but in implementations involving security gateways the clear-text header usually addresses the gateway, while the encrypted header's addressing point is the end-point host on an interior subnet. In transport mode only the transport layer (i.e., TCP, UDP) portion of the frame is encap-sulated into the ESP so the clear-text portions of the IP header retain their original values. Although the term "transport-mode" seems to imply a use limited to TCP and UDP protocols, this is a misnomer. Transport-mode ESP supports all IP client protocols. Processing for both modes takes place prior to fragmentation on output and after reassembly on input.

The Encapsulation Security Payload (ESP) header can be inserted any-where in the datagram after the IP header and before the transport layer protocol. It must appear after the AH header when used with the authenti-cation function (see Exhibit 14.3).

IPv4 Header	AH Header (optional)	Encapsulated Security Payload

Exhibit 14.3. IPv4 Placement Example

The header type is IANA-assigned number 50 and is identified in the next header or the protocol field of the preceding header structure. The ESP header contains three fields (Exhibit 14.4):

- The SPI field — the unique identifier for the SA used to process this datagram. This is the only mandatory ESP field.
- The opaque transform data field — additional parameters required to support the cryptographic transform used by this SA (e.g., an initial-ization vector). The data contained in this field is transform specific and therefore varies in length. The only IPSEC requirement is that the field be padded so it ends on a 32-bit boundary.
- The encrypted data field — the data output by the cryptographic transform.

Security Parameter Index		
Initialization Vector Data (variable number of 32-bit words)		
Payload Data (variable length)		
...Padding Data	Pad Length	Payload type
1 2 3 4 5 6 7 8	1 2 3 4 5 6 7 8	1 2 3 4 5 6 7 8 1 2 3 4 5 6 7 8

Exhibit 14.4. IP ESP Header Structure

IP version 4 or version 6 systems claiming ESP compliance must imple-ment the Encapsulation Security Protocol supporting the use of the DES CBC transform. All ESP implementations have an option to support other encryption algorithms. For instance, if no valid Security Associate exists for an arriving datagram (e.g., the receiver has no key), the receiver must discard the encrypted ESP and record the failure in a system or audit log. The recommended values to be logged are the SPI value, date/time, the sending and destination addresses, and the flow ID. The log entry may include other implementation-specific data. It is recommended that the receiving system not send immediate notification of failures to the send system because of the strong potential for easy-to-exploit denial of service attacks.

The calculation of the encrypted data by systems using the ESP does increase processing costs and communications latency. The overall impact depends upon the cryptographic algorithm and the implementation. Secret key algorithms require much less processing time than public key algorithms, and hardware-based implementations tend to be even faster with very little system impact.

The Encapsulation Security Payload function is more difficult to implement and subject to some international export and use restrictions, but its flexible structure, VPN capabilities, and strong confidentiality are ideal for businesses requiring secure communications across untrusted networks.

Key Management

Key management functions include the generation, authentication, and distribution of the cryptographic keys required to establish secure communications. The functions are closely tied to the cryptographic algorithms they are supporting, but in general, generation is the function that creates the keys and manages their life span and disposition; authentication is the process used to validate the hosts or gateways requesting keys services; and distribution is the process that transfers the keys to the requesting systems in a secure manner.

There are two common approaches to IP keying, host-oriented and user-oriented. Host-oriented keys have all users sharing the same key when transferring data between end point (i.e., hosts and gateways). User-oriented keying establishes a separate key for each user session that is transferring data between end points. The keys are not shared between users or applications. Users have different keys for Telnet and FTP sessions. Multilevel security (MLS) systems require user-oriented keying to maintain confidentiality between the different sensitivity levels. But it is not uncommon on non-MLS systems to have users, groups, or processes that do not trust each other. Therefore, the IETF Security Working Group strongly recommends the use of user-oriented keying for all IPSEC key management implementations.

Thus far we have only mentioned traditional cryptographic key management. However, traditional key management functions are not capable of supporting a full IPSEC implementation. IPSEC's transform independence requires that all the elements of the security association, not just the cryptographic keys, be distributed to the participating end points. Without all the security association parameters, the end points would be unable to determine how the cryptographic key is applied. This requirement led to the development of the Internet Security Association and Key Management Protocol (ISAKMP). ISAKMP supports the standard key management functions and incorporates mechanisms to negotiate, establish, modify, and delete security associations and their attributes. For the remainder of this section we will use the term SA management to refer to the management of the entire SA structure (including cryptographic keys) and key management to refer to just the cryptographic key parameters of an SA. It is important to note that key management can take place separate from SA management. For example, host-oriented keying would use SA management to establish both the session parameters and the cryptographic keys, whereas user-oriented keying would use the SA management function to establish the initial session parameters and the key management function to supply the individual use session keys.

The simplest form of SA or key management is manual management. The system security administrator manually enters the SA parameters and encryption keys for their system and the system(s) it communicates with. All IPv4 and IPv6 implementations of IPSEC are required to support the manual configuration of security associations and keys. Manual configuration works well in small, static environments but is extremely difficult to scale to larger environments, especially those involving multiple administrative domains. In these environments the SA and key management functions must be automated and centralized to be effective. This is the functionality ISAKMP is designed to provide.

Internet Security Association and Key Management Protocol (ISAKMP)

The ISAKMP protocol provides a standard, flexible, and scalable methodology for distributing security associations and cryptographic keys. The protocol defines the procedures for authenticating a communicating peer, creating and managing security associations, techniques for generating and managing keys and security associations, and ways to mitigate threats like replay and denial-of-service attacks. ISAKMP was designed to support IPSEC AH and ESP services, but it goes far beyond that. ISAKMP has the capability of supporting security services at the transport and applications layers for a variety of security mechanisms. This is possible because ISAKMP separates the security association management function from the key exchange mechanism. ISAKMP has key exchange protocol independence. It provides a common framework for negotiating, exchanging, modifying, and deleting SAs between dissimilar systems. Centralizing the management of the security associations with ISAKMP reduces much of the duplicated functionality within each security protocol and significantly reduces the connection set-up time because ISAKMP can negotiate an entire set of services at once.

A detailed discussion of ISAKMP is beyond the scope of this chapter so only the operations and functional requirements of a security association and key management system will be covered. A security association and key management system is a service application that mediates between systems establishing secure connections. It doesn't actively participate in the transfer of data between these systems. It only assists in the establishment of a secure connection by generating, authenticating, and distributing the required security associations and cryptographic keys.

Two parameters must be agreed upon for the system to work properly. First a trust relationship must be established between the end-point systems and the SA manager. The SA manager can be a third-party system — similar to a KERBEROS Key Distribution Center (KDC) — or integrated into the end point's IPSEC implementation. Each approach requires a manually configured SA for each manager and the end points it communicates with. The advantage is these few manual SAs can be used to establish a multitude of secure connections. Most vendors have chosen to integrate ISAKMP into the end-point systems and use a third-party (e.g. Certificate Authority) system to validate the initial trust relationship. The second requirement is for the end points to have a trusted third party in common. In other words, both end points must have an SA management system or Certificate Authority they both trust.

The operation is pretty straightforward. We'll use systems with integrated SAs for this scenario. System A wishes to establish a secure communications session with System B and no valid security association currently exists between them. System A contacts the SA management function on System B. The process then reverses itself (remember SAs are only established in one direction) as System B establishes a secure return path to System A. ISAKMP does have the capability of negotiating bidirectional SAs in a single transaction so a separate return path negotiation is usually not required.

The ISAKMP protocol has four major functional components. They are

- Authentication of communications peers
- Cryptographic key establishment and management
- Security association creation and management
- Threat mitigation

Authenticating the entity at the other end of the communication is the first step in establishing a secure communications session. Without authentication it is impossible to trust an entity's identification, and without a valid ID access control is meaningless. What value is there to secure communication with an unauthorized system?

ISAKMP mandates the use of public key digital signatures (e.g., DSS, RSA) to establish strong authentication for all ISAKMP exchanges. The standard does not specify a particular algorithm. Public key cryptography is a very effective, flexible, and scalable way to distribute shared secrets and session keys. However, to be completely effective there must be a means of binding public keys to a specific entity. In larger implementations, this function is provided by a trusted third party (TTP) like a Certificate Authority (CA). Smaller implementations may choose to use manually configured keys. ISAKMP does not define the protocols used for communication with trusted third parties.

Key establishment encompasses the generation of the random keys and the transportation of those keys to the participating entities. In an RSA public key system key transport is accomplished by encrypting the session key with the recipient's public key. The encrypted session key is then sent to the recipient system, which decrypts it with its private key. In a Diffie–Hellman system the recipient's public key would be combined with the sender's private key information to generate a shared secret key. This key can be used as the session key or for the transport of a second randomly generated session key. Under ISAKMP these key exchanges must take place using strong authentication. ISAKMP does not specify a particular key exchange protocol, but it appears that Oakley will become the standard.

Security association creation and management is spread across two phases of connection negotiation. The first phase establishes a security association between the two end-point SA managers. The second phase establishes the security associations for the security protocols selected for that session. Phase one constitutes the trust between the managers and end-points; the second phase constitutes the trust between the two end points themselves. Once phase two has been completed the SA manager has no further involvement in the connection.

The ISAKMP protocol integrates mechanisms to counteract threats like Denial of Service, Hijacking, and Man-in-the-Middle attacks. The manager service sends an anti-clogging token (cookie) to the requesting system prior to performing any CPU-intensive operation. If the manager does not receive a reply to this cookie, it assumes the request is invalid and drops it. Although this certainly isn't comprehensive anti-clogging protection, it is quite effective against most common flooding attacks. The anti-clogging mechanism is also useful for detecting redirection attacks. Since multiple cookies are sent during each session setup, any attempt to redirect the data stream to a different end point will be detected.

The ISAKMP protocol links the authentication process and the SA/key exchange process into a single data stream. This makes attacks which rely on the interception or modification of the data stream (e.g., Hijacking, Man-in-the-Middle) completely ineffective. Any interruption or modification of the data stream will be detected by the manager and further processing halted. ISAKMP also employs a built-in state machine to detect data deletions, thus ensuring that SAs based on partial exchanges will not be established. As a final anti-threat, ISAKMP specifies logging and notification requirements for all abnormal operations and limits the use of on-the-wire error notification.

SUMMARY

As a standard, IPSEC is quickly becoming the preferred method for secure communications on TCP/IP networks. Designed to support multiple encryption and authentication schemes and multivendor interoperability, IPSEC can be adapted to fit the security requirements of large and small organizations alike. Industries that rely on extranet technologies to communicate with their business partners will benefit from IPSEC's flexible encryption and authentication schemes; large businesses will benefit from IPSEC's scalability and centralized management; and every company can benefit from IPSEC's virtual private networking (VPN) capabilities to support mobile workers, telecommuters, or branch offices accessing company resources via the Internet.

The Internet Security Protocol Architecture was designed with the future in mind and is garnering the support it deserves from the security and computer communities. Recent endorsements by major manufacturing associations like the Automotive Industry Action Group, product commitments from major vendors like Cisco Systems, as well as the establishment of a compliance certification program through the International Computer Security Association are clear signs that IPSEC is well on its way to becoming the industry standard for business-to-business communications in the 21st century.

Domain 3.3
Risk Management

Chapter 53
Risk Management

Chapter 15
Risk Analysis and Assessment

Will Ozier

There are a number of ways to identify, analyze, and assess risk, and there is considerable discussion of "risk" in the media and among information security professionals. But, there is little real understanding of the process and metrics of analyzing and assessing risk. Certainly everyone understands that "taking a risk" means "taking a chance," but a risk or chance of what, is often not so clear.

When one passes on a curve or bets on a horse, one is taking a chance of suffering harm/injury or financial loss — undesirable outcomes. We usually give a degree of more or less serious consideration to such an action before taking the chance, so to speak. Perhaps we would even go so far as to calculate the odds (chance) of experiencing the undesirable outcome and, further, take steps to reduce the chance of experiencing the undesirable outcome.

To effectively calculate the chance of experiencing the undesirable outcome, as well as its magnitude, one must be aware of and understand the elements of risk and their relationship to each other. This, in a nutshell, is the process of risk analysis and assessment.

Knowing more about the risk, one is better prepared to decide what to do about it — accept the risk as now assessed (go ahead and pass on the blind curve or make that bet on the horse), or mitigate the risk. To mitigate the risk is to do something to reduce the risk to an acceptable level (wait for a safe opportunity to pass or put the bet money in a savings account with interest).

There is a third choice — to transfer the risk, i.e., buy insurance. However prudent good insurance may be, all things considered, having insurance will not prevent the undesirable outcome. Having insurance will only serve to make some compensation — almost always less than complete — for the loss. Further, some risks — betting on a horse — are uninsurable.

0-8493-9829-0/00/$0.00+$.50

The processes of identifying, analyzing and assessing, mitigating, or transferring risk are generally characterized as Risk Management.

There are a few key questions at the core of the risk management process:

1. What could happen (threat event)?
2. If it happened, how bad could it be (threat impact)?
3. How often could it happen (threat frequency, annualized)?
4. How certain are the answers to the first three questions (recognition of uncertainty)?

These questions are answered by analyzing and assessing risk.

Uncertainty is the central issue of risk. Sure, one might pass successfully on the curve or win big at the races, but does the gain warrant taking the risk? Do the few seconds saved with the unsafe pass warrant the possible head-on collision? Are you betting this month's paycheck on a long shot to win? Cost/benefit analysis would most likely indicate that both of these examples are unacceptable risks.

Prudent management, having analyzed and assessed the risks by securing credible answers to these four questions, will almost certainly find there to be some unacceptable risks as a result. Now what? Three questions remain to be answered:

1. What can be done (risk mitigation)?
2. How much will it cost (annualized)?
3. Is it cost effective (cost/benefit analysis)?

Answers to these questions, decisions to budget and execute recommended activities, and the subsequent and ongoing management of all risk mitigation measures — including periodic reassessment — comprise the balance of the Risk Management process.

Managing the risks associated with information in the information technology (IT) environment, information risk management, is an increasingly complex and dynamic task. In the budding Information Age, the technology of information storage, processing, transfer, and access has exploded, leaving efforts to secure that information effectively in a never-ending catch-up mode. For the risks potentially associated with information and information technology to be identified and managed cost-effectively, it is essential that the process of analyzing and assessing risk is well understood by all parties — and executed on a timely basis. This chapter is written with the objective of illuminating the process and the issues of risk analysis and assessment.

TERMS AND DEFINITIONS

To discuss the history and evolution of information risk analysis and assessment, several terms whose meanings are central to this discussion should first be defined.

Annualized Loss Expectancy (ALE) — This discrete value is derived, classically, from the following algorithm (see also the definitions for single loss expectancy [SLE] and annualized rate of occurrence [ARO] below):

$$\text{SINGLE LOSS EXPECTANCY} \times \text{ANNUALIZED RATE OF OCCURRENCE} = \text{ANNUALIZED LOSS EXPECTANCY}$$

To effectively identify the risks and to plan budgets for information risk management, it is helpful to express loss expectancy in annualized terms. For example, the preceding algorithm will show that the **ALE** for a threat (with an **SLE** of $1,000,000) that is expected to occur only about once in 10,000 years is ($1,000,000 divided by 10,000) only $100.00. When the expected threat frequency (**ARO**) is factored into the equation, the significance of this risk factor is addressed and integrated into the information risk management process. Thus, the risks are more accurately portrayed, and the basis for meaningful cost/benefit analysis of risk reduction measures is established.

Annualized Rate of Occurrence (ARO) — This term characterizes, on an annualized basis, the frequency with which a threat is expected to occur. For example, a threat occurring once in 10 years has an **ARO** of 1/10 or 0.1; a threat occurring 50 times in a given year has an **ARO** of 50.0. The possible range of frequency values is from 0.0 (the threat is not expected to occur) to some whole number whose magnitude depends on the type and population of threat sources. For example, the upper value could exceed 100,000 events per year for minor, frequently experienced threats such as misuse-of-resources. For an example of how quickly the number of threat events can mount, imagine a small organization — about 100 staff members — having logical access to an information processing system. If each of those 100 persons misused the system only once a month, misuse events would be occurring at the rate of 1,200 events per year. It is useful to note here that many confuse **ARO** or frequency with the term and concept of probability (defined below). While the statistical and mathematical significance of these frequency and probability metrics tend to converge at about 1/100 and become essentially indistinguishable below that level of frequency or probability, they become increasingly divergent above 1/100 to the point where probability stops — at 1.0 or certainty — and frequency continues to mount undeterred, by definition.

Exposure Factor (EF) — This factor represents a measure of the magnitude of loss or impact on the value of an asset. It is expressed as a percent, ranging from 0% to 100%, of asset value loss arising from a threat event.

This factor is used in the calculation of single loss expectancy (**SLE**), which is defined below.

Information Asset — This term, in general, represents the body of information an organization must have to conduct its mission or business. A specific information asset may consist of any subset of the complete body of information, i.e., accounts payable, inventory control, payroll, etc. Information is regarded as an intangible asset separate from the media on which it resides. There are several elements of value to be considered. First is the simple cost of replacing the information; second is the cost of replacing supporting software; and third through fifth is a series of values that reflect the costs associated with loss of the information's confidentiality, availability, and integrity. Some consider the supporting hardware and netware to be information assets as well. However, these are distinctly tangible assets. Therefore, using tangibility as the distinguishing characteristic, it is logical to characterize hardware differently than the information itself. Software, on the other hand, is often regarded as information.

These five elements of the value of an information asset often dwarf all other values relevant to an assessment of information-related risk. It should be noted that these elements of value are not necessarily additive for the purpose of assessing risk. In both assessing risk and establishing cost-justification for risk-reducing safeguards, it is useful to be able to isolate the value of safeguard effects among these elements.

Clearly, for an organization to conduct its mission or business, the necessary information must be present where it is supposed to be, when it is supposed to be there, and in the expected form. Further, if desired confidentiality is lost, results could range from no financial loss if confidentiality is not an issue, to loss of market share in the private sector, to compromise of national security in the public sector.

Qualitative/Quantitative — These terms indicate the (oversimplified) binary categorization of risk metrics and information risk management techniques. In reality, there is a spectrum across which these terms apply, virtually always in combination. This spectrum may be described as the degree to which the risk management process is quantified. If all elements — asset value, impact, threat frequency, safeguard effectiveness, safeguard costs, uncertainty, and probability — are quantified, the process may be characterized as fully quantitative.

It is virtually impossible to conduct a purely quantitative risk management project, because the quantitative measurements must be applied to the qualitative properties, i.e., characterizations of vulnerability, of the target environment. For example, "failure to impose logical access control" is a qualitative statement of vulnerability. However, it is possible to conduct a purely qualitative risk management project. A vulnerability analysis, for example, may identify only the absence of risk-reducing countermeasures, such as logical access controls. Even this simple qualitative process has an implicit quantitative element in its binary — yes/no — method of evaluation. In summary, risk analysis and assessment techniques should be described not as either qualitative or quantitative but in terms of the degree to which such elementary factors as asset value, exposure factor, and threat frequency are assigned quantitative values.

Probability — This term characterizes the chance or likelihood, in a finite sample, that an event will occur or that a specific loss value may be attained should the event occur. For example, the probability of getting a six on a single roll of a die is 1/6, or 0.16667. The possible range of probability values is 0.0 to 1.0. A probability of 1.0 expresses certainty that the subject event will occur within the finite interval. Conversely, a probability of 0.0 expresses certainty that the subject event will not occur within the finite interval.

Risk — The potential for harm or loss, best expressed as the answer to those four questions:

- What could happen? (What is the threat?)
- How bad could it be? (What is the impact or consequence?)
- How often might it happen? (What is the frequency?)
- How certain are the answers to the first three questions? (What is the degree of confidence?)

The key element among these is the issue of uncertainty captured in the fourth question. If there is no uncertainty, there is no "risk," per se.

Risk Analysis — This term represents the process of analyzing a target environment and the relationships of its risk-related attributes. The analysis should identify threat vulnerabilities, associate these vulnerabilities with affected assets, identify the potential for and nature of an undesirable result, and identify and evaluate risk-reducing countermeasures.

Risk Assessment — This term represents the assignment of value to assets, threat frequency (annualized), consequence (i.e., exposure factors), and other elements of chance. The reported results of risk analysis can be said to provide an assessment or measurement of risk, regardless of the degree to which quantitative techniques are applied. For consistency in this article, the term risk assessment hereafter is used to characterize both the process and the results of analyzing and assessing risk.

Risk Management — This term characterizes the overall process. The first phase, risk assessment, includes identification of the assets at risk and their value, risks that threaten a loss of that value, risk-reducing measures, and the budgetary impact of implementing decisions related to the acceptance, mitigation, or transfer of risk. The second phase of risk management includes the process of assigning priority to, budgeting, implementing, and maintaining appropriate risk-reducing measures. Risk management is a continuous process.

Safeguard — This term represents a risk-reducing measure that acts to detect, prevent, or minimize loss associated with the occurrence of a specified threat or category of threats. Safeguards are also often described as controls or countermeasures.

Safeguard Effectiveness — This term represents the degree, expressed as a percent, from 0 percent to 100 percent, to which a safeguard may be characterized as effectively mitigating a vulnerability (defined below) and reducing associated loss risks.

Single Loss Expectancy or Exposure (SLE) — This value is classically derived from the following algorithm to determine the monetary loss (impact) for each occurrence of a threatened event:

$$\text{ASSET VALUE} \times \text{EXPOSURE FACTOR} = \text{SINGLE LOSS EXPECTANCY}$$

The **SLE** is usually an end result of a business impact analysis (BIA). A BIA typically stops short of evaluating the related threats' **ARO** or their significance. The **SLE** represents only one element of risk, the expected impact, monetary or otherwise, of a specific threat event. Because the BIA usually characterizes the massive losses resulting from a catastrophic event, however improbable, it is often employed as a scare tactic to get management attention — and loosen budgetary constraints — often unreasonably.

Threat — This term defines an event (e.g., a tornado, theft, or computer virus infection), the occurrence of which could have an undesirable impact.

Uncertainty — This term characterizes the degree, expressed as a percent, from 0.0 percent to 100 percent, to which there is less than complete confidence in the value of any element of the risk assessment. Uncertainty is typically measured inversely with respect to confidence, i.e., if confidence is low, uncertainty is high.

Vulnerability — This term characterizes the absence or weakness of a risk-reducing safeguard. It is a condition that has the potential to allow a threat to occur with greater frequency, greater impact, or both. For example, not having a fire suppression system could allow an otherwise minor, easily quenched fire to become a catastrophic fire. The expected frequency (**ARO**) and the exposure factor (**EF**) for major and catastrophic fire are both increased as a consequence of not having a fire suppression system.

CENTRAL TASKS OF INFORMATION RISK MANAGEMENT

The following sections describe the tasks central to the comprehensive information risk management process. These tasks provide concerned management with credible decision support information regarding the identification and valuation of assets potentially at risk, an assessment of risk, and cost-justified recommendations for risk reduction. Thus, the execution of well-informed management decisions whether to accept, mitigate, or transfer risk cost-effectively is supported. The degree of quantitative orientation determines how the results are characterized, and, to some extent, how they are used. Each of these tasks is discussed below.

Establish Information Risk Management (IRM) Policy

A sound IRM program is founded on a well-thought-out IRM policy infrastructure that effectively addresses all elements of information security. Generally Accepted Information Security Principles (GASSP), currently being developed, based on an Authoritative Foundation of supporting documents and guidelines, will be helpful in executing this task.

IRM policy should begin with a high-level policy statement and supporting objectives, scope, constraints, responsibilities, and approach. This high-level policy statement should drive subordinate policy, from logical access control to facilities security to contingency planning.

Finally, IRM policy should be communicated effectively — and enforced — to all parties. Note that this is important for both internal control and external control — EDI, the Web, and the Internet — for secure interface with the rest of the world.

Establish and Fund an IRM Team

Much of IRM functionality should already be in place — logical access control, contingency planning, etc. However, it is likely that the central task of IRM, risk assessment, has not been built into the established approach to IRM or has, at best, been given only marginal support.

At the most senior management level possible, the tasks and responsibilities of IRM should be coordinated and IRM-related budgets cost-justified based on a sound integration and implementation of the risk assessment process. At the outset, the IRM team may be drawn from existing IRM-related staff. The person charged with responsibility for executing risk assessment tasks should be an experienced IT generalist with a sound understanding of the broad issues of information security and the ability to "sell" these concepts to management. This person will need the incidental support of one who can assist at key points of the risk assessment task, i.e., scribing a Modified Delphi information valuation (see below for details).

In the first year of an IRM program, the lead person could be expected to devote 50 to 75 percent of his/her time to the process of establishing and executing the balance of the IRM tasks, the first of which follows immediately below. Funds should be allocated (1) according to the above minimum staffing, and (2) to acquire, and be trained in the use of, a suitable automated risk assessment tool — $25 to 35K.

Establish IRM Methodology and Tools

There are two fundamental applications of risk assessment to be addressed (1) determining the current status of information security in the target environment(s) and ensuring that associated risk is managed (accepted, mitigated, or transferred) according to policy, and (2) assessing risk strategically. Strategic assessment assures that the risks associated with alternative strategies are effectively considered before funds are expended on a specific change in the IT environment, a change that could have been shown to be "too risky." Strategic assessment allows management to effectively consider the risks associated with various strategic alternatives in its decision-making process and weigh those risks against the benefits and opportunities associated with each alternative business or technical strategy.

With the availability of proven automated risk assessment tools, the methodology is, to a large extent, determined by the approach and procedures associated with the tool of choice. An array of such tools is listed at the end of this chapter. Increasingly, management is looking for quantitative results that support a credible cost/benefit analysis and budgetary planning.

Identify and Measure Risk

Once IRM policy, team, and risk assessment methodology and tools are established and acquired, the first risk assessment will be executed. This first risk assessment should be scoped as broadly as possible, so that (1) management is provided with a good sense of the current status of information security, and (2) management has a sound basis for establishing initial risk acceptance criteria and risk mitigation priorities.

Project Sizing. This task includes the identification of background, scope, constraints, objectives, responsibilities, approach, and management support. Clear project sizing statements are essential to a well-defined and well-executed risk assessment project. It should also be noted that a clear articulation of project constraints (what is not included in the project) is very important to the success of a risk assessment.

Threat Analysis. This task includes the identification of threats that may adversely impact the target environment. This task is important to the success of the entire IRM program and should be addressed, at least initially, by risk assessment experts to ensure that all relevant risks are adequately considered. One without risk management and assessment experience may fail to consider a threat, whether of natural causes or the result of human behavior, that stands to cause substantial harm or loss to the organization. Some risk assessment tools, such as BDSS™, help to preclude this problem by assuring that all threats are addressed as a function of expert system knowledge bases.

Asset Identification and Valuation. This task includes the identification of assets, both tangible and intangible, their replacement costs, and the further valuing of information asset availability, integrity, and confidentiality. These values may be expressed in monetary (for quantitative) or nonmonetary (for qualitative) terms. This task is analogous to a BIA in that it identifies the assets at risk and their value.

Vulnerability Analysis. This task includes the qualitative identification of vulnerabilities that could increase the frequency or impact of threat event(s) affecting the target environment.

Risk Evaluation. This task includes the evaluation of all collected information regarding threats, vulnerabilities, assets, and asset values in order to measure the associated chance of loss and the expected magnitude of loss for each of an array of threats that could occur. Results are usually expressed in monetary terms on an annualized basis (ALE) or graphically as a probabilistic "risk curve" for a quantitative risk assessment. For a qualitative risk assessment, results are usually expressed through a matrix of qualitative metrics such as ordinal ranking (low, medium, high or 1, 2, 3).

Interim Reports and Recommendations. These key reports are often issued during this process to document significant activity, decisions, and agreements related to the project:

- Project Sizing — This report presents the results of the project sizing task. The report is issued to senior management for their review and concurrence. This report, when accepted, assures that all parties understand and concur in the nature of the project before it is launched.
- Asset Identification and Valuation — This report may detail (or summarize) the results of the asset valuation task, as desired. It is issued to management for their review and concurrence. Such review helps prevent conflict about value later in the process. This report often provides management with their first insight into the value of the availability, confidentiality, or integrity of their information assets.
- Risk Evaluation — This report presents management with a documented assessment of risk in the current environment. Management may choose to accept that level of risk (a legitimate management decision) with no further action or to proceed with risk mitigation analysis.

Establish Risk Acceptance Criteria

With the results of the first risk assessment — through the risk evaluation task and associated reports (see below) — management, with the interpretive help from the IRM leader, should establish the maximum acceptable financial risk. For example, "Do not accept more than a 1 in 100 chance of losing $1,000,000," in a given year. And, with that, and possibly additional risk acceptance criteria, such as "Do not accept an ALE greater than $500,000," proceed with the task of risk mitigation.

Mitigate Risk

The first step in this task is to complete the risk assessment with the risk mitigation, costing, and cost/benefit analysis. This task provides management with the decision support information necessary to plan for, budget, and execute actual risk mitigation measures. In other words, fix the financially unacceptable vulnerabilities. The following risk assessment tasks are discussed in further detail under the section "Tasks of Risk Assessment" later in this chapter.

Safeguard Selection and Risk Mitigation Analysis. This task includes the identification of risk-reducing safeguards that mitigate vulnerabilities and the degree to which selected safeguards can be expected to reduce threat frequency or impact. In other words, this task comprises the evaluation of risk regarding assets and threats before and after selected safeguards are applied.

Cost Benefit Analysis. This task includes the valuation of the degree of risk mitigation that is expected to be achieved by implementing the selected risk-mitigating safeguards. The gross benefit less the annualized cost for safeguards selected to achieve a reduced level of risk, yields the net benefit. Tools such as present value and return on investment are often applied to further analyze safeguard cost-effectiveness.

Final Report. This report includes the interim reports' results as well as details and recommendations from the safeguard selection and risk mitigation analysis, and supporting cost/benefit analysis tasks. This report, with approved recommendations, provides responsible management with a sound basis for subsequent risk management action and administration.

Monitor Information Risk Management Performance

Having established the IRM program, and gone this far — recommended risk mitigation measures have been acquired/developed and implemented — it is time to begin and maintain a process of monitoring IRM performance. This can be done by periodically reassessing risks to ensure that there is sustained adherence to good control or that failure to do so is revealed, consequences considered, and improvement, as appropriate, duly implemented.

Strategic risk assessment plays a significant role in the risk mitigation process by helping to avoid uninformed risk acceptance and having, later, to retrofit (typically much more costly than built-in security or avoided risk) necessary information security measures.

There are numerous variations on this risk management process, based on the degree to which the technique applied is quantitative and how thoroughly all steps are executed. For example, the asset identification and valuation analysis could be performed independently. This task is often characterized as a business impact analysis. The vulnerability analysis could also be executed independently.

It is commonly but incorrectly assumed that information risk management is concerned only with catastrophic threats, that it is useful only to support contingency planning and related activities. A well-conceived and well-executed risk assessment can, and should, be used effectively to identify and quantify the consequences of a wide array of threats that can and do occur, often with significant frequency, as a result of ineffectively implemented or nonexistent IT management, administrative, and operational controls.

A well-run information risk management program — an integrated risk management program — can help management to significantly improve the cost-effective performance of its information technology environment, whether it is mainframe, client-server, Internet, or any combination, and to ensure cost-effective compliance with applicable regulatory requirements.

The integrated risk management concept recognizes that many often uncoordinated units within an organization play an active role in managing the risks associated with the failure to assure the confidentiality, availability, and integrity of information. The following quote from FIPSPUB-73, published June 30, 1980, is a powerful reminder that information security was long ago recognized as a central, not marginal issue:

> "Security concerns should be an integral part of the entire planning, development, and operation of a computer application. Much of what needs to be done to improve security is not clearly separable from what is needed to improve the usefulness, reliability, effectiveness, and efficiency of the computer application."

Resistance and Benefits

"Why should I bother with doing risk assessment?!" "I already know what the risks are!" "I've got enough to worry about already!" "It hasn't happened yet..." Sound familiar? Most resistance to risk assessment boils down to one of three conditions:

- Ignorance,
- Arrogance, and
- Fear.

Management often is ignorant, except in the most superficial context, of the risk assessment process, the real nature of the risks, and the benefits of risk assessment. Risk assessment is not yet a broadly accepted element of the management toolkit, yet virtually every "Big 5" consultancy, and other major providers of information security services, offer risk assessment in some form.

Arrogance of the bottom line often drives an organization's attitude about information security, therefore about risk assessment. "Damn the torpedoes, full speed ahead!" becomes the marching order. If it can't readily be shown to improve profitability, don't do it. It is commendable that IT has become so reliable that management could maintain that attitude for more than a few giddy seconds. Despite the fact that a well-secured IT environment is also a well-controlled, efficient IT environment, management often has difficulty seeing how sound information security can and does affect the bottom line in a positive way.

This arrogance is often described euphemistically as an "entrepreneurial culture."

Finally, there is the fear factor — fear of discovering that the environment is not as well-managed as it could be — and having to take responsibility for that; fear of discovering, and having to address, risks not already known; and fear of being shown to be ignorant or arrogant.

While good information security may seem expensive, inadequate information security will be not just expensive, but, sooner or later, catastrophic.

Risk assessment, while still a young science, with a certain amount of craft involved, has proven itself to be very useful in helping management understand and cost-effectively address the risks to their information and IT environments.

Finally, with regard to resistance, when risk assessment had to be done manually, or could be done only qualitatively, the fact that the process could take many months to execute (and that it was not amenable to revision or "what if" assessment) was a credible obstacle to its successful use. But that is no longer the case.

Some specific benefits are described below:

- Risk assessment helps management understand:
  1. What is at risk?
  2. The value at risk — as associated with the identity of information assets and with the confidentiality, availability, and integrity of information assets.

3. The kinds of threats that could occur and their financial consequences annualized.

4. Risk mitigation analysis. What can be done to reduce risk to an acceptable level.

5. Risk mitigation costs (annualized) and associated cost/benefit analysis. Whether suggested risk mitigation activity is cost-effective.

- Risk assessment enables a strategic approach to information risk management. In other words, possible changes being considered for the IT environment can be assessed to identify the least-risk alternative before funds are committed to any alternative. This information complements the standard business case for change and may produce critical decision support information that could otherwise be overlooked.

- "What if" analysis is supported. This is a variation on the strategic approach information to risk management. Alternative approaches can be considered and their associated level of risk compared in a matter of minutes.

- Information security professionals can present their recommendations with credible statistical and financial support.

- Management can make well-informed information risk management decisions.

- Management can justify, with credible quantitative tools, information security budgets/expenditures that are based on a reasonably objective risk assessment.

- Good information security, supported by quantitative risk assessment, will ensure an efficient, cost-effective IT environment.

- Management can avoid spending that is based solely on a perception of risk.

- An information risk management program based on the sound application of quantitative risk assessment can be expected to reduce liability exposure and insurance costs.

Qualitative vs. Quantitative Approaches

Background. As characterized briefly above, there are two fundamentally different metric schemes applied to the measurement of risk elements, qualitative and quantitative. The earliest efforts to develop an information risk assessment methodology were reflected originally in the National Bureau of Standards (now the National Institute of Standards & Technology [NIST] FIPSPUB-31 Automated Data Processing Physical Security and Risk Management, published in 1974. That idea was subsequently articulated in detail with the publication of FIPSPUB-65 Guidelines for Automated Data Processing Risk Assessment, published in August of 1979. This methodology provided the underpinnings for OMB A-71, a federal requirement for

259

conducting "quantitative risk assessment" in the federal government's information processing environments.

Early efforts to conduct quantitative risk assessments ran into considerable difficulty. First, because no initiative was executed to establish and maintain an independently verifiable and reliable set of risk metrics and statistics, everyone came up with their own approach; second, the process, while simple in concept, was complex in execution; and third, large amounts of data were collected that required substantial and complex mapping, pairing, and calculation to build representative risk models; fourth, with no software and desktop computers, the work was done manually — a very tedious and time-consuming process. Results varied significantly.

As a consequence, while some developers launched and continued efforts to develop credible and efficient automated quantitative risk assessment tools, others developed more expedient qualitative approaches that did not require independently objective metrics — and OMB A-130, an update to OMB A-71, was released, lifting the "quantitative" requirement for risk assessment in the federal government.

These qualitative approaches enabled a much more subjective approach to the valuation of information assets and the scaling of risk. In Exhibit 15.1, for example, the value of the availability of information and the associated risk were described as "low," "medium," or "high" in the opinion of knowledgeable management, as gained through interviews or questionnaires.

		Value		
		Low	Medium	High
Risk	Low			▓
	Medium		▓	█
	High	▓	█	

Exhibit 15.1.   Value of the Availability of Information and the Associated Risk

Often, when this approach is taken, a strategy is defined wherein the highest risk exposures (darkest shaded areas) require prompt attention, the moderate risk exposures (lightly shaded areas) require plans for corrective attention, and the lowest risk exposures (unshaded areas) can be accepted.

Elements of Risk Metrics

There are six primitive elements of risk modeling to which some form of metric can be applied:

- Asset Value
- Threat Frequency
- Threat Exposure Factor
- Safeguard Effectiveness
- Safeguard Cost
- Uncertainty

To the extent that each of these elements is quantified in independently objective metrics such as the monetary replacement value for Asset Value or the Annualized Rate of Occurrence for Threat Frequency, the risk assessment is increasingly quantitative. If all six elements are quantified with independently objective metrics, the risk assessment is fully quantified, and the full range of statistical analyses is supported.

Exhibit 15.2 relates both the quantitative and qualitative metrics for these six elements.

Note: The baseline approach makes no effort to scale risk or to value information assets. Rather, the baseline approach seeks to identify in-place safeguards, compare those with what industry peers are doing to secure their information, then enhance security wherever it falls short of industry peer security. A further word of caution is appropriate here. The baseline approach is founded on an interpretation of "due care" that is at odds with the well-established legal definition of due care. Organizations relying solely on the baseline approach could find themselves at a liability risk with an inadequate legal defense should a threat event cause a loss that could have been prevented by available technology or practice that was not implemented because the baseline approach was used.

The classic quantitative algorithm, as presented in FIPSPUB-65, that laid the foundation for information security risk assessment is simple:

$$(\text{Asset Value} \times \text{Exposure Factor} = \text{Single Loss Exposure})$$

$$\frac{\times \quad \text{Annualized Rate of Occurrence}}{= \quad \text{Annualized Loss Expectancy}}$$

For example, let's look at the risk of fire. Assume the asset value is \$1M, the exposure factor is 50%, and the annualized rate of occurrence is 1/10 (once in ten years). Plugging these values into the algorithm yields the following:

$$(\$1M \times 50\% = \$500K) \times 1/10 = \$50K$$

Using conventional cost/benefit assessment, the \$50K ALE represents the cost/benefit break-even point for risk mitigation measures. In other words, the organization could justify spending up to \$50K per year to prevent the occurrence or reduce the impact of a fire.

261

Risk Element	Quantitative Metrics				Qualitative Metrics			
	Monetary Value	Percent Factors (%)	Annualized Rate of Occurrence	Bounded Distribution (Range)	Low, Medium & High	Ordinal Ranking	Vital, Critical, Important, etc.	Baseline
Asset Value	x			x	x	x	x	
Threat Frequency (Annualized)			x	x	x	x		
Threat Exposure Factor		x		x	x	x		
Recommended Safeguard Effectiveness		x		x	x	x		
Safeguard Cost (Annualized)	x			x	x	x		
Uncertainty (Confidence Factor)		x		x	x	x		

Exhibit 15.2. Quantitative and Qualitative Metrics for the Six Elements

It is true that the classic FIPSPUB-65 quantitative risk assessment took the first steps toward establishing a quantitative approach. However, in the effort to simplify fundamental statistical analysis processes so that everyone could readily understand, the algorithms developed went too far. The consequence was results that had little credibility for several reasons, three of which follow:

- The classic algorithm addresses all but two of the elements, recommended safeguard effectiveness and uncertainty. Both of these must be addressed in some way, and uncertainty, the key risk factor, must be addressed explicitly.
- The algorithm cannot distinguish effectively between low frequency/high impact threats (such as "fire") and high frequency/low impact threats (such as "misuse of resources"). Therefore, associated risks can be significantly misrepresented.
- Each element is addressed as a discrete value, which, when considered with the failure to address uncertainty explicitly, makes it difficult to actually model risk and illustrate probabilistically the range of potential undesirable outcomes.

Yes, this primitive algorithm did have shortcomings, but advances in quantitative risk assessment technology and methodology to explicitly address uncertainty and support technically correct risk modeling have largely done away with those problems.

Pros and Cons of Qualitative and Quantitative Approaches

In this brief analysis, the features of specific tools and approaches will not be discussed. Rather, the pros and cons associated in general with qualitative and quantitative methodologies will be addressed.

Qualitative — Pros

- Calculations, if any, are simple and readily understood and executed.
- It is usually not necessary to determine the monetary value of information (its availability, confidentiality, and integrity).
- It is not necessary to determine quantitative threat frequency and impact data.
- It is not necessary to estimate the cost of recommended risk mitigation measures and calculate cost/benefit.
- A general indication of significant areas of risk that should be addressed is provided.

Qualitative — Cons

- The risk assessment and results are essentially subjective in both process and metrics. The use of independently objective metrics is eschewed.

- No effort is made to develop an objective monetary basis for the value of targeted information assets. Hence, the perception of value may not realistically reflect actual value at risk.
- No basis is provided for cost/benefit analysis of risk mitigation measures, only subjective indication of a problem.
- It is not possible to track risk management performance objectively when all measures are subjective.

Quantitative — Pros

- The assessment and results are based substantially on independently objective processes and metrics. Thus meaningful statistical analysis is supported.
- The value of information (availability, confidentiality, and integrity), as expressed in monetary terms with supporting rationale, is better understood. Thus, the basis for expected loss is better understood.
- A credible basis for cost/benefit assessment of risk mitigation measures is provided. Thus, information security budget decision-making is supported.
- Risk management performance can be tracked and evaluated.
- Risk assessment results are derived and expressed in management's language, monetary value, percentages, and probability annualized. Thus risk is better understood.

Quantitative — Cons

- Calculations are complex. If they are not understood or effectively explained, management may mistrust the results of "black box" calculations.
- It is not practical to attempt to execute a quantitative risk assessment without using a recognized automated tool and associated knowledge bases. A manual effort, even with the support of spread sheet and generic statistical software, can easily take ten to twenty times the work effort required with the support of a good automated risk assessment tool.
- A substantial amount of information about the target information and its IT environment must be gathered.
- As of this writing, there is not yet a standard, independently developed and maintained threat population and threat frequency knowledge base. Thus the users must rely on the credibility of the vendors who develop and support extant automated tools or do threat research on their own.

Business Impact Analysis vs. Risk Assessment

There is still confusion as to the difference between a Business Impact Analysis (BIA) and risk assessment. It is not unusual to hear the terms used interchangeably, but that is not correct. A BIA, at the minimum, is the equivalent of one task of a risk assessment — asset valuation, a determination of the value of the target body of information and its supporting IT resources. At the most, the BIA will develop the equivalent of a Single Loss Exposure, with supporting details, of course, usually based on a worst case scenario. The results are most often used to convince management that they should fund development and maintenance of a contingency plan.

Information security is much more than contingency planning. A BIA often requires 75 to 100 percent or more of the work effort (and associated cost) of a risk assessment, while providing only a small fraction of the useful information provided by a risk assessment. A BIA includes little if any vulnerability assessment, and no sound basis for cost/benefit analysis.

Target Audience Concerns

Risk assessment continues to be viewed with skepticism by many in the ranks of management. Yet those for whom a well-executed risk assessment has been done have found the results to be among the most useful analyses ever executed for them.

To cite a few examples:

- In one case, involving an organization with multiple large IT facilities — one of which was particularly vulnerable — a well-executed risk assessment promptly secured the attention of the Executive Committee, which had resisted all previous initiatives to address the issue. Why? Because IT management could not previously supply justifying numbers to support its case. With the risk assessment in hand, IT management got the green light to consolidate IT activities from the highly vulnerable site to another facility with much better security. This was accomplished despite strong union and staff resistance. The move was executed by this highly regulated and bureaucratic organization within three months of the quantitative risk assessment's completion! The quantitative risk assessment provided what was needed, credible facts and numbers of their own.
- In another case, a financial services organization found, as a result of a quantitative risk assessment, that they were carrying four to five times the amount of insurance warranted by their level of exposure. They reduced coverage by half, still retaining a significant cushion, and have since saved hundreds of thousands of dollars in premiums.
- In yet another case, management of a relatively young but rapidly growing organization had maintained a rather "entrepreneurial" attitude toward IT in general, until presented with the results of a risk assessment that gave them a realistic sense of the risks inherent to that posture. Substantial policy changes were made on the spot, and

information security began receiving real consideration, not just lip service.

- Finally, a large energy industry organization was considering relocating its IT function from its original facility to a bunkered, tornado-proof facility across town that was being abandoned by a major insurance company. The energy company believed that they could reduce their IT-related risk substantially. The total cost of the move would have run into the millions of dollars. Upon executing a strategic risk assessment for the alternatives, it was found that the old facility was sound, and relocating would not significantly reduce their risk. In fact, it was found that the biggest risks were being taken in their failure to maintain good management practices.

Some specific areas of concern are addressed below.

Diversion of Resources. That organizational staff will have to spend some time providing information for the risk assessment is often a major concern. Regardless of the nature of the assessment, there are two key areas of information gathering that will require staff time and participation beyond that of the person(s) responsible for executing the risk assessment:

1. Valuing the intangible information asset's confidentiality, integrity, and availability, and
2. Conducting the vulnerability analysis.

These tasks will require input from two entirely different sets of people in most cases.

Valuing the Intangible Information Asset. There are a number of approaches to this task, and the amount of time it takes to execute will depend on the approach as well as whether it is qualitative or quantitative. As a general rule of thumb, however, one could expect all but the most cursory qualitative approach to require one to four hours of continuous time from two to five key knowledgeable staff for each intangible information asset valued.

Experience has shown that the Modified Delphi approach is the most efficient, useful, and credible. For detailed guidance, refer to the "Guideline for Information Valuation" (GIV) published by the Information System Security Association (ISSA). This approach will require (typically) the participation of three to five staff members knowledgeable in various aspects of the target information asset. A Modified Delphi meeting routinely lasts four hours; so, for each target information asset, key staff time of 12 to 16 hours will be expended in addition to about 20 to 36 hours total for a meeting facilitator (4 hours) and a scribe (16 to 32 hours).

Providing this information has proven to be a valuable exercise for the source participants, and the organization, by giving them significant insight into the real value of the target body of information and the consequences of losing its confidentiality, availability, or integrity. Still, this information alone should not be used to support risk mitigation cost/benefit analysis.

While this "Diversion of Resources" may be viewed initially by management with some trepidation, the results have invariably been judged more than adequately valuable to justify the effort.

Conducting the Vulnerability Analysis. This task, which consists of identifying vulnerabilities, can and should take no more than five work days (about 40 hours) of one-on-one meetings with staff responsible for managing or administering the controls and associated policy, e.g., logical access controls, contingency planning, change control, etc. The individual meetings — actually guided interviews, ideally held in the interviewees' workspace — should take no more than a couple of hours. Often, these interviews take as little as five minutes. Collectively, however, the interviewees' total diversion could add up to as much as 40 hours. The interviewer will, of course, spend matching time, hour for hour. This one-on-one approach minimizes disruption while maximizing the integrity of the vulnerability analysis by assuring a consistent level-setting with each interviewee.

Credibility of the Numbers. Twenty years ago, the task of coming up with "credible" numbers for information asset valuation, threat frequency and impact distributions, and other related risk factors was daunting. Since then, the GIV was published, and significant progress has been made by some automated tools' handling of the numbers and their associated knowledge bases — the knowledge bases that were developed on the basis of significant research to establish credible numbers. And, credible results are provided if proven algorithms with which to calculate illustrative risk models are used.

However, manual approaches or automated tools that require the users to develop the necessary quantitative data are susceptible to a much greater degree of subjectivity and poorly informed assumptions.

In the past couple of years, there have been some exploratory efforts to establish a Threat Research Center tasked with researching and establishing:

1. a standard information security threat population,
2. associated threat frequency data, and
3. associated threat scenario and impact data;

and maintaining that information while assuring sanitized source channels that protect the providers of impact and scenario information from disclosure. As recognition of the need for strong information security and associated risk assessment continues to increase, the pressure to launch this function will eventually be successful.

267

Subjectivity. The ideal in any analysis or assessment is complete objectivity. Just as there is a complete spectrum from qualitative to quantitative, there is a spectrum from subjective to increasingly objective. As more of the elements of risk are expressed in independently objective terms, the degree of subjectivity is reduced accordingly, and the results have demonstrable credibility.

Conversely, to the extent a methodology depends on opinion, point of view, bias, or ignorance (subjectivity), the results will be of increasingly questionable utility. Management is loath to make budgetary decisions based on risk metrics that express value and risk in terms such as low, medium, and high.

There will always be some degree of subjectivity in assessing risks. However, to the extent that subjectivity is minimized by the use of independently objective metrics, and the biases of tool developers, analysts, and knowledgeable participants are screened, reasonably objective, credible risk modeling is achievable.

Utility of Results. Ultimately, each of the above factors (diversion of resources, credibility of the numbers, subjectivity, and, in addition, timeliness) plays a role in establishing the utility of the results. Utility is often a matter of perception. If management feels that the execution of a risk assessment is diverting resources from their primary mission inappropriately, if the numbers are not credible, if the level of subjectivity exceeds an often intangible cultural threshold for the organization, or if the project simply takes so long that the results are no longer timely, then the attention — and trust — of management will be lost or reduced along with the utility of the results.

A risk assessment executed with the support of contemporary automated tools can be completed in a matter of weeks, not months. Developers of the best automated tools have done significant research into the qualitative elements of good control, and their qualitative vulnerability assessment knowledge bases reflect that fact. The same is true with regard to their quantitative elements. Finally, in building these tools to support quantitative risk assessment, successful efforts have been made to minimize the work necessary to execute a quantitative risk assessment.

The bottom line is that it makes very little sense to execute a risk assessment manually or build one's own automated tool except in the most extraordinary circumstances. A risk assessment project that requires many work-months to complete manually (with virtually no practical "what-if" capability) can, with sound automated tools, be done in a matter of days, or weeks at worst, with credible, useful results.

TASKS OF RISK ASSESSMENT

In this section, we will explore the classic tasks of risk assessment and key issues associated with each task, regardless of the specific approach to be employed. The focus will, in general, be primarily on quantitative methodologies. However, wherever possible, related issues in qualitative methodologies will also be discussed.

Project Sizing

In virtually all project methodologies there are a number of elements to be addressed to ensure that all participants, and the target audience, understand and are in agreement about the project. These elements include:

- Background
- Purpose
- Scope
- Constraints
- Objective
- Responsibilities
- Approach

In most cases, it would not be necessary to discuss these individually, as most are well-understood elements of project methodology in general. In fact, they are mentioned here for the exclusive purpose of pointing out the importance of (1) ensuring that there is agreement between the target audience and those responsible for executing the risk assessment, and (2) describing the constraints on a risk assessment project. While a description of the scope, *what is included*, of a risk assessment project is important, it is equally important to describe specifically, in appropriate terms, *what is not included*. Typically, a risk assessment is focused on a subset of the organization's information assets and control functions. If what is not to be included is not identified, confusion and misunderstanding about the risk assessment's ramifications may result.

Again, the most important point about the project sizing task is to ensure that the project is clearly defined and that a clear understanding of the project by all parties is achieved.

Threat Analysis. In manual approaches and some automated tools, the analyst must determine what threats to consider in a particular risk assessment. Since there is not, at present, a standard threat population and readily available threat statistics, this task can require a considerable research effort. Of even greater concern is the possibility that a significant local threat could be overlooked and associated risks inadvertently accepted. Worse, it is possible that a significant threat is intentionally disregarded.

The best automated tools currently available include a well-researched threat population and associated statistics. Using one of these tools virtually assures that no relevant threat is overlooked, and associated risks are accepted as a consequence.

If, however, a determination has been made not to use one of these leading automated tools and instead to do the threat analysis independently, there are good sources for a number of threats, particularly for all natural disasters, fire, and crime (oddly enough, not so much for computer crime), even falling aircraft. Also, the console log is an excellent source for in-house experience of system development, maintenance, operations, and other events that can be converted into useful threat event statistics with a little tedious review. Finally, in-house physical and logical access logs (assuming such are maintained) can be a good source of related threat event data.

But, gathering this information independently, even for the experienced risk analyst, is no trivial task. Weeks, if not months, of research and calculation will be required, and, without validation, results may be less than credible.

For those determined to proceed independently, the following list of sources, in addition to in-house sources previously mentioned, will be useful:

- Fire — National Fire Protection Association (NFPA)
- Flood, all categories — National Oceanic and Atmospheric Administration (NOAA) and local Flood Control Districts
- Tornado — NOAA
- Hurricane — NOAA and local Flood Control Districts
- Windstorms — NOAA
- Snow — NOAA
- Icing — NOAA
- Earthquakes — U.S. Geological Survey (USGS) and local university geology departments
- Sinkholes — USGS and local university geology departments
- Crime — FBI and local law enforcement statistics, and your own in-house crime experience, if any
- Hardware failures — Vendor statistics and in-house records

Until an independent Threats Research Center is established, it will be necessary to rely on automated risk assessment tools, or vendors, or your own research for a good threat population and associated statistics.

Asset Identification and Valuation

While all assets may be valued qualitatively, such an approach is useless if there is a need to make well-founded budgetary decisions. Therefore, this discussion of asset identification and valuation will assume a need for the application of monetary valuation.

There are two general categories of assets relevant to the assessment of risk in the IT environment:

- Tangible assets, and
- Intangible assets

Tangible Assets. The tangible assets include the IT facilities, hardware, media, supplies, documentation, and IT staff budgets that support the storage, processing, and delivery of information to the user community. The value of these assets is readily determined, typically, in terms of the cost of replacing them. If any of these are leased, of course, the replacement cost may be nil, depending on the terms of the lease.

Sources for establishing these values are readily found in the associated asset management groups, i.e., facilities management for replacement value of the facilities, hardware management for the replacement value for the hardware — from CPUs to controllers, routers and cabling, annual IT staff budgets for IT staff, etc.

Intangible Assets. The intangible assets, which might be better characterized as information assets, are comprised of two basic categories:

- Replacement costs for data and software, and
- The value of the confidentiality, integrity, and availability of information.

Replacement Costs. Developing replacement costs for data is not usually a complicated task unless source documents don't exist or are not backed up, reliably, at a secure off-site location. The bottom line is that "x" amount of data represents "y" key strokes — a time-consuming, but readily measurable manual key entry process.

Conceivably, source documents can now be electronically "scanned" to recover lost, electronically stored data. Clearly, scanning is a more efficient process, but it is still time-consuming. However, if neither source documents nor off-site backups exist, actual replacement may become virtually impossible, and the organization faces the question of whether such a condition can be tolerated. If, in the course of the assessment, this condition is found, the real issue is that the information is no longer available, and a determination must be made as to whether such a condition can be overcome without bankrupting the private sector organization or irrevocably compromising a government mission.

Value of Confidentiality, Integrity, and Availability. In recent years, a better understanding of the values of confidentiality, integrity, and availability and how to establish these values on a monetary basis with reasonable credibility has been achieved. That understanding is best reflected in the ISSA-published GIV referenced above. These values often represent the most significant "at risk" asset in IT environments. When an organization is deprived of one or more of these with regard to its business or mission information, depending on the nature of that business or mission, there is a very real chance that unacceptable loss will be incurred within a relatively short time.

For example, it is well-accepted that a bank that loses access to its business information (loss of availability) for more than a few days is very likely to go bankrupt.

A brief explanation of each of these three critical values for information is presented below.

- *Confidentiality* — Confidentiality is lost or compromised when information is disclosed to parties other than those authorized to have access to the information. In the complex world of IT today, there are many ways for a person to access information without proper authorization, if appropriate controls are not in place. Without appropriate controls, that access or theft of information could be accomplished without a trace. Of course, it still remains possible to simply pick up and walk away with confidential documents carelessly left lying about or displayed on an unattended, unsecured PC.
- *Integrity* — Integrity is the condition that information in or produced by the IT environment accurately reflects the source or process it represents. Integrity may be compromised in many ways, from data entry errors to software errors to intentional modification. Integrity may be thoroughly compromised, for example, by simply contaminating the account numbers of a bank's demand deposit records. Since the account numbers are a primary reference for all associated data, the information is effectively no longer available. There has been a great deal of discussion about the nature of integrity. Technically, if a single character is wrong in a file with millions of records, the file's integrity has been compromised.

Realistically, however, some expected degree of integrity must be established. In an address file, 99 percent accuracy (only one out of 100 is wrong) may be acceptable. However, in the same file, if each record of 100 characters had only one character wrong — in the account number — the records would meet the poorly articulated 99 percent accuracy standard, but be completely compromised. In other words, the loss of integrity can have consequences that range from trivial to catastrophic.

Of course, in a bank with one million clients, 99 percent accuracy means at best that the records of 10,000 clients are in error. In a hospital, even one such error could lead to loss of life!

- *Availability* — Availability, the condition that electronically stored information is where it needs to be, when it needs to be there, and in the form necessary, is closely related to the availability of the information processing technology. Whether because the process is unavailable, or the information itself is somehow unavailable, makes no difference to the organization dependent on the information to conduct its business or mission. The value of the information's availability is reflected in the costs incurred, over time, by the organization, because the information was not available, regardless of cause. A useful tool (from the Modified Delphi method) for capturing the value of availability, and articulating uncertainty, is illustrated in Exhibit 15.3. This chart represents the cumulative cost, over time, of the best-case and worst-case scenarios, with confidence factors, for the loss of availability of a specific information asset.

INTERVAL	LO$	HI$	CF %	INTERVAL	LO$	HI$	CF %
O-1 HR				4 DAYS			
2 HR				8 DAYS			
4 HR				16 DAYS			
8 HR				1 MONTH			
16 HR				2 MONTHS			
1 DAY				3 MONTHS			
2 DAY				6 MONTHS			

Exhibit 15.3. Capturing the Value of Availability (Modified Delphi Method)

Vulnerability Analysis

This task consists of the identification of vulnerabilities that would allow threats to occur with greater frequency, greater impact, or both. For maximum utility, this task is best conducted as a series of one-on-one interviews with individual staff members responsible for developing or implementing organizational policy through the management and administration of controls. To maximize consistency and thoroughness, and to minimize subjectivity, the vulnerability analysis should be conducted by an interviewer who guides each interviewee through a well-researched series of questions designed to ferret out all potentially significant vulnerabilities.

It should be noted that establishment and global acceptance of Generally Accepted System Security Principles (GASSP), as recommended in the National Research Council report "Computers at Risk" (12/90), the National

Information Infrastructure Task Force (NIITF) findings, the Presidential National Security and Telecommunications Advisory Council (NSTAC) report (12/96), and the President's Commission on Critical Infrastructure Protection (PCCIP) report (10/97), all of which were populated with a strong private sector representation, will go far in establishing a globally accepted knowledge base for this task. The "Treadwell Commission" report published by the American Institute of Certified Public Accountants (AICPA) Committee of Sponsoring Organizations (COSO) in 1994, "Internal Control, Integrated Framework" now specifically requires that auditors verify that subject organizations assess and manage the risks associated with IT and other significant organizational resources. The guiding model characterized in the requirement represents quantitative risk assessment. Failure to have effectively implemented such a risk management mechanism now results in a derogatory audit finding.

Threat/Vulnerability/Asset Mapping

Without connecting — mapping — threats to vulnerabilities and vulnerabilities to assets and establishing a consistent way of measuring the consequences of their interrelationships, it becomes nearly impossible to establish the ramifications of vulnerabilities in a useful manner. Of course, intuition and common sense are useful, but how does one measure the risk and support good budgetary management and cost/benefit analysis when the rationale is so abstract?

For example, it is only good common sense to have logical access control, but how does one justify the expense? I am reminded of a major bank whose management, in a cost-cutting frenzy, came very close to terminating its entire logical access control program! With risk assessment, one can show the expected risk and annualized asset loss/probability coordinates that reflect the ramifications of a wide array of vulnerabilities. Exhibit 15.4 carries the illustration further with two basic vulnerabilities.

Applying some simple logic at this point will give the reader some insight into the relationships between vulnerabilities, threats, and potentially affected assets.

No Logical Access Control. Not having logical access control means that anyone can sign on the system, get to any information they wish, and do anything they wish with the information. Most tangible assets are not at risk. However, if IT staff productivity is regarded as an asset, as reflected by their annual budget, that asset could suffer a loss (of productivity) while the staff strives to reconstruct or replace damaged software or data. Also, if confidentiality is compromised by the disclosure of sensitive information (competitive strategies or client information), substantial competitive advantage and associated revenues could be lost, or liability suits for

VULNERABILITY	MAPPED THREAT(S)	AFFECTED ASSETS (At minimum)[a]
No Logical Access Control	Sabotage of Software	Software Goodwill
	Sabotage of Data/Information	Information Integrity Goodwill
	Theft of Software	Software Goodwill
	Theft of Data/Information	Information Confidentiality Goodwill
	Destruction of Software	Software Goodwill
	Destruction of Data/Information	Information Availability Goodwill
No Contingency Plan	Fire Hurricane Earthquake Flood Terrorist Attack	Facilities Hardware Media and Supplies IT Staff Budgets Software Information Availability Goodwill
	Toxic Contamination[b]	IT Staff Budgets Software Information Availability Goodwill

[a] In each case it is assumed that the indicated vulnerability is the only vulnerability, thus any impact on other information assets is expected to be insignificant. Otherwise, without current backups, for example, virtually every threat on this chart could have a significant impact on information availability

[b] Tangible assets are not shown as being impacted by a toxic contamination, aside from the IT staff budgets, because it is assumed that the toxic contamination can be cleaned up and the facilities and equipment restored to productive use.

Exhibit 15.4. Two Basic Vulnerabilities

---

disclosure of private information could be very costly. Both could cause company goodwill to suffer a loss.

Since the only indicated vulnerability is not having logical access, it is reasonable to assume monetary loss resulting from damage to the integrity of the information or the temporary loss of availability of the information is limited to the time and resources needed to recover with well-secured, off-site backups.

Therefore, it is reasonable to conclude, all other safeguards being effectively in place, that the greatest exposure resulting from not having logical access control is the damage that may result from a loss of confidentiality for a single event. But, without logical access control, there could be many such events!

What if there was another vulnerability? What if the information was not being backed up effectively? What if there were no usable backups? The loss of availability — for a single event — could become overwhelmingly expensive, forcing the organization into bankruptcy or compromising a government mission.

No Contingency Plan. Not having an effective contingency plan means that the response to any natural or man-made disaster will be without prior planning or arrangements. Thus, the expense associated with the event is not assuredly contained to a previously established maximum acceptable loss. The event may very well bankrupt the organization or compromise a government mission. This is without considering the losses associated with the tangible assets! Studies have found that organizations hit by a disaster and not having a good contingency plan are likely (4 out of 5) to be out of business within two years of the disaster event.

What if there were no usable backups — another vulnerability? The consequences of the loss of information availability would almost certainly be made much worse, and recovery, if possible, would be much more costly. The probability of being forced into bankruptcy is much higher.

By mapping vulnerabilities to threats to assets, we can see the interplay among them and understand a fundamental concept of risk assessment:

> *Vulnerabilities allow threats to occur with greater frequency or greater impact. Intuitively, it can be seen that the more vulnerabilities there are, the greater is the risk of loss.*

Risk Metrics/Modeling. There are a number of ways to portray risk, some qualitative, some quantitative, and some more effective than others.

In general, the objective of risk modeling is to convey to decision-makers a credible, usable portrayal of the risks associated with the IT environment, answering (again) these questions:

- What could happen (threat event)?
- How bad would it be (impact)?
- How often might it occur (frequency)?
- How certain are the answers to the first three questions (uncertainty)?

With such risk modeling, decision-makers are on their way to making well-informed decisions — either to accept, mitigate, or transfer associated risk.

The following brief discussion of the two general categories of approach to these questions, qualitative and quantitative, will give the reader a degree of insight into the ramifications of using one or the other approach:

Qualitative. The definitive characteristic of the qualitative approach is the use of metrics that are subjective, such as ordinal ranking — low, medium, high, etc. (see Exhibit 15.5). In other words, independently objective values such as objectively established monetary value, and recorded history of threat event occurrence (frequency) are not used.

		Value		
		Low	Medium	High
Risk	Low			
	Medium			
	High			

Exhibit 15.5.   Value of the Availability of Information and the Associated Risk

---

Quantitative. The definitive characteristic of quantitative approaches is the use of independently objective metrics and significant consideration given to minimizing the subjectivity that is inherent in any risk assessment. Exhibit 15.6 was produced from a leading automated tool, BDSS™, and illustrates quantitative risk modeling.

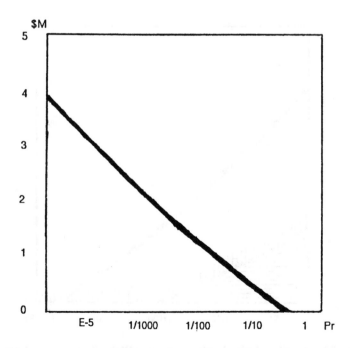

Exhibit 15.6.   Results of Risk Evaluation in BDSS™ Before Any Risk Mitigation

---

The graph shown in Exhibit 15.6 reflects the integrated "all threats" risk that is generated to illustrate the results of risk evaluation in BDSS™ before any risk mitigation. The combined value of the tangible and intangible assets at risk is represented on the "Y" axis, and the probability of financial loss is represented on the "X" axis. Thus, reading this graphic model, there is a 1/10 chance of losing about $0.5M over a one-year period.

The graph shown in Exhibit 15.7 reflects the same environment after risk mitigation and associated cost/benefit analysis. The original risk curve (Exhibit 15.6) is shown in Exhibit 15.7 with the reduced risk curve and associated average annual cost of all recommended safeguards superimposed on it, so the viewer can see the risk before risk mitigation, the expected reduction in risk, and the cost to achieve it. In Exhibit 15.7, the risk at 1/10 and 1/100 chance of loss is now minimal, and the risk at 1/1000 chance of loss has been reduced from about $2.0M to about $0.3M. The suggested safeguards are thus shown to be well justified.

Management Involvement and Guidance. Organizational culture plays a key role in determining, first, whether to assess risk, and second, whether to use qualitative or quantitative approaches. Many firms' management

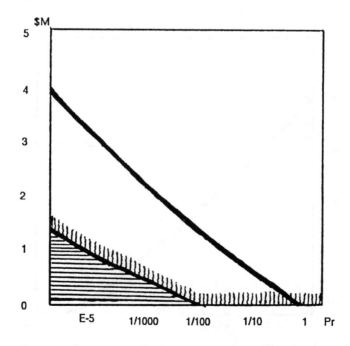

Exhibit 15.7. Results of Risk Evaluation After Risk Mitigation and Associated Cost/Benefit Analysis

organizations see themselves as "entrepreneurial" and have an aggressive bottom line culture. Their basic attitude is to minimize all costs, take the chance that nothing horrendous happens, and assume they can deal with it if it does happen.

Other firms, particularly larger, more mature organizations, will be more interested in a replicable process that puts results in management language such as monetary terms, cost/benefit assessment, and expected loss. Terms that are understood by business management will facilitate the creation of effective communication channels and support sound budgetary planning for information risk management.

It is very useful to understand the organizational culture when attempting to plan for a risk assessment and get necessary management support. While a quantitative approach will provide, generally speaking, much more useful information, the culture may not be ready to assess risk in significant depth.

In any case, with the involvement, support, and guidance of management, more utility will be gained from the risk assessment, regardless of its qualitative or quantitative nature. And, as management gains understanding of the concepts and issues of risk assessment and begins to realize the value to be gained, reservations about quantitative approaches will diminish, and they will increasingly look toward those quantitative approaches to provide more credible, defensible budgetary support.

Risk Mitigation Analysis

With the completion of the risk modeling and associated report on the observed status of information security and related issues, management will almost certainly find some areas of risk that they are unwilling to accept and for which they wish to see a proposed risk mitigation analysis. In other words, they will want answers to the last three questions for those unacceptable risks:

- What can be done?
- How much will it cost?
- Is it cost effective?

There are three steps in this process:

1. Safeguard Analysis and Expected Risk Mitigation
2. Safeguard Costing
3. Safeguard Cost/Benefit Analysis

Safeguard Analysis and Expected Risk Mitigation. With guidance from the results of the risk evaluation, including modeling and associated data collection tasks, and reflecting management concerns, the analyst will seek to identify and apply safeguards that could be expected to mitigate the vulnerabilities of greatest concern to management. Management will, of course, be most concerned about those vulnerabilities that could allow the greatest loss expectancies for one or more threats, or those subject to regulatory or contractual compliance. The analyst, to do this step manually, must first select appropriate safeguards for each targeted vulnerability; second, map or confirm mapping, safeguard/vulnerability pairs to all related threats; and third, determine, for each threat, the extent of asset risk mitigation to be achieved by applying the safeguard. In other words, for each affected threat, determine whether the selected safeguard(s) will reduce threat frequency, reduce threat exposure factors, or both, and to what degree.

Done manually, this step will consume many days or weeks of tedious work effort. Any "What if" assessment will be very time-consuming as well. When this step is executed with the support of a knowledge-based expert automated tool, however, only a few hours to a couple of days are expended, at most.

Safeguard Costing. In order to perform useful cost/benefit analysis, estimated costs for all suggested safeguards must be developed. While these cost estimates should be reasonably accurate, it is not necessary that they be precise. However, if one is to err at this point, it is better to overstate costs. Then, as bids or detailed cost proposals come in, it is more likely that cost/benefit analysis results, as shown below, will not overstate the benefit.

There are two basic categories of costing for safeguards:

- Cost per square foot, installed, and
- Time and materials

In both cases, the expected life and annual maintenance costs must be included to get the average annual cost over the life of the safeguard. An example of each is provided in Exhibits 15.8 and 15.9.

Cost per square foot	$165.00	
Total Square feet	50,000	
Total		$8,250,000
Safeguard Life expectancy	10 years	
Annualized cost (8,250,000/10)		$825,000
Annual Maintenance	$250,000	
Average Annual Cost		$1,075,000

Exhibit 15.8. Cost per Square Foot, Installed, for a Robust New IT Facility

Cost per labor hour	$65.00	
Labor hours	480	
Implementation cost, labor		$31,200
Purchase/materials for an automated DRP tool	$29,000	
Total acquisition and implementation cost		$70,200
Safeguard life expectancy	8 years	
Annualized acquisition and implementation cost ($70,200/8)		$8,775
Annual maintenance:	$4,350	
DRP license maintenance	$32,500	
DRP staff, .5 work year (65,000 x .5)		$36,850
Average Annual Cost		$45,625

Exhibit 15.9. Time and Materials for Acquiring and Implementing a Disaster Recovery Plan (DRP)

These average annual costs represent the break-even point for safeguard cost/benefit assessment for each safeguard. In these examples, discrete, single-point values have been used to simplify the illustration. At least one of the leading automated risk assessment tools, BDSS™, allows the analyst to input bounded distributions with associated confidence factors to articulate explicitly the uncertainty of the values for these preliminary cost estimates. These bounded distributions with confidence factors facilitate the best use of optimal probabilistic analysis algorithms.

Safeguard Cost/Benefit Analysis. The risk assessment is now almost complete, though this final set of calculations is, once again, not trivial. In previous steps, the expected value of risk mitigation — the annualized loss expectancy (ALE) before safeguards are applied, less the ALE after safeguards are applied, less the average annual costs of the applied safeguards — is conservatively represented individually, safeguard by safeguard, and collectively. The collective safeguard cost/benefit is represented first, threat by threat with applicable selected safeguards; and, second, showing the overall integrated risk for all threats with all selected safeguards applied. This may be illustrated as follows:

Safeguard 1 → Vulnerability 1→ n → Threat 1→ n

One safeguard may mitigate one or more vulnerabilities to one or more threats. A generalization of each of the three levels of calculation is represented below.

For the Single Safeguard. A single safeguard may act to mitigate risk for a number of threats. For example, a contingency plan will contain the loss for disasters by facilitating a timely recovery. The necessary calculation includes the integration of all affected threats' risk models before the safeguard is applied, less their integration after the safeguard is applied to define the gross risk reduction benefit. Finally, subtract the safeguard's average annual cost to derive the net annual benefit.

RB(T)1 RA(T)1

[( ) – ( ) = GRRB] — SGAAC = NRRB

RB(T)n RA(T)n

Where:

RB(T) = the risk model for threats 1-n *before* the safeguard is applied.
RA(T) = the risk model for threats 1-n *after* the safeguard is applied.
GRRB = Gross Risk Reduction Benefit
NRRB = Net Risk Reduction Benefit
SGAAC = Safeguard Average Annual Cost

This information is useful in determining whether individual safeguards are cost effective. If the net risk reduction (mitigation) benefit is negative, the benefit is negative, i.e., not cost effective.

For the Single Threat. Any number of safeguards may act to mitigate risk for any number of threats. It is useful to determine, for each threat, how much the risk for that threat was mitigated by the collective population of safeguards selected that act to mitigate the risk for the threat. Recognize at the same time that one or more of these safeguards may act as well to mitigate the risk for one or more other threats.

$$[(AALEB - AALEA = GRRB) - SGAACSG1-n] = NRRB$$

Where:

AALEB = Average Annual loss Expectancy *before* safeguards

AALEA = Average Annual Loss Expectancy *after* safeguards

In this case, NRRB refers to the combined benefit of the collective population of safeguards selected for a specific threat. This process should be executed for each threat addressed. Still, these two processes alone should not be regarded as definitive decision support information. There remains the very real condition that the collective population of safeguards could mitigate risk very effectively for one major threat while having only minor risk mitigating effect for a number of other threats relative to their collective SGAAC.

In other words, if looked at out of context, the selected safeguards could appear, for those marginally affected risks, to be cost prohibitive — their costs may exceed their benefit for those threats. Therefore, the next process is essential to an objective assessment of the selected safeguards overall benefits:

For All Threats. The integration of all individual threat risk models for before selected safeguards are applied and for after selected safeguards are applied shows the gross risk reduction benefit for the collective population of selected safeguards as a whole. Subtract the average annual cost of the selected safeguards, and the net risk reduction benefit as a whole is established.

This calculation will generate a single risk model that accurately represents the combined effect of all selected safeguards in mitigating risk for the array of affected threats. In other words, an executive summary of the expected results of proposed risk-mitigating measures is generated.

Final Recommendations. After the risk assessment is complete, final recommendations should be prepared on two levels: (1) A categorical set of recommendations in an executive summary, and (2) detailed recommendations in the body of the risk assessment report. The executive summary recommendations are supported by the integrated risk model reflecting all threats risks before and after selected safeguards are applied, the average annual cost of the selected safeguards, and their expected risk mitigation benefit.

The detailed recommendations should include a description of each selected safeguard and its supporting cost benefit analysis. Detailed recommendations may also include an implementation plan. However, in most cases, implementation plans are not developed as part of the risk assessment report. Implementation plans are typically developed upon executive endorsement of specific recommendations.

Automated Tools

The following products represent a broad spectrum of automated risk assessment tools ranging from the comprehensive, knowledge based expert system BDSS™, to RiskCalc, a simple risk assessment shell with provision for user-generated algorithms and a framework for data collection and mapping.

- ARES, Air Force Communications and Computer Security Management Office. Kelly AFB, TX
- @RISK. Palisade Corp. Newfield, NY
- Bayesian Decision Support System (BDSS™). OPA, Inc. — The Integrated Risk Management Group, Petaluma, CA
- Control Matrix Methodology for Microcomputers. Jerry FitzGerald & Associates. Redwood City, CA
- COSSAC. Computer Protection Systems Inc. Plymouth, MI
- CRITI-CALC. International Security Technology. Reston, VA
- CRAMM. Executive Resources Association. Arlington, VA
- GRA/SYS. Nander Brown & Co. Reston, VA
- IST/RAMP. International Security Technology. Reston, VA
- JANBER. Eagon. McAllister Associates Inc. Lexington Park, MD
- LAVA. Los Alamos National Laboratory. Los Alamos, NM
- LRAM. Livermore National Laboratory. Livermore, CA
- MARION. Coopers & Lybrand (UK-based). London, England
- Micro Secure Self Assessment. Boden Associates. East Williston, NY
- Predictor. Concorde Group International. Westport, CT
- PRISM. Palisade Corp. Newfield, NY
- QuikRisk. Basic Data Systems. Rockville, MD
- RA/SYS. Nander Brown & Co. Reston, VA
- RANK-IT. Jerry FitzGerald & Associates. Redwood City, CA
- RISKCALC. Hoffman Business Associates Inc. Bethesda, MD
- RISKPAC. Profile Assessment Corp. Ridgefield, CT

- RISKWATCH. Expert Systems Software Inc. Long Beach, Ca
- The Buddy System Risk Assessment and Management System for Microcomputers. Countermeasures, Inc. Hollywood, MD

SUMMARY

While the dialogue on risk assessment continues, management increasingly is finding utility in the technology of risk assessment. Readers should, if possible, given the culture of their organization, make every effort to assess the risks in the subject IT environments using automated, quantitatively oriented tools. If there is strong resistance to using quantitative tools, then proceed with an initial approach using a qualitative tool. But do start the risk assessment process!

Work on automated tools continues to improve their utility and credibility. More and more of the "Big Accounting Firms" and other major consultancies, including those in the insurance industry, are offering risk assessment services using, or planning to use, quantitative tools. Managing risk is the central issue of information security. Risk assessment with automated tools provides organizational management with sound insight on their risks and how best to manage them and reduce liability cost effectively.

Chapter 16

Protecting High-Tech Trade Secrets

William C. Boni

As business organizations enter the 21st century, it is vital that the managers and executives who lead them understand that there is a wide array of dark new threats. These threats strike at the core of what is increasingly the organization's most critical assets — the information, intellectual property and unique "knowledge value" which has been acquired in designing, producing, and delivering products and services. Many of these threats arise from the digital properties now associated with forms of critical information. The methods and techniques of acquiring sensitive information, which were previously available only to the world's leading intelligence services, are now widely available to anyone willing to engage "retired" professionals or acquire sophisticated electronic equipment. These capabilities create a host of new vulnerabilities that extend far beyond the narrow focus on computers and networks. The risk to company information increases as both people and technology, honed in the Cold War, now move into collecting business and technology secrets. Information protection programs for leading organizations must move beyond the narrow focus of physical security and legal agreements, to a program that safeguards their proprietary rights. A new awareness derived from assessing security implications of operational practices and applying a counter-intelligence mindset are essential to protect the enterprises' critical information assets against sophisticated and determined adversaries.

The new opponents of an organization may range from disgruntled insiders seeking revenge, to unethical domestic competitors, to a foreign nation's intelligence services operating on behalf of their indigenous "national flag" industry participant. Such opponents will not be deterred or defeated by boilerplate legal documents nor minimum-wage security guards. Defeating these opponents requires a well-designed and carefully implemented program to deter, detect, and if necessary, actively neutralize efforts to obtain information about the organization's plans, products, processes, people, and facilities capabilities, intentions, or activities.

0-8493-9829-0/00/$0.00+$.50
© 2000 by CRC Press LLC

The fact is that few in business truly appreciate the arsenal now available to "The Dark Side," which is how many protection professionals refer to those who steal the fruits of other's hard work. Understanding how "technology bandits" operate, their methods, targets, capabilities, and limitations, is essential to allow the organization to design safeguards to protect its own critical information against the new dangers. It is also important that managers understand they have a responsibility to help level the global playing field by encouraging foreign and domestic competitors to conform to a common ethical standard. The common theme must be fair treatment of the intellectual property of others. When an organization detects an effort to improperly obtain its intellectual property and trade secrets, it must use the full sanctions of relevant laws. In the U.S., companies now may benefit by seeking federal felony prosecutions under the Economic Espionage Act of 1996!

TRADE SECRET OVERVIEW AND IMPORTANCE

In any discussion of intellectual property and organizational information, it is first important to understand the distinction between trade secrets and patents. The U.S. (or any other national government) grants a patent to the inventor of a novel and useful product or process. In exchange for public disclosure of required information, the government grants the inventor exclusive benefits of ownership and profits derived from ownership for a period of time, commonly 17 years from date of issue or 20 years from date of application for a patent.

However, a business may decide that as a practical matter, it may ultimately derive more commercial advantages by maintaining as a "trade secret" the information, product, or process. The term "trade secret," for those from military or governmental backgrounds, is not the same as national security or "official" secrets. In identifying something as a trade secret, it qualifies as a special form of organizational property, which may be protected against theft or misappropriation. Essentially it means information, generally but not exclusively of a scientific or technical nature, which is held in confidence by the organization and which provides some sort of competitive advantage. The major advantage of protecting something as a trade secret rather than as a patent is that the company may, if it exercises appropriate oversight, continue to enjoy the profits of the "secret" indefinitely.

A practical example of a trade secret's potential for "unlimited" life is the closely guarded formula for Coca-Cola, which has been a carefully protected trade secret for over 80 years. However, there is a downside of protecting valuable discoveries as trade secrets. If the organization fails to take reasonable and prudent steps to protect the secret, they may lose some or all of the benefits of trade secret status for its information. This may allow another organization to profit from the originator's hard work!

Proprietary Information and Trade Secrets

As a practical matter, all of the information which a company generates or creates in the course of business operations and practices can be considered "proprietary." The dictionary defines proprietary as "used, made, or marketed by one having the exclusive legal rights" (*Webster's Collegiate*), which essentially means the company has an ownership right to its exclusive use. Although ALL trade secrets ARE proprietary information, not *all* proprietary information will meet the specific legal tests which are necessary to qualify them as trade secrets. Therefore, trade secrets are a specialized subset of proprietary information, which meet specific tests established in the law. Trade secrets statutes under U.S. laws provide the following three elements that must *all* be present for a specific piece or category of information to qualify for trade secret status:

- *The information MUST be a genuine, but not absolute or exclusive, "SECRET."* This means that an organization need not employ draconian protection measures and also that even though elements of the secret, indeed the secret itself, may be discoverable, through extraordinary (even legal means), it nonetheless is not generally apparent, and may thus qualify for trade secret status. The owner may even license the secret to others, and as long as appropriate legal and operational protections are applied, it remains a protected asset. It is also possible that a trade secret may be independently discoverable and usable by a competitor, and it can simultaneously be a trade secret for both developers!

- *It must provide the owner competitive or economic advantages.* This means the secret must have real (potential) business value to the holder/owner. A business secret that merely conceals inconsequential information from the general public cannot be protected as a trade secret.

- *The owner must take "reasonable" steps to protect the secret.* For those involved in both protection of an organization's trade secrets as well as those whose responsibility includes ferreting out the business strategies of competitors, *this* is the most crucial element in qualifying for trade secret status and attendant rights. Regrettably, neither courts nor legislatures have provided a convenient checklist of the minimum measures to qualify for the "reasonable" steps. Over the years, courts have applied the "reasonable" test and in a series of cases, defined commonly accepted minimum measures. In many cases the courts have ruled that a plaintiff's lack of a specific safeguard defeated their claim of trade secrets status for the information at issue. It is critical to understand that a court's decision as to what is necessary to protect an organization's trade secrets will depend on what is "reasonable" under the specific circumstances of a given situation, and therefore is extremely difficult to predict in advance of a trial. As a general standard, the protections that are "reasonable" will also reflect the common business practices of a particular industry.

Economic Espionage Act (EEA) of 1996

The single most significant development in trade secret protection in the U.S. was passage of the EEA in 1996. Title 18 USC sections 1831 and 1832 were added to the federal statutes after a series of disappointing cases became public which proved the need for new laws to deal with theft of technology and trade secrets. When President Clinton signed this act into law on October 11, 1996, American industry was given a strong weapon designed to combat the theft of trade secrets. The act created for the first time a *federal* law that criminalized the theft or misappropriation of organizational trade secrets, whether done by domestic or foreign competitors or by a foreign governmental entity. A key clause in the act defines trade secrets:

EEA Definition of Trade Secrets. The term "trade secret" means all forms and types of financial, business, scientific, technical, economic, or engineering information, including patterns, plans, compilations, program devices, formulas, designs, prototypes, methods, techniques, processes, procedures, programs, or codes, whether tangible or intangible, and whether or how stored, compiled, or memorialized physically, electronically, graphically, photographically, or in writing if:

1. the owner thereof has taken reasonable measures to keep such information secret; and
2. the information derives independent economic value, actual or potential, from not being generally known to, and not being readily ascertainable through proper means by, the public.

Value of Intellectual Property

In reviewing the definition as to what may qualify as a trade secret under the EEA, it seems that almost anything could be declared a trade secret. This seems to be a prudent approach because advanced business organizations in the developed world are largely based on the knowledge that such organizations have captured, for example, in their design, production, and operational systems. New and more advanced products and services derive from the aggregation of the learning organization knowledge, which is translated into "intellectual property" (abbreviated IP) to distinguish it from the tangible property of the organization. IP is generally considered to consist of the patents, copyrights, trademarks, and trade secrets of the organization, which are normally lumped into the overall category of "intangible assets" on the balance sheet. Although not reflected in traditional accounting practices, the IP of companies has increasingly become the source of competitive advantage. The significance of these assets is demonstrated by the fact that by some estimates over 50 percent or more of the market capitalization of a typical U.S. company is now subsumed under intangible assets, i.e., primarily intellectual property. Several industry segments are especially dependent on aggregating "knowledge" into their products in order to create valuable intellectual property.

Semiconductors. The most significant IP is not merely the designs (the specific masks or etchings) which are the road map of the chips, but also the exact assembly instructions. Although product lifecycles can be measured in months, the effort of thousands of highly educated engineers working in collaborative teams to design, debug, and manufacture leading-edge chips, should be measured in years. If a competitor has both the masks and the assembly instructions, they may anticipate the originator's target and "leap frog" over a current-generation product in price and performance. Alternatively they may merely join the originator in the market with a "me too" product. Such a strategy may be very attractive to an unethical competitor as it could allow them to remain competitive without investing as much time and resources in primary design as the originator.

Biotechnology and Pharmaceutical Products. Often developed over five to seven years and costing hundreds of millions of dollars each, a successful product will represent the work of hundreds of highly trained scientists, engineers, medical experts, physicians, nurses, and others. This highly educated workforce generates a product, which in the end may only be protected by a "production process" patent. The pure science which provides the foundation for such drugs is often public, so the organization's return on investment may well ride on safeguarding the various unique processes associated with development, production, or delivery of a therapeutic drug. Once again a competitor, especially one from a country where intellectual property rights are not well established or respected, may derive significant advantages by misappropriating or stealing product information early in a product's lifecycle. With luck or planning, such thefts may allow development of a competitive alternative that could be produced at minimum cost to the competitor and marketed locally with the encouragement or support of the national government.

Software Products. Without question, the rapid pace of information technology would not be as fast in the absence of sophisticated software products. Applications harness the raw horsepower of the silicon chip and deliver control to a user's business needs. Such tools benefit from highly skilled programmers working collaboratively to fashion new features and functionality. Their knowledge is captured in the product and becomes the source of an organization's ability to deliver new products.

Source code for new or unreleased software may be targeted by unscrupulous competitors or spirited away by employees lured away by better pay or working conditions. Too often, applications development staff will take with them copies of any new software they helped develop or to which they had access during their term of employment. This is an especially serious problem when contract programmers are employed, because by the nature of their assignments, they know their term is limited (e.g., Year 2000). Thus, they may be tempted to market a product developed for one client to another.

Sensitive Information Is Often Portable and Digital

Sensitive proprietary information and other valuable intellectual property including an organization's trade secrets are now often captured in some digital form. Critical trade secrets worth billions of dollars may be contained in CAD/CAM drawing files, a genetics database, or compiled source code for a breakthrough software application. This digital form creates a whole new class of problems that must be considered by protection professionals. Most new products owe their existence to the computers, networks, and users of those systems. However, in a digital state, and in a typical client-server-based systems environment, the "crown jewels" of organizational sensitive proprietary information are often poorly protected against unauthorized access. Such access may allow the hostile intruder or the malicious insider to purloin a duplicate of the original data, and perhaps corrupt or destroy the original. In a matter of seconds, a misappropriated copy of the corporate "crown jewels" can be sent to an exotic location on the other side of the planet. From there the thief may auction it off to the highest bidder or sell it to a competitor. This frightening possibility should, in and of itself, inspire the senior managers of leading companies to give increased priority to computer and network security. As we shall discuss a little later, it seems many organizations have not yet fully recognized the many risks to their intellectual property and trade secrets that poorly controlled systems and networks create.

Increased Potential for "Loss of Control"

As more organizations deploy network technology and as the IP crown jewels become more digital and portable, it's possible, perhaps even likely, that management will lose control of these key assets. Without constant attention, testing, and monitoring, the risk of a catastrophic loss of control and of the IP assets themselves is high.

Typical Confidential Information

Managers who apply themselves can quickly identify a list of the information about their organization that they consider confidential and which may be considered as sensitive and proprietary information that may also qualify for "trade secret" status. The difference between "confidential" and merely "proprietary" is often based on management's assessment of the competitive advantage that accrues to the organization by managing dissemination of the information. However, given the vast quantity of proprietary information created and stored by contemporary organizations, it is essential to stratify information. This essential step allows organization management to identify the truly critical proprietary information from items that are merely sensitive. Napoleon's maxim of war is appropriate to consider, "He who defends everything, defends nothing!" If an organization does not stratify or prioritize its information assets it is likely to spend too much time and money protecting the "crown jewels" (which typically also qualify as trade secrets), and mundane, low-value information equally. Alternatively, they may not invest sufficiently in protecting their core assets and lose considerable advantage when trade secrets and other critical information are compromised.

In a systematic and well-planned project, managers and corporate attorneys should consider what information, both by type and content, are of value and importance to the organization's business operations, capabilities, and intentions. From this list of valuable information the company should then identify those items or elements of information which are real sources of competitive advantage. Of this last group, the organization should determine which, if any, may qualify for trade secret status. Note that in this process it is likely that some very valuable and useful information will provide competitive advantage, but may not be protectable as a trade secret.

Unquestionably there will be trade secrets that have previously not been considered as such. The following list, while not all-inclusive, at least provides a point of departure for creating an organizational inventory which may be supplemented with industry and organization specific categories.

- Business plans and strategies
- Financial information
- Cost of research, development, and production
- New products: pricing, marketing plans, timing
- Customer lists, terms, pricing
- Research and development priorities, plans, activities
- Inventions and technology information
- Unique or exceptional manufacturing processes

- Facility blueprints, floor plans, layouts
- Employee records and human resources information

While any or all the above categories of information are likely to be considered "confidential," what does that really mean? Essentially "confidential" information if disclosed, modified, or destroyed, without appropriate controls or authorization, would likely have adverse consequences on the organization's business operations. However, any or all of the above information, plus any that is unique to your business could potentially be identified as a "trade secret" and benefit from additional legal protection providing it meets the previously discussed tests.

This "audit" or inventory procedure should then be taken to at least one more level of detail. In cooperation with the organization's information technology (IT) management and line managers, the specific documents, systems (servers, databases, work stations, document imaging/production, networks, etc.), file cabinets, and work areas (buildings) that contain the identified "trade secrets" and sensitive proprietary information should be identified. These environments should then be reviewed/inspected and the degree of compliance with trade secret protection requirements should be the standard for the inspection. At a minimum, all IT systems which contain trade secret and sensitive proprietary information must provide individual accountability for access to their contents and a secure audit trail of the access activity of specific users. Any systems, which do not provide at least these functions, should be upgraded to such functionality on a priority basis.

NEW THREATS TO SENSITIVE, PROPRIETARY INFORMATION

Threats to an organization's sensitive proprietary information have never been more formidable. Each of the following issues is significant and requires that any existing programs to safeguard the "crown jewels" be reassessed to ensure the risks have been appropriately managed.

Decline in Business Ethics and Loyalty

A recent newspaper headline declared "48% of Employees Lie, Cheat, Steal." However surprising such a statement may seem, the conclusions implied by the title were not fully justified in the supporting article, e.g., many employees engage in relatively innocuous acts of petty theft, such as office supplies. However, within the context of other studies, the conclusion is inescapable, there has been a substantial decline in employee loyalty and an increase in the range of actions that are considered acceptable business practices. As further proof of the overall change in business ethics, consider the story related by Staples' Chairman Thomas Stemberg in his book *Staples for Success*. In the book, the author describes how he asked his wife to apply for a job with arch rival Office Depot's Atlanta delivery-order center, apparently to gain insights concerning their training methods.

It's also important to appreciate the many changes in work force psychology, which grew out of the downsizing and outsourcing efforts of organizations in the late 1980s and early 1990s. Many workers and mid-level managers learned a harsh lesson: the organization will do without them, regardless of the consequences to the individuals. While such actions may have been necessary to survive in a global economy, many people drew the conclusion that the bond of loyalty between employer and employee had become a one-way street. As a consequence, some decided to do whatever they needed to survive. Once an individual reaches this point, it is easy to rationalize serious criminal behavior on the grounds that "everyone is doing it" or they are only getting their "fair share" before the organization eliminates their job. Although the U.S. economy now seems to have weathered the worst of this period, managers and executives must understand that the base of employee loyalty is often very shallow. Executives should consider the degree of employee loyalty as they design their protection measures, especially for the corporate crown jewels.

The Internet: Hacker Playground

One of the most remarkable changes in the late 20th century has been the explosive growth in the use of the Internet. Until the late 1980s it was the playground for hackers and computer nerds. Since that time, tens of millions of individuals have obtained personal accounts and hundreds of thousands of organizations have established Internet connections. As the number of businesses using "the net" has exploded, so too has the reported rate of computer and network intrusions.

Without question many network based "attacks" are not serious. However, the number and consequence of malicious activity are increasing. The 1997 Computer Security Institute/FBI Survey showed an increase of 36 percent in known instances of computer crime from the 1996 survey. The simple equation is increased network connectivity results in more computer crimes. Organizations that blindly hook up to the net without a well-thought-out protection plan place their sensitive intellectual property and trade secrets at serious risk.

The adverse impact on information protection of the global Internet and the rapid increases in Internet users should not be underestimated. Since the "net" now encompasses all continents and more than 100 countries, it is possible to reach anywhere from anywhere. The plans to circle the globe with low-orbiting satellites will increase both access and mobility. It is important to recognize that the Internet is essentially unregulated, and that there is NO central management or policing. When something happens, whether an attempted intrusion via the net or an unsolicited Spam storm, organizations often have few alternatives but to help themselves.

Growing Threat of Espionage

Perhaps the least appreciated new threat to organization information is the efforts by some companies and many countries to steal critical business information and trade secrets. Is this a real problem? According to the American Society of Industrial Security (ASIS), U.S. companies may have lost as much as $300 billion in trade secrets and other intellectual property in 1997.

A review of recent high-profile cases in the public domain shows that many well-known companies have been targets of industrial espionage and theft of technology and trade secrets. For example, a very short list would include:

- Intel, whose Pentium chip designs were stolen by an employee and offered to AMD.
- Representatives of a Taiwanese company who were willing to bribe a corrupt scientist to steal the secrets of Bristol Myers Taxol® production process information.
- In the another recent case, Avery-Denison learned that one of their research scientists was selling company information to a foreign competitor.
- In the most famous case in recent times, a former high-ranking executive of General Motors was accused of stealing literally box loads of highly confidential documents and offering them to his new employer, Volkswagen.
- Other cases include a retired engineer who sold Kodak trade secrets and a contract programmer who offered to sell key information concerning Gillette's new shaving system.

These scenarios indicate that the theft of trade secrets is a thriving business. According to the FBI, they have literally hundreds of investigations under way. It's important to note that these represent only some of the cases which are publicly known, and do not include cases which are quietly investigated and resolved by organizations fearful of the adverse publicity attendant to a litigation or prosecution. There are likely an even larger number of cases which go completely undetected and which may contribute to the potential failure of large and successful organizations.

Impact of Global Business Operations

Globalization of business operations is a major trend of the late 20th century. It is now a fact that most business organizations operate and compete throughout the world. An important factor to consider in global operations is that the standards of business and ethics, which prevail in the heartland of the Midwest, are not necessarily those which exist in remote areas of the world. Nations such as China and various Southeast Asian nations are real challenges, as they do not, at present, honor intellectual property rights to the extent common in much of Europe and North America. Unrelenting competition for survival and success may create situations where theft of trade secrets seems to promise the beleaguered executive an easy way to remain in business without the need to invest as much in developing new products or improving his operations.

Threats from Networks, Computers and Phones

Generally it has been argued that advanced nations have reaped increased productivity through many benefits of sophisticated communication. With regard to protecting trade secrets, such technologies raise a host of questions. First, as they proliferate throughout the organization, WHERE are the organization's secrets? This is more than just a question of primary physical storage. To properly answer the question, the organization must consider both hard copy documents, individual desktop microcomputers, file servers, databases, backup files/media, as well as imaging/document management and other computer and networking systems.

The myriad of locations and variety of forms and formats which may contain sensitive proprietary information makes it very difficult, sometimes impossible, to know with certainty WHO has access to company secrets! And in cases where management believes they have adequate control over access to sensitive proprietary information, HOW do they really know? Too often managers rely on simple assertions from the Management Information Systems (MIS) and Information Technology (IT) staff that the system and network controls are adequate to protect the organizational crown jewels. Given the importance of the topic and complexity of the environments, senior management is well advised to verify actual conditions of the security and control measures on a periodic basis.

The advent of inter-organizational networks, typically dubbed "extranets," should cause managers concerned with safeguarding their crown jewels to take a hard look at the function and features of the environment. Without careful attention to the configuration and management, it is possible that outsiders will be able to gain access to organization information that extends well beyond the legitimate scope of the relationship.

WHAT MUST BE DONE?

Managers who appreciate the full nature and scope of the threat to sensitive proprietary information and trade secrets must implement protective measures to mitigate the most likely vulnerabilities of their organizations. With regard to protecting trade secrets, there are some measures which have been found to be essential. There are now many additional security measures, which are highly recommended, even though they have not yet been held to be essential.

Required Protection Measures for Protecting Trade Secret Information

Although the courts in the U.S. have not published any sort of handbook which describes required protective measures to safeguard intellectual property, review of various case decisions provides various examples where judges have ruled in such a way that clearly indicated the desirability of the security measure.

Visitor Sign In and Escort. Common sense indicates all non-employees entering the company facility should be escorted by host employees, sign in at reception, and be retained until the host escort arrives. Too often, once inside the facility, host employees' excessive hospitality gives the visitor free reign of the site. In the absence of well-maintained internal perimeters, visitors may obtain accidental or deliberate access to sensitive areas, files, documents, and materials. Also, the unguarded conversations of co-workers unaware of the status of the listener may result in disclosure of sensitive information.

Identification Badges. Distinctive badges with photo provide good control over egress and exit. These are also so inexpensive that organization management would appear foolish if they failed to implement some sort of badging system.

Facility Access Control System. Often tied into the photo-ID badge system used by the organization, facility access control systems provide convenient and automated authentication technology. In the past, card readers alone were sufficient. However, many sophisticated organizations with significant assets are implementing biometric (voice, hand geometry, or retina) systems. Such systems dramatically curtail the potential for abuse.

Confidentiality/Nondisclosure Documents. These confidentiality and nondisclosure statements should specify invention assignments as well as an agreement to protect proprietary information.

Exit Interviews with Terminating Employees. Remind employees that are leaving the company of their continuing obligation to protect any trade secrets to which they had access during the time of their employment.

Other "Reasonable" Measures! The courts have a remaining variable, which can be very important. They may decide, entirely after the fact, that a given organization did or did not act "reasonably" by implementing or failing to implement a specific protective measure. The important fact for protection professionals to consider is that the outcome of a particular ruling is not possible to predict in advance of a trial and a specific set of circumstances.

Recommended Protection Measures

Develop and Disseminate Policies and Procedures. Although not strictly required, a policy that spells out the need for information protection and a procedural framework that addresses issues in both electronic and physical media is a useful tool.

Publication Approval Procedures. Disclosure of the trade secret information in publications will eliminate their trade secret status. Even if the proprietary information disclosed in an article, interview, or press release is not a trade secret, it may damage the company's competitive position. A publication screening procedure involving the company's patent staff or other knowledgeable attorneys, as well as other knowledgeable management, should consider not merely whether the content discloses trade secrets, but also whether it reveals competition-sensitive details. If available, the competitive intelligence group can render valuable service in advising on sensitivity. One must assume that the competitive intelligence analysts working for the most competent opponent will see the release /article and place it in appropriate context.

Contract Language for Vendors, Suppliers, etc. All vendors who provide products, services, even parts and supplies should be required to adhere to a basic confidentiality agreement concerning the nature and extent of the relationship with the company. Appropriate language should be inserted in the contract terms and conditions, specifying exactly how the vendor will act with regard to sensitive proprietary information to which they are granted access in the course of business. In the case of critical suppliers who provide unique or highly specialized elements which are essential to the company's success, it is appropriate to include a supplemental "security guidelines" document. This document should provide additional guidance and direction to the vendor describing (see example table of contents for a typical security guideline for a reprographic service provider).

1. Receipt
2. Storage
3. Handling
4. Work in process
5. Release of finished product
6. Destruction of overruns, QC failed copies, etc.
7. Reportable Incidents

Train Employees. Everyone who creates, processes, and handles company trade secrets and other sensitive proprietary information should be trained. This includes both regular (full-time) as well as contingent employees (temporaries, contractors, consultants, as well as part-time employees). They all need to know what is specifically considered trade secrets of the company, as well as what elements of information may not be trade secrets but are nonetheless considered critical and must not be disclosed outside the company without authorization from appropriate management. Training topics typically include the following:

- Identification of company trade secrets and sensitive proprietary information
- Marking
- Storage
- Physical transportation of hard copy documents and media
- Electronic transmission and storage of documents, materials
- Destruction of physical and electronic copies
- Reportable incidents

In addition a version of training should be tailored to the needs of the contingent employees, which commonly include temporary (clerical) staff as well as any on-site contractors, consultants, or vendor employees.

New-Hire Training Classes. One of the best ways to help people in an organization to change is to indoctrinate the newly hired staff. This way you get your message to the new people before they develop bad habits. This will gradually create a critical mass of supporters for the organization's program to protect information, trade secrets, and other valuable intellectual property. This class and supporting documentation should instruct all employees in the value of trade secrets and company IP, as well as correct procedures for safeguarding these assets.

Develop Incident Response Capability. Assume the worst and you will not be disappointed! There will come a time when the company knows or suspects trade secrets or other valuable intellectual property has been stolen or misappropriated. The statistics are very compelling: nearly 50% of high-technology companies experienced theft or misappropriation of trade secrets in a 1988 Institute of Justice study. Planning for that day is essential. Knowing who to call and what to do will maximize the company's chances for a successful prosecution or litigation.

Conduct Audits, Inspections, and Tests. One of the best ways to know the risks is to conduct a formal trade secret audit or inspection. The process, which must always be conducted under attorney-client privilege, should be a comprehensive review of the company's current inventory of trade secrets, including how well they are managed and protected. A useful extension to the basic review is to conduct a "valuation estimate" for trade secrets and other critical intellectual property. Such estimates, conducted prior to any possible losses, are a useful guide to management. When estimated values of IP are presented in dollars and cents, it will allow a more rational allocation of investment in protecting what may have seemed previously unsubstantial assets.

CONCLUSION: DON'T RELY EXCLUSIVELY ON THE COURTS TO PROTECT YOUR SECRETS!

If the reader takes only one lesson from this chapter it should be this: Although the legal system exists to provide redress for crimes and grievances through criminal prosecution and civil litigation, the process is laden with uncertainty and burdened with very high costs. It is estimated that General Motors spent millions of dollars pursuing Volkswagen and former executives for alleged theft of trade secrets. Even though in the end they prevailed, it was uncertain whether the German courts would find in favor of GM when the action was initiated. When the vagaries of international relations and politics are overlaid on top of the legal variables, it becomes obvious that prevention is a vastly preferable strategy.

Too often it seems that the organizations value more highly their capability to litigate and prosecute for theft or misappropriation of trade secrets. In the long run it is likely to be effective and more efficient to take reasonable steps to prevent incidents. It is important that management understand that a well-designed information protection program and aggressive, early intervention will often eliminate costly and uncertain legal conflicts. Of course, one could be cynical and assume that some attorneys relish the opportunity to showcase their awesome legal expertise on behalf of clients. There is the potential that such displays of capability will occur less frequently if organizations invest more in procedures and technologies designed to prevent and detect the attempts to steal sensitive proprietary information and trade secrets. However, it's more likely that many lawyers, the same as many executives, do not yet appreciate the vast scope of the problem and are merely applying their past experience.

In summary then, executive management should understand that:

1. Many thefts of sensitive proprietary information are preventable
2. Those that are not prevented can be detected earlier, thus minimizing potential losses
3. A well-designed protection program will enhance the organization's probability for successful prosecution and litigation.

Chapter 17
Information Security Management in the Healthcare Industry

Micki Krause

INTRODUCTION

Proper management of the information security program addresses two very important areas: technological, because many of the controls we implement are technical security mechanisms, and people, because security is first and foremost a people issue. However, the information security manager in the healthcare industry is forced to heed another very important area: federal and state regulations.

Recently enacted government legislation, such as the Balanced Budget Act and the Health Insurance Portability and Accountability Act (HIPAA), are adding immense pressure to healthcare organizations, the majority of which have not yet adopted the generally accepted system-security principles common to other regulated industries.

This chapter will address the following issues:

- History of healthcare information systems and the inherent lack of controls
- The challenges the healthcare organization faces, vis à vis its information systems
- The obstacles healthcare companies must overcome in order to implement consumer-centric systems in an environment of consumer distrust of both the healthcare industry and the technology
- The multitude of privacy laws proposed in the last 12 months
- E-commerce and the Internet
- An analysis of the HIPAA security standards

HISTORY OF HEALTHCARE INFORMATION SYSTEMS AND THE INHERENT LACK OF CONTROLS

The goal of today's healthcare organizations' information systems is open, interoperable, standards-compliant, and secure information systems. Unfortunately, this goal does not accurately reflect the state of healthcare's information systems today. We have some very real challenges to understand and overcome.

To begin, the healthcare industry has built information systems without the sufficient granularity required to adequately protect the information for which we are custodians. Many of the existing systems require no more than a three-character log-on ID; some have passwords that are shared by all users; and most have not implemented the appropriate classification of access controls for the jobs that users perform. One healthcare organization realized that their junior claims examiners were authorizing liposuction procedures, which ordinarily are not reimbursed. However, due to a lack of granularity, the junior examiners had the same privileges as the more senior personnel, and thus, the ability to perform inappropriate actions.

Because of this lack of appropriate controls, healthcare companies have recently come to the realization that they will have to invest in retrofitting security in order to be compliant with federal regulations. Not only will they be forced to expend incremental resources in this effort, but they lose the opportunity to utilize those resources for new application development.

Unfortunately, we don't see much of an improvement in many of the commercial product offerings on the market today. Consistently, from operating systems to off-the-shelf applications, too many new products lack sufficient controls. Products from large companies, with wide deployment, such as the Windows NT operating system or the Peoplesoft application, are not built to be compliant with best practices or generally accepted system-security principles. This is poor testimony to the quality of software today. In fact, many security practitioners find it unsettling to get blank stares from their vendor representatives when they ask whether the product has the most basic of controls. Worse yet is the null response security managers receive when they ask the vendor whether or not the manufacturers have a strategy for compliance with federal regulations.

There is no doubt that along with other industries, the healthcare industry must begin to collaborate with product vendors, to ensure that new products are built and implemented by default in a secure manner.

THE CHALLENGES THE HEALTHCARE ORGANIZATION FACES, VIS À VIS ITS INFORMATION SYSTEMS

Another challenge facing organizations today is the pressure of keeping their networked resources open and closed at the same time, a security paradox of doing electronic commerce. Healthcare companies are forced to allow their insecure systems to be accessible to outside constituencies, trading partners, vendors, and members. In these situations, more robust authentication and access controls are mandatory, especially for those users who are not employees of the company. To exacerbate the challenge, the security manager has to reconcile decisions vis à vis the correct balance between access and security, especially with regard to requests for access to internal resources by external trading partners. Questions plaguing the healthcare organization include: "Should an employer have a right to see the patient-identifiable data on their employees?" For example, if a healthcare company is custodian of John Smith's medical records, and John drives a dynamite truck, should the health plan acquiesce to the employer if John's medical records indicate he has epileptic seizures? Should the employer only have this right if the safety of the public is at risk? Should the employer have access only with John's permission? The answers to these dilemmas are not clear today. Thus, health plans struggle with the overriding challenge of maintaining confidentiality of patient information, while providing reasonable access to it. Further, this balance of access and security has to be maintained across a broadly diverse infrastructure of disparate platforms and applications.

Also, there are other business partners that consistently request access to internal resources, e.g., fulfillment houses, marketing organizations, pharmacy companies. Where does it stop? How can it stop — when the competitive imperative for healthcare companies today is providing the ability to connect quickly and meaningfully with business partners and customers to improve the movement and quality of information and services.

Then, of course, there is the new frontier, the Internet, and the challenges that new technologies present. Organizations tread lightly at first, opening up their networks to the Internet by providing the ability for their employees to surf the Web. It wasn't long before they discovered that if an employee using a company computer on company premises downloads pornographic materials, another of their employees could sue the company for sexual harassment. Once the barn door is open, however, it's hard to get the horses back in. Health plans faced increasing demand to accommodate electronic commerce. Surprisingly, the industry that, until very recently, considered sending files on a diskette the definition for electronic data interchange, rapidly found that they were losing membership because employers' benefits administrators were refusing to do business with plans that could not support file transfers over the Internet.

Of course, when the healthcare organization opens its kimono to the Internet, it introduces a multitude of threats to its internal network. Although most organizations implemented perimeter security with the installation of firewalls, business demands forced them to open holes in the defensive device, to allow certain types of inbound and outbound traffic. For example, one health plan encouraged its employees to enroll in courses offered on the Internet which required opening a specific port on the firewall and allowing traffic to and from the university's Internet address. In another instance, a health plan employee needed access to a nonprofit entity's Web site in order to perform Webmaster activities. In order to accomplish this, the employee utilized a service through the Internet, requiring access through the firewall. Thus, the firewall slowly becomes like Swiss cheese, full of holes. Ergo, health plans have the challenge of engaging in business with external partners while *effectively* managing the firewall.

More challenging than managing external connectivity is the security manager's task of hiring security practitioners with the necessary skills and knowledge to effectively manage the firewall. These individuals must have experience managing UNIX systems, since most firewalls are built on a UNIX operating system; must know how the Internet protocols such as file transfer protocol (FTP) work through the firewall; and must have the expertise to monitor network router devices and know how to write rules for those devices, in order to accommodate business requirements while protecting the enterprise. On the other hand, as healthcare organizations seek to outsource networked resources, for example, Web sites and firewalls, the security manager must be able to provide sufficient monitoring and security oversight, to ensure that the outsourcer is meeting its contractual obligations.

It's no wonder that insurance companies are offering a myriad of secure-systems insurance programs. Cigna Insurance, for example, recently developed a program to offer insurance policies of up to $25 million in liability per loss, reflecting the realization that companies are not only more reliant on information systems, but with the introduction of the Internet, the risk is that much greater.

THE OBSTACLES THAT HEALTHCARE COMPANIES MUST OVERCOME IN ORDER TO IMPLEMENT CONSUMER-CENTRIC SYSTEMS IN AN ENVIRONMENT OF CONSUMER DISTRUST OF BOTH THE HEALTHCARE INDUSTRY AND THE TECHNOLOGY

In this competitive industry, the healthcare organization's mandate is to increase customer intimacy while decreasing operational costs; grant external access to internal data and applications, while most existing applications don't have the appropriate controls in place; and secure the new technologies, especially for third-party access. With all of these issues to resolve, health plans are turning toward Web-based solutions, utilizing public key encryption and digital certificate technologies. But even though health plans have the motivation to move into the Internet mainstream, there are obstacles to overcome that have, for now, slowed the adoption of Web technologies.

First, there are technological weaknesses in the Internet infrastructure. Most organizations have service-level agreements for their internal resources, which guarantee to their employees and customers a certain level of availability and response time. In the Internet space, no one entity is accountable for availability. Also, there are five major electronic junctions where the Internet is extremely vulnerable. When one junction is down, many customers feel the pain of not having reliable service. Since the Internet is not owned or operated by any one person or organization, by its very nature, it cannot be expected to provide the same reliability, availability, and security as a commercial network service provider can. For example, commercial telecommunications companies provide outsourced wide area networks and deploy state of the art communications and security technologies with multiple levels of redundancy and circuitry. The Internet is like a Thomas' English muffin — a maze of nooks and crannies that no one entity controls.

Next, all of the studies show that a large majority of physicians are not comfortable with computers, let alone the Internet. The doctors are ambivalent about adopting information technology, and since there is no control over the content of the information on the net, physicians have been slow to adopt electronic mail communications with their patients on the Internet. They have legitimate concern since there is no positive assurance that we can know exactly who we are communicating with on the Internet. Thus, the healthcare providers distrust the Internet.

They are not the only persons with doubts and concerns. The perception of a lack of security and privacy by consumers is a tremendous challenge for healthcare organizations. Moreover, the media promulgates the paranoia. It's no wonder that consumers are fearful of losing their privacy when publications offer headlines such as "Naked Before the World: Will your Medical Records be safe in a new National Databank?" (*Newsweek* magazine) or "The Death of Privacy: You Have No Secrets." (*Time* magazine).

Therefore, if healthcare organizations are to successfully deploy consumer-intimate Web-based applications, the biggest hurdle they have to overcome is consumer fear, as depicted in the cartoon in Exhibit 17.1.

This consumer fear is not a new phenomenon. For many years, public polls have shown that consumers are increasingly distrustful of organizations that collect their private information. More disconcerting than this,

Exhibit 17.1.

from a healthcare perspective, is that this fear is manifesting itself in negative impacts to the quality of their personal health. More and more, consumers are going out of their local areas to obtain healthcare and lying or holding back information from their healthcare providers, primarily to maintain their sense of privacy and maintain some semblance of confidentiality. This reflects a real disconnect between the consumer and the custodians of the consumer data, the health plan and the doctor.

In early 1999, the Consumers Union, the largest consumer advocacy organization in the United States, sponsored a nationwide survey. They sampled 1000 adults in the U.S. and a separate 1000 adults in California. The survey asked people how willing they were to disclose their personal medical information.

In Exhibit 17.2, we can see that the survey found that although people do concede that persons other than their immediate provider require access to their personal medical records, they display a very strong preference for restricting access. Only four of every ten asked were willing to disclose their medical information to health plans. Roughly six in ten would explicitly refuse to grant access to their information to a hospital, even if the hospital were to offer preventive care programs. Also, consumers are not happy having their employers or potential employers view their personal healthcare information. Most are not willing to offer their information to a potential employer who may be considering them for a job. Further, the

**Percent of respondents willing to disclose
to following parties**

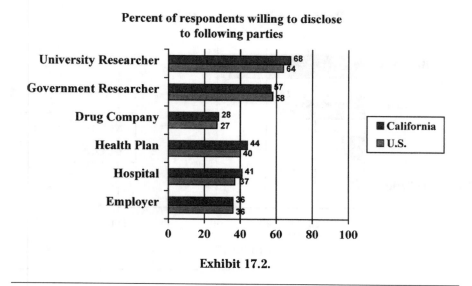

Exhibit 17.2.

drug companies are lowest on the totem pole because Americans do not want their medical data collected for the purposes of marketing new drugs.

In Exhibit 17.3, we see another interesting finding from the survey: most people consider electronic piracy, that is hackers, the biggest threat to their privacy. This is counter to the real threat, which is the disclosure of information by medical personnel, health plans, or other authorized users, but it's not surprising that the average consumer would be very worried about hackers, when we consider how the media exploits attempts by teenagers to hack in to the Pentagon's computers. Moreover, the vendors exacerbate these fears by playing up the evil hacker as they attempt to sell products by instilling fear, uncertainty, and doubt in our hearts and minds.

Exhibit 17.4 shows that most of the survey respondents perceive that if health plans and providers implement security provisions and information security management policies in order to protect medical information, it would make them more inclined to offer their personal information when it was requested. Americans believe that three specific policies should be adopted to safeguard their medical privacy:

1. Impose fines and punishments for violations
2. Require an individual's specific permission to release personal information
3. Establish security systems with security technologies, such as passwords and encryption

Perceived Threats to Privacy

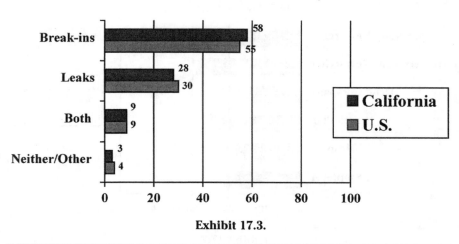

Exhibit 17.3.

Safeguards Rated as Very Effective to Protect Privacy

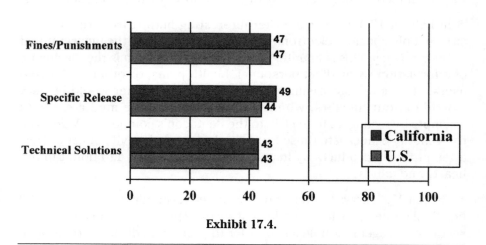

Exhibit 17.4.

Further, the survey respondents were very favorable about sending a health plan's Chief Executive Officer to prison in the event of willful or intentional disclosure of medical information.

The Consumers' Union survey also revealed that consumers are aware — they know that their information is stored in computer databases, and they perceive computerization as the greatest threat to their privacy. In fact, more than one-half of the respondents think that the shift from paper records to electronic systems makes it *more* difficult to keep personal medical information private and confidential. This should be of interest to any information systems manager, since computerization really provides more of an opportunity to secure data. However, perception *is* reality. Therefore, the lesson from this survey is threefold:

- Consumers do not trust health plans or providers
- Consumers do not trust computers
- Consumers will compromise the quality of their healthcare

all in the name of privacy.

This lesson can be an opportunistic one for the health plan security manager. Healthcare can turn those consumer fears around, and win over the public by showing them that health plans take their obligation for due diligence very seriously, and protecting consumer privacy is in perfect alignment with healthcare organizations' internal values.

Case in point: In December 1998, more people purchased goods on the Internet than ever before. The question is why? Price Coopers, the accounting firm, completed a survey early in 1999 which found that the leading factor that would persuade fearful consumers to log on to the Internet was *an assurance of improved privacy protection*. Healthcare can leverage the capabilities of security to garner that public trust. Privacy is not an arcane or a technical issue. It is, however, a major issue with consumers, and there is heightened urgency around healthcare privacy and security today, more so than ever before.

HISTORY REPEATS ITSELF

In 1972, in a similar environment of public distrust, then Department of Health and Human Services Secretary Elliot Richardson appointed an advisory board to assist the federal government in identifying approaches to protect the privacy of information in an ever-evolving computer age. The board issued a report detailing a code of fair information principles, which became the National Privacy Act of 1974.

The act outlines five separate and distinct practices:

Fair Information Privacy Principles
- "There must be a way ... to prevent information about a person that was obtained for one purpose from being used or made available for other purposes without that person's consent.
- There must be no personal data record-keeping systems whose very existence is secret.
- There must be a way for a person to correct or amend a record of identifiable information about that person.

- There must be a way for a person to find out what information about that person is in a record and how it is used.
- Any organization creating, maintaining, using, or disseminating records of identifiable personal data must ensure the reliability of the data for their intended use and must take steps to prevent misuse of the data."

Many bills and proposals concerning privacy of medical information have preceded the most prominent law, the Health Insurance Portability and Accountability Act (HIPAA), enacted in 1996. In 1995, Senator Robert Bennett (R-Utah) sponsored the Medical Records Confidentiality Act, designed to protect the privacy of medical records. Items addressed in the proposed legislation were:

1. Procedures for individuals to examine their medical records and the ability to correct any errors.
2. Identifies persons and entities with access to individually identifiable information as "health information trustees" and defines circumstances under which that information can be released, with or without patient authorization.
3. Establishes federal certification of health information services, which must meet certain requirements to protect identifiable information.
4. Provides both civil and criminal penalties, up to $500,000 and 10 years' imprisonment, for wrongful disclosure of protected information.

It is important to note that Bennett's bill would apply to medical information in any form, as compared to HIPAA legislation, which calls for the protection of *electronic* medical information. Bennett has indicated his resolve and declared his intention to reintroduce his bill, S.2609 in the 106th Congress in 1999.

Heightened interest in patient rights, sparked partially by tragic stories of individuals who died due to delays in medical treatment, led Senate Democratic Leader Tom Daschle to introduce the Patients' Bill of Rights in March of 1998. This law would guarantee patients greater access to information and necessary care, including access to needed specialists and emergency rooms, guarantee a fair appeals process when health plans deny care, expand choice, protect the doctor–patient relationship, and hold HMOs accountable for decisions that end up harming patients. Daschle's bill also:

- Requires plans and issuers to establish procedures to safeguard the privacy of any individually identifiable enrollee information.
- Maintains records and information in an accurate and timely manner.
- Assures the individual's timely access to such records and information.

Additionally, other organizations committed to strong privacy legislation, such as the Electronic Privacy Information Center (EPIC), have proposed multiple versions of similar bills. Most call for stringent controls over medical records. Many go beyond and call for advanced technical controls, including encryption and audit trails which record every access to every individual.

THE MULTITUDE OF PRIVACY LAWS PROPOSED IN RECENT MONTHS

The federal government, very aware of its citizens' concerns, is answering their outcry with no less than a dozen healthcare privacy laws, proposed in recent congressional sessions. Some of the most publicized are:

- McDermott Bill, a.k.a. "Medical Privacy in the Age of New Technologies Act" — 1997
- Jeffords–Dodd Bill, a.k.a. "Health Care Personal Information Non-Disclosure Act" — 1998
- Senate Bill S.2609, a.k.a. the Bennett Bill. This proposed legislation is important to note because it addresses information in all media, whereas the other bills address the protection of information in electronic format only.
- Kennedy–Kassebaum Bill, a.k.a. the Health Insurance Portability and Accountability Act (HIPAA) — 1996

  "Electronic medical records can give us greater efficiency and lower cost. But those benefits must not come at the cost of loss of privacy. The proposals we are making today will help protect against one kind of threat — the vulnerability of information in electronic formats. Now we need to finish the bigger job and create broader legal protections for the privacy of those records."

  — *The Honorable Donna E. Shalala, 1997*

Kennedy–Kassebaum Bill: Background

Several iterations of congressional hearings occurred where stories were told of citizens suddenly found to be uninsurable because they had changed jobs. These instances of insurance loss led to a plethora of tragic incidents, motivating Senators Edward M. Kennedy (D-Massachusetts) and Nancy Kassebaum (R-Kansas) to propose the legislation known as the Kennedy–Kassebaum Bill, also known as HIPAA. Because approximately two thirds of Americans are insured through their employers, the loss of a job often means the loss of health insurance — thus the justification for the term "portability," enabling individuals to port their health plan coverage to a new job. Legislators took this opportunity to incorporate privacy provisions into the bill, and thus, under HIPAA, the Health Care Financing

Administration (HCFA) has issued a series of proposed rules that are designed to make healthcare plans operate securely and efficiently.

"For the Record": The Report

In 1997, the government-sponsored National Research Council report, "For the Record: Protecting Electronic Health Information," captured the essence of the status of security in the healthcare industry. The report came to several conclusions, which laid the foundation for the call from Congress and the Department of Health and Human Service, to define security standards for the healthcare industry. The report concluded:

1. Improving the quality of healthcare and lowering its cost will rely heavily on the effective and efficient use of information technology; therefore, it is incumbent on the industry to maintain the security, privacy, and confidentiality of medical information while making it available to those entities with a need.
2. Healthcare organizations, including health maintenance organizations (HMOs), insurance companies, and provider groups, must take immediate steps to establish safeguards for the protection of medical information.
3. Vendors have not offered products with inherent protective mechanisms because customers are not demanding them.
4. Individuals must take a more proactive role in demanding that their personally identifiable medical information is protected adequately.
5. Self-regulation has not proven successful; therefore, the state and federal governments must intercede and mandate legislation.
6. Medical information is subject to inadvertent or malicious abuse and disclosure, although the greatest threat to the security of patient healthcare data is the authorized insider.
7. Appropriate protection of sensitive healthcare data relies on both organizational policies and procedures as well as technological countermeasures.

Satisfying these important security and privacy considerations is the basis for the administrative simplification provisions of HIPAA. At last, the healthcare industry is being tasked to heed the cry that the citizenry has voiced for years, "Maintain my privacy and keep my personal, sensitive information private."

HIPAA ADMINISTRATIVE SIMPLIFICATION: SECURITY STANDARDS

The specific rules that apply to security standards that protect healthcare-related information (code set 6 HCPR 1317) were issued August 17, 1998, for public comment. The deadline for comment was October 13, 1998. According to HCFA, the volume of comments received was extraordinary.

Plans and providers cried that implementation of the standards would be onerous and cost-prohibitive. HCFA essentially replied that "security is a cost of doing business" and the deadlines will stand. Those deadlines include adoption of security standards by 2002. Moreover, HIPAA requires Congress to pass comprehensive privacy legislation to protect individual health information by August 1999. If lawmakers fail to meet that deadline, then the responsibility falls to the Secretary of DHHS to promulgate protections by February 2000.

Throwing her full support behind HIPAA security standards, Shalala stated, "When Americans give out their personal health information, they should feel like they're leaving it in good, safe hands. ....Congress must pass a law that requires those who legally receive health information to take real steps to safeguard it."

President Bill Clinton has publicly supported privacy legislation for the healthcare industry since 1993. In a May 1997 speech at Morgan State University, the President reiterated that "technology should not be used to break down the wall of privacy and autonomy that [sic] free citizens are guaranteed in a free society."

Horror stories of inadvertent or malicious use or disclosure of medical information are held closely by healthcare organizations. No corporate officer wants to admit that information has "leaked" from his company. However, there are several publicized war stories in which sensitive patient healthcare information has been disclosed without proper authorization, resulting in misfortune and tragedy. For example, when former tennis star Arthur Ashe was admitted to a hospital due to chest pains, his HIV-positive status was discovered and leaked to the press, causing great embarrassment and strife not only to Ashe and his family, but to the medical institution as well.

In another instance, a claims processor brought her young teenager to work and sat her in front of a terminal to keep her occupied. The daughter accessed a database of patients who had been diagnosed with any number of maladies. The teenager concocted a game whereby she called several of the patients, pretended to be the provider, and misreported the diagnoses. One patient was told he had contracted AIDS. The man committed suicide before he could be told the report was the prank of a mischievous child.

In another instance, a healthcare maintenance employee, undergoing a nasty child custody battle with his wife's sister, gained access to his company's system, where he discovered some sensitive information about his sister-in-law, also covered by the health plan. He revealed this information in court in an attempt to discredit her. She sued the health plan for negligence and won the case.

These scenarios are not as rare as we would like to believe. The existing legal structure in healthcare does not provide for effective control of patient medical information. The federal government recognizes this and has attempted to forcefully impose stringent regulation over the protection of health information.

Under HIPAA, healthcare organizations must develop comprehensive security programs to protect patient-identifiable information or face severe penalties for noncompliance. Industry experts estimate that HIPAA will be the "next Y2K" in terms of resources and level of effort, and that annual healthcare expenditures for information security will increase from $2.2 million to $125 million over the next 3 years.

The HIPAA standards, designed to protect all electronic medical information from inadvertent or intentional improper use or disclosure, include provisions for the adoption of:

1. Organizational and administrative procedures
2. Physical security safeguards
3. Technological security measures

Health plans have until early 2002 to adopt these requirements. Although the intent of the standards should be uniform and consistent across the healthcare industry, considerable interpretation might alter the implementation of the controls from one organization to another. The HIPAA security requirements are outlined below.

1. Organizational and Administrative Procedures

1. Ensure that organizational structures exist to develop and implement an information security program. This formal, senior management-sponsored and supported organizational structure is required so that the mechanisms needed to protect information and computing resources are not overridden by a senior manager from another function, for example, Operations or Development, with their own "agendas" in mind. This requirement also includes the assignment of a Chief Security Officer responsible for establishing and maintaining the information security program. This program's charter should ensure that a standard of due care and due diligence is applied throughout the enterprise to provide an adequate level of assurance for data security (integrity/reliability, privacy/confidentiality, and availability).

2. The Chief Security Officer is responsible for the development of policies to control access to and for the release of, individually identifiable patient healthcare information. The over-arching information security policy should declare the organization's intent to comply with regulations and protect and control the security of its

information assets. Additional policies, standards, and procedures should define varying levels of granularity for the control of the sensitive information. For example, some of the policies may relate to data classification, data destruction, disaster recovery, and business continuity planning.

One of the most important organizational moves that a healthcare organization must make for HIPAA compliance is in appointing a Chief Security Officer (CSO). This person should report at a sufficiently high level in the organization so as to be able to ensure compliance with regulations. Typically, the CSO reports to the Chief Information Officer (CIO) or higher. This function is tasked with establishing the information security program, implementing best practices management techniques, and satisfying legal and regulatory requirements. Healthcare organizations seeking qualified, experienced security officers prefer or require candidates to be certified information system security professionals (CISSPs). This certification is offered solely by the non-profit International Information Systems Security Certification Consortium (ISC²) in Massachusetts. More information about professional certification can be obtained from the organization's Web site at www.isc2.org.

3. The organization is required to establish a security certification review. This is an auditable, technical evaluation establishing the extent to which the system, application, or network meets specified security requirements. The certification should also include testing to ensure that the controls actually work as advertised. It is wise for the organization to define control requirements up front and ensure that they are integrated with the business requirements of a system, application, or network. The certification documentation should include details of those control requirements, as well as how the controls are implemented. HIPAA allows for the certification to be done internally, but, it can also be done by an external agency.

4. Establish policies and procedures for the receipt, storage, processing, and distribution of information. Realizing that information is not maintained solely within the walls of an individual organization, HIPAA calls for an assurance that the information is protected as it traverses outside. For example, an organization should develop a policy that mandates authorization by the business owner prior to sending specific data to a third-party business partner.

5. Develop a contractual agreement with all business partners, ensuring confidentiality and data integrity of exchanged information. This standard may manifest itself in the form of a confidentiality clause for all contractors and consultants, which will bind them to maintain the confidentiality of all information they encounter in the performance of their employment.

6. Ensure access controls that provide for an assurance that only those persons with a need can access specific information. A basic tenet of information security is the "need to know." This standard requires that appropriate access is given only to that information an individual requires in order to perform his job. Organizations should establish procedures so that a business manager "owns" the responsibility for the integrity and confidentiality of the functional information, e.g., Claims, and that this manager authorizes approval for each employee to access said information.

7. Implement personnel security, including clearance policies and procedures. Several organizations have adopted human resources procedures that call for a background check of their employment candidates. This is a good practice and one that is recognized as an HIPAA standard. Employees, consultants, and contractors, who have authorized access to an organization's information assets, have an obligation to treat that information responsibly. A clearance of the employee can guarantee a higher degree of assurance that the organization can entrust that individual with sensitive information.

8. Perform security training for all personnel. Security education and awareness training is probably the most cost-effective security standard an organization can adopt. Information security analyses continually reflect that the greatest risk to the security of information is from the "insider threat."

9. Provide for disaster recovery and business resumption planning for critical systems, applications, and networks.

10. Document policies and procedures for the installation, networking, maintenance, and security testing of all hardware and software.

11. Establish system auditing policies and procedures.

12. Develop termination procedures which ensure that involuntarily terminated personnel are immediately removed from accessing systems and networks and voluntarily terminated personnel are removed from systems and networks in an expedient manner.

13. Document security violation reporting policies and procedures and sanctions for violations.

2. Physical Security Safeguards

1. Establish policies and procedures for the control of media (e.g., disks, tapes), including activity tracking and data backup, storage, and disposal.

2. Secure work stations and implement automatic logout after a specified period of nonuse.

3. Technological Security Measures

1. Assure that sensitive information is altered or destroyed only by authorized personnel.
2. Provide the ability to properly identify and authenticate users.
3. Create audit records whenever users inquire or update records.
4. Provide for access controls that are either transaction-based, role-based, or user-based.
5. Implement controls to ensure that transmitted information has not been corrupted.
6. Implement message authentication to validate that a message is received unchanged.
7. Implement encryption or access controls, including audit trails, entity authentication, and mechanisms for detecting and reporting unauthorized activity in the network.

One of the biggest challenges facing the organizations that must comply with HIPAA security standards is the proper interpretation of the regulation. Some of the standards are hazy at this time, but the fines for noncompliance are well-defined. HIPAA enforcement provisions specify financial and criminal penalties for wrongful disclosure or willful misuse of individually identifiable information at $250,000 and 10 years of imprisonment per incident.

SUMMARY

The reader can see that the security manager in the healthcare industry has an ominous task, and federal regulations make that task an urgent one. However, with the adoption of generally accepted system-security principles and the implementation of best-security practices, it is possible to develop a security program that provides for a reasonable standard of due care, and one that is compliant with regulations.

Domain 4
Application and Systems Development Security

Not very long ago, data access control was accomplished on an organization's mainframe with a centrally invoked and centrally administered access control utility. With the advent of client/server and distributed systems, application security and controls have become as diverse as the multi-tier architectures that house the data.

The chapter in this domain discusses the essence of data protection, that is, the integration and unity of the controls within the application design. The distributed system architecture demands that protection mechanisms be embedded into multiple layers of the system, and the author of this domain assists the practitioner in understanding the mechanics of doing just that.

Domain 4.1
Application Security

Chapter 18
Security Models for Object-Oriented Databases

James Cannady

Object-oriented (OO) methods are a significant development in the management of distributed data. Database design is influenced to an ever-greater degree by OO principles. As more DBMS products incorporate aspects of the object-oriented paradigm, database administrators must tackle the unique security considerations of these systems and understand the emerging security model.

INTRODUCTION

Object-oriented (OO) programming languages and OO analysis and design techniques influence database system design and development. The inevitable result is the object-oriented database management system (OODBMS).

Many of the established database vendors are incorporating OO concepts into their products in an effort to facilitate database design and development in the increasingly OO world of distributed processing. In addition to improving the process of database design and administration, the incorporation of OO principles offers new tools for securing the information stored in the database. This chapter explains the basics of database security, the differences between securing relational and object-oriented systems, and some specific issues related to the security of next-generation OODBMSs.

BASICS OF DATABASE SECURITY

Database security is primarily concerned with the secrecy of data. Secrecy means protecting a database from unauthorized access by users and software applications.

0-8493-9829-0/00/$0.00+$.50
© 2000 by CRC Press LLC

Secrecy, in the context of database security, includes a variety of threats incurred through unauthorized access. These threats range from the intentional theft or destruction of data to the acquisition of information through more subtle measures, such as inference. There are three generally accepted categories of secrecy-related problems in database systems:

1. *The improper release of information from reading data that was intentionally or accidentally accessed by unauthorized users.* Securing databases from unauthorized access is more difficult than controlling access to files managed by operating systems. This problem arises from the finer granularity that is used by databases when handling files, attributes, and values. This type of problem also includes the violations to secrecy that result from the problem of inference, which is the deduction of unauthorized information from the observation of authorized information. Inference is one of the most difficult factors to control in any attempts to secure data. Because the information in a database is semantically related, it is possible to determine the value of an attribute without accessing it directly. Inference problems are most serious in statistical databases where users can trace back information on individual entities from the statistical aggregated data.

2. *The improper modification of data.* This threat includes violations of the security of data through mishandling and modifications by unauthorized users. These violations can result from errors, viruses, sabotage, or failures in the data that arise from access by unauthorized users.

3. *Denial-of-service threats.* Actions that could prevent users from using system resources or accessing data are among the most serious. This threat has been demonstrated to a significant degree recently with the SYN flooding attacks against network service providers.

Discretionary vs. Mandatory Access Control Policies

Both traditional relational database management system (RDBMS) security models and OO database models make use of two general types of access control policies to protect the information in multilevel systems. The first of these policies is the discretionary policy. In the discretionary access control (DAC) policy, access is restricted based on the authorizations granted to the user.

The mandatory access control (MAC) policy secures information by assigning sensitivity levels, or labels, to data entities. MAC policies are generally more secure than DAC policies, and they are used in systems in which security is critical, such as military applications. However, the price that is usually paid for this tightened security is reduced performance of the database management system. Most MAC policies also incorporate DAC measures as well.

SECURING AN RDBMS VS. AN OODBMS: KNOW THE DIFFERENCES

The development of secure models for OODBMSs has obviously followed on the heels of the development of the databases themselves. The theories that are currently being researched and implemented in the security of OO databases are also influenced heavily by the work that has been conducted on secure relational database management systems.

Relational DBMS Security

The principal methods of security in traditional RDBMSs are through the appropriate use and manipulation of views and the structured query language (SQL) GRANT and REVOKE statements. These measures are reasonably effective because of their mathematical foundation in relational algebra and relational calculus.

View-Based Access Control. Views allow the database to be conceptually divided into pieces in ways that allow sensitive data to be hidden from unauthorized users. In the relational model, views provide a powerful mechanism for specifying data-dependent authorizations for data retrieval.

Although the individual user who creates a view is the owner and is entitled to drop the view, he or she may not be authorized to execute all privileges on it. The authorizations that the owner may exercise depend on the view semantics and on the authorizations that the owner is allowed to implement on the tables directly accessed by the view. For the owner to exercise a specific authorization on a view that he or she creates, the owner must possess the same authorization on all tables that the view uses. The privileges the owner possesses on the view are determined at the time of view definition. Each privilege the owner possesses on the tables is defined for the view. If, later on, the owner receives additional privileges on the tables used by the view, these additional privileges will not be passed on to the view. In order to use the new privileges within a view, the owner will need to create a new view.

The biggest problem with view-based mandatory access control is that it is impractical to verify that the software performs the view interpretation and processing. If the correct authorizations are to be assured, the system must contain some type of mechanism to verify the classification of the sensitivity of the information in the database. The classification must be done automatically, and the software that handles the classification must be trusted. However, any trusted software for the automatic classification process would be extremely complex. Furthermore, attempting to use a query language such as SQL to specify classifications quickly becomes convoluted and complex.

Even when the complexity of the classification scheme is overcome, the view can do nothing more than limit what the user sees — it cannot restrict the operations that may be performed on the views.

GRANT and REVOKE Privileges. Although view mechanisms are often regarded as security "freebies" because they are included within SQL and most other traditional relational database managers, views are not the sole mechanism for relational database security. GRANT and REVOKE statements allow users to selectively and dynamically grant privileges to other users and subsequently revoke them if necessary. These two statements are considered to be the principal user interfaces in the authorization subsystem.

There is, however, a security-related problem inherent in the use of the GRANT statement. If a user is granted rights without the GRANT option, he should not be able to pass GRANT authority on to other users. However, the system can be subverted by a user by simply making a complete copy of the relation. Because the user creating the copy is now the owner, he can provide GRANT authority to other users. As a result, unauthorized users are able to access the same information that had been contained in the original relation. Although this copy is not updated with the original relation, the user making the copy could continue making similar copies of the relation, and continue to provide the same data to other users.

The REVOKE statement functions similarly to the GRANT statement, with the opposite result. One of the characteristics of the use of the REVOKE statement is that it has a cascading effect. When the rights previously granted to a user are subsequently revoked, all similar rights are revoked for all users who may have been provided access by the originator.

Other Relational Security Mechanisms. Although views and GRANT/REVOKE statements are the most frequently used security measures in traditional RDBMSs, they are not the only mechanisms included in most security systems using the relational model. Another security method used with traditional relational database managers, which is similar to GRANT/REVOKE statements, is the use of query modification.

This method involves modifying a user's query before the information is retrieved, based on the authorities granted to the user. Although query modification is not incorporated within SQL, the concept is supported by the Cobb–Date relational database model.

Most relational database management systems also rely on the security measures present in the operating system of the host computer. Traditional RDMBSs such as DB2 work closely with the operating system to ensure that the database security system is not circumvented by permitting access to data through the operating system. However, many operating systems provide insufficient security. In addition, because of the portability of many newer database packages, the security of the operating system should not be assumed to be adequate for the protection of the wealth of information in a database.

Object-Oriented DBMS Characteristics

Unlike traditional RDBMSs, secure OODBMSs have certain characteristics that make them unique. Furthermore, only a limited number of security models have been designed specifically for OO databases. The proposed security models make use of the concepts of encapsulation, inheritance, information-hiding, methods, and the ability to model real-world entities that are present in OO environments.

The object-oriented database model also permits the classification of an object's sensitivity through the use of class (of entities) and instance. When an instance of a class is created, the object can automatically inherit the level of sensitivity of the superclass. Although the ability to pass classifications through inheritance is possible in object-oriented databases, class instances are usually classified at a higher level within the object's class hierarchy. This prevents a flow control problem, where information passes from higher to lower classification levels.

OODBMSs also use unique characteristics that allow these models to control the access to the data in the database. They incorporate features such as flexible data structure, inheritance, and late binding. Access control models for OODBMSs must be consistent with such features. Users can define methods, some of which are open for other users as public methods. Moreover, the OODBMS may encapsulate a series of basic access commands into a method and make it public for users, while keeping basic commands themselves away from users.

Proposed OODBMS Security Models

Currently only a few models use discretionary access control measures in secure object-oriented database management systems.

Explicit Authorizations. The ORION authorization model permits access to data on the basis of explicit authorizations provided to each group of users. These authorizations are classified as positive authorizations because they specifically allow a user access to an object. Similarly, a negative authorization is used to specifically deny a user access to an object.

The placement of an individual into one or more groups is based on the role that the individual plays in the organization. In addition to the positive authorizations that are provided to users within each group, there are a variety of implicit authorizations that may be granted based on the relationships between subjects and access modes.

Data-Hiding Model. A similar discretionary access control secure model is the data-hiding model proposed by Dr. Elisa Bertino of the Universita di Genova. This model distinguishes between public methods and private methods.

The data-hiding model is based on authorizations for users to execute methods on objects. The authorizations specify which methods the user is authorized to invoke. Authorizations can only be granted to users on public methods. However, the fact that a user can access a method does not automatically mean that the user can execute all actions associated with the method. As a result, several access controls may need to be performed during the execution, and all of the authorizations for the different accesses must exist if the user is to complete the processing.

Similar to the use of GRANT statements in traditional relational database management systems, the creator of an object is able to grant authorizations to the object to different users. The "creator" is also able to revoke the authorizations from users in a manner similar to REVOKE statements. However, unlike traditional RDBMS GRANT statements, the data-hiding model includes the notion of protection mode. When authorizations are provided to users in the protection mode, the authorizations actually checked by the system are those of the creator and not the individual executing the method. As a result, the creator is able to grant a user access to a method without granting the user the authorizations for the methods called by the original method. In other words, the creator can provide a user access to specific data without being forced to give the user complete access to all related information in the object.

Other DAC Models for OODBMS Security. Rafiul Ahad has proposed a similar model that is based on the control of function evaluations. Authorizations are provided to groups or individual users to execute specific methods. The focus in Ahad's model is to protect the system by restricting access to the methods in the database, not the objects. The model uses proxy functions, specific functions, and guard functions to restrict the execution of certain methods by users and enforce content-dependent authorizations.

Another secure model that uses authorizations to execute methods has been presented by Joel Richardson. This model has some similarity to the data-hiding model's use of GRANT/REVOKE-type statements. The creator of an object can specify which users may execute the methods within the object.

A final authorization-dependent model emerging from OODBMS security research has been proposed by Dr. Eduardo B. Fernandez of Florida Atlantic University. In this model the authorizations are divided into positive and negative authorizations. The Fernandez model also permits the creation of new authorizations from those originally specified by the user through the use of the semantic relationships in the data.

Dr. Naftaly H. Minsky of Rutgers University has developed a model that limits unrestricted access to objects through the use of a view mechanism similar to that used in traditional relational database management systems. Minsky's concept is to provide multiple interfaces to the objects within the database. The model includes a list of laws, or rules, that govern the access constraints to the objects. The laws within the database specify which actions must be taken by the system when a message is sent from one object to another. The system may allow the message to continue unaltered, block the sending of the message, send the message to another object, or send a different message to the intended object.

Although the discretionary access control models do provide varying levels of security for the information within the database, none of the DAC models effectively addresses the problem of the authorizations provided to users. A higher level of protection within a secure OO database model is provided through the use of mandatory access control.

MAC Methods for OODBMS Security. Dr. Bhavani Thuraisingham of MITRE Corp. proposed in 1989 a mandatory security policy called SORION. This model extends the ORION model to encompass mandatory access control. The model specifies subjects, objects, and access modes within the system, and it assigns security/sensitivity levels to each entity. Certain properties regulate the assignment of the sensitivity levels to each of the subjects, objects, and access modes. In order to gain access to the instance variables and methods in the objects, certain properties that are based on the various sensitivity levels must be satisfied.

A similar approach has been proposed in the Millen–Lunt model. This model, developed by Jonathan K. Millen of MITRE Corp. and Teresa Lunt of SRI/DARPA (Defense Advanced Research Projects Agency), also uses the assignment of sensitivity levels to the objects, subjects, and access modes within the database. In the Millen–Lunt model, the properties that regulate the access to the information are specified as axioms within the model. This model further attempts to classify information according to three different cases:

- The data itself is classified.
- The existence of the data is classified.
- The reason for classifying the information is also classified.

These three classifications broadly cover the specifics of the items to be secured within the database; however, the classification method also greatly increases the complexity of the system.

The SODA Model. Dr. Thomas F. Keefe of Pennsylvania State University proposes a model called Secure Object-Oriented Data Base (SODA). The SODA model was one of the first models to address the specific concepts in the OO paradigm. It is often used as a standard example of secure object-oriented models to which other models are compared.

The SODA model complies with MAC properties and is executed in a multilevel security system. SODA assigns classification levels to the data through the use of inheritance. However, multiple inheritance is not supported in the SODA model.

Similar to other secure models, SODA assigns security levels to subjects in the system and sensitivity levels to objects. The security classifications of subjects are checked against the sensitivity level of the information before access is allowed.

Polyinstantiation. Unlike many current secure object-oriented models, SODA allows the use of polyinstantiation as a solution to the multiparty update conflict. This problem arises when users with different security levels attempt to use the same information. The variety of clearances and sensitivities in a secure database system result in conflicts between the objects that can be accessed and modified by the users.

Through the use of polyinstantiation, information is located in more than one location, usually with different security levels. Obviously, the more sensitive information is omitted from the instances with lower security levels.

Although polyinstantiation solves the multiparty update conflict problem, it raises a potentially greater problem in the form of ensuring the integrity of the data within the database. Without some method of simultaneously updating all occurrences of the data in the database, the integrity of the information quickly disappears. In essence, the system becomes a collection of several distinct database systems, each with its own data.

CONCLUSION

The move to object-oriented DBMSs is likely to continue for the foreseeable future. Because of the increasing need for security in distributed processing environments, the expanded selection of tools available for securing information in this environment should be used fully to ensure that the data is as secure as possible. In addition, with the continuing dependence on distributed data the security of these systems must be fully integrated into existing and future network security policies and procedures.

The techniques that are ultimately used to secure commercial OODBMS implementations will depend in large part on the approaches promoted by the leading database vendors. However, the applied research that has been conducted to date is also laying the groundwork for the security components that will in turn be incorporated in the commercial OODBMSs.

Domain 5
Cryptography

The science of cryptography is complex and can be difficult to comprehend for those taking the certification examination. The chapters in this domain assist the reader in appreciating the intricacies of encryption technologies.

From symmetric to asymmetric to elliptical curve, encryption methodologies enable the protection of information, especially as it traverses traditionally unsafe waters, e.g., the Internet.

The chapters in this domain extend from the basics of cryptography to the details of public key infrastructure or PKI. Security practitioners will benefit from these chapters as the demand for encryption technologies and digital certificates becomes widespread.

Domain 5.1
Crypto Technology and Implementations

Chapter 19
Fundamentals of Cryptography and Encryption

Ronald A. Gove

This chapter presents an overview of some basic ideas underlying encryption technology. The chapter begins by defining some basic terms and follows with a few historical notes so the reader can appreciate the long tradition that encryption, or secret writing, has had. The chapter then moves into modern cryptography and presents some of the underlying mathematical and technological concepts behind private and public key encryption systems such as DES and RSA. We will provide an extensive discussion of conventional private key encryption prior to introducing the concept of public key cryptography. We do this for both historical reasons (private key did come first) and technical reasons (public key can be considered a partial solution to the key management problem).

SOME BASIC DEFINITIONS

We begin our discussion by defining some terms that will be used throughout the chapter. The first term is *encryption*. In simplest terms, encryption is the process of making information unreadable by unauthorized persons. The process may be manual, mechanical, or electronic, and the core of this chapter is to describe the many ways that the encryption process takes place. Encryption is to be distinguished from message-hiding. Invisible inks, microdots, and the like are the stuff of spy novels and are used in the trade; however, we will not spend any time discussing these techniques for hiding information. Exhibit 19.1 shows a conceptual version of an encryption system. It consists of a sender and a receiver, a message (called the "plain text"), the encrypted message (called the "cipher text"), and an item called a "key." The encryption process, which transforms the plain text into the cipher text, may be thought of as a "black box." It takes inputs (the plain text and key) and produces output (the cipher text). The

0-8493-9829-0/00/$0.00+$.50
© 2000 by CRC Press LLC

messages may be handwritten characters, electromechanical representations as in a Teletype, strings of 1s and 0s as in a computer or computer network, or even analog speech. The black box will be provided with whatever input/output devices it needs to operate; the insides, or cryptographic algorithm will, generally, operate independently of the external representation of the information.

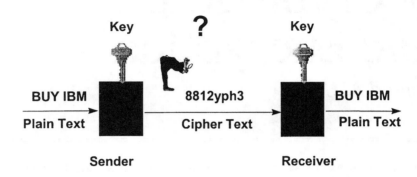

Exhibit 19.1. Conceptual Version of an Encryption System

The *key* is used to select a specific instance of the encryption process embodied in the machine. It is more properly called the "*cryptovariable.*" The use of the term "key" is a holdover from earlier times. We will discuss cryptovariables (keys) in more detail in later sections. It is enough at this point to recognize that the cipher text depends on both the plain text and the cryptovariable. Changing either of the inputs will produce a different cipher text. In typical operation, a cryptovariable is inserted prior to encrypting a message and the same key is used for some period of time. This period of time is known as a "cryptoperiod." For reasons having to do with cryptanalysis, the key should be changed on a regular basis. The most important fact about the key is that it embodies the security of the encryption system. By this we mean the system is designed so that complete knowledge of all system details, including specific plain and cipher text messages, is not sufficient to derive the cryptovariable.

It is important that the system be designed in this fashion because the encryption process itself is seldom secret. The details of the data encryption standard (DES), for example, are widely published so that anyone may implement a DES-compliant system. In order to provide the intended secrecy in the cipher text, there has to be some piece of information that is not available to those who are not authorized to receive the message; this piece of information is the cryptovariable, or key.

Inside the black box is an implementation of an algorithm that performs the encryption. Exactly how the algorithm works is the main topic of this chapter, and the details depend on the technology used for the message.

Cryptography is the study of the means to do encryption. Thus cryptographers design encryption systems. Cryptanalysis is the process of figuring out the message without knowledge of the cryptovariable (key), or more generally, figuring out which key was used to encrypt a whole series of messages.

SOME HISTORICAL NOTES

The reader is referred to Kahn[1] for a well-written history of this subject. We note that the first evidence of cryptography occurred over 4000 years ago in Egypt. Almost as soon as writing was invented, we had secret writing. In India, the ancients' version of Dr. Ruth's Guide to Good Sex, the *Kama-Sutra,* places secret writing as 45th in a list of arts women should know. The Arabs in the 7th century AD were the first to write down methods of cryptanalysis. Historians have discovered a text dated about 855 AD that describes cipher alphabets for use in magic.

One of the better known of the ancient methods of encryption is the Caesar Cipher, so called because Julius Caesar used it. The Caesar Cipher is a simple alphabetic substitution. In a Caesar Cipher, each plain text letter is replaced by the letter 3 letters away to the right. For example, the letter A is replaced by D, B by E, and so forth. (See Exhibit 19.2, where the plain-text alphabet is in lower case and the cipher text is in upper case.)

a b c d e f g h i j k l m n o p q r s t u v w x y z

D E F G H I J K L M N O P Q R S T U V W X Y Z A B C

Plain text: Omnia Gallia est divisa in partes tres … .

Cipher Text: RPQLD JDOOLD HVW GLYLVD LQ SDUWHV WUHV …

Exhibit 19.2. The Caesar Cipher

Caesar's Cipher is a form of a more general algorithm known as monoalphabetic substitution. While Julius Caesar always used an offset of 3, in principal one can use any offset, from one to 25. (An offset of 26 is the original alphabet.) The value of the offset is in fact the cryptovariable for this simplest of all monoalphabetic substitutions. All such ciphers with any offset are now called Caesar Ciphers.

There are many ways to produce alphabetic substitution ciphers. In fact, there are 26! (26 factorial or 26X25X24 . . . X2X1) ways to arrange the 26 letters of the alphabet. All but one of these yields a nonstandard alphabet. Using a different alphabet for each letter according to some well-defined rule can make a more complicated substitution. Such ciphers are called polyalphabetic substitutions.

Cryptography underwent many changes through the centuries often following closely with advances in technology. When we wrote by hand, encryption was purely manual. After the invention of the printing press various mechanical devices appeared such as Leon Batista Alberti's cipher disk in Italy. In the 18th century, Thomas Jefferson invented a ciphering device consisting of a stack of 26 disks each containing the alphabet around the face of the edge. Each disk had the letters arranged in a different order. A positioning bar was attached that allowed the user to align the letters along a row. To use the device, one spelled out the message by moving each disk so that the proper letter lay along the alignment bar. The bar was then rotated a fixed amount (the cryptovariable for that message) and the letters appearing along the new position of the bar were copied off as the cipher text. The receiver could then position the cipher text letters on his "wheel" and rotate the cylinder until the plain text message appeared.

By World War II very complex electromechanical devices were in use by the Allied and Axis forces. The stories of these devices can be found in many books such as Hodges.[2] The need for a full-time, professional cryptographic force was recognized during and after WWII and led to the formation of the National Security Agency by Presidential memorandum signed by Truman. See Bamford[3] for a history of the NSA.

Except for a few hobbyists, cryptography was virtually unknown outside of diplomatic and military circles until the mid-seventies. During this period, as the use of computers, particularly by financial institutions, became more widespread, the need arose for a "public," (non-military or diplomatic) cryptographic system. In 1973 the National Bureau of Standards (now the National Institute of Standards and Technology) issued a request for proposals for a standard cryptographic algorithm. They received no suitable response at that time and reissued the request in 1974. IBM responded to the second request with their Lucifer system, which they had been developing for their own use. This algorithm was evaluated with the help of the NSA and eventually was adopted as the Data Encryption Standard (DES) in 1976. See Federal Information Processing Standard NBS FIPS PUB 46.

The controversy surrounding the selection of DES[4] stimulated academic interest in cryptography and cryptanalysis. This interest led to the discovery of many cryptanalytic techniques and eventually to the concept of public key cryptography. Public key cryptography is a technique that uses distinct keys for encryption and decryption, only one of which need be secret. We will discuss this technique later in this chapter, as public key cryptography is more understandable once one has a firm understanding of conventional cryptography.

The 20 years since the announcement of DES and the discovery of public key cryptography have seen advances in computer technology and networking that were not even dreamed of in 1975. The Internet has created a demand for instantaneous information exchange in the military, government, and most importantly, private sectors that is without precedent. Our economic base, the functioning of our government, and our military effectiveness are more dependent on automated information systems than any country in the world. However, the very technology that created this dependence is its greatest weakness: the infrastructure is fundamentally vulnerable to attacks from individuals, groups, or nation-states that can easily deny service or compromise the integrity of information. The users of the Internet, especially those with economic interests, have come to realize that effective cryptography is a necessity.

THE BASICS OF MODERN CRYPTOGRAPHY

Since virtually all of modern cryptography is based on the use of digital computers and digital algorithms, we begin with a brief introduction to digital technology and binary arithmetic. All information in a computer is reduced to a representation as 1s and 0s. (Or the "on" and "off" state of an electronic switch.) All of the operations within the computer can be reduced to logical OR, EXCLUSIVE OR, and AND. Arithmetic in the computer (called binary arithmetic) obeys the rules shown in Exhibit 19.3 (represented by "addition" and "multiplication" tables):

$\oplus$	0	1		$\otimes$	0	1
0	0	1		0	0	0
1	1	0		1	0	1

Exhibit 19.3. Binary Arithmetic Rules

The symbol $\oplus$ is called modulo 2 addition and $\otimes$ is called modulo 2 multiplication. If we consider the symbol '1' as representing a logical value of TRUE and '0' as the logical value FALSE then $\oplus$ is equivalent to exclusive OR in logic (XOR) while $\otimes$ is equivalent to AND. For example, A XOR B is true only if A or B is TRUE but not both. Likewise, A AND B is true only when both A and B are TRUE.

All messages, both plain text and cipher text, may be represented by strings of 1s and 0s. The actual method used to digitize the message is not relevant to an understanding of cryptography so we will not discuss the details here.

We will consider two main classes of cryptographic algorithms:

- Stream Ciphers — which operate on essentially continuous streams of plain text, represented as 1s and 0s
- Block Ciphers — which operate on blocks of plain text of fixed size.

These two divisions overlap in that a block cipher may be operated as a stream cipher. Generally speaking, stream ciphers tend be implemented more in hardware devices, while block ciphers are more suited to implementation in software to execute on a general-purpose computer. Again, these guidelines are not absolute, and there are a variety of operational reasons for choosing one method over another.

STREAM CIPHERS

We illustrate a simple stream cipher in the table below and in Exhibit 19.4. Here the plain text is represented by a sequence of 1s and 0s. (The binary streams are to be read from right to left. That is, the right-most bit is the first bit in the sequence.) A keystream[5] generator produces a "random" stream of 1s and 0s that are added modulo 2, bit by bit, to the plain-text stream to produce the cipher-text stream.

The cryptovariable (key) is shown as entering the keystream generator. We will explain the nature of these cryptovariables later. There are many different mechanisms to implement the keystream generator, and the reader is referred to Schneier[6] for many more examples. In general, we may represent the internal operation as consisting of a finite state machine and a complex function. The finite state machine consists of a system state and a function (called the "next state" function) that cause the system to change state based on certain input.

The complex function operates on the system state to produce the keystream. Exhibit 19.5 shows the encryption operation. The decryption operation is equivalent; just exchange the roles of plain text and cipher text. This works because of the following relationships in modulo two addition: Letting p represent a plain-text bit, k a keystream bit, and c the cipher text bit

$$c = p \oplus k,$$

so, $\quad c \oplus k = (p \oplus k) \oplus k = p \oplus (k \oplus k) = p \oplus 0 = p,$

since in binary arithmetic $x \oplus x$ is always 0. ($1 \oplus 1 = 0 \oplus 0 = 0$).

Plain Text:	1	0	1	1	0	1	1	0	0
	⊕	⊕	⊕	⊕	⊕	⊕	⊕	⊕	⊕
Keystream	1	1	0	1	0	0	0	1	1
Cipher Text	0	1	1	0	0	1	1	1	1

Exhibit 19.4.   Stream Cipher

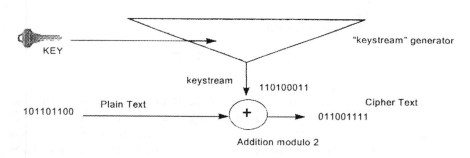

Exhibit 19.5.   Stream Ciphers

These concepts are best understood with examples. Exhibit 19.6 shows a simple linear feedback shift register (LFSR). A LFSR is one of the simplest finite state machines and is used as a building block for many stream ciphers (see Schneier's text). In Exhibit 19.6, the four-stage register (shown here filled with 1s) represents the state. During operation, at each tick of the internal clock, the 4 bits shift to the right (the right-most bit is dropped), and the last 2 bits (before the shift) are added (mod 2) and placed in the left-most stage. In general, an LFSR may be of any length, n, and any of the individual stages may be selected for summing and insertion into the left-most stage. The only constraint is that the right-most bit should always be one of the bits selected for the feedback sum. Otherwise, the length is really n − 1, not n. Exhibit 19.6 shows the sequence of system states obtained from the initial value of 1111. In some systems, the initial value of the register is part of the cryptovariable.

Note that if we started the sequence with 0000, then all subsequent states would be 0000. This would not be good for cryptographic applications since the output would be constant. Thus the all-0 state is avoided. Note also that this four-stage register steps through $15 = 2^4 − 1$ distinct

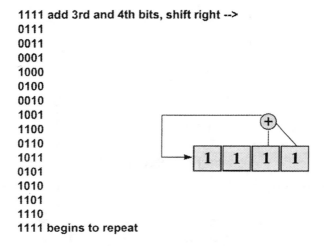

1111 add 3rd and 4th bits, shift right -->
0111
0011
0001
1000
0100
0010
1001
1100
0110
1011
0101
1010
1101
1110
1111 begins to repeat

Exhibit 19.6.   Simple LFSR

states before repeating. Not all configurations of feedback will produce such a maximal sequence. If we number the stages in Exhibit 19.6 from left to right as 1,2,3,4, and instead of feeding back the sum of stages 3 and 4 we selected 2 and 4, then we would see a very different sequence. This example would produce 2 sequences (we call them cycles) of length 6, one cycle of length 3, and 1 of length 0. For example, starting with 1111 as before will yield:

$$1111 \to 0111 \to 0011 \to 1001 \to 1100 \to 1110 \to 1111$$

It is important to have as many states as possible produced by the internal state machine of the keystream generator. The reason is to avoid repeating the keystream. Once the keystream begins to repeat, the same plain text will produce the same cipher text. This is a cryptographic weakness and should be avoided. While one could select any single stage of the LFSR and use it as the keystream, this is not a good idea. The reason is that the linearity of the sequence of stages allows a simple cryptanalysis. We can avoid the linearity by introducing some more complexity into the system. The objective is to produce a keystream that looks completely random.[7] That is, the keystream will pass as many tests of statistical randomness as one cares to apply. The most important test is that knowledge of the algorithm and knowledge of a sequence of successive keystream bits does not allow a cryptanalyst to predict the next bit in the sequence. The complexity can often be introduced by using some nonlinear polynomial $f(a_1, a_2, ..., a_m)$ of a selection of the individual stages of the LFSR. Nonlinear means that some of the terms are multiplied together such as $a_1a_2 + a_3a_4 + ...a_{m-1}a_m$. The selection of which register stages are

346

associated with which inputs to the polynomial can be part of the crypto-variable (key). The reader is encouraged to refer to texts such as Schneier[6] for examples of specific stream-cipher implementations. Another technique for introducing complexity is to use multiple LFSRs and to select output alternately from each based on some pseudorandom process. For example, one might have three LFSRs and create the keystream by selecting bits from one of the two, based on the output of a third.

Some of the features that a cryptographer will design into the algorithm for a stream cipher include:

1. Long periods without a repetition.
2. Functional complexity — each keystream bit should depend on most or all of the cryptovariable bits.
3. Statistically unpredictable — given n successive bits from the keystream it is not possible to predict the $n + 1^{st}$ bit with a probability different from $\frac{1}{2}$.
4. The keystream should be statistically unbiased — there should be as many 0s as 1s, as many 00s as 10s, 01s, and 11s, etc.
5. The keystream should not be linearly related to the cryptovariable.

We also note that in order to send and receive messages encrypted with a stream cipher the sending and receiving systems must satisfy several conditions. First, the sending and receiving equipment must be using identical algorithms for producing the keystream. Second, they must have the same cryptovariable. Third, they must start in the same state; and fourth, they must know where the message begins.

The first condition is trivial to satisfy. The second condition, ensuring that the two machines have the same cryptovariable, is an administrative problem (called key management) that we will discuss in a later section. We can ensure that the two devices start in the same state by several means. One way is to include the initial state as part of the cryptovariable. Another way is to send the initial state to the receiver at the beginning of each message. (This is sometimes called a message indicator, or initial vector.) A third possibility is to design the machines to always default to a specific state. Knowing where the beginning of the message is can be a more difficult problem, and various messaging protocols use different techniques.

BLOCK CIPHERS

A block cipher operates on blocks of text of fixed size. The specific size is often selected to correspond to the word size in the implementing computer, or to some other convenient reference (e.g., 8-bit ASCII text is conveniently processed by block ciphers with lengths that are multiples of 8 bits). Because the block cipher forms a one-to-one correspondence between input and output blocks it is nothing more or less than a permutation. If the blocks are n bits long, then there are 2^n possible input blocks and 2^n possible output blocks. The relationship between the input and output defines a permutation. There are $(2^n)!$ possible permutations, so theoretically there are $(2^n)!$ possible block cipher systems on n bit blocks.[8]

A simple block cipher on 4-bit blocks is shown in Exhibit 19.7.

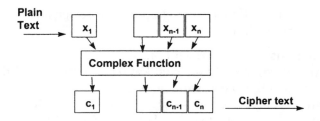

Exhibit 19.7. Block Ciphers

With such a prodigious number of possible block ciphers, one would think it a trivial matter to create one. It is not so easy. First of all, the algorithm has to be easy to describe and implement. Most of the $(2^n)!$ permutations can only be described by listing the entries in a table such as the one in Exhibit 19.8. For a 32-bit block cipher this table would have on the order of $10^{9.6}$ entries, which is quite impractical. Another consideration is that there needs to be a relation between the cryptovariable and the permutation. In most implementations, the cryptovariable selects a specific permutation from a wide class of permutations. Thus one would need as many tables as cryptovariables. We conclude from this that it is not easy to design good block ciphers.

The most well-known block cipher is the Data Encryption Standard, DES. The cryptovariable for DES is 64 bits, 8 of which are parity check bits. Consequently the cryptovariable is effectively 56 bits long. DES operates as follows: a 64-bit plain text block, after going through an initial permutation (which has no cryptographic significance) is split onto left and right halves, L_0 and R_0. These two halves are then processed as follows for i = 0, 1, ..., 15

$$L_i = R_{i-1}$$

$$R_i = L_{i-1} + f(R_{i-1}, K_i).$$

The blocks K_i are derived from the cryptovariable. The function f is a very complex function involving several expansions, compressions, and permutations by means of several fixed tables called the S-boxes and

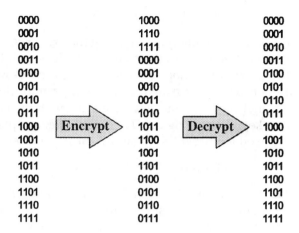

0000	1000	0000
0001	1110	0001
0010	1111	0010
0011	0000	0011
0100	0001	0100
0101	0010	0101
0110	0011	0110
0111	1010	0111
1000	1011	1000
1001	1100	1001
1010	1001	1010
1011	1101	1011
1100	0100	1100
1101	0101	1101
1110	0110	1110
1111	0111	1111

Exhibit 19.8. Simple Block Cipher

P-boxes. The reader is referred to FIPS PUB 46 for a detailed description of the S-boxes and P-boxes.

As was the case with the DES cryptovariable, there has been much discussion about the significance of the S-boxes. Some people have argued that the NSA designed the S-Boxes so as to include a "trap door" that would allow them to decrypt DES-encrypted messages at will. No one has been able to discover such a trap door. More recently it has been stated that the S-boxes were selected to minimize the danger from an attack called differential cryptanalysis.

Because of the widespread belief that the DES cryptovariable is too small, many have suggested that one encrypt a message twice with DES using two different cryptovariables. This "Double DES" is carried out in the following way. Represent the operation of DES encryption on message P and cryptovariable K as $C = E(P; K)$; and the corresponding decryption as $P = D(C; K) = D(E(P; K); K)$. The "Double DES" with cryptovariables K and K′ is

$$C = E(E(P; K); K')$$

Since each cryptovariable is 56 bits long, we have created an effective cryptovariable length of $56 + 56 = 112$ bits. However, we shall see in the section on cryptanalysis that there is an attack on double-DES that requires about the same amount of computation as that required to attack a single DES. Thus double DES is really no more secure than single DES.

A third variant is triple DES, which applies the DES algorithm three times with two distinct cryptovariables. Let K and K′ be DES cryptovariables. Then triple DES is

$$C = E(D(E(P; K); K'); K).$$

That is, apply the encrypt function to P using the first cryptovariable, K. Then apply the decrypt function to the result using the second cryptovariable, K'. Since the decrypt function is using a different cryptovariable, the message is not decrypted; it is transformed by a permutation as in any block cipher. The final step is to encrypt once again with the encrypt function using the first key, K. By using the D in the middle, a triple DES implementation can be used to encrypt a single DES message when K = K':

$$C = E(D(E(P; K); K); K) = E(P; K).$$

Thus, someone using triple DES is still able to communicate securely with persons using single DES. No successful attacks have been reported on triple DES that are any easier than trying all possible pairs of cryptovariables. In the next section we deal with cryptanalysis in more detail.

CRYPTANALYSIS

As we stated in the introduction, cryptography is the science of designing algorithms for encrypting messages. Cryptanalysis is the science (some would say art) of "breaking" the cryptographic systems. In the following we will try to explain just what "breaking" a cryptosystem means, as there are many misconceptions in the press.

There is an obvious analogy between cryptanalysis and cryptography and burglars and locks. As the locksmiths design better locks the burglars develop better ways to pick them. Likewise, as the cryptographer designs better algorithms the cryptanalyst develops new attacks. A typical design methodology would be to have independent design teams and attack teams. The design team proposes algorithms, and the attack teams tries to find weaknesses. In practice, this methodology is used in the academic world. Researchers publish their new algorithms, and the rest of the academic world searches for attacks to be published in subsequent papers. Each cycle provides new papers toward tenure.

Breaking or attacking a cryptosystem means recovering the plain-text message without possession of the particular cryptovariable (or key) used to encrypt that message. More generally, breaking the system means determining the particular cryptovariable (key) that was used. Although it is the message (or the information in the message) that the analyst really wants, possession of the cryptovariable allows the analyst to recover all of the messages that were encrypted in that cryptovariable. Since the cryptoperiod may be days or weeks, the analyst who recovers a cryptovariable will be able to recover many more messages than if he attacks a single message at a time.

Determining the specific details of the algorithm that was used to encrypt the message is generally not considered part of breaking an encryption system. In most cases, e.g., DES, the algorithm is widely known. Even many of the proprietary systems such as RC4 and RC5 have been published. Because it is very difficult to maintain the secrecy of an algorithm it is better to design the algorithm so that knowledge of the algorithm's details is still not sufficient to determine the cryptovariable used for a specific message without trying all possible cryptovariables.

Trying all cryptovariables is called a "brute force" or "exhaustion" attack. It is an attack that will always work as long as one is able to recognize the plain-text message after decryption. That is, in any attack you need to be able to decide when you have succeeded. One also has to be able to find the cryptovariable (and hence the message) in time for it to be of use. For example, in a tactical military environment, to spend one week to recover a message about an attack that will occur before the week is over will not be useful. Last, one has to be able to afford to execute the attack. One may often trade off time and computer power; an attack that may take one year on a PC might take only one day on 365 PCs. If one must have the message within a day for it to be valuable, but one does not have the funds to acquire or run 365 PCs, then one really doesn't have a viable attack.

Often a cryptanalyst might assume that she possesses matched plain and cipher text. This is sometimes possible in real systems because military and diplomatic messages often have stereotyped beginnings. In any case it is not a very restrictive condition and can help the cryptanalyst evaluate the cryptographic strength of an algorithm.

Let us look at a brute force attack on some system. We suppose that the cryptovariable has n binary bits (e.g., DES has n = 56). We suppose that we have a stream cipher and that we have matched plain and cipher text pairs P_i and C_i for $I = 1, 2, \ldots$. For each possible cryptovariable there is some fixed amount of computation ("work") needed to encrypt a P_i and see if it results in the corresponding C_i. We can convert this work into the total number, W, of basic bit operations in the algorithm such as shifts, mod 2 additions, compares, etc. Suppose for definiteness that $W = 1000$ or 10^3.

There is a total of 2^n n-bit cryptovariables. For $n = 56$, 2^{56} is about $10^{16.8}$ or 72,000,000,000,000,000. If we select one of the possible cryptovariables and encrypt P_1 we have a 50:50 chance of getting C_1 since the only choices are 1 and 0. If we do not obtain C_1 we reject the selected cryptovariable as incorrect and test the next cryptovariable. If we do get C_1 then we must test the selected cryptovariable on P_2 and C_2. How many tests do we need to make in order to be sure that we have the correct cryptovariable? The answer is: at least 56. The rationale is that the probability of the wrong cryptovariable successfully matching 56 or more bits is 2^{-56}. Since we potentially have to try 2^{56} cryptovariables the expected number of cryptovariables passing all the tests is $(2^{56})(2^{-56}) = 1$. With one "survivor" we may correctly assume it is the cryptovariable we want. If we tested only 2^{55} cryptovariables, then we would expect two survivors. (Cryptanalysts call a cryptovariable that passes all of the tests by chance a "non-causal survivor.") If we test a few more than 56, the expected number of non-causal survivors is much less than 1. Thus we can be sure that the cryptovariable that does successfully match the 56 P_i and C_i is the one actually used. In a block cipher, such as DES, testing one block is usually sufficient since a correct block has 64 correct bits.

A natural question is how long does it take to execute a brute force attack (or any other kind of attack for that matter). The answer depends on how much computational power is available to the analyst. And since we want cryptographic systems to be useful for many years we also need to know how much computational power will be available in years hence. Gordan Moore, one of the founders of Intel, once noted that processing speeds seem to double (or costs halved) every 18 months. This is equivalent to a factor of 10 increase in speed per dollar spent about every 5 years. This trend has continued quite accurately for many years and has come to be known as "Moore's law."

Using Moore's law we can make some predictions. We first introduce the idea of a MIPS year (M.Y.). This is the number of instructions a million-instruction-per-second computer can execute in one year. One M.Y. is approximately $10^{13.5}$ instructions. At today's prices, one can get a 50 MIPS PC for about $750. We can then estimate the cost of a MIPS year at about $750/50 or $15, assuming we can run the computer for one year.

Let's look at what this means in two examples. We consider two cryptographic systems. One with a 56-bit cryptovariable (e.g., DES) and the other a 40-bit cryptovariable. Note that 40 bits is the maximum cryptovariable length allowed for export by the U.S. government. We assume that each algorithm requires about 1000 basic instructions to test each cryptovariable. Statistics tells us that, on average, we may expect to locate the correct cryptovariable after testing about ½ of the cryptovariable space.

There are two perspectives: how much does it cost? And how long does it take? The cost may be estimated from:

$$(\text{½}) \ (1000N(15))/\text{M.Y.,}$$

where N equals the number of cryptovariables (in the examples, either 2^{56} or 2^{40}), and M.Y. = $10^{13.5}$. The elapsed time requires that we make some assumptions as to the speed of processing. If we set K equal to the number of seconds in one year, and R the number of cryptovariables tested per second, we obtain the formula:

$$\text{Time (in years)} = (\text{½}) \ (N/KR).$$

The results are displayed in Exhibit 19.9.

YEAR	M.Y. Cost	On 56 bit cryptovariable	On 40 bit cryptovariable
1998	$15	$17 Million	$260
2003	$1.50	$1.7Million	$26
2008	$0.15	$170 thousand	$2.60

Number of cryptovariables tested per second	On 56 bit cryptovariable	On 40 bit cryptovariable
1,000	300 million years	17.5 years
1,000,000	300,000 years	6.2 days
1,000,000,000	300 years	9 minutes
1,000,000,000,000	109 days	0.5 seconds

Exhibit 19.9. Cost and Time for Brute Force Attack

One of the first public demonstrations of the accuracy of these estimates occurred during the summer of 1995. At that time a student at Ecole Polytechnique reported that he had "broken" an encrypted challenge message posted on the Web by Netscape. The message, an electronic transaction, was encrypted using an algorithm with a 40-bit cryptovariable. What the student did was to partition the cryptovariable space across a number of computers to which he had access and set them searching for the correct one. In other words he executed a brute force attack and he successfully recovered the cryptovariable used in the message. His attack ran for about 6 days and processed about 800,000 keys per second. While most analysts did not believe that a 40-bit cryptovariable was immune to a brute force attack, the student's success did cause quite a stir in the press. Additionally the student posted his program on a Web site so that anyone could copy the program and run the attack. At the RSA Data Security Conference, January 1997, it was announced that a Berkeley student using the idle time on a network of 250 computers was able to break the RSA challenge message, encrypted using a 40-bit key, in three and one-half hours.

More recently a brute force attack was completed against a DES message on the RSA Web page. We quote from the press release of the DES Challenge team (found on www.frii.com/~rtv/despr4.htm):

> LOVELAND, COLORADO (June 18, 1997). Tens of thousands of computers, all across the U.S. and Canada, linked together via the Internet in an unprecedented cooperative supercomputing effort to decrypt a message encoded with the government-endorsed Data Encryption Standard (DES).
>
> Responding to a challenge, including a prize of $10,000, offered by RSA Data Security, Inc., the DESCHALL effort successfully decoded RSA's secret message.

According to Rocke Verser, a contract programmer and consultant who developed the specialized software in his spare time, "Tens of thousands of computers worked cooperatively on the challenge in what is believed to be one of the largest supercomputing efforts ever undertaken outside of government."

Using a technique called "brute-force," computers participating in the challenge simply began trying every possible decryption key. There are over 72 quadrillion keys (72,057,594,037,927,936). At the time the winning key was reported to RSADSI, the DESCHALL effort had searched almost 25% of the total. At its peak over the recent weekend, the DESCHALL effort was testing 7 billion keys per second.

... And this was done with "spare" CPU time, mostly from ordinary PCs, by thousands of users who have never even met each other.

In other words, the DESCHALL worked as follows. Mr. Verser developed a client-server program that would try all possible keys. The clients were available to any and all who wished to participate. Each participant downloaded the client software and set it executing on their PC (or other machine). The client would execute at the lowest priority in the client PC and so did not interfere with the participant's normal activities. Periodically the client would connect to the server over the Internet and would receive another block of cryptovariables to test. With tens of thousands of clients it only took 4 months to hit the correct cryptovariable.

Another RSA Data Security Inc.'s crypto-cracking contest, launched in March 1997, was completed in October 1997. A team of some 4000 programmers from across the globe, calling themselves the "Bovine RC5 Effort," has claimed the $10,000 prize for decoding a message encrypted in 56-bit -RC5 code. The RC5 effort searched through 47 percent of the possible keys before finding the one used to encrypt the message.

RSA Data Security Inc. sponsored the contest to prove its point that 128-bit encryption must become the standard. Under current U.S. policy, software makers can sell only 40-bit key encryption overseas, with some exceptions available for 56-bit algorithms.

A second DES challenge was solved in February 1998 and took 39 days (see Exhibit 19.10). In this challenge, the participants had to test about 90 percent of the keyspace.

This chapter has focused mostly on brute force attacks. There may be, however, other ways to attack an encryption system. These other methods may be loosely grouped as analytic attacks, statistical attacks, and implementation attacks.

Analytic attacks make use of some weakness in the algorithm that enables the attacker to effectively reduce the complexity of the algorithm

Start of contest:
 January 13, 1998 at 09:00 PST
Start of distributed.net effort: January 13, 1998 at 09:08 PST
End of Contest: February 23, 1998 at 02:26 PST

Size of keyspace: 72,057,594,037,927,936
Approximate keys tested: 63,686,000,000,000,000

Peak keys per second: 34,430,460,000

Exhibit 19.10. RSA Project Statistics

---

through some algebraic manipulation. We will see in the section on public key systems, that the RSA public key algorithm can be attacked by factoring with much less work than brute force. Another example of an analytic attack is the attack on double DES.

Double DES, you recall, may be represented by:

$$C = E(E(P; K); L),$$

where K and L are 56-bit DES keys. We assume that we have matched plain and cipher text pairs C_i, P_i. Begin by noting that if $X = E(P; K)$. Then $D(C; L) = X$. Fix a pair C_1, P_1, and make a table of all 2^{56} values of $D(C_1; L)$ as L ranges through all 2^{56} possible DES keys. Then try each K in succession, computing $E(P_1; K)$ and looking for matches with the values of $D(C_1; L)$ in the table. Each pair K, L for which $E(P_1; K)$ matches $D(C_1; L)$ in the table is a possible choice of the sought-for cryptovariable. Each pair passing the test is then tested against the next plain–cipher pair P_2, C_2.

The chance of a non-causal match (a match given that the pair K, L is not the correct cryptovariable) is about 2^{-64}. Thus of the 2^{112} pairs K, L, about $2^{(112-64)} = 2^{48}$ will match on the first pair P_1, C_1. Trying these on the second block P_2, C_2 and only $2^{(48-64)} = 2^{-16}$ of the non-causal pairs will match. Thus, the probability of the incorrect cryptovariable passing both tests is about $2^{-16} \sim 0$. And the probability of the correct cryptovariable passing both tests is 1.

The total work to complete this attack (called the "meet in the middle" attack) is proportional to $2^{56} + 2^{48} = 2^{56}(1+2^{-8}) \sim 2^{56}$. In other words an attack on double DES has about the same work as trying all possible single DES keys. So there is no real gain in security with double DES.

Statistical attacks make use of some statistical weakness in the design. For example, if there is a slight bias toward 1 or 0 in the keystream, one can sometimes develop an attack with less work than brute force. These attacks are too complex to describe in this short chapter.

The third class of attacks is implementation attacks. Here one attacks the specific implementation of the encryption protocol, not simply the cryptographic engine. A good example of this kind of attack was in the news in late summer 1995. The target was Netscape; and this time the attack was against the 128-bit cryptovariable. Several Berkeley students were able to obtain source code for the Netscape encryption package and were able to determine how the system generated cryptovariables. The random generator was given a seed value that was a function of certain system clock values.

The students discovered that the uncertainty in the time variable that was used to seed the random-number generator was far less than the uncertainty possible in the whole cryptovariable space. By trying all possible seed values they were able to guess the cryptovariable with a few minutes of processing time. In other words, the implementation did not use a randomization process that could, in principle, produce any one of the 2^{128} possible keys. Rather it was selecting from a space more on the order of 2^{20}. The lesson here is that even though one has a very strong encryption algorithm and a large key space, a weak implementation could still lead to a compromise of the system.

KEY (CRYPTOVARIABLE) MANAGEMENT

We have noted in the previous sections that each encryption system requires a key (or cryptovariable) to function and that all of the secrecy in the encryption process is maintained in the key. Moreover, we noted that the sending and receiving party must have the same cryptovariable if they are to be able to communicate. This need translates to a significant logistical problem.

The longer a cryptovariable is used the more likely it is to be compromised. The compromise may occur through a successful attack or, more likely, the cryptovariable may be stolen by or sold to an adversary. Consequently, it is advisable to change the variable frequently. The frequency of change is a management decision based on the perceived strength of the algorithm and the sensitivity of the information being protected.

All communicating parties must have the same cryptovariable. Thus you need to know in advance with whom you plan to exchange messages. If a person needs to maintain privacy among a large number of different persons, then one would need distinct cryptovariables for each possible communicating pair. In a 1000-person organization, this would amount to almost one million keys.

Next, the keys must be maintained in secrecy. They must be produced in secret, and distributed in secret, and held by the users in a protected area (e.g., a safe) until they are to be used. Finally they must be destroyed after being used.

For centuries, the traditional means of distributing keys was through a trusted courier. A government organization would produce the cryptovariables. And couriers, who have been properly vetted and approved, would distribute the cryptovariables. A rigorous audit trail would be maintained of manufacture, distribution, receipt, and destruction. Careful plans and schedules for using the keys would be developed and distributed.

This is clearly a cumbersome, expensive, and time-consuming process. Moreover the process was and is subject to compromise. Many of history's spies were also guilty of passing cryptovariables (as well as other state secrets) to the enemy.

As our communications systems became more and more dependent on computers and communication networks, the concept of a key distribution center was developed. The key distribution center concept is illustrated in Exhibit 19.11. The operation is as follows: Initially each user, A, B, ..., is given (via traditional distribution) a user-unique key that we denote by K_A, K_B, etc. These cryptovariables will change only infrequently, which reduces the key distribution problem to a minimum. The KDC maintains a copy of each user-unique key. When A calls B, the calling protocol first contacts the KDC and tells it that user A is sending a message to user B. The KDC then generates a random "session key," K, i.e., a cryptovariable that will be used only for this communicating session between A and B. The KDC encrypts K in user A's unique cryptovariable, $E(K; K_A)$ and sends this to A. User A decrypts this message obtaining K. The KDC likewise encrypts K in user B's unique cryptovariable, $E(K; K_B)$ and sends this result to B. Now A and B (and no other party) have K, which they use as the cryptovariable for this session.

A session here may be a telephone call or passing a message through a packet switch network; the principles are the same. In practice the complete exchange is done in seconds and is completely transparent to the user.

The KDC certainly simplifies the distribution of cryptovariables. Only the user-unique keys need to be distributed in advance, and only infrequently. The session key only exists for the duration of the message so there is no danger that the key might be stolen and sold to an unauthorized person at some later date. But the KDC must be protected, and one still has

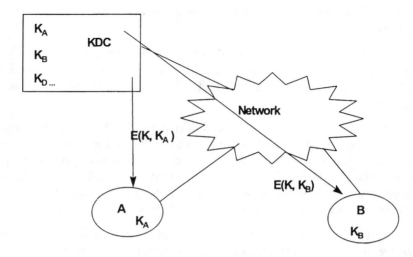

Exhibit 19.11. Key Distribution Center

to know with whom they will be communicating. The KDC will not help if one needs to send an electronic mail message to some new party (i.e., a party unknown to the KDC) for example.

It is clear that cryptovariable (or key) management is difficult and does not provide much in the way of flexibility. Many people have wondered if it would be possible to develop an encryption system that did not require secret keys; a system where one could have a directory of public keys. When you wanted to send an encrypted message to someone, you would look up that person's cryptovariable in a "telephone book," encrypt the message, and send it. And no one intercepting the message would be able to decrypt it except the intended recipient. Can such a system be designed? The answer is yes. It is called public key cryptography.

PUBLIC KEY CRYPTOGRAPHY

The concept of public key cryptography was first discovered and publicly announced by Whitfield Diffie and Martin Hellman (and independently by Ralph Merkle) in 1976. Adm. Bobby Inmann, a former director of the National Security Agency once stated publicly that NSA knew of the idea for many years prior to the publication by Diffie and Hellman.

The public key concept is rather simple (as are most great ideas, once they are explained). We assume that we have two special functions, E and D, that can operate on messages M. (In actual applications large integers will represent the messages, and E and D will be integer functions.) We assume that E and D satisfy the following conditions:

1. D(E(M)) = M
2. E(D(M)) = M
3. Given E it is not possible to determine D
4. Given D it is not possible to determine E.

The use of the function E in encryption is straightforward. We assume that each person, A, B, C, has pairs of functions E_A, D_A, E_B, D_B, ... that satisfy the conditions 1., 2., and 3. given above. Each user X makes their E_X publicly available but keeps their D_X secret and known only to themselves. When A wants to send a message, M, to B, A looks up E_B in the published list and computes $E_B(M)$. By property 2, $D_B(E_B(M)$ = M so B can decrypt the message. From property 3, no person can determine D_B from knowledge of E_B so no one but B can decipher the message.

The functions can also be used to sign messages. Perhaps A wants to send a message M to B and she does not care if anyone else sees the message, but she does want B to know that it really came from her. In this case A computes $D_A(M)$, called a signature, and sends it along with M. When B gets these two messages, he looks up A's function E_A and computes $E_A(D_A(M))$ and obtains M from property 2. If this computed M agrees with the message sent as M, then B is sure that it came from A. Why? Because no one else has or can compute D_A except A and the likelihood of someone producing a fictitious X such that $E_A(X)$ = M is infinitesimally small.

Now suppose A wants to send B a secret message and sign it. Let M be the message. A first computes a "signature" S = $D_A(M)$ and concatenates this to the message M, forming M, S. A then encrypts both the message and the signature, $E_B(M, S)$ and sends it to B. B applies D_B to $E_B(M, S)$ obtaining $D_B(E_B(M, S))$ = M, S. B then computes $E_A(S)$ = $E_A(D_A(M))$ = M and compares it to the message he decrypted. If both versions of M are the same, he can be assured that A sent the message.

The question the reader should be asking is "Do such functions exist?" The answer is yes, if we relax what we mean by conditions 3 and 4 above. If we only require that it be computationally infeasible to recover D from E (and vice versa) then the functions can be shown to exist. The most well-known example is the RSA algorithm, named for its discoverers, Rivest, Shamir, and Adleman.

A description of RSA requires a small amount of mathematics that we will explain as we proceed. We start with two large prime numbers, p and q. By large we mean they contain hundreds of digits. This is needed in order to meet conditions 3 and 4. A prime number, you recall, is a number that has no divisors except the number itself and 1. (In dealing with integers when we say a divides b we mean that there is no remainder; i.e., b = ac for some integer c.) The numbers 2, 3, 7, 11, 13, 17 are all prime. The number 2 is the only even prime. All other primes must be odd numbers.

We then define a number n as the product of p and q:

$$n = pq$$

We also define a number t as:

$$t = (p - 1)(q - 1)$$

As an example, take $p = 3$ and $q = 7$. (These are not large primes, but the mathematics is the same.) Then $n = 21$ and $t = 12$. The next step in the construction of RSA is to select a number e that has no common divisors with t. (In this case e and t are said to be relatively prime.) In our numerical example we may take $e = 5$ since 5 and 12 have no common divisors. Next we must find an integer d such that ed-1 is divisible by t. (This is denoted by $ed = 1 \mod t$.) Since $5*5 - 1 = 25 - 1 = 24 = 2*12 = 2*t$, we may take $d = 5$. (In most examples e and d will not be the same.)

The numbers d, p, and q are kept secret. They are used to create the D function. The numbers e and n are used to create the E function. The number e is usually called the public key and d the secret key. The number n is called the modulus. Once p and q are used to produce n and t, they are no longer needed and may be destroyed, but should never be made public.

To encrypt a message, one first converts the message into a string of integers, $m_1, m_2, \ldots$ all smaller than n. We then compute:

$$c_i = E(m_i) = m_i^e \mod n$$

This means that we raise m_i to the eth power and then divide by n. The remainder is $c_i = E(m_i)$. In our example, we suppose that the message is $m_1 = 9$. We compute:

$$c_1 = 9^5 \mod 21$$

$$= 59049 \mod 21$$

Because $59049 = 89979*21 + 18$, we conclude that $c_1 = 18 \mod 21$.

The decryption, or D function, is defined by:

$$D(c_i) = c_i^d \mod n$$

In our example,

$$18^d \mod n$$

$$= 18^5 \mod 21$$

$$= 1889668 \mod 21$$

As $1889568 = 889979*21 + 9$, we conclude that $D(18) = 9$, the message we started with.

To demonstrate mathematically that the decryption function always works to decrypt the message (i.e., that properties 1 and 2 above hold) requires a result from number theory called Euler's generalization of Fermat's little theorem. The reader is referred to any book on number theory for a discussion of this result.

The security of RSA depends on the resistance of n to being factored. Since e is made public, anyone who knows the corresponding d can decrypt any message. If one can factor n into its two prime factors, p and q, then one can compute t and then easily find d. Thus it is important to select integers p and q such that it is not likely that someone can factor the product n. In 1983, the best factoring algorithm and the best computers could factor a number of about 71 decimal (235 binary) digits. By 1994, 129 digit (428 bits) numbers were being factored. Current implementations of RSA generate p and q on the order 256 to 1024 bits so that n is about 512 to 2048 bits.

The reader should note that attacking RSA by factoring the modulus n is a form of algebraic attack. The algebraic weakness is that the factors of n lead to a discovery of the "secret key." A brute force attack, by definition, would try all possible values for d. Since d is hundreds of digits long, the work is on the order of 10^{100}, which is a prodigiously large number. Factoring a number, n, takes at most on the order of square root of n operations or about 10^{50} for a 100-digit number. While still a very large number it is a vast improvement over brute force. There are, as we mentioned, factoring algorithms that are much smaller, but still are not feasible to apply to numbers of greater than 500 bits with today's technology, or with the technology of the near future.

As you can see from our examples, using RSA requires a lot of computation. As a result, even with special purpose hardware, RSA is slow; too slow for many applications. The best application for RSA and other public key systems is as key distribution systems.

Suppose A wants to send a message to B using a conventional private key system such as DES. Assuming that B has a DES device, A has to find some way to get a DES cryptovariable to B. She generates such a key, K, through some random process. She then encrypts K using B's public algorithm, $E_B(K)$ and sends it to B along with the encrypted message $E_{DES}(M; K)$. B applies his secret function D_B to $E_B(K)$ and recovers K, which he then uses to decrypt $E_{DES}(M; K)$.

This technique greatly simplifies the whole key management problem. We no longer have to distribute secret keys to everyone. Instead, each person has a public key system that generates the appropriate E and D functions. Each person makes the E public, keeps D secret and we're done. Or are we?

The Man-in-the-Middle

Unfortunately there are no free lunches. If a third party can control the public listing of keys, or E functions, that party can masquerade as both ends of the communication.

We suppose that A and B have posted their E_A and E_B, respectively, on a public bulletin board. Unknown to them, C has replaced E_A and E_B with E_C, his own encryption function. Now when A sends a message to B, A will encrypt it as $E_C(M)$ although he believes he has computed $E_B(M)$. C intercepts the message and computes $D_C(E_C(M)) = M$. He then encrypts it with the real E_B and forwards the result to B. B will be able to decrypt the message and is none the wiser. Thus this man in the middle will appear as B to A and as A to B.

The way around this is to provide each public key with an electronically signed signature (a certificate) attesting to the validity of the public key and the claimed owner. The certificates are prepared by an independent third party known as a certificate authority (e.g., VeriSign). The user will provide a public key (E function) and identification to the certificate authority (CA). The CA will then issue a digitally signed token binding the customer's identity to the public key. That is, the CA will produce $D_{CA}(ID_A, E_A)$. A person, B, wishing to send a message to A will obtain A's public key, E_A and the token $D_{CA}(ID_A, E_A)$. Since the CA's public key will be publicized, B computes $E_{CA}(D_{CA}(ID_A, E_A)) = ID_A, E_A$. Thus B, to the extent that he can trust the certification authority, can be assured that he really has the public key belonging to A and not an impostor.

There are several other public key algorithms, but all depend in one way or another on difficult problems in number theory. The exact formulations are not of general interest since an implementation will be quite transparent to the user. The important user issue is the size of the cryptovariable, the speed of the computation, and the robustness of the implementation. However, there is a new implementation that is becoming popular and deserves some explanation.

ELLIPTIC CURVE CRYPTOGRAPHY

A new public key technique based on elliptic curves has recently become popular. To explain this new process requires a brief digression. Recall from the previous section, that the effectiveness of public key algorithms depend on the existence of very difficult problems in mathematics. The security of RSA depends, for example, on the difficulty of factoring large numbers. While factoring small numbers is a simple operation, there are only a few (good) known algorithms or procedures for factoring large integers, and these still take prodigiously long times when factoring numbers that are hundreds of digits long. Another difficult mathematical problem is called the discrete logarithm problem. Given a number b, the base, and x, the logarithm, one can easily compute b^x or b^x mod N for any N. It turns out to be very difficult to solve the reverse problem for large integers. That is, given a large integer y and a base b, find x so that b^x = y Mod N. The known procedures (algorithms) require about the same level of computation as finding the factors of a large integer. Diffie and Hellman[9] exploited this difficulty to define their public key distribution algorithm.

Diffie and Hellman Key Distribution

Suppose that Sarah and Tanya want to exchange a secret cryptovariable for use in a conventional symmetric encryption system, say a DES encryption device. Sarah and Tanya together select a large prime p and a base b. The numbers p and b are assumed to be public knowledge. Next Sarah chooses a number s and keeps it secret. Tanya chooses a number t and keeps it secret. The numbers s and t must be between 1 and p-1. Sarah and Tanya then compute (respectively):

$$x = b^s \text{ Mod p (Sarah)}$$

$$y = b^t \text{ Mod p (Tanya)}$$

In the next step of the process Sarah and Tanya exchange the numbers x and y; Tanya sends y to Sarah, and Sarah sends x to Tanya. Now Sarah can compute

$$y^s = b^{ts} \text{ Mod p}$$

And Tanya can compute

$$x^t = b^{st} \text{ Mod p}$$

But,

$$b^{ts} \text{ Mod p} = b^{st} \text{ Mod p} = K$$

which becomes their common key. In order for a third party to recover K, that party must solve the discrete logarithm problem to recover s and t. (To be more precise, solving the discrete logarithm problem is sufficient to recover the key, but it might not be necessary. It is not known if there is another way to find b^{st} given b^s and b^t. It is conjectured that the latter problem is at least as difficult as the discrete logarithm problem.) The important fact regarding the Diffie-Hellman key exchange is that it applies to any mathematical object known as an Abelian group. (See Exhibit 19.12.)

Now we can get into the idea of elliptic curve cryptography, at least at a high level. An elliptic curve is a collection of points in the x-y plane that satisfy an equation of the form

$$y^2 = x^3 + ax + b . \text{ (1)}$$

GROUPS:
A group is a collection of elements, G, together with an operation * (called a "product" or a "sum") that assigns to each pair of elements x, y in G a third element z = x*y. The operation must have an identity element e with e*x = x*e = x for all x in G. Each element must have an inverse with respect to this identity. That is, for each x there is an x' with x*x' = e = x'*x. Last, the operation must be associative. If it is also true that x*y = y*x for all x and y in G, the group is said to be commutative, or Abelian. (In this case the operation is often written as +.

Exhibit 19.12. Definition of Abelian Groups

The elements a and b can be real numbers, imaginary numbers, or elements from a more general mathematical object known as a field. As an example, if we take a = -1 and b = 0. The equation is:

$$y^2 = x^3 - x . (2)$$

A graph of this curve is shown in Exhibit 19.13. It turns out that the points of this curve (those pairs (x, y) that satisfy the equation 2) can form a group under a certain operation. Given two points P = (x, y) and Q = (x', y') on the curve we can define a third point R = (x," y") on the curve called the "sum" of P and Q. Furthermore this operation satisfies all of the requirements for a group. Now that we have a group we may define a Diffie-Hellman key exchange on this group. Indeed, any cryptographic algorithm that may be defined in a general group can be instantiated in the group defined on an elliptic curve. For a given size key, implementing an elliptic curve system seems to be computationally faster than the equivalent RSA. Other than the speed of the implementation there does not appear to be any advantage for using elliptic curves over RSA. RSA Data Security Inc. includes an elliptic curve implementation in their developer's kit (BSAFE) but they strongly recommend that the technique not be used except in special circumstances. Elliptic curve cryptographic algorithms have been

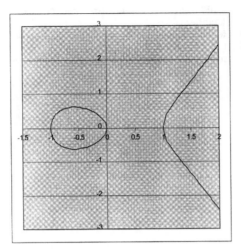

Exhibit 19.13.   Graph of Elliptic Curve

subjected to significantly less analysis than the RSA algorithm so it is difficult to state with any confidence that elliptic curves are as secure or more secure than RSA. See Koblitz[10] for a complete discussion.

CONCLUSIONS

This short chapter presented a quick survey of some basic concepts in cryptography. No attempt was made to be comprehensive; the object was to help the reader better understand some of the reports about encryption and "breaking encryption systems" that often appear in the trade press and newspapers. The reader is referred to any of the many fine books that are available for more detail on any of the topics presented.

Notes

1. Kahn, David: *The Codebreakers; The Comprehensive History of Secret Communication from Ancient Times to the Internet,* Scribner, 1996.
2. Hodges, A., *Alan Turing: The Enigma of Intelligence,* Simon and Schuster, 1983.
3. Bamford, J., *The Puzzle Palace,* Houghton Mifflin, 1982.
4. Many thought that NSA had implanted a "trap door" that would allow the government to recover encrypted messages at will. Others argued that the cryptovariable length (56 bits) was too short.
5. The reader is cautioned not to confuse "keystream" with key. The term is used for historical reasons and is not the "key" for the algorithm. It is for this reason that we prefer the term "cryptovariable."
6. Schneier, B., *Applied Cryptography,* John Wiley, 1996.
7. The output cannot be truly random since the receiving system has to be able to produce the identical sequence.

8. For $n = 7$, $2^n!$ is about 10^{215}. The case n=8 is more than I can calculate. Clearly, there is no lack of possible block ciphers.
9. Diffie, W. and M. E. Hellman, New directions in cryptography, *IEEE Transactions on Information Theory IT-22* (1976) 644-654.
10. Koblitz, Neil, *A Course in Number Theory and Cryptography*, Second Edition, Springer-Verlag, 1994.

Chapter 20
Principles and Applications of Cryptographic Key Management

William Hugh Murray

INTRODUCTION

The least appreciated of the (five) inventions that characterize modern cryptography is automated key management. This powerful mechanism enables us to overcome the lack of rigor and discipline that leads to the inevitable compromise of crypto systems. By permitting us to change keys frequently and safely, it overcomes the fundamental limitations of the algorithms that we use. It enables us to compensate for such human limitations as the inability to remember or transcribe long random numbers

This chapter will attempt to tell the information security professional the minimum that he needs to know about key management. It must presume that the professional already understands modern cryptography. This chapter will define key management, enumerate its fundamental principles and describe its use. It will make recommendations on the key choices that confront the user and manager.

CONTEXT

First a little context. Cryptography is the use of secret codes to hide data and to authenticate its origin and content. While public codes could be used to authenticate content, secret codes are necessary to authenticate origin. This latter use of cryptography has emerged only in the latter half of this century and has been surprising to all but a few.

Of all security mechanisms, cryptography is the one most suited to open and hostile environments, environments where control is otherwise limited, environments like the modern, open, flat, broadcast, packet-switched, heterogeneous networks.

It is broadly applicable. In the presence of cheap computing power, its uses are limited only by our imaginations. Given that most of the power of our computers goes unused, we could, if we wished, use secret codes by default, converting into public codes only for use. Indeed, the modern distributed computing systems and applications would be impossible without it.

It is portable; the necessary software to encode or decode the information can be distributed at or near the time of use in the same package and channel. Within minor limits, it is composable; we can put together different functions and algorithms without losing any strength. One can put together mechanisms in such a way as to emulate any environmental or media-based control that we have ever had.

Not only is cryptography effective, it is efficient. That is to say, it is usually the cheapest way to achieve a specified degree of protection. The cost of cryptography is low. Not only is it low in absolute terms, it is low in terms of the security value it delivers. It is low compared to the value of the data it protects. It is low compared to the alternative ways of achieving the same degree of security by such alternative means as custody, supervision, or automated access control.

Its low cost is the result in part of the low cost of the modern computer, and it is falling with the cost of that computing. The cost of a single cryptographic operation today is one ten thousandth of what it was as recently as 20 years ago and can be expected to continue to fall.

Another way of looking at it is that its relative strength is rising when cost is held constant; the cost to the user is falling relative to the cost to the attacker. As we will see, automated key management is one mechanism that permits us to trade the increasing power of computing for increased security.

Modern cryptography is arbitrarily strong; that is, it is as strong as we need it to be. If one knows what data he wishes to protect, for how long, and from whom, then it is possible to use modern cryptography to achieve the desired protection. There are limitations; if one wanted to encrypt tens of gigabytes of data for centuries, it is hard to know how to achieve that. However, this is a theoretical rather than a practical problem. In practice, there are no such applications or problems.

Cryptography is significantly stronger than other security mechanisms. Almost never will cryptography be the weak link in the security chain. However, in practice its strength is limited by the other links in the chain, for example, key management. As it is not efficient to make one link in a chain significantly stronger than another, so it is not necessary for cryptography to be more than a few hundred times stronger than the other mechanisms on which the safety of the data depends.

The cryptography component of a security solution is robust and resilient, not likely to break. While history suggests that advances in technology may lower the cost of attack against a particular cryptographic mechanism, it also suggests that the cost does not drop suddenly or precipitously. It is very unlikely to collapse. Given the relative effectiveness and efficiency of cryptography relative to other security measures, changes in the cost of attack against cryptography are unlikely to put security at risk. The impact is obvious, and there is sufficient opportunity to compensate.

Changes in technology reduce the cost to both the user of cryptography and the attacker. Because the attacker enjoys economies of scale, historically, advances such as the computer have favored him first and the user second. However, that probably changed forever when both the scale and the cost of the computer fell to within the discretion of an individual. Further advances in technology are likely to favor the cryptographer.

As we will see, as the cost of attack falls, the user will spend a little money to compensate. However, it is in the nature of cryptography that as his costs rise linearly, the costs to the attacker rise exponentially. For example, the cost of attack against the Data Encryption Standard (DES) has fallen to roughly a million MIPS years. While this is still adequate for most applications, some users have begun to use Triple DES-112. This may quadruple their cost but increase the cost of a brute force attack by 2.[55]

One way of looking at cryptography is that it changes the problem of maintaining the secrecy of the message to one of maintaining the secrecy of the keys. How we do that is called *key management.*

KEY MANAGEMENT DEFINED

Key management can be defined as the generation, recording, transcription, distribution, installation, storage, change, disposition, and control of cryptographic keys. History suggests that key management is very important. It suggests that each of these steps is an opportunity to compromise the cryptographic system. Further, it suggests that attacks against keys and key management are far more likely and efficient than attacks against algorithms.

Key management is not obvious or intuitive. It is very easy to get it wrong. For example, students found that a recent release of Netscape's SSL implementation chose the key from a recognizable subspace of the total key space. While the total space would have been prohibitively expensive to exhaust, the subspace was quite easy. Key management provides all kinds of opportunities for these kinds of errors.

As a consequence, key management must be rigorous and disciplined. History tells us that this is extremely difficult to accomplish. The most productive cryptanalytic attacks in history, such as ULTRA, have exploited poor key management. Modern automated key management attempts to use the computer to provide the necessary rigor and discipline. Moreover, it can be used to compensate for the inherent limitations in the algorithms we use.

KEY MANAGEMENT FUNCTIONS

This section will address the functions that define key management in more detail. It will identify the issues around each of these functions that the manager needs to be aware of.

Key Generation

Key generation is the selection of the number that is going to be used to tailor an encryption mechanism to a particular use. The use may be a sender and receiver pair, a domain, an application, a device, or a data object. The key must be chosen in such a way that it is not predictable and that knowledge of it is not leaked in the process.

It is necessary but not sufficient that the key be randomly chosen. In an early implementation of the Secure Socket Layer (SSL) protocol, Netscape chose the key in such a manner that it would, perforce, be chosen from a small subset of the total set of possible keys. Thus, an otherwise secure algorithm and secure protocol was weakened to the strength of a toy. Students, having examined how the keys were chosen, found that they could find the keys chosen by examining a very small set of possible keys.

In addition to choosing keys randomly it is also important that the chosen key not be disclosed at the time of the selection. While a key may be stored securely after its generation, it may be vulnerable to disclosure at the time of its generation when it may appear in the clear. Alternatively, information that is used in the generation of the key may be recorded at the time it is collected, thus making the key more predictable than might otherwise be concluded by the size of the key space. For example, some key-generation routines, requiring random numbers, ask the user for noisy data. They may ask the user to run his hands over the key board. While knowledge of the result of this action might not enable an attacker to predict the key, it might dramatically reduce the set of keys that the attacker must search.

Distribution

Key distribution is the process of getting a key from the point of its generation to the point of its intended use. This problem is more difficult in symmetric key algorithms, where it is necessary to protect the key from disclosure in the process. This step must be performed in a channel separate from the one that the traffic moves in.

During the Second World War, the Germans used a different key each day in their Enigma Machine but distributed the keys in advance. In at least one instance the table of future keys, recorded on water-soluble paper, was captured from a sinking submarine.

Installation

Key installation is the process of getting the key into the storage of the device or process that is going to use it. Traditionally this step has involved some manual operations. Such operations might result in leakage of information about the key, error in its transcription, or it might be so cumbersome as to discourage its use.

The German Enigma Machine had two mechanisms for installing keys. One was a set of three (later four) rotors. The other was a set of plug wires. In one instance, the British succeeded in inserting a listening device in a code room in Vichy France. The clicking of the rotors leaked information about the delta between key n and key n+1.

The plugging of the wires was so cumbersome and error prone as to discourage its routine use. The British found that the assumption that today's plug setting was the same as yesterday's was usually valid.

Storage

Keys may be protected by the integrity of the storage mechanism itself. For example, the mechanism may be designed so that once the key is installed in cannot be observed from outside the encryption machine itself. Indeed, some key-storage devices are designed to self-destruct when subjected to forces that might disclose the key or that are evidence that the key device is being tampered with.

Alternatively, the key may be stored in an encrypted form so that knowledge of the stored form does not disclose information about the behavior of the device under the key.

Visual observation of the Enigma Machine was sufficient to disclose the rotor setting and might disclose some information about the plug-board setting.

Change

Key change is ending the use of one key and beginning that of another. This is determined by convention or protocol. Traditionally, the time at which information about the key was most likely to leak was at key-change time. Thus, there was value to key stability. On the other hand, the longer the key is in use, the more traffic that is encrypted under it, the higher the probability that it will be discovered and the more traffic that will be compromised. Thus, there is value to changing the key.

The Germans changed the key every day but used it for all of the traffic in an entire theatre of operations for that day. Thus, the compromise of the key resulted in the compromise of a large quantity of traffic and large amount of information or intelligence.

Control

Control of the key is the ability to exercise a directing or restraining influence over its content or use. For example, selecting which key from a set of keys is to be used for a particular application or party is part of key control. Ensuring that a key that is intended for encrypting keys cannot be used for data is part of key control. This is such a subtle concept that its existence is often overlooked. On the other hand, it is usually essential to the proper functioning of a system.

The inventors of modern key management believe that this concept of key control and the mechanism that they invented for it, which they call the *control vector*, is one of their biggest contributions.

Disposal

Keys must be disposed of in such a way as to resist disclosure. This was more of a problem when keys were used for a long time and when they were distributed in persistent storage media than it is now. For example, Enigma keys for submarines were distributed in books with the keys for the future. In at least one instance such a book was captured.

MODERN KEY MANAGEMENT

Modern key management was invented by an IBM team in the 1970s.* It was described in the *IBM Systems Journal*** at the same time as the publication of the Data Encryption Standard (DES). However, while the DES has inspired great notice, comment, and research, key management has not gotten the recognition it deserves. While commentators were complaining

---

* Dr. Dorothy Denning has told me privately that she believes that automated key management was invented by the National Security Agency prior to IBM. Whether or not that is true is classified. In the absence of contemporaneous publication, it is unknowable. However, even if it is true, their invention did not ever make a difference; as far as we know, it never appeared in a system or an implementation. The IBM team actually implemented theirs, and it has made a huge difference. I remember being told by a member of the IBM team about the reaction of NSA to IBM's discussion of key management. He indicated that the reaction was as to a novel concept.

** R. Elander et al. *Systems Journal*, 1977; IBM pub G321-5066, *A Cryptographic Key Management Scheme*.

about the length of the DES key, IBM was treating it as a solved problem; they always knew how they would compensate for fixed key length and believed that they had told the world.

Modern key management is fully automated; manual steps are neither required nor permitted. Users do not select, communicate, or transcribe keys. Not only would such steps require the user to know the key and permit him to disclose it, accidentally or deliberately, they would also be very prone to error.

Modern key management permits and facilitates frequent key changes. For example, most modern systems provide that a different key will be used for each object, e.g., file, session, message, or transaction, to be encrypted. These keys are generated at the time of the application of encryption to the object and specifically for that object. Its life is no longer than the life of the object itself. The most obvious example is a session key. It is created at the time of the session, exchanged under a key-encrypting key, and automatically discarded at the end of the session. (Because of the persistence of TCP sessions, even this may result in too much traffic under a single key. The IBM proposal for secure-IP is to run two channels [TCP sessions], one for data and one for keys. The data key might change many times per session.)

One can compare the idea of changing the key for each object or method with the practices used during World War II. The Germans used the same key across all traffic for a service or theater for an entire day. Since the British were recording all traffic, the discovery of one key resulted in the recovery of a large amount of traffic.

Manual systems of key management were always in a difficult bind; the more frequently one changed the key, the greater the opportunity for error and compromise. On the other hand, the more data encrypted under a single key, the easier the attack against that key and the more data that might be compromised with that key. To change or not to change? How to decide?

Automating the system changes the balance. It permits frequent secure key changes that raise the cost of attack to the cryptanalyst. The more keys that are used for a given amount of data, the higher the cost of attack (the more keys to be found), and the lower the value of success (the less data for each key). As the number of keys increases, the cost of attack approaches infinity and the value of success approaches zero. The cost of changing keys increases the cost of encryption linearly, but it increases the cost of attack exponentially. All other things being equal, changing keys increases the effective key length of an algorithm.

Since many algorithms employ a fixed-length key, since one can almost always find the key in use by exhausting the finite set of keys, and since the falling cost and increasing speed of computers is always lowering the cost and elapsed time for such an attack, the finite length of the key might be a serious limitation on the effectiveness of the algorithm. In the world of the Internet, in which thousands of computers have been used simultaneously to find one key, it is at least conceivable that one might find the key within its useful life. Automatic key change compensates for this limit.

A recent challenge key* was found using more than 10,000 computers for months at the rate of billions of keys per second. The value of success was only $10,000. By definition, the life of a challenge key is equal to the duration of the attack. Automated key management enables us to keep the life of most keys to minutes to days rather than days to months.

However, modern key management has other advantages in addition to greater effective key length and shorter life. It can be used to ensure the involvement of multiple people in sensitive duties. For example, the Visa master key is stored in San Francisco inside a box called the BBN SafeKeyper. It was created inside that box and no one knows what it is. Beneficial use of the key requires possession of the box and its three physical keys. Since it is at least conceivable that the box could be destroyed, it has exported information about the key. Five trustees share that information in such a way that any three of them, using another SafeKeyper box, could reconstruct the key.

Key management can also be used to reduce the risk associated with a lost or damaged key. While in a communication application there is no need to worry about lost keys, in a file encryption application, a lost key might be the equivalent of loss of the data. Key management can protect against that. For example, one of my colleagues has information about one of my keys that would enable him to recover it if anything should happen to me. In this case he can recover the key all by himself. Since a copy of a key halves its security, the implementation that we are using permits me to compensate by specifying how many people must participate in recovering the key.

Key management may be a stand-alone computer application or it can be integrated into another application. IBM markets a product that banks can use to manage keys across banks and applications. The Netscape Navigator and Lotus Notes have key management built in.

Key management must provide for the protection of keys in storage and during exchange. Smart cards may be used to accomplish this. For example, if one wishes to exchange a key with another, one can put it in a smart card and mail it. It would be useless to anyone who took it from the mail.

* RSA $10,000 Challenge http://www.frii.com/~rcv/deschall.htm

PRINCIPLES OF KEY MANAGEMENT

A number of principles guide the use and implementation of key management. These are necessary, but may not be sufficient, for safe implementation. That is, even implementations that adhere to these principles *may be* weak, but all implementations that do not adhere to these principles *are* weak.

First, *key management must be fully automated.* There may not be any manual operations. This principle is necessary both for discipline and for the secrecy of the keys.

Second, *no key may ever appear in the clear* outside a cryptographic device. This principle is necessary for the secrecy of the keys. It also resists known-plain-text attacks against keys.

Keys must be randomly chosen from the entire key space. If there is any pattern to the manner in which keys are chosen, this pattern can be exploited by an attacker to reduce his work. If the keys are drawn in such a way that all possible keys do not have an equal opportunity to be drawn, then the work of the attacker is reduced. For example, if keys are chosen so as to correspond to natural language words, then only keys that have such a correspondence, rather than the whole space, must be searched.

Key-encrypting keys must be separate from data keys. Keys that are used to encrypt other keys must not be used to encrypt data, and vice versa. Nothing that has ever appeared in the clear may be encrypted under a key-encrypting key. If keys are truly randomly chosen and are never used to encrypt anything that has appeared in the clear, then they are not vulnerable to an exhaustive or brute force attack. In order to understand this, it is necessary to understand how a brute force attack works.

In a brute force attack, one tries keys one after another until one finds the key in use. The problem that the attacker has is that he must be able to recognize the correct key when he tries it. There are two ways to do this, corresponding clear- and cipher-text attacks, and cipher-text-only attacks. In the former, the attacker keeps trying keys on the cipher text until he finds the one that produces the expected clear text.

At a minimum, the attacker must have a copy of the algorithm and a copy of the cryptogram. In modern cryptography, the algorithm is assumed to be public. Encrypted keys will sometimes appear in the environment, and encrypted data, cipher text, is expected to appear there.

For the first attack, the attacker must have corresponding clear and cipher text. In historical cryptography, when keys were used widely or for an extended period of time, the attacker could get corresponding clear and cipher text by duping the cryptographer into encrypting a message that he already knew. In modern cryptography, where a key is used only once and then discarded, this is much more difficult to do.

In the cipher-text-only attack, the attacker tries a key on the cipher text until it produces recognizable clear text. Clear text may be recognized because it is not random. In the recent RSA DES Key Challenge the correct clear-text message could be recognized because the message was known to begin with the words, "The correct message is...." However, even if this had not been the case, the message would have been recognizable because it was encoded in ASCII.

To resist cipher-text-only attacks, good practice requires that all such *patterns* as format, e.g., file or e-mail message, language (e.g., English) alphabet (e.g., Roman), and public code (e.g., ASCII or EBCDIC) *in the clear text object must be disguised* before the object is encrypted.

Note that neither of these attacks will work on a key-encrypting key if the principles of key management are adhered to. The first one cannot be made to work because the crypto engine cannot be duped into encrypting a known value under a key-encrypting key. The only thing that it will encrypt under a key-encrypting key is a random value which it produced inside itself. The cipher-text-only attack cannot be made to work because there is no information in the clear text key that will allow the attacker to recognize it. That is, the clear text key is, by definition, totally random, without recognizable pattern, information, or entropy.

Keys with a long life must be sparsely used. There are keys, such as the Visa master key mentioned earlier, whose application is such that a very long life is desirable. As we have already noted, the more a key is used, the more likely is a successful attack and the greater the consequences of its compromise. Therefore, we compensate by using this key very sparsely and only for a few other keys. There is so little data encrypted under this key and that data is so narrowly held that a successful attack is unlikely. Since only this limited number of keys is encrypted under this key, changing it is not prohibitively expensive.

ASYMMETRIC KEY CRYPTOGRAPHY

In traditional and conventional cryptography, the key used for encrypting and the one used for decrypting have the same value; that is to say that the relationship between them is one of symmetry or equality. In 1976, Whitfield Diffie and Martin Hellman pointed out that though the relationship between these two numbers must be fixed, it need not be equality.

Other relationships could serve. Thus was born the idea of asymmetric key cryptography.

In this kind of cryptography the key has two parts; the parts are mathematically related to each other in such a way that what is encrypted with one part can only be decrypted by the other. The value of one of the keys does not necessarily imply the other; one cannot easily calculate one from the other. However, one of the keys, plus a message encrypted under it, does imply the other key. From a message and one part of the key, it is mathematically possible to calculate the other but it is not computationally feasible to do so.

Only one part, called the *private key*, need be kept secret. The other part, the *public key*, is published to the world. Anyone can use the public key to encrypt a message that can only be decrypted and read by the owner of the private key. Conversely, anyone can read a message encrypted with the private key, but only the person with beneficial use of that key could have encrypted it.

Note that if A and B share a symmetric key, then either knows that a message encrypted under that key originated with the other. Since a change in as little as one bit of the message will cause it to decode to garbage, the receiver of a good message knows that the message has not been tampered with. However, since each party has beneficial use of the key and could have created the cryptogram, they cannot demonstrate that it originated with the other. In asymmetric key cryptography only the possessor of the private key can have created the cryptogram. Any message that will decrypt with the public key is therefore known to all to have originated with the person who published it. This mechanism provides us with a *digital signature* capability that is independent of medium and far more resistant to forgery than marks on paper.

While key management can be accomplished using only symmetric key cryptography, it requires secret key exchange, a closed population, some prearrangement, and it benefits greatly from trusted hardware. Asymmetric key cryptography enables us to do key management without secret key exchange, in an open population, with a minimum of prearrangement. It reduces the need for trusted hardware for key distribution though it is still desirable for key storage and transcription.

However, when otherwise compared to symmetric key cryptography, asymmetric key cryptography comes up short. Exhibit 20.1 compares a symmetric key algorithm, DES, to an asymmetric key algorithm, RSA. Exhibit 20.1 shows that the asymmetric key algorithm requires much longer keys to achieve the same computational resistance to attack (i.e., to achieve the same security). It takes much longer to generate a key. It is much slower in operation, and its cost goes up faster than the size of the object to be encrypted.

CHARACTERISTIC	DES	RSA
Relative Speed	Fast	Slow
Functions Used	Transportation & Substitution	Multiplication
Key Length	56 bits	400–800 bits
Least Cost Attack	Exhaustion	Factoring
Cost of Attack	Centuries	Centuries
Time to Generate a Key	Microseconds	Tens of Seconds
Key Type	Symmetric	Asymmetric

Exhibit 20.1.

However, for keys that are to be used for a long period of time, the time required to generate a key is not an issue. For short objects to be encrypted, performance is not an issue. Therefore, asymmetric key cryptography is well suited to key management applications, and in practice its use is limited to that role. Most products use symmetric key cryptography to encrypt files, messages, sessions, and other objects, but use asymmetric key cryptography to exchange and protect keys.

HYBRID CRYPTOGRAPHY

If one reads the popular literature, he is likely to be gulled into believing that he has to make a choice between symmetric and asymmetric key cryptography. In fact and in practice, this is not the case. In practice we use a hybrid of the two that enables us to enjoy the benefits of each. In this style of use, a symmetric key algorithm is used to hide the object, while an asymmetric key mechanism is used to manage the keys of this symmetric algorithm.

The symmetric key algorithm is well suited for hiding the data object. It is fast and secure, even with a short key. Since keys are easily chosen, they can be changed for each object. The asymmetric key algorithm would not be suitable for this purpose since it is slow and requires a long key that is expensive to choose.

On the other hand, the asymmetric algorithm is well suited to managing keys. Since symmetric keys are short, one need not worry about the speed of encrypting them. Since key management keys are relatively stable, one need not worry about the cost of finding them.

Exhibit 20.2 illustrates a simple implementation of hybrid cryptography. A randomly selected 56-bit key is used to encrypt a message using the DES

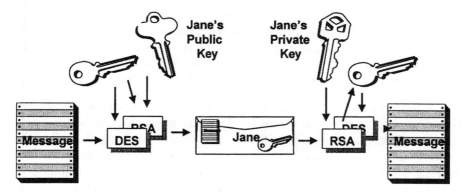

Exhibit 20.2. Hybrid Cryptography

algorithm. This key is then encrypted using Jane's public key. The encrypted message along with its encrypted key are now broadcast. While everyone can see these, their meaning is hidden from all but Jane. Jane uses her private key to recover the message key and the message key to recover the message.

PUBLIC KEY CERTIFICATES

As we have noted, by definition, there is no need to keep public keys secret. However, it is necessary to ensure that one is using the correct public key. One must obtain the key in such a way as to preserve confidence that it is the right key. Also, as already noted, the best way to do that is to obtain the key directly from the party. However, in practice we will get public keys at the time of use and in the most expeditious manner.

As we do with traditional signatures, we may rely on a trusted third party to vouch for the association between a particular key and a particular person or institution. For example, the state issues credentials that vouch for the bind between a photo, name and address, and a signature. This may be a driver's license or a passport. Similar credentials, called public key certificates, will be issued for public keys by the same kinds of institutions that issue credentials today: employers, banks, credit card companies, telephone companies, state departments of motor vehicles, health insurers, and nation states.

A public key certificate is a credential that vouches for the bind or join between a key pair and the identity of the owner of the key. Most certificates will vouch for the bind between the key pair and a legal person. It contains the identifiers of the key pair owner and the public half of the key pair. It is signed by the private key of the issuing authority and can be checked using the authority's public key. In addition to the identifiers of the owner and the key, it may also contain the start and end dates of its validity, and its intended purpose, use, and limitations. Like other credentials, it is revocable at the discretion of the issuer and used or not at the discretion of the key owner. Like other credentials, it is likely to be one of several and, for some purposes, may be used in combination with others.

Credential issuers or certification authorities (CAs) are legal persons trusted by others to vouch for the bind, join, or association between a public key and another person or entity. The CA may be a principal, such as the management of a company, a bank, or a credit card company. It may be the secretary of a "club" or other voluntary association, such as a bank clearing house association. It may be a government agency or designee, such as the post office or a notary public. It may be an independent third party operating as a fiduciary and for a profit.

The principal requirement for a certification authority is that it must be trusted by those who will use the certificate and for the purpose for which the certificate is intended. The necessary trust may come from its role, independence, affinity, reputation, contract, or other legal obligation.

USE OF CERTIFICATES FOR MANAGING KEYS

In one-to-one relationships, one knows that one is using the correct public key because one obtains it directly and personally from one's correspondent. However, for large populations and most applications, this is not feasible. In most such cases, it is desirable to obtain the key automatically and late, that is, at or near the time of use.

In a typical messaging application, one might look up one's correspondent in a public directory, using his name as a search argument. As a function, one would get an e-mail address, a public key, and a certificate that bound the key to the name and address.

Exhibit 20.3 illustrates looking up the address whmurray@sprynet.com in the public directory operated by VeriSign, Inc. In addition to the address, the directory returns a public key that goes with that name and address. It also returns a certificate for that key. As a rule, the user will never see nor care about the key or the certificate. They will be handled automatically by the application. However, if one clicked on the <properties> button, one would see the certificate shown in Exhibit 20.4.

If one now clicks <Encrypt> on the message options, the message will now be encrypted using this key. If one signs a message using a private key, the corresponding public key and its certificate will automatically be attached to the message. Other applications work in a similar manner. Tool

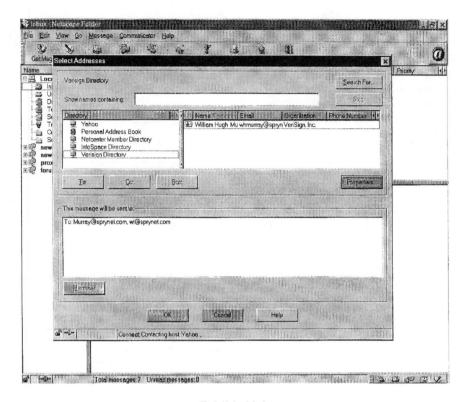

Exhibit 20.3.

kits can be purchased to incorporate these functions into enterprise-developed applications.

IMPLEMENTATIONS

In order to illustrate the power, use, and limitations of modern key management, this section discusses a number of implementations or products. Since the purpose of this discussion is to make points about key management, it will not provide a complete discussion of any of the products. The products are used only for their value as examples of key management. The order of presentation is chosen for illustrative purposes rather than to imply importance.

Kerberos Key Distribution Center

The Kerberos key distribution center (KDC) is a trusted server to permit any two processes that it knows about to obtain trusted copies of a key-session key. Kerberos shares a secret with every process or principal in the

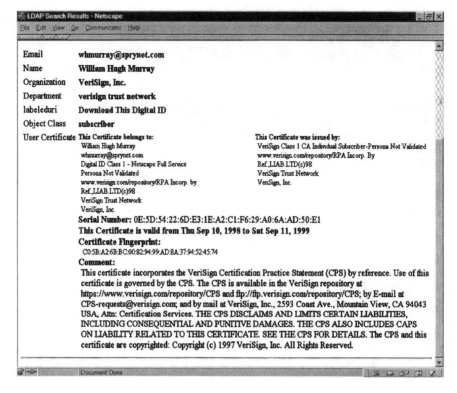

Exhibit 20.4.

population. When A wants to talk to B, it requests a key from the KDC. The KDC takes a random number and encrypts it under the secret it shares with B, appends a second copy of the key, and encrypts the result under the secret that it shares with A. It broadcasts the result into the network addressed to A.

A uses the secret it shares with the KDC to recover its copy of the key and B's copy (encrypted under the secret that B shares with the KDC). It broadcasts B's copy into the network addressed to B. While everyone in the network can see the messages, only A and B can use them. B uses its secret to recover its copy of the key. Now A and B share a key that they can use to talk securely to each other.

This process requires that the KDC be fully trusted to vouch for the identity of A and B, but not to divulge the secrets or the key to other processes or even to use it itself. If the KDC is compromised, all of the secrets will have to be changed, i.e., the principals must all be re-enrolled. These limitations could be reduced if, instead of keeping a copy of the secret shared with the principals, the KDC kept only its public key. Then whatever other remedies might be necessary if the KDC were compromised, there would be no secrets to change.

PGP

PGP stands for Phil's "Pretty Good Privacy." Phil Zimmerman, its author, has received honors and awards for this product, not so much because of its elegant design and implementation, as for the fact that it brought the power of encryption to the masses. It is the encryption mechanism of choice for confidential communication among individuals.

PGP is implemented exclusively in software. It is available in source code, and implementations are available for all popular personal computers. It is available for download from servers all over the world and is free for private use. It is used to encrypt files for protection on the storage of the local system and to encrypt messages to be sent across a distance.

It uses a block cipher, IDEA, with a 128-bit key to encrypt files or messages. It automatically generates a new block-cipher key for each file or message to be encrypted. It uses an asymmetric key algorithm, Rivest–Shamir–Adelman (RSA), to safely exchange this key with the intended recipient by encrypting it using the recipient's public key. Only the intended recipient, by definition the person who has beneficial use of the mathematically corresponding private key, can recover the symmetric key and read the message.

Since the principles of key management require that this key not be stored in the clear, it is stored encrypted under the block cipher. The key for this step is not stored but is generated every time it is needed by compressing to 128 bits an arbitrarily long pass-phrase chosen by the owner of the private key. Thus, beneficial use of the private key requires both a copy of the encrypted key and knowledge of the pass-phrase.

Of course, while PGP does not require secret exchange of a key in advance, it does require that the public key be securely acquired. That is, it must be obtained in a manner that preserves confidence that it is the key of the intended recipient. The easiest way to do this is to obtain it directly, hand-to-hand, from that recipient. However, PGP has features to preserve confidence while passing the public key via e-mail, public servers, or third parties.

Note that if the pass-phrase is forgotten, the legitimate owner will have lost beneficial use of the private key and all message or file keys that were hidden using the public key. For communication encryption the remedy is simply to generate a new key-pair, publish the new public key, and have the originator resend the message using the new key. However, for file encryption, access to the file is lost. As we will see, commercial products use key management to provide a remedy for this contingency.

PGP stores keys in files called "key-rings." These files associate user identifiers with their keys. It provides a number of mechanisms for ensuring that one is using the correct and intended public key for a correspondent. One of these is called the *key fingerprint*. This is a relatively short hash of the key that can be exchanged out of channel and used to check the identity of a key. Alice sends a key to Bob. On receiving the key, Bob computes the fingerprint and checks it with Alice. Note that while fingerprints are information about the public key, they contain even less information about the private key than does the public key itself. Therefore, the fingerprint need not be kept secret.

PGP also provides a record of the level of trust that was attributed to the source of the key when it was obtained. This information is available whenever the key is used. Of course, the existence of this mechanism suggests that all sources are not trusted equally nor equally trustworthy. In practice, entire key rings are often exchanged and then passed on to others. In the process, the provenance of and confidence in a key may be obscured; indeed, the confidence in a key is often no better than hearsay. The documentation of PGP suggests that the potential for duping someone into using the wrong key is one of the greatest limitations to the security of PGP.

ViaCrypt PGP, Business Edition

ViaCrypt PGP, Business Edition, is licensed for business or commercial use and includes *emergency key recovery* features to address some of the limitations of PGP noted above. Instead of encrypting the private key under a key generated on-the-fly from the pass-phrase, it introduces another level of key. This key will be used to encrypt the private key and will itself be hidden using the pass-phrases of the "owners" of the private key. This may be the sole user or it may be an employee and managers representing his employer. In the latter case, the employee is protected from management abuse of the private key by the fact that he has possession of it, while management only has possession of a copy of the key used to hide it. However, both the employee and management are protected from the consequences of loss of a single pass-phrase.

RSA Secure PC

RSA Secure PC is an add-in to the Windows file manager that is used for file encryption. It has features that extend the ideas in PGP BE and illustrate some other uses of key management. It encrypts specified files, directories, or folders, on command, that is, by marking and clicking; or by default, by marking a file or directory and indicating that everything in it is always to be encrypted. Marking the root of a drive would result in all files on the drive, except executables, always being stored in encrypted form.

The object of encryption is always the individual file rather than the drive or the directory. When a file is initially encrypted, the system generates a 64-bit block-cipher key to be used to encrypt the file. This file key is then encrypted using the public key of the system and is stored with the file.

The private key for the system is stored encrypted using a two-level key system and pass-phrase as in PGP BE. In order for a user to read an encrypted file, he must have the file key in the clear. To get that, he must have the private key in the clear. Therefore, when he opens a file, the system looks to see if the private key is in the clear in its memory. If not, then the user is prompted for his pass-phrase so that the private key can be recovered. At the time of this prompt, the user is asked to confirm or set the length of time that the private key is to be kept in the clear in system memory. The default is five minutes. Setting it to zero means that the user will be prompted for a second use. The maximum is 8 hours. The lower the user sets the time that the key may remain in memory, the more secure it is; the higher he sets it, the less often he will be prompted for the pass-phrase.

RSA SecurePC also implements emergency key-recovery features. These features go beyond those described above in that management may specify that multiple parties must be involved in recovering the private key. These features not only permit management to specify the minimum number of parties that must be involved but also permits them to specify a larger set from which the minimum may be chosen. *Multiparty emergency key recovery* provides both the user and management with greater protection against abuse.

BBN SafeKeyper

BBN SafeKeyper is a book-size hardware box for generating and protecting private keys. It generates a private-key/public-key pair. The private key cannot be removed from the box. Beneficial use of the key requires possession of the box and its three physical keys. SafeKeyper is intended for the root key for institutions.

The box has a unique identity and a public key belonging to BBN. After it generates its key pair, it encrypts its public key and its identity under the public key of BBN and broadcasts it into the network addressed to BBN. When BBN recovers the key, it uses its own private key to create a "certificate" for the SafeKeyper that vouches for the bind between the public key and the identity of the person or institution to whom BBN sold the box.

While the SafeKeyper box is very robust, it is still conceivable that it could be destroyed and its key lost. Therefore, it implements *emergency key recovery*. While it is not possible to make an arbitrary copy of its key, it will publish information about its key sufficient to enable another SafeKeyper box to recreate it. For example, information about the Visa masterkey is held by five people. Any three of them acting in concert can reproduce this key.

Secure Socket Layer (SSL)

SSL is both an API and a protocol intended for end-to-end encryption in client–server applications across an arbitrary network. The protocol was developed by NetScape, and the Navigator browser is its reference implementation. It uses public key certificates to authenticate the server to the client and, optionally, the client to the server.

When the browser connects to the secure server, the server sends its public key along with a certificate issued by a public certification authority. The browser automatically uses the issuer's public key to check the certificate, and manifests this by setting the URL to that of the server. It then uses the server's public key to negotiate a session key to be used for the session. It manifests this by setting a solid key icon in the lower-left-hand corner of the screen.

Optionally the client can send its public key and a certificate for that key issued by the management of the server or a certification authority trusted by the management of the server.

RECOMMENDATIONS FOR KEY MANAGEMENT

In order to ensure rigor and discipline, *automate all encryption, particularly including key management*; hide all encryption from users.

In order to resist disclosure or arbitrary copies of a key, *prefer trusted hardware for key storage*. Prefer evaluated (FIPS-140)* hardware, dedicated single-application-only machines (such as those from Atalla, BBN, Cylink, and Zergo), smart cards, PCMCIA cards, laptops, diskettes, and trusted desktops, in that order. As a general rule, one should discourage the use of multi-user systems for key storage except for keys that are the property of the system owner or manager (e.g., payroll manager key).

Prefer one copy of a key; avoid strategies that require multiple copies of a key. Every copy of a key increases the potential for disclosure. For example, rather than replicating a single key across multiple servers, use different keys on each server with a certificate from a common source.

Change keys for each file, message, session, or other object.

* Federal Information Processing Standard 140, http://csrc.ncsl.nist.gov/fips/fips1401.htm

Prefer one key per use or application rather than sharing a key across multiple uses. The more data that is encrypted under a single key, the greater the potential for successful cryptanalysis and the more damaging the consequences. With modern key management, keys are cheap.

In order to reduce the consequences of forgotten pass-phrases, *use emergency key recovery for file encryption applications.* Do not use emergency key recovery for communication encryption; change the key and resend the message.

Employ multiparty control for emergency key recovery; this reduces the potential for abuse, improves accountability, and increases trust all around. Consider requiring that the parties come from different levels of management and from different business or staff functions.

In order to ensure that keys are randomly selected from the entire key space, *prefer closed and trusted processes for key generation.* Avoid any manual operations in key selection.

Prefer encryption and key management that are integrated into the application. The easiest way to hide encryption from the user and to avoid errors is to integrate the encryption into the application.

Similarly, *prefer applications with integrated encryption and key management.* No serious business applications can be done in the modern network environment without encryption. Integrated encryption is a mark of good application design.

Finally, buy *key management code* from competent laboratories; do not attempt to write your own.

Chapter 21
Implementing Kerberos in Distributed Systems

Joe Kovara and Ray Kaplan

Kerberos is a distributed security system that provides a wide range of security services for distributed environments. Those services include authentication and message protection, as well as providing the ability to securely carry authorization information needed by applications, operating systems, and networks. Kerberos also provides the facilities necessary for delegation, where limited-trust intermediaries perform operations on behalf of a client. Entering its second decade of use, Kerberos is arguably the best tested and most scrutinized distributed security system in widespread use today.

Kerberos differs from many other distributed security systems in its ability to incorporate a very wide range of security technologies and mechanisms. That flexibility allows a mixture of security technologies and mechanisms to be used, as narrowly or broadly as required, while still providing the economies of scale that come from a common, reusable, and technology-neutral Kerberos security infrastructure. Technologies and mechanisms that have been incorporated into Kerberos and that are in use today include: certificate-based public key systems, smart cards, token cards, asymmetric-key cryptography, as well as the venerable user-ID and password.

Kerberos's longevity and acceptance in the commercial market are testament to its reliability, efficiency, cost of ownership, and its adaptability to security technologies past, present, and — we believe — future. Those factors have made Kerberos the *de facto* standard for distributed security in large, heterogeneous network environments. Kerberos has been in production on a large scale for years at a variety of commercial, government, and educational organizations, and for over a decade in one of the world's most challenging open systems environments: Project Athena[1] at MIT, where it protects campus users and services from what is possibly the security practitioner's worst nightmare.

HISTORY OF DEVELOPMENT

Many of the ideas for Kerberos originated in a discussion of how to use encryption for authentication in large networks that was published in 1978 by Roger Needham and Michael Schroeder.[2] Other early ideas can be attributed to continuing work by the security community, such as Dorothy Denning's and Giovanni Sacco's work on the use of time stamps in key distribution protocols.[3] Kerberos was designed and implemented in the mid-1980s as part of MIT's Project Athena. The original design and implementation of the first four versions of Kerberos were done by MIT Project Athena members Steve Miller (Digital Equipment Corp.) and Clifford Neuman, along with Jerome Salzer (Project Athena technical director) and Jeff Schiller (MIT campus network manager).

Kerberos versions 1 through 3 were internal development versions and, since its public release in 1989, version 4 of Kerberos has seen wide use in the Internet community. In 1990, John Kohl (Digital Equipment Corp.) and Clifford Neuman (University of Washington at that time and now with the Information Sciences Institute at the University of Southern California) presented a design for version 5 of the protocol based on input from many of those familiar with the limitations of version 4. Currently, Kerberos versions 4 and 5 are available from several sources, including freely distributed versions (subject to export restrictions) and fully supported commercial versions. Kerberos 4 is in rapid decline, and support for it is very limited. This discussion is limited to Kerberos 5.

Current Development

While there have been no fundamental changes to the Kerberos 5 protocol in recent years,[4] development and enhancement of Kerberos 5 continues today.[5] That development continues a history of incremental improvements to the protocol and implementations. Implementation improvements tend to be driven by commercial demands, lessons learned from large deployments, and the normal improvements in supporting technology and methodologies.

Standards efforts within the Internet Engineering Task Force (IETF) continue to play a predominant role in the Kerberos 5 protocol development, reflecting both the maturity of the protocol as well as the volatility of security technology. Protocol development is primarily driven by the emergence of new technologies, and standards efforts continue to provide an assurance of compatibility and interoperability between implementations as new capabilities and technologies are incorporated. Those efforts also ensure that new developments are vetted by the Internet community. Many additions to Kerberos take the form of separate standards, or IETF Request for Comments (RFCs).[6] Those standards make use of elements in the Kerberos protocol specifically intended to allow for extension and the addition and integration of new technologies. Some of those technologies and their integration into Kerberos are discussed in subsequent sections.

As of this writing, both Microsoft[7] and Sun[8] have committed to delivery of Kerberos 5 as a standard feature of their operating systems. Kerberos 5 has also been at the core of security for the Open Software Foundation's Distributed Computing Environment (OSF DCE) for many years.[9] Many application vendors have also implemented the ability to utilize Kerberos 5 in their products, either directly, or through the Generic Security Service Applications Programming Interface (GSS-API).

STANDARDS AND IMPLEMENTATIONS

When discussing any standard, care must be exercised in delineating the difference between what the standard defines, what is required for a solution, and what different vendors provide. As does any good protocol standard, the Kerberos 5 standard leaves as much freedom as possible to each implementation, and as little freedom as necessary to ensure interoperability. The basic Kerberos 5 protocol defines the syntax and semantics for authentication, secure messaging, limited syntax and semantics for authorization, and the application of various cryptographic algorithms within those elements.

The Kerberos 5 protocol implies, but does not define, the supporting infrastructure needed to build a solution that incorporates and makes useful all of the standard's elements. For example, the services that make up the logical grouping of the Kerberos security server are defined by the Kerberos 5 standard. The manifestation of those services — the underlying database that those services require, the supporting management tools, and the efficiency of the implementation — are not defined by the standard. Those elements make the difference between what is theoretically possible and what is real. That difference is a reflection of the state of technology, market demands, and vendor implementation abilities and priorities. In this discussion we have attempted to distinguish between the elements that make up the Kerberos 5 protocol, the elements that are needed to build and deploy a solution, and the variations that can be expected in different implementations.

PERCEPTIONS AND TECHNOLOGY

A review of perceptions about Kerberos will find many anecdotal and casual assertions about its poor usability, inferior performance, or lack of scalability. This appears to be inconsistent with the acceptance of Kerberos by major vendors and can be confusing to those tasked with evaluating security technologies. Much of that confusion is the result of the unqualified use of the term "Kerberos." Kerberos 4 and Kerberos 5 are very different, and any historical references must be qualified as to which version of Kerberos is the subject. As an early effort in distributed security, considerable study was devoted to the weaknesses, vulnerabilities, and limitations of Kerberos 4 and early drafts of the Kerberos 5 standard.[10] Modern implementations of Kerberos 5 address most, if not all, of those issues.

As a pioneering effort in distributed security, Kerberos exposed many new, and sometimes surprising, security issues. Many of those issues are endemic to distributed environments and are a reflection of organization and culture, and the changing face of security as organizations moved from a centralized to a distributed model. As a product of organization and culture, there is little if anything that technology alone can do to address most of those issues. While many of the resulting problems have been attributed to Kerberos, the vast majority of those problems are common to all distributed security systems, regardless of the technology used.

Various implementations of Kerberos have dealt with the broader organizational security issues in different ways, and with different degrees of success. The variability in the success of those implementations has also been a source of confusion. Enterprises that have a business need for distributed security and that understand the organizational, cultural, and security implications of distributed environments — or more accurately distributed business — tend to be most successful in deploying and applying Kerberos. Until very recently, organizations that fit that description have been in a small minority. Successes have also been achieved at other organizations, but those implementations tend to be narrowly focused on an application or a group within the organization. It should be no surprise that organizations that are in need of what Kerberos has to offer have been in the minority. Kerberos is a distributed security system. Distributed computing is still relatively young, and the technology and business paradigms are still far from convergence.

Outside of the minority of organizations with a business need for distributed security, attempts to implement broad-based distributed security systems such as Kerberos have generally failed. Horror stories of failed implementations tend to receive the most emphasis and are typically what an observer first encounters. Stories of successful implementations are more difficult to uncover. Those stories are rarely discussed outside of a small community of security practitioners or those directly involved, as there is generally little of interest to the broader community; "we're more secure than we were before" does not make for good press.

Whether drivers or indicators of change, the advent of the Internet and intranets bespeak a shift, as a greater number of enterprises move to more distributed organizational structures and business processes and discover a business need for solutions to distributed security problems. Those enterprises typically look first to the major vendors for solutions. Driven by customer business needs, those vendors have turned to Kerberos 5 as a key element in their security solutions.

Trust, Identity, and Cost

The vast majority of identity information used in organizations by computer systems and applications today is based on IDs and passwords. That identity information is bound to individuals. That is the result of years of evolution of our computer systems and applications. Any security based on that existing identity information is fundamentally limited by the trust placed in that information. In other words, security is limited by the level of trust we place in our current IDs and passwords as a means of identifying individuals.

Fundamentally increasing the level of trust placed in our identity information and the security of any system that uses those identities requires rebinding, or reverifying, individual identities. That is a very, very expensive proposition for all but the smallest organizations. In simple and extreme terms: any authentication technology purporting to improve the authenticity of individuals that is based on existing identity information is a waste of money; any authentication technology that is not based on existing identity information is too expensive to deploy on any but a small scale. This very simple but very fundamental equation limits all security technologies and the level of security that is practical and achievable.

We must use most of our existing identity information; the alternatives are not affordable. While the situation appears bleak, it is far from hopeless; we must simply be realistic about what can be achieved, and at what cost. There is no "silver bullet." The best that any cost-effective solution can hope to do is establish the current level of trust in individual identities as a baseline and not allow further erosion of that trust. Once that baseline is established, measures can be taken to incrementally improve the situation as needed and as budgets allow. The cheaper those goals can be accomplished, the sooner we will start solving the problem and improving the level of trust we can place in our systems.

Kerberos provides the ability to stop further erosion of our trust in existing identities. Kerberos also allows that level of trust to be improved incrementally, by using technologies that are more secure than IDs and passwords. Kerberos allows both of those to be achieved at the lowest possible cost. The ability for Kerberos to effectively utilize what we have today, stop the erosion, and allow incremental improvement is one of the key factors in the success of Kerberos in real-world environments.

Technology Influences

While technology continues to advance and provide us with the raw materials for improving Kerberos, many of the assumptions and influences that originally shaped Kerberos are still valid today. Although new security technologies may captivate audiences, the fundamentals have not changed. One fundamental of security that should never be forgotten is that a security system must be affordable and reliable if it is to achieve the goal of improving an organization's security.

An affordable and reliable security system makes the most of what exists, and does not require the use of new, expensive or unproven technologies as a prerequisite to improving security. A good security system such as Kerberos allows those newer technologies to be used but does not mandate them. With rapid advances in technology, single-technology solutions are also doomed to rapid obsolescence. Solutions that are predicated on new technologies will, by definition, see limited deployment until the cost and reliability of those solutions are acceptable to a broad range of organizations. The longer that evolution takes, the higher the probability that even newer technologies will render them, and any investment made in them, obsolete.

Moreover, history teaches us that time provides the only real validation of security. That is a difficult proposition for security practitioners when the norm in the information industry is a constant race of the latest and greatest. However, the historical landscape is littered with security technologies, most created by very smart people, that could not stand the test of time and the scrutiny of the security community. The technology influences that have shaped Kerberos have been based on simple and proven fundamentals that provide both a high degree of assurance and a continuing return on investment.

Protocol Placement

Kerberos is often described as an "application-layer protocol." While that description is nominally correct, and most descriptions of Kerberos are from the perspective of the application, the unfortunate result is a perception that Kerberos requires modification of applications in order to be useful. Kerberos is not limited to use at the application layer, nor does Kerberos require modification of applications. Kerberos can be, and is, used very effectively at all layers of the network, as well as in middleware. Placing Kerberos authentication, integrity, confidentiality, and access control services below the application layer can provide significant improvements in security without the need to modify applications. The most obvious example of security "behind the scenes" is the use of Kerberos for authentication and key management in a virtual private network (VPN).

However, there are limits to what can be achieved without the cooperation and knowledge of an application. Those limits are a function of the application and apply to all security systems. Providing an authenticated and encrypted channel (e.g., using a VPN) may improve the security of access to the application and the security of information flowing between a client and the application. However, that alone does nothing to improve the usability of the application and does not take advantage of Kerberos's ability to provide secure single sign-on. For example, an application that insists on a local user-ID for the users of that application will require mapping between the Kerberos identity and the application-specific user-ID. An application that insists on a password will typically require some form of "password stuffing" to placate the application — even if the password is null. Some applications make life easier by providing hooks, call-outs, or exits that allow augmenting the application with alternative security mechanisms. Other applications that do not provide this flexibility require additional and complex infrastructure in order to provide the appearance of seamless operation. Note that these issues are a function of the applications, and not the security system. All security systems must deal with identical issues, and they will generally be forced to deal with those issues in similar ways.

While we can formulate solutions to authentication, confidentiality, integrity, and access control that are useful and that are independent of a broad range of applications, the same cannot be said of delegation and authorization. In this context, the assertion that Kerberos requires modification of the application is correct. However, that requirement has little if any affect on the practical employment of Kerberos, because very few applications in use today need, or could make use of, those capabilities. Applications that can understand and make use of those capabilities are just starting to appear.

Passwords

One of the primary objectives of Kerberos has always been to provide security end-to-end. That is, all the way from an individual to a service, without the requirement to trust intermediaries. Kerberos can be, and is, also used to provide security for intermediate components such as computer systems, routers, and virtual private networks. However, humans present the most significant challenge for any security system, and Kerberos does an exemplary job of meeting that challenge.

The simple user-ID and password are far and away the most common basis for identification and authentication used by humans and applications today. Whatever their faults, simple IDs and passwords predominate the security landscape and will likely do so for the foreseeable future. They are cheap, portable, and provide adequate security for many applications — virtually all applications in use today. Kerberos is exceptional in its ability to provide a high level of security with nothing more than those IDs and passwords. Kerberos allows more sophisticated identification and authentication mechanisms to be used, but does not mandate their use.

Kerberos is specifically designed to eliminate the transmission of passwords over the network. Passwords are not transmitted in any form as a part of the Kerberos authentication process. The only case in which a password or a derivation of the password (i.e., a key derived from the password) is transmitted is during a password-change operation — assuming, of course, that passwords are being used for authentication, and not an alternative technology such as smart cards. During a password-change operation, the password or its derivation is always protected using Kerberos confidentiality services.

Cryptography

The need to provide effective security using nothing more than very low-cost methods such as an ID and password has had a significant influence on the Kerberos protocol and its use of cryptography. In particular, using a password as the sole means for identification and authentication requires that the password be the basis of a shared secret between the user and the Kerberos security server. That also requires the use of symmetric-key cryptography. While shared secrets and symmetric-key cryptography have been derided as "legacy" authentication technology, there are few if any alternatives to passwords if we want to provide an affordable and deployable solution sooner, rather than later.

The efficiency of cryptographic methods has also had a significant influence on the protocol and its use of cryptography. Although Kerberos can incorporate asymmetric-key cryptography, such as elliptic curve cryptography (ECC) and RSA, Kerberos can provide all of the basic security services using shared secrets and symmetric-key cryptography. Because of the CPU-intensive nature of asymmetric-key cryptography, the ability to use symmetric-key cryptography is extremely important for environments or applications that are performance-sensitive, such as high-volume transaction-processing systems, where each transaction is individually authenticated.

Online Operation

In a distributed environment, individuals and services are scattered across many computer systems and are geographically dispersed. Whatever their physical distribution, those individuals and services operate within a collective enterprise. Typically, the association between an individual and his access to enterprise services is reestablished at the beginning of each workday, such as through a login. Day-to-day work in the distributed enterprise requires an individual to make use of many different services, and an individual typically establishes an association with a service, performs work, and then terminates the association. All of these functions occur online.

The association between individual and service may be very short-lived, such as for the duration of a single transaction. In other cases that association is long-lived and spans the workday. Whatever the duration of the association, the vast majority of work is performed online. That is, the individual and the service interact in real-time. Offline operation, while sometimes necessary, is fast becoming a rarity. Notable exceptions are "road warriors," who must be capable of operating offline. However, that is a function of the limitations of connectivity, not of any desire to operate offline — as any road warrior will tell you.

The combined ability to provide both efficient and secure access to services, and the ability to serve as the basis for a collective security mechanism is one of Kerberos's major strengths. In order to deliver those capabilities, and deliver them efficiently, the Kerberos security server operates online. Extending that concept to an aggregate "enterprise security service" that incorporates Kerberos allows economies and efficiencies to be achieved across multiple security functions, including authentication, authorization, access control, and key management — all of which can be provided by, or built from, Kerberos. While the concept of an aggregate enterprise security service is not native to Kerberos, the union of the two is very natural. Moreover, given the direction of technology and the composition and conduct of modern distributed enterprises, online security services are both required and desirable. These attributes have much to do with the adoption of Kerberos as the basis for providing enterprise security, as opposed to Internet security.

ORGANIZATIONAL MODEL

There are many different approaches to distributed security, and each involves tradeoffs between scalability and resources. The only objective measure of a distributed security system is cost, as measured by the resources required to achieve a given level of security over a given scale. Resources include computational overhead, network bandwidth, and people. The resulting cost bounds the achievable security and the scalability of the system. The tradeoffs that must be made involve both the technology and the security model appropriate to an organization. The extremes of those organizational models are autocracy and anarchy.

Autocracy. All control flows from a central authority. That authority defines the association between itself and the individual and the level of trust it places in an individual. This model requires a level of control that is cost-prohibitive in today's distributed environments. The classic military or business models tend toward this end of the spectrum.

Anarchy. All authority flows from individuals. Each individual defines the association between himself and an enterprise and the level of trust they place in an enterprise. This model achieves no economies of scale or commonality. The Internet tends toward this end of the spectrum.

Where in that spectrum an enterprise lives depends on business practices and culture, and every enterprise is different. Within a single enterprise it is not unusual to find organizational units that span the entire spectrum. That variability places significant demands on a distributed security system, and in some cases those demands may conflict. Conflicting demands occur when multiple enterprises — or even different business units within the same enterprise — with very different business practices or cultures engage in a common activity, such as is typical in supplier and partner relationships. The extreme case of conflicting demands is most often seen when the enterprise meets the Internet. As enterprise boundaries continue to dissolve, the probability of conflicting demands increases, as does the need for security systems to cope with those conflicting demands.

Kerberos most naturally falls in the middle of the spectrum between the extremes of autocracy and anarchy. Depending on implementation and the technology that is incorporated, Kerberos can be applied to many points along that spectrum and can be used to bridge points along the spectrum. Kerberos's effectiveness drops as you approach the extreme ends of the spectrum. As a security system, Kerberos provides a means to express and enforce a common set of rules across a collective; by definition, that collective is not anarchy. As a distributed security system, Kerberos is designed to solve problems that result from autonomous (and hence untrusted) elements within the environment; by definition, that cannot be an autocracy. Note that "distributed" does not necessarily imply physically distributed. For example, if the LAN to which your computer is connected cannot ensure the confidentiality and integrity of data you send across it, then you are in a distributed security environment.

TRUST MODELS

The level of trust that is required between entities in a distributed system is a distinguishing characteristic of all distributed security systems, and affects all other services that are built on the system, as well as the scalability of the system. A prerequisite to trust is authentication: knowing the identity of the person (or machine) you are dealing with. In Kerberos, the entities that authenticate with one another are referred to as "principals," as in "principals to a transaction."

Direct Trust

Historically, users and applications have established direct trust relationships with one another. For example, each user of each application requires a user-ID and password to access that application; the user-ID and password represents a direct trust relationship between the user and the application. As the number of users and applications grows, the number of direct relationships, and the cost of establishing and managing those relationships, increases geometrically (Exhibit 21.1). A geometric increase in complexity and cost is obviously not sustainable and limits the scalability of such solutions to a small number of applications or users.

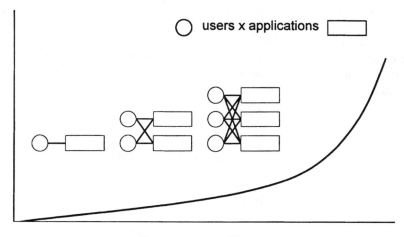

Exhibit 21.1. Direct Trust Relationships

A secure authentication system does not, in and of itself, reduce the complexity of this problem. The increase in complexity is a function of the number of direct trust relationships and has nothing to do with the security of the user-to-application authentication mechanism. An example of this is seen in Web-based applications that use IDs and passwords for authentication through the SSL (secure sockets layer) protocol. The SSL protocol can provide secure transmission of the ID and password from the client to the server. However, that alone does not reduce the number of IDs and passwords that users and servers must manage.

Mitigating the increasing cost and complexity of direct trust relationships in the form of many IDs and passwords is the same problem that single sign-on systems attempt to solve. One solution is to use the same user-ID and password for all applications. However, this assumes that all applications a user has access to are secured to the level of the most demanding application or user. That is required because an application has the information required to assume the identity of any of its users, and a compromise of any application compromises all users of that application. In a distributed environment, ensuring that all applications, their host computer systems, and network connections are secured to the required level is cost-prohibitive. The extreme case occurs with applications that are outside the enterprise boundaries. This is a nonscalable trust model.

Indirect Trust

Achieving scalable and cost-effective trust requires an indirect trust model. Indirect trust uses a third party, or parties, to assist in the authentication process. In this model, users and applications have a very strong trust relationship with a common third party, either directly or indirectly. The users and applications, or principals, trust that third party for verification of another principal's identity. The introduction of a third party reduces the geometric increase in complexity (shown in the previous section) to a linear increase in complexity (Exhibit 21.2).

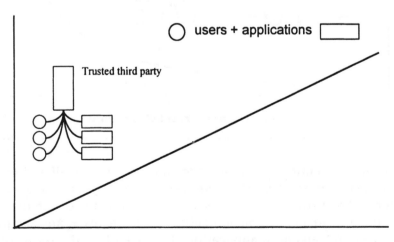

Exhibit 21.2. Indirect Trust Relationships

All scalable distributed security systems use a trusted third party. In the Kerberos system, the trusted third party is known as the Key Distribution Center (KDC). In public key systems, the trusted third party is referred to as a Certificate Authority (CA). In token card systems, the token card vendor's server acts as a trusted third party. Many other applications of third-party trust exist in the world, one of the most obvious being credit cards, where the bank acts as the trusted third party between consumer and merchant. Neither consumer nor merchant shares a high degree of trust with each other, but both trust the credit card issuer. Note that without a credit card, each consumer would have to establish a direct trust relationship with each merchant (i.e., to obtain credit). Credit cards have made it much easier for consumers and merchants to do business, especially over long distances.

Much like credit cards, a trusted third-party authentication system makes it easier for principals to do business — the first step of which is to verify each other's identity. In practical terms, that makes applications, information, and services more accessible in a secure manner. That benefits both consumers and providers of applications, information, and services, and reduces the cost to the enterprise.

SECURITY MODEL

The manner in which a trusted third party provides proof of a principal's identity is a distinguishing characteristic of trusted third party security systems. This has a significant effect on all other services provided by the security system, as well as the scalability of the system. Kerberos uses a credential-based mechanism as the basis for identification and authentication. Those same credentials may also be used to carry authorization information. Kerberos credentials are referred to as "tickets."

Credentials

Requiring interaction with the trusted third party every time verification of identity needs to be done would put an onerous burden on users, applications, the trusted third party, and network resources. In order to minimize that interaction, principals must carry proof of their identity. That proof takes the form of a credential that is issued by the trusted third party to a principal. The principal presents that credential as proof of identity when requested.

All scalable distributed security systems use credentials. The Kerberos credential, or ticket, is analogous to an X.509 certificate in a public key system. These electronic credentials are little different conceptually than physical credentials, such as a passport or driver's license, except that cryptography is used to make the electronic credentials resistant to forgery and tampering. As with physical credentials, an electronic credential is something you can "carry around with you," without the need for you to constantly go back to an authority to reassert and verify your identity, and without the need for services to go back to that authority to verify your identity or the authenticity of the credential. Note that the use of a trusted third party for authentication does not imply the use of credentials. Token card systems are an example of trusted third-party authentication without credentials. The result of the authentication using such a card is a simple yes–no answer, not a reusable credential, and every demand for authentication results in an interaction with both the user and the token card server.

The stronger a credential, the stronger the assurance that the principal's claimed identity is genuine. The strength of a credential is dependent on both technology and environmental factors. Since a credential is carried by each principal, the credential must be tamper-proof and not forgeable. A credential's resistance to tampering and forgery is contingent on the strength of the cryptography used. Assurance of identity is contingent on the diligence of the trusted third party in verifying the identity of the principal's identity prior to issuing the credential. Assurance of identity is also contingent on the secure management of the credential by the principal. As with physical credentials, electronic Kerberos credentials, and the information used to derive them must be protected, just as an individual's private key in a public key system must be protected.

As in the real world, all electronic credentials are not created equal. Simply possessing a credential does not imply universal acceptance or trust. As in the real world, the use and acceptance of a credential depends on the trust placed in the issuing authority, the integrity of the credential (resistance to forgery or tampering), and the purpose for which it is intended. For verification of identity, both passports and driver's licenses are widely accepted. A passport is typically trusted more than a driver's license, because the criteria for obtaining a passport are more stringent and a passport is more difficult to forge or alter. However, a passport says nothing about the holder's authorization or ability to operate a motor vehicle. A credential may also be single-purpose, such as a credit card. The issuing bank, as the trusted third party, provides protection to both the consumer and the merchant for a limited purpose: purchasing goods and services.

Credential Lifetime

As with physical credentials, the application and integrity of electronic credentials should limit the lifetime for which those credentials may be used. That lifetime may be measured in seconds or years, depending on the use of the credential. The strength of the cryptography that protects the integrity of the credential also effectively limits the lifetime of a credential. Credentials with longer lifetimes require stronger cryptography, because the credential is potentially exposed to attack for a longer period of time. However, cryptography is rarely the limiting factor in credential lifetime. Other issues, such as issuing cost and revocation cost, tend to be the determining factors for credential lifetime.

The distinguishing characteristic of credential-based systems is the lifetime of the credentials that they can feasibly accommodate. The longer the lifetime of a credential, the less often a new credential must be issued. However, the longer the life of a credential, the higher the probability that information embedded in the credential will change, or that the credential will be lost or stolen. The old "telephone book" revocation lists published by credit card companies is an example of the cost and complexity of revocation on a very large scale. Credit card companies have since moved to online authorization in order to lower costs and respond more rapidly.

Long-lived credentials reduce the credential-issuing cost but increase the credential-revocation cost. The shorter the lifetime of a credential, the more often a new credential must be issued. That increases the cost of the issuing process but reduces the cost of the revocation process. Credentials that are used only for authentication can have a relatively long lifetime. An individual's identity is not likely to change, and revocation would be necessary only if the credential was lost or stolen, or if the association between the individual and the issuing authority has been severed (e.g., such as when an employee leaves a company). Credentials that explicitly or implicitly carry authorization information generally require a shorter lifetime, because that information is more likely to change than identity information.

Different systems accommodate different lifetimes depending on the cost of issuing and revoking a credential and the intended use of the credential. While Kerberos credentials can have lifetimes of minutes or decades, they typically have lifetimes of hours or days. The process of constructing and issuing credentials is extremely efficient in Kerberos. That efficiency is key to Kerberos's ability to support authorization, capabilities, and delegation where new credentials may need to be issued frequently.

Capabilities

Credentials that carry authorization information are referred to as "capabilities," as they imply certain capabilities, or rights, upon the carrier of the credential. Kerberos supports capabilities by allowing authorization information to be carried within a Kerberos credential. As with other credentials, it is imperative that capabilities be resistant to tampering and forgery. We most often think of authorization information as coming from a central authorization service that provides commonly used information to various services (e.g., group membership information) where that information defines the limit of an individual's authorization. Kerberos supports this model by allowing authorization information from an authorization service to be embedded in a Kerberos credential when it is issued by the KDC; that authorization information is then available to services as a normal part of the Kerberos authentication process. Kerberos also supports a capability model based on "restricted proxies," in which the authorization granted to intermediate services may be restricted by the client.[11]

Delegation

There are also situations in which an individual authorizes another person to act on his behalf, thereby delegating some authority to that person. This is analogous to a power of attorney. Consider the simple example of a client who wants to print a file on a file server using a print server. The client wants to ensure that the print server can *print* (read) only the requested file, and not *write* on the file, or read any other files. The file server wants to ensure that the client really requested that the file be printed (and thus that the print server needs read-access to the file) and that the print server did not forge the request. The client should also limit the time for which the print server has access to the file, otherwise the print server would have access to the file for an indefinite period of time.

The extreme case is when an individual delegates unrestricted use of his identity to another person. As with an unrestricted power of attorney, allowing unrestricted use of another's identity can be extremely dangerous. (Obviously the authority that one individual can delegate to another must be limited by the authority of the delegating individual — we cannot allow an individual to grant authority they do not have, or the security of the entire system would crumble.) Unrestricted use of another's identity can also make end-to-end auditing much more difficult in many applications. Kerberos allows delegation of a subset of an individual's authority by allowing them to place authorization restrictions in a capability. The restricted proxy in Kerberos serves this function and is analogous to a restricted power of attorney. In the example above, the client would typically restrict the print server's right to read only the file that is to be printed using a restricted proxy. When the print server presents the resulting capability to the file server, the file server has all the information needed to ensure that neither the print server nor the client can exceed its authority, either individually or in combination.

In modern networks and business processes, it is common to find situations such as the above. Three-tier applications are another example. Here, the middle tier acts on the client's behalf for accessing back-end services. Delegation ensures the integrity and validity of the exchange and minimizes the amount of trust that must be placed in any intermediary. The need for delegation grows in significance as applications and services become more interconnected and as those connections become more dynamic. Without delegation, the identity and the rights of the originator, and the validity of a request, become difficult or impossible to determine with any degree of assurance. The alternative is to secure all intermediaries to the level required by the most sensitive application or user that makes use of the intermediary. This is cost-prohibitive on any but a very small scale.

SECURITY SERVICES

Many component security services are required to provide a complete distributed security service. The effectiveness of a distributed security system can be gauged by the component services it provides,[12] the degree to which those components operate together to provide a complete distributed security service, and the efficiency with which it provides those services.

Authentication

An authentication service permits one principal to determine the identity of another principal. The strength of an authentication service is the level of assurance that a principal's claimed identity is genuine. Put another way, the strength depends on the ease with which an attacker may assume the identity of another principal. For example, sending a person's ID and password across a network in the clear provides a very weak authentication, because the information needed to assume the identity of that person is readily available to any eavesdropper. Kerberos provides strong authentication by providing a high level of assurance that a principal's claimed identity is genuine. Kerberos also provides mutual authentication so that the identity of both client and service can be assured.

The reason for authentication is to ensure the identity of each principal prior to their conversing. However, without continuing assurance that their conversation has not been subverted, the utility of authentication alone is questionable. The Kerberos authentication protocol implicitly provides the cryptographic material, or "session keys," needed for establishing a secure channel that continues to protect the principal's conversation after authentication has occurred.

Secure Channels

A secure channel provides integrity and confidentiality services to communicating principals. Kerberos provides these services either directly through the use of Kerberos protocol messages, or indirectly by providing the cryptographic material needed by other protocols or applications to implement their own form of a secure channel.

Integrity

An integrity service protects information against unauthorized modification and provides assurance to the receiver that the information was sent by the proper party. Kerberos provides message integrity through the use of signed message checksums or one-way hashes using a choice of algorithms. Each principal in a Kerberos message exchange separately derives a checksum or hash for the message. That checksum or hash is then protected using a choice of cryptographic algorithms. The session keys needed for integrity protection are a product of the Kerberos authentication process.

Integrity applies not only to a single message, but to a stream of messages. As applied to a stream of messages, integrity also requires the ability to detect replays of messages. Simple confidentiality protection does not necessarily accomplish this. For example, recording and then replaying an encrypted message such as "Credit $100 to account X" several hundred times may achieve an attacker's goal without the need to decrypt or tamper with the message contents. The Kerberos protocol provides the mechanisms necessary to thwart replay attacks for both authentication and data.

Confidentiality

A confidentiality service protects information against unauthorized disclosure. Kerberos provides message confidentiality by encrypting messages using a choice of encryption algorithms. The session keys needed for confidentiality protection are a product of the Kerberos authentication process. Analysis based on message network addresses and traffic volume may also be used to infer information. An increase in the traffic between two business partners may predict a merger. Kerberos does not provide a defense against traffic analysis. Indeed, most don't since it is a very difficult problem.

Access Control

An access control service protects information from disclosure or modification in an unauthorized manner. Note that access control requires integrity and confidentiality services. Kerberos does not directly provide access control for persistent data, such as disk files. However, the Kerberos protocol provides for the inclusion and protection of authorization information needed by applications and operating systems in making access control decisions.

Authorization

An authorization service provides information that is used to make access control decisions. The secure transport of that authorization information is required in order to ensure that access control decisions are not subverted. Common mechanisms used to represent authorization information include access control lists (ACLs) and capabilities.

An ACL-based system uses access control lists to make access control decisions. An ACL-based system is built on top of other security services, including authentication, and integrity and confidentiality for distribution and management of ACLs. Kerberos does not provide an ACL-based authorization system but does provide all of the underlying services an ACL-based system requires.

Capability-based systems require the encapsulation of authorization information in a tamper-proof package that is bound to an identity. Capability-based authorization is a prerequisite to delegation in a distributed environment. Kerberos provides the facilities necessary for both capability-based authorization and delegation.

Nonrepudiation

Nonrepudiation services provide assurance to senders and receivers that an exchange between the two cannot subsequently be repudiated by either. That assurance requires an arbitration authority that both parties agree to; presentation of sufficient and credible proof by the parties to the arbitrator; and evaluation of that proof by the arbitrator in order to settle the dispute. For example, in the case of an electronic funds transfer between two business entities, a court of law would be the arbitrator that adjudicates repudiation-based disputes that arise between the two businesses.

The technological strength of a nonrepudiation service depends on the resistance to tampering or falsification of the information offered as proof and the arbitrator's ability to verify the validity of that information. Resistance to tampering or falsification must be sufficient to prevent modification of the proof for as long as a dispute might arise. While Kerberos offers the basic authentication and integrity services from which a nonrepudiation service could be built, the effectiveness of that service will depend on the required strength of the service, and it is dependent on what technologies are incorporated into a Kerberos implementation and the management of the implementation.

The symmetric-key cryptography as used by basic Kerberos implementations is generally not sufficient for nonrepudiation, because two parties share a key. Since that key is the basis of any technical proof, either party in possession of that key can forge or alter the proof. If augmented with strict process controls and protection for the KDC, symmetric-key cryptography may be acceptable. However, that process control and protection can be quite expensive. (Note that banks face this issue with the use of PINs, which use symmetric-key cryptography; and the fact that two parties share that key — the consumer and the bank — is rarely an issue, because the bank provides sufficient process controls and protection for management of the PIN.) Kerberos does not offer the arbitration services that are required for the complete implementation of such a service.

Availability

Availability services provide an expected level of performance and availability such as error-free bandwidth. Perhaps the best example of an availability problem is a denial-of-service attack. Consider someone simply disconnecting the cable that connects a network segment to its router. Kerberos does not offer any services to deal with this set of problems. Distributed security systems generally do not offer availability services.

FUNCTIONAL OVERVIEW

The ultimate objective of any Kerberos user is to gain access to application services. The process by which that occurs involves several steps, the last step being the actual authentication between the user and the application service. A key part of that process involves the trusted third party in the Kerberos system, the Kerberos security server (KDC). While descriptions of that process correctly focus on the interaction between users and the KDC, one of the key design elements of Kerberos is the ability for clients and services to securely interact, with little or no involvement of the KDC.

Kerberos is a trusted third-party, credentials-based authentication system. The KDC acts as the trusted third party for humans and services, or principals that operate on client or server computer systems. Kerberos principals authenticate with one another using Kerberos credentials, or tickets. These tickets are issued to principals by the KDC. A client principal authenticates to a service principal using a ticket. The Kerberos security server is not directly involved in that client–service authentication exchange. The result of an authentication exchange between a client and service is a shared session key that can be used to protect subsequent messages between the client and the service.

Components

The primary components of a Kerberos system are the client and server computer systems on which applications operate, and the Kerberos security server (KDC.) In addition to those physical components, there are a number of additional logical components and services that make up the

Kerberos system, such as the authentication service and the principals that make use of Kerberos services.

KDC. The keystone of the Kerberos system is the Kerberos security server, generally referred to as the "KDC," or Key Distribution Center. While the term KDC is not an accurate description of all the services provided, it has stuck. The KDC is the trusted third party in the Kerberos distributed security system. The KDC provides authentication services, as well as key distribution and management functions. There may be multiple KDCs, depending on the level of service and performance that is required. The KDC consists of a set of services and a database that contains information about principals.

Principal. The entities to which the KDC provides services are referred to as "principals." Principals share a very high degree of trust with the KDC. They may be human or may represent a service or a machine. Every principal has an identifier that is used by the KDC to uniquely identify a human or service and allow one principal to determine the identity of another during the Kerberos authentication process. Depending on the cryptographic mechanisms used, a principal may also share a secret key with the KDC, thus the high level of trust required between principals and the KDC.

The primary difference between human and service principals results from the available means for storing the password, or key, and the persistence of that key. A person can securely carry a password in his head, whereas services cannot. Services that use shared secrets for authentication require access to a key. Unlike keys that are used by humans — which are typically derived from a password — service keys are typically random bit strings. If unattended operation for services is required, that key must be kept in persistent storage that is accessible to the service. That key storage is referred to as a "key table" and is generally kept in a file on the host computer system on which the service operates. Key tables may contain keys for multiple services, or may be unique to a service. The security of key tables is dependent on the host computer system's security. This is identical to the problem of protecting private keys in public-key or asymmetric-key systems. More secure solutions for protection of key tables require tamper-proof hardware such as a smart card.

The most significant functional difference between a client and a service results from the difference in key persistence. Kerberos clients do not maintain the user's key in any form beyond a very short period of time during the initial authentication process (see below). However, services always have ready access to their key in the key table. The result is that clients generally can only initiate communications, whereas services may either initiate or accept communications (i.e., a service may also act as a client).

Ticket. A ticket is part of a cryptographically sealed credential issued by the KDC to a client. A ticket, along with other confidential information, allows a client to prove their identity to a service, without the client and service having any preestablished relationship. A ticket is specific to a client–service pair. That is, a ticket specifies both a client principal and the service principal: the client principal to whom the ticket was issued, and the service principal for which it is intended. A client may reuse tickets. Once a client obtains a ticket for a service, subsequent authentication of the client to the service does not require involvement of the KDC.

Realm. The KDC logically consists of a set of services and a database that contains information about principals. In Kerberos that collective is referred to as a "realm," and the authentication service within the KDC is the trusted third party for all principals in the realm. Realms may be defined based on either security requirements in order to separate domains of trust, or as an administrative convenience for grouping principals. Some implementations allow a single KDC to serve multiple realms to reduce the number of physical systems needed. Principals in different realms can interact using "cross-realm" (sometimes referred to as "inter-realm") authentication. Cross-realm authentication generally requires prior agreement between the administrators of the different realms.

Principal Identifier. Kerberos defines several principal identifier forms, including a native Kerberos form, as well as an X.500 distinguished-name form. We describe only the native Kerberos name form here. Simple principal identifiers take the form **name@REALM**. Principal identifiers are case sensitive. By convention, the realm name is the DNS domain name in upper case. For example, **hanley@Z.COM** refers to the principal named **hanley** in domain **z.com**. Principal identifiers may also contain an instance. Instances are typically used only for service principals (see *Names and Locations*, and *Operation* later in this chapter).

Authentication

The simplest and most basic form of the Kerberos protocol performs authentication using a shared secret and symmetric-key cryptography: the user and KDC share a secret key, and the service and KDC share a secret key. However, the user and service do not share a secret key. Providing the ability for a user and service to authenticate, and establish a shared secret, where none previously existed, is the fundamental purpose of the Kerberos protocol.

For this basic form of Kerberos authentication to work, users and services must first share a secret key with the KDC. Methods for first establishing that shared secret vary (see *Operation*). The steps of the basic authentication process are discussed below and shown in Exhibit 21.3.

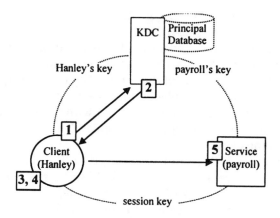

Exhibit 21.3. Basic Kerberos Authentication

1. A user, or more precisely, Kerberos client software on the user's work station acting on behalf of the user, prompts the user for his ID. The client then sends that ID to the KDC as an assertion of the user's identity, along with the name of a service that the client wishes to access, (for example, "I'm Hanley and I want access to the payroll service").

2. The authentication service (AS) of the KDC receives that request, constructs a reply, and sends that reply to the client.

   2.1. The AS checks to ensure that the requesting client (Hanley) and service (payroll) principals exist in the principal database maintained by the KDC. Assuming they exist, the AS constructs a "service ticket" for the requested service (payroll) and places the user's principal name (Hanley) into that service ticket.

   2.2. The AS then generates a random key, referred to as the "session key."

   2.3. The AS then places the session key into the service ticket. The service ticket is then encrypted, or "sealed," using the service's key, obtained from the principal database. That service key is a secret key the (payroll) service shares with the KDC. That key is held in the principal database, as well as by the service.

   2.4. The AS constructs the client part of the reply and places the same session key (from step 2.2) into the client part of the reply. The client part of the reply is then encrypted using the user's key, obtained from the principal database. That is, the secret key (i.e., password) the user (Hanley) shares with the KDC. That key is held in the principal database, as well as by the user.

3. The client receives the reply from the AS, and prompts the user for his password. That password is then converted to a key, and that

key is then used to decrypt, or "unseal," the client part of the reply from the AS (from step 2.4).

If that decryption succeeds, then the password/key entered by the user is the same as the user's key held by the KDC (i.e., the key used to encrypt the client part of the reply). The decryption process also exposes the session key placed into the reply by the AS (from step 2.4). Note that the client cannot tamper with the service ticket in the reply, because it is encrypted, or "sealed," using the service's key, not the client's key.

If the decryption does not succeed, then the password the user entered is incorrect, or the real AS did not issue the reply, or the user is not who he claims to be. In any case, the information in the AS's reply is useless because it cannot be decrypted without the proper password/key, and the process ends.

The following steps assume that the decryption process succeeded. Note that the AS has no knowledge of whether or not the decryption process on the client succeeded.

4. When the client (Hanley) wishes to authenticate to the service (payroll), the client constructs a request to the service. That request contains the service ticket for the payroll service issued by the AS (from step 2.3).

5. The service receives the request from the client, and uses its service key to decrypt the ticket in the request, i.e., the key that is the shared secret between the (payroll) service and the KDC, and that was used to encrypt the service ticket by the AS (from step 2.3).

   If the decryption succeeds, the service's key and the key that the ticket is encrypted in are the same. Since the KDC is the only other entity that knows the service's key, the service knows that the ticket was issued by the KDC, and the information in the ticket can be trusted. Specifically, the client principal name placed into the ticket by the AS (from step 2.1) allows the service to authenticate the client's identity. The decryption process also exposes the session key placed into the service ticket by the AS (from step 2.3).

   If the decryption fails, then the ticket is not valid. It was either not issued by the real AS, or the user has tampered with the ticket. In any case, the ticket is useless because it cannot be decrypted, and the process ends.

At this point, the service (payroll) has proof of the client's identity (Hanley), and both the client and the service share a common key: the session key generated by the AS (from step 2.2), and successfully decrypted by the client (from step 3) and by the service (from step 5). That common session key can then be used for protecting subsequent messages between the client and the service. Note that once the ticket is issued to the client, there is no KDC involvement in the authentication exchange between the client and the service. Also note that the user's password/key is held on the work station, and thus exposed on the work station, only for the period of time required to decrypt the reply from the KDC.

A thief could eavesdrop on the transmission of the reply from the KDC to the client. However, without the user's key, that reply cannot be decrypted. A thief could also eavesdrop on the transmission of the service's ticket. However, without the service's key, that ticket cannot be decrypted. Without knowledge of the user's or service's keys, the attacker is left with encrypted blobs that are of no use. There are other more sophisticated attacks that can be mounted, such as a replay attack, and there are other countermeasures in Kerberos to help thwart those attacks; those attacks and countermeasures are discussed in subsequent sections.

Credentials Caching

The authentication exchange described above allows a client and service to securely authenticate and securely establish a shared secret — the session key — without requiring a preestablished secret between the client and service. While those are useful and necessary functions of any distributed authentication service, it requires that the user obtain a service ticket each time access is required to a service. It also requires that the user enter a password each time a service ticket is obtained in order to decrypt the ticket. This behavior would obviously not be a very efficient use of people's time or network bandwidth.

A simple additional step to cache credentials — that is, the service ticket and session key — would allow the reuse of credentials without having to constantly go back to the AS or requiring user involvement. A "credentials cache" on the client serves this purpose, and all Kerberos implementations provide a credentials cache. Thus, as the user collects service tickets during the day, they can be placed into the credentials cache and reused. This eliminates involvement between the user and the AS when the same service is accessed multiple times. Note that a client requires both a ticket and the ticket's associated session key (a credential) to make use of a ticket. Thus the term "credentials cache," and not "ticket cache."

Kerberos can also limit the usable life of credentials by placing an expiration time into the ticket when the AS constructs the ticket. The ticket expires after that time, and the user must go back to the AS to obtain another ticket. While Kerberos tickets can have virtually any lifetime, the typical lifetime of a Kerberos ticket is the average workday.

Ticket-Granting

Even with credentials caching, interaction between the user and the authentication service (AS) would still be required every time the user wants another ticket. For environments in which a user may access dozens of services during the day, this is unacceptable. One possible solution would be to cache the user's password in order to obtain service tickets without user interaction. However, that exposes the user's password to theft by rogue client software. Note that rogue software could also steal credentials from the credentials cache. However, those credentials will typically expire after a day or less. So, while a thief may have a day's fun with stolen credentials, at least the thief doesn't get indefinite use of the user's identity. Thus, we can limit the duration of such a compromise to the lifetime of the credentials. The ability to limit a compromise in both space and time is an extremely important attribute of a distributed security system. However, if the user's password is stolen, it is much more difficult to limit such a compromise.

The solution to this problem builds on the three parts that we already have: the authentication service (AS), which can issue tickets for services to clients; the credentials cache on the client that allows reuse of a ticket; and the ability to authenticate a user to a service using an existing credential. Using those components, we can then build a service that issues tickets for other services, much like the AS. However, our new service accepts a ticket issued by the AS, instead of requiring interaction with the user.

Our new service is known as the "ticket-granting service," or TGS. The TGS operates as part of the KDC along with the authentication service (AS) and has access to the same principal database as the AS. We haven't dispensed with the AS, but the primary purpose of the AS is now to issue tickets for the TGS. A ticket issued by the AS for the TGS is known as a "ticket-granting ticket," or TGT. Using that ticket-granting ticket (TGT), a client can use the ticket-granting service (TGS) to obtain tickets for other services, or "service tickets." Thus, for example, instead of asking the authentication service (AS) for a ticket for the payroll service, the client first asks the AS for a ticket-granting ticket (TGT) for the ticket-granting service (TGS); then, using that TGT, asks the TGS for a service ticket for the payroll service. While that introduces an additional exchange between the client and the KDC, it typically need be done only once at the beginning of the workday. (See Exhibit 21.4.)

By using the AS only once at the beginning of the day to obtain a TGT, and then using that TGT to obtain other service tickets from the TGS, we can make the entire operation invisible to the user and significantly improve the efficiency and security of the process. Thus, the behavior becomes:

1. The first action of the day is to obtain a TGT from the AS as previously described (e.g., providing an ID and password). Only, instead

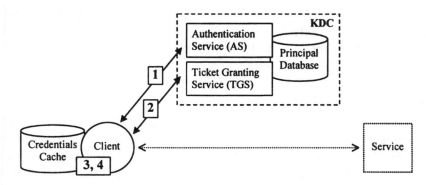

Exhibit 21.4. Authentication and Ticket-Granting Services

of the user specifying the name of a service, the client automatically requests a ticket for the TGS on behalf of the user.

2. The TGT and session key returned by the AS from the prior step is placed into the credentials cache, along with the TGT's session key.
3. When a service ticket is needed, the client sends a request to the TGS (instead of to the AS). That request includes the TGT and the name of the service for which a ticket is needed. The TGS authenticates the client using the TGT just like any other service and, just like the AS, constructs a service ticket for the requested service and returns that ticket and session key to the client.
4. The service ticket and session key returned from the TGS is placed into the credentials cache for reuse. The client may then contact the service and authenticate to the service using that service ticket.

A TGT is identical to any other service ticket and is simply shorthand for "a ticket for the TGS." The AS and TGS are virtually identical, and both can issue tickets for any other service. The primary difference between the AS and TGS is that the TGS uses a TGT as proof of identity, whereas the AS can be used to issue the first, or "initial" ticket. The proof the AS requires before that initial ticket is issued to a user can involves forms that aren't a Kerberos ticket, such as a token card, smart card, public key X.509 certificate, etc. Those various forms of proof are referred to as "preauthentication." Subsequent sections describe the AS and TGS exchanges, the client–service exchanges, and preauthentication in greater detail.

FUNCTIONAL DESCRIPTION

This section builds on the previous discussions and provides a description of both the Kerberos protocol and the interaction of various components in a Kerberos system. Application of the protocol to solve various distributed security problems is also used to illustrate concepts and

415

applications of the protocol. This description is not definitive or complete, and there are many details that have been omitted for clarity and brevity. For a complete description of the protocol, the official standard, Internet RFC 1510, should be consulted.

Initial Authentication

The Kerberos initial authentication process is the point in time when an individual proves his identity to Kerberos and obtains a ticket-granting ticket (TGT). Typical implementations integrate the initial authentication process with the host OS login, providing a single point of authentication for the user each morning. A variety of technologies can be brought to bear at this point, depending on the level of assurance that is needed for an individual's identity. Once initial authentication is completed, the TGT obtained as a result of that initial authentication can be used to obtain service tickets from the ticket-granting service (TGS) for other services. Those service tickets are the basis for client–service authentication, as well as the establishment of the keys needed to subsequently protect client–service interactions.

The simplest form of initial authentication uses an ID and password, as previously described:

1. The client asserts its identity by sending a Kerberos principal name to the KDC. The client sends no proof of its identity at this time. To put it another way, the proof offered by the client at this time is null.
2. The KDC then constructs a TGT and a reply that is encrypted in the user's key. That key is derived from the user's password and is a shared secret between the user and the KDC.
3. The KDC then sends the (encrypted) reply with the TGT back to the client.
4. The client receives the reply from the KDC, then prompts the user for his password and converts the password to a key. That key is then used to decrypt the reply from the KDC.
5. If the reply from the KDC decrypts properly, the user has authenticated. If the reply does not decrypt properly, the password provided by the user is incorrect.

Note that authentication actually occurs on the client, and the KDC has no knowledge of whether or not the authentication was successful. The KDC can infer that the authentication was successful only if the client subsequently uses the TGT that is part of the reply to obtain a service ticket. The drawback of this approach is that anyone can make a request to the KDC asserting any identity, which allows an attacker to collect replies from the KDC, and subsequently mount an offline attack on those replies. The

Kerberos preauthentication facility can be used to help thwart those attacks.

Preauthentication

The term "preauthentication" is used to describe an exchange in which the user sends some proof of his identity to the KDC as part of the initial authentication process. If that proof is unacceptable to the KDC, the KDC may demand more, or alternate, preauthentication information from the client, or may summarily reject or ignore the client. In essence, the client must authenticate prior to the KDC issuing a credential to the client; thus the term "preauthentication." The proof of identity used in preauthentication can take many forms and is how most technologies such as smart cards and tokens are integrated into the Kerberos initial authentication process.

What technologies are used depends on the level of assurance required for a user's identity and is typically associated with a user (or a role performed by a user). For example, Kerberos administrators might be required to use two-factor authentication, whereas a simple ID and password would suffice for other users. Implementations vary in the types of preauthentication they support. Preauthentication data may include a digital signature and an X.509 public key certificate; token card data; challenge–response; biometrics information; location information; or a combination of different types of those preauthentication data.

Preauthentication may require several messages between the client and KDC to complete the initial authentication process. For example, the challenge–response exchange used for some token cards may require additional messages for the challenge from the KDC and the response from the client. Only the simplest form of preauthentication is described here. The simplest form of preauthentication uses an ID and password, and an encrypted time-stamp:

1. The client prompts the user for his principal ID and password, and converts the password to a key.
2. The client then obtains the current time and encrypts that (along with a random confounder), attaches its principal ID, and sends the request to the KDC.
3. If the KDC can decrypt the time-stamp in the request from the client, it has some proof that the user is who he says he is. The KDC may also require that the time-stamp be within certain limits.

After this point the process is the same as the simple (non-preauthentication) exchange. Note that this approach affords greater protection by making it more difficult for an attacker to obtain a TGT for other users or otherwise attack a captured TGT.[13] However, an offline attack may still be mounted against replies sent from the KDC to other users that are sniffed off of the network. Thus, good passwords are still as important as ever, and most Kerberos implementations provide facilities for password policy enforcement to minimize the risk of weak passwords.

KDC–Client Exchanges

The exchanges used for initial authentication with the AS and the subsequent exchanges used to obtain service tickets with the TGS, are both built from the same basic mechanism. In this section we also identify the message names that Kerberos uses for the various requests and replies.

1. The client sends an authentication request (AS-REQ) message to the authentication service (AS). In that request, the client specifies that it wants a ticket for the ticket-granting service (TGS).
2. The AS sends a ticket-granting ticket (TGT) back to the client in an AS reply (AS-REP) message. That TGT is simply a service ticket for the ticket-granting service (TGS). The AS-REP contains both the TGT and the session key required in order for the client to use that TGT.
3. When the client wants a service ticket for another service, it requests a ticket from the TGS by placing the TGT into a TGS request (TGS-REQ) message. The TGS sends a service ticket for the requested service back to the client in a TGS reply (TGS-REP) message. The TGS-REP contains both the service ticket and the session key required in order for the client to use that service ticket.

Again, a TGT is functionally no different than any other ticket. Nor is the TGS conceptually any different than any other service. The only reason for using a special TGS-REQ message to talk to the TGS is to codify the conventions used by the ticket-granting service and optimize the protocol. However, if you look closely at the AS-REQ and TGS-REQ messages, they are very similar and are sometimes referred to collectively as a KDC request (KDC-REQ) message. The same is true of the AS-REP and TGS-REP messages, which are collectively referred to as a KDC reply (KDC-REP) message.

Initial Tickets

While the primary purpose of the AS is to issue TGTs, the AS may issue tickets for any service, not just TGTs for the TGS. The only real difference between tickets issued by the AS and tickets issued by the TGS are that tickets obtained from the AS are marked as "initial" tickets; tickets obtained from the TGS (using a TGT) are not marked "initial." Initial tickets can be useful if an application wants to ensure that the user obtained the ticket from the AS (i.e., the client went through initial authentication in order to obtain the service ticket) and did not obtain the service ticket using a TGT. For example, the change-password service requires that the user obtain an initial ticket for the change-password service. This requires that the user enter his password in order to obtain a ticket that is marked initial (i.e., a ticket that the change-password service will accept). A ticket for the change-password service obtained from the TGS using a TGT will not be marked initial and will be rejected by the change-password service. This precludes the use of a stolen TGT to change a user's password, or someone using an unlocked work station to change the work station user's password using a cached TGT.

Ticket Construction

Every ticket adheres to the same basic format and contains the same basic information. That information includes the name of the client principal, the name of the service principal, the ticket expiration time, and a variety of other attributes and fields. When a client requests a ticket for a service, the reply from the KDC contains the service ticket, encrypted in the key of that service. Most of the information in the service ticket is also exposed to the client as part of the reply. That information is provided to the client so that the client can ensure that what it received is what the client requested.

The KDC may also provide defaults for various fields in the ticket, which the client did not specify, but which the client may need to know. For example, each ticket has a lifetime; the client may or may not specify the ticket lifetime in a request. If the client does not specify a lifetime, the KDC will provide a default value. The KDC may also enforce maximum values for various fields. For example, if the site-wide maximum ticket lifetime is 8 hours, the KDC will not issue a ticket with a lifetime longer than 8 hours, regardless of what the client requests. Knowing the lifetime of a ticket is important for a client so that if the ticket is expired, a new ticket can be requested automatically from the TGS without user involvement. For instance, long-running batch jobs.

Most implementations also allow each service to specify a maximum ticket lifetime, and the KDC will limit the lifetime of a ticket issued for a service to the service-defined maximum. Some services, such as the change-password service, typically have maximum ticket lifetimes that are very short (e.g., 10 minutes), with the objective being to make those tickets "single use." Most password-change clients also do not cache such tickets, because holding on to them would be of no value.

Client–Service Exchanges

The authentication exchange that occurs between a client and a service is conceptually similar to the client–KDC exchanges. However, the messages used are different to accommodate specific needs of client–service authentication and to eliminate information that is required only for client–KDC exchanges. The messages used for client–service application authentication are collectively referred to as the application (AP), or client–server (CS), messages.

In the following example, we assume that the client already has a service ticket in its credentials cache and, if not, the client will obtain the required service ticket prior to beginning this exchange.

1. The client constructs an application request (AP-REQ) message and sends it to the service. The AP-REQ contains the service ticket as (previously issued by the KDC and stored in the credentials cache as part of a client-TGS exchange). The AP-REQ also contains an authenticator. The authenticator contains various information, including a time-stamp, and may be used by the service to ensure that the AP-REQ is not a replay. The client encrypts the authenticator, and some other information in the AP-REQ, with the session key that is associated with the service ticket (obtained originally from the KDC as part of the TGS-REP).

2. The service receives the AP-REQ and decrypts the ticket in the AP-REQ using its own service key. This exposes the information in the service ticket, including the client's identity, various flags, and the random session key generated by the KDC when the KDC issued the service ticket to the client. After this decryption process is completed, both the client and service are in possession of a common key: the random session key generated by the KDC when the service ticket was originally constructed and issued to the client by the KDC.

3. The session key obtained in the previous step is used to decrypt the authenticator. The authenticator contains information that allows the service to ensure that the AP-REQ message is not a replay. The authenticator may also contain a "subsession" key (see below).

4. If the client requests mutual authentication, the service is obliged to reply to the client with an application reply (AP-REP) message that is encrypted in either the session key from the ticket or a subsession key. The AP-REP allows the client to validate the identity of the service.

Other provisions of the AP-REQ and the AP-REP allow for the establishment of initial sequence numbers for data message sequencing, and the establishment of a new subsession key that is independent of the session key in the service ticket (which was generated by the KDC). Either the client or the service can generate a new subsession key. This allows a fresh session key, unknown to the KDC, to be used for every session between the client and the service.

Confidentiality and Integrity. Once the appropriate session keys are established, the Kerberos "safe" (SAFE) messages can be used for integrity protection, and "private" (PRIV) messages can be used for confidentiality protection. Those messages also provide for additional protection using sequence numbers, time-stamps, and address restrictions (see *Ticket Restrictions* later in this chapter). Alternatively, the application may choose to use its own form of integrity and confidentiality protection for data. For example, an IPSEC (Internet Protocol Security) implementation could use the basic AP-REQ and AP-REP exchange to establish the keys for two end points, where the end points are network stacks or systems, instead of a human and a service.

TGS AP-REQ. Examination of the protocol will show that an AP-REQ is also used in the TGS request (TGS-REQ). The AP-REQ is the client's way of authenticating and securely communicating with a service, and the TGS is simply another service, albeit with special capabilities. The AP-REQ used to authenticate to the TGS contains the TGT (the service ticket for the TGS), just as any AP-REQ for any service. Because the TGS-REQ requires more than just an AP-REQ, the AP-REQ in the TGS-REQ is carried in a pre-authentication element of the TGS-REQ.

Replay Protection

Replay protection ensures that an attacker cannot subvert the system by recording and replaying a previous message. As mentioned previously, confidentiality and integrity protection alone do not protect against replay attacks. Kerberos can use time-stamps, or a form of challenge response, to protect against replay attacks. The type of replay detection that is appropriate depends on whether a datagram-oriented protocol, such as UDP/IP, or a session-oriented protocol, such as TCP/IP, is used. Note that all protocols that provide replay protection will have mechanisms and requirements similar to those described here, regardless of the type of cryptography that is used.

Time-Stamps. Replay protection using time-stamps is most suited to datagram- or transaction-oriented protocols and requires loosely synchronized clocks based on a secure time service and the use of a "replay cache" by the receiver. A replay cache is simply a cache of messages previously seen by the receiver, or more likely, a hash of each of those messages. The receiver must check each received message against the replay cache to determine if the message is a replay. Note that the replay cache must be maintained in persistent storage if replay detection is to survive a restart of the service.

Obviously, the replay cache could grow forever unless it is bounded in some manner. Time-stamps help to limit the size of the replay cache. By defining a bounded window of time for the acceptance of messages, the replay cache can be limited to messages that are received within that window. A service will summarily reject any message with a time-stamp outside of that window, and messages outside that window can be discarded from the cache. Thus, the replay cache must be checked only for messages that fall within that window, and the size of the replay cache can be limited to messages received within that window.

That window of time over which the replay cache must operate is referred to as the acceptable "clock skew." Clock skew represents the maximum difference that is allowable between the clocks of two different systems. If the systems' clocks differ by more than the clock skew, all messages will be rejected. A typical value for clock skew is five minutes. Smaller clock skew values require closer synchronization of system clocks but reduce the overhead of maintaining and checking the replay cache. Larger clock skew values allow looser synchronization of system clocks, but increase the overhead of maintaining and checking the replay cache.

Datagram- or transaction-based applications must deal with duplicate, dropped, and out-of-sequence messages as a normal network occurrence. Thus, well-behaved datagram- or transaction-based applications should already have mechanisms for replay detection within the application, regardless of security considerations. If those applications protect their messages using Kerberos confidentiality or integrity services, there is usually no need to use Kerberos replay protection for the application data. While Kerberos can provide the necessary replay protection "out of the box" for those applications, the applications should be examined to ensure that the protection provided by Kerberos is not redundant and does not add unnecessary overhead.

Challenge–Response. Replay protection using a challenge–response exchange is most suited to session-oriented protocols, such as TCP/IP. The subsession key facility within the Kerberos AP-REQ and AP-REP messages provides a means to effect the challenge–response exchange. Challenge–response eliminates the requirement for clock synchronization between the client and the service, and the need for the service to maintain and check a replay cache. However, challenge–response adds an additional message from the service back to the client. Thus, challenge–response is typically suitable only for session-oriented communications where the cost of the messages can be amortized over an entire session, or where those messages can be piggybacked on the application's normal session-initiation messages. Individual messages within the session must then be protected using sequencing and confidentiality or integrity to ensure that the messages within the session are not subject to replay attacks.

Mechanisms similar to what are described here can also be used to minimize the need for clock synchronization between clients and the KDC.

Making use of the subsession key facility within the AP-REQ and AP-REP messages requires mutual authentication. Challenge–response also requires that the service respond with a new random subsession key in the AP-REP for each AP-REQ. In effect, the new random subsession key in the AP-REP generated by the service is the challenge. The client's ability to subsequently decrypt the AP-REP, extract the new subsession key, and protect subsequent messages to the service using that subsession key provide proof that the AP-REQ was not a replay and serves as the client's response to the service's challenge.

Note that the service cannot verify that the client has passed the challenge until the service receives the first data message from the client to the service protected by the subsession key. Thus, the client is technically not authenticated to the service until the first data message from the client is successfully received and decrypted by the service. By the same token, the service is technically not authenticated to the client until the first data message from the service in reply to the client is received and decrypted by the client (the AP-REP from the service could be a replay to the client). Whether that technical issue is a security issue depends on the behavior of the client and server. If the client or service engage in a significant and irreversible act prior to the completion of authentication on both sides, damage could result. Generally however, the worst that can happen is a denial of service attack that is difficult to diagnose.

Session Keys

Tickets may be sniffed off the network by an attacker during client–KDC or client–service exchanges. Thus, a ticket alone is insufficient to prove the identity of the client principal name embedded in a ticket or the right of the holder to use that ticket. The session key associated with a ticket provides the additional information necessary for that proof. Every ticket issued by the KDC has a unique session key (unless a client specifically requests otherwise). A Kerberos credential is a ticket and the associated session key. The following sections review the role session keys play in the various exchanges.

Authentication Service. During the initial authentication exchange, the client uses the key derived from the user's password to decrypt the reply (the AS-REP message issued by the AS). That reply, as do all KDC replies, contains a ticket (in this case, the TGT returned by the AS). When the client decrypts that reply, the decryption exposes a session key. All requests and replies between the client and the TGS from that point onward are protected using that session key from the AS-REP. Using the session key that results from the initial AS exchange eliminates the need to store the user's key in any form on the work station. That is, once the initial authentication exchange between the client and the AS is completed, subsequent exchanges use the session key returned by that exchange and not the key derived from the user's password. The TGT, as with any ticket, is sealed with the service key of the service for which the ticket is intended, which in this case is the TGS. The client typically places the TGT and the TGT's session key into a credentials cache for future use.

Ticket-Granting Service. When the KDC builds a TGS reply (TGS-REP), it first constructs a ticket for the requested service. As part of that construction process, the KDC generates a random session key that is placed into the ticket. The KDC then encrypts that ticket in the service's key (the key it shares with the service.) That ticket is then placed into the reply (TGS-REP) to the client, with the ticket ultimately destined for the service. That same random session key is also placed into the reply destined for the client. The reply is then encrypted with the session key associated with the TGT in the client's request to the TGS (TGS-REQ). When the construction of the reply (TGS-REP) is completed by the KDC, we have: (1) a service ticket containing the session key; (2) that service ticket encrypted in the service's key; (3) a reply containing the same session key; and (4) that reply encrypted in the session key associated with the TGT.

When the reply is received and decrypted by the client — using the TGT's session key — one copy of the ticket's session key, along with other relevant information about the ticket, is exposed to the client. The other copy of the session key, along with most of the same information exposed to the client, is still sealed in the service ticket. The content of that service ticket is not accessible to the client, because it is encrypted in the service's key (the key the service shares with the KDC), which is not known to the client. That prevents the client from tampering with the information in the ticket. The client typically places the ticket, along with the other ticket information, including the session key for that ticket, into a credentials cache for future use.

Client–Service Exchanges. Session keys play the same role in the client–service exchange as they do in the client–KDC exchanges. The authenticator constructed by the client as part of the application request (AP-REQ) message is encrypted using the session key associated with the service ticket. That same session key is accessible to the service when the service decrypts the service ticket using its own service key. That session key from the service ticket is then used to decrypt (and thus validate) the authenticator.

Cross-Real Authentication

A realm typically defines a collective trust, or common security domain. Obviously there are limits to the size of such a domain both in manageability and in the collective and common trust that domain represents. For example, collective or common trust usually drops precipitously at enterprise boundaries, and sometimes at organizational boundaries within an enterprise. However, it is often the case that those various domains, or realms, must still communicate securely.

Between realms, Kerberos provides cross-realm authentication services. Cross-realm authentication allows principals in one realm (e.g., clients) to authenticate with principals in another realm (e.g., services). Conceptually, cross-realm authentication treats each realm in the path between a client and a service as simply another service. The client's realm effectively issues a ticket for the ticket-granting service (TGS) in the service's realm; that ticket is referred to as a cross-realm or inter-realm TGT. For example, a client in realm X accessing a service in realm Y first goes to a KDC in realm X to obtain a cross-realm TGT for realm Y; that TGT is then presented to a KDC in realm Y in order to obtain a service ticket for the end, or "target" service.

Cross-realm authentication requires prior agreement between the administrators of the two realms in order to establish the keys on the respective KDCs. Those keys effectively allow one realm to issue cross-realm TGTs that will be honored by the other realm. As with other services, possession of a ticket does not ensure right of access; access is ultimately determined by the service and not the issuing realm or KDC. The trust established between realms for cross-realm authentication lies in the promise that the realms will not lie about the identity of their respective clients. The ability to issue a cross-realm TGT is not necessarily bilateral; this allows one-way cross-realm authentication, although this feature is rarely used.

The client may collect cross-realm TGTs obtained during cross-realm authentication, just as any other tickets, and hold them in its credential cache for reuse. Once the client obtains the cross-realm TGT for the target realm, the client can request tickets from the target realm's TGS directly, just as the client would request tickets directly from the TGS in its own realm. Once the client obtains the ticket for the target realm's TGS, the client–service authentication process is identical to the client–service authentication process within a single realm. Thus, cross-realm authentication between a client and any service in the other realm requires that the additional cross-realm authentication steps be performed only once. For example, given realms X and Y, where the realm administrators have previously established a cross-realm relationship, a client in realm X that wants to get to a service in realm Y must first obtain a cross-realm TGT from a KDC in realm X for realm Y. That cross-realm TGT may then be used to get a ticket from a KDC in realm Y for a service in realm Y and the KDC in realm X does not participate in the latter step.

Any number of realms can have a direct, or pair-wise, cross-realm relationship, in which case a client goes directly between those realms as described above. Where many realms are involved, direct relationships between every pair of realms can be a significant management overhead for establishing all of the necessary cross-realm keys. For example, with 10 realms, a direct relationship between every pair of realms requires that each realm maintain nine pairs of cross-realm keys (a key pair assumes a bilateral relationship), for a total of 90 cross-realm key pairs. While this is manageable for a relatively small number of realms, such as one might find within an enterprise, it becomes unmanageable for a large number of realms. Note that this is the geometric trust complexity problem discussed earlier (see *Trust Models* earlier in this chapter).

In order to reduce the complexity of cross-realm key management, realms may also be arranged in transitive relationships. This reduces the number of direct relationships that must be managed but may require a client to traverse, or transit, intermediate realms in order to get to the realm of the end service. For example, given realms X, Y, and Z, where X–Y has a direct relationship, Y–Z has a direct relationship, but X-Z does not have a direct relationship. In this case, X–Z has a transitive relationship through Y. In order for a client in X to get to a service in Z, the client must transit Y, because X and Z do not have a direct relationship. The client first obtains a cross-realm TGT from realm X to realm Y. That cross-realm TGT is then used to obtain a cross-realm TGT from realm Y to realm Z. The cross-realm process may be extended to as many steps as are necessary for a client to reach the target realm of a service. Each step in that process is identical and results in a cross-realm TGT for a realm that is "closer" to the realm of the service.

Within a collective, realms are typically organized as a tree, or "realm hierarchy," where each realm has a direct relationship with one parent and potentially several children. To get from one realm to another, the client may have to climb up the tree toward the root, and then down the tree to get to the desired service's realm, collecting inter-realm TGTs along the way. The tradeoff between direct and transitive realm structures is the key management overhead required for direct relationships vs. the network overhead required to transit intermediate realms. Both direct and transitive relationships can be used in combination. For example, the majority of realms may be arranged using transitive cross-realm relationships, as in a realm hierarchy. Where performance or trust is an issue for specific realms, those realms can also have direct cross-realm relationships, allowing clients to go directly to the target realm, thereby "short circuiting" the need to transit intermediate realms in the realm hierarchy.

Tickets issued as a result of cross-realm authentication have within them the names of the realms transited by the client within them. The list of transited realms is referred to as the "transited realms list." This allows a service (or any intermediate realm) to ensure that all the realms in the path that participated in cross-realm authentication can be trusted not to lie about the client's identity. However, in general, a realm will either be trusted or it won't. A trusted realm will be part of a cross-realm collective. Untrusted realms will be excluded from that collective or will not be placed in the path between critical clients and services. If principals or services must avoid the use of a less trusted realm due to the sensitivity of their work, direct relationships can be established between those realms, bypassing those less trusted realms.

Ticket Restrictions

If the client sends a credential — that is, a ticket and the associated session key — to another principal, the recipient's use of the client's identity is limited solely by the ticket's implicit restrictions. The lifetime of a ticket is one obvious implicit restriction that defines the time during which a ticket may be used. Another implicit restriction is the service name in the ticket; that service name is an implicit restriction on the use of the ticket. If the service name in that ticket is the ticket-granting service (TGS), and hence the ticket is a TGT, then the holder may obtain any other tickets. Obviously, handing over your TGT (along with the TGT's session key) to another principal requires a very high level of trust in that principal.

In some cases, the implicit restrictions in a ticket may be sufficient. For example, consider a client that wishes to print a file on a file server using a print server. If the client sufficiently trusts the print server, the client can simply send a credential (ticket and session key) for the file server to the print server. The print server can then use that credential to access the file server in the client's name. The service ticket (for the file server) in that credential only allows the print server to access the file server using the client's identity; it does not allow the print server to access any other services using the client's identity. However, the client must trust the print server sufficiently to allow the print server unrestricted use of the client's identity when accessing the file server. If that trust is not warranted, authorization data can be used to further restrict the print server's use of the client's identity (below).

In many cases we would like to restrict certain common uses of a credential by another principal without having to first agree on the syntax or semantics of authorization data. There are several common forms of restrictions provided by Kerberos to deal with these cases. (Most if not all of these cases could use authorization data to restrict the ticket's use.) The codification of these restrictions by Kerberos is in large part recognition of common use. These restrictions also allow common constraints on ticket usage that are based on site policies that are enforced by the KDC.

Address Restrictions. A ticket's use may be limited to specific network addresses, such as the originating client work station. Those address restrictions may be used to help restrict the use of credentials sent to another principal (below) and can also help to foil the use of stolen credentials. Multihomed systems (systems with more than one network address or interface) require special care to ensure that address restrictions include the appropriate addresses for the system. In some cases it may be appropriate to restrict use to a subset of the addresses or interfaces on the system (e.g., inbound or outbound interfaces on a firewall). In other cases there may be no control over, or any desire to control, which addresses or interfaces are used, such as on a high-performance server with many network interfaces. Address restrictions placed on a TGT are propagated to service tickets obtained with that TGT unless otherwise specified. Address restrictions may also be empty, in which case there are no restrictions on where a ticket may be used from. There are obvious security concerns with empty address restrictions. However, outside of a few uses, the use of address restrictions has fallen out of favor. This is due to the difficulty for clients and intermediaries to determine the addresses that a recipient may need.

Address restrictions provide the ability to restrict the use of credentials to a specific machine when those credentials are sent to an intermediary. It may also be desirable to restrict the intermediary's ability to propagate those credentials to other systems and services. (The term "propagation" used here means propagating the use of a credential; there is nothing that can be done to prohibit physical propagation of the ticket.) Ticket attributes known as "forwardable" and "proxiable" allow restricting the subsequent propagation of credentials by a recipient. Those restrictions are binary; they restrict further propagation of the credential by the recipient, or they do *not* restrict further propagation of the credential by the recipient. Finer-grained control must use restrictions in the authorization data. Sites may choose to limit the KDC's willingness to forward or proxy tickets. Similar indicators known as "forwarded" and "proxy" allow a service to determine if a ticket has been obtained in this manner. Services may modify their behavior based on the setting of those indicators. For example, a file server might choose to allow only read-access to certain files when presented with a ticket that has the proxy indicator set.

Proxiable. The proxiable attribute allows the holder of the ticket to ask the ticket-granting service (TGS) to modify the address or lifetime restrictions in the ticket. That results in another ticket with different address or lifetime restrictions. That resulting ticket always has the proxy attribute set. That proxy attribute may be checked by services to determine whether the ticket is from the original client or an intermediary. Proxiable tickets are used to restrict the use of a client's identity to a specific service; a proxiable ticket allows no changes to the ticket other than to the address restrictions. Sending a proxiable ticket to an intermediary allows that intermediary to propagate the ticket to other intermediaries.

For example, a client may provide an intermediary a service ticket for a file server where that ticket has the proxiable attribute set. This allows the intermediary to obtain another proxy or proxiable tickets for the file server and send that ticket to another intermediary, thus allowing other intermediaries access to the file server using the client's identity. Alternatively, the client may obtain a proxy ticket without the proxiable attribute set in the ticket. Lacking the proxiable attribute, that ticket can be used only by intermediaries that satisfy the address restrictions in the ticket. If there are no address restrictions in that ticket, there are effectively no restrictions on which intermediaries may use the ticket. However, what the ticket may be used for is still restricted implicitly by the ticket itself (e.g., the service name in the ticket). Client-specified authorization restrictions may further restrict the use of a credential (see below).

Forwardable. The forwardable attribute is similar to the proxiable attribute. The most significant difference is that the TGS will not issue another TGT based on a TGT with only the proxiable attribute set. A forwardable TGT effectively allows the holder (assuming they also have the TGT's session key) unrestricted use of the identity in the TGT: forwardable and forwarded tickets — including other TGTs — can be obtained by anyone holding such a TGT. A TGT that is only proxiable does not allow the holder to obtain another TGT.

A forwardable TGT is typically sent if unrestricted use of the client's identity is desirable. One of the few cases where this is desirable is when a user logs into another computer system using, e.g., telnet. In that case the use is effectively establishing the same identity on another remote system. While we could require the user to go through an initial authentication process again on that remote system (to obtain a TGT), that would provide little additional security and simply irritate the user. The difference in application between forwardable and proxiable tickets can be subtle, but important. In essence, there are three attributes that determine what requests the TGS will honor based on the ticket presented to it: forwardable, proxiable, and whether or not the ticket is a TGT.

Lifetime. A ticket's lifetime is an implied restriction. A proxiable or forwardable ticket's lifetime may be decreased but never increased.

Proxy Services

A proxy service is a service that performs a function on behalf of the client and that uses another end service in order to perform that function on behalf of the client (for example, a client wishing to print files using a print server where the files reside on a file server). The print server acts as a proxy for the client in order to access the files on the file server. The basic form of a proxy provides only implicit restrictions on the use of the client's identity by the intermediate service. This may be sufficient for some clients and services. In the previous example, the client must first obtain a proxy ticket for the print server. That ticket will show the requesting client as the client principal name, and the file server as the service principal name. That proxy ticket may be based on an existing service ticket the client holds for the file service, or it may be obtained directly using a TGT.

1. The client obtains a proxy service ticket for the file server. If the client possesses a ticket for the file server with the proxiable attribute set, that ticket may be used to request a proxy ticket from the TGS. The client sends the file server service ticket in its possession to the TGS, requesting a proxy ticket along with new address restrictions, if any. The TGS returns a service ticket for the file server with new address restrictions. That service ticket will, by default, have the proxiable attribute cleared and will always have the proxy indicator set.

   If the client does not possess a proxiable ticket for the file server, the client must obtain a proxy ticket for the file server using a TGT. That TGT must have the proxiable attribute set. This process is similar to the one described above, only it follows more typical TGS semantics.

2. The client authenticates to the print server using a conventional client–service authentication exchange. The client then sends the proxy credential (ticket and session key) obtained in the previous step to the print server. A variety of means may be used to send those credentials; the Kerberos "credentials" (CREDS) message is intended specifically for this purpose and ensures that the session key associated with the ticket is protected during the transfer of those credentials.

3. The print server uses the file server credential obtained in the previous step to authenticate to the file server, and obtain access to the file server, using the client's identity.

Note that when presented with such a ticket, the file server has no way of knowing that it is not really the client, but the print server, that is requesting access — the client name shown in the ticket is the originating client, not the print server. The file server may infer some information from the fact that the proxy indicator is set in the credential, for example. While useful, this does not provide very granular control and requires that the client must have an fairly high level of trust in the print server. Unless the file server places additional restrictions on access to files based on the setting of the proxy indicator, the print server has full access to any of the client's files. More granular restrictions require the use of client-provided authorization restrictions (see below).

Authorization

Kerberos defines the rules for packaging authorization data elements in tickets and the semantics for placing those elements into tickets. Kerberos does not define the interpretation of those authorization data elements. There are several points in time where authorization information may be provided or embedded into a ticket, ranging from the initial authentication exchange, to the client–service authentication exchange, and several points in between. There are also several possible sources of authorization information, including the client, as well as authorization services that may be a part of, or accessible to, the KDC. Authorization data provided by clients is referred to as restrictions, because the data restricts the authorized use of a client's identity. (Client-provided authorization data obviously should not be used to amplify the client's authorization, or clients could grant themselves any authority.)

Each authorization data element has a type associated with it. Kerberos defines the syntax of the type information, but does not generally define the interpretation of those types. Authorization data element types are application- or service-specific. Kerberos does not otherwise define the contents of the underlying authorization data elements, and KDCs generally do not interpret those elements, but treat them as opaque objects. Interpretation of authorization data elements is generally a function of each service. By convention or agreement, some elements may have meaning to a large number of services, and thus have a common syntax and interpretation for those services. In other cases, authorization data elements will be meaningful only to a single service, and thus the interpretation of those elements can be performed only by that service. Thus, the use of authorization data requires that the client and the end service (i.e., the applications) agree on the syntax and semantics of the authorization data.

In essence, Kerberos simply provides the ability to securely pass authorization data through intermediate services: the data is sealed (encrypted) in the ticket for the end service by the KDC using the end service's key; the data is unsealed (decrypted), by the end service using its service key. Since authorization data is sealed in a ticket, an intermediate service can not tamper with that information. However, an intermediate service may be able to modify certain implicit restrictions or may add authorization information to the ticket, depending on ticket attributes (see *Ticket Restrictions*).

During the initial authentication process between the client and the authentication service (AS), both the KDC and another authorization source may provide authorization data that is to be placed into the TGT. That data is generally propagated to all other tickets obtained using that TGT. That is, when the TGT is used to subsequently obtain a service ticket from the TGS, the authorization data in the TGT is copied to the service ticket as part of the service ticket construction by the TGS. KDC-supplied authorization data typically bounds the client's authorization. The authorization data placed into the TGT typically represents information that is widely applicable, and that would be of interest to most or all services. For example, KDC-supplied authorization data may include all of a client's group memberships.

The ticket-granting service (TGS) provides the same facilities as the AS for placing authorization data into a ticket. The KDC, or another authorization source, may provide authorization data that is to be placed into the service ticket. In addition, the client may also provide additional authorization data (i.e., restrictions) to be placed into the resulting ticket. That authorization data is in addition to the authorization data that is copied from the TGT used to obtain the service ticket. The authorization data placed into a service ticket as part of the TGS exchange typically represents information that is specific to a service; it may also represent information that is specific to a client–service pair.

Finally, the client–service authentication process provides an additional point at which the client can provide authorization data to the service. The client places additional authorization data into the authenticator that is part of the application request (AP-REQ) message. That authorization data represents restrictions that the client wishes to communicate to the service and that is specific to the session. Thus, at the point when a client authenticates to a service, the service has the sum of the authorization data and that is provided as part of the authenticator in the AP-REQ, the service ticket, and the TGT. That authorization data includes all client-specified restrictions.

Note that the AS does not define the ability for clients to specify authorization data (i.e., restrictions) in the authentication service request (AS-REQ) message, and thus place restrictions into the TGT. (The syntax of the AS-REQ allows this, but the semantics of the protocol preclude it, although it could be provided as preauthentication data if needed.) However, there is nothing that prevents a client from subsequently requesting a TGT from the TGS and placing restrictions into the resulting TGT at that time — for example, in the case of obtaining a proxy or forwarded TGT using an existing proxiable or forwardable TGT. The TGT is simply a ticket for the TGS, and there is nothing that precludes the TGS — or any service for that matter — from issuing a ticket for itself.

Capabilities and Delegation

A capability refers to a credential that has certain rights associated with its possession. Those rights may be both implicit in the fields of the associated ticket and explicit, using authorization data encapsulated in the ticket. A capability that has no address restrictions is sometimes referred to as a "bearer proxy," since it may be used by anyone (client or service) who possesses the credential.[14]

Anyone who possesses a credential with a ticket that is forwardable or proxiable can change or remove address restrictions from the ticket. Anyone who possesses a credential with a ticket that is forwardable or proxiable can also add to the authorization data. That authorization information should never be additive and thus allow the holder to amplify his privileges, thus the use of the term "restrictions" to refer to client-provided authorization information in such tickets. That is, it is acceptable for any holder to further restrict authorization by adding to the authorization data to the ticket; it is not acceptable for any holder to further amplify authorization by adding authorization data to the ticket.

To illustrate the use of capabilities, we again use the example of the client, print server, and file server. The approach illustrated in this example must be used carefully in order to guard against unwarranted amplification of privileges by intermediate services. For this example, we define authorization data with semantics that are similar to what one might find in an ACL with the triplet:

<id=principal><object=name><permissions=list>

In this triplet, "user" specifies who (a principal identifier); "object" specifies the name of the object to be acted on; and "permissions" specifies the allowable actions by the user on the object. If "id" is empty, then the implied ID is the client name listed in the associated ticket. An authorization data element is thus a triplet as defined above.

Once again, the client wishes to print a file using a print server (the intermediate, or proxy, service), where the file is on a file server (the end service). However, the client does not place a tremendous amount of trust in this print server, and therefore wants to restrict the print server's access. Specifically, the client wants to restrict the print server to read-access for a single file that is to be printed, and wants to restrict that access to a relatively short period of time. We assume that the client already has a service ticket for the print server and a proxiable service ticket for the file server.

1. The client requests a proxy ticket from the ticket-granting service (TGS) for the file server. In the TGS request, the client: provides the proxiable service ticket for the file server that is already in the client's possession; requests a lifetime of 30 minutes; specifies the proxy attribute; and has cleared the proxiable and forwardable attributes. If the client wishes to restrict the ticket to the use of a specific print server with a known network address, then the address restrictions in the TGS request specify only the print server's network address. The client could leave the address restrictions empty if the network address of the print server was unknown, or enumerate a list of addresses if the print server is multi-homed, or if any one of a pool of networked printers might be used to satisfy the request.

   The following element is specified in the authorization data field of the TGS request (or more accurately, the authorization data field of the AP-REQ that is part of the TGS request):

   <id=><object=/home/Hanley/thesis.ps><permissions=read>

   The interpretation of that triple is: id is null, and therefore interpreted as the client name in the ticket; object specifies the file "/home/Hanley/thesis.doc"; permissions specify read-access. The interpretation of that authorization is: "The client principal name specified in the ticket cannot perform any operation except to read the file '/home/Hanley/thesis.doc'."

2. The TGS constructs a new ticket and sends the new ticket back to the client. That new ticket is identical to the original proxiable service ticket for the file server (provided in the TGS request), except that the new ticket has: the client-specified authorization data sealed within it; the proxy indicator set; the proxiable and forwardable attributes clear; and a lifetime of 30 minutes (the new ticket may also have different address restrictions). The new ticket also has a new session key.

3. The client authenticates to the print server using a client–service authentication exchange.

4. The client sends the proxy credential (ticket and session key) obtained in step 2 to the print server using a credentials (CREDS) message.

5. The print server authenticates to the file server using the proxy credential, obtained from the client in the previous step, using a conventional client–service authentication exchange. The print

server is now communicating with the file server under the client's identity.

6. When the file server unseals the ticket received in the previous step, the authorization data in the ticket, placed there by the TGS in step 2, is exposed to the file server.

At this point, the print server and file server have authenticated, with the print server using the identity of the client. The file server has no knowledge of the fact that it is the print server actually acting on the client's behalf. However, the print server — through the authorization data in the ticket — knows that restrictions have been placed on the client's access and, we must assume, will enforce those restrictions. (If we can't trust the file server to properly enforce access controls on its own files, then it is of questionable use for storing controlled information. We can't solve that problem with Kerberos.) Also, since the ticket expires after 30 minutes, the print server will no longer be able to access the client's file on the print server after that time.

The conventions that control how authorization data is interpreted, the potential sources of that authorization data, and the ticket attributes used, are extremely important to ensure the integrity of this example. By convention, we have agreed that the presence of any authorization elements (i.e., authorization triples) in the authorization data implicitly restricts actions to those that are explicitly enumerated. While those enumerated elements are necessary, they are not sufficient for a complete and secure solution. If the ticket given to the print service had the proxiable or forwardable attribute set, the print service could go back to the TGS and obtain a new service ticket with different authorization. That would allow the print service to obtain access to any of the client's files. Note that this also implies that care should be exercised to ensure that no unwarranted authorization data is in the proxy ticket, as might be the case if the original (proxiable) ticket from which the proxy ticket was obtained had unwanted authorization information in it. Moreover, we cannot allow those tickets to be proxiable or forwardable, in order to eliminate the possibility of the print server amplifying its privileges by adding authorization data to a ticket.

Since the authorization data is created by the client, that authorization, while sufficient for the needs of the client, is not sufficient for the needs of the file server. The file server did not participate in the creation of the authorization data, and therefore should treat it as suspect. If the file server based all access control decisions only on the authorization data in the ticket, any client could grant itself any rights to any file. For example, there is nothing to stop the client from requesting a proxy with authorization data that specifies access to another user's files and using the resulting proxy ticket itself. This is one reason why proxiable and forwardable tickets should never be given out freely to untrusted intermediaries if authorization data could be used to amplify privileges.

If the file server blindly believed and obeyed the authorization data in the ticket, a client could use a proxy to gain access to any files. That would obviously not be very secure. Thus, this example is secure only if the file server has additional rules it applies to make authorization decisions, such as ACLs, to limit the authorization of the client. In other words, the file server must first check the authorization specified by its ACLs against the client's identity; with that as the authorized limits for the client, the file server can then determine if the authorization specified in the ticket is within those limits.

Note the temporal difference between capabilities and ACLs. To provide temporary, delegated access to a print server in an ACL-based system, the ACL on the file server would have to be modified temporarily to allow access by the file server. Constantly modifying ACLs could seriously degrade performance. However, there are practical limits to how much authorization data can be placed into a capability. This points to a need for both mechanisms: ACLs for long-lived and relatively static authorization information, and capabilities for more dynamic and context-specific information, as is found in delegation.

In the example above, the capability constructed by the client may be used by anyone who possesses the capability (subject to, for example, address restrictions). The client could also restrict the use of the capability to a specific principal using the "id" field in the authorization triplet. For example, by placing the print server's principal identifier into the ID field. This would require that the print server use two credentials to access the file server: the proxy credential provided by the client (showing the client identity in the ticket, and showing the print server's identity in the authorization data); and a credential for the print server itself (showing the print server's identity), to prove to the file server that the print server is the principal listed in the "id" field of the authorization triplet of the client proxy credential.

Identity-based restrictions, in conjunction with the other usage guidelines discussed above, would eliminate the possibility of the print server giving the client's proxy credential to another service, and of the other service subsequently using the credential to obtain unauthorized access to the client's files. This type of restriction would be preferable to address restrictions and also provides the ability for the file server to audit and control access based on the identity of both the client and the intermediate service. This would allow the file server to, for example, enforce additional restrictions based on the identity of the intermediate server. For example, the file server may choose to prohibit write-access to files by print servers, regardless of what permissions are specified in the authorization data. Another example might be to restrict access to certain files by "public" printers, regardless of the file specified in the authorization data.

MANAGEMENT

Management, performance, and operation are all reflections of one another. A system that makes many demands on the environment will require more resources to meet and maintain those demands, whether those demands be disk storage, CPU, network bandwidth, users, or support personnel. A system that makes many assumptions about the environment will require more resources to meet and maintain those assumptions. Those assumptions are simply implied demands the system places on its environment. Those demands have a direct influence on the cost of achieving an acceptable level of performance and the ability of the implementation to perform its intended function. The greater the demands, the higher the cost of operating and managing the system, or the supporting elements that the system depends on. If those demands are not satisfied, a system's performance and usability will suffer. In the extreme case, performance becomes so poor that the system cannot carry out its intended function.

The cost of satisfying demands and assumptions can rise very rapidly in a distributed environment. The more distributed an environment, the less likely that demands will be satisfied over a given number of systems, and the higher the cost of satisfying those demands. Of special concern is the ability of a system to function effectively in the face of changes in the environment. The more distributed an environment, the higher the probability that changes to the environment will occur over a given unit of time and that intervention will be required to compensate for those changes. Thus, the cost of maintaining assumptions increases.

Those problems are magnified in distributed security. The greater the demands placed on the environment by the security system, the more likely it is that performance problems will result and that the security system will fail to carry out its assigned function. The more assumptions that are made about the environment, the more likely it is that intervention will be required to compensate for those changes. Intervention increases the probability of errors, which can lead to security problems.

It is important to distinguish the demands made by Kerberos as a technology and the demands made by Kerberos as a security system. Kerberos technology makes modest demands on the environment, and satisfying those demands should be well within the means of most organizations. Kerberos as a security system can make very insignificant or very oppressive demands on the environment, depending on the level of security an organization needs or chooses to enforce. We use the term "appropriate" to describe that level of security and to qualify those elements that are outside the scope of Kerberos — or any security technology. If an organization decides that "appropriate security" means "very high security," then demands, assumptions, cost, and effort will all increase.

Users

One of the first concerns usually raised by network and system administrators is "What is this going to do to my users?" That is a justifiable concern, since any change that is visible to users will tend to produce a heavy influx of support calls. Kerberos can be virtually invisible and undemanding of users, or extremely visible and oppressive in its demands. That choice is a function of the level of security the site chooses to enforce using Kerberos. For the security needs of the vast majority of sites, Kerberos need not be visible to the user community.

Users are generally unaware of Kerberos, except during the initial authentication process (i.e., sign-on), when they must provide their Kerberos principal identifier and a password, or some other proof of identity. If the Kerberos sign-on is integrated into the host sign-on, Kerberos can be made invisible to the user. If the Kerberos sign-on is not integrated into the host sign-on, or the host has no concept of a sign-on, a separate Kerberos utility to allow the user to sign on and complete the initial authentication process is required.

The result of the Kerberos initial authentication is a ticket-granting ticket (TGT), which is placed into a credentials cache, and which applications may subsequently use for obtaining service tickets in order to authenticate to services. The process of obtaining service tickets using the TGT, and the subsequent authentication exchange between the client and the service, is invisible to the user. Kerberos utilities are typically provided to view the tickets contained in the credentials cache. However, with the exception of diagnostics and troubleshooting, those utilities are typically not used and are unnecessary.

One of the few times a user might encounter different behavior due to Kerberos is if their TGT expires. All tickets, including the TGT, have a lifetime. Applications will automatically request a new ticket if the old one has expired. However, an application cannot request a new TGT without user involvement. That is, the user must go through the initial authentication process to obtain a TGT. Whether the user community ever encounters that behavior will depend on the lifetime chosen for TGTs. If that lifetime is longer than the average workday, most users will never see this behavior.

Assumptions

Kerberos makes certain assumptions about the environment and the security of the various systems and individuals that make up the Kerberos environment. When discussing these assumptions it is important to distinguish what is required for any distributed or network environment, what is required for any distributed security system, what requirements are specific to Kerberos, and what requirements are specific to a Kerberos implementation.

Minimal assumptions and requirements necessary for any distributed environment include:

- A functional network in order for clients and services to interact.
- A functional network directory service in order for clients and services to locate each other.
- A functional software distribution system in order to distribute software to computer systems that host clients and services.

Assumptions and requirements that are common to virtually all distributed security systems are negotiable and depend on acceptable cost and risk. These include:

- Appropriately secure systems for hosting clients and services.
- Appropriately secure software distribution service.
- Appropriate protection of identity information by individuals (passwords, smart cards, tokens, etc.).

Assumptions and requirements that are Kerberos-specific are negotiable and depend on acceptable cost and risk. These include:

- Appropriately secure systems for hosting KDCs.
- Appropriately secure time service, with loosely synchronized clocks on all systems on which Kerberos operates.

The following discussion provides security recommendations for the assumptions and requirements enumerated above. These recommendations are common to virtually all implementations. However, they do not account for budget or other organizational constraints, and actual requirements will depend on cost–risk tradeoffs, which will be different for each deployment.

Directory Service. Kerberos typically requires the Internet domain name service (DNS) to construct the names of service-based principals and locate those principals on the network. An ineffective DNS or an inconsistent naming structure can make this job more cumbersome. Although many network services depend on a network naming system to function, a compromised name service does not present a security threat to Kerberos, other than possibly a denial-of-service attack. Note that such a denial-of-service attack would likely affect many network services, and not just Kerberos.

Software Distribution Service. Any large distributed environment requires a software distribution service for cost-effectively distributing and installing software on physically remote systems. That distribution system should be secure to ensure that the integrity of the security software itself is not compromised.

Secure Time Service. Loosely synchronized clocks are typically required between the KDCs, and between KDCs and application servers (e.g., within 5 minutes). Implementations vary in their requirements for clock synchronization. Unsynchronized clocks primarily represent a security threat due to replay attacks. Depending on the Kerberos implementation and the protocols used, clock synchronization may or may not be required. However, synchronized clocks are generally desirable in any large network, especially for auditing and network and system management in order to correlate activities and events across the network. If time-stamps are used as the basis for replay protection, the time service used to synchronize clocks should be secure.

KDCs. Because the KDC is the trusted third party for all principals in the realms it serves, the KDC should be both logically and physically secure. Failure to secure the KDC can result in the compromise of an entire realm. The KDC should support no applications, users, or protocols other than Kerberos. (That is, everything except Kerberos has been removed from the machine.) Ideally, the system will not support remote network access except by means of the Kerberos services it offers. Remote administration of KDCs and principals is a fact of life in today's environment. Most modern Kerberos implementations provide a secure remote administration facility.

Services. Systems that host services, or "application servers," should be secured to the level required by the most sensitive application or data on that server. Failure to adequately secure the application servers may result in the compromise of services that operate on that application server, and their data. Note that a compromise of an application server compromises only those applications on the server and does not compromise any other principals.

Clients. Client systems should be secured to the level required by the most sensitive user of the client or the most sensitive application that is accessed from that client. Failure to adequately secure client systems may result in the compromise of any users of the client system or compromise of data accessed from the system. A compromised client puts all users of the client at risk. For example, a password grabber on a client compromises anyone who uses the client; a virus potentially compromises the data of any application accessed from that client. A compromised client does not compromise principals that do not use that client. However a client compromise could spread if one of the users of that client has elevated privileges, e.g., a Kerberos administrator. Kerberos administrators (or anyone with elevated privileges) should not use a client system unless they have an appropriate level of trust in that system.

Identity Information. Identity information, no matter what the form, requires appropriate protection of that information by individuals. If passwords are used, those passwords should be sufficiently strong. Most modern Kerberos implementations provide password policy enforcement to minimize the use of weak passwords. If public key credentials are used, protection of those credentials is as important as password protection. If additional security is required, technologies that provide two-factor authentication, such as token cards or smart cards, may be used; appropriate care in protecting those devices must still be exercised by the individual. Note that a compromise of an individual does not implicitly compromise any other Kerberos component or principal. However, as with any system, administrative personnel who have elevated privileges should be of special concern. For those individuals, two-factor authentication may be appropriate.

Operation

In terms of operational management, clients are by far the most important, with services a distant second, followed by KDCs. Implicit in that ranking are the associated infrastructure elements that are required for each Kerberos component to perform its function. That ranking obtains from the relative numbers of the components. Clients are typically the most numerous by orders of magnitude, and their sheer numbers magnify even the smallest manageability problem. That is not to say that management of KDCs is unimportant, but if given the choice between a few skilled people trained and dedicated to managing a few KDCs, vs. 100,000 users and clients, the choice should be obvious.

Clients. Other than installation, the primary manageability concern with clients is locating KDCs and services (see *Names and Locations* later in this chapter).

Servers. The primary management overhead associated with service principals is the maintenance of the key table. As previously discussed, the key table holds a service principal's key. Communication of the key should be done securely, which means either manually communicating the key out-of-band or pulling the key from the KDC using a key management utility on the system on which the service operates. The latter method of pulling the key from the KDC is preferable.

For example, once Kerberos client software is installed on the application server, a key management utility can be used by an administrator to access the KDC, establish a secure session, generate the service key, and place the service key into the service's key table. The administrator effectively provides the secure channel for securely communicating the initial service key. Once the initial keys are established, secure key update, or "key rollover," can be automated. That key rollover can be initiated on the server to pull a new key from the KDC to the server, or a KDC can push a new key to the server. Implementations vary in the sophistication of the key management utilities available and the facilities for automating the key rollover process.

KDCs. A fully equipped KDC generally includes a variety of services for administration and management, database propagation, password change, etc. Some of those services can be quite complex. However, the main services provided by a KDC are for authentication and are quite simple. Those services do not, as a rule, maintain state or require write-access to the principal database.

Most implementations differentiate between "primary" and "secondary" (or "master" and "slave") KDCs depending on the services they provide. A primary KDC typically provides a reference copy of the principal database, as well as hosting services that require write-access to the database. Secondary KDCs typically maintain read-only copies of the database. Implementations vary tremendously in the mechanisms used to propagate information from primary to secondary KDCs. In the most primitive mechanisms, a bulk propagation of the entire database is performed at fixed intervals. More sophisticated mechanisms incrementally propagate only those database records that change in real time. The issues associated with periodic bulk propagation are numerous and significant. Incremental propagation is a prerequisite for any large-scale production implementation.

Services that require write access to the principal database include those required for day-to-day administration of the principal database, such as adding, deleting, and changing principals. Administrative functions are generally performed using a special administrative tool, either locally on the KDC, or remotely. Password-change operations also require write access to the principal database. Password-change is typically the only operation in which the general client population requires access to a service on the primary KDC — that is, a service that has write-access to the principal database. Although implementations vary, the inability of clients to access the primary KDC will typically preclude password-change operations. That argues for a primary KDC configuration that provides system and network redundancy and automatic failover. Beyond the administrative functions associated with principals, there is little additional work involved in managing a KDC.

The primary services used by clients — the authentication service (AS) and ticket-granting service (TGS) — do not generally require write-access to the database. Thus, secondary KDCs should, as a rule, be the client's first selection when locating a KDC to provide those services. It is not unusual for all AS and TGS requests to be serviced by secondary KDCs, and to dedicate the primary KDC to administrative services. This allows the resources of the primary KDC to be dedicated to services that only the primary KDC can provide, which allows it to serve a much larger client community.

Each entry in the principal database is typically encrypted in a "master key" that is defined when the database is created. That master key prevents compromise of the realm should a backup of the principal database be inadvertently released, for example. However, for unattended restart of the KDC and unattended operation of services that must manipulate the database, the master key must be kept in persistent storage. If unattended KDC restart is not required, the master key can be typed in on the console when the KDC starts. However, that typically does not make the master key available to other services that may require access to the database, such as administrative services. Because of those issues, virtually all implementations use a master key that is kept in persistent storage, such as a disk file. Obviously, keeping the master key secure is of paramount importance, and any backups should exclude storage containing a copy of the master key.

Realms. Most of the issues involved in the use of multiple realms revolve around the client's ability to locate KDCs and services in a realm (see *Names and Locations*). The ease or difficulty with which clients can perform those functions, and the associated management overhead, are usually the determining factors in whether or not an organization uses multiple realms.

If multiple realms are used, cross-realm keys must be established between realms, and appropriate entries placed into the principal database. Key generation and creation of the principal database entries require very little effort. However, those cross-realm keys must be communicated between realms in a secure fashion. Unless a secure channel already exists between realms, those keys should be communicated using a secure, out-of-band mechanism, such as physical mail. Once those initial keys are established, a secure channel can be formed to change the keys periodically.

Note that a user can have identities in multiple realms. For example, the same physical individual may have a principal identity in multiple realms. While those two identities may represent the same individual, Kerberos does not make that association. By the same token, there is nothing that prevents a client computer system from being used for authenticating an individual to any realm or accessing a service in any realm. That situation would not be unusual in an environment with multiple realms and a roving user community. While it is typical for client systems to define a default realm as a convenience for users, that default realm is only a convenience and, unless otherwise constrained, does not limit the use of the client by individuals in a single realm.

A service, or more precisely, the instantiation of an application on a host computer system, may also operate in multiple realms. While it is unusual, and there are security implications that must be considered, there is nothing that prevents one system from hosting applications that have identities in multiple realms. Nor is there anything that prevents the same application on the same system from having an identity in multiple realms. Having a common system or application that has an identity in multiple realms may be an alternative to cross-realm authentication. For example, consider a database that is shared between two groups in different realms. The database service can be placed into one realm, with the other group using cross-realm authentication to access it. Alternatively, the database can have an identity in both realms, with each group accessing the database as a service in their own realm, thus eliminating the need for cross-realm authentication. Again, there are security implications in such an approach that must be taken into account. Specifically, management of the service keys must be carefully considered.

Principals. Management of principals is similar to that of any system that maintains identity information. Principals must be added, removed, and modified. A principal identifier should not be reused until all services that may have local copies of the principal identifier have been notified. For example, if a service uses a principal identifier in a local access control list (ACL), the ACL must be updated before the principal identifier is reused to ensure that the new entity does not have unwarranted access to that service.

All implementations provide tools to perform administrative functions. For large-scale deployments, it may also be desirable to couple Kerberos administration to an enterprise administrative system. As with any system that uses passwords, resetting passwords is probably the most common administrative function performed in Kerberos. Some implementations allow administrative functions to be tightly constrained (for example, limiting help desk personnel to performing password resets and not allowing them to perform other administrative functions, such as adding, removing, or otherwise examining or modifying principal entries).

Key Strength and Rollover. As mentioned above, there are a number of keys that should be rolled over periodically. Those keys are generally randomly generated bit strings and are very resistant to any attack short of an exhaustive key search. Thus, the strength of the keys and the required rollover frequency depend almost entirely on the key length used. This suggests that the strongest possible key strength, such as triple-DES, should be used for critical keys. An exhaustive search of the triple-DES key space is well beyond the means of any organization today or for the foreseeable future, with the possible exception of a few government intelligence agencies.

As for all services, the key strength and rollover frequency for a service should be appropriate for the sensitivity of the service. One service stands out as demanding the highest possible level of protection: the ticket-granting service (TGS). All ticket-granting tickets (TGTs) received by clients are sealed in the key of the TGS, and all authentication with services is ultimately rooted in that TGT. If the TGS's key is compromised, the TGS can be impersonated, and with it the entire realm. Obviously, protecting the TGS's key is of paramount importance. Close behind the TGS in importance are the keys used for administrative services and cross-realm authentication.

Automation of the key-rollover process should eliminate virtually all management overhead associated with key rollover. For remote systems, rollover can be initiated from the KDC and pushed to the service, or it may be initiated by the service and pulled from the KDC. However it is done, automation of the rollover process for services on remote systems implies that an existing key is used to establish the secure channel for key rollover. If shared secrets and symmetric key cryptography are used as the basis for establishing that secure channel, the rollover process should strive to camouflage the key rollover sequence. That minimizes the probability of an attacker recording the sequence containing the new key and the subsequent compromise of the new key based on an old key.

Names and Locations

The majority of the management and operational issues with Kerberos revolve around names, the association of those names with physical or logical entities, and the location of those entities in the network. The naming and location issues faced by Kerberos are not unique to Kerberos and are faced by virtually all distributed environments.

Historically, services have been tied to machines, and those machines have a name that people know and understand, and the network software can be used to connect a client to that machine and implicitly a service. In many environments, a single system or service might be known by many names, and as long as the client is able to connect to the service, no one much cares. When a system such as Kerberos is introduced that relies on names to identify and authenticate unique entities, names start to matter much more. All of a sudden, the name may be used not only for location, but authentication, and the client, the service, and Kerberos must all agree on what those names are attached to, and the network naming or directory service must also agree with where they are located.

Name services such as DNS provide solutions to the simple client–server connection problem. However, as the coupling between physical systems and services becomes more tenuous, we are left with the problem of finding an instance of the service (i.e., a system on which the service is operating) somewhere in the network. That service name may or may not have any relationship to a computer system's network name. While there are many solutions to this problem, as of this writing there are no solutions that an implementation can rely on in most environments.

Name Spaces. Kerberos defines a name space consisting of realms and principals. Other than their own principal name, most users will have little or no knowledge of other Kerberos principal names, especially those associated with services. Thus it is left up to the Kerberos software and the environment to somehow map the names that people are familiar with to the corresponding Kerberos principal identities and locate those entities in the network. If Kerberos names are associated with an existing name space, such as DNS, and a name in one name space can be mapped trivially to another, most of the issues become relatively innocuous. If the names in the Kerberos name space are not associated with an existing name space, management effort and the probability of errors goes up significantly, as should be obvious from the discussion below.

Services. Services typically use an "instance" in the principal name to help distinguish different instances of the same service, e.g., **name/instance@REALM**. For example, the instance may distinguish the same service operating on different computer systems. Although it is generally the case that the same principal name would imply similar functions across different instances, that is by convention only. Different principal identifiers — the concatenation of the name, instance, and realm — are treated as completely different entities by Kerberos.

The instance is used by virtually all Kerberos implementations to locate the service on the network. For service principals, Kerberos clients by convention use the fully qualified DNS domain name of the host computer system on which a service operates as the instance. For example, **wadmin/www.z.com@Z.COM** might be a Web administrative service application on the system **www.z.com**. Other services may also be present on the same system, and each of those services could have its own name with the same instance. For example, **ccare/www.z.com@Z.COM** might be a customer care service application running on the same system.

By convention, there is a generic host principal used for authentication to generic host services, such as telnet. By convention, those generic services share the principal name "host." For example, telnet clients would use the service principal name **host/y.z.com@Z.COM** to access to a telnet server running on system **y.z.com**. The principal identifier **host/x.z.com@Z.COM** represents the same principal name (host) with a different instance (**x.z.com**). While **host/y.z.com@Z.COM** and **host/x.z.com@Z.COM** may imply a common service (i.e., a common function) on different systems, Kerberos makes no such implication. From the perspective of Kerberos, those principal identifiers are different, and therefore represent different entities; any implied similarity is by convention only.

Note that there is an implied relationship between the instance and the location of the service, and a client must know both in order to use a service. The location must be known in order to establish a connection with the service (regardless of whether Kerberos is used); and the principal name must be known in order for the client to form the correct service name for that service and obtain the correct service ticket. This implied relationship can be either a great convenience or a great pain, depending on whether the relationship holds true.

Within a single realm, the principal names used for services and the manner in which a client forms the identifier of a service principal have a significant effect on the usability of the implementation. Services that use the common and generic "host' principal name are well defined and not a problem. For other services, those services' principal identifiers must be defined and known to the client. The instance name used for service principals can also present a problem for the client. While the Kerberos convention is to use the fully qualified DNS domain name, or "long form," for the instance in the principal identifier, some DNS implementations return the "short form." This can present problems if one system uses the short form and another system uses the long form. From the perspective of Kerberos, those two identifiers are different, and hence different principals. Both of those identifiers must have a principal entry and an entry in the key table for the service — which increases management overhead — or an error will result when a client uses the wrong principal identifier to attempt to access the service.

KDCs. Before a client can do anything with Kerberos, it must locate a KDC in order to authenticate and obtain tickets for the individual using the client. Note that unlike service principals, which generally use the instance portion of the principal name to also locate the machine on which the service is operating, there is no implied KDC location based in the realm name. The only inference one can make from a realm name is that a KDC is operating on a system somewhere in the corresponding domain. For example, we can infer that a KDC for the realm **Z.COM** is probably located on a system somewhere in domain **z.com**.

If multiple KDCs are used for availability or performance, there must also be some means of directing the client to the appropriate KDC, or for the client to automatically locate a KDC should the first choices be unavailable. For systems that use primary and secondary KDCs, the client will also need to know how to locate the primary KDC for a realm for password-change operations (see below).

Different individuals in different realms may use the same client. It is unrealistic to expect those individuals to know the names or addresses of KDCs in their realm, and therefore the job of locating a KDC falls to the Kerberos client software. Applications on the client may also access different services in different realms. As with individual principals, it is unrealistic for those applications to have embedded within them knowledge as to the location of KDCs in different realms, and again that job falls to the Kerberos client software.

Traversing multiple realms can also present problems for the client. Kerberos defines a standard mechanism for traversing realms that are arranged in a hierarchy. For other realm structures, there is no defined mechanism. Moreover, the client must know the realm in which a service resides. If a service is in a different realm, the client must perform cross-realm authentication to get to that service. In order to perform that cross-realm authentication, the client again must locate a KDC in each of the realms it must traverse.

The basic KDC-realm location problem has a variety of solutions, and implementations vary in how they solve the problem. The simplest and most primitive solution is to use a configuration file on the client. Typically, that configuration file defines a default realm and KDC, which the client uses unless told otherwise. That solution is sufficient for basic implementations. That configuration file may also enumerate a list of alternate KDCs and realms, and the primary KDC for each realm. Thus, changes to the environment may require that configuration file to be updated on many clients. For a relatively static environment, that may be acceptable. For even a moderately dynamic environment, that is unacceptable.

To solve the KDC realm location problem in an effective manner, as much static configuration information as possible must be removed from the client. Solutions that address the problem may make use of naming conventions for KDCs and may include the use of DNS aliases, rotaries, and informational records. Other solutions may use "referrals" or "redirection" to direct the client to the appropriate source. This solution requires only that the client be able to contact at least one KDC; that KDC is assumed to have the knowledge of how to get to other KDCs and realms, and can refer or redirect the client as needed.

Interoperability

The Kerberos 5 protocol defines what is necessary for implementations to be "wire-level" interoperable, and different implementations tend to be quite good about wire-level interoperability. However, the Kerberos standard does not address many of the host-specific or environmental issues that every functional Kerberos implementation must deal with, and there is no guarantee that two implementations will deal with the same issue the same way. *De facto* standards have typically developed on different platforms to address these issues. If a platform vendor provides a Kerberos implementation, that vendor will generally set the standard on their platform. Thus, while these issues are generally not significant, they are worth noting.

- Locating a KDC within a realm may be done in different ways (see *Names and Locations*). This can result in duplicate management effort in order to maintain consistency between two different representations of that information.
- Credentials cache locations and formats may vary. The primary concern is the ability for applications to access the TGT for obtaining service tickets. Unless applications use a common credentials cache to hold the TGT, the user may be forced to go through an additional sign-on.

The most significant interoperability issues between KDCs and clients are not a function of the Kerberos protocol, but specific features that KDCs or clients may require or support. This usually manifests itself in the types of preauthentication mechanisms supported, such as token cards, public key X.509 certificates, etc.

While the standard defines client–KDC interactions, no standards, neither formal nor *de facto*, define KDC propagation mechanisms and administrative interfaces. Thus, those propagation mechanisms and administrative interfaces tend to be vendor-specific. The result is that, while it is quite feasible to use a mixture of clients and KDCs from different vendors, all KDCs within a realm must typically come from the same vendor. Between realms, cross-realm authentication couples the KDCs in those realms (not database propagation). Since cross-realm authentication is defined by the Kerberos standard, KDCs from different vendors in different realms should have no trouble interoperating.

Performance

Performance is the degree to which Kerberos can perform its intended function with a given level of resources. Kerberos will consume some resources, and the efficiency of Kerberos can be gauged by how effectively it uses those resources. Resources take the form of network bandwidth, and disk and CPU on clients, servers, KDCs, and personnel (see *Operation* and *Provisioning*)

For performance, the KDC is typically the most important component, with services a distant second and clients third. That order obtains from the relative concentration of work performed by each of those components and the effects of inefficiencies or failure on other components. An inefficient KDC can affect a large number of clients and services, whereas an inefficient client generally affects only that client. Implicit in that ranking are the infrastructure elements needed to support each component. The efficiency of a KDC, by any measure, makes little difference if the network or directory service needed for clients to communicate with the KDC is inefficient or inoperable.

Encryption. One of the first concerns that usually comes to mind with any security system that uses encryption is the additional CPU and network overhead. In Kerberos, the use of encryption for authentication in the authentication service (AS), ticket-granting service (TGS), and application (AP) messages is intentionally limited, and the resulting cryptographic overhead is minor.

For applications that encrypt and decrypt data, the overhead may be very noticeable (whether or not those applications use Kerberos). That overhead depends on the amount of data that is encrypted, the encryption algorithms used, the efficiency of the implementation's algorithms, and the availability and use of hardware cryptographic acceleration by the implementation. Data encryption and decryption overhead is generally not an issue on clients, as even moderately efficient software cryptographic implementations on today's client platforms are normally faster than the network. However, for servers the situation may be reversed, as those servers are typically the focal points for many clients. That is, the cost of encryption and decryption is spread over many clients, and a much smaller number of servers. Those servers may justify the investment in hardware cryptographic accelerators if performance is an issue.

Encryption of application data adds no measurable overhead to the network. The sole exception to this are protocols that exchange a very small amount of information in each message and that use a block cipher such as DES. This causes messages that are shorter than the block size of the cipher to be padded out to the block size of the cipher. For example, DES is a block cipher with a block size of 8 bytes; encrypting a single byte results in an output that is 8 bytes. However, the additional overhead added by Kerberos in this case will likely be unnoticeable, as it will be dwarfed by the overhead of the message envelope. Simply put, any protocol that transmits a few bytes of data in each message is, by definition, horribly inefficient at moving data — encrypted or not — and encryption will cause a very minor increase in that inefficiency.

Network. The demands Kerberos places on a network are modest and rarely an issue. Network demands will depend on several factors, including the behavioral pattern of clients, network topology, and the location of KDCs within the network. The KDC can communicate with clients using either UDP or TCP. Because of its greater efficiency, UDP is the preferred method. However, if firewalls are placed between clients and KDCs, UDP may not be feasible; for those clients, TCP may be used.

The additional network traffic produced by the Kerberos authentication process is simple to determine:

- Initial authentication. A single exchange between the client and a KDC at the beginning of the workday (AS-REQ and AS-REP). This exchange may involve more than one message in each direction, depending on the technology used for initial authentication. For example, a challenge–response token card typically requires an additional exchange between the client and a KDC.
- Obtaining a service ticket. A single exchange between the client and a KDC the first time an application service is accessed during the workday (TGS-REQ and TGS-REP). Different services require different service tickets, and thus each time a service is accessed the first time during the workday, this exchange will occur.
- Client-to-service authentication. A single message from the client to the service (AP-REQ). If the client requests mutual authentication, there is one additional message from the service to the client (AP-REP). The Kerberos authentication exchange between the client and service may be embedded in the application's session establishment messages and will not show up as an additional message, but rather as a nominal increase in size of the standard session establishment messages.

The size of the messages varies depending on various options and the amount of authorization information embedded in tickets. Assuming no authorization information, message sizes range from approximately 100 to 500 bytes.

KDCs. KDC performance is rarely an issue. The primary services provided by a KDC — those that are most used and have the greatest effect on performance — are the authentication service (AS) and ticket-granting service (TGS). The AS and TGS typically do not require local state, and typically require only read-access to the principal database. This allows liberal placement of KDCs within the network and eliminates the need to bind clients to specific KDCs. Moreover, because of the very simple and symmetric message exchanges and the reuse of common syntax and semantics in the protocol, KDC implementations tend to be quite compact and very efficient in their use of memory and CPU. Rates in excess of 20 AS and TGS exchanges per second for a KDC on a small system are not unusual.

The limiting factor on KDC performance is usually the I/O associated with the principal database. CPU overhead for encryption and decryption is usually a distant second (assuming that symmetric-key cryptography is being used), owing to the relatively small size of the messages processed by the KDC and the limited use of encryption for those messages. Disk resource requirements depend on the database used and the number of principals in the database; although requirements vary, a rule of thumb is 1Kb of disk for each principal in the database.

Clients and Services. Implementations vary in what they require of systems that host clients and services. Generally, the additional overhead imposed on clients, services, and the additional network overhead for an application is unobtrusive. Disk and memory usage on those systems is typically quite small; the primary variation and resource consumption is typically not in the implementation of the Kerberos protocol, but in ancillary facilities such as graphical user interfaces. Again, while the basic Kerberos authentication process is typically unobtrusive, applications that encrypt large amounts of data may see very visible effects on performance.

Provisioning

As discussed previously, the inherent demands Kerberos places on the network are quite modest. Most modern networks should have little or no trouble with the additional network traffic. However, the network topology, KDC placement, and the location of clients and servers relative to each other and KDCs can have either an insignificant or a very significant effect on the network. Most network operations groups have the knowledge and experience to properly provision and locate KDCs in the network, and those groups should be consulted when determining provisioning requirements.

Key Services. Many modern networks have the concept of "key services," which are required for the proper functioning of a modern enterprise network. Key services typically include naming services, such as DNS, and may include time services, such as NTP. The systems that host those services are typically located in facilities at key points in the network, and those facilities are intended to ensure the availability of key services to all users in the face of network outages and other failures.

Those key service facilities will typically have a higher level of physical security than many other facilities. Key services facilities will usually define the location of KDCs in the network, as well as secure time services, if used. Those key service facilities also provide a baseline for the physical security of the KDCs. That security may or may not be sufficient.

Primary KDC. The primary KDC should be dedicated to administrative functions and data distribution. The primary KDC should use a high-availability platform with no single point of failure. The number of secondary KDCs and their propagation requirements obviously contributes to sizing of the primary KDC. The most significant effect on sizing the primary KDC is client password-change frequency. For example, for a user population of 100,000, with a password expiration of three months (approximately 60 working days), the system will be required to handle an average of approximately 1700 password-change operations per day. Virtually all of those password changes will occur at sign-on (when the expiration is detected and the user is forced to change his password), and most will center on a narrow band at 8AM in any time zone. That can present a potentially significant load on the primary KDC. Network connectivity should be appropriate for that load. This also points out the need to distribute password expiration as evenly as possible when loading the principal database.

Secondary KDCs. Secondary KDCs should perform the vast majority of the day-to-day work: providing the authentication and ticket-granting services most used by clients. There is a great deal of freedom in the sizing and location of secondary KDCs. User communities of 5000 to 20,000 are within the performance range of a small to moderate-sized secondary KDC. Availability, not performance requirements, will be the major factor in determining secondary KDC provisioning. Clients should, as a rule, always be directed to a nearby secondary KDC as their first choice. This argues for a greater number of smaller secondary KDCs placed closer to clients.

If availability is a concern, large subnets, campuses, or other major user communities that may be separated by a network failure should have two secondary KDCs, in order to eliminate a single point of failure. Exact physical placement of that secondary pair will be determined by network topology. For example, the pair may be physically distant from each other and still provide a high level of redundancy and availability, depending on the network topology. On the other hand, placing both secondary KDCs on a single network segment that may fail increases cost and does little for redundancy.

If Kerberos is used for local work station access control, availability to the client is critical. If clients and application servers are separated, and if access to those application servers is the predominant factor, then secondary KDCs should be close to the application servers, and not to the clients. Simply put, if the network between the client and the application server is inoperable, a secondary KDC local to the client will not do much good if the objective is to allow the client to securely communicate with the application server.

Clients and Servers. Client and server platforms will not, as a rule, require any additional resources for Kerberos. However, if large amounts of application data are encrypted, servers may require additional CPU capability or hardware cryptographic accelerators. Encryption of application data does not add any measurable overhead to the network. Additional CPU requirements should scale linearly with the amount of data and will depend on the strength of the cryptographic algorithm, and the key size used. Thus, the additional CPU required to meet the demands of the application can be determined with simple timing tests. If hardware cryptographic accelerators are used, scheduling overhead and key setup time for the accelerator may put an upper bound on performance for small messages. Simple metrics such as the number of bytes per second that can be encrypted or decrypted are not sufficient to determine the real-world performance of hardware accelerators.

Deployment

The appropriate deployment strategy for Kerberos depends both on the intended application and the infrastructure that is in place. Typically, the application will define what demands are placed on Kerberos, and that will, in turn, define the demands on the organization and infrastructure. Other than client software distribution and configuration, those organizational and infrastructure demands are typically the gating factor in any Kerberos deployment. For narrowly focused applications, deployment is generally not an issue and is driven exclusively by the application requirements, with Kerberos simply a component embedded in, and deployed with, that application. For broad-based applications, such as secure single sign-on or enterprise access control, the deployment strategy is typically much more complex. That complexity arises not so much from the technology, but from the more complex and varied organizational and environmental requirements of those deployments.

Deployment stakeholders typically include the user community, security groups, network operations groups, and user administration groups, among others. All will be affected by any large-scale deployment, and all will have a say, directly or indirectly, in a deployment. The introduction of a broad-based security system will, by definition, cross organizational and functional boundaries, and friction is usually the result. If pushed too far and too fast, that deployment friction can generate heat sufficient to incinerate even a well-oiled machine. Unless the organization has a demonstrated need and desire to take big steps, small steps should be the rule. That applies to all security systems.

Successful large-scale deployments tend to be done in two phases: partial infrastructure deployment, followed by incremental client deployment, along with any incremental requirements in the supporting infrastructure. Supporting infrastructure, including any KDCs required for availability and performance, can occur in tandem with deployment of pockets of clients. Alternatively, a KDC "backbone" can be deployed prior to any client deployments (see *Provisioning*).

DNS. The identifier space for DNS should be a concern. While rationalizing the DNS structure for many organizations was an issue 5 years ago, it tends to be a much smaller issue now. Because of the growth in TCP/IP and intranets, most organizations have already been forced to deal with that issue over the past years. That said, if the DNS machine name space is chaotic, the DNS structure should be rationalized.

The DNS subdomains that are rationalized must consider the relative locations of clients and services and their interaction. Putting Kerberos into two different subdomains — where clients and servers cross between those subdomains — without first rationalizing the name space in both domains will usually result in problems. Again, this is usually best done incrementally, one subdomain at a time, with rationalization preceding deployment within a subdomain. However, it is not unusual to find that rationalizing one subdomain causes unexpected problems elsewhere. It would be wise to let those perturbations settle before embarking on a Kerberos deployment.

Identities. Typically, the most significant problem encountered in large-scale deployments is rationalizing the identifier spaces for people. Everyone in most organizations has at least one, and typically many more than one, ID. Rationalizing those spaces in the form of secure single sign-on can itself be the justification for a Kerberos deployment. However, no technology provides a solution to the fundamental problem: people are known by different identities within different and discrete name spaces within the enterprise, and the binding of those multiple identities to a specific individual cannot be known. That problem is the result of years of evolution. Binding of multiple identities to a specific individual can be inferred in some cases. The cost and effort of solving this problem, and level of trust in the resulting environment, depend on the level of assurance provided by that inference.

If there is at least one identifier that is relatively universal, and that identity can be trusted, or there are discrete sets of identifiers with little or no overlap, then the job is much easier. If, on the other hand, the identifier space is chaotic, then more time and energy will be required to rationalize IDs. That time and energy can be due to several factors, including: the need to change some names; the need to gain user acceptance when names are changed; and the need to rectify any problems caused by name changes (e.g., systems or applications that are hard-wired with specific names or groups). The actual implementation of the solution is best performed incrementally. This implies an extended deployment, or at least an extended period over which the system is enabled and visible to users. While possible, changing even a relatively small fraction of 100,000 user or system identifiers all at once will likely result in chaos and mass hysteria.

The problem is not eliminated if identity mapping is used to map local identifiers (e.g., a local host or application user ID) to a more uniform identifier, such as a Kerberos principal identifier. Identity mapping may obscure or hide that uniform identifier from users, and thus obviate at least some of the issues with changing identifiers. However, while this approach has an intuitive appeal, it does not eliminate the need for someone or something to go through and map identifiers between different name spaces (the uniform name space being one of those). Building such an "identity map" can be a labor-intensive, time-consuming, and error-prone process. The cost and effort of such a solution should be weighed against the cost and effort in promoting a visible uniform identifier before an approach is selected. Note that Kerberos does not provide implicit capabilities for identifier mapping. Using multiple realms may help but can bring additional issues (below). Also note that when mapping identities, more-trusted identities should always be used to derive less-trusted identities; less-trusted identities should never be used to derive more-trusted identities.

Enrollment. Even with a rational identifier space, users must still be enrolled in the Kerberos database. That is, the principal database must be populated with the names and the passwords of users. There are several ways of populating the principal database depending on what information is available from existing sources, such as legacy user databases, and the form of that information. Depending on what is available, initially populating the principal database can be either a very trivial or a very significant effort.

If a legacy database exists with IDs and passwords, that legacy database can be used to bulk-load the principal database. That database must have clear-text passwords, or keys that are based on an algorithm that is compatible with Kerberos. If clear-text passwords exist in the legacy database, bulk loading is a simple and straightforward process. If the password algorithm used for the legacy database is incompatible with Kerberos, the keys must be transformed to an algorithm that is acceptable to Kerberos, which can be difficult or impossible, depending on the legacy algorithm used.

If keys that use a standard Kerberos algorithm are unavailable, an alternative is to add support for the legacy algorithms to Kerberos, specifically for the purpose of deployment or initially loading the principal database. This requires creating local-use encryption types within the Kerberos implementation (which the protocol allows for). The Kerberos principal database is then loaded with the existing password values from the legacy databases. Those principal entries would also be flagged to require a change-password operation the first time the user logs in. As part of that change-password operation, the new password would be used to update the principal database entry using a standard Kerberos algorithm. After all users have been registered in this manner, support for the legacy algorithm should be removed.

The use of a legacy algorithm as the basis for initial authentication can reduce the security of the system, and thus its use should be limited to enrollment or deployment. While this approach may expose a weak derivation of the password on the network, that exposure is limited. Moreover, if clear-text passwords or a weak derivation is currently being used and transmitted across the network, this approach does not make the situation any worse and allows us to rapidly improve the situation. If no legacy databases exist, an existing interface (e.g., the existing login process) can be modified to capture and use passwords to enroll those users and populate the principal database with their passwords. As a last resort, new passwords/keys can be issued to users.

Realm Design. Other than environmental factors and provisioning requirements discussed previously, the greatest effect on the operation and deployment of a Kerberos implementation will depend on realm design. As always, the rule should be to keep it simple. Unless there is a reason for multiple realms, a single realm should be used. The reasons for using multiple realms might include separation of duties or trust between realms, or the need to distribute the number of primary KDCs (one per realm) for availability of administrative services.

The ability of clients to automatically determine the realm of a service, locate a KDC within a realm, and traverse realms will determine the additional management overhead of a multiple-realm design (see *Names and Locations*). If services are available to automate those client needs, multiple realms will not add measurable management overhead. Performance issues due to additional cross-realm authentication operations may also affect the design, but that is usually a distant second behind management overhead. DNS informational records and redirection and referral capability by KDCs can be used to significantly reduce the management overhead of multiple realms. The following discussion assumes that those facilities are unavailable to, or unused by, the Kerberos implementation.

If automated services are not available to mitigate client realm issues, multiple realms should be arranged in a hierarchy, or tree, and that tree should follow the organization's existing DNS domain structure in order to simplify the association of a service name with, or locating a KDC within, a realm. This argues for realms that map directly to each and every subdomain that provides services that clients in other domains (and hence realms) access. This also implies that when a new subdomain is created, a new realm is created as well. This typically implies a large number of realms, which may not be feasible due to the number of KDCs required. An implementation that allows multiple realms to be serviced by a single KDC can mitigate KDC provisioning issues but does not address separation of security or trust, or the availability of a primary KDC.

The key to the success of this strategy is maintaining congruency between realms and DNS domains to whatever depth of the DNS hierarchy is appropriate. This is required in order to minimize the amount of information required by clients and to maximize the amount of information that can be inferred by clients. For example, if congruency to first-level subdomains is appropriate, then each and every first-level subdomain must have a realm; if congruency to second-level subdomains is appropriate, then each and every second-level subdomain must also have a realm. This also implies that creation or removal of a subdomain implies creation or removal of the corresponding realm.

Maintaining realm–domain congruency allows clients to infer a realm implicitly given a DNS name; the client would have to be explicitly told to what depth the realm–domain structure is congruent (e.g., first, second, etc., level of subdomains). Note that this does not provide any information as to the name of a KDC within a realm. KDC-location by clients can be handled using appropriate naming conventions. For example, using KDC's with names such as "kerberos.sub.domain" might be used to locate KDCs within "sub.domain," and implicitly "sub.realm." If secondary KDCs are used, a DNS rotary can be used, or additional conventions such as "kerberos$n$.sub.domain" (where n denotes secondary KDCs).

ONGOING DEVELOPMENT

This section gives a snapshot of ongoing development efforts surrounding Kerberos and related technologies. Given the rapid development of security technology today, this discussion can only be illustrative and is by no means complete or definitive.

Standards

This section provides an overview of standards efforts relating to Kerberos. Some of these efforts are ongoing and have not yet been approved by the IETF.

Authorization. Ongoing standards efforts are intended to define commonly used authorization data types for identifying the source of authorization information[15] (for example, to distinguish between client- and KDC-supplied authorization information). This effort is also aimed at standardizing the behavior of servers in the presence, or absence, of certain authorization information.

PKINIT. The Public Key Initial Authentication (PKINIT) effort is designed to standardize the use of Public Key credentials (certificates and key pairs) and asymmetric-key cryptography for authentication as part of the Kerberos initial authentication exchange.[16] Using PKINIT, users with Public Key credentials can gain access to Kerberos services within the enterprise. Simple public–private key pairs, without credentials (i.e., issued by a CA), may also be used. PKINIT uses the preauthentication facility of the initial authentication process to incorporate public key capabilities.

PKCROSS. The Public Key Cross-Realm (PKCROSS) effort is based on the PKINIT effort and is designed to standardize the use of Public Key credentials and asymmetric-key cryptography for cross-realm authentication.[17] PKCROSS allows *ad hoc* and direct trust relationships to be established between different realms, thus eliminating the key management required of current implementations, as well as minimizing trust issues associated with transited realms for clients. This minimizes the need for clients or transited realms to have information about realm topology or relationships.

PKTAPP. Public Key Utilizing Tickets for Application Servers (PKTAPP) allows the use of the Kerberos ticketing mechanism without the requirement for a central KDC.[18] PKTAPP proposes a variation of the PKINIT mechanism for allowing application servers to issue tickets for themselves, instead of having the tickets issued by a KDC.

Related Technologies

These technologies are related to Kerberos or are commonly integrated with, or interact with, Kerberos implementations. As of this writing, all of these technologies have ongoing Kerberos-related development efforts associated with them, either within the standards community or by specific vendors.

Public Key. Public Key may describe a system that uses certificates or the underlying public key (i.e., asymmetric-key) cryptography on which such a system is based, or both. A Public Key system implies asymmetric-key cryptography; asymmetric-key cryptography does not imply a Public Key system. (By the same token, Kerberos implies support for DES, whereas DES does not imply Kerberos.)

In the traditional Public Key (PK) model, clients are issued credentials, or "certificates," by a "Certificate Authority" (CA). The CA is a trusted third party. PK certificates contain the user's name, the expiration date of the certificate, etc. The most prevalent certificate format is X.509, which is an international standard. PK certificates typically have lifetimes measured in months or years. Because of the long-lived nature of PK certificates, certificate revocation is a key element in PK infrastructures (PKIs). The authentication process in PK authentication systems also provides the information necessary for a client and server to establish a session key for subsequent data encryption (that is, encryption of application data).

PK credentials, in the form of certificates and public–private key pairs, can provide a strong, distributed authentication system. The private key, which is the most important secret possessed by an individual, runs to hundreds or thousands of bits in length. Thus, a persistent storage system is required to hold the private key, and access to this storage must be protected using a more mundane and conventional mechanism, such as a password. Conventional PK systems still suffer from lack of tools and techniques for managing client credentials. Smart cards hold some promise for secure and mobile private key storage. However, that technology is still relatively new and expensive to deploy on any but a limited scale. Lower-cost solutions, which store the credentials on a local (e.g., work station) disk file, have mobility or security issues. Revocation of PK credentials is still a problem, and standard, scalable and efficient solutions have yet to be provided.

The Kerberos and PK trust models are very similar. A Kerberos ticket is analogous to a PK certificate. However, Kerberos tickets usually have lifetimes measured in hours or days, instead of months or years. Because of their relatively short lifetime, Kerberos tickets are typically allowed to expire instead of being explicitly revoked. The Kerberos session key is analogous to the private key associated with the public key contained in a PK certificate. Possession of the private key is required to prove the authenticity of the sender in a PK system. That is typically done by signing, or encrypting, information with the private key. That signed or encrypted information, along with the certificate, allows a receiver to verify the association between that information and the certificate. As with Kerberos, the trust the receiver places in the identity of the sender is a function of the trust the receiver places in the issuing authority. In the public key systems, that issuing authority is the certificate authority (CA); in Kerberos, that issuing authority is the KDC.

The use of authentication mechanisms such as public key has the potential for minimizing the need for a central online authentication service such as Kerberos. However, authentication is only one of the functions required of an enterprise security service, and the removal of authentication is unlikely to affect Kerberos's role in supporting access control, authorization, and delegation. Moreover, applications where the performance of asymmetric-key cryptography is unacceptable will still require the use of a system that can provide robust services based on symmetric-key cryptography. Advances in cryptography, such as optimizations of elliptic curve algorithms and hardware acceleration, promise improvements in the performance and cost-effectiveness of asymmetric-key cryptography. When the cost will reach a level that allows wide-scale adoption is unclear. In any case, Kerberos can incorporate that technology today for those who can afford it.

PK systems have been integrated into Kerberos using the preauthentication facility of the initial authentication exchange (see *PKINIT*). For example, the client can provide a signed message, with or without an X.509 certificate, as a preauthentication element in the request to the Kerberos authentication service. The result of that exchange is a standard Kerberos 5 credential.

OSF DCE. The Open Software Foundation, Distributed Computing Environment (OSF DCE) uses Kerberos 5 as the underlying security mechanism.[19] DCE extends the basic Kerberos credential to include other information, such as authorization, and defines an authorization system that is separate but typically co-located with the authentication and ticket-granting services on the DCE security server. DCE clients also use RPC (Remote Procedure Call) as their basic communication mechanism, which requires that both client and server utilize the same secure RPC to be interoperable; the RPC is secured using Kerberos 5.

DCE applications are not interoperable with Kerberos 5 applications. However, many DCE implementations also provide support for standard Kerberos 5 clients. That is, the DCE security server may also provide a standard Kerberos 5 authentication service (AS) and ticket-granting service (TGS). That support for standard Kerberos 5 clients does not make DCE and Kerberos 5 applications interoperable; authorization and RPC transport are still barriers to interoperability between applications. As the term "computing environment" implies, DCE requires additional infrastructure components beyond the basic security service, such as a cell directory service, time service, etc.

Kerberos 4. Kerberos 4 is the predecessor of Kerberos 5. Kerberos 5 addresses many Kerberos 4 security issues, as well as other scalability and portability issues associated with Kerberos 4. While conceptually similar, Kerberos 5 and Kerberos 4 are quite different. Kerberos 4 has seen fairly extensive use in educational and commercial environments, and in a few key applications. One of the most widely used applications is AFS (Andrew File System), which is a secure distributed file system (similar to the OSF DCE distributed file service, DFS).

Kerberos 5 and Kerberos 4 applications are not interoperable. Some Kerberos 5 implementations also include support for Kerberos 4 and provide facilities to improve interoperation between Kerberos 4 and Kerberos 5 environments. Interoperation may be achieved by direct support for Kerberos 4 authentication and ticket-granting services by the KDC, or by allowing a Kerberos 4 ticket to be used to obtain a Kerberos 5 ticket (or vice versa).

GSS-API. The Generic Security Service Applications Programming Interface (GSS-API) is a standard that provides applications with a standard API for using different security mechanisms. The objective of the GSS-API is to shield applications from variations in the underlying security mechanisms. In its simplest form, the GSS-API is a thin veneer that sits above an underlying mechanism; that mechanism, such as Kerberos 5, provides the actual security services. While applications are shielded from the underlying mechanism, the infrastructure for each security mechanism is still required.

The original GSS-API specification is referred to as V1.[20] V1 of the GSS-API does not support mechanism negotiation (see *SNEGO*). V2 of the GSS-API specification provides the ability for implementations to support multiple mechanisms.[21] As an API, the GSS-API must define specific language bindings, and there are separate standards for each language binding, such as Java.[22] As of this writing, only "C" language bindings are standardized.[23] GSS-API mechanism specifications may also encapsulate existing mechanisms, in which case a protocol, and not just an API, is defined as part of the GSS-API mechanism standard.

Kerberos 5 was one of the first mechanisms implemented under the GSS-API. Several other mechanisms have also been implemented, including SPKM[24] (Simple Public Key Mechanism) and IDUP[25] (Independent Data Unit Protocol). Two GSS-API applications are compatible only if the underlying GSS-API mechanisms are compatible. GSS-API applications using a Kerberos 5 mechanism and "native" Kerberos 5 applications are not interoperable, because the GSS-API defines not only an API, but a protocol as well.[26] While the GSS-API Kerberos 5 mechanism uses messages that are the same as Kerberos 5, those messages are encapsulated in a protocol that is different from Kerberos 5.

Microsoft SSPI. The Microsoft Security Service Provider Interface (SSPI) is the Microsoft equivalent of the GSS-API.[27] A mechanism such as Kerberos 5 is a "security provider," and applications use security providers through the "provider interface" (the API). The SSPI Kerberos 5 mechanism is wire-level compatible with the GSS-API Kerberos 5 mechanism. The SSPI API is not compatible with the GSS-API. Thus, while the APIs differ, clients and servers written to use either SSPI or GSS-API can interoperate using a common Kerberos 5 mechanism.

SNEGO. The Simple and Protected GSS-API Negotiation Mechanism (SNEGO), is a special GSS-API mechanism that allows the secure negotiation of the mechanism to be used by two different GSS-API implementations.[28] In essence, SNEGO defines a universal but separate mechanism, solely for the purpose of negotiating the use of other security mechanisms. SNEGO itself does not define or provide authentication or data protection, although it can allow negotiators to determine if the negotiation has been subverted, once a mechanism is established. GSS-API implementations that do not support SNEGO cannot negotiate, and therefore the client and server must agree *a priori* what mechanism or mechanisms will be used.

SSL. Secure Sockets Layer (SSL), and the related Transport Layer Security (TLS), are secure point-to-point protocols that define both authentication and message confidentiality protection.[29] SSL uses Public Key authentication. Because SSL is point-to-point, it is suitable only as a low-level transport protocol. An SSL authentication exchange results in the establishment of a shared secret key on both the client and server. That key, and conventional symmetric-key cryptography, is used to provide message confidentiality protection.

SSL has also been used to provide an initial authentication exchange between a client and a Kerberos KDC. In essence, SSL is used to replace the standard Kerberos initial authentication exchange, and a special authentication service (AS) is used on the KDC. SSL authentication is used in place of the client's initial authentication request, which may or may not involve the use of a password by the client. SSL is then used to securely transport the TGT back to the client. SSL is presently one of the few protocols that do not have a standard way of integrating Kerberos authentication to provide message integrity and confidentiality, although such integration has been proposed.[30]

SASL. Simple Authentication and Security Layer (SASL) is a framework for negotiating a security mechanism for session-oriented protocols.[31] SASL specifies a naming convention for registered mechanisms, as well as profile information required for clients and servers to use a mechanism to protect a specific protocol. Registered SASL mechanisms include Kerberos 4 and GSS-API, among others.

IPSEC. Internet Protocol Security (IPSEC), provides integrity or confidentiality services at the network layer.[32] All data protection is performed using symmetric-key cryptography. Establishment of the session keys for data protection is also defined by IPSEC, and may use both symmetric- and asymmetric-key cryptography.

While IPSEC provides data protection, it does not provide the key management infrastructure necessary for a large number of IPSEC systems to authenticate and establish the session keys needed for data protection. As a network layer protection service, IPSEC is targeted primarily at machine-to-machine security; authentication of individuals and applications is outside the scope of IPSEC, and depends entirely on the key management infrastructure used, and the integration of that key management infrastructure with the IPSEC implementation.

Kerberos can provide key management for IPSEC implementations, and this has been proposed through the use of the GSS-API mechanism.[33] In essence, the Kerberos principals are simply machines, or more accurately, the service on each machine that provides IPSEC network layer protection. Kerberos can also provide the key management for binding individuals and applications to IPSEC implementations.

RADIUS. The Remote Authentication Dial-In User Service (RADIUS) allows a RADIUS client (typically a network access device, such as a terminal server), to authenticate a user on a remote computer and control that user's access to the network.[34] The RADIUS client uses the RADIUS protocol to talk to a RADIUS server to authenticate the user. The RADIUS server may contain a simple database containing IDs and passwords, or may use another server to authenticate the client, such as a token card server, or a Kerberos KDC. RADIUS has gained significant acceptance among network and token card vendors.

RADIUS protects the communication between a RADIUS client (e.g., a terminal server), and a RADIUS server. RADIUS does not protect the communications between a remote client and a RADIUS client. Thus, information passed between the remote client (e.g., a laptop computer) and the RADIUS client is unprotected. RADIUS does not have the concept of a credential, and the result of authentication using RADIUS is a yes–no answer. Thus, RADIUS is primarily used as a simple access control mechanism. DIAMETER, part of the AAA (Authentication, Authorization, and Accounting) effort in the IETF, is working to address some of the limitations of RADIUS.[35]

RADIUS has been integrated with Kerberos by using the RADIUS server as a surrogate Kerberos client. That is, the RADIUS server acts as a client to verify an ID and password against a KDC; that ID and password come from the end user at the remote computer system. While the RADIUS server obtains a Kerberos credential as the result of that authentication, there is no way to send that credential back to the end client through the RADIUS client. The benefit of using RADIUS in this manner is that a single authentication database can be used (the KDC's principal database), even though the result of authentication does not provide the client a credential. Note that RADIUS does not protect the user's password between the end client and the RADIUS, and the RADIUS client and server have access to the user's Kerberos ID and password. Thus, use of RADIUS as part of a Kerberos implementation should ensure that the resulting exposure is acceptable.

CDSA. Common Data Security Architecture (CDSA) provides a standard API for many security services, including encryption, authentication, and credential storage and management.[36] CDSA also defines standard methods for incorporating a variety of security service providers, both hardware and software, and a variety of mechanisms, including public key and biometrics. CDSA is similar to Microsoft's Cryptographic API (MS CAPI) in purpose. CDSA was originally developed by Intel and has now been adopted by the Open Group.[37]

Token Cards. Token cards are an example of a very simple trusted third party authentication system. A user, in possession of a token, keys in information from the token. That information is then sent to the application, which verifies the information with a token card server (the trusted third party) provided by the token card vendor. Typically, the value presented by the token is usable only once (to prevent replays) or has a very limited life, and is generated using a key contained within the token card (which is tamper-proof) and a key known to the vendor's token card server.

Token cards secure only the authentication to the application and do not provide any security for the application's data. That is, no information in the authentication process is available for establishing a session key for subsequently encrypting application data. Moreover, token cards must be used for authentication to each application, just as a password is. While the user is not required to remember passwords — the token card in effect generates the passwords — the user must still key a "password" in for each application authentication.

There are three basic types of token cards: challenge–response, time synchronous, and event synchronous. Regardless of type, all have a common attribute: the card is (or should be) tamper-proof, and the card contains a secret key shared between the card and the security server. Use of the card typically requires both physical possession of the card (something you have) and a PIN (something you know). The requirement that those two factors be present for authentication to succeed is the basis for the term "two-factor authentication." Software may also be used to achieve the same effect as a hardware token card. Obviously a software "token card" does not provide the two factors provided by a hardware token.

A variety of token card systems have been integrated into Kerberos using the preauthentication facility of the initial authentication service. The KDC then contacts the token card server, instead of the client contacting the token card server. This allows a mix of token card technologies to be used. The result of the initial authentication exchange is a standard Kerberos 5 credential.

Smart Cards. Smart cards are so named because they have processing intelligence on a card that is the same form factor as a credit card. The processing power and memory capacity varies depending on the card. Smart cards have received prominent attention recently, primarily because of the promise they hold for addressing Public Key client credential management and security issues, by holding the user's private key in tamper-proof storage, and performing cryptographic operations on the card. Thus, the user's private key never leaves the card.

Smart card costs are dropping rapidly. However, a wide-scale smart card deployment requires not only cards, but also readers. As of this writing, cards with the necessary processing power and storage, and the associated readers, are still too expensive for wide-scale deployment. Although smart cards are most often associated with Public Key systems, smart cards are also used to provide symmetric-key cryptography. Symmetric-key smart cards may provide secure key storage and associated cryptographic functions for use as challenge–response devices, for example.

Public Key smart cards have been integrated into Kerberos using the preauthentication mechanism. This allows users with smart cards to authenticate to the Kerberos authentication service using the Public Key credentials on a smart card (see *PKINIT*).

Encryption Algorithms. The two broad classifications of cryptographic systems are symmetric-key and asymmetric-key. Both Kerberos and Public Key systems (as well as other authentication systems) may incorporate one or both cryptographic systems. Common symmetric-key systems include DES (Data Encryption Standard), and the triple-DES variant.[38] Common asymmetric-key systems include ECC[39] (elliptic curve) and RSA[40] (Rivest Shamir Adleman). The strength of these different systems is difficult to compare and is only one element that determines their application. For example, based on exhaustive key search, a triple-DES (112-bit) key is approximately equal to a 1792-bit RSA key (i.e., key modulus);[41] and a 1024-bit RSA key is approximately equal to a 160-bit ECC key.[42]

The distinguishing characteristic of these systems is the symmetry of the keys used for encryption and decryption. Symmetric-key systems use the same key for encryption and decryption. Thus, two parties must share the same key (presumably secret) in order to encrypt and decrypt information. Asymmetric-key systems use different, but related, keys for encryption and decryption: information encrypted with one key can only be decrypted with the other key. That key pair is typically referred to as a public–private key pair. One of the keys is public and known to many people; the other key is private (presumably secret) and known to only one person.

Another distinguishing characteristic of these systems is the CPU speed or hardware complexity for encryption and decryption operations. Symmetric-key systems tend to be quite fast. Asymmetric-key systems tend to be CPU intensive and are typically used only for encrypting small amounts of data — typically only that needed for authentication (as with digital signatures). Because of its speed advantages, symmetric key cryptography is still used by all security systems for encrypting application data. Symmetric- and asymmetric-key are often used together. For example, asymmetric-key is used to establish a session key for symmetric-key by encrypting a symmetric session key (that symmetric-key usually being a very a small amount of data). Higher-performance symmetric-key is then used to encrypt and decrypt the application data. The speed of cryptographic operations in symmetric-key systems is typically symmetric. That is, encrypt and decrypt speeds are generally the same (for the same implementation running on the same hardware). The speed of cryptographic operations in asymmetric-key systems is typically asymmetric, and depends on what function is being performed.

Cryptographic systems alone do not constitute a secure authentication system. Kerberos and Public Key are secure, distributed, authentication systems that use cryptographic systems, define the rules of how cryptography is used, and that define the syntax and semantics for various protocol messages and data formats. Although the rules and protocols for different authentication systems tend to be very different, the problems that must be solved to build a practical, secure, distributed, authentication system are largely invariant.

Kerberos defines the use of symmetric-key cryptography, including both DES and triple-DES, for both authentication and data encryption. Asymmetric-key cryptography has also been integrated into Kerberos using the preauthentication facility of the initial authentication service (see *PKINIT*).

Secure Hash Algorithms. Secure distributed authentication systems require secure hash functions and not just encryption and decryption, although secure hash functions are often built using a cryptographic algorithm. A secure hash function takes a large amount of data and hashes it down to a small amount of data (e.g., 128 bits), or the "hash value." The attributes of a secure hash function are: no two inputs should produce the same output ("collision proof"), and you can't work backwards from the hash value to the input. Think of the secure hash value as a fingerprint: the hash value uniquely defines the input but doesn't tell you anything about the input. Note that a simple checksum, such as CRC32, is not a secure hash function — too many inputs produce the same output. A secure hash is sometimes referred to as a message digest or cryptographic checksum.

A secure hash is typically used to provide integrity protection and is also used in digital signature applications. The hash value of a document is generated, and that value is encrypted using an individual's key. Encrypting only the hash value, or signature, eliminates the need to encrypt the entire document for integrity protection. That encrypted value is also the digital signature of the individual applied to a document. Verifying the signature against the document simply regenerates the hash value of the document, decrypts the encrypted hash value, and compares the two. If someone changes either the signature or the document, the hash will change, and verification will fail. The most common hash functions are MD5[43] (Message Digest 5), and SHA-1[44] (Secure Hash Algorithm 1).

Kerberos defines the use of several secure hash functions, including DES and triple-DES message authentication code (MAC) hashing functions, as well as MD5 and SHA-1.

LESSONS LEARNED

As discussed in previous sections, most of the technical issues surrounding the implementation and deployment of Kerberos are tractable, and when properly understood, those issues should not present serious problems. The significant technical issues that remain — such as fragmented or dysfunctional namespaces — and their solutions are dependent on the environment. Various methods can minimize those issues, but there is little that Kerberos, or any security system, can do to fix the underlying problems. And as with all security systems, the primary obstacles to success are not technical, but fundamental to the role of information security in today's business and organizational environments. Kerberos does what it can technically by providing a robust and cost-effective distributed security system. The rest is up to us.

Risk, Fear and Value

Kerberos is fundamentally a strong distributed authentication system. It can be used for a single application within a single group or a set of applications that span an enterprise. Whatever the use, successful deployments usually address applications that can benefit from what Kerberos has to offer. That applies whether Kerberos is being used for a single application or to implement enterprise-wide secure single sign-on. As obvious as it may seem, the security that Kerberos brings with it must be perceived to be of value to the organization. While security practitioners may appreciate the intrinsic value of strong authentication, the broader community within most organizations generally does not perceive that value. Without perceived value, cost and effort will be viewed as wasted. To put it another way, without perceived value, any deployment problems will be magnified, and the probability of success will rapidly approach zero.

Applications that can benefit from a distributed security system such as Kerberos are growing more common than in the past. However, the fundamentals still hold true. As enterprises move to more distributed environments, services are often pushed out toward the consumer. For example, providing on-demand access to human resources data (typically some of the most sensitive information in an organization) by employees from individual desktops. Such "self-service" applications require a strong, distributed authentication system that can also provide data encryption, and provide those capabilities at reasonable cost. The cost of the security infrastructure can often be justified by the cost savings obtained by removing the "human firewall" of clerks that typically guard access to those applications' data.

Because the intrinsic value of a system such as Kerberos is not always appreciated, it is up to security practitioners to identify the applications that can benefit. That requires more than an understanding of security. It also requires understanding the application, and the business needs that surround the application. It requires knowledge sufficient to make the benefits of security intrinsically obvious to the application owners, or sufficient knowledge to quantify the risks and costs to the application owners. Risk and cost are a business decision. Making an informed decision requires understanding both. Risk is often difficult to quantify, and unquantified risk, in the form of fear, can sometimes be a great motivator. However, decisions based on fear are often subject to reversal and second-guessing, and are poor substitutes for informed decision-making.

Security based on value and informed decisions will find a more accepting audience, and much easier deployment, than those based on fear.

Distributed Security

The rules that a security system enforces represent demands and assumptions made of the environment. If those rules are too onerous, the security implementation will fail as predictably, and for the same reasons, as any technology that makes unrealistic assumptions or resource demands on its environment. As a security *technology*, Kerberos provides very good performance and makes relatively modest demands and assumptions on its environment. As a security *system*, the demands and assumptions made by Kerberos are entirely dependent on an organization's definition of acceptable security.

The tradeoff between acceptable security and what is practical in an organization, is the first question that the security practitioner must answer. The answer to that question varies from organization to organization, and technology generally plays a minor role in the equation. Moreover, the organic nature of most distributed environments is not receptive to the introduction of a broad-based security system. Introduction of such a system into those environments — with implicitly greater uniformity and rigidity — will cause friction. If Kerberos is used to enforce draconian security measures in environments that have previously had very informal or isolated security practices, problems are very likely to occur. Technology cannot solve those problems.

The very nature of distributed environments increases diversity and indeterminacy. That introduces a greater degree of uncertainty into the security equation. That uncertainty is something the security community has historically been very uncomfortable with. Probabilistic models of security require quantification and analysis. Today, that quantification and analysis are extremely difficult at best, impossible at worst, and so rare as to be nonexistent. Thus we are left to make a value judgment, and for most it is far easier to retreat into the absolutes of the past than to risk uncertainty. After all, risk reduction and aversion is what security is all about.

While the level of certainty that we are historically accustomed to is achievable in distributed environments, it is not achievable at a cost that any organization can afford. That is extremely unlikely to change. Diversity and indeterminacy are increasing with every passing day. Successful distributed security implementations recognize and embrace those changes, making incremental improvements as organizations and technology adapt and converge on an acceptable paradigm. Unsuccessful distributed security implementations shun those changes and attempt to impose unrealistic demands based on time-worn assumptions about what is feasible, necessary, or desirable.

The one lesson that stands out from years of Kerberos implementations is that uncertainty is a fact of life in distributed security. Learn to deal with it.

References

1. Project Athena is a model of "next-generation distributed computing" in the academic environment. It began in 1993 as an eight-year project with DEC and IBM as its major industrial) sponsors. Their pioneering model is based on client–server technology and it includes such innovations as authentication based on Kerberos and X Windows. An excellent reference — George Champine, *MIT Project Athena, A Model for Distributed Campus Computing*, Digital Press, 1991. Other definitive works on Kerberos include B. Clifford Neuman and Theodore Ts'o. Kerberos: an authentication service for computer networks, *IEEE Communications* 32(9):33-38. September 1994 - available at http://gost.isi.edu/publications/kerberos-neuman-tso.html and http://nii.isi.edu/publications/kerberos-neuman-tso.html
2. R. Needham and M. Schroeder, Using encryption for authentication in large networks of computers, *Communications of the ACM 21*, December 1978.
3. D.E. Denning and G.M. Sacco, Time-stamps in key distribution protocols, *Communications of the ACM 24*, August 1981.
4. J. Kohl, C. Neuman, "The Kerberos Network Authentication Service(V5)," Internet Request for Comments 1510, September 1993. http://www.rfc-editor.org
5. Current revisions to the Kerberos protocol can be found in: C. Neuman, J. Kohl, T. Ts'o, "The Kerberos Network Authentication Service (V5)," Internet Draft, November 1998.
6. IETF RFC information can be found at various Internet sites. The reference sites are ds.internic.net (US East Coast), nic.nordu.net (Europe), ftp.isi.edu (US West Coast), and munnari.oz.au (Pacific Rim).
7. Microsoft Corporation, "Microsoft Windows 2000 Product Line Summary," http://www.microsoft.com/presspass/features/1998/winntproducts.htm.
8. Sun Microsystems, "Sun Enterprise Authentication Mechanism for Solaris Enterprise Server Datasheet," http://www.sun.com/solaris/ds/ds-seamss.
9. B. Blakley, "Security Requirements for DCE", Open Software Foundation Request for Comments 8.1, October 1995.
10. S. M. Bellovin and M. Merritt, Limitations of the Kerberos authentication system, *Proceedings of the Winter 1991 Usenix Conference*, January 1991.
11. B. Clifford Neuman, Proxy-based authorization and accounting for distributed systems, in *Proceedings of the 13th International Conference on Distributed Computing Systems*, Pittsburgh, May 1993.
12. In his treatise on distributed systems security, Morrie Gasser categorizes the security services that a distributed system can provide for its users and applications as: secure channels, authentication, confidentiality, integrity, access control. nonrepudiation, and availability. M. Gasser, Security in distributed systems, in *Recent Developments in Telecommunications*, North-Holland, Amsterdam, The Netherlands, Elsevier Science Publishers, 1992.
13. J. Pato, "Using Pre-Authentication to Avoid Password Guessing Attacks," Open Software Foundation DCE Request for Comments 26, December 1992.
14. See Reference 11.
15. C. Neuman, J. Kohl, T. Ts'o, "The Kerberos Network Authentication Service (V5)," Internet Draft, November 1998.
16. C. Neuman, J. Wray, B. Tung, J. Trostle, M. Hur, A. Medvinsky, S. Medvinsky, "Public Key Cryptography for Initial Authentication in Kerberos," Internet Draft, November 1998.
17. G. Tsudik, C. Neuman, B. Sommerfeld, B. Tung, M. Hur, T. Ryutov, A. Medvinsky, "Public Key Cryptography for Cross-Realm Authentication in Kerberos," Internet Draft, November 1998.

18. C. Neuman, M. Hur, A. Medvinsky, Alexander Medvinsky, "Public Key Utilizing Tickets for Application Servers (PKTAPP)," Internet Draft, March 1998. See also: M. Sirbu, J. Chuang. "Distributed Authentication in Kerberos Using Public Key Cryptography," Symposium On Network and Distributed System Security, 1997.

19. B. Blakley, "Security Requirements for DCE," Open Software Foundation Request for Comments 8.1, October 1995.

20. J. Linn, "Generic Security Service Application Program Interface," Internet Request for Comments 1508, September 1993. http://www.rfc-editor.org

21. J. Linn, "Generic Security Service Application Program Interface, Version 2," Internet Request for Comments 2078 (January 1997). http://www.rfc-editor.org

22. J. Kabat, "Generic Security Service API Version 2: Java bindings," Internet Draft, August 1998.

23. J. Wray, "Generic Security Service API: C-bindings," Internet Request for Comments 1509, September 1993. http://www.rfc-editor.org

24. C. Adams, "The Simple Public-Key GSS-API Mechanism (SPKM)," Internet Request for Comments 2025, October 1996. http://www.rfc-editor.org

25. C. Adams, "Independent Data Unit Protection Generic Security Service Application Program Interface (IDUP-GSS-API)," Internet Request for Comments 2479, December 1998. http://www.rfc-editor.org

26. J. Linn, "The Kerberos Version 5 GSS-API Mechanism," Internet Request for Comments 1964, June 1996.

27. D. Chappell, NT 5.0 in the enterprise, *Byte Magazine*, May 1997.

28. E. Baize, D. Pinkas, "The Simple and Protected GSS-API Negotiation Mechanism," Internet Request for Comments 2478, December 1998. http://www.rfc-editor.org

29. T. Dierks, C. Allen, "The TLS Protocol Version 1.0," Internet Request for Comments 2246, January 1999. http://www.rfc-editor.org

30. M. Hur, A. Medvinsky, "Addition of Kerberos Cipher Suites to Transport Layer Security (TLS)," Internet Draft, September 1998.

31. J. Myers, "Simple Authentication and Security Layer (SASL)," Internet Request for Comments 2222, October 1997. http://www.rfc-editor.org

32. R. Thayer, N. Doraswamy, R. Glenn, "IP Security Document Roadmap," Internet Request for Comments 2411, November 1998. http://www.rfc-editor.org

33. D. Piper, "A GSS-API Authentication Mode for IKE", Internet Draft, December 1998.

34. C. Rigney, A. Rubens, W. Simpson, S. Willens. "Remote Authentication Dial In User Service (RADIUS)," Internet Request for Comments 2138, April 1997. http://www.rfc-editor.org

35. A. Rubens, P. Calhoun, "DIAMETER Base Protocol," Internet Draft, November 1998.

36. Intel Corporation, "Making PC Interaction Trustworthy for Communications, Commerce and Content," Intel Security Program, July 1998.

37. The Open Group, "New Security Standard from The Open Group Brings the Realization of High-Value E-Commerce for Everyone a Step Further" Press Release January 6, 1998.

38. National Bureau of Standards, U.S. Department of Commerce, "Data Encryption Standard (DES)," Federal Information Processing Standards Publication 46-2, Washington, DC (December 1993). National Bureau of Standards, U.S. Department of Commerce, "DES Modes of operation," Federal Information Processing Standards Publication 81 (December 1980). Information on triple-DES can be found in: National Institute of Standards and Technology, U.S. Department of Commerce, "Data Encryption Standard (DES)," Draft Federal Information Processing Standards Publication 46-3, (January 1999).

39. V.S. Miller, Use of elliptic curves in cryptography, *Advances in Cryptology — Proceedings of CRYPTO85,* (Springer Verlag Lecture Notes in Computer Science 218, pp. 417-426, 1986). For a more contemporary treatment, see: Jurisic and A.J. Menezes, Elliptic curves and cryptography, *Dr. Dobb's Journal*, pages 26-35, (April 1997).

40. R.L. Rivest, A. Shamir, and L.M. Adleman, A method for obtaining digital signatures and public-key cryptosystems, *Communications of the ACM 21*, February 1978.

41. B. Schneier, *Applied Cryptography*, John Wiley & Sons, NY, 1996.

42. "Remarks on the Security of the Elliptic Curve Cryptosystem," Certicom Corporation ECC whitepaper (September 1997).
43. R. Rivest, "The MD5 Message Digest Algorithm," Internet Request for Comments 1321, MIT Laboratory for Computer Science, April 1992.
44. National Institute of Standards and Technology, U.S. Department of Commerce, "Secure Hash Standard (SHS)," Federal Information Processing Standard Publication 180-1, April 1995.

Chapter 22

Getting Started with PKI

Harry DeMaio

In the recent history of information protection there has been an ongoing parade of technologies that loudly promises new and total solutions but frequently does not make it past the reviewing stand. In some cases, it breaks down completely at the start of the march. In others, it ends up turning down a side street. Is Public-Key Infrastructure (PKI) just another gaudy float behind more brass bands, or is there sufficient rationale to believe that this one might make it? There are some very good reasons for optimism in this case, but optimism has been high before.

To examine PKI, one needs to know more than just the design principles. Many a slick and sophisticated design has turned embarrassingly sour when implemented and put into application and operational contexts. There are also the questions of economics, market readiness, and operational/technological prerequisites, all of which can march a brilliant idea into a blind alley.

APPROACH AND PRELIMINARY DISCUSSION

We'll start with a short review of the changing requirements for security. Is there really a need, especially in networking, that didn't exist before for new security technologies and approaches?

- We'll (very) briefly describe encryption, public-key encryption and PKI.
- We'll see how well PKI satisfies today's needs from a design standpoint.
- We'll look at what's involved in actually making PKI a cost-effective reality.
- Finally, we'll ask whether PKI is an exceptional approach or just one of many alternatives worth looking at.

0-8493-9829-0/00/$0.00+$.50

THE CHANGING WORLD OF NETWORKED SYSTEMS

First a few characteristics of yesterday's and today's network-based information processing need to be considered. If the differences can be summed up in a single phrase, it is "accelerated dynamics." The structure and components of most major networks are in a constant state of flux — as are the applications, transactions, and users that traverse its pathways. This has a profound influence on the nature, location, scope, and effectiveness of protective mechanisms.

Exhibit 22.1 illustrates some of the fundamental differences between traditional closed systems and open (often Internet-based) environments. These differences do much to explain the significant upsurge in interest in encryption technologies.

	LEGACY/CLOSED NETWORK	MODERN OPEN NETWORK
User Environments	Known and stable	Mobile/variable
End Points	Established	Dynamic/open
Network Structure	Established/known	Dynamic/open
Processing	Mainframe/internally distributed	Multisite/Multienterprise
Data Objects	Linked to defined process	Often independent

Exhibit 22.1. Open vs. Closed Networks

Clearly, each network is unique, and most display a mix of the above characteristics. But the trends toward openness and variability are clear. The implications for security can be profound. Security embedded in or "hard-wired" to the system and network infrastructure cannot carry the entire load in many of the more mobile and open environments, especially where dial-up is dominant. A more flexible mode that addresses the infrastructure, user, work station, environment, and data objects is required.

An example: Envision the following differences:

- A route salesperson who returns to the office work station in the evening to enter the day's orders (online batch)
- That same worker now entering on a laptop through a radio or dial-up phone link those same orders as they are being taken at the customer's premises (dial-up interactive)
- Third-party operators taking orders at an 800/888 call center
- Those same orders being entered by the customer on a Web site
- A combination of the above

The application is still the same: order entry. But the process is dramatically different, ranging from batch entry to Web-based electronic commerce.

In the first case, the infrastructure, environment, process, and user are known, stable, and can be well controlled. The classic access control facility or security server generally carries the load.

In the second (interactive dial-up) instance, the employee is still directly involved. However, now there is a portable device and its on-board functions and data, the dial-up connections, the network, the points of entry to the enterprise, and the enterprise processes to protect if the level of control that existed in the first instance is to be achieved.

The third instance involves a third party, and the network connection may be closed or open.

The fourth (Web-based) approach adds the unknowns created by the customer's direct involvement and linkage through the Internet to the company's system.

The fifth, hybrid scenario calls for significant compatibility adjustments on top of the other considerations. By the way, this scenario is not unlikely. A fallacious assumption in promoting Web-based services is that one can readily discontinue the other service modes. It seldom happens.

Consider the changes to identification, authentication, and authorization targets and processes in each instance. Consider monitoring and the audit trail. Then consider the integrity and availability issues. Finally, the potential for repudiation begins to rear its ugly head. The differences are real and significant.

THE EVOLVING BUSINESS NETWORK

Remember, too, that most network-based systems in operation today have evolved, or in many cases, accreted into their current state — adding infrastructures and applications on demand and using the technology available at the time. Darwin notwithstanding, some of the currently surviving networks are not necessarily the fittest. In most of the literature, networks are characterized as examples of a specific class — open–closed; intranet–extranet; LAN–WAN–Internet; protocol-X or protocol-Y. Although these necessary and valuable distinctions can be used to describe physical and logical infrastructures, remember that when viewed from the business processes they support supply chain, order entry, funds transfer, and patient record processing. Most "business process" networks are technological and structural hybrids.

The important point is that today security strategy and architecture decisions are being driven increasingly by specific business requirements, not just technology. This is especially true in the application of encryption-related techniques such as PKI. Looking again at the order entry example above, the application of consistent protective mechanisms for a hybrid order entry scenario will undoubtedly require compatibility and interoperability across platform and network types unless the entire system is rebuilt to one specification. This seldom happens unless the enterprise is embarking on a massive reengineering effort or deploying major application suites such as the SAP AG R/3 or PeopleSoft.

The Disintegration and Reintegration of Security Mechanisms

To be effective, a protective mechanism must appropriately bind with the object and the environment requiring protection. In open networks, the connection, structure, and relationship of the components are more loosely defined and variable. Therefore, the protective mechanisms must be more granular, focused, and more directly linked to the object or process to be protected than was the case with legacy systems. Formerly, protection processes operated primarily at a "subterranean plumbing" level, surfacing only in password and authorization administration and log-ons. Now the castle moat is being supplemented with "no-go" zones, personal bodyguards posted at strategic spots, food tasters, and trusted messengers.

Encryption mechanisms fit this direct, granular requirement often ideally, since they can protect individual files, data elements (including passwords), paths (tunneling and Virtual Private Networks) and manage access management requirements. (Identification and authentication through encryption is easier than authorization.) But saying that encryption is granular is not the same as saying that a PKI system is interoperable, portable, or scalable. In fact, it means that most encryption-related systems today are still piece parts, although some effective suites such as Entrust are in the market and several others, such as IBM SecureWay and RSA/SD Keon, are just entering.

This "disintegrated" and specialized approach to providing security function creates a frustrating problem for security professionals accustomed to integrated suites. Now the user becomes the integrator or must use a third-party integrator. The products may not integrate well or even be able to interface with one another. At the 1999 RSA Conference in San Jose, CA, the clarion call for security suites was loud and clear.

Encryption Defined

Encryption is a process for making intelligible information unintelligible through the application of sophisticated mathematical conversion techniques. Obviously, to be useful the process must be reversible (decryption). The three major components of the encryption/decryption process are as follows:

1. *The information stream in clear or encrypted form.*
2. *The mathematical encryption process* — the algorithm. Interestingly, most commercial algorithms are publicly available and are not secret. What turns a public process into a uniquely secret one is the encryption key.
3. *The encryption key.* The encryption key is a data string that is mathematically combined with the information (clear or encrypted) by the algorithm to produce the opposite version of the data (encrypted or clear). Remember that all data on computers is represented in binary number coding. Binary numbers can be operated upon by the same arithmetic functions as those that apply to decimal numbers. So by combining complex arithmetic operations, the data and key are converted into an encrypted message form and decrypted using the same process and *same key — with one critical exception.*

Before explaining the exception, one more definition is required. The process that uses the *same key* to decrypt and encrypt is called *symmetric* cryptography. It has several advantages, including exceptional speed on computers. It has a serious drawback. In any population of communicating users (n), in order to have *individually unique* links between each pair of users, the total number of keys required is n (n + 1)/2. Try it with a small number and round up. If the population of users gets large enough, the number of individual keys required rapidly becomes unmanageable. This is one (but not the only) reason why symmetric cryptography has not had a great reception in the commercial marketplace in the last 20 years.

The salvation of cryptography for practical business use has been the application of a different class of cryptographic algorithms using *asymmetric* key pairs. The mathematics is complex and is not intuitively obvious, but the result is a *pair of linked keys* that must be used together. However, only one of the pair, the private key, must be kept secret by the key owner. The other half of the pair — the public key — can be openly distributed to anyone wishing to communicate with the key owner. A partial analogy is the cash depository in which all customers have the same key for depositing through a one-way door, but only the bank official has a key to open the door to extract the cash. This technique vastly reduces the number of keys required for the same population to communicate safely and uniquely.

ENTER PKI

If the public key is distributed openly, how do you know that it is valid and belongs with the appropriate secret key and the key owner? How do you manage the creation, use, and termination of these key pairs. That is the foundation of PKI. Several definitions follow:

> The comprehensive system required to provide public-key encryption and digital signature services is known as the *public-key infrastructure* (PKI). The purpose of a public-key infrastructure is to manage keys and certificates.
>
> *Entrust Inc.*

> A public-key infrastructure (PKI) consists of the programs, data formats, communications protocols, institutional policies, and procedures required for enterprise use of public-key cryptography.
>
> *Office of Information Technology, University of Minnesota*

> In its most simple form, a PKI is a system for publishing the public-key values used in public-key cryptography. There are two basic operations common to all PKIs:
>
> 1. Certification is the process of binding a public-key value to an individual organization or other entity, or even to some other piece of information such as a permission or credential.
>
> 2. Validation is the process of verifying that a certificate is still valid.
>
> How these two operations are implemented is the basic defining characteristic of all PKIs.
>
> *Marc Branchaud*

The Digital Certificate and Certificate Authorities

Obviously, from these definitions, a digital certificate is the focal point of the PKI process. What is it? In simplest terms, a digital certificate is a credential (in digital form) in which the public key of the individual is embedded along with other identifying data. That credential is encrypted (signed) by a trusted third party or certificate authority (CA) who has established the identity of the key owner (similar to but more rigorous than notarization). The "signing key" ties the certificate back to the CA and ultimately to the process that bound the certificate holder to his or her credentials and identity proof process.

By "signing" the certificate, the CA establishes and takes liability for the authenticity of the public key contained in the certificate and the fact that it is bound to the named user. Now total strangers who know or at least trust a common CA can use encryption not just to *conceal* the data but also to *authenticate* the other party. The *integrity* of the message is also ensured.

If you change it once encrypted, it will not decrypt. The message *cannot be repudiated* because it has been encrypted using the sender's certificate.

Who are CAs? Some large institutions are their own CAs, especially banks (private CAs). There are some independent services (public CAs) developing, and government, using the licensing model as a take off point, is moving into this environment. It may become a new security industry. In The Netherlands, KNB, the Dutch notary service, supplies digital certificates.

As you would expect, there has been a move by some security professionals to include more information in the certificate, making it a multipurpose "document." There is one major problem with this. Consider a driver's license, which is printed on special watermarked paper, includes the driver's picture and is encapsulated in plastic. If one wished to maintain more volatile information on it, such as current make of car(s), doctor's name and address, or next of kin, the person would have to get a new license for each change.

The same is true for a certificate. The user would have to go back to the CA for a new certificate each time he made a change. For a small and readily accessible population, this may be reasonable. However, PKI is usually justified based on large populations in open environments, often across multiple enterprises. The cost and administrative logjam can build up with the addition of authorization updates *embedded in the certificate*. This is why relatively changeable authorization data (permissions) are seldom embedded in the certificate but rather attached. There are several certificate structures that allow attachments or permissions that can be changed independently of the certificate itself.

To review, the certificate is the heart of the PKI system. A given population of users who wish to intercommunicate selects or is required to use a specific CA to obtain a certificate. That certificate contains the public-key half of an asymmetric key pair as well as other indicative information about the target individual. This individual is referred to as the "distinguished name" — implying that there can be no ambiguities in certificate-based identification — all Smiths must be separately distinguished by ancillary data.

Where are Certificates Used?

Certificates are used primarily in open environments in which closed network security techniques are inappropriate or insufficient for any or all of the following:

- Identification/authentication
- Confidentiality

- Message/transaction integrity
- Nonrepudiation

Not all PKI systems serve the same purposes or have the same protective priorities. This is important to understand when one is trying to justify a PKI system for a specific business environment.

How Does PKI Satisfy Those Business Environment Needs?

Market Expectation. As PKI becomes interoperable, scalable, and generally accepted, companies will begin to accept the wide use of encryption-related products. Large enterprises such as government, banks, and large commercial firms will develop trust models to easily incorporate PKI into everyday business use.

Current Reality. It is not that easy. Thus far, a significant number of PKI projects have been curtailed, revised, or temporarily shelved for reevaluation. The reasons most often given include the following:

- Immature technology
- Insufficient planning and preparation
- Underestimated scope
- Infrastructure and procedural costs
- Operational and technical incompatibilities
- Unclear cost-benefits

Apparent Conclusions about the Marketplace

PKI has compelling justifications for many enterprises, but there are usually more variables and pitfalls than anticipated. Broadside implementation, though sometimes necessary, has not been as cost-effective. Pilots and test beds are strongly recommended.

A properly designed CA/RA administrative function is always a critical success factor.

CERTIFICATES, CERTIFICATE AUTHORITIES (CA), AND REGISTRATION AUTHORITIES (RA)

How do they work and how are they related?

First look at the PKI certificate lifecycle. It is more involved than one may think. A digital certificate is a secure and trustworthy credential, and the process of its creation, use, and termination must be appropriately controlled.

Not all certificates are considered equally secure and trustworthy, and this is an active subject of standards and industry discussion. The strength of the cryptography supporting the certificate is only one discriminating factor. The degree to which the certificate complies with a given standard, X.509, for example, is another criterion for trustworthiness. The standards cover a wide range of requirements, including content, configuration, and process. The following is hardly an exhaustive list, but it will provide some insight into some of the basic requirements of process.

- *Application* — How do the "certificate owners to be" apply for a certificate? To whom do they apply? What supporting materials are required? Must a face-to-face interview be conducted, or can a surrogate act for the subject? What sanctions are imposed for false, incomplete, or misleading statements? How is the application stored and protected, etc?
- *Validation* — How is the applicant's identity validated? By what instruments? By what agencies? For what period of time?
- *Issuance* — Assuming the application meets the criteria and the validation is successful, how is the certificate actually issued? Are third parties involved? Is the certificate sent to the individual or, in the case of an organization, some officer of that organization? How is issuance recorded? How are those records maintained and protected?
- *Acceptance* — How does the applicant indicate acceptance of the certificate? To whom? Is nonrepudiation of acceptance eliminated?
- *Use* — What are the conditions of use? Environments, systems, and applications?
- *Suspension or Revocation* — In the event of compromise or suspension, who must be notified? How? How soon after the event? How is the notice of revocation published?
- *Expiration and Renewal* — Terms, process, and authority?

Who and What Are the PKI Functional Entities That Must Be Considered?

Certification Authority (CAs)

- A person or institution who is trusted and can vouch for the authenticity of a public key
- May be a principal (e.g., management, bank, credit card issuer)
- May be a secretary of a "club" (e.g., bank clearing house)
- May be a government agency or designee (e.g., notary public, Department of Motor Vehicles, or post office)
- May be an independent third party operating for a profit (e.g., VeriSign)
- Makes a decision on evidence or knowledge after due diligence
- Records the decision by signing a certificate with its private key
- Authorizes issuance of certificate

Registration Authority (RA)

- Manages certificate life cycle, including Certificate Directory maintenance and Certificate Revocation List (s) maintenance and publication
- Thus can be a critical choke point in PKI process and a critical liability point, especially as it relates to CRLs
- An RA may or may not be CA

Other Entities

- *Other Trusted Third Parties* — These may be service organizations that manage the PKI process, brokers who procure certificates from certificate suppliers, or independent audit or consulting groups that evaluate the security of the PKI procedure
- *Individual Subscribers*
- *Business Subscribers* — In many large organizations, two additional constructs are used:
    1. *The Responsible Individual* (RI) — The enterprise certificate administrator
    2. *The Responsible Officer* (RO) — The enterprise officer who legally assures the company's commitment to the certificate. In many business instances, it is more important to know that this certificate is backed by a viable organization that will accept liability than to be able to fully identify the actual certificate holder. In a business transaction, the fact that a person can prove he or she is a partner in Deloitte & Touche LLP who is empowered to commit the firm usually means more than who that person is personally.

PKI policies and related statements include the following:

- Certificate policy
- Named set of rules governing certificate usage with common security requirements tailored to the operating environment within the enterprise
- Certificate practices statement (CPS)
- Detailed set of rules governing the Certificate Authority's operations
- Technical and administrative security controls
- Audit
- Key management
- Liability, financial stability, due diligence
- CA contractual requirements and documents
- Subscriber enrollment and termination processes

The Certificate Revocation List (CRL)

Of all the administrative and control mechanisms required by a PKI, the CRL function can be one of the more complex and subtle activities. The CRL is an important index of the overall trustworthiness of the specific PKI environment. Normally it is considered part of the RA's duties. Essentially the CRL is the instrument for checking the continued validity of the certificates for which the RA has responsibility. If a certificate is compromised, if the holder is no longer authorized to use the certificate or if there is a fault in the binding of the certificate to the holder, it must be revoked and taken out of circulation as rapidly as possible. All parties in the trust relationship must be informed. The CRL is usually a highly controlled online database (it may take any number of graphic forms) at which subscribers and administrators may determine the currency of a target partner's certificate. This process can vary dramatically by the following:

- *Timing/frequency of update.* Be careful of the language here. Many RAs claim a 24-hour update. That means the CRL is refreshed every 24 hours. It does not necessarily mean that the total cycle time for a particular revocation to be posted is 24 hours. It may be longer.
- *Push-pull.* This refers to the way in which subscribers can get updates from the CRL. Most CRLs require subscribers to pull the current update. A few private RAs (see below) employ a push methodology. There is a significant difference in cost and complexity and most important the line of demarcation between an RA's and subscriber's responsibility and liability. For lessened liability alone, most RAs prefer the pull mode.
- *Up link/down link.* There are two transmissions in the CRL process. The link from the revoking agent to the CRL and the distribution by the CRL to the subscribing universe. Much work has been exerted by RAs to increase the efficiency of the latter process, but because it depends on the revoking agency, the up link is often an Achilles' heel. Obviously, the overall time is a combination of both processes, plus file update time.
- *Cross domain.* The world of certificates may involve multiple domains and hierarchies. Each domain has a need to know the validity status of all certificates that are used within its bounds. In some large extranet environments, this may involve multiple and multilayer RA and CRL structures. Think this one through very carefully and be aware that the relationships may change each time the network encompasses a new environment.
- *Integrity.* One major way to undermine the trustworthiness of a PKI environment is to compromise the integrity of the CRL process. If the continued validity of the certificate population cannot be assured, the whole system is at risk.

- *Archiving.* How long should individual CRLs be kept and for what purposes?
- *Liabilities and commitments.* These should be clearly, unambiguously, and completely stated by all parties involved. In any case of message or transaction compromise traceable to faulty PKI process, the RA is invariably going to be involved. Make very sure you have a common understanding.

As you might expect, CAs and RAs come in a variety of types. Some of the more common include the following:

- *Full-service public CA* providing RA, certificate generation, issuance, and life-cycle management. Examples: VeriSign, U.S. Postal Service, TradeWave
- *Branded public CA* providing RA, certificate issuance and lifecycle management
- *Certificates generated by a trusted party*, e.g., VeriSign, GTE CyberTrust. Examples: IDMetrix/*GTE CyberTrust*, Sumitomo Bank/*VeriSign*
- *Private CAs* using CA turn-key system solutions internally. Examples: ScotiaBank (*Entrust*), Lexis–Nexis (*VeriSign On-Site*)
- *IBM Vault Registry*

There are also wide variations in trust structure models. This is driven by the business process and network architecture:

- Hierarchical trust (a classical hierarchy that may involve multiple levels and a large number of individual domains)
- VeriSign, Entrust
- X.509v3 certificates
- One-to-one binding of certificate and public key
- Web of Trust (a variation on peer relationships between domains)
- PGP
- Many-to-one binding of certificates and public key
- Constrained or Lattice of Trust structures
- Hybrid of hierarchical and Web models
- Xcert

There are several standards, guidelines, and practices that are applicable to PKI. This is both a blessing and a curse. The most common are listed below. Individual explanations can be found at several Web sites. Start at the following site, which has a very comprehensive set of PKI links — http://www.cert.dfn.de/eng/team/ske/pem-dok.html. This is one of the best PKI link sites available.

- X.500 Directory Services and X.509 Authentication
- Common Criteria (CC)
- ANSI X9 series

- Department of Defense Standards
- TCSEC, TSDM, SEI CMM
- IETF RFC — PKIX, PGP
- S/MIME, SSL, IPSEC
- SET
- ABA Guidelines
- Digital Signatures, Certification Practices
- FIPS Publications 46, 140-1, 180-1, 186

CA/RA Targets of Evaluation. To comprehensively assess the trustworthiness of the individual CA/RA and the associated processes, Deloitte & Touche has developed the following list of required evaluation targets:

- System level (in support of the CA/RA process and certificate usage if applicable)
- System components comprising an CA/RA environment
- Network devices
- Firewalls, routers, and switches
- Network servers
- IP addresses of all devices
- Client work stations
- Operating systems and application software
- Cryptographic devices
- Physical security, monitoring, and authentication capabilities
- Data object level (in support of the CA/RA process and certificate usage)
- Data structures used
- Critical information flows
- Configuration management of critical data items
- Cryptographic data
- Sensitive software applications
- Audit records
- Subscriber and certificate data
- CRLs
- Standards compliance where appropriate
- Application and operational level (repeated from above)
- Certificate policy
- Named set of rules governing certificate usage with common security requirements tailored to the operating environment within the enterprise
- Certificate practices statement (CPS)
- Detailed set of rules governing the CA operations
- Technical and administrative security controls
- Audit
- Key management

- Liability, financial stability, and due diligence
- CA contractual requirements and documents
- Subscriber enrollment and termination processes

How Well Does PKI Satisfy Today's Open Systems Security Needs?

In a nutshell, PKI is an evolving process. It has the fundamental strength, granularity, and flexibility required to support the security requirements outlined. In that respect, it is the best available alternative. But wholesale adoption of PKI as the best, final, and global solution for security needs is naïve and dangerous. It should be examined selectively by business process or application to determine whether there is sufficient "value-added" to justify the direct and indirect cost associated with deployment. As suites such as Entrust become more adaptive and rich interfaces to ERP systems such as the SAP R/3 become more commonplace, PKI will be the security technology of choice for major, high-value processes. It will never be the only game in town. Uncomfortable or disillusioning as it may be, the security world will be a multisolution environment for quite a while.

What Is Involved in Making PKI a Cost-Effective Reality?

The most common approach to launching PKI is a pilot environment. Get your feet wet. Map the due diligence and procedural requirements against the culture of the organization. Look at the volatility of the certificates that will be issued. What is their life expectancy and need for modification? Check the interface issues. What is the prospective growth curve for certificate use? How many entities will be involved? Is cross-certification necessary? Above all else, examine the authorization process requirements that must co-exist with PKI. PKI is not a full-function access-control process. Look into the standards and regulations that affect your industry. Are there export control issues associated with the PKI solution being deployed? Is interoperability a major requirement? If so, how flexible is the design of the solutions being considered?

CA PILOT CONSIDERATIONS

Type of Pilot

- *Proof of concept* — May be a test bed or an actual production environment
- *Operational* — A total but carefully scoped environment. Be sure to have a clear statement of expectations against which to measure functional and business results.
- *Interenterprise* — Avoid this as a start-up if possible. But sometimes it is the real justification for adopting PKI. If so, spend considerable time and effort getting a set of procedures and objectives agreed upon by

all of the partners involved. An objective third-party evaluation can be very helpful.

- Examine standards alternatives and requirements carefully — especially in a regulated industry.
- Check product and package compatibility, interoperability, and scalability *very carefully*.
- Develop alternative compatible product scenarios. At this stage of market maturity, a Plan B is essential. Obviously not all products are universally interchangeable. Develop a backup suite and do some preliminary testing on it.
- Investigate outsourced support as an initial step into the environment. Although a company's philosophy may dictate an internally developed solution, the first round may be better deployed using outside resources.
- What are the service levels explicitly or implicitly required?
- Start internally with a friendly environment. You need all the support you can get, especially from business process owners.
- Provide sufficient time and resources for procedural infrastructure development, including CA policy, CPS, and training
- Do not promise more than you can deliver.

Is PKI an Exceptional Approach or Just One of Many Alternatives Worth Looking At?

The answer depends largely on the security objectives of the organization. PKI is ideal (but potentially expensive) for extranets and environments in which more traditional identification and authentication are insufficient. Tempting as it may be, resist the urge to find the *single solution*. Most networked-based environments and the associated enterprises are too complex for one global solution. Examine the potential for SSL, SMIME, Kerberos, single sign-on, and VPNs. If you can make the technical, operational and cost-justification case for a single, PKI-based security approach, do so. PKI is a powerful structure, but it is not a religious icon. Leave yourself room for tailored multi-solution environments.

Harry DeMaio is president of Deloitte & Touche Security Services LLC, (DTS) a wholly owned subsidiary of Deloitte & Touche LLP, Deerfield, IL. In addition to his current assignment, he is a director in Deloitte & Touche (D&T) Enterprise Risk Services, delivering the D&T family of information security and continuity planning services to major clients globally.

Domain 6
Security Architecture and Models

At this time, this domain is focusing on microcomputer and LAN security. In essence, this is a microcosm of the whole subject of information security. Working from the desktop, the author covers a wide spectrum of pertinent topics. These include: physical security, viruses, access controls, and encryption, as well as operational issues, such as backup and recovery.

The bottom line is that while mainframes and minicomputers continue to anchor many systems, particularly in areas such as online transaction processing, the major shift into client/server solutions based on microcomputer technology continues to expand. Therefore, the focus of information security needs to make the shift as well.

Domain 6.1
Microcomputer and LAN Security

Chapter 23
Microcomputer and LAN Security
Stephen Cobb

INTRODUCTION

This chapter focuses on preserving the confidentiality, integrity, and availability of information in the microcomputer and local area network (LAN) environment. We often refer to this as the desktop environment, desktop computing, or PC-based computing.

Why Desktop Computing Matters

Although mainframe computers continue to be used extensively for such tasks as large-scale batch processing and online transaction processing, for many organizations today, computer security is, in effect, desktop computer security. Networked desktop computers are the dominant computing platform of the late 1990s, from the Microsoft Windows-based computers that some airlines use to check in passengers at airports, to the stock transaction and account inquiry systems used in banking and financial institutions, from personal computer-controlled assembly lines to PC-based medical information systems.

In many of these applications the personal computer may appear to be working as a terminal access device for a larger system. But from a security perspective it is important to understand that every personal computer system is a complete computer system, capable of input, output, storage, and processing. As such, a PC poses a much more significant threat than a dumb terminal, should the PC be subverted or illegally accessed. Furthermore, with very few exceptions, none of the desktop computing devices deployed today were designed with security in mind. Add to this the enormous increase in both the depth and the breadth of computer literacy within society over the last 10 years and you have a recipe for serious security headaches.[1]

0-8493-9829-0/00/$0.00+$.50
© 2000 by CRC Press LLC

The Approach Taken

All major aspects of desktop security will be addressed in this chapter, beginning with the need to address desktop issues within the organization's information security policies. Security awareness on the part of both users and managers is stressed. The need for, and implementation of, data backup systems and regimes is outlined. Passwords and other forms of authentication for desktop users are discussed, along with the use of encryption of information on desktop machines and LANs. There is a section on malicious code. The network dimensions of desktop computing security are explored, together with the problems of remote access.

Centralized, Layered, and Design-Based Approaches

A good case can be made for saying that desktop computer security is best handled through automated background processes, preferably centrally managed on a network.[2] Desktop computer users, so the argument goes, should not be expected to worry about backups and virus scanning and access controls. These security mechanisms should be handled for them as part of the operating system.

This sounds appealing, but there are several practical reasons why an understanding of the security weaknesses of stand-alone PCs and under-managed LANs remains critical, and why, in at least some cases, it is necessary to implement piecemeal solutions that lack the elegance and obvious efficiency of the automated, centrally managed approach:

- A lot of desktop computers are currently connected to networks that have little hope of ever being centrally managed, yet the information they handle is still important and so warrants protection.
- Many of the methods for automating and managing security will only be applicable to, or compatible with, newer hardware and software. Older systems will remain in use and will still need to be protected.[3]
- Mature tools with which to automate and centrally manage security on local area networks are only just coming to market, and many organizations are only just realizing that they need them and will have to pay for them.
- A fairly high level of security can be achieved on both current and older personal computers with the layered approach, described next.

The layered approach to desktop security maximizes existing, but underutilized, security mechanisms, plus low-cost add-ons, through policy, awareness, and training. For example, the floppy disk drive of a PC is a major security problem. Confidential and proprietary data can be copied to a floppy diskette and smuggled out.[4] Incoming diskettes may introduce pirated software, Trojan code, and viruses to the company network. Yet the BIOS in most of today's PCs allows you to tightly control use of the floppy drive, for example, disabling boot from, read from, or write to. PC security is considerably enhanced by implementing this type of control, which is essentially free. The layered approach would extend this protection by also requiring antivirus software on the PC and putting in place a company policy governing the use of floppy disks in the office. When employees understand the threat that a serious virus outbreak or data theft poses to their jobs, most are apt to support the policy.

DESKTOP SECURITY: PROBLEMS, THREATS, ISSUES

The problems, threats, and issues of desktop security need to be placed in perspective. A common, but dangerous, mistake is to underestimate the seriousness of this aspect of information system security. A clear understanding of desktop system architecture and its security implications is required.

The Ubiquitous Micro

Historically, desktop computers have been on the fringe of information security, which has its roots in the protection of very expensive, highly centralized, multi-user information processing systems. Today, desktop computers performing distributed computing are no longer on the fringe. Failure to realize this will undermine your ability to protect any information system, big or small, for four reasons:

1. A significant percentage of mission-critical computing is now performed on personal computers deployed as LAN work stations and network file servers.[5]
2. Most large-scale computer systems are at some point connected to one or more desktop systems. Even when PC connectivity is not specifically provided to a large system, PC access may be possible, for example, via a remote maintenance line.
3. Inexpensive and widely available desktop systems now have the power to mount attacks that endanger the security of large-scale systems, such as brute force cryptanalysis, password-cracking, and denial-of-service attacks.[6]
4. Knowledge about how to use, and abuse, desktop computers is widely dispersed throughout most areas of society and most countries of the world. This is a far less homogeneous, and thus less predictable, population than previous generations of computer users.[7]
5. Such knowledge, particularly new developments in software techniques that can be abused to compromise security, is instantly accessible via the Internet.[8]

Clearly, an understanding of desktop security is more important than ever. Desktop machines are an integral part of the client–server distributed computing paradigm that dominates the late 1990s. In the vast majority of systems, the clients to which servers serve up data are microcomputers;

the primary topology by which they do this is the local area network. Furthermore, in an increasing number of systems, the servers themselves are essentially beefed-up microcomputers. This is particularly true of the Internet, which is beginning to rival leased lines and private value-added networks as the data communication channel of choice.

Desktop System Architecture

Although you may be familiar with the following definitions they are stated here because they have important security implications which are not always understood.[9] A microcomputer is a computer system in miniature, a collection of hardware and software that is small enough to fit on a desk (or into a briefcase or even a shirt pocket) but able to perform the four major functions that define a computer system: input, processing, storage, and output. Note that processing requires both a processor and random access memory (RAM). Also note that RAM is different from storage (data that are stored remains accessible after system reset or reboot, data held in RAM are typically not accessible after system reset or reboot).

Soon after microcomputers were developed, the term "personal computer" was coined to describe these self-contained computer systems. This was later shortened to "PC" although this term is often used to refer to a specific type of personal computer, that is, one based on the nonproprietary architecture developed by IBM around the Intel 8086 family of processors (including the 80286, 80386, 80486, and Pentium chips).

Today, the majority of personal computers conform to the IBM/Intel architecture, and most of these run the DOS/Microsoft Windows operating systems (a small but significant percentage still adhere to the proprietary Apple Macintosh architecture). A separate class of desktop machines are those using the UNIX operating system. Often referred to as "work stations," these UNIX machines are typically more expensive, more powerful, and confined to specialized areas such as engineering and scientific research. While the DOS and Windows 95 operating systems use an open file system, with no provision for separate user accounts on a single machine, UNIX offers tight control of file permissions and multiple accounts. UNIX machines are often used as high-performance back-room database hosts and World Wide Web servers.

Recently, a new category of machine, the network computer or NC, has been making headlines. In many ways this is simply the re-birth of the diskless PC, several models of which were unsuccessfully marketed in the late 1980s. Both the NC and the diskless PC are machines that have their own processor and random access memory and so perform local processing, but possess no local storage devices. Their operating system is a combination of a ROM-based boot process and server-based network operating system. However, whereas the diskless PC was aimed at solving security, management, and support problems on local area networks, the NC concept has been developed in a wide area context, specifically the Internet, and in particular, the World Wide Web.

Strict categorization of desktop systems is seldom helpful. For example, IBM/Intel-based machines can run powerful versions of UNIX, such as SCO UNIX. Both BSDI UNIX and Linux run on Intel chips and are very popular as Web servers. Furthermore, Microsoft Windows NT and IBM OS/2 both offer a multi-user, multitasking alternative to UNIX, with a familiar graphical user interface (GUI). They also allow you to use a closed file system. What may be helpful is further clarification of the terms PC, work station, terminal, server, and client.

- PC: a self-contained computer system with its own processor, storage, and output devices (the screen is perhaps the most basic of output devices). Typically, it is small enough to fit on or under a desk.
- Work station: a self-contained computer system with its own processor that is also connected to a server. A work station does at least some of its own processing and may have its own storage, but may also use or rely on the server for storage.
- Terminal: a computer access device with screen and keyboard that does not have its own processing or storage capabilities.
- Server: any computer system that is providing access to its resources to another computer system, for example, a Web server provides a browser/client with access to Web pages stored on the server.
- Client: any computer system that is accessing resources made available to it by another computer system, for example, a Web browser/client accesses to Web pages stored on a Web server.

DESKTOP SECURITY POLICY AND AWARENESS

Every organization should have an information security policy. However, field experience suggests that these policies often fail to address desktop computing issues appropriately or adequately. For example, it is common for companies to have comprehensive policies for mainframe systems that address all contingencies, but only a few specific desktop policies such as antivirus procedures written in response to specific incidents such as a virus infection.

From the Top Down

Effective information security policies are created from the top down, beginning with the organization's basic commitment to information security formulated as a general policy statement. Here is a good example of a general policy statement:

1. Timely access to reliable information is vital to the continued success of Megabank.
2. Protection of Megabank's information assets and facilities is the responsibility of each and every employee and officer of Megabank.
3. The information assets and processing facilities of Megabank are the property of Megabank and may only be used for Megabank business as authorized by Megabank management.

When a general policy like this has been agreed to by top management, each employee should be required to sign, upon hiring and each year thereafter, a document consisting of the policy statement and words to this effect:

> I have read and understood the company's information security policy and agree to abide by it. I realize that serious violations of this policy are legitimate grounds for dismissal.

Once you have a general policy like this in place, you can elaborate upon particulars. In the case of desktop systems these include:

- Password policies (e.g., minimum length, storage of passwords)
- Backup duties (for individual PCs as well as the network server)
- Data classification (rating each document for sensitivity)
- Removable media handling (e.g., who can take diskettes in or out)
- Encryption (what data will be encrypted, which algorithms to use)
- Physical security (how is equipment protected against theft/tampering)
- Access policies (who is allowed to access which machines/files)

There will also need to be policies for specific systems, for example, the accounting department LAN. These can be promulgated by the staff who have responsibility for those systems provided there is oversight and sign-off by the managers of those departments and the security staff.

The Fine Print

The task of developing detailed policy is often avoided because it is seen as too daunting. It is sometimes postponed because "there is no way to predict where information technology will go next." While this is true, you need specific policies as soon as they become feasible, plus a general policy to deal with emerging areas of concern. For example, consider the fairly recent ability to browse the World Wide Web with a desktop computer attached to the company's Internet connection. It is now possible to formulate specific policy such as "employees must not use company systems to visit Web sites that contain sexually explicit material."

However, in companies where employees have, for a time at least, enjoyed unrestricted Web access, such specific policies may be resisted (as though browsing the Web on the company's dime is a right, just like selecting your own desktop design or installing your own games). But if the company has a preexisting general policy statement that asserts ownership of information processing assets, any restrictions on how PCs may be used can immediately be vindicated and enforced because it is clearly in keeping with that policy.

On the other hand, you have to be realistic. The desktop computing environment is inherently difficult to control and so the most effective policies are those which are understood and accepted by those who must abide by them. Developing policy by consensus is clearly more effective in this environment than policy by decree. To this end, high-level policy statements which establish the company's right to control its own computers play an important psychological role.

Desktop Security Awareness

It is not enough to develop security policies for desktop systems. Users must be told what the policies are and trained to support them. The ideal situation is a self-regulating workforce so that, for example, when Fred in engineering brings to work a game on a floppy disk that his son brought home from school the night before, Mary will refuse to put it in her PC because she knows that (1) it is a violation of security policy, and (2) it exposes her PC, and thus the company LAN, to the risk of virus infection; and (3) LAN downtime and person-hours consumed by virus disinfection have a negative effect on company profitability, which in turn has a negative effect on her earnings and employment prospects.

Raising employee security awareness to this level requires a significant training effort, but it is money well spent relative to more technology-oriented solutions. In an age of universal computer literacy it would be foolish to rely solely upon high-tech security systems, since there will always be people with the skills to challenge such defenses. You can reduce the incentive to mount such challenges by eschewing policy dictation in favor of consensus-based policy making. If employees understand and thus "buy-in" to the policy, the technical defenses can be concentrated in the areas of greatest effectiveness.

Determining those areas is an ongoing process which depends upon a different type of security awareness: that which you cultivate as a security professional. It involves staying current with the latest trends in computer insecurity, for example, new virus outbreaks, newly discovered operating system vulnerabilities, and so on. You maintain this awareness by subscribing to industry publications, participating in online forums and mailing lists, attending security conferences, and networking with fellow security professionals.

PHYSICAL SECURITY: DESKTOPS AND LAPTOPS

Efforts to thwart computer equipment theft are a good illustration of the importance of security awareness. For example, do you know the total value of desktop computer equipment that is stolen every year in North America? The answer, according to SAFEWARE, the Columbus, Ohio-based computer insurance specialist, is quite staggering: more than $1 billion. Consider some of the security implications of desktop computer theft:

- All data on a stolen hard drive that was not backed up is now lost.
- No data can be accessed in a timely manner while backups are restored to replacement equipment.
- Certain components, such a custom cables, are hard to replace if stolen.
- Most PC-based systems depend upon a very specific configuration of hardware and software which may be difficult to replicate on replacement systems.
- Unless it was encrypted, anyone who receives a stolen PC has access to the data stored on it.
- If the stolen PC is recovered it is very hard to know whether or not someone made a copy of the data that was stored on it.

Obviously, your information security policy should mandate that backups of all data be available at all times (this typically requires off-site backup storage as a defense against backup media being stolen along with the systems backed up thereon). However, even if you are in compliance with this lofty goal, backups cannot solve every security problem. If a competitor obtains copies of your trade secrets by stealing your computers, having a backup copy is not much consolation.[10]

Awareness of current trends in computer theft will not only help you plan countermeasures, but also help you refine policy and provide timely security awareness training. The first point to note is that personal computers are now a commodity, like VCRs, camcorders, and stereos. This means they can be turned into cash very quickly, making them a target for casual thieves and those supporting drug habits. Because of their higher value-to-weight ratio, notebook computers are very popular with this type of thief.

More organized felons will target notebooks at locations such as airports, where there are rich pickings. For example, a popular tactic in recent years has been for two-person teams to steal notebooks at security check points. One thief waits until a notebook-bearing bag is placed on the conveyor belt to the X-ray machine, then holds up the line going through the metal detector (not hard to do). The accomplice waiting on the other side of the check point simply picks up the bag and departs.

While desktop systems in offices are sometimes targeted by the "smash and grab for cash thief," the more serious risk may be sophisticated criminals stealing to order. Such thieves tend to target high-end equipment like graphics work stations, large monitors, and production-quality typesetters and color scanners. European offices seem to be particularly vulnerable due to the high demand and relative lack of resources in former Eastern bloc countries. On occasion, Scotland Yard has recovered trucks full of expensive Apple Macintosh desktop publishing equipment stolen to order and destined for Eastern Europe.

A slightly different combination of factors led to a rash of chip heists in the early 1990s. Shortages of memory chips resulted in high prices and led to several types of theft. Europe experienced a rash of thefts in which chips were removed from office systems. Employees arrived in the morning to find desktop computers torn apart (none too gracefully) and the memory chips removed. This represents a major blow to any organization (a charity for the elderly and the Automobile Association were two of the victims). No data processing can occur until the chips are replaced. Specification of chips for used equipment is no simple matter (there are many different types and many compatibility issues). Even if you can afford the high replacement cost there may be delays obtaining chips. After all, the motive for the theft was high prices caused by a shortage.

A different type of theft occurred in chip producing areas such as America's Silicon Valley and Scotland's Silicon Glen. This involved direct, and sometimes violent, attacks on chip factories and shipping facilities. However, the motivating factors were the same: memory chips are easily resold, hard to trace, and they can have a higher value-to-weight ratio than gold or platinum.

The point of these examples is that as an information systems security professional you need to be keenly aware of the current economics of both crime and computing. As this chapter is being written, memory prices are at an all-time low, reducing the incentive for chip theft, and possibly impacting your spending on countermeasures, relative to other threats. However, if prices suddenly rise again you will need to tighten security measures in this particular area.[11] Some specific microcomputer physical security measures to consider include:

1. Good site security: this not only protects against theft, but also against vandalism, unauthorized access, and media removal.
2. Case locks: these not only deter theft of internal components, but also protect BIOS-based security services, described elsewhere in this chapter.
3. Documentation: you need to keep detailed records of all your hardware and software, including serial numbers, purchase dates, invoices, and so on. These records will be invaluable if you ever have to prove loss or reclaim stolen items that have been recovered.
4. Insurance: computer equipment typically requires separate insurance or a special rider in your business insurance or office contents

policy. Note that home contents policies often exclude computers used for work.

5. Access controls and encryption: if a computer is stolen you would like to make it as difficult as possible for the person who ends up trying to use it to access the data that are stored on the system.

DESKTOP DATA BACKUP

Clearly, the single most effective technical strategy you can employ to defend the integrity and availability of computer-based data is making backup copies, often simply referred to as backup. This is standard doctrine for most information systems professionals, particularly those familiar with the mainframe environment, where backup is an integral part of computing. However, in the desktop environment, which is based on systems that have their origins in casual, even recreational use, the task of backing up is all too often neglected until it is too late.[12]

Backup Types and Devices

Most "live" data in use today are stored on hard disk drives. While the reliability of the hard disk devices found in desktop and laptop systems has steadily improved over the last decade, they are nevertheless mechanical devices quite capable of wearing out, sometimes prematurely, sometimes without warning. Furthermore, users are only human, often lacking in formal training. Sometimes they erase important files or records within files by mistake. Sometimes they delete data out of malice. Viruses and other malicious programs can destroy files. Making backup copies of all of the files that are on a hard disk is the best, and often the only, means of recovery from mechanical failure, user error, malevolent software, natural disaster, and physical theft.

Hard drives have finite storage capacity. Eventually you have to erase files from the hard disk to make way for more. You may need to keep copies of those "surplus" files, such as last year's bookkeeping ledger. These days some people use two computers, one on the desk at work, another that travels with the user or resides in the user's home. Thus we can identify at least four different types of file copying, as listed in Exhibit 23.1.

Backups=Copies of files made to defend against loss/corruption of originals
Archives=Copies of files made to relieve overcrowding on primary storage devices
Updates=Copies of files made to synchronize files between two machines
Duplicates=Copies of files made to provide other users with copies of programs or data

Exhibit 23.1. Four Different Types of File Copying

The main focus in this section is backups, but the other categories are also important. Updates that synchronize files between desktops and portable machines are a relatively recent concern and have implications for data integrity. An archive is a set of files that has been copied as an historical record. Typically these are files containing data that will not change, and immediate access to which is no longer required, such as properly aged accounting records. When the archive copy has been created the original can be erased, thus freeing up storage space. Several terms that are useful at this point are

- Primary storage — where frequently used software and data reside.
- Online storage — storage that is immediately available and randomly accessible; this includes removable media such as floppy diskettes.
- Removable media — any media that can be physically removed from the system, such as diskettes and CD-ROMs.
- Magnetic media — storage based on magnetic properties, such as hard drives, tapes, and floppies.
- Optical media — storage based on optical properties, such as CD-ROMs.
- Magneto-optical — storage based on a combination of magnetic and optical properties, like some high-capacity cartridge drives.
- Random vs. linear access — the ability to immediately access data regardless of their physical location on the media (e.g., a hard drive) as opposed to access which requires reading preceding data (e.g., a tape drive).
- Read only — the ability to read stored data but not change it.
- Write once, read many — the ability to record data in read only form and then read it multiple times (e.g., burning a CD-ROM).
- RAID — redundant array of inexpensive disks — a storage system which combines multiple disks managed as a single storage device, allowing disks to be "hot swapped," i.e., replaced without powering down or losing data.
- Jukebox — a storage system which combines multiple tapes or CD-ROM drives managed as a single storage device with automated media switching, providing large-scale storage or backup.

In the early days of personal computing the primary means of backup, software duplication, and archiving, was the floppy diskette. A floppy diskette can be described as randomly accessible removable media, with write many/read many, as well as read only capability (by physically adjusting the write-protect setting on the disk jacket you can write-protect the contents, although this is a reversible procedure, distinguishable from

Type	Capacity	Comments
Floppy diskettes	1.44 Mb	Standard equipment Low capacity, slow, cheap, tedious.
Tape drives e.g., Travan, Exabyte, DAT	400 Mb–9 Gb	Low media cost, highly automated, most widely used.
Removable cartridges e.g., Syquest, Jaz, Zip	200 Mb–4.6 Gb	High media cost, very fast, good for online systems.
CD-ROM	650 Mb	Low media cost, slow to make, convenient access.

Exhibit 23.2.   Backup Options

WORM media that is physically impossible to overwrite). The floppy diskette has several benefits:

- Low cost for both drives and media
- Included as standard equipment on all machines
- Widespread compatibility between systems

Unfortunately, hard drive capacities and the complexity of both software and data have far outstripped the capacity of standard diskettes, while possible alternatives such as high-capacity cartridge drives and read/write optical media have so far failed to achieve anything like the same level of acceptance as standard equipment. The current options for backup are listed in Exhibit 23.2. Note that some of these removable media devices also work as primary storage, for active software and live data, as well as secondary or backup storage.

While constant improvements in performance, capacity, and pricing make "best buy" statements about storage devices imprudent, there are clearly some practical points that can be made. First of all, you need to match capacity and speed to need. For example, if a desktop machine uses about 600 megabytes of hard drive storage, 5 megabytes of which is updated every day, a CD-R drive might be worth considering as an alternative to tape. But tape would be better for a system that regularly stores twice as much data and updates data at a faster daily rate. For a network file server that stores several gigabytes of constantly changing data, you will probably want to use RAID for primary storage and a jukebox for constant backup.[13]

Boosting Backup

If desktop users are on a network, part of the backup problem has been solved. Any data they store on the file server will be backed up as part of normal network management (any network file server worthy of the name will have a built-in backup device, typically tape, and any network administrator worthy of the name will use it diligently). But unless the network

work stations are diskless, there will be a residual problem of local backup. It is possible to back up local work station storage through the file server, but this is not always practical (typically the work station must be on with the user logged in but not using the machine, an arrangement that has security implications). Besides, users may be keeping some data locally on removable media, such as diskettes.

What is required is a clear policy on local backup (as well as on the use of removable media). But how do you persuade users to do better in the backup department? Make it easier to do and make people want to do it. Making people want to do something is mainly a question of education. People need to be told why backups are important, and this means more than simply saying, "Because it is company policy." A positive approach is to educate, using scenarios in which backup saves the day. Users should be made aware of the variety of ways in which data can be lost or damaged. But don't dwell too long on the negative — emphasize the comfortable feeling that comes from knowing that you have current backups.

Making backup easy to do involves some decisions about hardware and software. What backup media will be used — floppy disks, tape, optical disks, cartridges? What backup software will be used? Will computers attached to a network be backed up independently or by the network? Will macros, batch files, or automated schedule programs be used to simplify the procedures? If so, who is responsible for creating and configuring these? Beyond these are questions such as how often backup should be done, what files should be backed up, and where will the backup media be stored? You should establish explicit guidelines on these matters so that users are clear about what their backup responsibilities are. Such rules and regulations can be incorporated into an education campaign. To summarize, a general improvement in backup habits is likely to occur if you:

1. Make backup a policy, not an option.
2. Make backup desirable.
3. Make backup easy.
4. Make backup mandatory.
5. Make sure users comply with backup policy.

Backup Strategy

There is no universal path to quick and easy backup. If there was, everyone would be taking it and cheerfully doing their daily backup. The user with unlimited resources has some excellent options, the most attractive probably being optical disks. But the whole culture of personal computers is shaped by economics and the inescapable fact is that most individuals and organizations do not have unlimited resources. To make effective use of time and money devoted to backup, a backup strategy should be developed. Consider what files need to be backed up, and how often the backup should be performed. Begin by considering the type of backup that is needed.

Image Backup. Early personal computer tape drives could only perform a complete and total backup of every file on the hard disk, referred to as an image backup. This is a "warts and all" image, a track-by-track reading of the surface of the hard disk, including hidden and system files, even unused areas and cross-linked files. This caused problems when restoring data; for example, if the hard drive to which the data were being restored was not exactly the same make and model as the original. Some systems only allowed an image backup to be restored in its entirety, meaning that bad sectors were restored along with the good. But image backup has some advantages, such as speed. By treating the contents of the hard disk as a continuous stream of data bits, a lot of time that would otherwise be spent searching the disk for parts of specific files is saved. Recently, the use of image backup has been revived by more intelligent software that eliminates the shortcomings of early systems.

File-By-File. The alternative to an image backup is a file-by-file backup in which the user selects the directories and files to be backed up. The software then reads and writes each one in turn. While this may take longer than an image backup, it allows quick restoration of a single file or group of files. A file-by-file backup can also be faster than an image backup when only a small percentage of the hard disk has been used, or if the data on the hard disk are "optimized."[14] A file-by-file backup can be complete, including all of the files on the hard disk, but this is different from an image backup. In a file-by-file backup, the files are read individually rather than as a pattern on the disk.

Data Vs. Disk. When choosing the files to include in a backup, there is some logic in omitting program files because these already exist on the original program distribution disk(s). However, a fully functioning personal computer is constantly changing. Software is fine-tuned, utility programs are added, batch files and macros created, tool bars and icons are customized, and system files are tweaked for optimum performance. Recreating a system after a major crash involves a lot more than just copying back the data and reinstalling the programs. Numerous parameters, the right combinations of which were previously determined by considerable trial and error, need to be recreated. If you have no backup of configuration or user-preference files, getting the system back to normal can be quite a challenge. A good compromise is to make a complete backup at longer intervals, while backing up changing data files more frequently.

Now consider what you want to include when performing a data file backup. For example, are font files to be included? They seldom change but can take up a lot of space. You might want to omit them from a data file backup. The same applies to spelling dictionaries and thesauri, which do not change. However, user-defined spelling supplements that are regularly updated might need to be included.

The method you use to include or exclude files from a backup operation will depend on the backup software you are using. For example, on the Macintosh, the operating system itself distinguishes between data/document files and program/application files, so backup software on the Mac often has a simple check box to include or exclude programs. Backup software on the PC often has include and exclude parameters based on file extensions. Program files can be excluded by specifying the extensions EXE and COM, plus BAT and SYS (as well as DLL on Windows systems). If you are consistent in your file naming, you might be able to group data files by specifying extensions such as DBF, XLS, DOC, and so on.

Incremental and Differential. An incremental backup involves backing up only those files that have changed since the last backup. The idea is that successive "all data files" backups are likely to include files that were already backed up. This slows down the backup process. Interim backups can be performed that only apply to files that have been added or modified since the last backup. Operating systems can do this by checking the status of files stored along with names and other directory information. Some backup software makes a distinction between incremental and differential backups; the latter is defined as all files that are new or modified since the last full backup. This differs from an incremental backup, which is all files that are new or modified since the last backup, either full or incremental.

Note that restoring from an incremental backup, as opposed to a full backup, may require more work. Several sets of media may be required, namely the previous full backup plus all incremental backups since then. On the other hand, restoring from a differential backup requires only the last full backup plus the last differential backup. However, differential backups take up more space and take longer to perform than incrementals. Basically, incrementals are better to systems that are heavily used, like file servers on a network, whereas differentials are more appropriate for single-user systems.

Backup Regimen

The timing of backups depends on how often the information on a system changes. A personal computer might operate purely as an information bank, perhaps used to look up pricing information that seldom changes — such a system only needs to be backed up when the information is updated. But a PC that records customer orders coming in as fast as they can be typed might have to be backed up at least once a day. Most systems are somewhere between these two extremes, but remember that frequency of file changes may not be a constant factor. For example, spreadsheets in the accounting department might change quite often while the annual budget is being prepared, but remain unchanged the rest of the year. So, the backup regimen you implement will depend on how you use your computer. The three factors that need to be weighed against each other are:

- The amount of time and effort represented by changes to files.
- The amount of time and effort represented by backing up the files.
- The value of the contents of the files.

Careful consideration of work patterns is necessary to establish an appropriate backup regimen. You can combine the three levels of backup described earlier, based on three different intervals:

Interval 3	Total backup
Interval 2	Data file backup
Interval 1	Incremental data file backup

For example, you could do a total backup once a month, a total data file backup once a week, and an incremental data file backup every day. The main point is that every backup does not have to be complete or lengthy, and a schedule mixing complete and partial backups will require less time and so stand more chance of being adhered to. One important factor to bear in mind when designing your backup schedule is the ease with which the state of your data at a specific point in the past can be recreated. For example, suppose that a virus is discovered on a hard drive and many files have been infected. A process of deduction determines that the virus was probably introduced on Monday when an employee brought in a game on a floppy disk. If incremental backup is done daily with a full backup on Friday and today is Wednesday, then one option of dealing with the virus is to erase the hard disk and then restore the previous Friday's backup. Since viruses do not infect true data files you can then restore the data files from the Monday and Tuesday incremental backups.

But what if records were accidentally erased from a database on Tuesday, and this affected spreadsheets and reports created on Wednesday, yet the error was not discovered until the following Monday? You could not use the complete backup from the immediately preceding Friday to correct this problem. You would need the complete backup from the preceding Friday, plus the following Monday's incremental backup. If this sort of problem sounds challenging, that's because it is. Getting people to create backups is only part of the problem. Restoring systems and data from those backups is quite another.

Backup Handling and Storage

Consider the physical handling of the backup media. Where will it be stored? How many copies will there be? What makes a good off-site storage location? One possible media management program is to place backup copy 1 off-site (a bank, the manager's home, a different office of the same company). Note that simply using a fireproof safe designed for important papers is not enough. Magnetic tapes give up the digital ghost at much lower temperatures than paper ignites — you want a safe that prevents internal temperature from rising above 125°F for at least 1 hour during exposure to fire at 1500°F. After a suitable interval you make backup copy 2, which is placed off-site, while backup 1 moves to on-site storage. After another interval, you reuse the backup 1 media to make backup 3, which is placed off-site while backup 2 is moved on-site. This means the off-site backup is always the most up-to-date.

For data-intensive operations, such as order processing where large amounts of data are added or altered every day, you can use a day-by-day backup schedule such as the six-way system. You begin by labeling six sets of media as Friday1, Friday2, Monday, Tuesday, Wednesday, and Thursday. On Friday afternoon, the operator goes to the backup storage cabinet and takes out the media marked Friday1. This is used to make a complete backup of the hard disk. The media is locked away over the weekend. On Monday afternoon, the operator goes to the media cabinet and gets out media marked Monday. This is used to make an incremental backup, over-writing the previous data on the media. The same thing happens on Tuesday through Thursday. Incremental backups are made each day on media marked for that day of the week.

When Friday rolls around again, the Friday2 media is used for a new complete backup. On Monday the incremental backup is made onto the Monday media, and so on, until Friday comes around again and you overwrite Friday1 with another complete backup. This system gives you a maximum archive period of two weeks. For example, on Fridays before you perform the Friday backup you have the ability to restore data from one or two Friday's ago. On any day of the week you can restore things to the way they were on same day of the previous week.

This system has several advantages. The time required for an incremental backup is generally far less than that for a full backup, making the daily routine less burdensome. Nevertheless, if restoration is required, a full set of data can be put together. If you simply use the same backup media every day, this type of recovery is not possible. A variation of this six-way routine, sometimes referred to as the father/son backup cycle, requires eight sets of media with the additional ones being called Friday3 and Friday4 so that your archive goes back a whole month.

Yet another backup cycle is the ten-way or grandfather/father/son system. This covers 12 weeks and allows you to delete data from your hard disk and retrieve it up to 3 months later. A variation of this scheme involves removing some of the complete backups from circulation at regular intervals for archive purposes, for example, once a month or once a quarter.

One advantage of this is a gradual replacement of media, which have a natural tendency to wear out from repeated use.

Give some thought to the time of day that backups are performed. It seems natural to do the backup at the end of the day, then lock the media away or take it off-site. Because some backup systems, such as tape units, allow backups to be triggered automatically, some people leave systems on overnight and have the backup performed under software control. This minimizes inconvenience to users, and leaving systems running is not considered detrimental to their health or reliability (although monitors should be turned down or off). However, even if the hardware performs reliably, there is a problem because the backup is being performed during a period of high risk.

Theft of computers, tampering with files, or disasters such as fires can progress with less chance of detection during the night. An unsupervised overnight backup operation is no protection against these threats. Indeed, if the backup media sits in the computer until a human operator arrives in the morning, it can make a nice present to someone looking to steal data. Doing backup first thing in the morning might seem like the answer, but again, an overnight attack threatens a whole day's worth of work. Besides, backup operations tend to tie up processing time and thus prevent systems from being used, which can make backing up in the morning counterproductive. One solution available to companies with an evening shift is to have them perform the backup and lock up the media before leaving. Indeed, with larger networks it will be necessary to budget staff specifically for this task.

Remote Backup Strategies

Off-site storage of backups is a strong defense against two serious threats, physical theft and natural disaster. However, some off-site storage options pose practical or tactical problems. Requiring staff to take backup media home with them imposes a considerable burden of responsibility, and requires a high degree of trust. Most banks are not set up to receive magnetic media for safe deposit outside normal banking hours. Fortunately, numerous companies now specialize in off-site storage of media, such as Arcus Data Security, DataVault, and Safesite Records Management.

Safesite's SafeNet service provides off-site storage and rotation of file server backup tapes. Outgoing tapes are placed in foam shipping trays and air-freighted overnight to secure vaults where they are bar coded and stored in a halon-protected environment that is fully temperature and humidity controlled. You pay a weekly fee for this service. Other companies operate at a local level, offering daily pickup and delivery of backup media according to standard rotation schedules. This has the added benefit of reinforcing backup regimes.

One step beyond physical off-site collection and delivery of backup media is remote off-site backup. In other words, your computers are backed up automatically, over phone lines, to a remote location, a strategy known as televaulting. This not only provides protection against theft and natural disasters at your site, it also provides insurance against errors and failures in your normal on-site backup systems. A pioneer and leading supplier of this type of service is Minneapolis-based Rimage Corporation (while the company headquarters are in Minneapolis, all its eggs are not in one basket — Rimage operates backup sites in New York and Atlanta, plus one near Los Angeles and another near San Francisco).

DEFEATING VIRUSES AND OTHER MALICIOUS CODE

One of the most persistent threats to the confidentiality, integrity, and availability of data entrusted to desktop systems, is malicious code, the most common form of which is the virus. A computer virus is self-replicating code designed to spread from system to system. Thousands of different viruses have been identified, although only a few hundred are active. This is software which can erase files, bring down networks, and waste a lot of person power and processing time. There are several types of programs, besides viruses, that can be grouped together as malicious code, or MC, although each type poses a different threat to the integrity and availability of your data.

The Malicious Code Problem

Based on numerous studies it is possible to say that malicious code has caused billions of dollars worth of damage and disruption over the last five years.[15] Malicious code has affected everything from corporate mainframes and networks to computers in homes, schools, and universities. Despite impressive advances in defensive measures, malicious programs continue to pose a major threat to information security. A key member of IBM's antivirus team, Alan Fedeli, uses the following as simple, working definitions of the three main problems for PC and LAN users:

- Virus: a program which, when executed, can add itself to another program, without permission, and in such a way that the infected program, when executed, can add itself to still other programs.
- Worm: a program which copies itself into nodes in a network, without permission.
- Trojan horse: a program which masquerades as a legitimate program, but does something other than what was expected, (as in the deceptive wooden horse used by the Greek army to achieve the fall of Troy).

Note that while viruses and worms replicate themselves, Trojan horses do not. Viruses and worms both produce copies of themselves but worms do so without using host files as carriers.

A fourth category of malicious code, the logic bomb, has historically been associated with mainframe programs but can also appear in desktop and network applications. A logic bomb can be defined as dormant code, the activation of which is triggered by a predetermined time or event. For example, a logic bomb might start erasing data files when the system clock reaches a certain date or when the application has been loaded × number of times. In practice, these various elements can be combined, so that a virus could gain access to a system via a Trojan, then plant a logic bomb, which triggers a worm.

The practical objection to viruses and worms, Trojan horses, and logic bombs, is that no programmer, however smart, can write code that will run benignly on every computer it encounters. Commercial software developers like Microsoft, which spend millions on software development and testing, cannot create such code, even when an elaborate installation program is used. The number of hardware permutations alone is staggering (with 12 alternatives in 12 categories you get 8,916,100,448,256 possible combinations). Quite simply, you cannot write benign code which can insert itself unannounced into every system without causing problems for at least some of those systems.

About Viruses

According to Dr. Peter Tippett, President of the National Computer Security Association, even if virus code does not try to cause harm, "most of the damage that viruses cause, day in and day out, relates to the simple fact that contamination by them must be cleaned up. The problem is that unless you search through all the personal computers at your site, as well as all the diskettes at your site, you can have no assurance that you have found all copies of the virus that may have actually infected only four or five PCs. Since viruses are essentially invisible the engineer must actually go looking for them on all 1000 PCs and 35,000 diskettes in an average corporate computer site. And if even a single instance of the virus is missed, then other computers will eventually be reinfected and the whole clean-up process must start again."

Further light is shed by IBM's Al Fedeli who notes that "While viruses exhibit many other characteristic behaviors, such as causing pranks, changing or deleting files, displaying messages or screen effects, hiding from detection by changing or encrypting themselves, modifying programs and spreading are the necessary and sufficient conditions for a program to be considered a virus." The very act of modifying files means that the presence of a virus causes disruption to normal operation, in addition to which the virus program can be written to carry out a specific task, like playing a tune at a certain time every day. In a mix of metaphors, such a virus task is referred to as a payload, and the event that releases or invokes it is referred to as a trigger. This might be a date or action, such as booting up the machine. Some payloads are very nasty, such as corrupting the file allocation table (FAT) on a disk and thus rendering files inaccessible.

A lot of viruses attack operating system files, meaning that they have the potential to disrupt a wide range of users. Other viruses attack a particular application. Consider the virus that attacks dBASE data files, stored with the DBF extension. The virus reverses the order of bytes in the file as it is written to disk. The virus reverses them back to normal when the file is retrieved, making the change transparent to the casual user. However, if the file is sent to an uninfected user, or if the virus is inadvertently removed from the host system, the data are left in a scrambled state.

Before moving on to Trojan horses, it is important to point out that although some people say there are thousands of viruses to worry about, as of early 1997, only a few hundred were "in the wild." This term is reserved for viruses that have actually infected someone, somewhere. It is important to distinguish this small number of "in the wild" viruses from the much larger number of "in the zoo" viruses. We use this term to describe a virus that has never been seen in a real-world situation (believe it or not, some people who write viruses send them to antivirus researchers, which is one reason the population of the zoo far outnumbers that of the wild).[16]

The Trojan Horse

According to Rosenberger and Greenberg, "Trojan horse is a generic term describing a set of computer instructions purposely hidden inside a program. Trojan horses tell programs to do things you don't expect them to do." The original Trojan horse held enemy soldiers in its belly who thus gained entrance to the fortified city of Troy. In computer terms, a seemingly legitimate program is loaded by the user, but at some point thereafter malicious code goes to work, possibly capturing password keystrokes or erasing data.

An example appeared in 1995 when someone started distributing a file described as PKZIP 3.0, the long-awaited update of PKZIP version 2.04g, an excellent file archiving tool. Naturally, since the purpose of PKZIP is to compress and decompress files, version 2.04g was distributed as a self-extracting file. That is, it was executed as a program at the DOS prompt. PKZIP 3.0 was also made available on bulletin boards as an executable file, but it was not a self-extracting archive. Instead it was a Trojan horse that attempted to execute the DELTREE and FORMAT commands. Although clumsily written, it sometimes worked and some people lost data (one defense against such programs is to rename, remove, or relocate potentially destructive commands like FORMAT and DELTREE).

The Worm

According to virus experts Rosenberger and Greenberg, a worm is similar to a Trojan horse, but there is no "gift" involved: "If the Trojans had left that wooden horse outside the city, they wouldn't have been attacked from inside the city. Worms, on the other hand, can bypass your defenses without having to deceive you into dropping your guard." The classic example is a program designed to spread itself by exploiting bugs in a network operating software, spreading parts of itself across many different computers that are connected into a network. The parts remain in touch with, or related to, each other, thus giving rise to the term *worm*, a segmented insect. Naturally, this has a disruptive effect on the host computers, eating up empty space in memory and storage, and wasting valuable processing time.

The best-known example is the Internet worm which consumed so much memory space and processor time that eventually several thousand computers ground to a halt (the Morris/Internet worm has been exhaustively analyzed and documented on the Web). More destructive worms might erase files. Even without malicious intent, communications on the network are likely to be disrupted by any worm as it attempts to grow from one area to another. Most people agree that a worm is typified by independent growth rather than modification of existing programs. The difference between a worm and a virus might be characterized by saying a virus reproduces, while a worm grows.

The Code Bomb

One of the oldest forms of malicious programming is the creation of dormant code that is later activated or triggered by specific circumstances. Typical triggers are events such as a particular date or a certain number of system starts. Stories abound of disgruntled programmers planting logic bombs to get back at employers deemed to have been unfair. Several logic bombs have been planted in order to extort money. You have to pay up or find the malicious code and remove it. The latter option can be extremely costly when the system is a large mainframe computer.

Defenses Against MC

The layered approach to security that we advocate can provide a head start in defending against malicious code. To briefly reiterate the elements of this layered approach, they are

- Access control
  - Site — controlling who can get near the system.
  - System — controlling who can use the system.
  - File — controlling who can use specific files.

- System support
  - Power — keeping supply of power clean and constant.
  - Backup — keeping copies of files current.

The three access control items provide positive protection against infection, while the last item under System Support, backup, allows you to recover from a virus attack. However, we now add a third layer of System Support, namely Vigilance — keeping tabs on what enters or attempts to enter the system. By exercising vigilance, users and administrators alike can prevent, or at least minimize, the effects of malicious programming. To be vigilant, users need to know what they are defending against. This means:

- General training in malicious code awareness.
- Constant updating of defenses to remain effective against a threat which continues to evolve.
- An ongoing program of security checking, review, and retraining.

In the case of the most prevalent malicious code threat, viruses, vigilance means:

- Knowing what viruses are, the methods of attack they use, and what constitutes a healthy regimen of computer operation and maintenance.
- The use of hardware and/or software that prevents or warns of virus attacks (typically, software of this type needs to be updated on a regular basis in order to remain effective).
- Hardware and software buying choices might be affected, with systems and programs that are more inherently virus-free being preferred.

Staying Abreast

To be effective against malicious code you must keep abreast of the latest threats. Fortunately, this is now a lot easier than it used to be. There are a number of online sources that are sure to report new developments:

- NCSA forums on CompuServe
- NCSA pages on the Web
- Forum/Web page/BBS hosted by your antivirus vendor
- VIRUS-L news group

For the small/home office user we recommend checking in with one or more of these sources once a week. After all, it only takes a few minutes. For larger organizations we suggest that someone, probably on the support staff, be assigned the task of making a daily check.

Basic Rules

Being vigilant about the files that enter your system will go a long way towards protecting it from malicious code. If you use access controls to extend that vigilance to the times when you are not around to oversee what is happening to your computer, you should avoid the immediate effects of malicious code attacks. To sum up the defensive measures discussed here, the following rules can be promulgated, first for the individual user, and then for the manager of users.

1. Observe site, system, and file access security procedures.
2. Always perform a backup before installing new software.
3. Only use reputable software from reputable sources.
4. Know the warning signs of a malicious program.
5. Use antivirus products to watch over your system.
6. Use an isolated machine to test software that might be suspect.

Rules for managers of users:

1. Make sure that access control and backup procedures are observed by all users.
2. Check all new software installations, floppy disks, and file transfers with an antivirus product.
3. Forbid the use of unchecked or unapproved software, floppy disks, or online connections.
4. Stay informed of latest developments in malicious programming, either through an alert service or by tasking in-house staff.
5. Keep all staff informed of latest trends in malicious code so that they know what to look for.
6. Make use of activity/operator logging systems so that you know who is using each system and what it is being used for.
7. Encourage the reporting of all operational anomalies and match these against known attacks.

Boot Sector Viruses

This type of infection hits your computer just as it loads the operating system. Most common on IBM-compatible machines, boot sector viruses can also be created for other systems (the "first" virus was an Apple II boot sector virus). Boot sectors are what get the operating system loaded into memory after you power-up the system (cold boot), or perform a hard reset (usually using a button on the front of the machine). On IBM-compatible machines, the instructions stored in the BIOS, which cannot themselves be infected by a virus since they are burned into ROM (Read Only Memory), load information from the Master Boot Sector and DOS Boot Sector into RAM, after performing the POST (Power On Self Test) and reading data, such as the time, from CMOS (which can be corrupted by viruses).

According to Virus Bulletin's description "boot sector viruses alter the code stored in either the Master Boot Sector or the DOS Boot Sector. Usually, the original contents of the boot sector are replaced by the virus code.... Once loaded, the virus code generally loads the original boot code into memory and executes it, so that as far as the user is concerned, nothing is amiss." This might be accomplished by virus code in the boot sector that points to a different section of the disk. So the virus code is in memory and the user is none the wiser. The virus may then infect the boot sector of any floppy disk that is used in the machine's floppy disk drive, thus passing the infection on. While this is rather clever, it would seem to be an inefficient means of replicating now that so many people boot from a hard disk. If everyone cleaned their hard disk boot sector it would appear that extermination of boot sector viruses would be achievable.

Unfortunately, this overlooks the fact that there are boot sectors on ALL floppy disks, not just those that are bootable system disks. And we have all made the mistake of turning on or resetting a system with a floppy in drive A. If the floppy disk is not bootable, for example, if it is a data or program installation disk, we get the "Non-System disk or disk error. Replace and strike any key when ready" message. Alas, at that point the boot sector virus is already in memory. Indeed, that message is read onto the screen from the boot sector. Taking the floppy out and pressing "any key" will not clear the virus from memory, and besides, it may have already infected the hard disk. Note that the Macintosh uses a combination of hardware design and operating system software to spit out floppy disks when booting, thus considerably reducing the chances of this type of infection.

Even without the Mac's method of handling floppies, the solution appears quite simple: don't leave floppies in drive A, and if you do get the Non-System error message, reset the system instead of pressing "any key" when you get the message. Better still, if you have a newer BIOS that allows you to adjust the drive boot sequence, tell it to boot from C before A (this still allows you boot from a floppy if something happens to drive C). Well-known boot sector viruses include Michelangelo, Monkey.B, and perhaps the most widely occurring viruses of all time, Stoned and Form.

While at first it sounds like you could only catch a boot sector virus from a floppy disk, the threat is slightly more complex thanks to the folks who enjoy placing boot sector viruses in Trojan horse or "bait" files and then uploading them to bulletin boards. These files are designed to place the boot sector virus on your system when you execute them (ironically, these programs accomplish this task with a routine known as a "dropper," originally developed to allow the transfer of boot sector viruses between legitimate researchers and antivirus programmers).

Parasitic Viruses

More numerous than boot sector viruses but less prevalent, parasitic viruses are also referred to as file infectors, because they infect executable files. According to Virus Bulletin "they generally leave the contents of the host program relatively unchanged, but append or prepend their code to the host, and divert execution flow so that the virus code is executed first. Once the virus code has finished its task, control is passed to the original program which, in most cases, executes normally." While such a complex operation sounds at first like it would be immediately noticeable to the user, this is often not the case since virus code is typically very compact. The temporary diversion of program flow is often indiscernible from normal operations.

Multipartite and Companion Viruses

You now know what boot sector and file infector viruses do. Put the two together and you have multipartite viruses, such as Tequila, which are capable of spreading by both methods. At the other end of the sophistication scale are companion viruses which take advantage of this simple fact about DOS: if you launch a program at the DOS prompt by entering its name, as in FORMAT, and DOS finds that there are two program files in the current directory, one called FORMAT.COM and the other called FORMAT.EXE, the COM file will be executed before the EXE file. A companion virus thus hides and spreads as a COM variant of a standard EXE file. Examples include the rare AIDS II and Clonewar viruses.

Other Types of Virus

Link viruses are a type of virus rare in the wild, despite the fact that they have considerable potential for spreading rapidly owing to the way they manipulate the directory structure of the media on which they are stored, pointing the operating system to virus code instead of legitimate programs. Academic viruses researchers and underground virus writers both spend a lot of time thinking about new ways in which viruses may be spread. This leads to many "in the zoo" or "in theory" viruses which exist more on paper than in practice. Several approaches to infection that fit into this category are source code and object code viruses. The idea behind a source code virus is to insert virus instructions into programs at the source code level, rather than through the compiled program.

A source code virus would add itself to the source code file, then get compiled into the executable file when the program code was compiled. From the complied program the virus code then seeks out further source code files to infect. This method of infection could be quite effective in some environments since most source code files have common and easily identifiable attributes, such as file extensions (like .C and .BAS). There is little evidence of such viruses on desktop machines, but widespread use of an interpreted language, like Microsoft Visual Basic, could make this an appealing path for infection.

To understand the object code virus, of which at least one example, Shifting_Objectives, has been discovered, you need to know that all of the source code for a complex program, such as Microsoft Windows or Microsoft Excel, is not compiled into one large EXE or COM file. Instead, these programs use sections of code, called objects, that are loaded into RAM and linked together only when they are needed. Programmers like to write code in the form of objects because these can be recycled very easily. For example, if treated as an object, the code required to create a dialog box can also be used in many places within a program, without the programmer having to code each dialog box individually. By infecting an object rather than an executable, the object code virus makes itself less open to normal methods of detection (for example, many antivirus strategies concentrate on protecting and monitoring executable files).

The term *kernel* is used to describe the core of the operating system. In DOS, for example, the kernel is stored in the hidden file IO.SYS. The idea behind a kernel infector, of which there are currently very few, is to operate at one level above the boot sector, but within the heart of the operating system, replacing the instructions in the real IO.SYS with its own agenda. This makes the virus more difficult to track than if it infected visible COM files such as COMMAND.COM. By loading its own code into memory ahead of the operating system the virus can achieve "stealthing" to avoid many traditional forms of virus detection.

Stealth and Polymorphism

Stealth viruses use traditional techniques for infection, such as boot sectors and executable files, but they have code which stays in memory to monitor and intercept operating system calls, thus disguising its presence. As Jonathan Wheat, one of the antivirus experts at NCSA puts it, "When the system seeks to open an infected file, the stealth virus leaps ahead, uninfects the file and allows the operating system to open it, so that all appears normal. When the operating system closes the file, the stealth virus reverses the actions, reinfecting the file. If you look at a boot sector on a disk infect by a stealth boot sector virus what you see looks normal, but it is not the real boot sector." Stealth viruses pose numerous problems for traditional antivirus products, which may even propagate the virus as they examine files when looking for infections.

The term *polymorphic* is used to describe computer viruses that mutate to escape detection by traditional antivirus software which compares suspect code to an inventory of known viruses. Polymorphic viruses can infect any type of host software. Polymorphic file viruses are most common, but polymorphic boot sector viruses have also been discovered (virus writers use a free piece of software called the Mutation Engine to transform simple viruses into polymorphic ones, which ensures that polymorphic viruses are likely to further proliferate).

Some polymorphic viruses have a relatively limited number of variants or disguises, making them easier to identify. The Whale virus, for example, has 32 forms. Antivirus tools can detect these viruses by comparing them to an inventory of virus descriptions that allows for wildcard variations. Polymorphic viruses derived from tools such as the Mutation Engine are tougher to identify, because they can take any of four billion forms!

Macro Viruses

Viruses do not need to be written in assembly code or a higher language such as C. They can be written using any instruction set. Ask anyone who has worked with macros in programs such as 1-2-3 or Excel, WordPerfect, or Word, and you will discover that these work just like a programming language. As macros evolved from their origins in the 1970s in word processing (storing multiple keystrokes under one key) to spreadsheets in the early 1980s (enabling complex menu branches of conditional commands) they acquired a vital ingredient for virus making, automatic execution.

Of course, the purpose of automated operation was to enable the creation of easy-to-use, macro-driven applications for less-experienced users. In the mid to late 1980s this became a major activity within some organizations. Macro power increased, driven by power users of programs like 1-2-3 who worked hard to reduce complex operations, such as invoicing, to simple macro menus. Macros acquired the ability to execute operating system commands and further extended their power in the early 1990s when software designers introduced cross-application macro languages, such as WordBasic. The result is a class of computer file which appears at first to be a data file, but which may actually contain a program of macro commands.

This further blurred the distinction embodied in the oft-repeated advice that "your computer cannot be infected by a document" and "you can only be infected by programs." These statements only remain true if we carefully define documents to exclude those containing macros (and any other pseudo-language such as PostScript, which can trigger hardware events when transmitted to a printer) and define programs to include executable code in the widest sense (including ANSI codes, which could execute some unwanted actions if placed in e-mail that was displayed in text mode).

Ironically, Microsoft's domination of the software market in the mid 1990s provided the final ingredient for a "document" virus outbreak, that is, a universal, transplatform application — Microsoft Word. In late August of 1995 people learned that there was a dark side to the compatibility benefits of a *de facto* standard for word processing. A new virus came to light, capable of being spread through the exchange of Microsoft Word documents.

The virus, named Winword.Concept, replicates by adding internal macros to Word documents. If the virus is active on a system, an uninfected document can become infected simply by opening it and saving it using the "File Save As" menu option. Although Winword.Concept does not cause any intentional damage to the system, some users have reported problems when saving documents.

The macro virus becomes active when you open an infected document, doing so via Microsoft Word's "AutoOpen" macro, which executes each time you open a document. If you open an infected document with Word, the first thing the macro virus does is check the global document template, typically NORMAL.DOT, for the presence of either a macro named PayLoad or FileSaveAs. If either macro is found, the routine aborts and no infection of the global document template occurs. However, if these macros are not found, then several macros are copied to your global document template. During the course of copying the macros a small dialog box with an "OK" button appears on the screen. The dialog box simply contains the number "1" as its only text. The title bar of the dialog box indicates it is a Microsoft Word dialog box. This dialog will only be shown during the initial infection.

Once these macros are added to the global document template, they replicate by means of the virus version of "File Save" command. Consequently any document created using File Save As will contain this macro virus. An uninfected user can simply open the document and become infected. This can even happen while you are online to the World Wide Web, if you have your Web browser configured to use Word as the viewer for DOC files (the remedy is to use a viewer program such as Word Viewer, instead, as described later in this chapter). Note that the "PayLoad" macro contains the following text:

Sub MAIN

>REM That's enough to prove my point

End Sub

However, "PayLoad" is not executed at any time. Because of the flexibility of Microsoft's WordBasic macro language, almost anything could be performed here (including a file delete or other potentially damaging operating system commands). Also note that Word is available in many different languages, and in some versions the macro language commands have also been translated. This has the effect that macros written with the English version of Word will not work in, for example, the Finnish version of Word. The result is that users of such a national version of Word will not get infected by this virus. However, using an infected document in a translated version of Word will not produce any errors, and the infection will stay intact even if the document is re-saved. Under these circumstances you should check for the presence of the virus in any case, in order not to spread infected DOC files further.

There are some preventative measures built into Word that are supposed to control automatic macros. For example, the Word for Windows manual states that if you hold down Shift while double-clicking the Word icon in Program Manager, then Word will start up with file-related "auto-execute" macros disabled. However, while this ought to inhibit the actuation of some macro viruses like WinWord.Nuclear, which relies on this feature, many users have found that it doesn't work. They also found that starting up Word with the command line WINWORD.EXE/m, which is supposed to achieve a similar effect, failed as well, as did holding down Shift while opening a document to disable any automatic macros in that file. Furthermore, many companies have invested a lot of development time in automatic Word macros to automate routine tasks. The best strategy for preventing infection is thus to scan all incoming documents. All products that achieve the NCSA's antivirus certification (listed at www.ncsa.com) are capable of spotting macro viruses.

ACCESS CONTROLS AND ENCRYPTION

Earlier it was noted that access controls and encryption are a defense against the compromise of data on stolen systems and storage media. For example, if a laptop system is stolen but the bulk of the data on the machine are stored in encrypted files, it is unlikely that the thief, or the person to whom the machine is fenced and ultimately sold, will gain access to the data.

Unfortunately, encryption is an example of security's two-edged sword. For example, the very feature that makes a notebook easier to secure physically (the small size — it can be locked away in an office drawer or a hotel-room safe) also makes it easier to run off with. Similarly, the technology that renders files inaccessible to the wrong people, encryption, can be abused to deny access to legitimate users (in the last 12 months we have received several calls from companies wanting help in retrieving their own data, encrypted by a disgruntled employee who refuses to share the password — payment is sometimes demanded, leading to the term *data ransoming*).

Nevertheless, it is better to use the digital protection schemes that are available than risk data loss or compromise. Start with the BIOS. Most laptops and desktops produced in recent years have a decent set of BIOS-based security features. For example, the trusty three-year-old Compaq Concerto on which this chapter is being written allows the user to "hot lock" with a single keystroke, preventing anyone from using the mouse or keyboard unless they can enter the correct PIN. This can be set to kick in at system startup, thus defending against a reboot attack. Beyond this, you can disable the floppy drive, even block the ports, and all with a security program that has a Windows interface. Getting around this protection would require taking the machine apart and knowing just how to drain current from the CMOS.

Beyond BIOS-based protection you have the option of installing encryption software to scramble the contents of files so that they are useless to anyone who doesn't have the password/key. Encryption programs can operate at different levels. You can choose to encrypt just a few very valuable files on a file-by-file basis. This is simple and straightforward with something like Nortel Entrust Lite, McAfee's PC Secure, RSA's SecurPC, or Cobweb Application's KeyRing. These programs are particularly useful when you want to transmit files by e-mail, which remote users often need to do. If you routinely need to encrypt your e-mail messages, as opposed to file attachments, then PGPMail or ConnectSoft's Email Connection may be the way to go (the latter supports the S/MIME standard and requires a password before you can even run the program).

The next level of encryption is a designated area on the hard disk, in which all files stored are automatically encrypted. This is possible with programs like Utimaco's Safe Guard Easy products, which perform on-the-fly encryption. In other words, encryption and decryption are made part of the normal file save and open process. This can be more convenient in that constant entering of passwords is not required, but then again, if the master password is compromised the attacker may gain access to more data than if each file had a separate password. Program's like Symantec's Norton Your Eyes Only can actually encrypt everything on the entire hard disk, if that is what you want to do.

If you do use encryption you will need to take passwords seriously. The use of a master password, which unlocks all files you have encrypted, can simplify this, but it also increases the amount you have riding on one single password. Separate passwords for each file presents a management problem. Then there is the dilemma of easy-to-remember passwords, like your name, being easy for interlopers to guess, vs. long, obscure, and hard to crack passwords that you are tempted to write down, and thus compromise, just because they are hard to remember.

Also, there is the temptation to use the same password in different situations, which can lead to compromise. For example, it is relatively easy to crack the standard Windows 95 screen-saver password. So, you shouldn't use the same password for the screen-saver that you use for network log-in or sensitive file encryption (alternatively, you can use a more powerful screen-saver, such as Cobweb Application's HideThat).

Several encryption solutions attempt to go beyond passwords. For example, Fischer International offers a hardware key that fits inside a floppy disk drive. Companies like Chrysalis and Telequip make PCMCIA cards that not only store encryption keys but also perform encryption calculations, thus mitigating some of the performance hit that encryption can impose. Encryption programs like Entrust can store passwords on floppy disks, which allows them to be kept separate from the computer where the encrypted files are stored. Keep that in your pocket when you leave your laptop behind and at least you will know that nobody can get to your files, even if they steal your machine.

DEFENDING THE LAN

The first personal computer networks were installed in the mid 1980s, allowing users to share, for purposes of efficiency, productivity and cost-saving, their storage devices, printers, and software. Naturally, these networks started out small, hence the term local area network. They were often informal, employed by a group of users who knew and trusted each other, and so people paid little attention to the security implications of this new type of computing.

Peer-to-Peer Networks

Typical of this phase of networking is the peer-to-peer network, in which each computer on the network has an equal ability to make its resources available to all the others. Examples are Appletalk, standard on the Apple Macintosh since 1984, Microsoft Windows for Workgroups, and Novell Personal NetWare. Microsoft continues to provide peer-to-peer networking in Windows 95 and Windows NT Workstation. The ease with which users of peer-to-peer networks can share files and printers is both appealing and alarming.

If you work with a small group of trusted colleagues, this approach to networking can be both convenient and efficient. But as such networks grow, systems become harder to manage, and trust is spread thinner. Access is difficult to control, because the network operating system was not designed with control in mind. All connections between a peer-to-peer network and other systems, such as the Internet or a dial-up line for a remote user are a security threat. For example, unless specific and nonobvious precautions are taken, any machine on a Windows 95 peer-to-peer network which dials out to the Internet immediately creates a path by which any other system on the Internet can access your shared resources.[17]

Server-Based Networks

Novell's main Netware product has always been a server-based network operating system and this path was followed by IBM, and later Microsoft (in the form of Microsoft LAN Manager which has evolved into Windows NT Server). Note that PCs connected to a network file server as clients act as work stations, not terminals. In other words, they do not give up their ability to locally input, process, store, and output. Furthermore, unless they are logged onto the network, the network cannot have any effect on their security, which has serious implications. For example, when a PC has been logged off, the network operating system cannot control access to directories on its hard drive or prevent the user running locally stored applications.

Similarly, the network file server may scan both server and client directories for malicious code, but it cannot scan clients when they are not clients, that is, when they are logged off. This means that viruses can still infect machines that are part of the network. When an infected local machine later logs onto the network, it can spread the virus to the server.

While it is typical for the network file server to require that only authorized users, with valid users name and passwords, be allowed to use network resources, the network itself cannot identify users who do not log on. Theft, destruction, or corruption of data that are stored locally on a client is thus entirely possible, unless additional controls are in place. However, some interesting variations are possible when PCs are networked. For example, it is possible to configure desktop machines so that they cannot be operated unless they are logged onto the network. This can be achieved by extending the BIOS-based security described earlier (other examples of enhanced BIOS include alerting the network if the PC is logged off or disconnected).

Network Computers

If access to local storage is also blocked at the BIOS level, or removed completely, then the desktop computer becomes a truly dedicated client, useless without its properly authenticated network connection. Of course, some might argue that the machine is no longer a "personal computer," but from a security perspective the response is likely to be "so what?" In fact, today's networking technology allows the network to provide users with their own server-based storage and their own customized applications and settings, without the need for local storage. This facilitates centralized management of security tasks such as backup, authentication, and malicious code scanning.

The personal computer (PC) is thus transformed into the network computer (NC), a reincarnation of the diskless work stations that flopped in the 1980s. Back then, server-based software was far less exciting than the code you could run on stand-alone desktop machines, which were first adopted by eager do-it-yourself programmers who were people with a natural aptitude for productive use of the technology. Now that more than 50% of the workers in America have to use a computer of some kind, there is less need for each one of those computers to be personally managed and controlled.

From a security and management perspective, the NC is clearly a step forward, a cost-effective one at that. It is not unreasonable to suggest that individuals who still need or want a truly personal computer can either use their own machine at home, or use a nonnetworked system at the office. In any event, organizations should not lose sight of the fact that the "personal" computers it provides to its employees are actually the property of the organization, which is free to control the manner in which they are used, particularly when some uses such as Web surfing can increase risks to valuable data, not to mention the negative impact on productivity.

Network Security Implications

Constant improvements in hardware and software enabled LANs to grow in size and power. By the early 1990s some LANs had evolved into mission-critical information systems. The security implications increased dramatically but, even when network managers have had time to think about these implications, they have often lacked the resources and tools with which to address them. Furthermore, because many of these PC-based networks resembled the familiar paradigm of a powerful central computer supporting numerous, less powerful machines, many people assumed that the security problems could be solved in familiar ways, such as (1) give users password protected network accounts and don't let anyone log onto the network unless they can supply a valid account name and password; and (2) perform regular backups.

In practice, (2) has been easier to achieve than (1), but in a typical LAN environment (2) offers less protection than you might expect. The reason is simple. As was noted earlier, desktop computers are computers, they are not terminals. A desktop computer runs its own operating system under local control, does its own processing, has its own storage and its own input and output capabilities. Of course, you can try and make a desktop computer emulate a terminal, but unless you turn it into a terminal it will still be a computer.

Of course, there are many positive reasons for increased intercomputer communications, such as:

- Cost savings from sharing resources
- Productivity gains from faster, better communications and information sharing.

There are also potential security benefits. Any serious network operating system, or NOS, contains security features, and every NOS is more mindful of security than the popular desktop operating systems. The centralized storage of information that comes with server-based networking makes that information easier to protect, at least in terms of backup.

But these gains come with risks attached. Connecting two computers opens up a new front for the attacker who can exploit the connection, either to get at the data being transferred, or to penetrate one or more of the connected systems. Simply put, establishing a connection between two or more computers means:

- More to lose.[18]
- More ways to lose it.

The increase in potential gains from a single successful penetration of security makes the connected computer a far more promising target for the attacker. You still have to worry about in-house interlopers, both the merely curious and the seriously fraudulent, as well as disgruntled employees for whom intercomputer connections are a target for belligerence. But you also need to consider outside hackers, both amateur and professional, who live and breathe intercomputer communications.[19] The security implications of networking personal computers can be assessed as two different factors:

- The multiplication factor: normal security problems associated with an unconnected computer system are multiplied by a factor, roughly equal to the number of computer systems connected together.
- The channel factor: a new security area created by opening up channels of communications between computer systems, providing access into a computer through one port or another.

Taken together the multiplication and channel factors create the unique set of security problems normally referred to as network security. However, the term "manifold security" might better describe the situation confronting those responsible for securing personal computers which need to communicate, because, despite the existence of a substantial body of knowledge that deals with the protection of networks of large computer systems, much of it cannot be applied directly to personal computers. There are major differences in design and application. Personal computers are rarely located in secure or controlled environments. Neither personal computer hardware, nor the operating systems that control it, offer much in the way of built-in access control, particularly when it comes to connections with other hardware.

The Multiplication Factor

The security of computers that are connected has to start with individual computer security. You cannot combine a number of insecure computers into a network and create a secure system from the top down (unless you remove all local storage and processing, which in effect reduces the personal computer to a dumb terminal). While the network operating system will provide security measures, these are defeated or weakened if the individual systems are not secure. If someone has uncontrolled use of a PC connected to a network, they have an excellent platform from which to attack the network, not to mention data that have already been transferred from the network to your PC (after all, the whole point of client/server computing is to make valuable data available on the desktop).

Even if the network is securely configured it cannot protect the PC that is not logged on. This problem is not likely to disappear any time soon, given that the default as-delivered state of most PCs continues to be unlocked and unprotected. Consider Windows 95, the first major new desktop operating system in many years. It contains plenty of hooks to which network security features can be attached, but it offers no serious stand-alone security. The point is clear: intercomputer security begins with everything in the chapter so far, from boot protection to backups, theft prevention to power conditioning, access control to virus prevention. According to the layered approach that this book advocates, each computer connected to another must be

- Protected by site, system, and file access control.
- Supported by suitable power and data backup facilities.
- Watched over by a vigilant operator/administrator.

The multiplication factor implies that protecting two computers is at least twice as difficult at protecting one. For example, a network can actually increase the damage and disruption that a virus can cause. The potential fall-out from the errors, omissions, and malicious actions of individual users is magnified when they are network users. Typically, a higher degree of user supervision is required; however, this is not always forthcoming. Users accustomed to the freedom and independence of stand-alone computing may find it irksome to submit to the rules for network users.

The Channel Factor

In previous chapters, you have seen how the layered approach to security is built up. So far, the concern has been the protection of personal computers as separate entities, vulnerable to abuse by users putting information in or taking it out via disk, screen, and keyboard. The layered approach to stand-alone security can be summarized like this:

- Access control
  - Site — controlling who can get near the system.
  - System — controlling who can use the system.
  - File — controlling who can use specific files.
- System support
  - Power — keeping supply of power clean and constant.

- Backup — keeping copies of files current.
- Vigilance — keeping tabs on what enters and leaves the system.

This arrangement needs to be expanded whenever a computer system is connected to another system. Intercomputer connection opens a channel of communication between machines. This adds a third layer, channel protection, which can be divided into three areas:

- Channel control
- Channel verification
- Channel support

Channel Control

A connection between two computers is one more way for an attacker to steal, delete, and corrupt information, or otherwise undermine normal operations. To prevent a channel of communication from becoming an avenue of attack, you need to control who can:

- Open a channel.
- Use a channel.
- Close a channel.

Clearly the first step is to ensure that proper site and system access controls are in place. The next step is to decide who needs to use a particular channel and then restrict access to authorized users. In network terms, this might be a matter of using password-controlled log-on procedures, or two-part token authentication. Password protection can be used for mainframe connections as well. Most commercial online services require an account number and password for access, and these should be closely guarded. However, system access control should be particularly tight on all personal computers equipped with modems.

Channel Verification

To be on the safe side, you should think of a channel of communication as a path through enemy territory. Whatever passes along that route runs the risk of being ambushed. Secure communications involves ongoing verification of:

- The identity of users.
- The integrity of data.
- The integrity of the channel.

Users of a communication channel should be required to identify themselves, whether the connection is a network hookup, a modem, or a mainframe link. When you are on the receiving end of intercomputer communications, that is, acting as the host for users calling in, you need to be able to verify the claimed identity. Network nodes need to be able to verify the legitimacy of packets received.

One of the most important requirements for secure communications between computers is verification of identity. On a local area network, this might mean that each user has an ID number and a password, both of which must be entered before log-in can be completed. Of course, entry of a valid ID number/password combination does not guarantee the identity of the person using them, but the network software will tell the administrator who claims to be using the system. In small sites, a tour of the LAN can provide visual verification of these claims. In large installations, where the administrator might not be expected to put a name to every face, assistance might be provided in the form of photo-ID tags or biometric controls.

When data are being transferred via a communications channel, they are subject to possible distortion, tampering, or theft. Verifying the integrity of the channel means making sure that this does not happen. Most communications software includes some form of error checking. At a rudimentary level, this can check that the amount of data received matches the amount transmitted. More sophisticated methods confirm details of the transmission.

Verifying the integrity of the channel also means making sure nobody is listening in, or preventing the theft of anything useful if someone is. This is best accomplished by encryption. You will need to assess the likelihood of anyone attempting to intercept or overhear your communications. If the risk is high enough, then you can encrypt important communications, using a variety of devices. Some software systems encrypt all network and telephone line traffic. Hardware encryption/decryption devices can be placed at each end of a communications link. Some of these are combined with data verification systems.

Channel Support

Intercomputer communications can only be established when a large number of different parameters are properly coordinated. Once established, communications need to be maintained. This requires a high degree of reliability in communications hardware and software. The need for reliability and protection centers on those components that serve more than one user, in proportion to the number of users served. For example, in a local area network where one personal computer is acting as a file server for others, disruption or failure of the server can have far greater consequences than the breakdown of a single personal computer working on its own. Once established, channels of communication must be supported, or else those tasks that depend upon them will be jeopardized.

Business Recovery for LANs and Desktop Systems

One of the biggest challenges facing information systems professionals today is the recovery of desktop/LAN-based systems following disasters such as fires and floods (for more about the topic of business continuity planning, see Domain 8). As noted earlier in this chapter, a significant percentage of mission-critical applications are now running on desktop systems, which are inherently more complex when it comes to recovery. Unlike mainframe systems, which tend to conform to certain standards as far as equipment and code are concerned, and can thus be duplicated by a hot site with relative ease, each LAN represents a unique configuration of hardware and software.

The configuration of a particular LAN server, and the personal computer clients that it serves, may have been tweaked and fine-tuned over a long period of time. It is seldom possible to simply take the server backup tapes, load them onto a different server, and bring up the system. There are simply too many variables. There are some steps you can take to minimize these problems:

1. Carefully document the current LAN hardware and software, including all configuration settings.
2. Use "standard" equipment and configurations wherever possible.
3. Document the minimum configuration required to restore essential data and services on a replacement LAN.
4. Use server-mirroring, fault-tolerant hardware, and redundant disk arrays.

SECURE REMOTE ACCESS AND INTERNET CONNECTION

One of the most revolutionary, and largely unforeseen, implications of personal computer technology has been the emergence of the home office and the mobile worker. Invariably, users who are on the road need to call home, and so do their computers. Laptops like to link up with head office systems to update databases and download e-mail. A growing army of work-at-home telecommuters need some sort of remote access to their employer's systems. The technology with which to create these connections has been around for some time, and so has the subtle art of subverting it for nefarious purposes, or mere curiosity.

It might be hard to understand, but some people get a genuine thrill simply being "in" someone else's computer system. Remote access points are still a popular way of getting in. (Given the number of frustrating hurdles that you sometimes have to clear in order to establish a legitimate connection, it might be hard to imagine someone doing this for fun; however, at that precise moment when you finally get your own e-mail after hours of dropped connections and redials, it is possible to sense something of the kick you get from hacking into someone else's system.)

Recent publicity about computer break-ins over the Internet has tended to overshadow hacking in through remote access points such as those provided for telecommuters, maintenance people, and field staff. However, this form of penetration is still used. Typically, it starts with a war dialer, a piece of software running on a modem-equipped PC, which automatically calls all of the phone numbers in a certain range, such as 345-0000, 345-0001 to 347-9999. The software records which numbers are answered by a modem. This gives the hacker a list of numbers worth testing for further access.

One technique that can reduce the risk of being found by such a technique is to set your modem to answer only after four or five rings — since the default operation of war dialers is geared toward speed, they may not linger that long at unanswered numbers. Of course, there are less technically sophisticated ways of getting phone numbers for computers, such as downloading lists of such numbers that are routinely shared on hacker bulletin boards, or digging through company trash for discarded phone directories.

Technically speaking you have several options for remote access. The most basic is a modem on your desktop machine which answers calls from the modem on your laptop. With "remote control" software running at both ends, the laptop user can operate the desktop machine as though seated at it. This remote control technology was popular early on in PC development since it kept to a minimum the data that needed to be sent over the phone at slow modem speeds. Later, when desktop machines were networked, the remote laptop user was able to control the desktop machine while it was logged into the network, thus giving network access.

With faster modems it became possible to log a remote caller directly into the network as a remote node. In other words, the laptop becomes a work station on the network. This is typically more convenient for the user, but it may be more expensive since the laptop needs to have its own licensed copy of the networked applications (instead of borrowing them from the desktop). However, network managers have tended to prefer remote node access because it is easier to manage, and this in turn provides security benefits. The remote machine has to prove its identity to the more demanding network server, rather than a mere desktop work station.

Recently, we have seen big strides towards consolidating remote network access, with special servers designed to run either remote node or remote control access in a tightly controlled manner. Typical methods for protecting a modem connection that is providing remote access are password protection and call-back. A simple form of the latter approach is for the remote user to dial into the modem at the office, which then hangs up and calls the remote user back. The idea is to prevent people establishing connections from unauthorized numbers, but hackers have found that it is possible to fool the modem at the office into thinking it has dropped the connection, so that the call-back never really takes place. The addition of a password requirement at the time of call-back reduces the chances of this type of hack succeeding.

The call-back approach can be hard to scale when the number of remote users starts to grow, and the cost of long distance calls to all those users starts to add up. An alternative is to provide a toll-free number for remote users to dial into, which is answered by a remote access server. This is a combined hardware and software solution that creates a special node on the network with the ability to receive and authenticate multiple incoming calls. The connection should be authenticated by something stronger than an ordinary password, such as a one-time password generated by a smart card.

For example, modem-maker U.S. Robotics uses the SecurID system on its Total Control Enterprise Network Hub remote access server. To access the server the user enters a PIN followed by the code displayed on the SecurID card issued to that user. The code displayed on the card changes every 60 seconds, in sync with the company's ACE/Server authentication server at the office. Other options for two-factor authentication (something you know, like a PIN, plus something you have, like a token) include requiring special PCMCIA cards holding encrypted keys to be present in the remote laptop before the connection can be made.

The number of users who dial into the office is bound to increase as companies expand the use of telecommuting and virtual offices. This will continue to provide a possible channel for penetration of internal systems. But improvements in remote access servers supported by two-factor authentication systems have the potential to make such penetration increasingly difficult. Two developments that need to be watched carefully are the shift towards using the Internet for remote access to in-house databases, and public key-based digital certificates as a means of authentication.

SUMMARY

In less than two decades the microcomputer has risen from the basement workshop and the garage benchtop to become the dominant force in computer hardware. While mainframes and minicomputers continue to anchor many systems, particularly in areas such as online transaction processing, the shift towards client/server solutions based on what are, in essence, microcomputers, shows no signs of abating.

We are only just beginning to come to terms with the information security implications of this phenomenon.[20] The process starts with an understanding of the desktop computer environment. Experience has shown that you cannot simply take big-system security practices and impose them on desktop machines. We have to develop security policies and procedures that are appropriate for the desktop. We have to implement those policies and procedures by educating users about security. We might not like it, but the fact is personal computers will never be secure unless the personnel who use them also secure them.

There are alternative strategies. For example, you can emasculate the PC and make it an NC, controlled and secured by a server that is treated like a mainframe, even if it is just a beefed up PC. Whether this option will find favor, either in corporate information systems or cubicle-land, remains to be seen.

Footnotes

1. As someone you call when you get one of these headaches, I can attest to the increased frequency of the calls and the growing severity of the headaches. The opening comments in this chapter were shaped by participation in security assessments at a number of major U.S. and international corporations during the last 12 months. For a collection of recent infosec-related statistics, visit http://www.theroyfamily.com/security.html.
2. For more detailed statement of this position and its weaknesses, see *The NCSA Guide to PC and LAN Security*, McGraw-Hill, New York, 1996.
3. For example, many new PCs today have BIOS-based boot protection, but there are plenty still in use that do not.
4. Examples of this are legion, from Aldrich Ames, the CIA spy, to lists of AIDS patients made public in Florida, to company secrets valued at millions of dollars in cases brought by American Airlines and Merrill-Dow.
5. About 76% of survey respondents said they were running "mission critical" applications on local area networks. Ernst & Young survey of 1,271 technology and business executives, January, 1995.
6. For example, a modest 486 and a modem is all it takes to mount a very effective denial of service attack on a Web site, mail gateway, or even an Internet Service Provider such as the New York provider, PANIX, which was disrupted for more than a week in 1996.
7. "After 1998, the widespread availability of inexpensive disruptive technology and the broadening base of home computer users will put threat capabilities into the hands of a wider, less-privileged class, dramatically increasing the risk for intermediate-size organizations (0.8 probability)." Gartner Group.
8. For example, instructions for mounting the type of attack suffered by PANIX were posted on the Internet and recently an easy-to-use Windows attack program was released.
9. For example, it is relatively easy to configure a dumb terminal so that the screen is the only output device which is ideal for transitory lookup access to confidential data, such as medical records. But it is relatively difficult to lobotomize a PC so that it cannot retain or redirect whatever data it receives. I still meet mainframe-oriented systems people who have not yet grasped this distinction.
10. "Someone broke into the offices of Interactive Television Technologies, Inc. in Amherst, New York, and stole three computers containing the plans, schematics, diagrams and specifications for proprietary Internet access technology still in development but conservatively valued at $250 million." Reuters, 1996.
11. For example, case locks, building locks, increase surveillance.

12. A few years ago a manufacturer of data backup tapes, 3M Corp., did a survey about backup regimes and found that, of those respondents who regularly performed backups, some 80 percent only started to do so *after* they had lost data through lack of backup.
13. A tape jukebox can cycle through multiple tapes and backup RAID data that is mirrored and not being accessed.
14. The term "optimized" refers to organizing data on the disk so that files are stored in contiguous sectors, in logical order for the most efficient retrieval. The term "defragmented" is used to describe the process of rearranging files so that they are stored in contiguous sectors.
15. One of the most comprehensive studies is the one performed by NCSA, available at their Web site, www.ncsa.com.
16. A list of current "in the wild" viruses can be found at www.ncsa.com/virus/wildlist.html. The list is maintained independently for the computing community by Joe Wells, with the help of over 40 volunteers around the world.
17. For a test, point your Web browser to www.omna.com/yes/mwc/info, a page that tells you how your Windows 95 machine is configured.
18. A 1993 study by Infonetics Research of San Jose, California found that when companies experienced losses due to LAN outages, the average amount per company, including lost revenues and productivity, was $7.5 million.
19. Remember that hacker Kevin Mitnik's first arrest was for stealing manuals from a Pacific Bell switching station — that was in 1981, when he was 17.
20. See footnote 7.

Domain 7
Computer Operations Security

The two most difficult problems facing those in the operations environment is how to protect their systems from the potential ravages of mobile code and what countermeasures to employ to control attacks by intruders. The first chapter gives us a look at the security available in Java. While some of the latest firewalls can help protect against unwanted activities perpetrated by mobile code through data inspection techniques, it is useful to know also how Java security can help. Many believe that the term "Java security" is an oxymoron, but this is not necessarily true. Knowing your vulnerabilities as well as employing active content protection can remove many concerns.

The second chapter provides some ideas on how to deal with those intruders known as "hackers." Although new types of attacks keep emerging from the active minds of the intruders of the world, having a plan to control them provides some operational comfort.

Domain 7.1
Threats

Chapter 24
How to Trap the Network Intruder

Jeff Flynn

The job of securing networks is quite difficult. Probably the most significant reason is system complexity. Networks are complicated. They are so complicated no one person can fully comprehend exactly how they work. The models that govern the designs were developed with this concept in mind and provide a layered view of networks that hide the true complexity. This makes it possible for programmers to work on various layers without understanding all the details of the other layers. Of course, programmers on occasion make mistakes, and these mistakes accumulate. Consequently, the Internet we have come to rely on is vulnerable to a wide variety of attacks. Some of the vulnerabilities are well known. Others are known only to a few or are yet to be discovered.

As the Internet grows, so too does the complexity. The growth of the Internet is still accelerating. Every year, more systems are connected to it than were connected the year before. These systems contain increasing amounts of memory. Larger memories allow programmers to develop larger and more complex programs, which provides the programmers with more opportunities to make mistakes. Larger programs also provide intruders with more places to hide malicious code.

Thus, a good network security manager must be very good indeed. The best network security managers may find themselves performing against the unrealistic expectation that they cannot be overwhelmed. These experts must keep up with all the latest attacks and countermeasures. Attackers, on the other hand, need to know only one or a small combination of attacks that will work against their opponents.

A common response to this situation is to simply fix the known problems. This involves closely monitoring reports from organizations such as

CERT or CIAC. As new vulnerabilities are discovered, the system manager responds appropriately. Unfortunately, the list of problems is also growing at an increasing rate. This can be a frustrating experience for the system manager who is forced to fight a losing battle. Likewise, financial managers are caught. They recognize that there are significant risks, yet no investment in safeguards can guarantee immunity from disaster.

It is hard to assess the extent to which tools have improved the situation. The Internet is a highly dynamic environment and does not provide good control samples for making such observations. The common-sense view might be, "However bad it is, it would be worse if we didn't have these devices." Unfortunately, the tools are not always applied properly and can lull management into thinking the situation is under control when it is not. In this situation, there is no benefit. The impact on the intruders is also quite difficult to assess. Serious intruders go to great lengths to keep their identities and approaches secret. Assessing the threat is, hence, a difficult aspect of evaluating the effectiveness of tools.

ASSESSING THE THREAT

There are many ways to gain a perspective on the threat. Most professionals in the field of network security use more than one. Some ways are more subjective than others. Yet there are several popular choices.

Reading

Several written information sources are available on the subject of network security. These include books, technical articles, newspaper articles, trade journal articles, newsgroups, and mailing lists. Each of these mediums has its strengths. Each also has its weaknesses. Trade journal articles, for example, can be biased and may attempt to use fear, uncertainty, and doubt to motivate buyers. Newspaper articles, although less biased, are driven by readership and limited in technical detail. Technical articles are many times too technical, sometimes describing threats that were not threats before publication. The information found in books is quickly dated. Finally, newsgroups and mailing lists, while providing timely information, are transmitted via networks that are subject to the same attacks we are attempting to prevent.

Experimentation

One way to see how difficult it is for someone to break into your system is to attempt to break into it yourself. The Self-Hack Audit, sometimes called Penetration Testing, is a useful means for finding weaknesses and is likely to improve awareness. Similarly, information warfare games provide true insight into how sophisticated intrusions can occur. Still, both of these methods are contrived and do not necessarily represent the actual threat.

Surveys

The 1997 CSI/FBI Computer Crime and Security Survey summarizes the anonymous responses of security professionals from a wide variety of industry segments. Respondents were asked, "If your organization has experienced computer intrusion(s) within the last 12 months, which of the following actions did you take?" Only 29.3% answered that they reported the incident to law enforcement or their own legal counsel. The remainder answered that they did not report the intrusion, or they did their best to "patch security holes." In fact, although 4,899 questionnaires were distributed, only 563 (11.5%) were returned. Of these security professionals, 99 acknowledged detecting "system penetrations," 101 acknowledged detecting "theft of proprietary information," 407 acknowledged detecting viruses, and 338 acknowledged detecting "insider abuse of net access." Security surveys produce statistics that provide managers with useful information for making decisions. Still, many computer incidents go undetected or unreported. This prevents surveys from being as valuable as they would be otherwise.

Firsthand Experience

Human nature seems to dictate that this is the path that most will follow. Firsthand experience occurs, for example, when a person buys a better lock after he detects a burglary. Firsthand experience involves a real threat, but the response comes after the fact. If the initial attack is sufficiently hostile, a response may be of limited use.

There is also a good chance the initial intrusion may go undetected. Network intruders are quite adept at installing back doors. The process is quite simple and may be the first act taken by an attacker after a successful intrusion. Consequently, it is far more difficult to restore security after a network intrusion than it is to prevent an intrusion. Before an individual decides to make firsthand experience his primary approach, he should ask himself, "Is this the kind of experience I want to have?" If the answer is, "I'm willing to take that risk," he should ask himself, "Is it morally responsible for me to make that decision on behalf of all those who may be affected?" What happens on networks can often affect more than the keepers of a network. A 911 emergency system in Florida that was taken down by network intruders provides a compelling example of this fact.

Measuring

Another option for network security managers is to measure the threat. This is critical, because one certainly cannot well manage what one cannot measure. This chapter has two purposes. The first is to suggest that the use of traps can be an effective way to gain a realistic assessment of the threat without exposing individuals and organizations to unreasonable risks. The second is to identify some of the qualities of a "good" trap.

THE BENEFIT OF TRAPS

Traps are attractive for three reasons. First, traps provide real-world information. If designed properly, the activation of the trap is highly correlated to real intrusions. This is not a contrived threat. The intruders detected are real, and they are targeting a particular organization. Second, well-designed traps can provide these measurements safely. Finally, traps can be used to deter future attacks. The trap response to a triggering event is part of the trap design. This goes beyond what intrusion detection systems provide, which may be considered components of traps. There are only three components to a trap: the bait, the trigger, and the snare.

THE QUALITIES OF A "GOOD" TRAP

It is obvious that a good trap is one that actually catches its prey. Good traps share other qualities too.

A Good Trap is Hidden

A hunter would not expect to catch his quarry if he simply left his trap lying on the ground. Animals are too smart or sensitive for this to work. The hunter must hide the trap, perhaps under a pile of leaves. Similarly, hacker traps should be invisible to the network intruder. Of course, one does not need to hide the bait portion of the trap. One only needs to ensure that characteristics of the bait do not betray the presence of the trap. There are many ways to make traps hard to detect. Devices such as in-circuit emulators, SCSI analyzers, and network protocol analyzers can monitor activities without affecting the behavior of the systems being monitored. Alternatively, log information can be transmitted via one-way connections to systems performing real-time intrusion detection functions. In tracking the activities of German hackers, Cliff Stoll transparently monitored modem ports with dramatic results.

A Good Trap Has Attractive Bait

If a trap is to be effective at luring its prey, it must have attractive bait. The trapper has several options in this area, and great care should be used in the selection. Just as a fly fisherman attempts to "match the hatch," the trapper must select a lure that is appropriate for the environment. In some cases, the bait might be a file or directory entitled "ops_planning." In other cases, it might be a file containing the words "security" or "intrusion detection." A continuous indecipherable sequence of bytes transmitted between two hosts may be sufficient. When selecting the bait, the network security manager should consider the possible goals of the intruder. The goals may have much to do with the business of the targeted organization, although this is not necessarily so. If previous intrusions were detected, the network manager might determine what sort of things the intruder found interesting. Again, care should be taken to prevent the bait from betraying the trap. If it looks too good to be true, the intruder may decide to look elsewhere and thus avoid detection.

A Good Trap Has an Accurate Trigger

A good trap should trap intruders. It should not trap innocent souls who stumble across it in the course of their normal duties. Consequently, the trigger should be designed so that the probability of a false detection is very low. This is extremely important. The loss of trust and the dissension caused by false suspicions or accusations can be considerable. These events can quite possibly cause more damage to an organization than an actual intruder. Of course, real intrusions can result in serious damage too. Hence, if an actual intruder goes for the bait, the probability of detection should be very close to 100 percent. Trap placement can be a useful means to improve the selectivity of a trigger. If the trigger is positioned in a place where no one should legitimately be, false detections can be greatly reduced. Ideally, a trap should be designed so that the intruder has violated a law before he can activate the trigger.

A Good Trap Has a Strong Snare

If a hunter's trap does not have a strong snare, the quarry may simply destroy the device. Animal traps are effective because they are strong enough to hang onto the animal. Similarly, an effective intruder trap should hang onto the intruder. Admittedly, this is one of the most difficult aspects of designing an effective trap.

The identity of an intruder can be known, and the victim organization can have arrest powers. But if the location of the intruder is outside the jurisdiction of that organization, an arrest may not be practical. Currently, the best intruder traps are those that preserve evidence, involve law enforcement, and, in certain circumstances, attempt to bring the intruder into a jurisdiction where action can be taken.

Complicating matters is the hacker modus operandi of weaving (sometimes referred to as looping or hopping) through the Internet. During this process, the hacker may impersonate one or more individuals, systems, or processes. Thus, the path back to the intruder's lair can take many twists and turns. In some cases, the process of following this path might require penetration of a third-party organization's network. Although this is beyond what most would attempt, it is possible that such action could be deemed legal if done with the proper authority.

By way of analogy, one might compare the situation to that of a police officer in "hot pursuit" or acting under "exigent circumstances." If an officer is in immediate pursuit of a criminal, and that criminal enters a residence, the officer does not wait for someone to grant him access. The officer does not wait for a warrant. He follows the criminal into the residence, breaking the lock on his way if necessary. If that criminal weaves in and out of one property after another, so too will the officer. This process continues until the criminal is apprehended, the criminal is lost, or the pursuit crosses a jurisdictional boundary. In the case of a jurisdictional border crossing, the officer might continue the pursuit, or he could pass the responsibility to another organization according to preexisting agreements between the various parties involved. Unfortunately, the present situation in the Internet is not so well organized. Perhaps, in time, as more laws and law enforcement personnel find their way into the Internet, the situation will improve.

Good Traps Are Used in Combination

To maximize the effectiveness of a trap, the trapper simply needs to add more traps. Just as a good fisherman keeps more than one line in the water, and perhaps more than one lure per line, the trapper should have more than one trap set. A good rule of thumb might be to count the number of targets an organization presents to a would-be intruder. The number of traps that are set should exceed that number. If the traps set are "good," it is more likely that an intruder will be detected than it is a target will be compromised. The approach scales nicely, allowing the trapping organization to select a security stance appropriate for its particular situation.

Good Traps Are Original

Once an intruder becomes aware of a particular type of trap, it is less likely that he can be fooled again in the same way. Hence, good traps should be unique. This is particularly true for the visible bait component of the trap. Other trap components should also be unique. If an intruder suspects a trap, he might try to trigger it from a safe circumstance. Likewise, he may know how to escape from a snare he encountered previously. The less an intruder can surmise about a trap, the better the trap. Originality in design then becomes the hallmark of a good trap. This fact should be viewed as good news for the network security administrator whose job has become an endless loop of applying patches. By developing traps, the network security administrator can have many opportunities to be creative.

Good Traps Do Not Entrap

Trapping and entrapping are two separate things. The difference is in the relation between the trap and the intruder. If the trap somehow induces someone to commit a crime, entrapment occurs, which adversely effects the strength of the trap's snare. Entrapment can prevent prosecution in many legal systems, which is an important component of an effective snare. Entrapment is also counterproductive. One of the goals of trapping is to deter intruders. Entrapment techniques produce the opposite result by encouraging intrusions. To keep a trap from becoming an entrapping device, the trapper should make the bait invisible to those who have not yet committed a crime. It should be obvious to the intruder and the trapper that a crime has been committed before the bait has the effect of drawing the intruder to the trigger. Notifications and banners should be used to make this point clear. These should indicate the boundaries of legality. Good caveats should include words to the effect that intrusion is not invited or welcome, various laws will be broken by those who proceed without authorization, use of the system implies acknowledgment of this, and use of the system implies consent to monitoring. The name of the organization being protected is not necessary, but a number to contact for clarification should be provided.

When complete, a trap should resemble the situation encountered with silent burglar alarms found in banks. These are traps too. Banks contain such traps, and there is usually no question as to whether entrapment was involved.

PSYCHOLOGY AT WORK

As mentioned previously, one of the benefits of a trap is that it deters. When a hacker realizes that he is in a situation where he is as likely to encounter a trap as he is to obtain his objective, he is likely to slow his pace. When his partners in crime are trapped (i.e., prosecuted), he may consider abandoning the craft. Few things deter more than well-designed traps. Consider the psychological impact on soldiers knowing they are about to cross a minefield. How much slower do they proceed? How much more effective is this deterrent after a mine is detonated?

AN EXAMPLE TRAP

Once network security administrators are aware of the benefits and attributes of good traps, they should consider a working example. Imagine a host set up behind the perimeter of a networked organization. This system is on a network that is protected by banners and other methods (perhaps a firewall). On the host is a file that contains a short list of phone numbers with corresponding passwords. The passwords are long random sequences of alphanumeric characters. These phone numbers and passwords are the bait. To the intruder, they represent additional access. The trigger is a computer (with software) connected to one of these phone numbers. When an intruder attempts to access the trigger with the correct password, the trigger is activated. The probability that the trap was activated by an actual intruder is quite high. The probability that the trap can be triggered by someone who did not break the rules is quite low. The telephone line is configured with caller ID (CNID) or automatic number identification, so that once triggered, the source of the call can be determined. This information can be used to draft an affidavit that might allow law enforcement to search the premises for the source of the attack. If the intruder was foolish enough to use his own line to make the call, there may be an opportunity for an arrest. If the intruder is not so foolish, at least the designer of the trap is aware that his barrier was penetrated. He does not need to know how it happened for this to be useful information. The mere fact that the intrusion occurred can be enough to justify investigation and additional investment in protective measures. It should be noted that intruders have circumvented CNID systems.

As an alternative to the snare just described, network security administrators could also imagine a trap that might physically capture an intruder, or someone acting on his behalf. By replacing the password bait with an electronic lock combination, a map, and a street address, one might be able to lure an intruder into a holding area disguised as a wiring closet. The use of the correct combination would notify authorities of the intrusion and allow entry. Once inside, the door would lock again and not allow exit. Great care would be required in the planning of such a trap to avoid physical risk to the intruder. Significant liability would result if harm were to come to the prisoner. It would not be reasonable to leave an intruder locked in a closet any significant length of time. Only when the safety of the prisoner can be guaranteed should such a trap be considered. Still, ideas like this may be attractive. In the event an intruder were to fall for this trap, the authorities would not only have a suspect; they would have probable cause for an arrest.

CONCLUSION

The network intruder can be quite clever and may attempt attacks that have not been previously encountered. Techniques are needed for detecting and deterring such intrusions. Although the use of traps will not necessarily free a network security administrator from the burden of simply patching one hole after another, it may help him to focus his efforts in the areas that are most important. It may also give him the well-needed opportunity to be creative. Perhaps the time has come for the network security manager to become more clever than the network intruder.

Chapter 25
A Look at Java Security

Ben Rothke

INTRODUCTION

Why should Java security concern you? Many push-based applications are being ported to Java. In addition, Java is one of the cornerstones of active content and an understanding of Java security basics is necessary for understanding the implications of push security issues.

A lot of people ask: "Why do I need Java security? I thought it was safe." Java as a language is basically safe and is built on top of a robust security architecture. But security breaches related to bugs in the browser, poorly written Java code, malicious Java programs, poorly written CGI scripts and Javascript code, and others often occur. Moreover, placing the enforcement of a security policy in the browser, and thus in the hands of end users, opens up many opportunities for security measures to be defeated. In addition, many push vendors are relatively new startups that do not always understand mission-critical software and security needs. Such circumstances only exacerbate the security predicament.

While some people might opine that Java is too insecure to be used in production environments and that it should be completely avoided, doing so creates the situation where a tremendous computing opportunity is lost. While the company that decides to bypass Java relieves itself of Java security worries, that means that they also relinquish the myriad benefits that Java affords. In addition, a significant number of cutting-edge Internet-based activities, such as E-commerce, online trading, banking, and more, are all written in Java. Also, many firewall and router vendors are writing their management front-end application in Java. When a company cuts itself off from Java, it may likely cut itself off from the next generation of computing technology.

Push-based programs are powerful and flexible Web tools, and where the Web is directed, but these programs, by their nature, are inherently buggy and untrustworthy. Now take a look at the Java security model.

A QUICK INTRODUCTION TO THE JAVA PROGRAMMING LANGUAGE

The essence of Java is to be a portable and robust programming language for development of write-once programs. Java was created to alleviate the quandary of writing the same applications for numerous platforms that many large organizations faced in developing applications for large heterogeneous networks. To achieve this, the Java compiler generates class files, which have an architecturally neutral, binary intermediate format. Within the class file are Java bytecodes, which are implementations for each of the class's methods, written in the instruction set of a virtual machine. The class file format has no dependencies on byte-ordering, pointer size, or the underlying operating system, which allows it to be platform independent. The bytecodes are run via the runtime system, which is an emulator for the virtual machine's instruction set. It is these same bytecodes that enable Java to be run on any platform. Finally, two significant advantages that increase Java's security is that it is a well-defined and openly specified language.

While many systems subscribe to the *security through obscurity* model, Java achieves a significant level of security through being published. Anyone can download the complete set of Java source code and examine it for themselves. In addition, numerous technical security groups and universities have done their own audits of Java security.

The second area where Java security is increased is through its architectural definitions. Java requires that all primitive types in the language are guaranteed to be a specific size and that all operations defined must be performed in a specified order. This ensures that two correct Java compilers will never give different results for execution of a program, as opposed to other programming languages in which the sizes of the primitive types are machine- and compiler-dependent, and the order of execution is undefined except in a few specific cases.

OVERVIEW OF THE JAVA SECURITY MODEL

The Java applet[1] security model introduced with the 1.0 release of Java SDK considers any Java code running in a browser from a remote source to be untrusted. The model anticipates many potential attacks, such as producing Java code with a malicious compiler (one that ignores any protection boundaries), tampering with the code in transit, etc. The goal of the Java security model is to run an applet under a set of constraints (typically referred to as a sandbox) that ensures the following:

- No information on the user's machine, whether on a hard disk or stored in a network service, is accessible to the applet.

- The applet can only communicate with machines that are considered to be as trusted as itself. Typically, this is implemented by only allowing the applet to connect back to its source.
- The applet cannot permanently affect the system in any way, such as writing any information to the user's machine or erasing any information.

From a technical perspective, this sandbox is implemented by a layer of modules that operate at different levels.

Language Layer

The language layer operates at the lowest layer of the Java language model and has certain features that facilitate the implementation of the security model at the higher levels.

Memory Protection. Java code cannot write beyond array boundaries or otherwise corrupt memory.

Access Protection. Unlike C++, Java enforces language-level access controls such as private classes or methods.

Bytecode Verifier. When a Java applet is compiled, it is compiled all the way down to the platform-independent Java bytecode where the code is verified before it is allowed to run. The function of bytecode verification is to ensure that the applet operates according to the rules set down by Java and ensures that untrusted code is snared before it can be executed.

While the language restrictions are implemented by any legal Java compiler, there is still the possibility that a malicious entity could craft its own bytecode or use a compromised compiler. To deal with this possibility, Sun Microsystems architected the Java interpreter to run any applet bytecode against a verifier program that scans the bytecode for illegal sequences. Some of the checks performed by the verifier are done statically before the applet is started. However, because the applet can dynamically load more code as it is running, the verifier also implements some checks at runtime.

The bytecode verifier is the mechanism that ensures that Java class files conform to the rules of the Java application. While not all files are subject to bytecode verification, those that are have their memory boundaries enforced by the bytecode verifier.

Security Manager. The function of the Java security manager is to restrict the ways in which an applet uses the available interfaces, and the bulk of Java's security resources are implemented via the security manager.

At the highest level, the security manager implements an additional set of checks. The security manager is the primary interface between the core

Java API and the operating system and has the responsibility for allowing or denying access to the system resources it controls.

This security manager can be customized or subclassed, which allows it to refine or change the default security policy. Changing the security manager at runtime is disallowed because an applet could possibly discover a way to install its own bogus security manager. All of the Java class libraries that deal with the file system or the network call the security manager to ensure that accesses are controlled.

From a technology perspective, the security manager is a single interface module that performs the runtime checks on potentially dangerous methods that an applet could attempt to execute.

Security Package. The security package is the mechanism that allows for the authentication of signed Java classes. Those are the classes that are specified in the *java.security* package.

Signed applets were introduced in version 1.1 of the Java SDK and specifically are collections of class files and their supporting files that are signed with a digital signature.

The way in which a signed applet operates is that a software developer obtains a certificate from a certificate authority (CA) and uses that certificate to sign their applications. When an end user browses a Web page the developer has signed, the browser informs the end user who signed the applet and allows the user to determine if he wants to run that applet.

Key Database. The key database works with the security manager to manage the keys used by the security manager to control access via digital signatures.

The Java Standard Applet Security Policy

The exact set of policies that are enforced by Java in a specific environment can be modified by creating a custom version of the security manager class. However, there is a standard policy that has been defined by Sun and is implemented by all Web browsers that implement Java applets. The standard policy basically states[2]:

- An applet can only connect back to its source. This means, for example, that if the applet source is outside a company firewall, the applet is only allowed to talk to a machine that is also outside the firewall.
- An applet cannot query system properties because these properties could hold important information that could be used to compromise the system or invade the user's privacy.
- An applet cannot load native libraries because native code cannot be restricted by the Java security model.

- An applet cannot add classes to system packages because it might violate some access-control restrictions.
- An applet cannot listen on socket connections. This means that an applet can connect to a network service (on its source machine), but it cannot accept connections from other machines.
- An applet cannot start another program on the client work station. This way, an applet cannot then spawn some other program or rogue process on the work station. From a programming perspective, an applet is not allowed to manipulate threads outside its own thread group.
- An applet cannot read or write to any files on the user's machine.
- An applet can only add threads to its own thread group.

Java Language Security

This is not the place to detail the security features of the Java programming language, but a few of its most significant security-based features include the following:

Lack of Pointer Arithmetic. Java security is extended through lack of pointer arithmetic since Java programs do not use explicit pointers. Pointers are simply memory locations in applications. Consequently, no one can program (either maliciously or accidentally) a forged pointer to memory. The mishandling of pointers is probably one of the largest sources of bugs in most programming languages. To get around the lack of pointers, all references to methods and instance variables in the Java class file are via symbolic names.

Garbage Collection. Java garbage collection is the process by which Java deallocates memory that it no longer needs. Most languages such as C and C++ simply allocate and deallocate memory on the fly. The use of garbage collection requires Java to keep track of its memory usage and to ensure that all objects are properly referenced. When objects in memory are no longer needed, the memory they use is automatically freed by the garbage collector so that it can be used for other applets. The Java garbage collection engine is a multithreaded application that runs in the background and complements the lack of memory pointers in that they prevent problems associated with bad pointers.

Compiler Checks. The Java compiler checks that all programming calls are legitimate.

E-Commerce and Java

Sun Microsystems has entered the E-commerce arena in a big way and envisions having Java at the forefront of E-commerce. To assist in that attempt, Sun has created a Java E-commerce architecture to promote it.

Components of the architecture are the Java Wallet, Commerce Client, Commerce API, and Commerce JavaBeans.

The Java Wallet is a family of products written in Java that enable secure electronic commerce operations. The Java Wallet combines the Java Commerce Client, Commerce JavaBeans components, the gateway security model, and the Java Commerce Messages to create a single platform for E-commerce. It should be noted that the components can be used independently of one another. The Java wallet is written in Java; thus, it can run in any Java-capable browser.

THREATS

In *Java Security: Hostile Applets, Holes & Antidotes,* McGraw and Felten describe four classes of threats that Java is susceptible to:

- System modification: This is the most severe class of threats where an applet can significantly damage the system on which it runs. While this threat is the most severe, the defenses Java has to defend against it are extremely strong.
- Invasion of privacy: This is the type of attack where private information about host, file, or user is disclosed. Java defends against this type of attack rather well because it monitors file access and applets can only write back to the channel in which they were originally opened.
- Denial of service: Denial-of-service attacks are written to deny users legitimate access to system resources. Denial-of-service attacks take many forms, but are primarily applications or malicious applets that take more processes or memory allocation area than they should use, such as filling up a file system or allocating all of a system's memory. Denial-of-service attacks are the most commonly encountered Java security concern and, unfortunately, Java has a weak defense against it.
- Antagonism: An antagonistic threat is one in which the applet simply annoys the user, such as by playing an unwanted sound file or displaying an undesired image. Many antagonistic attacks are simply programming errors. Most denial-of-service attacks can be classified as antagonistic threats, but the ones defined here are less annoying than their denial-of-service counterpart. Like their counterpart, Java has a weak defense against them.

USING JAVA SECURELY

By following some generic guidelines, and then customizing those guidelines for an environment's unique needs, Java can be safely used in most environments. Java security, like most computer security, is built on a lot of common sense. A few of the major issues are:

- Make sure that your browser is up to date: Many Java vulnerabilities have originated in browser design flaws. Staying with a relatively new release of a browser hopefully ensures that discovered security flaws have been ameliorated.
- Stay on top of security alerts: Keep track of advisories from CERT (www.cert.org), CIAC (www.ciac.llnl.gov), and the appropriate browser vendor.
- Think before you visit a Web site: If visiting www.whitehouse.gov, chances of downloading a hostile Java applet are much less than if visiting www.hackers.subterfuge.org. The bottom line, use your head when surfing the Web.
- Know your risks: Every company must assess its risks before it can really understand how to deal with the security risks involved with Java. If the risk of Java is too great (i.e., nuclear control centers), do not use Java; if the risks are more minimal (i.e., home), one can pretty much use Java with ease.

THIRD-PARTY SOFTWARE PROTECTION

There are numerous third-party software tools available to further secure Java and add protection against the potential security threats that Java can produce. Such products are a necessity for running push and active content applications.

- Finjan — SurfinGate & SurfinGate (www.finjan.com)
- eSafe Technologies — eSafe Protect (www.esafe.com)
- Digitivity — Cage (www.digitivity.com)
- Security7 — SafeGate (www.security7.com)

CONCLUSIONS ABOUT JAVA SECURITY

Java has an impressive security architecture and foundation, but one cannot rely on the sandbox model exclusively. Combined with poorly written PERL and CGI scripts, browser vulnerabilities, operating system holes, Web server holes, and more, there are plenty of potential openings in which a malicious or poorly written application could wreak havoc.

Knowing what one's risks are, combined with an understanding of Java's vulnerabilities and active protection of content, will prove that *Java security* is not an oxymoron.

Notes

1. An applet is defined as a Java program that is run from inside a Web browser. The html page loaded into the Web browser contains an <applet> tag, which tells the browser where to find the Java .class files. For example, the URL http://cnn.com/TECH/computing/JavaNews.html starts a Java applet in the browser windows since the source code contains the entry <applet code=Ticker.class>.

2. This article cannot list all of the details of the standard policy. For a thorough listing, view the Java SDK documentation set.

References

Frequently Asked Questions — Java Security, http://java.sun.com/sfaq/index.html.
Under Lock and Key: Java Security for the Networked Enterprise, http://java.sun.com/features/1998/01/security.html.
The Java Commerce FAQ, http://java.sun.com/products/commerce/faq.html.
The Gateway Security Model in the Java Commerce Client, http://java.sun.com/products/commerce/docs/whitepapers/security/gateway.pdf.
Low Level Security in Java by Frank Yellin, http://www.javasoft.com/sfaq/verifier.html

Ben Rothke, CISSP, is a New Jersey-based consultant with the Information Security Services group of Ernst & Young, L.L.P. He can be reached via e-mail at bennett.rothke@ey.com.

Domain 8
Business Continuity Planning and Disaster Recovery Planning

Business continuity and disaster recovery are crucial components used to ensure that systems critical to the operation of the organization are available when needed. We address both of these areas in this domain. The first chapter provides some guidance on how to improve the difficult process of business continuity planning. Perhaps employing the recommended improvements will result in a more cost-effective operation. The second chapter addresses the issues, often overlooked, that enable an organization to quickly and efficiently restore operations to a normal state after a prolonged outage. Fast reaction from professional restoration teams can save important documents, files, and equipment.

Domain 8.1
Business Continuity Planning

Chapter 26
Reengineering the Business Continuity Planning Process

Carl B. Jackson

The failure of organizations to accurately measure the contributions of the BCP process to its overall success has led to the downward spiraling cycle of the total business continuity program. The recurring downward spin or decomposition includes planning, testing, maintenance, decline → re-planning, testing, maintenance, decline → re-planning, testing, maintenance, decline, etc. The most recent (1998) *Contingency Planning and Management/Ernst and Young LLP Business Continuity Planning Survey*[1] clearly supports this observation. According to the latest survey results, 63 percent of the respondents ranked BCP as being either *extremely important* or *very important* to senior management. This study indicates that decision makers have a high level of awareness regarding the importance of BCP. These findings contrast with other survey results which illustrate that execution and follow-through of the BCP mission is often lacking. These statistics include:

1. 82 percent of the respondents do not measure the cost/benefit of their BCP programs;
2. Only 27 percent of the respondents' organizations train their people on how to execute the BCP;
3. 33 percent of the organizations responding do not test their BCPs;
4. Only 3.6 percent of the organizations' base pay increases for BCP personnel on the success of the BCP program.

0-8493-9829-0/00/$0.00+$.50
© 2000 by CRC Press LLC

Business Continuity Planning Measurements

These results also suggest a disconnect between top management's perceptions of BCP objectives and the manner in which they measure its value. In the past, BCP effectiveness was usually measured in terms of a pass/fail grade on a mainframe recovery test or on the perceived benefits of backup sites and redundant telecommunications capabilities weighed against the expense for these capabilities. The trouble with these types of metrics is that they only measure BCP direct costs and/or indirect perceptions as to whether a test was effectively executed. These metrics do not indicate whether a test validates the appropriate infrastructure elements or even whether it is thorough enough to test a component until it fails, thereby extending the reach and usefulness of the test scenario.

So, one might inquire as to what the correct measures to use are. While financial measurements do constitute *one* measure of the BCP process, others measure the BCP's contribution to the organization in terms of quality and effectiveness, which are not strictly weighed in monetary terms. The contributions that a well-run BCP Process can make to an organization include:

1. Sustaining growth and innovation;
2. Enhancing customer satisfaction;
3. Providing for people needs;
4. Improving overall mission-critical process quality; and
5. Providing for practical financial metrics.

Each of these measurements is discussed later in this chapter.

A RECIPE FOR RADICAL CHANGE: BCP PROCESS IMPROVEMENT

During the 1970s and 1980s experts in organizational management efficiency began introducing *performance process improvement disciplines*. These process improvement disciplines have been slowly adopted across many industries and companies for improvement of *general manufacturing* and *administrative business processes*. The basis of these and other improvement efforts was the concept that an organization's *processes* (Process — see Definitions in Exhibit 26.1) constituted the organization's fundamental lifeblood and, if made more effective and efficient, could dramatically decrease errors and increase organizational productivity.

An organization's processes are a series of successive activities, and when they are executed in the aggregate, they constitute the foundation of the organization's mission. These processes are intertwined throughout the organization's infrastructure (individual business units, divisions, plants, etc.) and are tied to the organization's supporting structures (data processing, communications networks, physical facilities, people, etc.).

Activities — Activities are things that go on within a process or sub-process. They are usually performed by units of one (one person or one department). An activity is usually documented in an instruction. The instruction should document the tasks that make up the activity.

Benchmarking — Benchmarking is a systematic way to identify, understand, and creatively evolve superior products, services, designs, equipment, processes, and practices to improve the organization's real performance by studying how other organizations are performing the same or similar operations.

Business Process Improvement (BPI) — Business Process Improvement is a methodology that is designed to bring about self-function improvements in administrative and support processes using approaches such as FAST, process benchmarking, process redesign, and process reengineering.

Comparative Analysis — Comparative Analysis is the act of comparing a set of measurements to another set of measurements for similar items.

Enabler — An enabler is a technical or organizational facility/resource that makes it possible to perform a task, activity, or process. Examples of technical enablers are personal computers, copying equipment, decentralized data processing, voice response, etc. Examples of organizational enablers are enhancement, self-management, communications, education, etc.

FAST — Fast Analysis Solution Technique is a breakthrough approach that focuses a group's attention on a single process for a one- or two-day meeting to define how the group can improve the process over the next 90 days. Before the end of the meeting, management approves or rejects the proposed improvements.

Future State Solution — Future State Solution is a combination of corrective actions and changes that can be applied to the item (process) under study to increase its value to its stakeholders.

Information — Information is data that has been analyzed, shared, and understood.

Major Processes — A major process is a process that usually involves more than one function within the organization structure, and its operation has a significant impact on the way the organization functions. When a major process is too complex to be flowcharted at the activity level, it is often divided into sub-processes.

Organization — An organization is any group, company, corporation, division, department, plant, or sales office.

Process — A process is a logical, related, sequential (connected) set of activities that takes an input from a supplier, adds value to it, and produces an output to a customer.

Sub-process — A sub-process is a portion of a major process that accomplishes a specific objective in support of the major process.

System — A system is an assembly of components (hardware, software, procedures, human functions, and other resources) united by some form of regulated interaction to form an organized whole. It is a group of related processes that may or may not be connected.

Tasks — Tasks are individual elements and/or subsets of an activity. Normally, these tasks are related to how an item performs a specific assignment.

Exhibit 26.1. Definitions[5]

A key concept of the **Process Improvement and Reengineering** movement revolves around identification of process enablers and barriers (see Definitions in Exhibit 26.1). These enablers and barriers take many forms (people, technology, facilities, etc.) and must be understood and taken into consideration when introducing radical change into the organization.

The preceding narration provides the backdrop for the idea of focusing on business continuity planning not as a **project**, but as a **continuous process** that must be designed to support the other mission-critical processes of the organization. Therefore, the idea was born of adopting a continuous process approach to BCP, along with understanding and addressing the people, technology, facility, etc., enablers and barriers. This constitutes a *significant* or even *radical change* in thinking from the manner in which we have traditionally viewed and executed recovery planning. An example of a BCP process is presented in Exhibit 26.2.

Radical Changes Mandated

High management awareness and low BCP execution effectiveness, coupled with the lack of consistent and meaningful BCP measurements, call for radical changes in the manner in which we execute recovery planning responsibilities. The techniques used to develop mainframe-oriented disaster recovery (DR) plans of the '70s and '80s consisted of six distinct stages which required the recovery planner to:

1. Establish a project team and a supporting infrastructure to develop the plans;
2. Conduct a threat or risk management review to identify likely threat scenarios to be addressed in the recovery plans;
3. Conduct a business impact analysis (BIA) to understand time-critical applications/networks and determine maximum-tolerable-downtimes;
4. Select an appropriate recovery alternative that effectively addresses the recovery priorities and time-frames mandated by the BIA;
5. Document the recovery plans; and
6. Establish and adopt an ongoing testing and maintenance strategy.

Shortcomings of the Traditional Disaster Recovery Planning Approach

This approach worked well when disaster recovery of *glass house* mainframe infrastructures were the norm. It even worked fairly well when it came to integrating the evolving distributed/client–server systems into the overall recovery planning infrastructure. However, when organizations became concerned with **business unit** recovery planning, the traditional DR methodology was ineffective in designing and implementing business

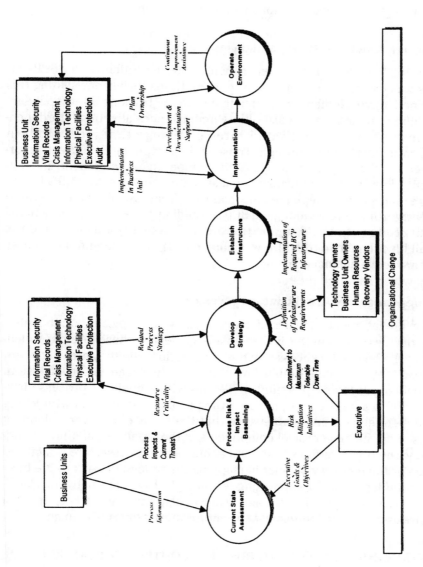

Exhibit 26.2. The BCP Process

unit/function recovery plans. Of primary concern when attempting to implement enterprise-wide recovery plans was the issue of **functional interdependencies**. Recovery planners became obsessed with identification of interdependencies between business units and functions, and the interdependencies between business units and the technological services supporting time-critical functions within these business units.

Losing Track of the Interdependencies

The ability to keep track of departmental interdependencies for BCP purposes was extremely difficult, and most methods for accomplishing this were ineffective. Numerous circumstances made tracking interdependencies difficult to achieve consistently. Circumstances affecting interdependencies revolve around rapid rates of change that most modern organizations are going through. These include reorganization/restructuring, personnel relocation, changes in the competitive environment, and outsourcing. Every time an organizational structure changes, the BCPs had to change, and the interdependencies had to be reassessed. The more rapid the change, the more daunting the BCP reshuffling. Because many functional interdependencies could not be tracked, BCP integrity was lost, and the overall functionality of the BCP was impaired. There seemed to be no easy answers to this dilemma.

Interdependencies Are Business Processes

Why are interdependencies of concern and what, typically, are the interdependencies? The answer is that, to a large degree, these interdependencies are the **business processes** of the organization, and they are of concern because they must function in order to fulfill the organization's mission. Approaching recovery planning challenges with a business process viewpoint can, to a large extent, mitigate the problems associated with losing interdependencies, and also ensure that the focus of recovery planning efforts is on the most crucial components of the organization. Understanding how the organization's time-critical business processes are structured will assist the recovery planner in mapping the processes back to the business units/departments, supporting technological systems, networks, facilities, vital records, people, etc., and also will help the planner keep track of the processes during reorganizations and/or during times of change.

THE PROCESS APPROACH TO BUSINESS CONTINUITY PLANNING

Traditional approaches to mainframe focused disaster recovery planning emphasized the need to recover the organization's technological and communications platforms. Today, many companies have shifted away from technology recovery and toward continuity of prioritized business processes and the development of specific business process recovery plans. Many large corporations use the process reengineering/improvement disciplines to increase overall organizational productivity. BCP itself should also be viewed as such a process. The following figure provides a graphical representation of how the enterprise-wide BCP Process framework (see Exhibit 26.3) should look:

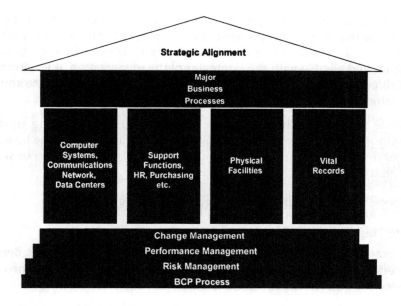

Exhibit 26.3. The BCP Process Framework

At the base or foundation of the business continuity planning structure are the business continuity planning support sub-processes. These sub-processes are relevant and necessary to ensure that:

- business continuity plans are complete
- plans address all business issues
- business process owners take responsibility for their area's BCP
- staff are trained and capable of executing the recovery plans effectively

The four pillars are the core infrastructure and service elements required to effectively support the business processes of the organization.

- Basic infrastructure includes supporting resources/services (i.e., technological platforms, voice and data communications networks, etc.).

- Support functions include HR, Purchasing, etc., support mechanisms and external service providers (the virtual organization).
- Facilities refer to locations where the business may be carried out.
- Vital records are those records, manual and electronic, that are used to support time-critical business processes in the relevant business units, in addition to the traditional legal obligations pertaining to government and other statutory record-keeping requirements.

Resting on the four supporting pillars are the key business processes which are required to keep the organization operating effectively after a disruption. The roof of the structure shows all these elements brought together and aligned with the strategies of the organization. It is within the overall context of the business strategies that BCP solutions are sought, evaluated, and prioritized.

While the base, columns, and roof of the continuity planning strategy are important and provide the strength of the structure, it is the business processes they support that determine the effectiveness of the business continuity plan.

MOVING TO A BCP PROCESS IMPROVEMENT ENVIRONMENT

Route Map Profile and High-Level BCP Process Approach

A practical, high-level approach to *BCP Process Improvement* is demonstrated by breaking down the BCP process into individual sub-process components, as shown in Exhibit 26.4.

While this route map appears complex, it goes far beyond the BCP approaches which have been used in traditional DR planning methodologies, including:

- Business Impact Assessment
- Strategy Selection
- Plan Development, Testing, and Maintenance

Within this route map, it is important to note that:

- Provision is made for the identification and initiation of immediate "quick hits," which are BCP-related recommendations that require urgent and immediate attention to provide protection in the short term) that can jump-start BCP initiatives. These initiatives can be effectively addressed without waiting until the end of the BCP process implementation project;
- Provision is made for introduction of Organizational Change Management components which will help facilitate deployment of the BCP Process;
- Emphasis is placed on Co-development of recovery strategies;

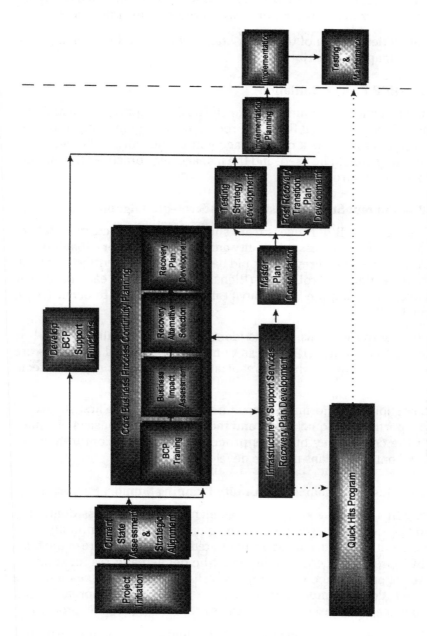

Exhibit 26.4. Sub-Process Components of BCP

- Development of business continuity plans must be business-process driven; and
- Development of process-oriented recovery plans independently for each time-critical business process is critical to overall success.

The activities in each of the major stages of the BCP Process Improvement route-map are described below.

Stage 1 — BCP Process Initiation

During this stage, the foundation for the business continuity planning is established by developing the BCP Process plan and obtaining approval. The BCP Process plan is a detailed account of the work to be done, the resources that should be used, and the management practices that should be followed to control it.

Stage 2 — Current State Assessment and Strategic Alignment

In this stage the BCP Process team should analyze the current state of the organization's Business Continuity and Disaster Recover capabilities. A threat/risk management review should be conducted to identify threat categories, the estimated probability (High, Medium, Low) of each particular threat occurring, and the likely impact if the threat were to occur (High, Medium, Low).

Another activity of this stage is identifying strategic alignments. It is imperative that whatever Business Continuity Plans and strategies are developed are aligned with the organization's overall business and technology plans.

Two portfolios of information result from this stage. The first stage consists of a portfolio of "quick hits," and the second stage consists of a portfolio of the core or key business processes for which comprehensive Business Continuity Plans must be developed.

Stage 3 — Develop Business Continuity Planning Support Processes

During this stage the key support elements of the Business Continuity Planning process are developed. To ensure that Business Continuity Planning is institutionalized, it must be integrated into the structure of the business. BCP program accountability must be defined and responsibilities allocated. Performance measurement criteria and processes must be developed. Policies and procedures must define how the organization plans to manage and execute the business continuity planning process.

A risk management framework should be developed that monitors business continuity risk factors and ensures that appropriate risk management and contingency action plans are maintained. Change management plans should also be developed that focus on how business and technical changes are incorporated into the Business Continuity Planning process.

Core Business Process Continuity Planning. The following four stages that make up this phase should be repeated for each *core business process* identified during the Current State Analysis.

Stage 4 — Business Continuity Planning Training

Business Process Owners and staff participating in this BCP Process should be trained in the fundamentals of Business Continuity Planning and receive basic instruction in:

- Conducting Business Impact Assessments, and
- Recovery Plan Development.

The use of a knowledgeable and experienced person(s) from each of the organization's departments/business processes is vital to the success of this process. This should facilitate the preparation of viable continuity plans and procedures for each critical business process. It is also important to have these people involved during all stages of planning because they are most likely to be called upon to execute the user aspects of the continuity plan in the event of disruption.

Stage 5 — Business Impact Assessment

The purpose of the Business Impact Assessment stage is to understand the impact of a loss of business functionality due to an interruption of computing and/or infrastructure support services. Through an interview and information-gathering process these impacts should be measured quantitatively (financially) and qualitatively (operationally), such as confidence in the ability to deliver and track service to member institutions. The goal of the business assessment impact stage is twofold.

- *Resource Priorities for Recovery* — each business process is identified and business impact information is gathered. Attention is then focused on those "time-critical business processes" requiring recovery within the maximum tolerable downtime (MTD), while placing non-time-critical business processes at a lower priority for recovery. Resource requirements for continuity of critical processes are determined.
- *Maximum-Tolerable Downtime* — The BIA helps to estimate the longest period of time a business process can remain interrupted before it risks its ability to ever adequately recover. Those business processes that require continuity within shorter time periods are defined as "time-critical," with the assumption they should receive priority attention following a disruption.

Once the analysis is complete, the BCP Process team should ensure that business units or support services management agree with the results. These results should then be formalized and presented to the responsible senior executive authority with recommendations and a request for authorization to proceed to the next BCP Process stage.

Stage 6 — Recovery Alternative Selection

Once the BIA is completed, the BCP Process team should identify available continuity strategy alternatives. Risk management options are considered during the strategy selection process, and issues such as risk avoidance, risk limitation, risk sharing, and risk transfer are analyzed. Criteria for evaluating available continuity strategies are determined. The primary objective of this stage is the development of a recovery alternatives matrix with an appropriate business case presented for the recommended continuity strategy.

Stage 7 — Recovery Plan Development

This stage involves documenting the continuity strategies that were determined in the steps above and organizing the information in a convenient format that can be used following a business interruption. The plans should address business process recovery team structures, emergency control center location(s), inventory information (i.e., people, equipment, documentation, supplies, hardware/software, vendors, critical applications, data processing reports needed, communications capabilities required, vital records, etc.), and high-level procedures to be followed. Business process managers and staff are responsible for providing additional detailed procedures, as required, to the continuity plan.

Vital records backup, storage strategies and plans are also reviewed during this stage.

Stage 8 — Infrastructure and Support Services Continuity Plan Development

During this stage, continuity plans are developed for the key support services and complex infrastructure services. The key drivers of the development of these plans are the infrastructure and service requirements identified and validated during the development of the business process recovery plans.

Stage 9 — Master Plan Consolidation

During this stage the individual Core Business Process Recovery Plans and the Infrastructure and Support Services Continuity Plans are consolidated and integrated into the organization's overall Crisis Management/

Continuity Plan. This acts as the central control and launch point in the event of a major service interruption or disaster. During the development of the overall Crisis Management/Continuity Plan, certain "global" issues are considered and planned for (e.g., Damage Assessment and Disaster Declaration Procedures, location of emergency control centers, etc.).

Stage 10 — Testing Strategy Development

During this stage, an appropriate Testing Strategy is developed, ensuring the business continuity capability is periodically tested and evaluated. Testing strategies generally include definition of test scope and objectives, measurement criteria, test scripts, test schedules, post-mortem reviews, and test reporting.

Stage 11 — Post Recovery Transition Plan Development

After an interruption occurs and the business continuity plan is implemented, organizations find themselves operating in a non-normal mode and environment with no plans for resumption of normal operating procedures. During this BCP Process stage, a high-level plan is developed to facilitate the transition back to a normal operating environment as quickly and efficiently as possible.

Stage 12 — Implementation Planning

During this stage, comprehensive implementation plans are developed for the Core Business Process Recovery Plans and Infrastructure and Support Services Recovery Plans that have been integrated into the overall Crisis Management/Contingency Plan. Implementation plans include the acquisition and installation of facilities and resources required to facilitate the continuity strategy.

Stage 13 — Quick Hits Program

The quick hits program identifies critical business continuity initiatives that require addressing in the short term in order to provide a level of comfort. This program enables organizations to provide partial services in the event of major service disruption or disaster. Solutions developed during this phase may be temporary or stop-gap solutions, until the enterprise-wide business continuity planning process is fully functional.

Stage 14 — Implementation and Testing and Maintenance Stages

These stages should become integral parts of the organization's business continuity program. The regular maintenance and testing of the business continuity plans and strategy help to ensure that:

- The continuity strategy stays viable;
- Plan documentation is current and accurate; and
- Team leaders are trained in the execution of continuity plan procedures.

HOW DO WE GET THERE? THE CONCEPT OF THE BCP VALUE JOURNEY

The **BCP Value Journey** is a helpful mechanism for co-development of BCP expectations by the organization's top management group and those responsible for recovery planning. In order to achieve a successful and measurable recovery planning process, the following checkpoints along the *BCP Value Journey* should be considered and agreed upon. The checkpoints include:

- *Defining Success* — Define what a successful BCP implementation will look like. What is the Future State?
- *Aligning the BCP with Business Strategy* — Challenge objectives to ensure that the BCP effort has a business-centric focus.
- *Charting an Improvement Strategy* — Benchmark where the organization and the organization's peers are, the organization's goals based upon their present position as compared to their peers, and which critical initiatives will help the organization achieve its goals.
- *Becoming an Accelerator* — Accelerate the implementation of the organization's BCP strategies and processes. In today's environment, fast beats slow, and speed is a critical success factor for most companies.
- *Creating a Winning Team* — Build an internal/external team that can help lead the company through BCP assessment, development, and implementation.
- *Assessing Business Needs* — Assess time-critical business processes' dependence on the supporting infrastructure.
- *Documenting the Plans* — Develop continuity plans that focus on assuring that time-critical business processes will be available.
- *Enabling the People* — Implement mechanisms that can help to enable rapid reaction and recovery in times of emergency, such as training programs, a clear organizational structure, and a detailed leadership and management plan.
- *Completing the Organization's BCP Strategy* — Position the organization to complete the operational and personnel-related milestones necessary to ensure success.
- *Delivering Value* — Focus on achieving the organization's goals while also envisioning the future and handling all organizational changes which occur simultaneously.
- *Renewing/Recreating* — Challenge the new BCP process structure and organizational management to continue to adapt and meet the challenges of demonstrating availability and recoverability.

The Value Journey Facilitates Meaningful Dialogue

This *Value Journey* technique for raising the awareness level of management helps to both facilitate meaningful discussions about the BCP Process and to ensure that the resulting BCP strategies truly add *value*. As will be discussed later, this value-added concept will also provide additional metrics by which the success of the overall BCP process can be measured.

THE NEED FOR ORGANIZATIONAL CHANGE MANAGEMENT

In addition to the approaches of *BCP Process Improvement*, and the *BCP Value Journey* mentioned above, the need to introduce people-oriented *Organizational Change Management* (OCM) concepts becomes an important component in implementing a successful BCP process.

Mr. H. James Harrington, et al., in their book *Business Process Improvement Workbook*,[2] point out that applying process improvement approaches can often cause trouble unless the organization manages the change process. They state that, "Approaches like reengineering only succeed if we challenge and change our paradigms and our organization's culture. It is a fallacy to think that you can change the processes without changing the behavior patterns or the people who are responsible for operating these processes."[3]

Organizational change management concepts, including the identification of people enablers and barriers and the design of appropriate implementation plans which change behavior patterns, play an important role in shifting the BCP project approach to one of *BCP Process Improvement*. The authors also point out that, "There are a number of tools and techniques that are effective in managing the change process, such as pain management, change mapping, and synergy. The important thing is that every *BPI* (Business Process Improvement) program must have a very comprehensive change management plan built into it, and this plan must be effectively implemented."[4]

Therefore, it is incumbent on the recovery planner to ensure that, as the concept of the BCP Process evolves within the organization, appropriate OCM techniques are considered and included as an integral component of the overall deployment effort.

HOW DO WE MEASURE SUCCESS? BALANCED SCORECARD CONCEPT

A complement to the *BCP Process Improvement* approach is the establishment of meaningful measures or metrics that the organization can use to weigh the success of the overall BCP process. Traditional measures include:

- How much money is spent on hotsites?
- How many people are devoted to BCP activities?
- Was the hotsite test a success?

Instead, the focus should be on measuring the **BCP Process** contribution to achieving the overall goals of the organization. This focus helps us to:

- Identify agreed-upon BCP development milestones
- Establish a baseline for execution
- Validate BCP Process delivery
- Establish a foundation for management satisfaction in order to successfully manage expectations

The *BCP Balanced Scorecard* includes a definition of the:

- Value Statement
- Value Proposition
- Metrics/Assumptions on reduction of BCP risk
- Implementation Protocols
- Validation Methods

Exhibit 26.5 illustrates the *Balanced Scorecard* concept and shows examples of the types of metrics that can be developed to measure the success of the implemented BCP Process. Included in this *Balance Scorecard* approach are the new metrics upon which the BCP Process will be measured.

Following this *Balanced Scorecard* approach, the organization should define what the *Future State* of the BCP Process should look like (see the preceding *BCP Value Journey* discussion). This *Future State* definition should be co-developed by the organization's top management and those responsible for development of the BCP Process infrastructure. Once the *Future State* is defined, then the BCP Process development group can outline the BCP Process implementation critical success factors in the areas of:

- Growth and innovation
- Customer satisfaction
- People
- Process quality
- Financial state

These measures must be uniquely developed based upon the specific organization's culture and environment.

SUMMARY

The failure of organizations to measure the success of their BCP implementations has led to an endless cycle of plan development and decline. The primary reason for this is that a meaningful set of BCP measurements

Balanced Scorecard

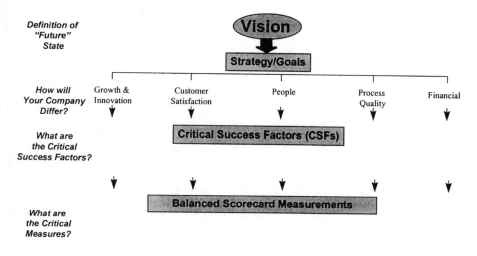

Exhibit 26.5. The Balanced Scorecard Concept

---

has not been adapted to fit the organization's future state goals. Because these measurements are lacking, expectations of both top management and those responsible for BCP often go unfulfilled. Statistics gathered in the *Contingency Planning and Management/Ernst and Young LLP Business Continuity Planning Survey* support this assertion. Based on this, a radical change in the manner in which organizations undertake BCP implementation is necessary. This change should include adapting and utilizing the *Business Process Improvement* (BPI) approach for BCP. This BPI approach has been implemented successfully at many *Fortune 1000* companies over the past 20 years. Defining BCP as a process, applying the concepts of the *BCP Value Journey*, expanding BCP measurements utilizing the *BCP Balanced Scorecard*, and exercising the *Organizational Change Management* (OCM) concepts will facilitate a radically different approach to BCP.

References

1. *Contingency Planning and Management*, April 1998. (The survey was conducted in the U.S. and consisted of 482 respondents drawn from *Contingency Planning and Management* magazine's domestic subscription list. Industries represented by respondents include "financial/banking" [20%]; "manufacturing/industrial" [14%]; and "government" [10%]).
2. H. James Harrington, Erick K. C. Esseling, Harm Van Nimwegen, *Business Process Improvement Workbook*, McGraw-Hill, 1997.
3. Harrington, p 18.
4. Harrington, p 19.
5. Harrington, pp. 1-20.

Domain 8.2
Disaster Recovery Planning

Chapter 27
Restoration Component of Business Continuity Planning

John Dorf and Marty Johnson

Everyone understands the importance of developing a Business Continuity Plan (BCP) to ensure the timely recovery of mission-critical business processes following a damaging event. There are two objectives, however, and often, the second objective is overlooked. That is: Return to normal operations as soon as possible. The reason for the urgency to return to normal operations is that backup and work-around procedures are certainly not "business as usual." Backup capabilities, whether it is due to the loss of primary premises or primary data, probably only include those business activities that are critical to getting by. The longer a company must operate in this mode, the more difficult the catch-up will be. There are several steps that can be taken in advance to prepare for the timely, efficient return to normalization. The purpose of this chapter is to discuss the steps and resources to ensure total recovery. In addition, it is important to understand how to handle damaged equipment and media in order to minimize the loss associated with a disaster.

Restoration includes the following:

1. Handling damaged equipment and media in order to minimize the loss
2. Salvaging hard copy and electronic media
3. Performing damage assessment and the resulting disposition of damaged facilities and equipment
4. Determining and procuring appropriate property insurance

0-8493-9829-0/00/$0.00+$.50
© 2000 by CRC Press LLC

5. Identifying internal and external resources to perform restoration activities

6. Developing, maintaining, and testing your restoration plan

This chapter will help you understand the issues related to each of these items and be a resource for developing the necessary information for inclusion in your BCP program.

The more time that passes before the salvation of hard copy and electronic media, the greater the chance that the data or archival records will be permanently lost. However, if you rush to handle, move, dry, etc., media and do not do so in the correct manner, you may worsen the situation. Therefore, to ensure minimizing the damage you must act quickly and correctly to recover data and restore documents. This also applies to the facilities and infrastructure damage.

Having telephone numbers for restoration companies is not enough. The primary reason is in the event of a regional problem like flooding, ice storms, etc., you will have to wait for those companies that have advance commitments from other companies.

Another important issue associated with restoration is insurance. It is imperative you understand what is covered by your insurance policy and what approval procedures must be completed before any restoration work is performed. There are many stories about how insurance companies challenged claims because of disagreements concerning coverage or restoration procedures. Challenges from insurance carriers can hold up restoration for extended periods of time. Below are two examples showing the importance and magnitude of effort involved with restoration following a disaster.

> The 1993 World Trade Center bombing illustrates the potential magnitude of a cleanup effort. Over a 16-day period, 2700 workers hired by a restoration contractor, working round the clock in three shifts, cleaned over 880,000 square feet of space in the twin towers and other interconnected facilities. Ninety percent of the floors in the 110-story towers had light amounts of soot, while 10 percent suffered heavier damage.

> In 1995 Contra Costa County, California, suffered almost $15 million in arson-related fire damage to four county court houses over a three-week period. In all, 124,000 files had to be freeze dried and restored at an estimated cost of $50 per document.

A good restoration program will not guarantee you will not have a problem with your insurance carrier. The following is an example of how a disagreement between an insured and insurer can delay restoration of your business:

In 1991, a 19-hour fire at One Meridian Plaza in Philadelphia destroyed eight of the 38 floors in the building. It took 6 years of legal maneuvering to settle the claim between the building owners and the insurers. Each party disagreed with the other over the extent of the restoration. For most of the 6 years, the parties' difference amounted to almost $100 million. The owners believed that the floors above the 19th floor had to be torn down because the steel beams supporting the structure had moved 4 inches and could not be certified as safe. The insurance company disagreed and argued that the building could be repaired without tearing down the floors. The owner and insurer also disagreed over the extent of environmental cleanup caused by the fire. Eventually, the matter was settled out of court for an undisclosed sum.

UNDERSTANDING THE ISSUES

For all damaged or destroyed property a company must understand when they need to try to restore the property, and when it can just be replaced. A critical issue concerning restoration is really the handling of documents and electronic media. Handling of the physical damage is more easily accomplished and more straightforward. The handling of vital records, however, is more difficult. The vital records may only be needed if an original contract is challenged, or is needed from a corporate entity standpoint. How a company deals with this exposure is not an easy determination. Some companies build facilities that are protected from most hazards to critical documents and data. The issue concerning having both a protected environment and duplication becomes a business issue; how much insurance is enough. Therefore, any time a company only has a single copy of vital documents and data, you must develop a strategy of what you would do if those records are damaged. This is a dilemma for many companies where duplicate copies cannot be maintained. Insurance companies have millions of pages of archived contracts and other legal documents that may not be feasibly copied. Other industries such as financial services handle equity certificates and other legal tender that perhaps cannot be copied as a normal course of business.

A company should develop a restoration plan in conjunction with performing a vital records review. This way the restoration of business-critical items can be assessed along with the alternatives of providing replication. Insurance coverage must be evaluated and coordinated with the restoration plan and other components of your Business Continuity Planning.

HOW TO SELECT RESTORATION SERVICE PROVIDERS

It is not difficult to find a service provider to clean up the rubble following a flood or fire. It is much more difficult to find a service provider that knows how to dry the soaked documents to best ensure their usability. It also takes a lot of expertise to handle fire-damaged documents and magnetic media to restore information.

The normal care for selecting any critical supply chain partner should be used. For a restoration company, however, you don't have the ability to ask for a pilot program. There are many sources of information to identify restoration companies, including local, state, and federal agencies. In addition, the Internet is an excellent source for both planning information, and resources.

Your own insurance carrier is also a good source of service provider information. Additionally, many insurance carriers have a partnership with recovery firms so that a firm is authorized to do certain work and deal directly with the insurance carrier to ensure there are no misunderstandings about the work to be performed.

WHERE DOES INSURANCE COVERAGE FIT INTO YOUR RESTORATION PROGRAM?

The subjects of restoration and insurance are closely intertwined as, in most cases, property insurers are expected to pay for the majority of the cost of any restoration. The settlement of a property insurance claim can be a complex, time-consuming, and vexing issue, even for a seasoned insurance professional. The insured often do not understand their coverage and routinely overestimate the amount of the loss or assume that a claim is covered when it is not. Insurers and their representatives may communicate poorly with the insured as to the nature of the coverage, the information required to adjust the claim, and the timetable to be expected. Both sides need to cooperate and communicate clearly so that reasonable expectations are established quickly and conflicts can be resolved in a timely manner.

The discussion on insurance will include a brief overview of standard commercial property insurance policies and common problems during the claim settlements process.

Property Insurance Overview

Property insurance can be purchased with many options, which serve to tailor the standard policy language to the specific needs of the policyholder. Therefore, it is important that business owners take the time to review their needs with their insurance agent, broker, or advisor, so that the resulting insurance purchase reflects those needs before a loss occurs. This will help avoid future misunderstandings with the insurance company in the event of a claim.

Property insurance can be purchased on either a named perils or All Risks form. The All Risk form covers all causes of loss that are not specifically excluded in the policy form and provides broader protection to the insured than a named perils form. Under a named perils form, the insured bears the responsibility of proving that damage to their property was caused by one of the enumerated causes of loss. Use of the All Risk form shifts the burden of proof onto the insurer to prove that a particular loss was not covered by the policy. Insurers avoid the use of the phrase "All Risk" and use the phrase "Special Form" to describe this same coverage.

The property policy valuation clause is a second area of frequent misunderstanding by policyholders. That is, if a loss occurs, on what basis will the policyholder be compensated for the loss or damage to their property. Insurers offer two basic valuation choices: actual cash value (ACV) or replacement cost coverage. ACV is defined as the cost to repair or replace the lost or damaged property with property of like kind and quality *less physical depreciation*. For example, suppose that a commercial refrigerator purchased 5 years ago and expected to have a useful working life of 10 years is burned up in a fire. Assuming that the refrigerator had been well maintained up to the time of the loss, the insurance company adjuster might offer to settle the claim for 50 percent of the cost today of a new refrigerator of similar design, quality, and capacity. It should be noted that the lost or damaged property will be valued as of the date of the loss and not on the basis of the original cost.

Replacement cost valuation means that the policyholder will be compensated on the basis of new for old. That is, the policyholder is entitled to compensation on the basis of the cost to repair or replace the lost or damaged property with property of like kind and quality with no deduction for physical depreciation. As noted above, the determination of the replacement cost of the damaged or lost property takes place as of the actual date of loss.

Regardless of whether ACV or replacement cost valuation is chosen, the policyholder needs to make sure that the amount of insurance purchased accurately reflects the current replacement cost value of the insured property. This is necessary to avoid a Coinsurance penalty being applied that could reduce any loss adjustment.

If replacement cost coverage is chosen, then in the event of loss or damage to the covered property, the insured must actually repair or replace the lost or damaged property. Otherwise, the insurance company is usually only required to reimburse the insured on an ACV basis.

Finally, the insurance company will never pay more than the applicable amount of insurance that has been purchased by the policyholder. This last provision underscores the need for business owners to adequately assess the replacement cost value of their property at the time the policy is placed.

We have not included an in-depth discussion of the topics of Business Interruption or Extra Expense insurance in our discussion of property insurance because it is beyond the scope of this chapter. These coverages go hand in hand with adequate property insurance coverage. Business interruption coverage pays for lost earnings and continuing expenses during the period of time the business is shut down. Extra expense coverage pays for the additional costs to maintain business during the shut-down period. The absence or insufficiency of either of these coverages can jeopardize the survival of the business that is jeopardized because of a lack of financial resources during the restoration period. Detailed records of all expenditures to maintain the operations of the business (extra expense) should be kept and included in the claim. The business interruption portion of the claim will be based on the lost earnings of the business as compared with periods preceding the loss.

In addition to standard property insurance coverage, business owners should discuss with their insurance advisors the need for additional insurance coverage in the following areas:

- Boiler and machinery
- Valuable papers
- Accounts receivable
- Electronic data processing (EDP)

Property insurance policies exclude coverage for damage caused by:

- Explosion of steam boilers, steam pipes, steam engines, or steam turbines
- Artificially generated electric current, including electric arcing, that affects electrical devices, appliances, or wire
- Mechanical breakdown, including rupture or bursting caused by centrifugal force.

Such damage may be covered under boiler and machinery insurance policies. Boiler and machinery policies have many characteristics similar to property policies. In the event of a loss, these insurers often provide assistance in the repair or replacement of the damaged equipment. They also provide statutorily required inspection services.

Valuable papers coverage under a standard commercial property insurance policy is limited to $2500. Valuable papers coverage may be important for businesses where the destruction of documents would cause the business to suffer a monetary loss or to expend large sums in reconstructing the documents. The limit of insurance under a standard property policy can be increased to meet a desired need. The ISO (Insurance Services

Office) valuable papers form defines valuable papers and records as "inscribed, printed, or written documents, manuscripts, or records." Money and securities, data processing programs, media, and converted data are not covered. Coverage for loss or destruction to money and securities can be found in Crime insurance policies. Data processing programs, media, and data can be covered under EDP policies. Care needs to be exercised in estimating the cost of reconstructing documents so that adequate limits of insurance can be purchased.

If Accounts Receivable records are damaged by an insured cause of loss, this type of coverage will pay the business owner amounts due from customers that he is unable to collect as a result of the damage to his records, collection expenses in excess of normal collection costs, and other reasonable expenses incurred to reestablish records of accounts receivable. This coverage can be purchased as an endorsement to a commercial property insurance policy. Again, care must be exercised in setting an adequate amount of insurance.

Electronic data processing (EDP) coverage is a must for organizations that rely heavily on data processing or electronic means of information storage. EDP coverage can provide All Risk coverage for equipment and data, software and media, including the perils of electrical and magnetic injury, mechanical breakdown, and temperature and humidity changes, which are important to computer operations. In addition, the coverage can include the cost of reproducing lost data, which is not available under a standard commercial property insurance policy.

Property Insurance Claims Settlement Process

Exhibit 27.1 provides a broad overview of the claim settlement process. The last row underscores the importance of complete and well-organized documentation and open communication during the claim settlement process. These two factors are major reasons why claims settlements are delayed or even end up in litigation. The items shown in this table are important steps to include in your restoration plan.

The claims settlement process is adversarial by its nature. The insured party is intent on maximizing its potential recovery under its insurance policy, while the insurance company is trying to minimize its exposure to the insured's claim. This does not mean that the claim settlement process must be nasty or unpleasant. The parties should work together in good faith in arriving at a reasonable settlement of a claim. The insurance carrier will be less likely to raise substantive issues if they believe that the insured is not trying to take advantage of the situation. Likewise, if the insurer establishes reasonable ground rules at the beginning of the process, they should expect the insured to be forthcoming with the information requested in a timely manner. While it is usually in the insured's best interests to provide complete and well-organized documentation, the insured should not overwhelm the insurance company and should only provide the documentation necessary to substantiate the amounts requested, keeping ancillary documentation available in the event that the insurance carrier requests additional information.

- Report the event to the property insurance company immediately. Depending on the specific items damaged and the nature of the damage it may be appropriate to notify the boiler and machinery insurer as well.
- Prevent further damage to covered property.
- Obtain property repair/replacement estimates or appraisals and prepare and document the claim. If business interruption and/or extra expense are going to be claimed, extensive additional documentation may be needed. (If a business interruption loss exceeds $1 million, the insured should consider hiring accountants experienced in documenting such claims.)
- Submit documentation to the insurance company adjuster and cooperate with the adjuster in his investigation and adjustment of the claim.
- Request authorization to proceed with repairs or the purchase of major items.
- If appropriate, request a partial payment of the claim from the insurance company.
- Negotiate the final claim settlement with the insurance company adjuster.
- Submit a sworn proof of loss to the insurance company.
- Receive claim settlement.

Exhibit 27.1.

The insurance adjuster is an individual assigned by the insurance company to handle a claim on its behalf. The adjuster may be an employee of the insurance company or may work for an independent firm hired by the insurance company. Adjusters will be the key contact between the insurer and the insured. Their responsibilities include determining the cause of a loss, the nature and scope of damage to the property, whether the policy covers the damages claimed, to what extent property should be repaired or replaced and the corresponding cost, and finally the amount that the insurance carrier is willing to pay in settlement of the claim. The adjuster also acts as a quarterback in determining whether other specialists need to become involved.

Depending on the size and complexity of the claim, the insurance carrier may selectively involve accountants, lawyers, and other specialists in the claim settlement process. These specialists are working on behalf of the insurance carrier and not the insured. While the insured should not be unduly alarmed if the insurance company employs such specialists, the insured may be well advised to consider employing his own specialists to work on his behalf in calculating the claim in order to be on a more equal footing with the insurance company.

The agent or broker who placed the insurance can provide guidance and assistance to the insured in handling the claim. This should be expected, since the broker or agent has received compensation to arrange the insurance. Smaller brokers sometimes lack the capability to be of much assistance in a claim situation.

The responsibilities of the policyholder in the event of a loss are spelled out in most insurance policies. They include prompt notification of the insurer, protecting the covered property from further damage, providing detailed inventories of the damaged and undamaged property, allowing the insurance company to inspect the damaged property, take samples, and examine the pertinent records of the company, providing a sworn proof of loss, cooperating with the insurer in the investigation and settlement of the claim, and submitting to examination under oath concerning any matter relating to the insurance or the claim.

Willis Corroon, a large multinational insurance broker, recommends that the following steps be taken immediately following a loss:

- Make sure that the loss area is safe to enter.
- Report the claim to the agent and to the insurer.
- Restore fire protection.
- Take immediate action to minimize the loss.
- Protect undamaged property from loss.
- Take photographs of the damage.
- Identify temporary measures needed to resume operations and maintain safety and security, and the costs of those measures.
- Consult with engineering, operations, and maintenance personnel as well as outside contractors for an initial estimate of the scope and cost of repairs.
- Make plans for repairing the damage.

WHAT'S INCLUDED IN A RESTORATION PLAN?

After a disaster such as a fire or hurricane, the natural inclination is to assume that documents, computer records, equipment and machinery, and high-tech computers and other data processing equipment that appear to be unusable or severely damaged should be scrapped and replaced. However, before anything is done, experts should be brought in to assess the damage and determine short- and long-term courses of action. The short-term course of action is intended to stabilize the situation at the disaster location so as to prevent further damage from occurring. The long-term strategy is to determine which items can be salvaged and repaired and what items should be replaced.

Although notification to the insurance company should be one of the first steps taken after a disaster has occurred; do not wait for the insurance adjuster to show up before implementing stabilization procedures. It is a common insurance policy requirement that the insured take steps to prevent additional damage from occurring after a disaster. Such post-loss disaster mitigation should be part of a comprehensive business continuity plan. If no plan exists, then common sense should prevail.

Your restoration plan should include the following:

- Ensure life safety at the disaster location.
- Reactivate fire protection and other alarm/life safety systems.
- Establish security at the site to keep out intruders, members of the public, the press, as well as employees who should not be allowed in the disaster area unless they are directly involved in damage assessment or mitigation efforts.
- Cover damaged roofs, doors, windows, and other parts of the structure.
- Arrange for emergency heat, dehumidification, or water extraction.
- Separate damaged components that may interfere with restoration, but do not dispose of these components because restoration experts and the insurance adjuster will want to inspect them.
- Take photographs or videotape of the disaster site as well as damaged and undamaged property.
- Bring in experts in document/records restoration and qualified technical personnel to work on computer and communications equipment and systems, machinery and furniture, wall and floor coverings, and structural elements.
- Maintain a log of all steps taken after a disaster, noting time, location, what has been done, who did it, as well as work orders and invoices of all expenditures relating to the disaster.

After the disaster site has been secured and stabilized and the extent of damage assessed, contracts should be negotiated with qualified restoration contractors. The insurance company adjuster may be able to recommend qualified contractors. The adjuster should be consulted before any contracts are awarded.

The extent of the restoration possible depends on the type of property damaged, the nature of the damage, and the extent and speed of post-disaster damage minimization. Another factor is the level of expertise brought in to assess and recommend restoration strategies as well as the quality of the restoration contractors brought in to do the work.

Here are some generalized comments on the restoration of paper documents, magnetic media (computer disks and tape), and electronic equipment and machinery.

Water damage is one of the most prevalent forms of damage to paper-based documents. Restoration efforts need to begin immediately if documents are to be saved. Water should be pumped out of the area as quickly as possible. The area also needs to be vented to allow air to circulate. Cool temperatures will help preserve water-soaked documents until actual restoration work can begin. Bringing in a freezer unit such as a refrigerated trailer (capable of being held at 0 degrees F) to store the documents will help slow down mold damage. Before freezing, documents should be cleaned and handled with extreme care. Documents should be kept in blocks (i.e., not pulled apart) as this will prevent additional deterioration. Documents that are not thoroughly soaked can be dried using dehumidification. Freeze-drying water-soaked documents will produce good results. Sterilization and application of a fungicidal buffer will help prevent further mold damage. Dehumidification and freeze-drying can take from one to two weeks to be completed.

Damaged computer tapes and diskettes need to be restored within 72 to 96 hours of a disaster to be effective. Water-damaged diskettes can be opened and dried using isopropyl alcohol and put into new jackets. Then the information is transferred onto new disks. Tapes can be freeze-dried or machine-dried using specialized machinery. The data on the tapes is then transferred to new media. Soot- and smoked-damaged diskettes need to be cleaned by hand, and then data transfer can take place.

Equipment and machines need to be evaluated on a case-by-case basis. There are specialist firms that can evaluate and recommend repair/restoration strategies for equipment. These firms may also do the repairs, or they may recommend shipping the damaged equipment to the manufacturer or utilize other shops to do the restoration. In general, insurance companies will not authorize replacement of damaged equipment with new or refurbished equipment unless the cost to repair the item exceeds 50 percent of its replacement cost. Smoke, soot, and other contaminants can be removed from equipment and replacement parts when damaged parts cannot be adequately cleaned. Occasionally, the original manufacturer may balk at substantially repairing damaged equipment, claiming that the repair will prove inadequate or will void the manufacturer's warranty. They are usually interested in selling new equipment. In such cases, insurance companies may be able to purchase replacement warranties (to replace the original manufacturer's warranty) from a warranty replacement company to satisfy the insured. The replacement warranty will be for the period of time remaining on the original manufacturer's warranty.

WHAT ARE THE COSTS FOR A RESTORATION PROGRAM?

The costs associated with restoration are more "at time of disaster" costs and would be covered by insurance. Having a thorough restoration strategy and plan will help to scope the insurance needed, and may even save money for those who are over-insured due to the lack of knowledge.

The primary cost of a program are the people resources necessary to develop and maintain the capability.

An approach to matching insurance needs with the potential cost to restore data and infrastructure is to start with your insurance carrier. Determine the types of restoration covered with different policies and then compare the coverage with restoration company estimates. Costs are usually based on square feet, type of media, etc.

Restoration of critical equipment is usually procured through the source of the equipment. This may include staged replacement parts or quick-ship components. Sometimes there is an incremental charge to maintenance fees to guarantee expedited service or replacement.

ENSURING PROVIDER CAN AND WILL PERFORM AT TIME OF DISASTER

Restoration is a service not dissimilar to maintenance for critical IT and facility operations. In the event of an emergency, any delay can cause a significant financial impact. You should view restoration in this same light. Therefore, expand the same diligence you would to selecting a service provider for ensuring business *continuation*, to selecting one for ensuring timely business *resumption*.

TESTING YOUR RESTORATION PLAN

Once a restoration plan has been implemented, it should be tested as part of a company's BCP program. The purpose of testing will be to validate that the plan:

1. Meets the business needs in terms of timeframe
2. Reduces the exposure to the loss of documents and data to an acceptable level
3. Remains in compliance with insurance requirements
4. Is current and the level of detail is sufficient to ensure a timely, efficient recovery

Testing is a primary means of keeping the restoration plan current. Regular tests with varying scope and objectives prevent the program from becoming too routine. As with any testing program, you start out simple and build on successes. Initially, it may involve contacting your service providers and verifying the following:

- You would be able to reach them at any hour, on any day
- They should be able to respond within the expected timeframes

Other tests may involve your restoration team members' awareness of the plan, ability to perform the tasks, and coordination with other "recovery and return to normal" activities.

In some cases, a company's need for restoration services actually diminishes. As IT solutions become more robust and the need for nonstop processing increases, more and more companies employ remote, replicated data. In this case, if the primary copy of data is lost, a second, equally current, copy is available. Therefore, if a company had services for the restorations of electronic media, it may not be necessary.

RESTORATION PLAN WITHOUT A BCP PLAN

Even if your company does not have a BCP program, it is still prudent to have ready resources to provide restoration services if needed. A company that does not understand the need for a BCP program will not allocate resources to develop a restoration strategy. A fallback would be to coordinate with your insurance carrier so they understand the critical nature of your vital records and single points of processing failure so they can procure the appropriate resources to get the job done.

CONCLUSION

A restoration strategy is one that can be implemented relatively easily and at minimal cost. Have your insurance carrier explain the types of hazards and restoration techniques, and if in a bind, work with their approved service partners.

Since time is of the essence when it comes to recovering damaged vital records and sensitive equipment, a BCP team should be assigned specific restoration responsibilities. Restoration should be a close second when it comes to recovering your business following a disaster.

GETTING SUPPORT FOR YOUR RESTORATION PROGRAM

The most difficult task in developing a restoration capability and plan is to get internal manpower resources approved to help with the work. There may be some reluctance to go to management and suggest there is a need to prepare for the potential damage to critical property after management has spent money to supposedly eliminate the risk.

Everyone has seen news reports of damage due to floods, fires, and explosions. What most people do not know is that there is significant technology available to recover the critical data from damaged vital records. In addition, there are service providers who will guarantee replacement equipment within pre-established timeframes for a fixed subscription fee.

The important task is for the owner of critical business data and processing equipment to educate himself and his management that preplanning can significantly reduce the impact from potential loss of data.

NEXT STEPS TO PLANNING FOR RESTORATION

Below is an outline of steps to be performed to design and implement a restoration strategy to further protect a company's informational and physical assets.

I. Assess the needs
   A. What insurance coverage currently exists for the recovery and restoration of vital records following an event?
   B. What are the coverage options available for restoration of archival data and documents, as well as data needed to fully recover business processing?
   C. What are the business risks in terms of single copies of vital records?
   D. What are the business risks associated with the loss of equipment and facilities?
II. Develop a restoration strategy
   A. Identify alternatives to either eliminate single points of failure or reduce the impact of lost or damaged property.
   B. Perform a cost/benefit analysis of viable alternatives.
   C. Obtain approval and funding for appropriate alternatives.
   D. Implement the preventative and restoration strategies.
III. Develop a restoration plan and ongoing quality assurance
   A. Incorporate restoration into the existing BCP program.
   B. Assign restoration roles and responsibilities.
   C. Coordinate restoration with the risk management department and other BCP efforts.
   D. Develop ongoing plan maintenance tasks and schedules.
   E. Perform periodic tests of restoration capability.

Domain 9
Law, Investigation, and Ethics

The topics encompassed by law, investigation, and ethics are of immediate concern to those taking the CISSP examination but also can be very important to security practitioners working through the daily challenges of their jobs. Although these three topics are somewhat related, they are different areas of expertise. The first chapter deals with the chore of investigating computer security incidents. Although not all security officers are frequently involved in conducting investigations, they are close enough to the problems that they should know how an investigation should proceed.

The second chapter deals with ethics involved with the use of the Internet. With so many millions of Internet users, it is increasingly important that the ethics we expect from each other are well established.

The third chapter focuses on the moving target of international law that controls the flow of information across borders between countries. This issue is becoming more important as E-commerce continues to expand and becomes a way of life for many enterprises throughout the world.

Domain 9.1
Investigation

Chapter 28

Computer Crime Investigation and Computer Forensics

Thomas Welch

Incidents of computer-related crime and telecommunications fraud have increased dramatically over the past decade, but due to the esoteric nature of this crime there have been very few prosecutions and even fewer convictions. The same technology that has allowed for the advancement and automation of many business processes has also opened the door to many new forms of computer abuse. While some of these system attacks merely use contemporary methods to commit older, more familiar types of crime, others involve the use of completely new forms of criminal activity that have evolved along with the technology.

Computer crime investigation and computer forensics are also evolving sciences which are affected by many external factors: continued advancements in technology, societal issues, legal issues, etc. There are many gray areas that need to be sorted out and tested through the courts. Until then, the system attackers will have a clear advantage, and computer abuse will continue to increase. We, as computer security practitioners, must be aware of the myriad of technological and legal issues that affect our systems and its users, including issues dealing with investigations and enforcement.

This chapter will take the security practitioner and investigator through each of the areas of computer crime investigation and computer forensics, so that they are better prepared to respond to both internal and external attacks.

0-8493-9829-0/00/$0.00+$.50
© 2000 by CRC Press LLC

COMPUTER CRIME

According to the *American Heritage Dictionary* a "crime" is any act committed or omitted in violation of the law. This definition causes a perplexing problem for law enforcement when dealing with computer-related crime, since much of today's computer-related crime is without violation of any formal law. This may seem be a contradictory statement, but traditional criminal statutes, in most states, have only been modified throughout the years to reflect the theories of modern criminal justice. These laws generally envision applications to situations involving traditional types of criminal activity, such as burglary, larceny, fraud, etc. Unfortunately, the modern criminal has kept pace with the vast advancements in technology, and he has found ways to apply such innovations as the computer to his criminal ventures. Unknowingly and probably unintentionally, he has also revealed the difficulties in applying older traditional laws to situations involving "computer-related crimes."

In 1979 the United States Department of Justice established a definition for "computer crime," stating that "a computer crime is any illegal act for which knowledge of computer technology is essential for its perpetration, investigation, or prosecution." This definition was too broad and has since been further refined by new or modified, state and federal criminal statutes.

Criminal Law

Criminal law identifies a crime as being a wrong against society. Even if an individual is victimized, under the law, society is the victim. A conviction under criminal law normally results in a jail term or probation for the defendant. It could also result in a financial award to the victim as restitution for the crime. The main purpose for prosecuting under criminal law is punishment for the offender. This punishment is also meant to serve as a deterrent against future crime. The deterrent aspect of punishment only works if the punishment is severe enough to discourage further criminal activity. This is certainly not the case in the United States, where very few computer criminals ever go to jail. In other areas of the world there are very strong deterrents. For example, in China in 1995, a computer hacker was executed after being found guilty of embezzling $200,000 from a national bank. This certainly will have a dissuading value for other hackers in China!

To be found guilty of a criminal offense under criminal law, the jury must believe, beyond a reasonable doubt, that the offender is guilty of the offense. The lack of technical expertise, combined with the many confusing questions posed by the defense attorney, may cause doubt for many jury members, thus rendering a "not guilty" decision. The only short-term solution to this problem is to provide simple testimony in layman's terms and to use demonstrative evidence whenever possible. Even with this, it will be difficult for many juries to return a guilty verdict.

Criminal conduct is broken down into two classifications depending on severity. A felony is the more serious of the two, normally resulting in a jail term of more than one year. Misdemeanors are normally punishable by a fine or a jail sentence of less than a year. It is important to understand that if we wish to deter future attacks, we must push for the stricter sentencing, which only occurs under the felonious classification. The type of attack and/or the total dollar loss has a direct relationship to the crime classification. As we cover investigation procedures, we will see why it is so important to account for all time and money spent on the investigation.

Criminal law falls under two main jurisdictions: federal and state. Although there is a plethora of federal and state statutes which may be used against traditional criminal offenses, and even though many of these same statutes may apply to computer-related crimes with some measure of success, it is clear that many cases fail to reach prosecution or fail to result in conviction because of the gaps which exist in the Federal Criminal Code and the individual state criminal statutes.

Because of this, every state in the United States, with the exception of one, along with the federal government, have adopted new laws specific to computer-related abuses. These new laws, which have been redefined over the years to keep abreast of the constant changes in the technological forum, have been subjected to an ample amount of scrutiny due to many social issues, which have been impacted by the proliferation of computers in society. Some of these issues, such as privacy, copyright infringement, and software ownership are yet to be resolved, thus we can expect many more changes to the current collection of laws. Some of the computer-related crimes, which are addressed by the new state and federal laws, are

- Unauthorized access
- Exceed authorized access
- Intellectual property theft or misuse of information
- Child pornography
- Theft of services
- Forgery
- Property theft (i.e., computer hardware, chips, etc.)
- Invasion of privacy
- Denial of services
- Computer fraud
- Viruses
- Sabotage (data alteration or malicious destruction)
- Extortion
- Embezzlement
- Espionage
- Terrorism

All but one state, Vermont, have created or amended laws specifically to deal with computer-related crime. Twenty-five of the states have enacted specific computer crime statutes, while the other twenty-four states have merely amended their traditional criminal statutes to confront computer crime issues. Vermont has announced legislation under Bill H.0555, which deals with theft of computer services. The elements of proof, which define the basis of the criminal activity, vary from state to state. Security practitioners should be fully cognizant of their own state laws, specifically the elements of proof. Additionally, traditional criminal statutes, such as theft, fraud, extortion and embezzlement, can still be used to prosecute computer crime.

Just as there has been much new legislation at the state level, there have also been many new federal policies, such as the:

- Electronic Communications Privacy Act
- Electronic Espionage Act of 1996
- Child Pornography Prevention Act of 1996
- Computer Fraud and Abuse Act of 1986, 18 U.S.C. 1001

These laws and policies have been established, precisely to deal with computer and telecommunications abuses at the federal level. Additionally, many modifications and updates have been made to the Federal Criminal Code, Sections 1029 and 1030, to deal with a variety of computer-related abuses. Even though these new laws have been adopted for use in the prosecution of a computer-related offense, some of the older, proven federal laws, identified below, offer a "simpler" case to present to judges and juries:

- Wire Fraud
- Mail Fraud
- Interstate Transportation of Stolen Property
- Racketeer Influenced & Corrupt Organizations (RICO)

The Electronic Communications Privacy Act (ECPA) is being tested more today than ever before. The ECPA prohibits all monitoring of wire, oral, and electronic communications unless specific statutory exceptions apply. This includes monitoring of e-mail, network traffic, keystrokes, or telephone systems. The ECPA was not meant to prohibit network providers from monitoring and maintaining their networks and connections, thus the ECPA provides an exception for monitoring network traffic for legitimate businesses purposes. Additionally, the ECPA also allows monitoring when the network users are notified of the monitoring process.

The two new Acts enacted in 1996, the Child Pornography Prevention Act (CPPA) and the Electronic Espionage Act (EEA) have proved that the legislative process is working, albeit a bit more slowly than one would like.

The CPPA is especially impressive in that it eradicates many of the loopholes afforded by newer technology. The CPPA was enacted specifically to combat the use of computer technology to produce pornography that conveys the impression that children were used in the photographs or images, even if the participants are actually adults. The Court held that any child pornography, including simulated or morphed images, stimulates the sexual appetites of pedophiles and that the images themselves may persuade a child to engage in sexual activity by viewing other children. The CPPA was contested by the Freedom of Speech Coalition (FSC), but was upheld by the Court in FSC v. Reno.

The EEA hopefully will curtail some of the industrial espionage that is going on today, but it will also have an impact on how business is conducted in the United States, especially intelligence gathering. According to the EEA, it is a criminal offense to take, download, receive, or possess trade secret information obtained without the owner's authorization. Penalties can reach $10 million in fines, up to 15 years in prison, and forfeiture of property used in the commission of the crime. This could have tremendous, far-reaching consequences for businesses should an employee improperly use information gained from any previous employment.

Civil Law

Civil law (or tort law) identifies a tort as a wrong against an individual or business, which normally results in damage or loss to that individual or business. The major differences between criminal and civil law are the type of punishment and the level of proof required to obtain a guilty verdict. There is no jail sentence under the civil law system. A victim may receive financial or injunctive relief as restitution for his loss. An injunction against the offender will attempt to thwart any further loss to the victim. Additionally, a violation of the injunction may result in a Contempt of Court order, which would place the offender in jeopardy of going to jail. The main purpose for seeking civil remedy is for financial restitution, which can be awarded as follows:

- Compensatory Damages
- Punitive Damages
- Statutory Damages

In a civil action, if there is no culpability on the part of the victim, the victim may be entitled to compensatory (restitution), statutory, and punitive damages. Compensatory damages are actual damages to the victim and include attorney fees, lost profits, investigation costs, etc. Punitive damages are just that — damages set by the jury, with the intent to punish the offender. Even if the victim is partially culpable, an award may be made on the victim's behalf, but may be lessened due to the victim's culpable negligence. Statutory damages are damages determined by law. Mere violation of the law entitles the victim to a statutory award.

Civil cases are much easier to convict under because the burden of proof required for a conviction is much less. To be found guilty of a civil wrong, the jury must believe, based only upon the preponderance of the evidence, that the offender is guilty of the offense. It is much easier to show that the majority (51%) of the evidence is pointing to the defendant's guilt.

Finally, just as a Search Warrant is used by law enforcement as a tool in the criminal investigation, the Court can issue an Impoundment Order or Writ of Possession, which is a court order to take back the property in question. The investigator should also keep in mind that the criminal and civil case could take place simultaneously, thus allowing items seized during the execution of the Search Warrant to be used in the civil case.

Insurance

An insurance policy is generally part of an organization's overall risk mitigation/management plan. The policy offsets the risk of loss to the insurance company in return for an acceptable level of loss (the insurance premium). Since many computer-related assets (software and hardware) account for the majority of an organization's net worth, they must be protected by insurance. If there is a loss to any of these assets, the insurance company is usually required to pay out on the policy. One important factor to bear in mind is the principle of culpable negligence. This places part of the liability on the victim if the victim fails to follow a "standard of due care" in the protection of identified assets. If a victim organization is held to be culpably negligent, the insurance company may be required to pay only a portion of the loss. Also, an insurance company can attempt to deny coverage, arguing that an employee's "dishonest" acts caused the damage.

Two important insurance issues related to the investigation are prompt notification of the loss and understanding that the insurance company has a duty to defend. Regarding prompt notification, insurance companies may deny coverage by arguing that the claim was received too late. Some states even allow insurance companies to void its insurance obligations if the notice or claim is proven to be late.

RULES OF EVIDENCE

Before delving into the investigative process and computer forensics, it is essential that the investigator have a thorough understanding of the Rules of Evidence. The submission of evidence in any type of legal proceeding generally amounts to a significant challenge, but when computers are involved, the problems are intensified. Special knowledge is needed to locate and collect evidence, and special care is required to preserve and transport the evidence. Evidence in a computer crime case may differ from traditional forms of evidence inasmuch as most computer-related evidence is intangible—in the form of an electronic pulse or magnetic charge.

Before evidence can be presented in a case, it must be competent, relevant, and material to the issue, and it must be presented in compliance with the rules of evidence. Anything which tends to prove directly or indirectly that a person may be responsible for the commission of a criminal offense may be legally presented against him. Proof may include the oral testimony of witnesses or the introduction of physical or documentary evidence.

By definition, **evidence** is any species of proof or probative matter, legally presented at the trial of an issue, by the act of the parties and through the medium of witnesses, records, documents, objects, etc., for the purpose of inducing belief in the minds of the court and jurors as to their contention. In short, evidence is anything offered in court to prove the truth or falsity of a fact at issue. This section will cover each of the Rules of Evidence as it relates to computer crime investigations.

Types of Evidence

There are many types of evidence that can be offered in court to prove the truth or falsity of a given fact. The most common forms of evidence are direct, real, documentary, and demonstrative. Direct evidence is oral testimony, whereby the knowledge is obtained from any of the witness's five senses and is, in itself, proof or disproof of a fact in issue. Direct evidence is called to prove a specific act (i.e., Eye Witness Statement). Real Evidence, also known as associative or physical evidence, is made up of tangible objects that prove or disprove guilt. Physical evidence includes such things as tools used in the crime, fruits of the crime, perishable evidence capable of reproduction, etc. The purpose of the physical evidence is to link the suspect to the scene of the crime. It is this evidence which has material existence and can be presented to the view of the court and jury for consideration. Documentary evidence is evidence presented to the court in the form of business records, manuals, printouts, etc. Much of the evidence submitted in a computer crime case is documentary evidence. Finally, demonstrative evidence is evidence used to aid the jury. It may be in the form of a model, experiment, chart, or an illustration offered as proof.

It should be noted that in order to aid the court and the jury in their quest to understand the facts at issue, demonstrative evidence is being used more often, especially in the form of simulation and animation. It is very important to understand the difference between these two types of evidence because the standard of admissibility is affected. A computer simulation is a prediction or calculation about what will happen in the future given known facts. A traffic reconstruction program is a perfect example of computer simulation. There are many mathematical algorithms used in this type of program that must be either stipulated to or proven to the court to be completely accurate. It is generally more difficult to admit a simulation as evidence, because of the substantive nature of the process.

Computer animation, on the other hand, is simply a computer-generated sequence, illustrating an expert's opinion. Animation does not predict future events. It merely supports the testimony of an expert witness through the use of demonstrations. An animation of a hard disk spinning while the read/write heads are reading data can help the court or jury understand how a disk drive works. There are no mathematical algorithms that must be proven. The animation solely aids the court and jury through visualization. The key to having animation admitted as evidence is in the strength of the expert witness. Under Rule 702, the expert used to explain evidence must be qualified to do so through skill, training, or education.

When seizing evidence from a computer-related crime, the investigator should collect any and all physical evidence, such as the computer, peripherals, notepads, documentation, etc., in addition to computer-generated evidence. There are four types of computer-generated evidence. They are

- Visual output on the monitor
- Printed evidence on a printer
- Printed evidence on a plotter
- Film recorder — Includes magnetic representation on disk, tape, or cartridge, and optical representation on CD

Best Evidence Rule

The Best Evidence Rule, which had been established to deter any alteration of evidence, either intentionally or unintentionally, states that the court prefers the original evidence at the trial, rather than a copy, but they will accept a duplicate under the following conditions:

- Original lost or destroyed by fire, flood, or other acts of God. This has included such things as careless employees or cleaning staff.
- Original destroyed in the normal course of business
- Original in possession of a third party who is beyond the court's subpoena power

This rule has been relaxed to now allow duplicates unless there is a genuine question as to the original's authenticity, or if admission of the duplicate would, under the circumstances, be unfair.

Exclusionary Rule

Evidence must be gathered by law enforcement in accordance with court guidelines governing search and seizure or it will be excluded (Fourth

Amendment). Any evidence collected in violation of the Fourth Amendment is considered to be "Fruit of the Poisonous Tree," and will not be admissible. Furthermore, any evidence identified and gathered as a result of the initial inadmissible evidence will also be held to be inadmissible. Evidence may also be excluded for other reasons, such as violations of the Electronic Communications Privacy Act (ECPA) or violations related to provisions of Chapters 2500 and 2700 of Title 18 of the United States Penal Code.

Private citizens are not subject to the Fourth Amendment's guidelines on search and seizure, but are exposed to potential exclusions for violations of the ECPA or Privacy Act. Therefore, internal investigators, private investigators, and Computer Emergency Response Team (CERT) members should take caution when conducting any internal search, even on company computers. For example, if there were no policy in place explicitly stating the company's right to electronically monitor network traffic on company systems, then internal investigators would be well advised not to set up a sniffer on the network to monitor such traffic. To do so may be a violation of the ECPA.

Hearsay Rule

A legal factor of computer-generated evidence is that it is considered hearsay. Hearsay is second-hand evidence; evidence which is not gathered from the personal knowledge of the witness but from another source. Its value depends on the veracity and competence of the source. The magnetic charge of the disk or the electronic bit value in memory, which represents the data, is the actual, original evidence. The computer-generated evidence is merely a representation of the original evidence.

Under the US Federal Rules of Evidence, all business records, including computer records, are considered "hearsay" because there is no first-hand proof that they are accurate, reliable, and trustworthy. In general, hearsay evidence is not admissible in court. However, there are some well-established exceptions (Rule 803) to the hearsay rule for business records. In Rosenberg v. Collins, the court held that if the computer output is used in the regular course of business, then the evidence shall be admitted.

Business Record Exemption to the Hearsay Rule

US Federal Rules of Evidence 803(6) allows a court to admit a report or other business document made at or near the time by, or from information transmitted by, a person with knowledge, if kept in the course of regularly conducted business activity, and if it was the regular practice of that business activity to make the [report or document], all as shown by testimony of the custodian or other qualified witness, unless the source of information or the method or circumstances of preparation indicates lack of trustworthiness.

609

To meet Rule 803 (6) the witness must:

- Have custody of the records in question on a regular basis
- Rely on those records in the regular course of business
- Know that they were prepared in the regular course of business

Audit trails would meet the criteria if they were produced in the normal course of business. The process to produce the output will have to be proven to be reliable. If computer-generated evidence is used and admissible, the court may order disclosure of the details of the computer, logs, maintenance records, etc., in respect to the system generating the printout, and then the defense may use that material to attack the reliability of the evidence. If the audit trails are not used or reviewed (at least the exceptions — i.e., failed log-on attempts) in the regular course of business, then they may not meet the criteria for admissibility.

US Federal Rules of Evidence 1001 (3) provides another exception to the Hearsay Rule. This rule allows a memory or disk dump to be admitted as evidence, even though it is not done in the regular course of business. This dump merely acts as statement of fact. System dumps (in binary or hexadecimal) would not be hearsay because they are not being offered to prove the truth of the contents, but only the state of the computer.

Chain of Evidence (Custody)

Once evidence is seized, the next step is to provide for its accountability and protection. The Chain of Evidence, which provides a means of accountability, must be adhered to by law enforcement when conducting any type of criminal investigation, including a computer crime investigation. It helps to minimize the instances of tampering. The Chain of Evidence must account for all persons who handled or who had access to the evidence in question.

The Chain of Evidence shows:

- Who obtained the evidence
- Where and when the evidence was obtained
- Who secured the evidence
- Who had control or possession of the evidence

It may be necessary to have anyone associated with the evidence testify at trial. Private citizens are not required to maintain the same level of control of the evidence as law enforcement although they would be well advised to do so. Should an internal investigation result in the discovery and collection of computer-related evidence, the investigation team should follow the same, detailed chain of evidence as required by law enforcement. This will help to dispel any objection by the defense that the evidence is unreliable should the case go to court.

Admissibility of Evidence

The admissibility of computer-generated evidence is, at best, a moving target. Computer-generated evidence is always suspect because of the ease with which it can be tampered—usually without a trace! Precautionary measures must be taken in order to ensure that computer-generated evidence has not been tampered with, erased, or added to. In order to ensure that only relevant and reliable evidence is entered into the proceedings, the judicial system has adopted the concept of admissibility.

- *Relevancy of Evidence* — evidence tending to prove or disprove a material fact. All evidence in court must be relevant and material to the case.
- *Reliability of Evidence* — The evidence and the process to produce the evidence must be proven to be reliable. This is one of the most critical aspects of computer-generated evidence.

Once computer-generated evidence meets the Business Record Exemption to the hearsay rule, is not excluded for some technicality or violation, follows the Chain of Custody, and is found to be both relevant and reliable, then it is held to be admissible. The defense will attack both the relevancy and reliability of the evidence, so great care should be taken to protect both.

Evidence Life Cycle

The Evidence Life Cycle starts with the discovery and collection of the evidence. It progresses through the following series of states until it is finally returned to the victim or owner:

- Collection and Identification
- Analysis
- Storage, Preservation, and Transportation
- Presented in Court
- Returned to Victim (Owner)

Collection and Identification. As the evidence is obtained or collected, it must be properly marked so that it can be identified as being the particular piece of evidence gathered at the scene. The collection must be recorded in a logbook identifying the particular piece of evidence, the person who discovered it, and the date, time, and location discovered. The location should be specific enough for later recollection in court. All other types of identifying marks, such as make, model, or serial number, should also be logged. It is of paramount importance to list any type of damage to the particular piece of evidence. This is not only for identification purposes, but it will also limit any potential liability should a claim be made later that you damaged the evidence. When marking evidence, the following guidelines should be followed:

- Mark the actual piece of evidence if it will not damage the evidence, by writing or scribing your initials, the date, and the case number if known. Seal this evidence in the appropriate container and, again, mark the container by writing or scribing your initials, the date, and the case number, if known.
- If the actual piece of evidence cannot be marked, then seal the evidence in an appropriate container, then mark the container by writing or scribing your initials, the date, and the case number, if known.
- The container should be sealed with evidence tape, and your marking should write over the tape, so that if the seal is broken it can be noticed.
- Be extremely careful not to damage the evidence while engraving or marking the piece.

When marking glass or metal, a diamond scriber should be used. For all other objects, a felt-tip pen with indelible ink is recommended. Dependent on the nature of the crime, the investigator may wish to preserve latent fingerprints. If so, static-free gloves should be used if working with computer components, instead of standard latex gloves.

Try to always mark evidence the same way, because you will be asked to testify to the fact that you are the person identified by the evidence markings. Keep in mind, that the defense is going to try to discredit you as a witness or try some way to keep the evidence out of court, so something as simple as quick, positive identification of your mark is largely beneficial to your case.

Storage, Preservation, and Transportation. All evidence must be packed and preserved to prevent contamination. It should be protected against heat, extreme cold, humidity, water, magnetic fields, and vibration. The evidence must be protected for future use in court and for return to the original owner. It the evidence is not properly protected, the person or agency responsible for the collection and storage of the evidence may be held liable for damages. Therefore, the proper packing materials should be used whenever possible. Documents and disks (hard, floppy, optical, tapes, etc.) should be seized and stored in appropriate containers to prevent their destruction. For example, hard disks should be packed in a sealed, static-free bag, within a cardboard box with a foam container. The box should be sealed with evidence tape and an Electromagnetic Field (EMF) warning label should be affixed to the box. It may be wise to defer to the system administrator or a technical advisor on how to best protect a particular type of system, especially mini-systems or mainframes.

Finally, evidence should be transported to a location where it can be stored and locked. Sometimes the systems are too large to transport, thus the forensic examination of the system may need to take place on site.

Presented in Court. Each piece of evidence that is used to prove or disprove a material fact needs to be presented in court. After the initial seizure, the evidence is stored until needed for trial. Each time the evidence is transported to and from the courthouse for the trial, it needs to be handled with the same care as with the original seizure. Additionally, the Chain of Custody must continue to be followed. This process will continue until all testimony related to the evidence is completed. Once the trail is over, the evidence can be returned to the victim (owner).

Returned to Victim (Owner). The final destination of most types of evidence is back with its original owner. Some types of evidence, such as drugs or paraphernalia (i.e., contraband) are destroyed after the trial. Any evidence gathered during a search, even though maintained by law enforcement, is legally under the control of the courts. Even though a seized item may be yours and may even have your name on it, it may not be returned to you unless the suspect signs a release or after a hearing by the court. Unfortunately, many victims don't want to go to trial. They just want to get their property back.

Many investigations merely need the information on a disk to prove or disprove a fact in question, thus there is no need to seize the entire system. Once a schematic of the system is drawn or photographed, the hard disk can be removed and then transported to a forensic lab for copying. Mirror copies of the suspect disk are obtained using forensic software, and then one of those copies can be returned to the victim so that business operations can resume.

COMPUTER CRIME INVESTIGATION

The computer crime investigation should start immediately following the report of any alleged criminal activity. Many processes ranging from reporting and containment to analysis and eradication need to be accomplished as soon as possible after the attack. An Incident Response Plan should be formulated and a Computer Emergency Response Team (CERT) should be organized prior to the attack. The Incident Response Plan will help set the objective of the investigation and will identify each of the steps in the investigative process.

The use of a Corporate CERT Team is invaluable. Due to the numerous complexities of any computer-related crime, it is extremely advantageous to have a single group that is acutely familiar with the Incident Response Plan to call upon. The CERT team should be a technically astute group, knowledgeable in the area of legal investigations, the Corporate Security Policy (especially the Incident Response Plan), the severity levels of various attacks, and the company position on information dissemination and disclosure.

The Incident Response Plan should be part of the overall Corporate Computer Security Policy. The plan should identify reporting requirements, severity levels, guidelines to protect the crime scene and preserve evidence, etc. The priorities of the investigation will vary from organization to organization but the issues of containment and eradication are reasonably standard, that is to minimize any additional loss and resume business as quickly as possible. The following sections describe the investigative process starting with the initial detection.

Detection and Containment

Although intrusion detection is covered elsewhere in this manual, it must be mentioned that before any investigation can take place, the system intrusion or abusive conduct must first be detected. The closer the detection is to the actual intrusion event will not only help to minimize system damage, but will also assist in the identification of potential suspects.

To date, most computer crimes have either been detected by accident or through the laborious review of lengthy audit trails. While audit trails can assist in providing user accountability, their detection value is somewhat diminished because of the amount of information that must be reviewed and because these reviews are always post-incident. Accidental detection is usually made through observation of increased resource utilization or inspection of suspicious activity, but again, is not effective due to the sporadic nature of this type of detection.

These types of reactive or passive detection schemes are no longer acceptable. Proactive and automated detection techniques need to be instituted in order to minimize the amount of system damage in the wake of an attack. Real-time intrusion monitoring can help in the identification and apprehension of potential suspects, and automated filtering techniques can be used to make audit data more useful.

Once an incident is detected it is essential to minimize the risk of any further loss. This may mean shutting down the system and reloading clean copies of the operating system and application programs. It should be noted, that failure to contain a known situation (i.e., system penetration) might result in increased liability for the victim organization. For example, if a company's system has been compromised by an external attacker and the company failed to shut down the intruder, hoping to trace him, the company may be held liable for any additional harm caused by the attacker.

Report to Management

All incidents should be reported to management as soon as possible. Prompt internal reporting is imperative in order to collect and preserve potential evidence. It is important that information about the investigation be limited to as few people as possible. This should be done on a need-to-know basis. This limits the possibility of the investigation being leaked. Additionally, all communications related to the incident should be made via an out-of-band method to ensure the intruder does not intercept any incident-related information. In other words, do not use e-mail to discuss the investigation on a compromised system. Based on the type of crime and type of organization it may be necessary to notify:

- Executive Management
- Information Security Department
- Physical Security Department
- Internal Audit Department
- Legal Department

Preliminary Investigation

A preliminary internal investigation is necessary for all intrusions or attempted intrusions. At a minimum, the investigator must ascertain if a crime has occurred; and if so, he must identify the nature and extent of the abuse. It is important for the investigator to remember that the alleged attack or intrusion may not be a crime at all. Even if it appears to be some form of criminal conduct, it could merely be an honest mistake. Most internal losses occur from errors, not from overt criminal acts. There is no quicker way to initiate a lawsuit than to mistakenly accuse an innocent person of criminal activity.

The preliminary investigation usually involves a review of the initial complaint, inspection of the alleged damage or abuse, witness interviews, and, finally, examination of the system logs. If during the preliminary investigation, it is determined that some alleged criminal activity has occurred, the investigator must address the basic elements of the crime to ascertain the chances of successfully prosecuting a suspect either civilly or criminally. Additionally, the investigator must identify the requirements of the investigation (dollars and resources). If it is believed that a crime has been committed, neither the investigator nor any other company personnel should confront or talk with the suspect. Doing so would only give the suspect the opportunity to hide or destroy evidence.

Determine if Disclosure is Required

It must be determined if a disclosure is required or warranted, due to laws or regulations. Disclosure may be required by law or regulation or may be required if the loss affects a corporation's financial statement. Even if disclosure is not required, it is sometimes better to disclose the attack to possibly deter future attacks. This is especially true if the victim organization prosecutes criminally and/or civilly. Some of the following attacks would probably result in disclosure:

- Large Financial Loss of a Public Company
- Bank Fraud
- Public Safety Systems (i.e., Air Traffic Control)

The Federal Sentencing Guidelines also require organizations to report criminal conduct. The stated goals of the Commission were to "provide just punishment, adequate deterrence, and incentives for organizations to maintain internal mechanisms for preventing, detecting, and reporting criminal conduct." The Guidelines also state that organizations have a responsibility to "maintain internal mechanism for preventing, detecting, and reporting criminal conduct." The Federal Sentencing Guidelines do not prevent an organization from conducting preliminary investigations to ascertain if, in fact, a crime has been committed. One final note of the Federal Sentencing Guidelines is that they were designed to punish computer criminals for acts of recidivism and using their technical skills and talents to engage in criminal activity.

If the decision is made to disclose an alleged incident or intrusion, be sure to be especially careful when dealing with the media. The media has a history of sensationalizing these types of events and can easily distort the facts that could portray the victim organization as the "Goliath," using the "David v. Goliath" analogy. Make sure that you have all the facts and provide the media with the "slant" that best serves your purposes. Do not lie to the media! A "No Comment" is better then lying.

Investigation Considerations

Once the preliminary investigation is complete and the victim organization has made a decision related to disclosure, the organization must decide on the next course of action. The victim organization may decide to do nothing or it may attempt to eliminate the problem and just move on. Deciding to do nothing is not a very good course of action as the organization may be held to be culpably negligent should another attack or intrusion occur. The victim organization should at least attempt to eliminate the security hole that allowed the breach, even if it does not plan to bring the case to court. If the attack is internal, the organization may wish to conduct an investigation that might only result in the dismissal of the subject. If it decides to further investigate the incident, it must also determine if it is going to prosecute criminally or civilly, or merely conduct the investigation for insurance purposes. If an insurance claim is to be submitted, a police report is usually necessary.

When making the decision to prosecute a case, the victim must clearly understand the overall objective. If the victim is looking to make a point by punishing the attacker, then a criminal action is warranted. This is one of the ways to deter potential future attacks. If the victim were seeking financial restitution or injunctive relief, then a civil action would be appropriate. Keep in mind that a civil trial and criminal trial can happen in parallel. Information obtained during the criminal trial can be used as part of the civil trial. The key is to know what you want to do at the outset, so all activity can be coordinated.

The evidence or lack thereof, may also hinder the decision to prosecute. Evidence is a significant problem in any legal proceeding, but the problems are compounded when computers are involved. Special knowledge is needed to locate and collect the evidence, while special care is required to preserve the evidence.

There are many factors to consider when deciding upon whether or not to further investigate an alleged computer crime. For many organizations, the primary consideration will be the cost associated with an investigation. The next consideration will probably be the impact to operations or the impact to business reputation. The organization must answer the following questions:

- Will productivity be stifled by the inquiry process?
- Will the subject system have to be shut down to conduct an examination of the evidence or crime scene?
- Will any of the system components be held as evidence?
- Will proprietary data be subject to disclosure?
- Will there be any increased exposure for failing to meet a "standard of due care"?
- Will there be any adverse publicity related to the loss?
- Will a disclosure invite other perpetrators to commit similar acts, or will an investigation and subsequent prosecution deter future attacks?

The answers to these questions may have an impact on how the investigation is handled and who is called in to conduct the investigation. Furthermore, these issues must be addressed early on, so that the proper authorities can be notified if required. Prosecuting an alleged criminal offense is a very time-consuming task. Law enforcement and the prosecutor will expect a commitment of time and resources for the following:

- Interviews to prepare crime reports and search warrant affidavits
- Engineers or computer programmers to accompany law enforcement on search warrants
- Assistance of the victim company to identify and describe documents, source code, and other found evidence
- A company expert who may be needed for explanations and assistance during the trial

617

- Discovery — Documents may need to be provided to the defendant's attorney for discovery. They may ask for more than you want to provide. Your attorney will have to argue against broad-ranging discovery. Defendants are entitled to seek evidence they need for their defense.
- You and other company employees will be subpoenaed to testify.

Who Should Conduct the Investigation?

Based upon the type of investigation (i.e., civil, criminal, insurance, or administrative) and extent of the abuse, the victim must decide who is to conduct the investigation. This used to be a fairly straightforward decision, but high-technology crime has altered the decision-making process. Inadequate and untested laws, combined with the lack of technical training and technical understanding, has severely hampered the effectiveness of our criminal justice system when dealing with computer-related crimes.

In the past, society would adapt to change, usually at the same rate of that change. Today, this is no longer true. The information age has ushered in dramatic technological changes and achievements, which continue to evolve at exponential rates. The creation, the computer itself, is being used to create new technologies or advance existing ones. This cycle means that changes in technology will continue to occur at an ever-increasing pace. What does this mean to the system of law? It means we have to take a look at how we establish new laws. We must adapt the process to account for the excessive rate of change. Unfortunately, this is going to take time! In the meantime, if they are to launch an investigation, the victim must choose from the following options:

- Conduct an internal investigation
- Bring in external private consultants/investigations
- Bring in local/state/federal law enforcement

Exhibit 28.1 identifies each of the tradeoffs.

Law enforcement officers have greater search and investigative capabilities than private individuals, but they also have more restrictions than private citizens. For law enforcement to conduct a search, a warrant must first be issued. No warrant is needed if the victim or owner of compromised system gives permission to conduct the search. Issuance of the search warrant is based upon probable cause (reason to believe that something is true). Once probable cause has been identified, law enforcement officers have the ability to execute search warrants, subpoenas, and wire taps. The warrant process was formed in order to protect the rights of the people. The Fourth Amendment to the Constitution of the United States established the following:

Group	Cost	Legal Issues	Information Dissemination	Investigative Control
Internal Investigators	Time/People Resources	Privacy Issues Limited Knowledge of Law and Forensics	Controlled	Complete
Private Consultants	Direct Expenditure	Privacy Issues	Controlled	Complete
Law Enforcement Officers	Time/People Resources	Fourth Amendment Issues Jurisdiction Miranda Privacy Issues	Uncontrolled Public Information (FOIA)	None

Exhibit 28.1. Tradeoffs for Three Options Compensating for Rate of Change

---

The right of the people to be secure in their persons, houses, papers, and effects, against unreasonable searches and seizures, shall not be violated, and no Warrants shall issue, but upon probable cause, supported by oath or affirmation, and particularly describing the place to be searched, and the persons or things to be seized.

There are certain exceptions to this. The "exigent circumstances" doctrine allows for a warrantless seizure, by law enforcement, when the destruction of evidence is impending. In United States v. David, the court held that "When destruction of evidence is imminent, a warrantless seizure of that evidence is justified if there is probable cause to believe that the item seized constitutes evidence of criminal activity."

Internal investigators (non-government) or private investigators, acting as private citizens, have much more latitude in conducting a warrantless search, due to a ruling by the Supreme Court in Burdeau v. McDowell. In this case, the Supreme Court held that evidence obtained in a warrantless search could be presented to a grand jury by a government prosecutor, because there was no unconstitutional government search and hence no violation of the Fourth Amendment.

Normally, a private (party) citizen is not subject to the rules and laws governing search and seizure, but a private citizen becomes a police agent, and the Fourth Amendment applies, when:

- the private party performs a search which the government would need a search warrant to conduct;
- the private party performs that search to assist the government, as opposed to furthering its own interest; and
- the government is aware of that party's conduct and does not object to it.

The purpose of this doctrine is to eliminate the opportunity for government to circumvent the warrant process by eliciting the help of a private citizen. If a situation required law enforcement to obtain a warrant, due to the subject's expectations of privacy, and the government knowingly allowed a private party to conduct a search in order to disclose evidence, the court would probably rule that the private citizen acted as a police agent. A victim acting to protect its property by assisting police to prevent or detect a crime does not become a police agent.

Law enforcement personnel are not alone in their ability to obtain a warrant. A private party can also obtain a warrant, albeit a civil one, to search and seize specifically identified property which they make claim to. This civil warrant, also known as a Writ of Possession, allows the plaintiff to seize property that is rightfully theirs. In order to obtain such a court order, the plaintiff must prove to a judge or magistrate that the property in question is his and that an immediate seizure is essential to minimizing any collateral monetary loss. Additionally, the plaintiff must also post a bond, double the value of the property in question. This places an enormous burden on the plaintiff, should he be unsuccessful in his endeavor, but it also protects individuals and businesses against frivolous requests made to the court.

The biggest issues affecting the decision on who to bring in (in order of priority) are information dissemination, investigative control, cost, and the associated legal issues. Once an incident is reported to law enforcement, information dissemination becomes uncontrolled. The same holds true for investigative control. Law enforcement controls the entire investigation, from beginning to end. This is not always bad, but the victim organization may have a different set of priorities. Cost is always a concern, and the investigation costs only add to the loss initially sustained by the attack or abuse. Even law enforcement agencies, which are normally considered "free," add to the costs because of the technical assistance they require during the investigation.

Another area that affects law enforcement is jurisdiction. Jurisdiction is the geographic area where the crime had been committed and any portion of the surrounding area over, or through which the suspect passed, is enroute to, or going away from, the actual scene of the crime. Any portion of this area adjacent to the actual scene over which the suspect, or the victim, might have passed, and where evidence might be found, is considered part of the crime scene. When a system is attacked remotely, where did the crime occur? Most courts submit that the crime scene is the victim's location. But what about "enroute to"? Does this suggest that a crime scene may also encompass the telecommunications path used by the attacker? If so, and a theft occurred, is this interstate transport of stolen goods? There seem to be more questions than answers but only through cases being presented in court can precedence be set. It will take time for the answers to shake out.

There are advantages and disadvantages to each of the groups identified above. Internal investigators will know your systems the best, but may lack some of the legal and forensic training. Private investigators who specialize in high-technology crime also have a number of advantages, but usually result in higher costs. Private security practitioners and private investigators are also private businesses and may be more sensitive to business resumption than law enforcement. If you elect to retain the services of a private investigator or computer consultant, it is best if your corporate counsel retains them. This protects the victim organization from unwarranted or untimely disclosure. All communications are treated as privileged communications, under the Attorney-Client Privilege. Additionally, all work product is protected by the same privilege and is protected from disclosure. This includes details of the investigation, witness interviews, forensic analysis, etc. It also includes any past criminal activity by the victim organization which may be uncovered during the investigation.

Should you decide to contact your local police department, call the detective unit directly. Chances are you will get someone who is more experienced and knowledgeable and someone who can be more discreet. If you call 911, a uniformed officer will arrive on your doorstep and possibly alert the attacker. Furthermore, the officer must create a report of the incident that will become part of a public log. Now the chances for a discretionary dissemination of information and a covert investigation are gone.

Ask the detective to meet with you in plain clothes. When he arrives at your business have him announce himself as a consultant. If you decide that you would like federal authorities to be present, do so, but you should inform the local law enforcement authorities. Be aware that your local law enforcement agency may not be well equipped to handle high-tech crime. The majority of law enforcement agencies have limited budgets and, as such, place an emphasis on problems related to violent crime and drugs.

Also, with technology changing so rapidly, most law enforcement officers lack the technical training to adequately investigate an alleged intrusion.

The same problems hold true for the prosecution and the judiciary. To successfully prosecute a case, both the prosecutor and the judge must have a reasonable understanding of high-tech laws and the crime in question. This is not always the case. Additionally, many of the current laws are woefully inadequate. Even though an action may be morally and ethically wrong, it is still possible that no law is violated (i.e., LaMacchia case). Even when there is a law that has been violated, many of these laws remain untested and lack precedence. Because of this many prosecutors are reluctant to prosecute high-tech crime cases.

Many recent judicial decisions have indicated that judges are lenient towards techno-criminals just as with other white-collar criminals. Furthermore, the lack of technology expertise may cause "doubt," thus rendering "not guilty" decisions. Since many of the laws concerning computer crime are new and untested, many judges have a concern with setting precedents, which may later be overturned in an appeal. Some of the defenses that have been used, and accepted by the judiciary, are:

- If you have no system security or lax system security, then you are implying that there is no company concern. Thus there should be no court concern.
- If a person is not informed that access is unauthorized, then it can be used as a defense.
- If an employee is not briefed and does not acknowledge understanding of policy and procedures, then they can use it as a defense.

The Investigative Process

As with any type of criminal investigation the goal of the investigation is to know who, what, when, where, why, and how. It is important that the investigator logs all activity and accounts for all time spent on the investigation. The amount of time spent on the investigation has a direct impact on the total dollar loss for the incident. This may result in greater criminal charges and, possibly, stiffer sentencing. Finally, the money spent on investigative resources can be reimbursed as compensatory damages in a successful civil action.

Once the decision is made to further investigate the incident, the next course of action for the investigative team is to establish a detailed investigative plan, including the search and seizure plan. The plan should consist of an informal strategy that will be employed throughout the investigation, including the search and seizure:

- Identify any potential suspects
- Identify potential witnesses
- Identify what type of system is to be seized
- Identify the Search and Seizure Team Members
- Obtain a Search Warrant (if required)
- Determine if there is risk of the suspect destroying evidence or causing greater losses

Identify Any Potential Suspects. The type of crime and the type of attacker will set the stage for the overall investigation. Serious attacks against government sites, military installations, financial centers, or a telecommunications infrastructure must be met with the same fervor as that of a physical terrorist attack. Costs will not be the issue. On the other hand, when an organization plans to conduct an investigation pertaining to unauthorized access or a violation of company policy all the factors should be considered. This includes the anticipated cost and the chances of success. In either case, there will always be the usual suspects: insiders and outsiders.

Insiders are usually trusted users who abuse their level of authorized access to the system. They are normally the greatest source of loss. They know the value of your assets! They are usually motivated by greed, need (i.e., drug habit, gambling problem, divorce, etc.), or perceived grievance. Most importantly that have the access and the opportunity. Outsiders, as the name implies, attack your systems and networks from the outside. They attack systems for a variety of reasons, with attacks increasing at alarming rates because of advancements such as the Internet. Some examples of outsiders are as follows:

- Hackers and crackers
- Organized crime
- Terrorists
- Pedophiles
- Industrial/corporate spies

While, individually, each of these groups continues to be a problem, it is especially disturbing to realize the potential for collaboration between any two or more of the groups. When organized crime groups or terrorist factions gain access to the technical expertise provided by hackers and crackers, the potential for widespread harm and exorbitant financial losses is intensified. Albert Einstein said it best when he said, "Technological progress is like an axe in the hands of a pathological criminal."

When commencing with the investigation, it is important to understand how and why a system is being attacked. The how will provide you with information pertaining to technical expertise required to conduct the attack. The why will potentially indicate motive. The how and why together, along with the when and the where, may provide the who.

Identify Potential Witnesses. It is important to identify potential witnesses early on in the investigation. It is just as important not to alert the suspect to the investigation. Therefore selecting whom will be interviewed, and when, may have an impact on the investigation. The key to obtaining good witness statements is to ascertain the facts in the case, not opinions. Also, it is wise not to ask leading questions. Sources of information may be staff members, expert witnesses, associates, etc. Interviews are not the same as interrogations, and great care should go into not confusing the two. If a hostile witness does not want to be interviewed, then the process should cease immediately. If a witness or potential witness is detained against his will, there may be criminal and/or civil liability to the individuals and business responsible for the investigation. Never intimidate, coerce, or harass a potential witness.

Technically competent personnel should conduct interviews of technical witnesses or suspects. A potential suspect who is technically competent will have a field day if interviewed by a non-technical investigator. Many times these individuals are arrogant to start with. If they feel that they have the upper hand, because of their "esoteric knowledge," they may be less inclined to provide a truthful statement. Also, it is sometimes better to interview a technical suspect (i.e., programmer) first, before seizing his system. If you advise the suspect that you will be seizing his systems if he does not cooperate, he may assist in the investigation.

One final note on conducting interviews. It is always a good idea to have the witness write out and sign his statement, in his own handwriting. This statement can then be typed for better readability, but you can always point to the original. This helps to counter statements made by the witness in court, that that is not what he meant.

Identify the Type of System That Is to Be Seized. It is imperative to learn as much as possible about the target computer system(s). If possible, obtain the configuration of the system, including the network environment (if any), hardware, and software. The following data should be acquired prior to the seizure:

- Identify system experts. Make them part of the team.
- Is a security system in place on the system, If so, what kind? Are passwords used? Can a root password be obtained?
- Where is the system located? Will simultaneous raids be required?
- Obtain the required media supplies in advance of the operation
- What law has been violated? Discuss the elements of proof. These should be the focus of the search and seizure.

- What is your Probable Cause? Obtain a warrant if necessary.
- Determine if the analysis of the computer system will be conducted on site or back in the office or forensics lab.

Identify the Search and Seizure Team Members. There are different rules for Search and Seizure based upon who's conducting the search. Under the Fourth Amendment, law enforcement must obtain a warrant, which must be based on probable cause. Regardless of who's conducting the Search and Seizure, a team should be identified and should consist of the following members:

- Lead Investigator
- Information Security Department
- Legal Department
- Technical Assistance — System Administrator as long as he is not a suspect

If a Corporate CERT Team is already organized, then this process is already complete. A Chain of Command needs to be established and it must be determined who is to be in charge. This person is responsible for delegating assignments to each of the team members. A media liaison should be identified if the attack is to be disclosed. This will control the flow of information to the media.

Obtaining and Serving Search Warrants. If it is believed that the suspect has crucial evidence at his home or office, then a search warrant will be required to seize the evidence. If a search warrant is going to be needed, then it should be done as quickly as possible before the intruder can do further damage. The investigator must establish that a crime has been committed and that the suspect is somehow involved in the criminal activity. He must also show why a search of the suspect's home or office is required. The victim may be asked to accompany law enforcement when serving the warrant to identify property or programs.

If you must take along documents with you when serving the Search Warrant, consider copying them onto a colored paper to prevent the defense from inferring that what you might have found was left by you.

Is the System at Risk. Prior to the execution of the plan, the investigative team should ascertain if the suspect, if known, is currently working on the system. If so, the team must be prepared to move swiftly, so that evidence is not destroyed. The investigator should determine if the computer is protected by any physical or logical access control systems and be prepared to respond to such systems. It should also be decided early on, what will be done if the computer is on at the commencement of the seizure. The goal of this planning is to minimize any risk of evidence contamination or destruction.

Executing the Plan

The first step in executing the plan is to secure and control the scene. This includes securing the power, network servers, and telecommunications links. If the suspect is near the system, it may be necessary to physically remove him. It may be best to execute the search and seizure after normal business hours to avoid any physical confrontation. Keep in mind, that even if a search is conducted after hours, the suspect may still have remote access to the system via a LAN-based modem connection, PC-based modem connection, wireless modem connection, or Internet connection. Many times it is required to seize a disk from the suspect's computer, mirror image a copy of the disk, and then replace the original with a copy of the disk, all without the suspect knowing what is happening. This allows the investigative team to protect the evidence and continue with the investigation, while retaining secrecy of the investigation.

Enter the area slowly so as not to disturb or destroy evidence. Evaluate the entire situation. In no other type of investigation can evidence be destroyed more quickly. Do not touch the keyboard as this may invoke a Trojan Horse or some other rogue or malicious program. Do not turn off the computer unless it appears to be active (i.e., formatting the disk, deleting files, initiating some I/O process, etc.). Look for the disk activity light and listen for disk usage. If you must turn off the computer, pull the plug from the wall, rather than using the on/off switch. Look for notes, documentation, passwords, encryption codes, etc. The following questions must be answered in order to effectively control the scene:

- Is the subject system turned on?
- Is there a modem attached? If so,
  - Check for internal and wireless modems
  - Check for telephone lines connected to the computer
- Is the system connected to a LAN?

The investigator may wish to videotape the entire evidence collection process. There are two schools of thought on this. The first is that if you videotape the search and seizure, any mistakes can nullify the whole operation. The second school of thought is that if you videotape the evidence collection process, many of the claims by the defense can be silenced. In either case, be careful what you say if the audio is turned on!

Sketch and photograph the crime scene before touching anything. Sketches should be drawn to scale. Take still photographs of critical pieces of evidence. At a minimum, the following should be captured:

- The layout of desks and computers (include dimensions and measurements)
- The configuration of the all computers on the network
- The configuration of the suspect computer, including network connections, peripheral connections, internal and external components, and system backplane
- The suspect computer display

A drawing package, such a Visio — Technical Edition, is excellent for these types of drawings. Visio allows the investigator to sketch the scene using a drag and drop graphical user interface (GUI). Most computer and network graphics, desk and furniture graphics, etc., are included with the application. The output is a professional product that is made part of the report and can be used later to recreate the environment or to present the case in court.

If the computer is on, the investigator should capture what is on the monitor. This can be accomplished by videotaping what is on the screen. The best way to do this, without getting the "scrolling effect" caused by the video refresh, is to use a National Television Standards Committee (NTSC) adapter. Every monitor has a specific refresh rate (i.e., Horizontal: 30-66 KHz, Vertical: 50-90 Hz), which identifies how frequently the screen's image is redrawn. It is this redrawing process that causes the videotaped image to appear as if the vertical hold is not properly adjusted. The NTSC adapter is connected between the monitor and the monitor cable, and directs the incoming signal into the camcorder directly. The adapter converts the computer's analog signal (VGA) to an NTSC format. Still photos are a good idea too. Do not use a flash, because it can "white out" the image. Even if the computer is off, check the monitor for burnt-in images. This does not happen as much with the new monitors, but it may still help in the discovery of evidence.

Once you have reviewed and captured what's on the screen, pull the plug on the system. This is for PC-based systems only. Mini-systems or mainframes must be logically powered-down. It is best to conduct a forensic analysis (technical system review with a legal basis focused on evidence gathering) on a forensic system, in a controlled environment. If necessary, a forensic analysis can be conducted on site, but never using the suspect system's operating system or system utilities. See the section on forensic analysis for the process that should be followed.

Once the computer is turned off, remove the cover and photograph and sketch the inside of the computer. The analyst or investigator should use a static-dissipative grounding kit when working inside of the computer. You should note any peculiarities, such as booby traps. Identify each drive and its logical ID (i.e., C: drive) by tracing the ribbon cables to the I/O board.

Also identify any external drives. Once this has been completed, remove, label, and pack all drives. Check the floppy drives for any media. If a disk is in the drive, remove the disk, and mark on the evidence label where it was found. Next, place a blank diskette into the floppy drive(s). Place evidence tape over the floppy drives and the on/off switch, once it is placed in the off position.

Identify, mark, and pack all evidence according to the collection process under the Rules of Evidence. Identify and label all computer systems, cables, documents, disks, etc. The investigator should also seize all diskettes, backup tapes, PCMCIA disks, magnetic cartridges, optical disks, and printouts. All diskettes should be write protected. Make an entry for each in the evidence log. Check the printer. If it uses ribbons, make sure it (or at least the ribbon) is taken as evidence. Keep in mind that many of the peripheral devices may contain crucial evidence in their memory and/or buffers. Some items to consider are LAN servers, routers, printers, etc. You must check with the manufacturer on how to output the memory buffers for each device. Also, keep in mind that most buffers are stored in volatile memory. Once the power is cut, the information may be lost.

Additionally, check all drawers, closets, and even the garbage for any forms of magnetic media (i.e., hard drives, floppy diskettes, tape cartridges, optical disks, etc.) or documentation. It seems that many computer literate individuals conduct most of their correspondence and work product on a computer. This is an excellent form of leads, but take care to avoid an invasion of privacy. Even media that appear to be destroyed can turn out to be quite useful. One case involved an American serviceman who contracted to have his wife killed and wrote the letter on his computer. In an attempt to destroy all the evidence, he cut up the floppy disk, containing the letter, into 17 pieces. The Air Force Office of Special Investigations (AFOSI) was able to reconstruct the diskette and read almost all the information.

Don't overlook the obvious, especially hacker tools and any ill-gotten gains (i.e., password or credit card lists). This will help your case when trying to show motive and opportunity. The State of California has equated hacker tools with burglary tools; the mere possession constitutes a crime. Possession of a Red Box, or any other telecommunications instrument that has been modified with the intent to defraud, is also prohibited under U.S.C. Section 1029. Some of the hacker tools that you should be aware of are:

- Password crackers
- Network sniffers
- Automated probing tools (i.e., SATAN)
- Anonymous remailers

- War dialers
- Encryption and steganography tools

Finally, phones, answering machines, desk calendars, day-timers, fax machines, pocket organizers, electronic watches, etc. are all sources of potential evidence. If the case warrants, seize and analyze all sources of data, both electronic and manual. Document all activity in an Activity Log, and if necessary secure the crime scene.

Surveillance

There are two forms of surveillance used in computer crime investigations. They are physical surveillance and computer surveillance. The physical surveillance can be generated at the time of the abuse, via CCTV security camera, or after the fact. When done after the fact, physical surveillance is usually performed undercover. It can be used in an investigation to determine a subject's personal habits, family life, spending habits, or associates.

Computer surveillance is achieved in a number of ways. It is done passively through audit logs or actively by way of electronic monitoring. Electronic monitoring can be accomplished via keyboard monitoring, network sniffing, or line monitoring. In any case, it generally requires a warning notice and/or explicit statement in the security policy, indicating that the company can and will electronically monitor any and all systems or network traffic. Without such a policy or warning notice, a warrant is normally required.

Before you conduct electronic monitoring, make sure you review Chapters 2500 & 2700 of the Electronic Communications Privacy Act, Title 18 of the US Code as it relates to keystroke monitoring or system administrators looking into someone's account. If you do not have a banner or if the account holder has not been properly notified, the system administrator and the company can be guilty of a crime and liable for both civil and criminal penalties. Failure to obtain a warrant could result in the evidence being suppressed or worse yet, litigation by the suspect for invasion of privacy or violation of the ECPA.

One other method of computer surveillance that is used are "sting operations." These operations are established so as to continue to track the attacker, online. By baiting a trap or setting up "Honey Pots," the victim organization lures the attacker to a secured area of the system. This is what was done in the Cuckoo's Egg. The system attackers were enticed into accessing selected files. Once these files or their contents are downloaded to another system, their mere presence can be used as evidence against the suspect. This enticement is not the same as entrapment as the intruder is already predisposed to commit the crime. Entrapment only occurs when a law enforcement officer induces a person to commit a crime that the person had not previously contemplated.

INVESTIGATION

It is very difficult to track and identify a hacker or remote intruder, unless there is a way to trace the call (i.e., Caller ID, wiretap, etc.). Even with these resources, many hackers meander through communication networks, hopping from one site to the next, via a multitude of telecommunications gateways and hubs, such as the Internet! Bill Cheswick, author of Firewalls and Internet Security, refers to this a "connection laundering." Additionally, the organization cannot take the chance of allowing the hacker to have continued access to its system and potentially cause any additional harm.

Telephone traps require the equivalent of a search warrant. Additionally, the victim will be required to file a criminal report with law enforcement and must show probable cause. If sufficient probable cause is shown, a warrant will be issued and all incoming calls can be traced. Once a trace is made, a pen register is normally placed on the suspect's phone to log all calls placed by the suspect. These entries can be tied to the system intrusions based upon the time of the call and the time the system was accessed.

Investigative and Forensic Tools

Exhibit 28.2, although not exhaustive, identifies some of the investigative and forensic tools that are commercially available. The first table identifies the hardware and software tools that should be part of the investigator's toolkit, while the second table identifies forensic software and utilities.

Other Investigative Information Sources

When conducting an internal investigation it is important to remember that the witness statements and computer-related evidence are not the only sources of information useful to the investigation. Personnel files provide a wealth of information related to an employee's employment history. It may show past infractions by the employee or disciplinary action by the company. Telephone and fax logs can possibly identify any accomplices or associates of the subject. At a minimum they will identify the suspect's most recent contacts. Finally, security logs, time cards, and check-in sheets will determine when a suspected insider had physical access to a particular system.

Investigative Reporting

The goal of the investigation is to identify all available facts related to the case. The investigative report should provide a detailed account of the incident, highlighting any discrepancies in witness statements. The report should be a well-organized document that contains a description of the incident, all witness statements, references to all evidentiary articles, pictures of the crime scene, drawings and schematics of the computer and the computer network (if applicable), and finally, a written description of the forensic

Investigative Tools	
Investigation and Forensic Toolkit Carrying Case	Static Charge Meter
Cellular Phone	EMF/ELF Meter (Magnetometer)
Laptop Computer	Gender Changer (9 Pin and 25 Pin)
Camcorder w/NTSC adapter	Line Monitor
35mm Camera (2)	RS232 Smart Cable
Wide Angle & Telephoto Lens	Nitrile Anti-static Gloves
Night Vision Adapter for Camera and Camcorder	Alcohol Cleaning Kit
Polaroid Camera	CMOS Battery
Tape Recorder (VOX)	Extension Cords
Scientific Calculator	Power Strip
Label Maker	Keyboard Key Puller
Crime Scene/Security Barrier Tape	Cable Tester
PC Keys	Breakout Box
IC Removal Kit	Transparent Static Shielding Bags (100 Bags)
Compass	Anti-Static Sealing Tape
Diamond Tip Engraving Pen Extra Diamond Tips	Serial Port Adapters (9 Pin—25 Pin & 25 Pin—9 Pin)
Felt Tip Pens	Foam-Filled Carrying Case
Evidence Seals (250 Seals/Roll)	Static-Dissipative Grounding Kit w/Wrist Strap
Plastic Evidence Bags (100 Bags)	Foam-Filled Disk Transport Box
Evidence Labels (100 Labels)	Computer Dusting System (Air Spray)
Evidence Tape—2″ X 165′	Small Computer Vacuum
Tool Kit containing: Screwdriver Set (inc. Precision Set) Torx Screwdriver Set 25′ Tape Measure Razor Knife Nut Driver Pliers Set LAN Template Probe Set Neodymium Telescoping Magnetic Pickup Allen Key Set Alligator Clips Wire Cutters Small Pry Bar Hammer Tongs and/or Tweezers	Printer and Ribbon Cables 9 Pin Serial Cable 25 Pin Serial Cable Null Modem Cable Centronics Parallel Cable 50 Pin Ribbon Cable LapLink Parallel Cable Telephone Cable for Modem
Cordless Driver w/Rechargeable Batteries (2)	Batteries for Camcorder, Camera, Tape Recorder, etc. (AAA, AA, 9-volt)
Pen Light Flashlight	
Magnifying Glass 3 1/4″	
Inspection Mirror	

Exhibit 28.2. Investigative and Forensic Tools (continues)

Computer Supplies	Software Tools
Diskettes: 3 1/2" Diskettes (Double & High Density Format) 5 1/4" Diskettes (Double & High Density Format)	Sterile O/S Diskettes
Diskette Labels	Virus Detection Software
5 1/2" Floppy Diskette Sleeves	SPA Audit Software
3 1/2" Floppy Diskette Container	Little-Big Endian Type Application
CD-ROM Container	Password Cracking Utilities
Write Protect labels for 5 1/4" Floppies	Disk Imaging Software
Tape and Cartridge Media 1/4" Cartridges 4mm & 8mm DAT Travan 9-Track/1600/6250 QIC Zip Drives Jazz Drives	Auditing Tools Test Data Method Integrated Test Facility (ITF) Parallel Simulation Snapshot Mapping Code Comparison Checksum
Hard Disks IDE SCSI	File Utilities (DOS, Windows, 95, NT, UNIX)
Paper 8 1/2 x 11 Laser Paper 80 Column Formfeed 132 Column Formfeed	Zip/Unzip Utilities
Miscellaneous Supplies	**Miscellaneous Supplies**
Paper Clips	MC60 Microcassette Tapes
Scissors	Camcorder Tapes
Rubber Bands	35mm Film (Various Speeds)
Stapler and Staples	Polaroid Film
Masking Tape	Graph Paper
Duct Tape	Sketch Pad
Investigative Folders	Evidence Checklist
Cable Ties/Labels	Blank Forms—Schematics
Numbered and Colored Stick-on Labels	Label Maker Labels

Exhibit 28.2. (continued)

---

analysis. The report should state final conclusions, based solely on the facts. It should not include the investigator's opinions, unless he is an expert. Keep in mind that all documentation related to the investigation is subject to discovery by the defense, so be careful about what is written down!

COMPUTER FORENSICS

Computer forensics is the study of computer technology as it relates to the law. The objective of the forensic process is to learn as much about the suspect system as possible. This generally means analyzing the system using a variety of forensic tools and processes. Bear in mind that the examination of the suspect system may lead to other victims and other suspects. The actual forensic process will be different for each system analyzed, but the following guidelines should help the investigator/analyst conduct the forensic analysis.

There are many tools available to the forensic analyst to assist in the collection, preservation, and analysis of computer-based evidence. The make-up of a forensic system will vary from lab to lab, but at a minimum, each forensic system must have the ability to:

- Conduct a Disk Image Backup of the Suspect System
- Authenticate the File System
- Conduct Forensic Analysis in a Controlled Environment
- Validate Software and Procedures

Before analyzing any system it is extremely important to protect the systems and disk drives from static electricity. The analyst should always use an anti-static or static-dissipative wristband and mat before conducting any forensic analysis.

Conduct a Disk Image Backup of the Suspect System

A disk image backup is different from a file system backup in that it conducts a bit level copy of the disk, sector by sector, rather than merely copying the system files. This process provides the capability to back up deleted files, unallocated clusters, and slack space. The backup process can be accomplished by using either disk imaging hardware, such as the ImageMaster 1000, or through a variety of software programs. Most of these programs run under DOS or Windows and will back up most any type of hard disk or floppy disk, regardless of the operating system. The image backup process is conducted as depicted in Exhibit 28.3.

Authenticate the File System

File system authentication helps to ensure the integrity of the seized data and the forensic process. Before actually analyzing the suspect disk, a message digest is generated for all system directories, files and disk sectors. A message digest is a signature that uniquely identifies the content of a file or disk sector. It is created using a one-way hashing algorithm. In the past a 32-bit CRC32 algorithm was used, but due to the advancements in cryptographic research and along with more powerful machines, two more advanced, one-way hashing algorithms are now being used. MD5 is a 128-bit hash, while SHA is a 160-bit hash. These strong cryptographic hashing algorithms virtually guarantee the integrity of the processed data. Doing

Step	Disk Image Backup Procedure
1	Remove the internal hard disk(s) from suspect machine and label (if not already done). Make a note of which logical disk you are removing. Follow the ribbon cables from the disk to the I/O board to accomplish this task. It is a good idea to photograph the inside of the system including the connections to the I/O boards and disk drives.
2	Identify the type of disk (i.e. IDE or SCSI). Identify the make and model.
3	Identify the disk capacity. Make a note of cylinders, heads and sectors.
4	Place each disk, one at a time, in a clean forensic examination machine as the next available drive. Beware that the suspect disk may have a virus (keep only the minimal amount of software on the forensic examination machine). Note, if you are using a hardware-based disk duplication method (i.e. ImageMaster 1000), then this step is not necessary.
5	Backup (Disk Image) the suspect disk(s) to tape—Make at least 4 copies of each suspect disk
6	Check the disk image backup logs to make sure that there were no errors during the backup process.
7	Place the original suspect disk(s), along with one of the backup tapes, and backup logs, in the appropriate container. Seal, mark and log into evidence.
8	Return a copy of the original disk to the victim (if applicable)
9	Use the last two copies for the forensic analysis (one is used for file authentication)

Exhibit 28.3.   Image Backup Process

---

this now will help refute any argument by the defense, that the evidence was tampered with.

The concept of a one-way hash, using MD5 for example, is that a file is read into memory. The file is then processed, bit by bit, until it reaches the end of the file. The hashing process creates a 128-bit signature for the file that is based upon the file content. Even the change of a single bit will change the signature produced by the hashing algorithm. The significance of the one-way hash is that it only works one way. Knowledge of the hash value cannot produce the file content itself.

The only problem with executing the authentication process is that it will change the file's last access time. The mere process of reading the file to produce the hash value will change this time. That is why a separate backup is used for the authentication process.

Conduct Forensic Analysis in a Controlled Environment

After restoring at least one of the backup tapes to a disk, of equal capacity to the original disk (identical disk, if possible), the restored data should be analyzed. This should be done in a controlled environment on a forensic system. Everything on the system must be checked, starting with the file system and directory structure. The analyst should create an organizational chart of the disk file system and then inventory all files on the disk.

There are a number of commercially available utilities that allow the analyst to quickly create a directory tree, list system files, identify hidden files, and to conduct keyword searches. The analyst should make notes during each step in the process, especially when restoring hidden or deleted files, or modifying the suspect system (i.e., repairing a corrupted disk sector w/Norton Utilities). The analyst should also note that what may have happened on the system may have resulted from error or incompetence rather than from a malicious user. It is a good idea to check for viruses at this point to, first, note their existence, and secondly, to avoid potential contamination.

Since forensic analysis can be a laborious and time-consuming process, it is sometimes better to distribute the workload to other analysts and case agents. Since it would be too costly to have multiple forensic systems and to have to replicate the suspect data on multiple hard drives, it may be more effective to make CD copies of the hard disk contents that can be distributed and analyzed by different individuals. This is certainly more cost effective and may possibly accelerate the analysis process.

When using CD-R or WORM (Write Once Read Many) technology, the data should be structured in a way that will enhance the forensic process. One method of data organization that works quite well is to create a logical directory structure that will store and organize all data from the target disk. This should include all files and directories from the original file structure, deleted files, hidden files, data in slack space, data in unallocated space, compressed data, encrypted data, and data generated from search results.

To initiate this process, the analyst should copy (file copy) the complete file structure, starting from the root directory, from the image copy to a newly created hard disk partition. This type of copy will not pick up deleted files, data in slack space, or data in unallocated space, therefore the analyst must manually copy this data from the target system to the new disk partition. Before copying this data, individual sub-directories must be created for each data type: DELETED, SLACK, UNALLOC. The file copy process will copy the swap file, but it may be best to move the file to a SWAP sub-directory. The next step in the process is to review the information in the original file system, looking for files with hidden file attributes, compressed files, encrypted files, and files that meet the criteria of keyword searches. These, too, should be copied to specific directories, so that later it is understood where the data came from. The following directories should be created to store and organize this data: HIDDEN, COMPRESS, ENCRYPT, and SEARCH.

The final process is to use a disk editor utility to look for "BAD" clusters that have data in them and to run keyword searches at the disk editor level (below the operating system). Any data found during this analysis should be copied to the newly created file system. A BAD sub-directory can be created under the HIDDEN sub-directory, and an EDITOR sub-directory can be created under the SEARCH sub-directory. Once the new file system is populated with all the data, the information can be burnt into a CD-R or WORM drive. This information can then be made available to other forensic analysts or case agents. If damaging evidence is discovered upon review of the data stored on the CD-R or WORM drive, the original information can easily be recovered from the original image copy.

A quick background on file times should be given before continuing on. Most computer systems, including Windows 95, NT, and UNIX store three values for file times: creation time, update time, last access time. Any or all of these file times may have an impact on the investigation. The access time is the one most susceptible to modification because any read to access to the file changes this time. The image backup will not change this time, but the file authentication process will! The creation time is the time the file was originally created. It is not accessible from the file manager or the DIR command. The update time is the time the file was last modified (written to). This is the time the file manager displays. The last access time is recorded whenever any other program or command, including read, copy, etc., touches the file. This time is also not accessible from the file manager but can be seen in the file properties.

When searching through files and directories, the first things to look for are file names or document content that have case-relevant names. For example, if the case you are working is an espionage or theft of trade secrets case, then look for file names with the word (or partial word) of the trade secret item itself. If trade secret was related to the release of a new, database software product, called SplitDB, then look for files with the name "split.xls," "db.doc," or "database.ppt." Another search may find the word "split," "db," or "database" in the body of a word processing document (i.e., a hidden file named sys.dll with the following phase, "For this database structure to work effectively..."). Another indicator that something is afoul, is when the file extension doesn't match the file signature. All files have a signature, which identifies the type of file, somewhere in the first 50 characters of the file. This file signature normally correlates to a particular file extension. For example, a bitmap graphic file normally has a file extension of .bmp and a file signature of BM as the first two bytes of the file. If these two items do not match up, then it may mean that someone modified the file extension to hide the presence of the file. A pedophile can use this technique to hide a bitmap image containing child pornography in the c:\windows\system directory as system.dll. A cursory review of the system may miss this file completely, thinking that it is a Windows system file, when in fact it is damaging evidence.

Search Tools. There are many search tools that can assist the forensic analyst in his endeavor to locate damaging evidence. Most of these tools are commercial off-the-shelf (COTS) applications that were created for some reason other than forensics. It just so happens that these applications work well in a forensic environment. Norton Utilities, although not the end all, is a must for all forensic investigators. Norton provides file searching utilities, disk editor functions, data recovery, etc. Some other tools are listed below:

- Quick View Plus
- Expert Witness
- Computer Forensics Laboratory
- Drag and View
- Rescue Professional
- Super Sleuth
- Outside/In

Searching for Obscure Data. Once the basic analysis is complete, the next step is to conduct a more detailed analysis of more obscure data. It may be necessary to use forensic data recovery techniques to locate and recover:

- Hidden files
  - Hidden by attributes
  - Hidden through steganography
  - Hidden in slack space
  - Hidden in good clusters marked as BAD
- Modifying the size of the file in the directory entry
- Hidden directories
- Erased or deleted files
- Reformatted media
- Encrypted data
- Overwritten (wiped) files

The fact that a file is hidden is a good indicator of its evidentiary value. If someone took the time to hide the file, it was probably hidden for a reason. The simplest way to hide a file is to alter the file attribute to Hidden, System, or Volume Label. Files with these attributes do not normally appear in a DIR listing or even in the Windows file manager. Simply changing the attribute back will make the file accessible. Files with the Hidden attribute set are usually further hidden in a hidden directory. An example of a hidden directory would be the .directory in UNIX or creating a directory with the ALT 255 character in a Windows or DOS system. Many times these hidden directories are deeply nested to avoid discovery. The "chkdsk" utility will display the number of hidden files on the DOS system, while Norton Utilities will display a listing of the hidden file and its location.

A file can also be hidden in slack space. Slack space is the area left over in a cluster that is not utilized by a file. For example, if a 2K file is stored in a 32K cluster, then there is 30K of slack space, which may contain data from a previous file. This area can also be used to hide data. A cluster, which is the basic allocation unit, is the smallest unit of space that DOS uses for a file. The amount of slack space for a given file varies based upon the file size and cluster size. The cluster size usually expands as hard disk capacity increases.

Another, more elaborate way to hide data is to first write data to a file in the normal way. When this is complete, the suspect can use a disk editor to ascertain the sector and cluster of the newly created file, go to that cluster and mark the cluster as BAD. When the operating system sees a BAD cluster, it simply ignores the area. The data is still present on the disk even though it cannot be accessed. The analyst will need to locate the cluster by using a sector-searching utility, then go to the specific cluster and remove the BAD label.

Files and directories can also be deleted. But when DOS or Windows deletes a file, it only changes the first character of the file name to 0xE5, which merely makes the file space available. The file is not actually removed. The data in the cluster previously allocated by the file is still available until overwritten by a new file. On DOS and Windows systems, the analyst can use the un-erase utility to recover deleted files. These utilities only recover the first cluster that the file occupied. If the file occupied multiple clusters, this data may be lost, as the cluster chain is no longer available. Cluster chains can be rebuilt, although not reliably.

If the disk is formatted, the analyst can attempt to use the "un-format" command in the DOS or Windows environment. If the disk has been wiped, which is also known as shredding, the data is not easily recoverable. The cost of recovery is usually exorbitant, far exceeding the initial loss.

Steganography. Steganography is the art of hiding communications. Unlike encryption, which utilizes an algorithm and a seed value to scramble or encode a message in order to make it unreadable, steganography makes the communication invisible. This takes concealment to the next level — that is to deny that the message even exists. If a forensic analyst were to look at an encrypted file, it would be obvious that some type of cypher process has been used. It is even possible to determine what type of encryption process was used to encrypt the file, based upon a unique signature. However, steganography hides data and messages in a variety of picture files, sound files, and even slack space on floppy diskettes. Even the most trained security specialist or forensic analyst may miss this type of concealment during a forensic review.

Steganography simply takes one piece of information and hides it within another. Computer files, such as images, sound recordings, and slack space contain unused or insignificant areas of data. For example, the least significant bits of a 24-bit bitmap image can be used to hide messages, usually without any material change in the original file. Only through a direct, visual comparison of the original and processed image can the analyst detect the possible use of steganography. Since many times the suspect system only stores the processed image, the analyst has nothing to use as a comparison and generally has no way to tell that the image in question contains hidden data. There is research under way that will help in the forensic process when dealing with steganography. New tools are being developed that will look at the file contents to determine if there is a steganographic signature within the file. But with over 25 different types of steganography being used today, this new research may take some time.

Review Communications Programs. A good source of contact and associate information can many times be found online. Since many technically competent individuals use technology for the same reasons businesses do, electronic Rolodexes, databases of contacts, and communication programs should be searched. Applications like Microsoft Outlook, ACT, and others can be tremendously beneficial during an investigation to link your suspect to other individuals or businesses. Some computers store Caller ID files, while others may contain war dialer (or demon dialer) logs. Review communications programs, such as Procomm, to ascertain if any numbers are stored in the application.

Microprocessor Output. One final note, before moving on to the next step in the forensic process, is to understand that not all microprocessors are created equal. If a forensic analyst is forced to dump the contents of a file in binary or hexadecimal format, he must not only understand how to read these hieroglyphic notations, but must know the type of microprocessor that produced the output. For example, the Intel 30286 is a 16-bit, little endian processor. A 16-bit microprocessor is capable of working with binary numbers of up to 16 places or bits. That translates to the decimal number 65,536. The Intel 30486 and newer Pentium processors are 32-bit computers, capable of handling binary numbers of up 32 bits or up to the decimal number 4,294,967,296. The little endian attribute of the Intel chip signifies the byte, not bit, ordering sequence. In this case the bytes are reversed, where the high-order byte(s) is stored in a low-order byte location. A big endian processor does not reverse the byte order. It is important to understand that the same value dumped out on two different systems may produce different results.

Reassemble and Boot Suspect System
(with Clean Operating System)

The next step in the process is to reassemble the suspect system, using one of the copies of the suspect disk. Place a clean copy of the forensic operating system (usually DOS or Windows) into the floppy drive. Start the boot process and enter the CMOS setup. Check the CMOS to make sure that the boot sequence looks to the floppy drive first, then the hard disk second. This will allow the investigator to boot from the clean operating system diskette. Also, if the system is password protected at the CMOS level, remove and reinstall or short out the CMOS battery. Continue with the boot process and pay particular attention to the Boot-up process, looking for a modified BIOS or EPROM.

It is very important to boot from a clean operating system, as the target system utilities may contain a Trojan Horse or Logic Bomb that will do other than what's intended. (e.g., Modified command.com—conducting a Delete with the Dir command). The first thing to do once the system is booted is to check the system time. This time, even if not accurate, will give the analyst or investigator a reference for all file times. After the system time is obtained, run a complete Systems Analysis Report. This report should, at a minimum, provide the following:

- System Summary—contains basic system configuration
- Disk Summary
- Memory Usage w/Task List
- Display Summary
- Printer Summary
- TSR Summary
- DOS Driver Summary
- System Interrupts
- CMOS Summary
- Listing of all environment variables as set by Autoexec.bat, config.sys, win.ini, system.ini, etc.

Audit trails can be viewed any time subsequent to the image backup, but before a thorough analysis can be completed, the analyst will need a time reference, which is obtained from booting the suspect system. Check the audit logs for system and account activity. Check with the victim organization to ascertain if the Audit logs are used in the normal course of business. The following questions must be asked:

- Is there a corporate security policy on how the logs are to be used? If so, has the policy been followed?
- What steps have been taken to ensure the integrity of the audit trail?
- Has the audit trail been tampered with? If so, when?

Boot Suspect System (with Original Operating System)

The next step in the forensic process is to boot the target system using the original, target system operating system. This is done to see if any rouge programs were left on the system. The analyst should let the system install all background programs (set by autoexec.bat and config.sys). Once this has been done, the analyst should check what programs (including TSRs) are running and what system interrupts have been set. The goal is to learn if there are any Trojan Horses or other rouge programs, such as keystroke monitors, activated. Execute some of the basic operating system commands to see if the command.com file has been altered.

Searching Backup Media

Remember that if the data is not on the hard disk, it may be on backup tapes or some other form of backup media. Even if the data was recently deleted from the hard disk, there may be a backup that has all of the original data. Many times a "snapshot" of the system is taken on a weekly or monthly basis and saved in the long-term archives for disaster contingency purposes. Search for PCMCIA flash disks, floppy diskettes, optical disks, Ditto tapes, Zip and Jazz cartridges, Kangaroo drives, or any other form of backup media. Restore and review all data. Many organizations store backups off-site, and although a warrant may be required to obtain the media, don't forget to ascertain if this practice is being done. Before analyzing floppy diskettes, always write-protect the media.

Searching Access Controlled Systems and Encrypted Files

During a search the investigator may be confronted with a system which is secured physically and/or logically. Some physical security devices, such as CPU key locks, prevent only a minor obstacle, whereas other types of physical access control systems may be harder to break.

Logical access control systems may pose a more challenging problem. The analyst may be confronted with a software security program that requires a unique user-name and password. Some of these systems can be simply bypassed by entering a control-c or some other interrupt command. The analyst must be cautious that any of these commands may invoke a Trojan Horse routine that may destroy the contents of the disk. A set of "password cracker" programs should be part of the forensic tool-kit. The analyst can always try to contact the publisher of the software program in an effort to gain access. Most security program publishers leave a back door into their systems.

The investigator should look around the suspect's work area for documents that may provide him with a clue to the proper user-name/password combination. Check desk drawers, the suspect's Rolodex, acquaintances, friends, etc. It may be possible to compel a suspect to provide access information. It is a good idea to first ask the suspect for his password, before going through the process of compelling him to do so. The following cases set precedence for ordering a suspect, whose computer is in the possession of law enforcement, to divulge password or decryption key:

- Fisher v US (1976), 425 US 391, 48 LED2 39
- US v Doe (1983), 465 US 605, 79 LED2d 552
- Doe v US (1988), 487 US 201, 101 LED2d 184
- People v Sanchez (1994) 24 CA4 1012

The caveat is that the suspect might use this opportunity to command the destruction of potential evidence. The last resort may be that the system needs to be hacked. This can be done as follows:

- Search for passwords written down (it may be part of the evidence collected)
- Try words, names, or numbers that are related to the suspect
- Call the software vendor and request their assistance (some charge for this)
- Try to use password cracking programs which are readily available on the net
- Try a brute force or dictionary attack

LEGAL PROCEEDINGS

A brief description of the legal proceedings that occur subsequent to the investigation is necessary so the victim and the investigative team understand the full impact of their decision to prosecute. The post-incident legal proceedings generally result in additional cost to the victim, until the outcome of the case, at which time they may be reimbursed.

Discovery and Protective Orders

Discovery is the process whereby the prosecution provides all investigative reports, information on evidence, list of potential witnesses, any criminal history of witnesses, and any other information except how they're going to present the case to the defense. Any property or data recovered by law enforcement will be subject to discovery if a person is charged with a crime. However, a protective order can limit who has access, who can copy, and the disposition of the certain protected documents. These protective orders allow the victim to protect proprietary or trade secret documents related to a case.

Grand Jury and Preliminary Hearings

If the defendant is held to answer in a preliminary hearing or the grand jury returns an indictment, a trial will be scheduled. If the case goes to trial, interviews with witnesses will be necessary. The victim company may have to assign someone to work as the law enforcement liaison.

The Trial

The trial may not be scheduled for some time based upon the backlog of the court that has jurisdiction in the case. Additionally, the civil trial and criminal trial will occur at different times, although much of the investigation can be run in parallel. The following items provide tips on courtroom testimony:

- The prosecutor does not know what the defense attorney will ask.
- Listen to the questions carefully to get the full meaning and to determine that this is not a multiple part or contradictory question.
- Do not answer quickly; give the prosecutor time to object to the defense questions that are inappropriate, confusing, contradictory, or vague.
- If you do not understand the question, ask the defense attorney for an explanation, or answer the question by stating, "I understand your question to be . . ."
- You cannot give hearsay answers. This generally means that you cannot testify to what someone has told you.
- Do not lose your temper and get angry as this may affect your credibility.
- You may need to utilize expert witnesses.

Recovery of Damages

To recover the costs of damages, such as reconstructing data, re-installing an uncontaminated system, repairing a system, or investigating a breach, you can file a civil law suit against the suspect in either Superior Court or Small Claims Court.

Post Mortem Review

The purpose of the Post Mortem review is to analyze the attack and close the security holes that led to the initial breach. In doing so, it may also be necessary to update the corporate security policy. All organizations should take the necessary security measures to limit their exposure and potential liability. The security policy should include an:

- Incident Response Plan
- Information Dissemination Policy
- Incident Reporting Policy
- Electronic Monitoring Statement
- Audit Trail Policy

- Inclusion of a Warning Banner—This should:
  - Prohibit unauthorized access and;
  - Give notice that all electronic communications will be monitored

One final note is that many internal attacks can be avoided by conducting background checks on potential employees and consultants.

SUMMARY

As you probably gleaned from this chapter, computer crime investigation is more an art than a science. It is a rapidly changing field that requires knowledge in many disciplines. But although it may seem esoteric, most investigations are based on traditional investigative procedures. Planning is integral to a successful investigation. For the internal investigator, an Incident Response Plan should be formulated prior to an attack. The Incident Response Plan will help set the objective of the investigation and will identify each of the steps in the investigative process. For the external investigator, investigative planning may have to happen post incident. It is also important to realize that no one person will have all the answers and that teamwork is essential. The use of a Corporate CERT Team is invaluable, but when no team is available, the investigator may have the added responsibility of building a team of specialists.

The investigator's main responsibility is to determine the nature and extent of the system attack. From there, with knowledge of the law and forensics, the investigative team may be able to piece together who committed the crime, how and why the crime was committed, and maybe more importantly, what can be done to minimize the potential for any future attacks. For the near term, convictions will probably be few, but as the law matures and as investigations become more thorough, civil and criminal convictions will increase. In the meantime, it is extremely important that investigations be conducted so as to better understand the seriousness of the attack and the overall impact to business operations

Finally, to be successful, the computer crime investigator must, at a minimum, have a thorough understanding of the law, the rules of evidence as they relate to computer crime, and computer forensics. With this knowledge, the investigator should be able to adapt to any number of situations involving computer abuse.

Domain 9.2
Information Ethics

Chapter 29
Ethics and the Internet
Micki Krause

The research for this chapter was done entirely on the Internet. The net is a powerful tool. This author dearly hopes that the value of its offerings is not obviated by those who would treat the medium in an inappropriate and unethical manner.

Ethics: Social values; a code of right and wrong

INTRODUCTION

The ethical nature of the Internet has been likened to "a restroom in a downtown bus station," where the lowest of the low congregate and nothing good ever happens. This manifestation of antisocial behavior can be attributed to one or more of the following:

- The relative anonymity of those who use the net
- The lack of regulation in cyberspace
- The fact that one can masquerade as another on the Internet
- The fact that one can fulfill a fantasy or assume a different persona on the net, thereby eliminating the social obligation to be accountable for one's own actions

Whatever the reason, the Internet, also known as the "wild west" or the "untamed frontier," is absent of law and therefore is a natural playground for illicit, illegal, and unethical behavior.

In the ensuing pages, we will explore the types of behavior demonstrated in cyberspace, discuss how regulation is being introduced and by whom, and illustrate the practices that businesses have adopted in order to minimize their liability and encourage their employees to use the net in an appropriate manner.

0-8493-9829-0/00/$0.00+$.50
© 2000 by CRC Press LLC

THE GROWTH OF THE INTERNET

When the Internet was born approximately 30 years ago it was a medium used by the government and assorted academicians, primarily to perform and share research. The user community was small and mostly self-regulated. Thus, although a useful tool, the Internet was not considered "mission-critical," as it is today. Moreover, the requirements for availability and reliability were not as much a consideration then as they are now, since Internet usage has grown exponentially since the late 1980s.

The increasing opportunities for productivity, efficiency and world-wide communications brought additional users in droves. Thus, it was headline news when a computer worm, introduced into the Internet by Robert Morris, Jr., in 1988, infected thousands of net-connected computers and brought the Internet to its knees.

In the early 1990s, with the advent of commercial applications and the World Wide Web (WWW), a graphical user interface for Internet information, the number of Internet users soared. Sources such as the *Industry Standard*, "The Newsmagazine of the Internet Economy," published the latest Nielsen Media Research Commerce Net study in late 1998, which reported the United States Internet population at 70.5 million (out of a total population of 196.5 million).

Today, the Internet is a utility, analogous to the electric company, and "dot com" is a household expression. The spectrum of Internet users extends from the kindergarten classroom to senior citizenry, although the GenX generation, users in their 20s, are the fastest adopters of net technology (see Exhibit 29.1).

A Higher Percentage of Gen-Xers Use the Web...

	Used the Web in the past 6 months
Generation X	61%
Total U.S. Adults	49%

... More Regularly...

	Use the Web regularly
Generation X	82%
Baby Boomers	52%

... Because it's the Most Important Medium

	Most Important Media
Internet	55%
Television	39%

Source: *The Industry Standard*, M.J. Thompson, July 10, 1998.

Exhibit 29.1. GenX Internet Use

Because of its popularity, the reliability and availability of the Internet are critical operational considerations, and activities that threaten these attributes, e.g., spamming, spoofing, hacking and the like, have grave impacts on its user community.

UNETHICAL ACTIVITY DEFINED

Spamming, in electronic terminology, means electronic garbage. Sending unsolicited junk electronic mail, for example, such as an advertisement, to one user or many users via a distribution list, is considered spamming.

One of the most publicized spamming incidents occurred in 1994, when two attorneys (Laurence Carter and Martha Siegel) from Arizona, flooded the cyber-waves, especially the Usenet newsgroups,* with solicitations to the immigrant communities of the U.S. to assist them in the green card lottery process to gain citizenship. Carter and Siegel saw the spamming as "an ideal, low-cost and perfectly legitimate way to target people likely to be potential clients" (*Washington Post*, 1994). Many Usenet newsgroup users, however, saw things differently. The lawyers' actions resulted in quite an uproar among the Internet communities primarily because the Internet has had a long tradition of noncommercialism since its founding. The attorneys had already been ousted from the American Immigration Lawyers' Association for past sins, and eventually they lost their licenses to practice law.

There have been several other spams since the green card lottery, some claiming "MAKE MONEY FAST," others claiming "THE END OF THE WORLD IS NEAR." There have also been hundreds, if not thousands, of electronic chain letters making the Internet rounds. The power of the Internet is the ease with which users can forward data, including chain letters. More information about spamming occurrences can be found on the net in the Usenet newsgroup alt.folklore.urban.

Unsolicited Internet e-mail has become so widespread that lawmakers have begun to propose sending it a misdemeanor. Texas is one of 18 states considering legislation that would make spamming illegal. In February 1999, Virginia became the fourth state to pass an anti-spamming law. The Virginia law makes it a misdemeanor for a spammer to use a false online identity to send mass mailings, as many do. The maximum penalty would be a $500 fine. However, if the spam is deemed malicious and results in damages to the victim in excess of $2500 (e.g., if the spam causes unavailability of computer service), the crime would be a felony, punishable by up to 5 years in prison. As with the Virginia law, California law allows for the jailing of spammers. Laws in Washington and Nevada impose civil fines.

* Usenet newsgroups are limited communities of net users who congregate online to discuss specific topics.

This legislation has not been popular with everyone, however, and has led organizations such as the American Civil Liberties Union (ACLU), to complain about its unconstitutionality and threat to free speech and the First Amendment.

Like spamming, threatening electronic mail messages have become pervasive in the Internet space. Many of these messages are not taken as seriously as the one that was sent by a high school student from New Jersey, who made a death threat against President Clinton in an electronic mail message in early 1999. Using a school computer which provided an option to communicate with a contingent of the U.S. government, the student rapidly became the subject of a Secret Service investigation.

Similarly, in late 1998, a former investment banker was convicted on eight counts of aggravated harassment when he masqueraded as another employee and sent allegedly false and misleading Internet e-mail messages to top executives of his former firm.

Increasingly, businesses are establishing policy to inhibit employees from using company resources to perform unethical behavior on the Internet. In an early 1999 case, a California firm agreed to pay a former employee over $100,000 after she received harassing messages on the firm's electronic bulletin board, even though the company reported the incident to authorities and launched an internal investigation. The case is a not so subtle reminder that businesses are accountable for the actions of their employees, even actions performed on electronic networks.

Businesses have taken a stern position on employees surfing the web, sending inappropriate messages, and downloading pornographic materials from the Internet. This is due to a negative impact on productivity, as well as the legal view that companies are liable for the actions of their employees. Many companies have established policies for appropriate use and monitoring of computers and computing resources, as well as etiquette on the Internet, or "Netiquette."

These policies are enhancements to the Internet Advisory Board's (Request for Comment) RFC 1087, "Internet Ethics," January 1989, which proposed that access to and use of the Internet is a privilege and should be treated as such by all users of the system. The IAB strongly endorsed the view of the Division Advisory Panel of the National Science Foundation Division of Network Communications Research and Infrastructure. That view is paraphrased below.

Any activity is characterized as unethical and unacceptable that purposely:

- Seeks to gain unauthorized access to the resources of the Internet
- Disrupts the intended use of the Internet

- Wastes resources (people, capacity, computers) through such actions
- Destroys the integrity of computer-based information
- Compromises the privacy of users
- Involves negligence in the conduct of Internet-wide experiments

Source: RFC 1087, "Ethics and the Internet," Internet Advisory Board, January 1989.

A sample "Appropriate Use of the Internet" policy is attached as Appendix A. Appendix B contains the partial contents of RFC 1855, "Netiquette Guidelines," a product of the Responsible Use of the Network (RUN) Working Group of the Internet Engineering Task Force (IETF).

In another twist on Internet electronic mail activity, in April 1999 Intel Corporation sued a former employee for doing a mass e-mailing to its 30,000 employees, criticizing the company over workers' compensation benefits. Intel claims the e-mail was an assault and form of trespass, as well as an improper use of its internal computer resources. The former employee contends that his e-mail messages are protected by the First Amendment. "Neither Intel nor I can claim any part of the Internet as our own private system as long as we are hooked up to this international network of computers," said Ken Hamidi in an e-mail to *Los Angeles Times* reporters. The case was not settled as of this writing. ("Ruling is Due on Mass E-mail Campaign Against Intel," Greg Miller, *Los Angeles Times*, April 19, 1999.)

Using electronic media to stalk another person is known as "cyberstalking." This activity is becoming more prevalent, and the law has seen fit to intercede by adding computers and electronic devices to existing stalking legislation. In the first case of cyberstalking in California, a Los Angeles resident, accused of using his computer to harass a woman who rejected his romantic advances, is the first to be charged under a new cyberstalking law that went into effect in 1998. The man was accused of forging postings on the Internet, on America Online (AOL) and other Internet services, so that the messages appeared to come from the victim. The message provided the woman's address and other identifying information, which resulted in at least six men visiting her home uninvited. The man was charged with one count of stalking, three counts of solicitation to commit sexual assault, and one count of unauthorized access to computers.

In another instance where electronic activity has been added to existing law, the legislation for gambling has been updated to include Internet gambling. According to recent estimates, Internet-based gambling and gaming has grown from about a $500 million-a-year industry in the late 1990s, to what some estimate could become a $10 billion-a-year enterprise by 2000. Currently, all 50 states regulate in-person gambling in some manner. Many conjecture that the impetus for the regulation of electronic gambling is financial, not ethical or legal.

PRIVACY ON THE INTERNET

For many years, American citizens have expressed fears of invasion of privacy, ever since they realized that their personal information is being stored on computer databases by government agencies and commercial entities. However, it is just of late that Americans are realizing that logging on to the Internet and using the World Wide Web threatens their privacy as well. Last year, the Center for Democracy and Technology (CDT), a Washington, D.C. advocacy group, reported that only one third of federal agencies tell visitors to their Web sites what information is being collected about them.

AT&T Labs conducted a study early last year, in which they discovered that Americans are willing to surrender their e-mail address online, but not much more than that. The study said that users are reluctant to provide other personal information, such as a phone number or credit card number.

The utilization of technology offers the opportunity for companies to collect specific items of information. For example, Microsoft Corporation inserts tracking numbers into its Word program documents. Microsoft's Internet Explorer informs Web sites when a user bookmarks them by choosing the "Favorites" option in the browser. In 1998, the Social Security Administration came very close to putting a site on line that would let anyone find out another person's earnings and other personal information. This flies in the face of the 1974 Privacy Act, which states that every agency must record "only such information about an individual as is relevant and necessary to accomplish a purpose of the agency required to be accomplished by statute or by executive order of the President."

There is a battle raging between privacy advocates and private industry aligned with the U.S. government. Privacy advocates relate the serious concern for the hands-off approach and lack of privacy legislation, claiming that citizens are being violated. Conversely, the federal government and private businesses, such as American Online, defend current attempts to rely on self-regulation and other less government-intrusive means of regulating privacy, for example, the adoption of privacy policies. These policies, which state intent for the protection of consumer privacy, are deployed to raise consumer confidence and increase digital trust. The CDT has urged the federal government to post privacy policies on each site's home page, such as is shown in Exhibit 29.2 from the Health and Human Services web site from the National Institute of Health (www.nih.gov).

HHS Web Privacy Notice

(as of April 13, 1999)

Thank you for visiting the Department of Health and Human Services Website and reviewing our Privacy Policy. Our Privacy Policy for visits to **www.hhs.gov** is clear:

We will collect no personal information about you when you visit our website unless you choose to provide that information to us.

Here is how we handle information about your visit to our website:

Information Collected and Stored Automatically

If you do nothing during your visit but browse through the website, read pages, or download information, we will gather and store certain information about your visit automatically. This information does not identify you personally. We automatically collect and store only the following information about your visit:

- The Internet domain (for example, "xcompany.com" if you use a private Internet access account, or "yourschool.edu" if you connect from a university's domain), and IP address (an IP address is a number that is automatically assigned to your computer whenever you are surfing the Web) from which you access our website
- The type of browser and operating system used to access our site,
- The date and time you access our site,
- The pages you visit, and
- If you linked to our website from another website, the address of that website.

We use this information to help us make our site more useful to visitors – to learn about the number of visitors to our site and the types of technology our visitors use. We do not track or record information about individuals and their visits.

Links to Other Sites

Our website has links to other federal agencies and to private organizations. Once you link to another site, it is that site's privacy policy that controls what it collects about you.

Information Collected When You Send Us an E-mail Message

When inquiries are e-mailed to us, we again store the text of your message and e-mail address information, so that we can answer the question that was sent in, and send the answer back to the e-mail address provided. If enough questions or comments come in that are the same, the question may be added to our Question and Answer section, or the suggestions are used to guide the design of our website.

We do not retain the messages with identifiable information or the e-mail addresses for more than 10 days after responding unless your communication requires further inquiry. If you send us an e-mail message in which you ask us to do something that requires further inquiry on our part, there are a few things you should know.

The material you submit may be seen by various people in our Department, who may use it to look into the matter you have inquired about. If we do retain it, it is protected by the Privacy Act of 1974, which restricts our use of it, but permits certain disclosures.

Also, e-mail is not necessarily secure against interception. If your communication is very sensitive, or includes personal information, you might want to send it by postal mail instead.

Exhibit 29.2.

ANONYMITY ON THE INTERNET

Besides a lack of privacy, the Internet promulgates a lack of identity. Users of the Internet are virtual, meaning that they are not speaking with, interacting with, or responding to others, at least not face to face. They sit behind their computer terminals in the comfort of their own home, office, or school. This anonymity makes it easy to masquerade as another, since there is no way of proving or disproving who you are or who you say you are.

Moreover, this anonymity lends itself to the venue of Internet chat rooms. Chat rooms are places on the net where people congregate and discuss topics common to the group, such as sports, recreation, or sexuality. Many chat rooms provide support to persons looking for answers to questions on health, bereavement, or disease and, in this manner, can be very beneficial to society.

Conversely, chat rooms can be likened to sleazy bars, where malcontents go seeking prey. There have been too many occurrences of too-good-to-be-true investments that have turned out to be fraudulent. Too many representatives of the dregs of society lurk on the net, targeting the elderly or the innocent, or those who, for some unknown reason, make easy marks.

A recent *New Yorker* magazine ran a cartoon showing a dog sitting at a computer desk, the caption reading "On the Internet, no one knows if you're a dog." Although the cartoon is humorous, the instances where child molesters have accosted their victims by way of the Internet are very serious. Too many times, miscreants have struck up electronic conversations with innocent victims, masquerading as innocents themselves, only to lead them to meet in person with dire results. Unfortunately, electronic behavior mimics conduct that has always occurred over phone lines, through the postal service, and in person. The Internet only provides an additional locale for intentionally malicious and antisocial behavior. We can only hope that advanced technology, as with telephonic caller ID, will assist law enforcement in tracking anonymous Internet "bad guys."

Attempts at self-regulation have not been as successful as advertised, and many question whether the industry can police itself. Meanwhile, there are those within the legal and judicial systems that feel more laws are the only true answer to limiting unethical and illegal activities on the Internet. How it will all play out is far from known at this point in time. The right to freedom of speech and expression has often been at odds with censorship. It is ironic, for example, that debates abound on the massive amounts of pornography available on the Internet, and yet, in early 1999, the entire transcript of the President Clinton impeachment hearings was published on the net, complete with sordid details of the Monica Lewinsky affair.

INTERNET AND THE LAW

The Communications Decency Act of 1996 was signed into law by President Clinton in early 1996 and has been challenged by civil libertarian organizations ever since. In 1997, the United States Supreme Court declared the law's ban on indecent Internet speech unconstitutional.

The Childrens' Internet Protect Act (S.97, January 1999), introduced before last year's Congress, requires "the installation and use by schools and libraries of a technology for filtering or blocking material on the Internet on computers with Internet access to be eligible to receive or retain universal service assistance."

MONITORING THE WEB

Additionally, many commercial businesses have seen the opportunity to manufacture software products that will provide parents the ability to control their home computers. Products such as Crayon Crawler, FamilyConnect, and KidsGate are available to provide parents with control over what Internet sites their children can access, while products like WebSense, SurfControl and Webroot are being implemented by companies that choose to limit the sites their employees can access.

SUMMARY

Technology is a double-edged sword, consistently presenting us with benefits and disadvantages. The Internet is no different. The net is a powerful tool, providing the ability for global communications in a heartbeat; sharing information without boundaries; a platform for illicit and unethical shenanigans.

This chapter has explored the types of behavior demonstrated in cyberspace, antisocial behavior, which has led to many discussions about whether or not this activity can be inhibited by self-regulation or the introduction of tougher laws. Although we don't know how the controversy will end, we know it will be an interesting future in cyberspace.

APPENDIX A
"APPROPRIATE USE AND MONITORING OF COMPUTING RESOURCES"

Policy

The Company telecommunications systems, computer networks, and electronic mail systems are to be used only for business purposes and only by authorized personnel. All data generated with or on the Company's business resources are the property of the Company; and may be used by the Company without limitation; and may not be copyrighted, patented, leased, or sold by individuals or otherwise used for personal gain.

Electronic mail and voice mail, including pagers and cellular telephones, are not to be used to create any offensive or disruptive messages. The Company does not tolerate discrimination, harassment, or other offensive messages and images relating to, among other things, gender, race, color, religion, national origin, age, sexual orientation, or disability.

The Company reserves the right and will exercise the right to review, monitor, intercept, access, and disclose any business or personal messages sent or received on Company systems. This may happen at any time, with or without notice.

It is the Company's goal to respect individual privacy, while at the same time maintaining a safe and secure workplace. However, employees should have no expectation of privacy with respect to any Company computer or communication resources. Materials that appear on computer, electronic mail, voice mail, facsimile and the like, belong to the Company. Periodically, your use of the Company's systems may be monitored.

The use of passwords is intended to safeguard Company information, and does not guarantee personal confidentiality.

Violations of company policies detected through such monitoring can lead to corrective action, up to and including discharge.

APPENDIX B
NETIQUETTE

RFC 1855
NETIQUETTE GUIDELINES

Status of This Memo

This memo provides information for the Internet community. This memo does not specify an Internet standard of any kind. Distribution of this memo is unlimited.

Abstract

This document provides a minimum set of guidelines for Network Etiquette (Netiquette) which organizations may take and adapt for their own use. As such, it is deliberately written in a bulleted format to make adaptation easier and to make any particular item easy (or easier) to find. It also functions as a minimum set of guidelines for individuals, both users and administrators. This memo is the product of the Responsible Use of the Network (RUN) Working Group of the IETF.

1.0 Introduction

In the past, the population of people using the Internet had "grown up" with the Internet, were technically minded, and understood the nature of the transport and the protocols. Today, the community of Internet users includes people who are new to the environment. These "Newbies" are unfamiliar with the culture and don't need to know about transport and protocols. In order to bring these new users into the Internet culture quickly, this Guide offers a minimum set of behaviors which organizations and individuals may take and adapt for their own use. Individuals should be aware that no matter who supplies their Internet access, be it an Internet Service Provider through a private account, or a student account at a University, or an account through a corporation, that those organizations have regulations about ownership of mail and files, about what is proper to post or send, and how to present yourself. Be sure to check with the local authority for specific guidelines.

We've organized this material into three sections: One-to-one communication, which includes mail and talk; One-to-many communications, which includes mailing lists and NetNews; and Information Services, which includes ftp, WWW, Wais, Gopher, MUDs and MOOs. Finally, we have a Selected Bibliography, which may be used for reference.

2.0 One-to-One Communication (Electronic Mail, Talk)

We define one-to-one communications as those in which a person is communicating with another person as if face-to-face: a dialog. In general, rules of common courtesy for interaction with people should be in force for any situation and on the Internet it's doubly important where, for example, body language and tone of voice must be inferred. For more information on Netiquette for communicating via electronic mail and talk, check references [1,23,25,27] in the Selected Bibliography.

2.1 User Guidelines

2.1.1 For mail:

- Unless you have your own Internet access through an Internet provider, be sure to check with your employer about ownership of electronic mail. Laws about the ownership of electronic mail vary from place to place.
- Unless you are using an encryption device (hardware or software), you should assume that mail on the Internet is not secure. Never put in a mail message anything you would not put on a postcard.
- Respect the copyright on material that you reproduce. Almost every country has copyright laws.
- If you are forwarding or re-posting a message you've received, do not change the wording. If the message was a personal message to you and you are re-posting to a group, you should ask permission first. You

may shorten the message and quote only relevant parts, but be sure you give proper attribution.

- Never send chain letters via electronic mail. Chain letters are forbidden on the Internet. Your network privileges will be revoked. Notify your local system administrator if your ever receive one.
- A good rule of thumb: Be conservative in what you send and liberal in what you receive. You should not send heated messages (we call these "flames") even if you are provoked. On the other hand, you shouldn't be surprised if you get flamed and it's prudent not to respond to flames.
- In general, it's a good idea to at least check all your mail subjects before responding to a message. Sometimes a person who asks you for help (or clarification) will send another message which effectively says "Never Mind". Also make sure that any message you respond to was directed to you. You might be cc:ed rather than the primary recipient.
- Make things easy for the recipient. Many mailers strip header information which includes your return address. In order to ensure that people know who you are, be sure to include a line or two at the end of your message with contact information. You can create this file ahead of time and add it to the end of your messages. (Some mailers do this automatically.) In Internet parlance, this is known as a ".sig" or "signature" file. Your .sig file takes the place of your business card. (And you can have more than one to apply in different circumstances.)
- Be careful when addressing mail. There are addresses which may go to a group but the address looks like it is just one person. Know to whom you are sending.
- Watch cc's when replying. Don't continue to include people if the messages have become a 2-way conversation.
- In general, most people who use the Internet don't have time to answer general questions about the Internet and its workings. Don't send unsolicited mail asking for information to people whose names you might have seen in RFCs or on mailing lists.
- Remember that people with whom you communicate are located across the globe. If you send a message to which you want an immediate response, the person receiving it might be at home asleep when it arrives. Give them a chance to wake up, come to work, and log in before assuming the mail didn't arrive or that they don't care.
- Verify all addresses before initiating long or personal discourse. It's also a good practice to include the word "Long" in the subject header so the recipient knows the message will take time to read and respond to. Over 100 lines is considered "long".
- Know whom to contact for help. Usually you will have resources close at hand. Check locally for people who can help you with software and system problems. Also, know whom to go to if you receive anything questionable or illegal. Most sites also have "Postmaster" aliased to a

knowledgeable user, so you can send mail to this address to get help with mail.

- Remember that the recipient is a human being whose culture, language, and humor have different points of reference from your own. Remember that date formats, measurements, and idioms may not travel well. Be especially careful with sarcasm.
- Use mixed case. UPPER CASE LOOKS AS IF YOU'RE SHOUTING.
- Use symbols for emphasis. That *is* what I meant. Use underscores for underlining. _War and Peace_ is my favorite book.
- Use smileys to indicate tone of voice, but use them sparingly. :-) is an example of a smiley (Look sideways). Don't assume that the inclusion of a smiley will make the recipient happy with what you say or wipe out an otherwise insulting comment.
- Wait overnight to send emotional responses to messages. If you have really strong feelings about a subject, indicate it via FLAME ON/OFF enclosures. For example:
FLAME ON:
This type of argument is not worth the bandwidth it takes to send it. It's illogical and poorly reasoned. The rest of the world agrees with me.
FLAME OFF
- Do not include control characters or non-ASCII attachments in messages unless they are MIME attachments or unless your mailer encodes these. If you send encoded messages make sure the recipient can decode them.
- Be brief without being overly terse. When replying to a message, include enough original material to be understood but no more. It is extremely bad form to simply reply to a message by including all the previous message: edit out all the irrelevant material.
- Limit line length to fewer than 65 characters and end a line with a carriage return.
- Mail should have a subject heading which reflects the content of the message.
- If you include a signature keep it short. Rule of thumb is no longer than 4 lines. Remember that many people pay for connectivity by the minute, and the longer your message is, the more they pay.
- Just as mail (today) may not be private, mail (and news) are (today) subject to forgery and spoofing of various degrees of detectability. Apply common sense "reality checks" before assuming a message is valid.
- If you think the importance of a message justifies it, immediately reply briefly to an e-mail message to let the sender know you got it, even if you will send a longer reply later.
- "Reasonable" expectations for conduct via e-mail depend on your relationship to a person and the context of the communication. Norms learned in a particular e-mail environment may not apply in general to

your e-mail communication with people across the Internet. Be careful with slang or local acronyms.

- The cost of delivering an e-mail message is, on the average, paid about equally by the sender and the recipient (or their organizations). This is unlike other media such as physical mail, telephone, TV, or radio. Sending someone mail may also cost them in other specific ways like network bandwidth, disk space or CPU usage. This is a fundamental economic reason why unsolicited e-mail advertising is unwelcome (and is forbidden in many contexts).
- Know how large a message you are sending. Including large files such as Postscript files or programs may make your message so large that it cannot be delivered or at least consumes excessive resources. A good rule of thumb would be not to send a file larger than 50 Kilobytes. Consider file transfer as an alternative, or cutting the file into smaller chunks and sending each as a separate message.
- Don't send large amounts of unsolicited information to people.
- If your mail system allows you to forward mail, beware the dreaded forwarding loop. Be sure you haven't set up forwarding on several hosts so that a message sent to you gets into an endless loop from one computer to the next to the next.

5.0 SELECTED BIBLIOGRAPHY

This bibliography was used to gather most of the information in the sections above as well as for general reference. Items not specifically found in these works were gathered from the IETF-RUN Working Group's experience.

1. Angell, D., and B. Heslop, *The Elements of E-mail Style,* New York: Addison-Wesley, 1994.
2. Answers to Frequently Asked Questions about Usenet" Original author: jerry@eagle.UUCP (Jerry Schwarz) Maintained by: netannounce@deshaw.com (Mark Moraes) Archive-name: usenet-faq/part1
3. Cerf, V., "Guidelines for Conduct on and Use of Internet," at: http://www.isoc.org/policy/conduct/conduct.html
4. Dern, D., *The Internet Guide for New Users,* New York: McGraw-Hill, 1994.
5. "Emily Postnews Answers Your Questions on Netiquette" Original author: brad@looking.on.ca (Brad Templeton) Maintained by: netannounce@deshaw.com (Mark Moraes) Archive-name: emily-postnews/part1
6. Gaffin, A., *Everybody's Guide to the Internet,* Cambridge, Mass., MIT Press, 1994.
7. "Guidelines for Responsible Use of the Internet" from the US house of Representatives gopher, at: gopher://gopher.house.gov:70/OF-1%3a208%3aInternet%20Etiquette
8. How to find the right place to post (FAQ) by buglady@bronze.lcs.mit.edu (Aliza R. Panitz) Archive-name: finding-groups/general
9. Hambridge, S., and J. Sedayao, "Horses and Barn Doors: Evolution of Corporate Guidelines for Internet Usage," LISA VII, Usenix, November 1-5, 1993, pp. 9-16. ftp://ftp.intel.com/pub/papers/horses.ps or horses.ascii>
10. Heslop, B., and D. Angell, *The Instant Internet Guide: Hands-on Global Networking,* Reading, Mass., Addison-Wesley, 1994.
11. Horwitz, S., "Internet Etiquette Tips," ftp://ftp.temple.edu/pub/info/help-net/netiquette.infohn
12. Internet Activities Board, "Ethics and the Internet," RFC 1087, IAB, January 1989. ftp://ds.internic.net/rfc/rfc1087.txt

13. Kehoe, B., *Zen and the Art of the Internet: A Beginner's Guide*, Netiquette information is spread through the chapters of this work. 3rd ed. Englewood Cliffs, NJ., Prentice-Hall, 1994.
14. Kochmer, J., *Internet Passport: NorthWestNet's Guide to Our World Online*, 4th ed. Bellevue, WA, NorthWestNet, Northwest Academic Computing Consortium, 1993.
15. Krol, Ed, *The Whole Internet: User's Guide and Catalog*, Sebastopol, CA, O'Reilly & Associates, 1992.
16. Lane, E. and C. Summerhill, *Internet Primer for Information Professionals: A Basic Guide to Internet Networking Technology*, Westport, CT, Meckler, 1993.
17. LaQuey, T., and J. Ryer, The Internet companion, Chapter 3 in *Communicating with People*, pp 41-74. Reading, MA, Addison-Wesley, 1993.
18. Mandel, T., "Surfing the Wild Internet," SRI International Business Intelligence Program, Scan No. 2109. March, 1993. gopher://gopher.well.sf.ca.us:70/00/Communications/surf-wild
19. Martin, J., "There's Gold in them thar Networks! or Searching for Treasure in all the Wrong Places," FYI 10, RFC 1402, January 1993. ftp://ds.internic.net/rfc/rfc1402.txt
20. Pioch, N., "A Short IRC Primer," Text conversion by Owe Rasmussen. Edition 1.1b, February 28, 1993. http://www.kei.com/irc/IRCprimer1.1.txt
21. Polly, J., "Surfing the Internet: an Introduction," Version 2.0.3. Revised May 15, 1993. ftp://ftp.nysernet.org/pub/resources/guides/surfing.2.0.3.txt
22. "A Primer on How to Work With the Usenet Community" Original author: chuq@apple.com (Chuq Von Rospach) Maintained by: netannounce@deshaw.com (Mark Moraes) Archive-name: usenet-primer/part1
23. Rinaldi, A., "The Net: User Guidelines and Netiquette," September 3, 1992. http://www.fau.edu/rinaldi/net/index.htm
24. "Rules for posting to Usenet" Original author: spaf@cs.purdue.edu (Gene Spafford) Maintained by: netannounce@deshaw.com (Mark Moraes) Archive-name: posting-rules/part1
25. Shea, V., *Netiquette*, San Francisco: Albion Books, 1994?.
26. Strangelove, M., with A. Bosley, "How to Advertise on the Internet," ISSN 1201-0758.
27. Tenant, R., "Internet Basics," ERIC Clearinghouse of Information Resources, EDO-IR-92-7. September, 1992. gopher://nic.merit.edu:7043/00/introducing.the.Internet/Internet.basics.eric-digest gopher://vega.lib.ncsu.edu:70/00/library/reference/guides/tennet
28. Wiggins, R., *The Internet for Everyone: A Guide for Users and Providers*, New York, McGraw-Hill, 1995.

7.0 AUTHOR'S ADDRESS

Sally Hambridge
Intel Corporation
2880 Northwestern Parkway
SC3-15
Santa Clara, CA 95052
Phone: 408-765-2931
Fax: 408-765-3679
EMail: sallyh@ludwig.sc.intel.com

Domain 9.3
Information Law

Chapter 30
Jurisdictional Issues in Global Transmissions

Ralph Spencer Poore

In the information age where teleconferences replace in-person meetings, where telecommuting replaces going to the office, and where international networks facilitate global transmissions with the apparent ease of calling your neighbor, valuable assets change ownership at the speed of light. Louis Jionet, secretary-general of the French Commission on Data Processing and Liberties stated: "Information is power and economic information is economic power." Customs officials and border patrols cannot control the movement of these assets. But does this mean companies may transmit the data which either represents or is *the* valuable asset without regard to the legal jurisdictions through which they pass? To adequately address this question we will discuss both the legal issues and the practical issues involved in transnational border data flows.

LEGAL ISSUES

All legally incorporated enterprises have Official Books of Record. Whether these are in manual or automated form, they are the records governmental authorities turn to when determining the status of an enterprise. The ability to enforce a subpoena or court order for these records reflects the effective sovereignty of the nation in which the enterprise operates. Most countries require enterprises incorporated, created, or registered in their jurisdiction to maintain official books of record physically within their borders. For example, a company relying on a service bureau in another country for data processing services may cause the official records to exist only in that other country. This could occur if the printouts reflected only a historic position of the company, perhaps month-end conditions, where the current position of the company — the position on which management relies — exists only through online access to the company's executive information system. From a nation's perspective, two issues of sovereignty arise:

1. That other country might exercise its rights and take custody of the company's records — possibly forcing it out of business — for actions alleged against the company that the company's "home" nation considers legal.
2. The company's "home" nation may be unable to enforce its access rights.

Another, usually overriding factor, is a nation's ability to enforce its tax laws. Many nations have value added taxes (VATs) or taxes on "publications," "computer software," and "services." Your organization's data may qualify as a "publication" or as "computer software" or even as "services" in some jurisdictions. Thus, many nations have an interest in the data that flows across their borders because it may qualify for taxation. In some cases, the tax is a tariff intended to discourage the importation of "computer software" or "publications" in order to protect the nation's own emerging businesses. More so than when the tax is solely for revenue generation, protective tariffs may carry heavy fines and be more difficult to negotiate around. With the advent of Internet businesses, determining a business' nexus for tax purposes has become even more complex. Such business may have income, franchise, and inventory or property tax issues in addition to sales tax, excise tax, and import or export duties. Business taxes, registration or license fees, and even reporting requirements depend on the applicability of a given jurisdiction.

National security interests may include controlling the import and export of information. State secrecy laws exist for almost all nations. The United States, for example, restricts government classified data (e.g., Confidential, Secret, Top Secret) but also restricts some information even if it is not classified (e.g., technical data about nuclear munitions, some biological research, some advanced computer technology, and, to varying degrees, cryptography).

Among those nations concerned with an individual's privacy rights, the laws vary greatly. Laws like the United States Privacy Act of 1974 (5 USC 552a) have limited applicability (generally applying only to government agencies and their contractors). The United Kingdom's Data Protection Act of 1984 (1984 c 35 [*Halsbury's Statutes 4th Edition*, Butterworths, London, 1992, Vol. 6, pp. 899-949]), however, applies to the commercial sector as does the 1981 Council of Europe's Convention for the Protection of Individuals with Regard to Automatic Processing of Personal Data. (An excellent discussion of this can be found in Anne W. Brandscomb's *Toward a Law of Global Communications Networks*, The Science and Technology section of the American Bar Association, Longman, New York, 1986.) Privacy laws generally have at least the following three characteristics:

1. They provide notice to the subject of the existence of a database containing the subject's personal data (usually by requiring registration of the database).
2. They provide a process for the subject to inspect and to correct the personal data.
3. They provide a requirement for maintaining an audit trail of accessors to the private data.

The granularity of privacy law requirements also varies greatly. Some laws, e.g., the U.S. Fair Credit Reporting Act of 1970 (see 15 USC 1681 *et seq.*), require only the name of the company that requested the information. Other laws require accountability to a specific office or individual. Because the granularity of accountability may differ from jurisdiction to jurisdiction, organizations may need to develop their applications to meet the most stringent requirements, i.e., individual accountability. In my experience, few electronic data interchange (EDI) systems support this level of accountability. (*UNCID Uniform Rules of Conduct for Interchange of Trade Data by Teletransmission*, ICC Publishing Corporation, New York, 1988. All protective measures and audit measures are described as options with granularity left to the discretion of the parties.)

To further complicate data transfer issues, patent, copyright, and trade secrets laws are not uniform. Although international conventions exist, e.g., General Agreement on Tariffs and Trade (GATT), not all nations subscribe to these conventions, and the conventions often allow for substantial differences among signatories. Rights you may have and can enforce in one jurisdiction may not exist (or may not be enforceable) in another. In some cases, the rights you have in one jurisdiction constitute an infringement in another jurisdiction. For example, you may hold a United States registered trademark on a product. A trademark is a design (often a stylized name or monogram) showing the origin or ownership of merchandise and reserved to the owner's exclusive use. The Trade-Mark Act of 1946 (see 15 USC 1124) provides that no article shall be imported which copies or simulates a trademark registered under U.S. laws. A similar law protecting, for example, trademarks registered in India might prevent your using the trademark in India if a similar or identical trademark is already registered there.

Disclosure of information not in accordance with the laws of the jurisdictions involved may subject the parties to criminal penalties. For example, the U.K.'s Official Secrets Act of 1989 clearly defines areas wherein disclosure of the government's secrets is a criminal offense. Most nations have similar laws (of varying specificity) making the disclosure of state secrets a crime. However, technical information considered public in one jurisdiction may be considered a state secret in another. Similarly, biographical information on a national leader may be mere background information for a news story in one country but be viewed as espionage by another. These areas are particularly difficult since most governments will not advise you in advance what constitutes a state secret (as this might compromise the secret). Unless your organization has a presence in each jurisdiction sensitive to these political and legal issues to whom you can turn for guidance, you should seek competent legal advice before transmitting text or textual database materials containing information about individuals or organizations.

From a business perspective, civil law rather than criminal law may take center stage. Although the U.S. probably has the dubious distinction as the nation in which it is easiest to initiate litigation, law suits are possible in most jurisdictions worldwide. No company wants to become entangled in litigation, especially in foreign jurisdictions. However, when information is transmitted from one nation to another, the rules may change significantly. For example, what are the implied warranties in the receiving jurisdiction? What constitutes profanity, defamation, libel, or similar actionable content? What contract terms are unenforceable (e.g., can you enforce a non-disclosure agreement of 10 years' duration)?

In some jurisdictions ecclesiastical courts may have jurisdiction for offenses against a state-supported religion. Circumstances viewed in one jurisdiction as standard business practices (e.g., "gifts") may be viewed in another as unethical or illegal. Even whether an organization has standing (i.e., may be represented in court) varies among nations. An organization's rights to defend itself, for example, vary from excellent to nil in jurisdictions ranging from Canada to Iran.

Fortunately, companies may generally choose the jurisdictions in which they will hold assets. Most countries enforce their laws (and the actions of their courts) against corporations by threat of asset seizure. A company with no seizable assets (and no desire to conduct future business) in a country is effectively judgment-proof. The reverse can also be true, i.e., a company may be unable to enforce a contract (or legal judgment) because the other party has no assets within a jurisdiction willing to enforce the contract or judgment. When you contract with a company to develop software, for example, and that company exists solely in a foreign country, your organization should research the enforceability of any contract and, if you have any doubt, require a bond be posted in your jurisdiction to ensure at least bond forfeiture as recourse.

SPECIFIC AND GENERAL JURISDICTION

In September 1997, in Bensusan Restaurant Corp. v. King (1997 U.S. App. Lexis 23742 (2d Cir. Sept. 10, 1997)), the 2d U.S. Circuit Court of Appeals held that a Missouri resident's Web site, accessed in New York, did not give rise to jurisdiction under New York's long arm statute. The court ruled there was no jurisdiction because the defendant was not physically in New York when he created the offending Web page. However, a similar case in California with a similar ruling was reversed on appeal (Hall v. LaRonde, 1997 Cal. App. Lexis 633 (Aug. 7, 1997)). Citing the changing "role that electronic communications plays in business transactions," the court decided that jurisdiction should not be determined by whether the defendant's communications were made physically within the state, instead concluding: "[t]here is no reason why the requisite minimum contacts cannot be electronic."

To comply with due process, the exercise of specific jurisdiction generally requires that the defendant took advantage of the benefits of the jurisdiction intentionally, and so could have expected to be hauled into court there. The nature of electronic communications and their growing role in commerce have contributed to findings that defendants' Internet communications constitute "purposeful availment" (legalese for intentionally taking advantage of the benefits) and establish jurisdiction. For example, in California Software Inc. v. Reliability Research Inc. (631 F. Supp. 1356 (C.D. Cal. 1986)) the court held that a nonresident's defamatory e-mail to a resident was sufficient to establish specific jurisdiction. The court noted that, as modern technology makes nationwide commercial transactions more feasible, it broadens the scope of jurisdiction.

Courts have also pointed out the distinguishing features of the Internet when holding that a Web site gives rise to specific jurisdiction for infringement claims arising out of the site's content. In Maritz Inc. v. Cybergold Inc., (947 F. Supp. 1328, 1332, 1334 (E.D. Mo. 1996)) the court suggested that Web site advertising more likely amounts to purposeful availment than advertising by direct mail or an "800" telephone number, noting the "different nature" of electronic communications.

Conceivably, a Web site could reflect contacts with a state's residents that were sufficiently continuous and systematic to establish general jurisdiction over the site owner. Courts have held, however, that the mere creation of a Web site does not create general jurisdiction. See, for example, McDonough v. Fallon McElligott, Inc., 1996 U.S. Dist. Lexis 15139 (S.D. Cal. Aug. 6, 1996). Further, courts have held in more traditional contexts that merely placing advertisements in nationally distributed periodicals or communicating through a national computer-based information system does not subject a nonresident to jurisdiction. See, for example, Federal Rural Elec. Ins. Corp. v. Kootenai Elec. Corp., 17 F.3d 1302, 1305 (10th Cir. 1994).

This area of law is evolving rapidly, with many jurisdictions asserting what amounts to extraterritorial jurisdiction on the basis of electronic transactions into, through, or out of their territory. The Council of Europe's Convention for the Protection of Individuals with Regard to Automatic Processing of Personal Data is but one of many examples. The entire area of cryptography, for example, is another. In January of 1999, the French dramatically eased their long-standing restriction on the use of cryptography within its jurisdiction. This announcement came only six weeks after France joined with 32 other countries to sign an update of a document known as the Wassenaar Agreement. Signatories to this agreement promised to tighten restrictions on the import or export of cryptography. The so-called "Long Arm" provisions of many laws and the lack of consensus among nations on important issues including privacy, intellectual property rights, communications security, and taxes will challenge (or plague) us for the foreseeable future.

TECHNICAL ISSUES

Any nation wishing to enforce its laws with regard to data transmitted within or across its borders must have (1) the ability to monitor/intercept the data and (2) the ability to interpret/understand the data. Almost all nations can intercept wire (i.e., telephone/telegraph) communications. Most can intercept radio, microwave, and satellite transmissions. Unless your organization uses exotic technologies (e.g., point-to-point laser, extremely low frequency (ELF), super high frequency, spread spectrum), interception will remain likely.

The second requirement, however, is another matter. Even simple messages encoded in accordance with international standards may have meaning only in a specific context or template not inherent in the message itself. For example: "142667456043052" could be a phone number (e.g., 1-426-674-5604 x3052), or it could be a social security number and birthday (e.g., 142-66-7456 04/30/52), or it could be dollar amounts ($14,266.74 $560,430.52), or inventory counts by part number (PN) (e.g., PN 142667 Quantity 45, PN 604305 Quantity 2), or zipcodes (e.g., 41266, 74560, 43052). Almost limitless possibilities exist even without using codes or ciphers. And this example used human-readable digits. Many transmissions may be graphic images, object code, or compressed text files completely unintelligible to a human "reading" the data on a datascope.

From the preceding, you might conclude that interception and interpretation by even a technologically advanced nation was too great a challenge. This is, however, far from true. Every "kind" of data has a signature or set of attributes which, when known, permits its detection and identification. This includes encrypted data where the fact of encryption is determinable. Where transmitting or receiving encrypted messages is a crime, a company using encryption risks detection. Once the "kind" of data is determined, applying the correct application is often a trivial exercise. Some examples of such strong typing of data include:

- Rich text format (RTF) documents and most word processing documents
- SQL transactions
- Spreadsheets (e.g., Lotus 1-2-3, Microsoft Excel)
- DOS, Windows, UNIX, and other operating system executables
- Standardized EDI messages
- ASCII vs. EBCDIC

If this were not the case, sending data from one computer to another would require extensive advanced planning at the receiving computer — severely impacting data portability and interoperability, two attributes widely sought in business transactions.

Countries with sufficient technology to intercept and interpret your organization's data may pose an additional problem beyond their law enforcement: government-sponsored industrial espionage. Many countries have engaged in espionage with the specific objective of obtaining technical or financial information of benefit to the countries' businesses. A search of news accounts of industrial espionage resulted in a list including the following countries: Argentina, Cuba, France, Germany, Greece, India, Iran, Iraq, Israel, Japan, North Korea, Peoples Republic of China, Russia, South Korea, and Turkey. Most of these countries have public policies against such espionage, and countries like the United States find it awkward to accuse allies of such activities (both because the technical means of catching them at it may be a state secret and because what one nation views as counter-espionage another nation might view **as** espionage!).

PROTECTIVE TECHNOLOGIES

For most businesses, the integrity of transmitted data is more important than its privacy. Cryptographic techniques a business might otherwise be unable to use because of import or export restrictions associated with the cryptographic process or the use of a privacy-protected message may be used in some applications for data integrity. For example, the Data Encryption Standard (DES), when used for message authentication in accordance with the American National Standard X9.9 for the protection of electronic funds transfers between financial institutions, may be approved by the U.S. Department of the Treasury without having to meet the requirements of the International Trade in Arms Regulations

(ITAR). (Note that technological advances may also impact this. For example, the key space exhaustion attack in January 1999 of a DES Challenge was successful in 22.25 hours. Both the U.S. and French governments made policy changes that permit stronger cryptography for export and import that had previously been permitted.)

Integrity measures generally address one or both of the following problems:

- Unauthorized (including accidental) modification or substitution of the message
- Falsification of identity or repudiation of the message

The techniques used to address the first problem are generally called Message Authentication techniques. Those addressing the second class of problems are generally called Digital Signature techniques.

Message authentication works by applying a cryptographic algorithm to a message in such a way as to produce a resulting message authentication code (MAC) which has a very high probability of being affected by a change to any bit or bits in the message. The receiving party recalculates the MAC and compares it to the transmitted MAC. If they match, the message is considered authentic (i.e, received as sent); otherwise, the message is rejected.

Because international standards include standards for message authentication (e.g., ISO 9797), an enterprise wanting to protect the integrity of its messages can find suitable algorithms which should be (and historically have been) acceptable to most jurisdictions worldwide. With some exceptions, even the Data Encryption Algorithm (DEA), also known as the Data Encryption Standard (DES), may be used in hardware implementations of message authentication. For digital signature this may also be true, although several excellent implementations (both public key and secret key) rely on algorithms with import/export restrictions. The data protected by digital signature or message authentication, however, is not the problem, as both message authentication and digital signature leave the message in plaintext. Objections to their use center primarily on access to the cryptographic security hardware or software needed to support these services. If the cryptographic hardware or software can be obtained legally within a given jurisdiction without violating export restrictions, then using these services rarely poses any problems.

Digital signature techniques exist for both public key and secret key algorithm systems (also known respectively as asymmetric- and symmetric-key systems). The purpose of digital signature is to authenticate the sender's identity and to prevent repudiation (where an alleged sender claims not to have sent the message). The digital signature implementation may or may not also authenticate the contents of the signed message.

Privacy measures address the concern for unauthorized disclosure of a message in transit. Cipher systems, e.g., DEA, transform data into what appear to be random streams of bits. Some ciphers, e.g., a Vernam cipher with a keystream equal to or longer than the message stream, provide almost unbreakable privacy. As such, the better cipher systems almost always run afoul of export or import restrictions. The United States is currently working on the Advanced Encryption Standard (AES) to replace DES. One of the policy issues with AES will be its exportability, as it will allow 128-, 192-, and 256-bit encryption keys. (The National Institute of Standards and Technology expects AES to be available by 2003.)

In some cases, the use of codes is practical and less likely to run into restrictions. As long as the "codebook" containing the interpretations of the codes is kept secret, an organization could send very sensitive messages without risk of disclosure if intercepted in route. For example, an oil company preparing its bid for an off-shore property might arrange a set of codes as shown in Exhibit 30.1.

CODE	MEANING
Red Sun	Highest authorized bid is
Blue Moon	Stall, we aren't ready
White Flower	Kill the deal; we aren't interested
June	1
April	2
July	3
December	4
August	5
January	6
March	7
September	8
November	9
May	0

Exhibit 30.1. Sample Codebook

The message "RED SUN NOVEMBER MAY MAY" would make little sense to an eavesdropper but would tell your representative the maximum authorized bid is 900 (the units would be prearranged, so this could mean $900,000).

Other privacy techniques that do not rely on secret codes or ciphers include:

1. Continuous stream messages (the good message is hidden in a continuous stream of otherwise meaningless text). For example: "THVSTOPREAXZTRECEEBNKLLWSYAINNTHELAUNCHGBMEAZY" contains the message "STOP THE LAUNCH." When short messages are sent as part of a continuous, binary stream, this technique (one of a class known as steganography) can be effective. This technique is often combined with cipher techniques where very high levels of message security are needed.

2. Split knowledge routing (a bit pattern is sent along a route independent of another route on which a second bit pattern is sent; the two bit streams are exclusive-OR'ed together by the receiving party to form the original message). For example: if the bit pattern of the message you wished to send was 0011 1001 1101 0110, a random pattern of equal length would be exclusive-OR'ed with the message, e.g., 1001 1110 0101 0010, to make a new message 1010 0111 1000 0100. The random pattern would be sent along one telecommunication path, and the new message would be sent along another, independent telecommunication path. The recipient would exclusively OR the two messages back together, resulting in the original message. Since no cryptographic key management is required and because the exclusive-OR operation is very fast, this is an attractive technique where the requirement of independent routing can be met.

3. The use of templates (which must remain secret) that permit the receiver to retrieve the important values and ignore others in the same message. For example, our string used above: "THVSTOPRE-AXZTRECEEBNKLLWSYAINNTHELAUNCHGBMEAZY" used with the following template reveals a different message: "XXXXXXXNNXXXNNNXXXXXXXXXXX-NXXXNXXXXXXXXXXXXXXX" where only the letters at the places marked with "N" are used: RETREAT.

The first technique may also be effective against traffic analysis. The second technique requires the ability to ensure independent telecommunication routes (often infeasible). The third technique has roughly the same distribution problems that codebook systems have, i.e., the templates must be delivered to the receiver in advance of the transmission and in a secure manner. These techniques do, however, avoid the import and export problems associated with cryptographic systems.

In addition to cryptographic systems, most industrialized nations restrict the export of specific technologies, including those with a direct military use (or police use) and those advanced technologies easily misused by other nations to suppress human rights, improve intelligence gathering, or counter security measures. Thus, an efficient relational database product might be restricted from export because oppressive third-world nations might use it to maintain data on their citizens (e.g., "subversive activities lists"). Restrictions on software export can sometimes be averted by finding a nation in which the desired product is sold legally without the export restriction. (Note: check with your legal counsel in your enterprise's official jurisdiction as this work-around may be illegal — some countries claim extraterritorial jurisdiction, or claim that their laws take precedence for legal entities residing within their borders.) For example, the Foreign Corrupt Practices Act (see 15 USC 78) of the United States prohibits giving gifts (i.e., paying graft or bribes) by U.S. corporations even if such practice is legal and traditional in a country within which you are doing business. Similarly, if the Peoples Republic of China produces clones of hardware and software which violate intellectual property laws of other countries but which are not viewed by China as a punishable offense, using such a product to permit processing between the United States and China would doubtlessly be viewed by U.S. authorities as unacceptable.

THE LONG VIEW

New technologies (e.g., Software Defined Digital Network (SDDN) and Frame Relay) will make our networks increasingly intelligent, capable of enforcing complex compliance rules and allowing each enterprise to carefully craft the jurisdictions from which, through which, and into which its data will flow. North America, the European Community, Japan, and similar "information age" countries will see these technologies before the turn of the century. But many nations will not have these capabilities for decades.

Most jurisdictions will acquire the ability to detect cryptographic messages and to process cleartext messages even before they acquire the networking technologies that would honor an enterprise's routing requests. The result may be a long period of risk for those organizations determined to send and to receive whatever data they deem necessary through whatever jurisdictions happen to provide the most expeditious routing.

The use of public key infrastructures (PKI) and the reliance on certificate authorities (CA) for electronic commerce will force many changes in international law. The jurisdictional location of a registration authority (RA), for example, may dictate whose personal data may be captured for registration. In a ruling by the EC Privacy Council early in 1999 with regard to IP addresses, they determined that a static IP address constituted privacy-protected data, just as a name and mailing address would. The existence of a CA in a jurisdiction may constitute a nexus for an assertion of general jurisdiction or for taxation if the certificates signed by this CA are used for commercial purposes. Although this technology promises solutions to many problems — including restricting access to data on a selective basis that could bound jurisdictions — it also introduces rapid change and complexity with which societies (and legal systems) are already struggling.

SUMMARY

Data daily flows from jurisdiction to jurisdiction with most organizations unaware of the obligations they may incur. As nations become more sophisticated in detecting data traffic transiting their borders, organizations will face more effective enforcement of laws, treaties, and regulations ranging from privacy to state secrets, and from tax law to intellectual property rights. The risk of state-sponsored industrial espionage will also increase. Because organizations value the information transferred electronically, more and more will turn to cryptography to protect their information. Cryptography, however, has import and export implications in many jurisdictions worldwide. The technology required to intelligently control the routing of communications is increasingly available, but will not solve the problems in the short term. Rather, the advancing technology will complicate matters further in two ways:

1. Where the controls become available, it will make their nonuse indefensible.
2. Where the controls are used, it will make the jurisdictions intentional, thereby strengthening the state's case that it has jurisdiction.

With more legal entities asserting jurisdiction, conflict of laws cases will increase. Implicit contracts will become extremely hazardous (e.g., an e-mail message may be sufficient to constitute a contract, but what are its default terms?). Ultimately, the need for effective commerce will prevail and jurisdictional issues will be resolved. But for the near term, jurisdictional issues in global transmissions remains a growth industry for legal professionals, politicians, lobbyists, tax accountants, and electronic commerce consultants.

Companies will need to exercise care when they place their data on open networks, the routings of which they cannot control. They will need to understand the jurisdictions in which and through which their global information infrastructure operates. The information security professional will want to have competent legal assistance on her team and to stay well informed. The effectiveness of the enterprise's information security program is now irreversibly intertwined with the jurisdictional issues of global electronic commerce.

Domain 10
Physical Security

Physical security, difficult to implement because of the microcomputers that proliferate in today's business establishments, is nonetheless critical to the success of the technical security being implemented. We focus on the capabilities of intrusion detection systems in this edition. Statistics show that for every intruder discovered by a system administrator 10 are detected by today's off-the-shelf intrusion detection systems.

Domain 10.1
Threats and Facility Requirements

Chapter 31

Intrusion Detection: How to Utilize a Still Immature Technology

E. Eugene Schultz and Eugene Spafford

Defending one's systems and networks is an arduous task indeed. The explosive growth of the Internet combined with the ever-expanding nature of networks makes simply keeping track of change nearly an overwhelming challenge. Add the task of implementing proper security-related controls and the problem becomes of far greater magnitude than even the most visionary experts could have predicted 20 years ago. Although victories here and there in the war against cybercriminals occur, reality echoes the irrefutable truth that "cyberspace" is simply too big a territory to adequately defend. Worse yet, security-related controls that work today will probably fail tomorrow as the perpetrator community develops new ways to defeat these controls. Also, the continuing rush to market software with more new features is resulting in poorly designed and poorly tested software being deployed in critical situations. Thus, the usual installation is based on poorly designed, buggy software that is being used in ways unanticipated by the original designers and that is under continuing attack from all over.

Schultz and Wack (SCHU96) have argued that InfoSec professionals need to avoid relying on an approach that is overly reliant on security-related controls. Determining the controls that most effectively reduce risk from a cost-benefit perspective, then implementing and maintaining those controls is an essential part of the risk management process. Investing all of one's resources in controls is, however, not wise because this strategy does not leave resources for detecting and responding to the security-related incidents that invariably occur. The so-called "fortress mentality" (implementing security barrier after security barrier but doing nothing else) in the InfoSec arena does not work any better than did castles in the United Kingdom when Oliver Cromwell's armies aimed their cannons at them. It is far better to employ a layered, defense-in-depth strategy that includes protection, monitoring, and response (cf. Garfinkel and Spafford [GARF96, GARF97]).

Merely accepting the viewpoint that it is important to achieve some degree of balance between deploying controls and responding to incidents that occur, unfortunately, does little to improve the effectiveness of an organization's InfoSec practice. An inherent danger in the incident response arena is the implicit assumption that if no incidents surface, all is well. Superficially this assumption seems logical. Studies by the U.S. Defense Information Systems Agency (DISA) in 1993 and again in 1997, however, provide statistics that prove it is badly flawed. Van Wyk (VANW94) found that of nearly 8800 intrusions into Department of Defense systems by a DISA tiger team, only about one in six was detected. Of the detected intrusions, approximately only 4 percent were reported to someone in the chain of command. This meant that of all successful attacks, less than 1 percent were both noticed and reported. A similar study by the same agency 3 years later produced nearly identical results.

One could argue that perhaps many Department of Defense personnel do not have as high a level of technical knowledge as their counterparts in industry because industry (with its traditionally higher salaries) can attract top technical personnel who might more readily be able to more readily recognize the symptoms of attacks. In industry, therefore, according to this line of reasoning, it would be much more likely that some technical "guru" would notice intrusions that occurred. This reasoning is at best only partially true, however, in that in the DISA studies little attempt was made to cover up the intrusions in the first place. In what might be called "more typical" intrusions, in contrast, attackers typically devote a large proportion of their efforts to masquerade the activity they have initiated to avoid being noticed. This is further supported by the latest CSI/FBI survey (POWER99) that indicated that many firms are unable to determine the number or nature of intrusions and losses to their enterprise from IT system attacks, but that losses and number of incidents are continuing to increase.

The main point here is that effective incident response is important and necessary, but it hardly does any good if people do not notice incidents that occur in the first place. Human efforts to notice incidents, as good as they may be, are in many if not most operational settings inadequate. InfoSec professionals often need something more, an automated capability that enables them to be able to discover incidents that are attempted or actually succeed. The solution is intrusion detection. This chapter covers

the topic of intrusion detection, discussing what it is, the types of requirements that apply to intrusion detection systems, and ways that intrusion
detection systems can be deployed.

ABOUT INTRUSION DETECTION

What is Intrusion Detection?

Intrusion detection refers to the process of discovering unauthorized
use of computers and networks through the use of software designed for
this purpose. Intrusion detection software in effect serves a vigilance function. An effective intrusion detection system both discovers and reports
unauthorized activity, such as log-on attempts by someone who is not the
legitimate user or an account and unauthorized transfer of files to another
system. Intrusion detection may also serve a role of helping to document
the (attempt at) misuse so as to provide data for strengthening defenses,
or for investigation and prosecution after the fact.

Intrusion detection is misnamed. As a field, it started as a form of misuse
detection for mainframe systems. The original idea behind automated
intrusion detection systems is often credited to James P. Anderson for his
1980 paper on how to use accounting audit files to detect inappropriate
use. Over time, systems have become more connected via networks; attention has shifted to penetration of systems by "outsiders," thus including
detection of "intrusion" as a goal. Throughout our discussion, we will use
the common meaning of "intrusion detection" to include detection of both
outsider misuse and insider misuse; users of ID systems should likewise
keep in mind that insider misuse must be detected, too.

Why Utilize Intrusion Detection?

One possible approach to intrusion detection would be to deploy thousands of specially trained personnel to continuously monitor systems and
networks. This approach would in almost every setting be impossible to
implement because it would be impractical. Few organizations would be
willing to invest the necessary level of resources and time required to train
each "monitor" to obtain the needed technical expertise. Running one or
more automated programs, designed effectively to do the same thing but
without the involvement of thousands of people, is a more logical
approach, provided of course that the program yields acceptable results in
detecting unauthorized activity. Additionally, although many people with
high levels of technical expertise could be deployed in such a monitoring
role, it may not be desirable to do so from another perspective. Even the
most elite among the experts might miss certain types of unauthorized
actions given the typically gargantuan volume of activity that occurs

683

within today's systems and networks. A suitable intrusion detection program could thus uncover activity that experts miss.

Detection *per se* is not the only purpose of intrusion detection. Another very important reason to use IDSs is that they often provide a reporting capability. Again, the worst-case scenario would be relying on a substantial number of human beings to gather intrusion data when each person uses a different format to record the data, in addition to using terms and descriptions ambiguous to everyone but that person. Trying to combine each observer's data and descriptions to derive patterns and trends would be virtually impossible; making sense out of any one observer's data would be very challenging. An effective intrusion detection system provides a reporting capability that not only produces human-friendly information displays but also interfaces with a central database or other capability that allows efficient storage, retrieval, and analysis of data.

How IDSs Work

IDSs work in a large variety of ways related to the type of data they capture as well as the types of analysis they perform. At the most elementary level, a program that runs on one or more machines receives audit log data from that machine. The program combs through each entry in the audit logs for signs of unauthorized activity. This type of program is part of a host or system-based IDS. At the other extreme, an IDS may be distributed in nature (MUKH94). Software (normally referred to as agent software) resides in one or more systems connected to a network. Manager software in one particular server receives data from the agents it knows about and analyzes the data (CROS95). This second approach characterizes a network-based IDS (see Exhibit 31.1).

Note that if the data that each agent sends to the manager has not been tampered with, the level of analysis possible is more powerful than with host or system-based IDSs for several reasons:

1. Although a host-based IDS may not depend upon audit data (if it has its own data-capturing service independent of auditing), audit and other types of data produced within single systems are subject to tampering and/or deletion. An attacker who disables auditing and/or an intrusion data collection service on a given machine effectively disables the IDS that runs on that machine. This is not true, however, in the case of a network-based IDS, which can gather data from individual machines and from passive devices (e.g., protocol analyzers) and other, more difficult-to-defeat machines such as firewalls. In other words, network-based IDSs are not as dependent on data from individual systems.

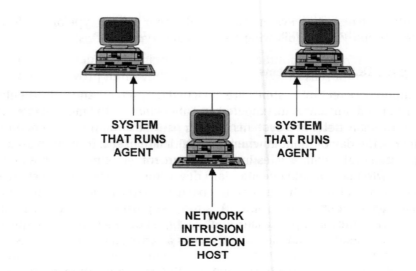

SYSTEM
THAT RUNS
AGENT

SYSTEM
THAT RUNS
AGENT

NETWORK
INTRUSION
DETECTION
HOST

Exhibit 31.1. A Deployment of an IDS in Which Agent Software Running on Hosts Sends Data to a Central Network Intrusion Detection Capability for Analysis

2. Network-based IDSs, furthermore, can utilize data that are not available in system-based IDSs (HERR97). Consider, for example, an attacker who logs on to one system as user "BROWN," then logs on to another system on the same network as "SMITH." The manager software can assign a net ID to each user, thus enabling it to know that the user who has a log-on shell in both systems is the same user. This IDS can then generate an alarm based on the fact that the user in this example has logged on to different accounts with different names. This level of analysis is not possible if an IDS does not have data from multiple machines on the net.

A third form of ID system, currently quite popular, involves one or more systems that observe network traffic (usually at a border location such as near a firewall) and scan for packet traffic that indicates misbehavior. These "network intrusion detection systems" are easy to deploy to protect an enterprise from attack from the outside, but they have the drawback of missing internal behavior that may also be of interest.

APPROACHES TO INTRUSION DETECTION

Not only do different implementations of IDSs work using fundamentally different kinds of data and analysis methods, but they also differ in the types of approaches to intrusion detection that have been incorporated into their design. The correct question here is not "do you want to deploy an intrusion detection system (IDS)," but rather "which type of IDS do you want to deploy?" The following are the major types of IDSs:

Anomaly Detection Systems

Anomaly Detection Systems are designed to discover anomalous behavior, i.e., behavior that is unexpected and abnormal. At the most elementary level, anomaly detection systems look for use of a computer system during a time of the day or night in which the legitimate user hardly ever uses the computer. Statistical profiles indicating percentiles of measurable behavior and what falls within one standard deviation of the norm, two standard deviations, and so forth are often the basis for determining whether or not a given user action is anomalous. At a more sophisticated level, one might profile variables and processes such as types of usage by each specific user. One user, for example, might access a server mostly to read e-mail; another may balance usage time between e-mail and using spreadsheet-based applications; and a third might mostly write and compile programs. If the first user suddenly starts compiling programs, an anomaly detection system should flag this type of activity as suspicious.

Misuse Detection Systems

The main focus of misuse detection systems is upon symptoms of misuse by authorized users. These symptoms include unauthorized log-ons or bad log-on attempts to systems in addition to abuse of services (e.g., Web-based services, file system mounts, and so on) in which users do not need to authenticate themselves. In the latter case, therefore, good misuse detection systems will identify specific patterns (called "signatures") of anomalous actions. If an anonymous FTP user, for example, repeatedly enters cd .., cd .., cd .. from a command line, there is a good chance that the user is attempting a "dotdot" attack to reach a higher-level directory than FTP access is supposed to allow. It is very unlikely that a legitimate user would repeatedly enter these keystrokes.

Target Monitoring Systems

Target monitoring systems represent a somewhat radical departure from the previously discussed systems in that they do not attempt to discover anomalies or misuse. Instead they report whether certain target objects have been changed; if so, an attack may have occurred. In UNIX systems, for example, attackers often change the /sbin/login program (to cause a pseudo-login to occur in which the password of a user attempting to login is captured and stored in a hidden file) or the /etc/passwd file (which holds names of users, privilege levels, and so on). In Windows NT systems someone may change .DLL (dynamically linked library) files to alter system behavior. Most target monitoring systems use a cryptographic algorithm to compute a cryptochecksum for each target file. Then if the cryptochecksum is calculated later in time and the new cryptochecksum is different from the previous one, the IDS will report the change. Although this type of IDS superficially does not seem as sophisticated as the previous ones, it has several advantages over anomaly and misuse detection systems:

1. When intruders break into systems, they frequently make changes (sometimes accidentally, sometimes on purpose). Therefore, changed files, executables that are replaced with Trojan Horse versions, and so forth are excellent potential indications that an attack has occurred.

2. Target monitoring systems are not based on statistical norms, signatures, and other indicators that may or may not be valid. These systems are, therefore, not as model-dependent. They are simple and straightforward. Furthermore, they do not really need to be validated because the logic behind them is so obvious.

3. They do not have to be continuously run to be effective. All one has to do is run a target monitoring program at one point in time, then another. Target monitoring systems thus do not generally result in as much performance overhead as do other types of IDSs.

Systems that Perform Wide-Area Correlation of Slow and "Stealth" Probes

Not every attack that occurs is an all-out attack. A fairly typical attack pattern is one in which intruders first probe remote systems and network components such as routers for security-related vulnerabilities, then actually launch attacks later. If attackers were to launch a massive number of probes all at once, the likelihood of noticing the activity would increase dramatically. Many times, therefore, attackers probe one system, then another, then another at deliberately slow time intervals. The result is a substantial reduction in the probability that the probes will be noticed. A fourth type of IDS performs wide-area collection of slow and stealth probes to discover the type of attacks mentioned in this section.

MAJOR ADVANTAGES AND LIMITATION OF INTRUSION DETECTION TECHNOLOGY

Advantages

Intrusion detection is potentially one of the most powerful capabilities that an InfoSec practice can deploy. Much of attackers' ability to perpetrate computer crime and misuse depends on their ability to escape being noticed until it is too late. The implications of the DISA statistics cited earlier are potentially terrifying; in the light of these findings, it might be more reasonable to ask how an InfoSec practice that claims to observe the principle of "due diligence" could avoid using an IDS enterprise-wide. We strongly assert that any InfoSec practice that does not utilize IDS technology at least to some degree is not practicing due diligence because it will necessarily overlook a large percentage of the incidents that occur. Any practice that remains unaware of incidents does not understand the real risk factor; sadly, it only mimics the behavior of an ostrich with its head in the sand. Simply put, an effective IDS can greatly improve the capability to discover and report security-related incidents.

We also note that the complexity of configuration of most systems and the poor quality of most commercial software effectively guarantees that new flaws will be discovered and widely reported that can be used against most computing environments. Patches and defenses are often not as quickly available as attack tools, and defenses based on monitoring and response are the only way to mitigate such dangers. A failure to use such mechanisms is a failure to adequately provide comprehensive security controls.

In addition to increasing an organization's capability to notice and respond to incidents, intrusion detection systems offer several other major benefits. These include:

1. Cost reduction. Automated capabilities over time generally cost less than humans performing the same function. Once an organization has paid the cost of purchasing and installing one or more IDSs, the cost of an intrusion detection capability can be quite reasonable.
2. Increased detection capability. As mentioned earlier, an effective IDS is able to perform more sophisticated analysis (e.g., by correlating data from a wide range of sources) than are humans. The epitome of the problem of reading and interpreting data through human inspection is reading systems' audit logs. These logs typically produce a volume of data that system administrators seldom have time to inspect, at least in any detail. Remember, too, that attackers often have the initial goal of disabling auditing once they compromise a system's defenses. IDSs do not necessarily rely on audit logs.
3. Deterrent value. Attackers who know intrusion detection capabilities are in place are often more reluctant to continue unauthorized computer-related activity. IDSs thus serve to deter unauthorized activity to some degree.
4. Reporting. An effective IDS incorporates a reporting capability that utilizes standard, easy-to-read and understand formats and database management capabilities.

5. Forensics. A few IDSs incorporate forensics capabilities. Forensics involves the proper handling of evidence that may be used in court. A major goal of forensics is to collect and preserve evidence about computer crime and misuse that will be admissible in a court of law.
6. Failure detection and recovery. Many failures exhibit features similar to misuse or intrusion. Deployment of good IDSs may result in advance notice of these symptoms before they result in full failures. Furthermore, some IDSs can provide audit data about changes, thus allowing failed components to be restored or verified more quickly.

Disadvantages

Intrusion detection is also beset with numerous limitations. Some of the most critical of these drawbacks include:

1. Immaturity. Most (but not all) IDSs available today have significant limitations regarding the quality of functionality they provide. Some are little more than prototypes with a sophisticated user interface. Others purport to compare signatures from a signature library to events that occur in systems and/or networks, but the vendors or developers refuse to allow potential customers to learn how complete and how relevant these libraries are. Equally troubling is the fact that new types of attacks occur all the time; unless someone updates the signature library, detection efficiency will fall. Still other IDSs rely on statistical indicators such as "normal usage patterns" for each user. A clever perpetrator can, however, patiently and continuously engage in activity that does not fall out of the normal range but comes close to doing so. The perpetrator thus can adjust the statistical criteria over time. Someone who normally uses a system between 8 a.m. and 8 p.m. may want to attack the system at midnight. If the perpetrator were to simply attack the system at midnight, alarms might go off because the IDS may not consider midnight usage within the normal range for that user. But if the perpetrator keeps using the system from, say, 11 a.m. to 11 p.m. every day for one week, usage at midnight might no longer be considered statistically deviant.
2. False positives. Another serious limitation of today's IDSs is false positives (Type I errors). A false positive occurs when an IDS signals that an event constitutes a security breach, but that event in reality does not involve such a breach. An example is multiple, failed logins by users who have forgotten their passwords. Most IDS customers today are concerned about false alarms because they are often disruptive and because they sidetrack the people who investigate the false intrusions away from other, legitimately important tasks.

3. Performance decrements. Deploying IDSs results in system and/or network performance hits. The actual amount of decrement depends on the particular IDS; some are very disruptive to performance. Anomaly-based systems are often the most disruptive because of the complexity of matching required.

4. Initial cost. The initial cost of deploying IDSs can be prohibitive. When vendors of IDS products market their products, they often mention only the purchase cost. The cost to deploy these systems may require many hours of consultancy support, resulting in a much higher cost than originally anticipated.

5. Vulnerability to attack. IDSs themselves can be attacked to disable the capabilities they deliver. The most obvious case is when a trusted employee turns off every IDS, engages in a series of illegal actions, then turns every IDS on again. Any attacker can flood a system used by IDS capability with superfluous events to exceed the disk space allocated for the IDS data, thereby causing legitimate data to be overwritten, systems to crash, and a range of other, undesirable outcomes.

6. Applicability. IDSs are designed to uncover intrusions, unauthorized access to systems. Yet a large proportion of the attacks reported during the past year (at the time this chapter was written) were either probes (e.g., use of scanning programs to discover vulnerabilities in systems) or denial-of-service attacks. Suppose that an attacker wants to cause as many systems in an organization's network to crash as possible. Any IDSs in place may not be capable of discovering and reporting many denial-of-service attacks in the first place. Even if they are capable of doing so, knowing that "yes, there was a denial-of-service attack" hardly does any good if the attacked systems are already down! Additionally, many (if not most) of today's IDSs do a far better job of discovering externally initiated attacks than ones that originate from inside. This is unfortunate given that expected loss for insider attacks is far higher than for externally originated attacks.

7. Vulnerability to tampering. IDSs are vulnerable to tampering by unauthorized as well as authorized persons. Many ways to defeat IDSs are widely known within both the InfoSec and perpetrator communities. In a highly entertaining article, Cohen describes 50 of these ways (COHE97).

8. Changing technology. Depending on a particular technology may result in loss of protection as the overall computing infrastructure changes. For instance, network-based intrusion detection is often foiled by switch-based IP networks, ATM-like networks, VPNs, encryption, and alternate routing of messages. All of these technologies are becoming more widely deployed as time goes on.

The advantages and disadvantages of intrusion detection technology are summarized in Exhibit 31.2.

ADVANTAGES	DISADVANTAGES
Cost reduction (at least over time) resulting from automation	Many IDSs do not deliver the functionality that is needed
Increased efficiency in detecting incidents	Unacceptably high false alarm rates
Can deter unauthorized activity	Generally produce performance decrements
Built-in reporting, data management, and other functions	Initial cost may be prohibitive
Built-in forensics capabilities	May yield superfluous data
	IDSs themselves are vulnerable to attack

Exhibit 31.2. Summary of Advantages and Disadvantages of Intrusion Detection Technology

ASSESSING INTRUSION DETECTION REQUIREMENTS

The Relationship of Intrusion Detection to Risk

A large number of organizations go about the process of risk management by periodically performing risk assessments, determining the amount of resources available, then allocating resources according to some method of priority-based risk mitigation strategy, i.e., introducing one or more controls that counter the risk with the greatest potential for negative impact, then implementing one or more measures that address the risk with the second greatest negative impact, and so on until the resources are spent. Regardless of whether or not one agrees with this mode of operation, it tends to guarantee that intrusion detection will be overlooked. In simple terms, intrusion detection does not address any specific risk as directly as measures such as encryption and third-party authentication solutions.

Developing Business-Related Requirements

Developing specific, business-related requirements concerning intrusion detection is anything but an easy process. The difficulty of doing so is, in all likelihood, one of the major detractors in organizations' struggles in dealing with intrusion detection capabilities. Business units, furthermore, may be the most reluctant to utilize intrusion detection technology because of the typical level of resources (personnel and monetary) required and because this technology may superficially seem irrelevant to the needs of fast-paced business units in today's commercial environments.

On the other hand, obtaining buy-in from business units and developing business requirements for intrusion detection at the business unit level is probably not the primary goal anyway. In most organizations if intrusion detection technology is to be infused successfully, it must be introduced as a central capability. Business requirements and the business rationale for intrusion detection technology are likely to be closely related to the requirements for an organization's audit function. The ultimate goal of intrusion detection technology in business terms is the need to independently evaluate the impact of system and network usage patterns in terms of the organization's financial interests. As such, it is often easiest to put intrusion detection technology in the hands of an organization's audit function.

Decision Criteria

Suppose that your organization decides to introduce intrusion detection technology. After you derive the business requirements that apply to your organization, the next logical step is to determine whether your organization will build a custom IDS or buy a commercial, off-the-shelf version. The latter is generally a much wiser strategy — building a custom IDS generally requires far more time and resources than you might ever imagine. Additionally, maintenance of custom-built IDSs is generally a stumbling block in terms of long-term operations and cost. The exception to the rule is deploying very simple intrusion detection technology. Setting up and deploying "honey pot" servers, for example, is one such strategy. Honey pot servers are alarm servers connected to a local network. Normally nobody uses a honey pot server, but this host is assigned an interesting but bogus name (e.g., patents.corp.com). If anyone logs in or even attempts to login, software in this type of server alerts the administrator, perhaps by having the administrator paged. The major function of honey pot servers is to indicate whether an unauthorized user is "loose on the net" so that one or more individuals can initiate suitable incident response measures. This strategy is not elegant in terms of the intrusion detection capability that it provides, but it is simple and very cost effective. Better yet, an older, reasonably low-ended platform (e.g., a Sparcstation 5) is generally more than sufficient for this type of deployment.

Buying a commercial IDS product is easier when one systematically evaluates the functionality and characteristics of each candidate product against meaningful criteria. We suggest that at a minimum you apply the following criteria:

1. Cost. This includes both short- and long-term costs. As mentioned previously, some products may appear to cost little because their purchase price is low, but life-cycle deployment costs may be intolerable.
2. Functionality. The difference between a system- versus network-based IDS is very important here. Many intrusion detection experts assert that system-based IDSs are better for detecting insider activity, whereas network-based IDSs are better for detecting externally

originated attacks. This consideration is, however, only a beginning point with respect to determining whether or not a product's functionality is suitable. The presence or absence of functions, such as reporting capabilities, data correlation from multiple systems, and near real-time alerting, is also important to consider.

3. Scalability. Each candidate tool should scale not only to business requirements but also to the environments in which it is to be deployed. In general, it is best to assume that whatever product one buys will have to scale upward in time, so obtaining a product that can scale not only to the current environment, but also to more complex environments is frequently a good idea.

4. Degree of automation. The more features of an IDS product that are automated, the less human intervention is necessary.

5. Accuracy. An IDS product should not only identify any *bona fide* intrusion that occurs but should also minimize the false alarm rate.

6. Interoperability. Effective IDSs can interoperate with each other to make data widely available to the various hosts that perform intrusion detection management and database management.

7. Ease of operation. An IDS that is easy to deploy and maintain is more desirable than one that is not.

8. Impact on ongoing operations. An effective IDS causes little disruption in the environment in which it exists.

DEVELOPING AN INTRUSION DETECTION ARCHITECTURE

After requirements are in place and the type of IDS to be used is selected, the next logical phase is to develop an architecture for intrusion detection. In the current context, the term "architecture" is defined as a high-level characterization of how different components within a security practice are organized and how they relate to each focus within that practice. Consider, for example, the components of an InfoSec practice shown in Exhibit 31.3.

To develop an intrusion detection architecture, one should start at the highest level, ensuring that the policies include the appropriate provisions for deploying, managing, and accessing intrusion detection technology. For example, some policy statement should include the provision that no employee or contractor shall access or alter any IDS that is deployed. Another policy statement should specify how much intrusion detection data are to be captured and how they must be archived. It is also important to ensure that an organization's InfoSec policy clearly states what constitutes "unauthorized activity" if the output of IDSs is to have any real meaning.

At the next level down, one might write specific standards appropriate to each type of IDS deployed. For IDSs with signature libraries, for example,

Exhibit 31.3. A Simple Framework for a Security Architecture

it is important to specify how often the libraries should be upgraded. At the lowest level one might include recommendations such as how much disk space to allocate for each particular IDS installation. It is important to realize that an intrusion detection capability does not work well in isolation; it needs to be part of the inner fabric of an organization's culture. As such, developing an intrusion detection architecture is a very important step in successfully deploying intrusion detection technology. Note also that developing such an architecture is not as simple as diagrams such Exhibit 31.3 might imply; it requires carefully analyzing exactly what intrusion detection requires for each component of the architecture and how to embody the solution for each need within that component. Equally important, it requires consensus among organizations that will or may be affected by the rollout of intrusion detection technology in addition to buy-in from senior-level management.

CONCLUSION

We have examined intrusion detection and its potential role in an InfoSec practice, arguing against the "fortress mentality" that results in implementation of security control measures such as password checkers without realizing that no defense measure is 100 percent effective anyway. It is important, therefore, to devote a reasonable portion of an organization's resources to detecting incidents that occur and effectively responding to them. We have taken a look at its advantages and disadvantages, then discussed how one can effectively introduce intrusion detection technology into an organization. Finally, we explained considerations related to deploying IDSs.

Intrusion detection in many ways stands at the same crossroads that firewall technology did nearly a decade ago. The early firewalls were really rather crude and most organizations viewed them as interesting but impractical. Intrusion detection technology has been available before the first firewall was ever implemented, but the former has always faced more of an uphill battle. The problem can be characterized as due to the mystery and evasiveness that has surrounded IDSs. Firewalls are more straightforward — the simplest firewalls simply block or allow traffic destined for specific hosts. You can be reasonably sure when you buy a firewall product how this product will work. The same has not been true in the intrusion detection arena. Yet at the same time, intrusion detection is rapidly gaining acceptance among major organizations around the world. Although the technology surrounding this area is far less than perfect, it is now sufficiently reliable and sophisticated to warrant its deployment. To ignore and avoid deploying this technology now, in our judgment, constitutes a failure to adopt the types of measures responsible organizations are now putting in place, which in simple terms is a failure to observe "due care" standards.

The good news is that intrusion detection technology is becoming increasingly sophisticated every year. Also encouraging is the fact that performance-related problems associated with IDSs are becoming relatively less important because operating systems and the hardware platforms on which they run are constantly improving with respect to performance characteristics. The research community, additionally, is doing a better job in pioneering the way for the next generation of intrusion detection technology. Some current advances in intrusion detection research include areas such as interoperability of IDSs, automatic reporting, and automated response (in which the IDS takes evasive action when it determines that an attack is in progress).

The bad news is that if your organization does not currently use intrusion detection technology, it is badly behind the intrusion detection "power curve." Consider, furthermore, that an organization that buys, then rolls out a new IDS product is by no means ready to reap the benefits immediately. A definite, steep learning curve for using intrusion detection technology exists. Even if you start deploying this technology now, it takes time to assimilate the mentality of intrusion detection and the technology associated with it into an organization's culture. It is important, therefore, to become familiar with and start using this technology as soon as possible to avoid falling behind even further. The alternative is to continue to function as the proverbial ostrich with its head beneath the sand.

References

COHE97 Cohen, F., Managing network security - Part 14: 50 ways to defeat your intrusion detection system. *Network Security*, December, 1997, pp. 11 – 14.

CROS95 Crosbie, M. and Spafford, E.H., Defending a computer system using autonomous agents. *Proceedings of 18th National Information Systems Security Conference*, 1995, pp. 549 – 558.

GARF96 Garfinkel, S. and Spafford, G., *Practical Unix and Internet Security,* O'Reilly & Associates, inc., 1996.

GARF97 Garfinkel, S. and Spafford, G., *Web Security & Commerce*, O'Reilly & Associates, inc., 1997.

HERR97 Herringshaw, C. Detecting attacks on networks. *IEEE Computer,* 1997, Vol. 30 (12), pp. 16 – 17.

MUKH94 Mukherjee, B., Heberlein, L.T., and Levitt, K.N., Network intrusion detection. *IEEE Network*, 1994, Vol. 8 (3), pp. 26 – 41.

POWER99 Power Richard, Issues and Trends: 1999 CSI/FBI computer crime and security survey, *Computer Security Journal*, Vol. XV, No. 2, Spring 1999

SCHU96 Schultz, E.E. and Wack, J., Responding to computer security incidents, in M. Krause and H.F. Tipton (Eds.), *Handbook of Information Security.* Boston: Auerbach, 1996, pp. 53 – 68.

VANW94 Van Wyk, K.R., Threats to DoD Computer Systems. Paper presented at 23rd Information Integrity Institute Forum. (Cited with author's permission.)

Index